Suicide Bereavement and Postvention: Advances in Research, Practice and Policy

Suicide Bereavement and Postvention: Advances in Research, Practice and Policy

Editors

Karl Andriessen
Karolina Krysinska
Yossi Levi-Belz

MDPI • Basel • Beijing • Wuhan • Barcelona • Belgrade • Manchester • Tokyo • Cluj • Tianjin

Editors

Karl Andriessen
The University of Melbourne
Parkville, VIC, Australia

Karolina Krysinska
The University of Melbourne
Parkville, VIC, Australia

Yossi Levi-Belz
Ruppin Academic Center
Emek Hefer, Israel

Editorial Office
MDPI
St. Alban-Anlage 66
4052 Basel, Switzerland

This is a reprint of articles from the Special Issue published online in the open access journal *International Journal of Environmental Research and Public Health* (ISSN 1660-4601) (available at: https://www.mdpi.com/journal/ijerph/special_issues/suicide_bereavement_postvention).

For citation purposes, cite each article independently as indicated on the article page online and as indicated below:

LastName, A.A.; LastName, B.B.; LastName, C.C. Article Title. *Journal Name* **Year**, *Volume Number*, Page Range.

ISBN 978-3-0365-8018-0 (Hbk)
ISBN 978-3-0365-8019-7 (PDF)

Contents

About the Editors

Karl Andriessen

Karl Andriessen, PhD, is a Senior Research Fellow at the Centre for Mental Health, Melbourne School of Population and Global Health, the University of Melbourne. Having a broad and longstanding interest in suicide prevention, his research is focused on ethical issues in suicide research, and suicide bereavement and postvention.

Karolina Krysinska

Karolina Krysinska, PhD, is an experienced research psychologist and Senior Research Fellow at the Centre for Mental Health, Melbourne School of Population and Global Health, the University of Melbourne. She has conducted various studies and published widely on suicide prevention, including studies on lived experiences of suicide, and research on suicide bereavement and postvention.

Yossi Levi-Belz

Yossi Levi-Belz, PhD, is a clinical psychologist and the chair of the Lior Tsfaty Center for Suicide and Mental Pain Studies at Ruppin Academic Center. His research interests include moral injury, psychological mechanisms of suicidal behavior as well as growth and depression processes among suicide-bereaved individuals. He has published over a hundred articles in scientific journals in the fields of suicide prevention, moral injury, and post-traumatic growth from suicide-loss. He is the editor-in-chief of the book "*Illuminating the Mountains of Darkness: Suicide among adolescents*" and the new book "*Under the Dark Black Sky- dialogues about mental pain, suicide and hope*".

International Journal of
Environmental Research and Public Health

MDPI

Editorial

What Do We Know about Suicide Bereavement, and What We Can Do to Help Suicide-Loss Survivors?

Yossi Levi-Belz [1,*], Karolina Krysinska [2] and Karl Andriessen [2]

1 The Lior Tsfaty Center for Suicide and Mental Pain Studies, Ruppin Academic Center, Emek Hefer 40250, Israel
2 Centre for Mental Health, Melbourne School of Population and Global Health, The University of Melbourne, Parkville, VIC 3010, Australia
* Correspondence: yossil@ruppin.ac.il

Citation: Levi-Belz, Y.; Krysinska, K.; Andriessen, K. What Do We Know about Suicide Bereavement, and What We Can Do to Help Suicide-Loss Survivors? *Int. J. Environ. Res. Public Health* **2023**, *20*, 5577. https://doi.org/10.3390/ijerph20085577

Received: 31 March 2023
Accepted: 18 April 2023
Published: 19 April 2023

"Suicide is not only the end of life for the deceased but also the beginning of a highly challenging life for those left behind". While most efforts and scientific studies concerning suicide focus on prevention [1], these touching words of Edwin Shneidman remind us that the societal toll of suicide reaches well beyond human loss. Recent studies [2–4] noted that each suicide affects, on average, five family members and up to 135 community members. Considering that approximately 700,000 people worldwide die by suicide annually [5], estimates are that 60 million people are added to the suicide-loss survivors' population each year. These numbers alone underscore the importance of understanding how we can help those bereaved by suicide in their psychosocial journey of dealing with their grief.

A large body of data has found that suicide-loss survivors are at greater risk than other bereaved individuals and the general population for many severe psychological and health problems. Research has revealed that suicide-loss survivors present higher levels of depression, and suicidal ideation and behavior [6,7] than other bereaved individuals. Moreover, those bereaved by suicide can experience adverse grief reactions such as prolonged grief disorder symptoms [8,9] which can persist even several years following the loss.

Suicide loss has also been associated with other deleterious psychosocial consequences. The turmoil of guilt, shame, anger, and embarrassment that follow the suicide of a loved one (e.g., [10]) seems to facilitate social withdrawal and efforts to conceal the cause of the significant other's death [11,12]. These behaviors, along with low self-disclosure [13], low perceived social support [14], and high levels of thwarted belongingness [15], have all been found to characterize suicide-loss survivors. Together, these features can be viewed as a call to action to devise ways to help those bereaved by suicide.

We have co-edited a Special Issue which focuses on suicide bereavement and postvention, with the aim to highlight the current knowledge and advances in the research, practices, and policies regarding suicide bereavement. The Special Issue includes 19 papers which cover a wide range of topics, including (a) the impact of suicide on individuals and communities, and adverse grief reactions, (b) the impact of suicide on health professionals, and (c) coping and support for those bereaved by suicide. The findings of these studies are an important step forward in our understanding of additional approaches to support those bereaved by suicide in their healing journey.

1. Impact of Suicide and Adverse Grief Reactions

Macdonald and colleagues [16] conducted a qualitative study with participants who had lost a male family member by suicide. The participants reported on their perception of the suicide and their struggles with meaning making and finding closure. Mathieu and colleagues [17] compared bereavement after different modes of death six months after the loss and did not find a difference in coping styles. However, having a previous mental health diagnosis was associated with increased avoidant and problem-focused coping, and stigma and shame were associated with increased avoidant coping. Women were more likely to report using adaptive coping than men. Goodall and colleagues [18] conducted a systematic review on continuing bonds in suicide bereavement and found that continuing bonds can be experienced in various ways and that most people bereaved by suicide tended to perceive it primarily as a positive experience that may help with coping and meaning making.

Little is known about suicide bereavement in later life, and to address this gap Hafford-Letchfield and colleagues [19] explored how suicide loss can intersect with ageing and what supports are needed for this population. Interestingly, several participants had guided their social network to receive the necessary support. In another important study, Tiech Fire and colleagues [20] focused on school staff, with the aim of understanding the impact of student suicides on post-trauma and grief symptoms among teachers, counsellors, and school principals. The authors found that homeroom teachers suffered more from complicated grief and post-traumatic stress disorder (PTSD) compared to psychologists and counsellors and, as such, should receive more preparatory training. Additionally, in the context of schools, Khalid and colleagues [21] found encouraging results from a training program that increased preparedness and skills in school staff to respond to student suicides. Rivant and colleagues [22] focused on suicide bereavement among ethnic minority groups. They found that this population suffers from a lack of support and high prevalence of stigma in the aftermath of suicide loss. These preliminary results broaden our understanding of a minority population which requires special attention, more visibility, and better access to support services.

Andriessen and colleagues [23] examined the experiences of adolescents who participate in qualitative research interviews about suicide-related experiences, as there is a perception of risk regarding asking young people about these topics. Importantly, the findings indicated that bereaved adolescents, as well as parents and clinicians, could safely participate in research interviews regarding their experiences of grief after suicide, and they highly valued this opportunity to share their experiences. These findings can be used to build future study designs to help us to better understand the processes of grief after suicide among adolescents.

Several studies in our Special Issue examined deleterious and long-term effects of suicide bereavement. In a latent class analysis, Grafiadeli and colleagues [24] found that about half of the examined population showed elevated prolonged grief disorder symptoms, and one-third of the sample also showed PTSD symptoms. In a six-year longitudinal study, Levi-Belz and Brinbaum [15] highlighted that suicide bereavement facilitated higher levels of depression and suicide ideation. Other studies also emphasized the moderators of these negative outcomes. Levi-Belz and Brinbaum [15] found that the sense of belongingness can serve as a buffer against depression, as suicide-loss survivors with higher levels of belongingness were less vulnerable to depression at later assessments. Levi-Belz and Ben-Yaish [9] highlighted interpersonal factors, such as social support and self-disclosure, that serve as moderators of prolonged grief symptoms following suicide bereavement. Pitman and colleagues [25] examined whether bereavement by various causes had a deterrent effect on alcohol and drug use in bereaved individuals. They found no group differences regarding reduced alcohol use, but a significantly greater proportion of people bereaved by sudden unnatural causes, including suicide, reduced/stopped drug use post-bereavement compared to people bereaved by sudden natural causes.

2. Impact of Suicide on Mental Health Professionals

Both health and mental health professionals are at risk of losing a client or a colleague to suicide. The integrated review of 17 articles conducted by Causer and colleagues [26] emphasized the impact that a suicide by a colleague may have on workers in healthcare and other settings. They found that the perceptions of grief are complicated by professional identities and workplace cultures. Tamworth and colleagues [27] revealed that losing a patient to suicide can be a profoundly traumatic experience for psychiatrists. Peer support was key in processing their grief. Pisnoli and Van der Hallen [28] focused on mental health professionals who had a client die by suicide. These authors examined the relationships between attitudes toward (client) suicide and the psychological impact of client suicide as perceived by the therapists. It was found that those who believe that "suicide can and should be prevented" reported a higher impact in the form of short-term emotional and long-term professional impacts. Together, these studies indicate a need for systemic postvention, enhanced peer support, and promotion of self-care among mental health professionals.

3. Coping and Support for Those Bereaved by Suicide

Agnietė Čepulienė and Skruibis [29] conducted a qualitative interview study and analyzed the data using reflexive thematic analysis. They found that spirituality can function as a resource after a loved one's suicide and can even contribute to post-traumatic growth after the loss, while spirituality-related issues, such as stigmatization and a lack of personally meaningful traditions, can contribute to higher distress among suicide-loss survivors. In a scoping review, Higgins and colleagues [30] indicated the potential effectiveness of peer-led suicide bereavement support, but also highlighted a need for rigorous design and evaluation of peer-led interventions in this field. Hybholt and colleagues [31] explored the experiences of members of peer-led support groups in Denmark and Ireland. Although some participants found it difficult to participate in a peer support group, most participants described them as safe and supportive spaces that aided in their grief process. Griffin and colleagues [32] surveyed participants of peer-led support groups and found a significant improvement in wellbeing and grief reactions, adjusting for time since bereavement. The participants reported that the groups provided a sense of belonging and hope. This study underscored the enduring mental health challenges for those bereaved by suicide and the need for the ongoing availability of peer-led support in postvention.

In conclusion, the studies included in this Special Issue emphasize the short- and long-term impact of suicide loss, the needs of those bereaved by suicide, and appropriate interventions in the aftermath of suicide loss. The included studies showed that suicide bereavement impact various populations, far beyond the nuclear family of the deceased. Moreover, these studies highlight the risk of long-term mental health challenges and adverse grief reactions among those bereaved by suicide. Health professionals, often involved in suicide prevention, should not be overlooked with regard to support after a loss by suicide.

4. Public Health Approach to Postvention

As individuals and population groups may experience suicide loss differently, and their needs for support may evolve over time, various support options must be available. A recent review of the literature indicates that adjusting the support to the level of the impact of the bereavement, and focusing the support on the grief rather than on other outcomes are key characteristics of effective suicide bereavement support [33]. As indicated by studies on peer-led support in this Special Issue, the involvement of trained peers who may serve as role models or community members enhancing the social support network, may contribute to the effectiveness of suicide bereavement support [33].

According to the public health model, universal interventions target those who experience little impact from a death by suicide. Such interventions may include, for example, leaflets, fact sheets, or online information about suicide bereavement for wide audiences. Selective interventions target people with moderate grief reactions and include support groups, community and educational support, and training for health professionals. Indicated interventions, focusing on people with adverse grief and mental health reactions, may include specific grief therapy, and psychological and psychiatric support [33]. Adopting a public health approach to postvention can help to better tailor service delivery to the needs of the bereaved individuals and to align postvention with suicide prevention programs, which are also often based on this public health model. The training of service providers, including peers, volunteers, and health professionals, is paramount. Further evaluation and research will strengthen the evidence of effectiveness of the interventions and service delivery in this important field.

Author Contributions: Conceptualization, Y.L.-B. and K.A.; investigation, Y.L.-B., K.A. and K.K. writing—original draft preparation, Y.L.-B., K.A. and K.K.; writing—review and editing, Y.L.-B., K.A. and K.K. All authors have read and agreed to the published version of the manuscript.

Conflicts of Interest: The author declares no conflict of interest.

References

1. Mann, J.J.; Michel, C.A.; Auerbach, R.P. Improving suicide prevention through evidence-based strategies: A systematic review. *Am. J. Psychiatry* **2021**, *178*, 611–624. [CrossRef] [PubMed]
2. Cerel, J.; Brown, M.M.; Maple, M.; Singleton, M.; Van de Venne, J.; Moore, M.; Flaherty, C. How many people are exposed to suicide? Not six. *Suicide Life-Threat. Behav.* **2019**, *49*, 529–534. [CrossRef] [PubMed]
3. Andriessen, K.; Rahman, B.; Draper, B.; Dudley, M.; Mitchell, P.B. Prevalence of exposure to suicide: A meta-analysis of population-based studies. *J. Psychiatr. Res.* **2017**, *88*, 113–120. [CrossRef] [PubMed]
4. Levi-Belz, Y.; Feigelman, W. Pulling together–The protective role of belongingness for depression, suicidal ideation and behavior among suicide-bereaved individuals. *Crisis* **2021**, *43*, 278–288. [CrossRef] [PubMed]
5. WHO (World Health Organization). Suicide Prevention–Overview. 2019. Available online: https://www.who.int/health-topics/suicide#tab=tab_1 (accessed on 1 April 2022).
6. Maple, M.; Cerel, J.; Sanford, R.; Pearce, T.; Jordan, J. Is exposure to suicide beyond kin associated with risk for suicidal behavior? A systematic review of the evidence. *Suicide Life-Threat. Behav.* **2017**, *47*, 461–474. [CrossRef] [PubMed]
7. Levi-Belz, Y.; Gilo, T. Emotional distress among suicide survivors: The moderating role of self-forgiveness. *Front. Psychiatry* **2020**, *11*, 341. [CrossRef]
8. Levi-Belz, Y.; Aisenberg, D. Interpersonal predictors of suicide ideation and complicated-grief trajectories among suicide bereaved individuals: A four-year longitudinal study. *J. Affect. Disord.* **2022**, *282*, 1030–1035. [CrossRef]
9. Levi-Belz, Y.; Ben-Yaish, T. Prolonged Grief Symptoms among Suicide-Loss Survivors: The Contribution of Intrapersonal and Interpersonal Characteristics. *Int. J. Environ. Res. Public Health* **2022**, *19*, 10545. [CrossRef]
10. Sveen, C.A.; Walby, F.A. Suicide survivors' mental health and grief reactions: A systematic review of controlled studies. *Suicide Life-Threat. Behav.* **2008**, *38*, 13–29. [CrossRef]
11. Oexle, N.; Feigelman, W.; Sheehan, L. Perceived suicide stigma, secrecy about suicide loss and mental health outcomes. *Death Stud.* **2020**, *44*, 248–255. [CrossRef]
12. Jordan, J.R. Lessons learned: Forty years of clinical work with suicide loss survivors. *Front. Psychol.* **2020**, *11*, 766. [CrossRef]
13. Levi-Belz, Y.; Lev-Ari, L. "Let's talk about it": The moderating role of self-disclosure on complicated grief over time among suicide survivors. *Int. J. Environ. Res. Public Health* **2019**, *16*, 3740. [CrossRef]
14. Levi-Belz, Y. With a little help from my friends: A follow-up study on the contribution of interpersonal characteristics to posttraumatic growth among suicide-loss survivors. *Psychol. Trauma: Theory Res. Pract. Policy* **2019**, *11*, 895–904. [CrossRef]
15. Levi-Belz, Y.; Birnbaum, S. Depression and Suicide Ideation among Suicide-Loss Survivors: A Six-Year Longitudinal Study. *Int. J. Environ. Res. Public Health* **2022**, *19*, 16561. [CrossRef]
16. Macdonald, D.; Nicolopoulos, A.; McLachlan, K.; Habak, S.; Christensen, H.; Boydell, K.M. Tragedies, Fates, Furies and Fuels: Narratives of Individuals Bereaved by Suicide. *Int. J. Environ. Res. Public Health* **2022**, *19*, 8715. [CrossRef]
17. Mathieu, S.; Todor, R.; De Leo, D.; Kõlves, K. Coping Styles Utilized during Suicide and Sudden Death Bereavement in the First Six Months. *Int. J. Environ. Res. Public Health* **2022**, *19*, 14709. [CrossRef]
18. Goodall, R.; Krysinska, K.; Andriessen, K. Continuing Bonds after Loss by Suicide: A Systematic Review. *Int. J. Environ. Res. Public Health* **2022**, *19*, 2963. [CrossRef]
19. Hafford-Letchfield, T.; Hanna, J.; Grant, E.; Ryder-Davies, L.; Cogan, N.; Goodman, J.; Rasmussen, S.; Martin, S. "It's a Living Experience": Bereavement by Suicide in Later Life. *Int. J. Environ. Res. Public Health* **2022**, *19*, 7217. [CrossRef]
20. Tiech Fire, N.; Gvion, Y.; Alkalay, S.; Zalsman, G. The "Forgotten Grievers": The Impact of Pupil Suicide on Post-Trauma and Grief Symptoms in School Staff. *Int. J. Environ. Res. Public Health* **2022**, *19*, 12160. [CrossRef]
21. Khalid, N.; Zapparrata, N.; Loughlin, K.; Albright, G. Postvention as Prevention: Coping with Loss at School. *Int. J. Environ. Res. Public Health* **2022**, *19*, 11795. [CrossRef]
22. Rivart, P.; Wainwright, V.; Flynn, S.; Hunt, I.M.; Shaw, J.; Smith, S.; McGale, B.; McDonnell, S. Ethnic Minority Groups' Experiences of Suicide Bereavement: A Qualitative Exploratory Study. *Int. J. Environ. Res. Public Health* **2021**, *18*, 11860. [CrossRef] [PubMed]
23. Andriessen, K.; Krysinska, K.; Rickwood, D.; Pirkis, J. The Reactions of Adolescents, Parents and Clinicians to Participating in Qualitative Research Interviews Regarding Adolescents Bereaved by Suicide and Other Traumatic Death. *Int. J. Environ. Res. Public Health* **2022**, *19*, 452. [CrossRef] [PubMed]
24. Grafiadeli, R.; Glaesmer, H.; Wagner, B. Loss-Related Characteristics and Symptoms of Depression, Prolonged Grief, and Posttraumatic Stress Following Suicide Bereavement. *Int. J. Environ. Res. Public Health* **2022**, *19*, 10277. [CrossRef] [PubMed]

25. Pitman, A.; Stevenson, F.; Osborn, D. Investigating Whether Bereavement by Suicide and Other Unnatural Causes Has a Deterrent Effect on Alcohol or Drug Use in Young Adults. *Int. J. Environ. Res. Public Health* **2022**, *19*, 13245. [CrossRef]
26. Causer, H.; Spiers, J.; Efstathiou, N.; Aston, S.; Chew-Graham, C.A.; Gopfert, A.; Grayling, K.; Maben, J.; van Hove, M.; Riley, R. The Impact of Colleague Suicide and the Current State of Postvention Guidance for Affected Co-Workers: A Critical Integrative Review. *Int. J. Environ. Res. Public Health* **2022**, *19*, 11565. [CrossRef]
27. Tamworth, M.; Killaspy, H.; Billings, J.; Gibbons, R. Psychiatrists' Experience of a Peer Support Group for Reflecting on Patient Suicide and Homicide: A Qualitative Study. *Int. J. Environ. Res. Public Health* **2022**, *19*, 14507. [CrossRef]
28. Pisnoli, I.; Van der Hallen, R. Attitudes toward Suicide and the Impact of Client Suicide: A Structural Equation Modeling Approach. *Int. J. Environ. Res. Public Health* **2022**, *19*, 5481. [CrossRef]
29. Čepulienė, A.A.; Skruibis, P. The Role of Spirituality during Suicide Bereavement: A Qualitative Study. *Int. J. Environ. Res. Public Health* **2022**, *19*, 8740. [CrossRef]
30. Higgins, A.; Hybholt, L.; Meuser, O.A.; Eustace Cook, J.; Downes, C.; Morrissey, J. Scoping Review of Peer-Led Support for People Bereaved by Suicide. *Int. J. Environ. Res. Public Health* **2022**, *19*, 3485. [CrossRef]
31. Hybholt, L.; Higgins, A.; Buus, N.; Berring, L.L.; Connolly, T.; Erlangsen, A.; Morrissey, J. The Spaces of Peer-Led Support Groups for Suicide Bereaved in Denmark and the Republic of Ireland: A Focus Group Study. *Int. J. Environ. Res. Public Health* **2022**, *19*, 9898. [CrossRef]
32. Griffin, E.; O'Connell, S.; Ruane-McAteer, E.; Corcoran, P.; Arensman, E. Psychosocial Outcomes of Individuals Attending a Suicide Bereavement Peer Support Group: A Follow-Up Study. *Int. J. Environ. Res. Public Health* **2022**, *19*, 4076. [CrossRef]
33. Andriessen, K.; Krysinska, K.; Kõlves, K.; Reavley, N. Suicide postvention service models and guidelines 2014–2019: A systematic review. *Front. Psychol.* **2019**, *10*, 2677. [CrossRef]

International Journal of
Environmental Research and Public Health

MDPI

Article

Ethnic Minority Groups' Experiences of Suicide Bereavement: A Qualitative Exploratory Study

Pauline Rivart [1,*], Verity Wainwright [1], Sandra Flynn [1], Isabelle M. Hunt [1], Jenny Shaw [1,2,3], Shirley Smith [4,5], Barry McGale [5,6] and Sharon McDonnell [1,6]

1 The Centre for Mental Health and Safety, Faculty of Biology, Medicine and Health, University of Manchester, Manchester M13 9PL, UK; verity.wainwright@manchester.ac.uk (V.W.); sandra.m.flynn@manchester.ac.uk (S.F.); isabelle.m.hunt@manchester.ac.uk (I.M.H.); jennifer.j.shaw@manchester.ac.uk (J.S.); sharon.mcdonnell@suicidebereavementuk.com (S.M.)
2 Greater Manchester Mental Health NHS Foundation Trust, Manchester M25 3BL, UK
3 Independent Advisory Panel on Deaths in Custody, London SW1H 9AJ, UK
4 If U Care Share Foundation, Chester-le-Street, Chester DH2 2EY, UK; shirley@ifucareshare.co.uk
5 Support After Suicide Partnership, London SE1 7NQ, UK; mcgaleb@aol.com
6 Suicide Bereavement UK, Ramsbottom BL0 9EX, UK
* Correspondence: pauline.rivart@manchester.ac.uk

Abstract: It is estimated that between 36,000 and 360,000 people are affected by suicide every year in the UK, and a proportion may develop depression and post-traumatic stress disorder, or engage in high-risk behaviours. Recent systematic analyses have revealed a clear gap in research on suicide bereavement in minority ethnic groups. This study aimed to understand the experiences and support needs of individuals from ethnic minority backgrounds bereaved by suicide and was the first in the UK to investigate this matter. The study was a secondary analysis of data. Participants were 7158 people residing in the UK who completed an online survey about their experiences of suicide. Free-text qualitative responses of 227 participants who did not identify as White British were analysed using thematic analysis. Four themes were identified: maladaptive coping strategies, emotional processes following suicide, lack of support from agencies, and the importance of mental health awareness. Ethnic minority groups reported a lack of support despite attempts to engage with services, noted the prevalence of stigma within ethnic minority groups, and expressed a need to tackle this. These preliminary results suggest that ethnic minority individuals require visible and accessible services that can successfully engage with and support them.

Keywords: suicide; bereavement; ethnic minority; support; stigma; postvention

Citation: Rivart, P.; Wainwright, V.; Flynn, S.; Hunt, I.M.; Shaw, J.; Smith, S.; McGale, B.; McDonnell, S. Ethnic Minority Groups' Experiences of Suicide Bereavement: A Qualitative Exploratory Study. *Int. J. Environ. Res. Public Health* **2021**, *18*, 11860. https://doi.org/10.3390/ijerph182211860

Academic Editors: Karl Andriessen, Karolina Krysinska and Yossi Levi-Belz

Received: 22 October 2021
Accepted: 9 November 2021
Published: 12 November 2021

1. Introduction

Every year, around 6000 people die by suicide in the United Kingdom [1] and it is estimated that between six and 60 individuals are affected by each suicide [2]. However, more recent evidence suggests that up to 135 individuals could be affected [3] and it is possible that the number of people bereaved by suicide every year in the UK has been underestimated. Data from the past few years also indicate that suicide rates are increasing in the UK [1].

People bereaved by suicide experience physical and mental health issues, including a higher risk of attempting suicide and dying by suicide, developing depression and post-traumatic stress disorder (PTSD), and engaging in high-risk behaviours (such as substance abuse) [4,5]. In the UK, around 10% of individuals bereaved by suicide will attempt to take their own lives, whilst 8% will withdraw from education or resign from their job [6]. Compared to people bereaved by other sudden modes of death, higher levels of stigma, shame, and guilt are also reported in this group [7]. As a result, suicide bereavement is considered to be a highly stigmatizing type of bereavement, limiting the help-seeking behaviour of those bereaved [7,8].

Support in the UK for those bereaved by suicide, known as postvention, is limited and inconsistent [9], despite the breadth of research showing that postvention is highly valued by people bereaved by suicide and can assist in the grieving process [4,10]. Therefore, the National Institute of Care Excellence (NICE) recommended that support be made more available across the UK and that the bereaved should be fully involved in the development of postvention programs [9]. This was further acknowledged by the latest NHS Long-Term Plan which highlighted the importance of putting into place consistent support for those bereaved by suicide in the UK [11]. As part of this plan, the Department of Health and Social Care announced that funding would be provided across England to develop services offering individual or group support sessions or referrals to appropriate mental health services for the bereaved [12]. Similar strategies exist in the devolved nations of the UK [13–15].

Whilst postvention needs are individual, certain specific groups (e.g., children or ethnic minority groups) may have particular needs [16,17]. Understanding how and why these may differ would be beneficial to the development of postvention, for example by considering how the support needs of these individuals may be influenced by cultural beliefs (e.g., religion and spirituality [18]). Yet, there has been very little research on these groups [19]. Whilst there seems to be no significant differences between ethnic groups in terms of grieving processes [20], bereaved Black Caribbean individuals in the UK reported poorer health outcomes compared to their White counterparts, following the loss of a relative or friend to a progressive disease [21]. This outcome was associated with housing and legal issues following the loss of a loved one and suggested that individuals belonging to a minority ethnic group may have different support needs [20,21].

Additional barriers to help-seeking that are not found among White British individuals also need to be acknowledged when considering postvention interventions. Shefer et al. [22] argued that minority ethnic groups face two types of stigma when seeking help for mental health support: perceived or external stigma (i.e., perceived inequalities and discrimination within medical institutions), which can lead to feelings of mistrust towards professionals, as well as internal stigma regarding perceptions of mental health and associated feelings of shame and guilt within their community. In the UK, people from ethnic minority groups have reported that their cultural identity can be an obstacle to identifying psychological distress and seeking help for the latter [23]. As a result, general mental health provision in the UK has taken some steps towards tackling inequalities in mental health among ethnic minority groups, notably by increasing representation and diversity in mental health professionals [24]. Finally, there is evidence that ethnic minority groups are heterogeneous and differ from one another in terms of help-seeking [25] and this needs to be considered by postvention interventions.

Research has highlighted that individuals bereaved by suicide are a high-risk, vulnerable group, specifically regarding suicide ideation, but it is largely unknown how ethnic minority groups experience suicide bereavement. As a result, it is also unknown how these groups can be supported to reduce the impact of suicide bereavement on physical and mental health outcomes. This study aimed to address these gaps in knowledge by exploring the experiences of individuals bereaved by suicide in people from a minority ethnic background. Ultimately, furthering our knowledge has the potential to inform research and practice in the suicide bereavement field with regards to ethnic minorities in the UK, notably to support the development of specialized postvention services if required.

2. Materials and Methods

The current study presents a secondary analysis of qualitative survey data. This analysis was undertaken as part of the first author's Master of Science degree.

2.1. Materials

The survey designed for the primary study included 71 questions, of which 41 were checkbox questions, 26 were free-text questions, and 4 were both checkbox and free-text questions. The questions revolved around three main topics: suicide bereavement in general and in the workplace, the impact of suicide on the bereaved, and access to support following suicide bereavement. For the current study, seven free-text questions (see Table 1) were selected for analysis by the lead researcher (first author) and reviewed by the wider research team. This selection was guided by previous literature on the impact of suicide bereavement and research on grief outcomes and help-seeking among ethnic minority groups. Questions which could potentially inform future practice and the development of postvention with these groups were also retained. The questions, the range of response length (i.e., shortest answer to longest answer), the mean response length in words, and the response frequency (i.e., how many participants responded) for each question can be found in Table 1.

Table 1. Free-text questions and response characteristics.

Question	Range of Response Length (in Words)	Mean Response Length (in Words)	Response Frequency *N* (%)
36. After the person had died by suicide did you feel this led to you engaging in high risk behavior? (Examples of high risk behaviors might include fighting, driving dangerously, unprotected sexual activities, excessive spending, or adopting behaviors that were similar to how the person died.) If yes, please tell us about the high risk behavior in the space provided below.	2–25	6	35 (15%)
37. If you have any other comments on how the death of this person affected you, please tell us in the space provided below.	2–642	52	103 (45%)
52. Are there any other organizations that you feel could have offered you help? If so, please tell us in the space provided below.	1–92	18	53 (23%)
53. From your experience, how and when would you like to be approached when being offered support by organizations?	1–122	14	73 (32%)
58. Please tell us about your experience of using support services in the space provided below.	1–145	33	68 (30%)
60. Please provide further information on why you did not access support services.	1–114	28	37 (16%)
64. Please tell us anything else you think might help to improve support for people bereaved or affected by suicide.	1–353	41	55 (24%)

2.2. Participants

The primary study recruited 7158 participants using convenience and snowball sampling. Participants were eligible to take part if they were aged 18 or older, lived in the UK, and perceived themselves as affected and/or bereaved by suicide. For the secondary analysis, the sample included all participants identifying as non-White British. The current study included 227 participants (3.2% of the primary sample): 174 females (77%), 48 males (21%), and 1 non-binary individual. The mean age of participants was 38.79 years old (SD = 12.44) and ranged from 18 to 72 years old. In terms of ethnicity, 106 (46.7%) participants identified as multiple/Mixed race, 73 (32.2%) as Asian, 32 (14.1%) as Black Caribbean or African, and 16 (7%) as belonging to any other ethnic background (including Arab and Middle Eastern). Further information on the ethnic background of participants can be found in Table 2. For nearly a fifth (18.5%) of the sample, suicide had occurred between two and five years ago, and for around a sixth (15%), it had occurred between ten and twenty years ago. The rest of the sample had been bereaved for less than six months (8.8%), between six months and a year (7.5%), between one year and two years (8.4%), between five and ten years (10.1%), and over 20 years (6.6%). One participant in six had lost a friend (17.6%), one in seven a sibling (14.1%), and one in ten (9.3%) a relative other than a parent, child, or sibling (e.g., aunt/uncle, grandparent, cousin). The rest of the sample had lost a parent (6.6%), a spouse or partner (5.3%), or a child (4.4%).

Table 2. Ethnic background of participants.

Ethnic Group	*N*	Frequency
Mixed/Multiple ethnic groups	106	46.7%
White and Black Caribbean	36	15.9%
White and Black African	8	3.5%
White and Asian	39	17.2%
Other Mixed/Multiple ethnic background	23	10.1%
Asian/Asian British	73	32.2%
Indian	48	21.1%
Pakistani	9	4%
Bangladeshi	2	0.9%
Chinese	4	1.8%
Other Asian background	10	4.4%
Black/African/Caribbean/Black British	32	14.1%
African	9	4%
Caribbean	19	8.4%
Other Black/African/Caribbean background	4	1.8%
Other ethnic group	16	7%
Arab	2	0.9%
Any other ethnic background	14	6.2%

2.3. Procedure

The primary study advertised the survey on the Centre for Mental Health and Safety, University of Manchester, UK website and the Support After Suicide Partnership website between July 2017 and August 2018, as well as newspapers, social media, on radio and TV, conferences and by word of mouth. Participants could complete the survey online or using a paper version. The survey was preceded by the participant information sheet. The latter informed participants that completing the survey would be taken as informed consent, and that they could withdraw at any time without penalty. However, due to the anonymity of the responses, participants were informed that, once the survey was completed, it would not be possible to identify and withdraw their responses from the collected data. Information signposting individuals to support organizations was provided at the end of the survey which was designed to provide participants with support and to minimise any potential distress as much as possible. The survey was expected to take 30 min to complete.

2.4. Data Analysis

Thematic analysis was used to identify themes and patterns in the data. This analysis technique was chosen over other qualitative approaches as the focus of this study was on the experiences associated with suicide bereavement, rather than how participants made sense of or narrated these experiences [26]. As this was an exploratory study, the data were analyzed using an inductive approach where the experiences of the participants led to patterns and potential theory [26].

The thematic analysis was conducted using NVivo (Version 12; QSR International, 2020) and was guided by the steps described by Braun and Clarke [26]. The coding of the data was undertaken by the first author. Once all data were analyzed, codes were reviewed and similar concepts merged whilst broader ones were split into more specific codes. A codebook was created to document this process and was shared with the research team. Codes were then organized into prevalent patterns found in the sample and to answer the research question with as accurate an interpretation of the data as possible.

3. Results

Four themes were identified: maladaptive coping strategies, emotional processes following suicide, lack of support from agencies, and the importance of mental health awareness. Each theme will be discussed using illustrative quotes.

3.1. Maladaptive Coping Strategies

Participants reported engaging in maladaptive coping strategies as a consequence of suicide bereavement. This was first reflected in a number of participants recalling they had engaged in harmful behaviors, such as self-harm, suicide ideation, or suicide attempts, to try and cope with their loss. One participant reported that "in the years after her death, I have had thoughts of self-harm and thoughts of suicide although I do not think I ever would have done either of these things, the thoughts were very distressing" (participant 190). Another participant reported experiences of suicide ideation: "I have had fleeting thoughts of not wanting to go on myself" (participant 184). Experiencing harmful behaviors as a consequence of suicide bereavement was one of the most reported experiences in the sample.

Another maladaptive coping strategy adopted by suicide loss survivors was increased alcohol use. One participant explained engaging in "excessive drinking and drugs" (participant 134) and another reported that their loss had "increased my alcoholism" (participant 225). Whilst this was not as prevalent as experiences of suicide ideation or self-harm, it was one of the most reported high-risk behaviors.

These high-risk behaviors seemed at times to be related to the initial emotional reactions of participants to the death. Indeed, a majority reported anger as a significant experience associated with suicide bereavement. One participant reported feeling "awful angry at the situation" (participant 65) whilst another explained that they "felt very angry that he had done it" (participant 144). Experiences of anger in the sample seemed to be particularly intense and at times overwhelming. In some cases, this intense anger resulted in other maladaptive coping behaviors: one participant reported that their "upset and anger about the suicide as well as other problems led to dangerous driving" (participant 226). Overall, these maladaptive coping strategies seemed to be an initial response to the experienced loss, similar to acute grief.

3.2. Emotional Processes following Suicide

Participants reported experiencing guilt associated with their own behavior towards the deceased before the suicide, feeling that they could have done more to help or could have been more present for the deceased:

> *I have a sense of guilt and shame—that is not overpowering but always lingers. I wonder what I could have done to help. I feel like I could have reached out in better ways. I knew that he was going through a tough time—and I feel like I didn't do enough to help when I knew (participant 163).*

Several participants also reported feeling guilt regarding their inability to notice the distress the deceased had been experiencing before their death, and as a consequence felt that they had failed them: "Overriding guilt of not having known more deeply about how he was feeling or done more to help" (participant 106). As such, guilt was one of the main feelings reported by participants.

In addition, a significant number of participants reported feelings of abandonment. They felt as if they had been left behind by the deceased and were having difficulties making sense of the world without them. One participant explained that "there was no one left for me or to be proud of me because he was the only person who really parented [sic] me, so I felt hopeless in living because there was no one to make proud or happy" (participant 197). Such feelings were especially heightened in participants who reported experiencing suicide ideation before the death: "It affected me because having had my own suicidal thoughts it felt like the option had now been removed" (participant 64). This participant reported experiencing feelings of anger and resentment, as their own issues were minimized and not being attended to following the suicide. On the other hand, another participant reported that: "I think it has made me feel a bit more likely to act on suicidal feelings as I think of him having done it and not feeling in pain when I am in a lot of emotional pain" (participant 137). This participant reported having experienced severe mental health issues in the past, and their experience of losing someone to suicide seemed to have enabled them to draw parallels between their own mental health difficulties and that of their loved one. Ultimately, this resulted in them feeling increasingly vulnerable to suicide. Feelings of abandonment were reported by many participants but manifested themselves in different ways from one participant to another.

These feelings of guilt and abandonment seemed to influence the participants' understanding of the suicide and how they made sense of it, known as 'meaning-making' in the literature [27]. For most participants, this was manifested by a need to replay potential scenarios. Indeed, participants reported attempts to construct a narrative to try and understand the suicide due to their feelings of guilt: "often [I] would try and replay scenarios and put myself in his shoes but found it really hard to understand how this could happen" (participant 12). Another participant who also experienced this phenomenon described it as a distressing experience: "Nothing prepares you to lose someone that way. You go insane thinking of all the times that you could have helped or done more and it consumes you" (participant 98). Arguably, the need to replay scenarios could be explained by the shock and disbelief usually associated with suicide deaths. Participants may have felt they needed to try and make sense of the decision-making of the deceased. This can also be seen as an attempt to make sense of their own perceived responsibility for the death, and to resolve issues of guilt.

The distress associated with these emotional processes suggested an obvious need for support; yet, support following suicide bereavement was found to be lacking.

3.3. Lack of Support from Agencies

The majority of participants reported a clear lack of support which was manifested through different scenarios. First, most participants reported a lack of awareness regarding support provision. They explained that they did not receive any support information from agencies and, as a result, had to seek support on their own. One participant reported that "if there were any support services around suicide, they were invisible to me (or very low profile)" (participant 194), suggesting that the taboo around suicide impacted the visibility and accessibility of support. This was supported by another participant who reported that "there was not much indication of what help/support was available" (participant 178). These accounts suggest that participants were proactive in attempting to access support; however, the inability to find appropriate support may have led them to experience a sense of helplessness and hopelessness, which, in turn, may have put them at an increased risk of suicide themselves.

On the other hand, although some participants reported having received some form of support information, their attempts to access support were unsuccessful. One participant reported trying to access support by calling a number of different agencies:

> *There was no help for me. Charities [sic] couldn't deal with bereavement. Other charity [sic] who are supposed to deal with bereavement just gave me phone numbers and I was constantly calling different number [sic] and it was getting me nowhere (participant 130).*

Another participant described a similar experience: "asked for help but was ignored, by many organizations, people push you from pillar to post" (participant 208). Participants reported limited empathy and compassion from agencies throughout the process of seeking help, and subsequently described having very little faith in them. This, once again, may have led to feelings of hopelessness and helplessness. Overall, the experiences reported by the participants suggested that there was no structured and coordinated approach to support provision between agencies.

Few participants accessed support and had negative experiences with professionals. Indeed, a number of these participants reported that professionals providing support for suicide bereavement had behaved in an inconsiderate manner. When asked about their experience of receiving support, one participant described it as very negative: "Dreadful—the visitor just kept saying 'no wonder he killed himself, he had so many problems'" (participant 90). Another participant who reached out to their GP and asked to be put on medication to cope with their loss reported that "one doctor actually said to me, 'Well, pills won't bring your brother back will they'" (participant 203). Overall, participants explained that such experiences served to invalidate their difficulties and made them even less likely to access support.

The police were cited numerous times by participants as an agency which provided insufficient support. Participants believed that, as police officers are usually among the first responders when a suicide occurs, they should provide more support for people bereaved by suicide: "I believe the police are the first people who have contact with you when you experience suicide and they don't give you any information where to seek support" (participant 176). Similar to other agencies, there did not seem to be a straightforward procedure following a suicide death. One participant explained that "apparently I should have had more support from the police and should have an assigned officer but [I] had nothing. I did receive a call from the police who said they were sending me a booklet which never arrived" (participant 214). This may have reinforced feelings of abandonment and isolation in participants, especially since the police are usually regarded as an agency that can provide help in times of crisis.

Overall, the lack of coordinated support made help-seeking after suicide bereavement difficult at a time when participants already felt severely distressed and, as a result, often felt unable to seek help.

3.4. Importance of Mental Health Awareness

A large proportion of the sample mentioned the need for mental health awareness when asked what could be improved regarding suicide bereavement support. This suggestion was the most common in the sample when participants were asked about potential areas of improvement for suicide bereavement support. This seemed to reflect the participants' belief that there was a need for prevention before postvention. In the sample, the importance of mental health awareness was reported to serve two main purposes.

First, participants believed that increased mental health awareness could help people experiencing suicide ideation. One participant explained there is a need for "more openly available information on the importance of mental health and that there are people who have suffered the same and come through to the other side" (participant 12). There was also a belief that such awareness could also help bereaved individuals, who themselves may be at an increased risk of suicide ideation/attempt following suicide bereavement. This was reported by another participant: "there was (still is) some taboo around discussing suicide, so some education to prepare people for if/when it happens around them; an awareness issue" (participant 194). Overall, participants suggested that increased mental health awareness could help both people with mental health issues and bereaved individuals.

Second, participants suggested that mental health awareness could reduce the stigma experienced by individuals bereaved by suicide. Indeed, a number of participants reported experiencing stigma following suicide bereavement and they believed that talking more openly about mental health issues could help. One participant suggested: "have people talk and share, there is so much stigma around this from the place I come from" (participant 151, of Indian ethnicity). This was highlighted by another participant: "have to remove the stigma around the word suicide" (participant 156). More importantly, a few participants mentioned that this was even more needed among certain ethnic minority groups. Indeed, participants explained that suicide is rarely discussed in some communities and that this can reinforce stigma: "There seems to be a lack of support groups within minority ethnic groups and a lack of faith led support groups as suicide is often not talked about and the individual can feel isolated" (participant 79, of Pakistani ethnicity). This was also reported by another participant from an Asian background: "I think there should be support offered within the British Asian Community who still see it as something to hide and shameful" (participant 86, of Indian ethnicity). Participants suggested that stigma is an even more prevalent issue among people from a minority ethnic background; therefore, the need for awareness was considered more critical in this group. The words "hide", "shameful", and "not talked about" particularly suggested the taboo around suicide for minority ethnic groups. Several participants reported being told to get on with their lives and to not dwell on the suicide death for too long. Consequently, participants felt rejected by and isolated from their own community, which may have further impacted their ability to seek help.

4. Discussion

4.1. Findings

This study aimed to explore and understand the experiences of individuals bereaved by suicide in ethnic minority groups, specifically in relation to support needs and access to support. Four themes were identified. Participants reported a range of maladaptive coping strategies including harmful behaviors, increased alcohol use, and anger issues as a result of suicide bereavement. Participants also reported that their understanding of the suicide had been largely influenced by emotional processes following the latter which, for most participants, was guided by feelings of guilt and abandonment, leading to further distress. A lack of support was identified. Overall, participants reported that they had sought help but had received very limited support or none at all. This suggested that participants were proactive in seeking support and willing to engage with services. The need for increased mental health awareness within ethnic minority communities was also expressed, notably to tackle the stigma experienced by people bereaved by suicide, which was perceived as more significant in some communities. This finding suggested that these groups may need culture-specific support, including mental health support, to prevent issues of stigma and isolation.

The maladaptive behaviors evidenced here have been reported previously in studies looking at individuals bereaved by suicide in general. McDonnell et al. [4] reported an increased risk of engaging in suicidal behaviors, such as self-harm, and high-risk behaviors including substance abuse, unsafe driving, or sexual promiscuity. Guilt and stigma have also been found to be significant experiences of suicide bereavement, whereby individuals blame themselves for death and experience social rejection from others [8]. Previous studies in the UK have revealed that accessing support is difficult and often not immediate, and that many bereaved individuals are not offered any formal or informal support [28]. Wainwright et al. [10] have also reported that people bereaved by suicide often feel helpless and hopeless when trying to access professional help. In our sample, participants felt that professionals were not well-equipped to support them. General practitioners in the UK have previously reported that they did not feel they had adequate training to support individuals bereaved by suicide [29]. This evident need for specialized support for individuals bereaved by suicide demonstrated by existing literature was also apparent in this sample.

The experiences reported in this study seem to be in line with the literature on individuals bereaved by suicide, especially with regards to coping behaviors, poor access to support, and associated feelings of helplessness [4,10]. Whilst there may be some variation within different ethnic minority communities, the findings suggest that, overall, these groups report very similar experiences and support needs to the ethnic majority. Ethnic specific factors only emerged in the last theme when participants expressed potentially higher levels of shame and stigma. Shefer et al. [22] argued that ethnic minority groups experience more stigma and shame within their community than the ethnic majority regarding mental health issues, which in turn affects help-seeking behavior for such issues [23]. A previous study by Barnes [16] in the US revealed that African American individuals bereaved by suicide often had no support system due to the stigma associated with suicide. Participants reported that, in order to avoid stigma, they would not discuss the suicide further [16]. However, the data collected as part of the current study could not indicate whether lack of support was linked to the ethnic background of participants or was simply a reflection of the overall lack of support offered to individuals bereaved by suicide. Indeed, the current analysis did not directly compare the sample used in this study to a White British sample.

4.2. Limitations

This is the first study in the UK looking at the experiences and needs of minority ethnic groups in relation to suicide bereavement. This specific focus constitutes the main strength of the study. However, some of its limitations should be addressed. This study discussed the experiences of ethnic minority communities as a homogeneous group and doing so may have led to a failure to identify differences between specific groups (e.g., between Asian and Black communities). It could be that certain experiences (e.g., heightened stigma) were specific to one group, which the design of this study could not identify. In addition, there were no specific questions on the views and needs of minority groups which may have elicited further material on differences between groups. No data on immigration was collected as part of this study, although previous research has evidenced that immigrant populations may present different help-seeking patterns from the majority population for mental health issues [30]. Our data also did not allow us to draw conclusions regarding the presence of external stigma as defined by Shefer et al. [22]. Future research could thus benefit from investigating how immigration and external stigma may impact the needs of individuals bereaved by suicide in ethnic minority groups. Finally, it is important to note that snowball sampling may have limited the representativeness of the sample and that 21.6% of the sample had been bereaved for over ten years. Thus, their experiences may not reflect current support provision in the UK.

4.3. Future Research and Practical Implications

This study begins to explore potential differences in experiences of suicide bereavement and support needs between the ethnic majority and ethnic minority groups but it was, nonetheless, unclear if aspects of suicide bereavement were more specific to or more prevalent in ethnic minority groups, as well as differences between these groups. The experiences of these communities would benefit from further research to ensure that our understanding of their experiences and needs is comprehensive and accurate.

The findings suggest that ethnic minority groups require services that are accessible and visible, and that can address their specific needs, especially to tackle stigma. Some participants felt that professionals failed to engage with them and, therefore, that there may be a need to develop support and services that are culture-specific. It is important to note that participants did report engaging with services when given the opportunity. This is a significant finding in relation to the development of postvention services. In October 2019, the Department of Health and Social Care revealed that, as part of the NHS Long-Term Plan, the government would provide GBP 1 million to ten areas across England to develop suicide bereavement support [12]. Such support will be made available to relatives and friends of the deceased shortly after the death. It could include individual sessions with trained counsellors or volunteers, support groups, or referrals to appropriate mental health services. The support offer will differ between areas to link with already available services, such as local charities, the police, coroners, and healthcare professionals. Further research will need to clarify whether support for the ethnic majority in the UK is appropriate for people from a minority ethnic background. However, the preliminary findings of this study suggest that offering immediate accessible support, as described in the NHS Long-Term Plan, to the bereaved could be a first solid step towards better support provision for ethnic minority groups. It is hoped that similar policies will be adopted in Wales, Scotland, and Northern Ireland.

The Support After Suicide Partnership and their recently published *Core Standards for Developing and Running a Suicide Bereavement Support Service* [31] may also further support the development of postvention services for ethnic minority groups in the UK. One of these

Core Standards, "Awareness and Access", aims to ensure that services are accessible to all, and address equality and diversity issues within suicide bereavement support [31]. This study provides an insight into the needs of ethnic minority groups and, along with future research, could provide a basis for the development of evidence-based support for individuals from an ethnic minority background.

5. Conclusions

This is the first study in the UK to engage with ethnic minority groups and provide a preliminary understanding of their experiences and needs in relation to suicide bereavement. The data suggested that experiences reported by these communities were similar to those described in previous research on predominantly White samples. Participants reported a clear lack of support despite attempts to seek help and engage with services, and expressed the need for a coordinated and structured approach to suicide bereavement support. These initial findings suggest that providing support that is accessible and visible, tackles stigma, and enables professionals to successfully engage with these groups could make a significant difference to the experiences of people bereaved by suicide.

Author Contributions: Conceptualization, P.R. and V.W.; data curation, S.F. and S.M.; formal analysis, P.R.; funding acquisition, S.M.; investigation, S.F., I.M.H., J.S., S.S., B.M. and S.M.; methodology, P.R. and V.W.; project administration, S.M.; resources, S.F., I.M.H., J.S., S.S., B.M. and S.M.; supervision, V.W. and S.M.; validation, P.R. and V.W.; visualization, P.R.; writing—original draft, P.R.; writing—review & editing, P.R., V.W., S.F., I.M.H., J.S., S.S., B.M. and S.M. All authors have read and agreed to the published version of the manuscript.

Funding: The current study did not receive any funding. The primary study was supported by the Monument Trust (£10,000).

Institutional Review Board Statement: Ethical approval for the primary study was obtained from the University of Manchester Research Ethics Committee (reference number: 2017-1818-2599). The current study was covered by the ethical approval for the primary study.

Informed Consent Statement: Informed consent was obtained from all subjects involved in the study.

Data Availability Statement: Research data are not shared.

Acknowledgments: We would like to thank the participants who took part in the study and shared their experiences. We would also like to thank the advisory group for their guidance and expertise, and the Support After Suicide Partnership (SASP).

Conflicts of Interest: The authors declare no conflict of interest.

References

1. Office for National Statistics. Suicide in England and Wales: 2019 Registrations. 2020. Available online: https://www.ons.gov.uk/peoplepopulationandcommunity/birthsdeathsandmarriages/deaths/bulletins/suicidesintheunitedkingdom/2019registrations (accessed on 20 September 2021).
2. Pitman, A.L.; Hunt, I.M.; McDonnell, S.J.; Appleby, L.; Kapur, N. Support for Relatives Bereaved by Psychiatric Patient Suicide: National Confidential Inquiry into Suicide and Homicide Findings. *Psychiatr. Serv.* **2016**, *68*, 337–344. [CrossRef] [PubMed]
3. Cerel, J.; Brown, M.M.; Maple, M.; Singleton, M.; Van de Venne, J.; Moore, M.; Flaherty, C. How Many People Are Exposed to Suicide? Not Six. *Suicide Life Threat. Behav.* **2018**, *49*, 529–534. [CrossRef] [PubMed]
4. McDonnell, S.; Hunt, I.M.; Flynn, S.; Smith, S.; McGale, B.; Shaw, J. From Grief to Hope: The Collective Voice of Those Bereaved or Affected by Suicide in the UK. 2020. Available online: https://supportaftersuicide.org.uk/resource/from-grief-to-hope-the-collective-voice-of-those-bereaved-or-affected-by-suicide-in-the-uk/ (accessed on 22 September 2021).
5. Young, I.T.; Iglewicz, A.; Glorioso, D.; Lanouette, N.; Seay, K.; Ilapakurti, M.; Zisook, S. Suicide bereavement and complicated grief. *Dialogues Clin. Neurosci.* **2012**, *14*, 177–186. [CrossRef]
6. Pitman, A.L.; Osborn, D.P.J.; Rantell, K.; King, M.B. Bereavement by suicide as a risk factor for suicide attempt: A cross-sectional national UK-wide study of 3432 young bereaved adults. *BMJ Open* **2016**, *6*, e009948. [CrossRef] [PubMed]
7. Pitman, A.L.; Osborn, D.P.J.; Rantell, K.; King, M.B. The stigma perceived by people bereaved by suicide and other sudden deaths: A cross-sectional UK study of 3432 bereaved adults. *J. Psychosom. Res.* **2016**, *87*, 22–29. [CrossRef] [PubMed]
8. Pitman, A.L.; Stevenson, F.; Osborn, D.P.J.; King, M.B. The stigma associated with bereavement by suicide and other sudden deaths: A qualitative interview study. *Soc. Sci. Med.* **2018**, *198*, 121–129. [CrossRef]

9. National Institute for Health and Care Excellence. Suicide Prevention Quality Standard [QS189]. 2019. Available online: Nice.org.uk/guidance/qs189 (accessed on 20 September 2021).
10. Wainwright, V.; Cordingley, L.; Chew-Graham, C.; Kapur, N.; Shaw, J.; Smith, S.; McGale, B.; McDonnell, S. Experiences of support from primary care and perceived needs of parents bereaved by suicide: A qualitative study. *Br. J. Gen. Pract.* **2020**, *70*, e102–e110. [CrossRef] [PubMed]
11. National Health Service. The NHS Long Term Plan. 2019. Available online: Longtermplan.nhs.uk/wp-content/uploads/2019/08/nhs-long-term-plan-version-1.2.pdf (accessed on 20 September 2021).
12. Department of Health and Social Care. Suicide Bereavement Support to Be Made Available across England. 2019. Available online: https://www.gov.uk/government/news/suicide-bereavement-support-to-be-made-available-across-england (accessed on 20 September 2021).
13. Department of Health. Protect Life 2—Suicide Prevention Strategy. 2019. Available online: Health-ni.gov.uk/protectlife2 (accessed on 20 September 2021).
14. Scottish Government. Scotland's Suicide Prevention Action Plan. 2018. Available online: https://www.gov.scot/binaries/content/documents/govscot/publications/strategy-plan/2018/08/scotlands-suicide-prevention-action-plan-life-matters/documents/00539045-pdf/00539045-pdf/govscot%3Adocument/00539045.pdf (accessed on 20 September 2021).
15. Welsh Parliament. NDM7211 Member Debate under Standing Order 11.21 (iv) Suicide Bereavement Support. 2020. Available online: https://business.senedd.wales/mgIssueHistoryHome.aspx?IId=27512&Opt=0 (accessed on 20 September 2021).
16. Barnes, D.H. The Aftermath of Suicide among African Americans. *J. Black Psychol.* **2006**, *32*, 335–348. [CrossRef]
17. Cerel, J.; Fristad, M.A.; Weller, E.B.; Weller, R.A. Suicide-Bereaved Children and Adolescents: A Controlled Longitudinal Examination. *J. Am. Acad. Child Adolesc. Psychiatry* **1999**, *38*, 672–679. [CrossRef]
18. Andriessen, K.; Castelli Dransart, D.A.; Cerel, J.; Maple, M. Current Postvention Research and Priorities for the Future. *Crisis* **2017**, *38*, 202–206. [CrossRef]
19. Maple, M.; Pearce, T.; Sanford, R.; Cerel, J.; Castelli Dransart, D.A.; Andriessen, K. A Systematic Mapping of Suicide Bereavement and Postvention Research and a Proposed Strategic Research Agenda. *Crisis* **2018**, *39*, 275–282. [CrossRef] [PubMed]
20. Klein, S.; Alexander, D.A. Good grief: A medical challenge. *Trauma* **2003**, *5*, 261–271. [CrossRef]
21. Koffman, J.; Donaldson, N.; Hotopf, M.; Higginson, I.J. Does ethnicity matter? Bereavement outcomes in two ethnic groups living in the United Kingdom. *Palliat. Supportive Care* **2005**, *3*, 183–190. [CrossRef]
22. Shefer, G.; Rosem, D.; Nellums, L.; Thornicroft, G.; Henderson, C.; Evans-Lacko, S. 'Our community is the worst': The influence of cultural beliefs on stigma, relationships with family and help-seeking in three ethnic communities in London. *Int. J. Soc. Psychiatry* **2013**, *59*, 534–544. [CrossRef]
23. Memon, A.; Tayler, K.; Mohebati, L.M.; Sundin, J.; Cooper, M.; Scanlon, T.; de Visser, R. Perceived barriers to accessing mental health services among black and minority ethnic (BME) communities: A qualitative study in Southeast England. *BMJ Open* **2016**, *6*, e012337. [CrossRef] [PubMed]
24. NHS England. Advancing Mental Health Equalities Strategies. 2020. Available online: England.nhs.uk/wp-content/uploads/2020/10/00159-advancing-mental-health-equalities-strategy.pdf (accessed on 3 August 2021).
25. Hunt, I.M.; Robinson, J.; Bickley, H.; Meehan, J.; Parsons, R.; McCann, K.; Flynn, S.; Burns, J.; Shaw, J.; Kapur, N.; et al. Suicides in ethnic minorities within 12 months of contact with mental health services: National clinical survey. *Br. J. Psychiatry* **2003**, *183*, 155–160. [CrossRef]
26. Braun, V.; Clarke, V. Using thematic analysis in psychology. *Qual. Res. Psychol.* **2006**, *3*, 77–101. [CrossRef]
27. Cerel, J.; Sanford, R.L. It's Not Who You Know, It's How You Think You Know Them: Suicide Exposure and Suicide Bereavement. *Psychoanal. Study Child* **2018**, *71*, 76–96. [CrossRef]
28. Pitman, A.L.; Rantell, K.; Moran, P.; Sireling, L.; Marston, L.; King, M.; Osborn, D. Support received after bereavement by suicide and other sudden deaths: A cross-sectional UK study of 3432 young bereaved adults. *BMJ Open* **2017**, *7*, e014487. [CrossRef]
29. Foggin, E.; McDonnell, S.; Cordingley, L.; Kapur, N.; Shaw, J.; Chew-Graham, C. GPs' experiences of dealing with parents bereaved by suicide: A qualitative study. *Br. J. Gen. Pract.* **2016**, *66*, e737–e746. [CrossRef]
30. Markova, V.; Sandal, G.M.; Pallesen, S. Immigration, acculturation, and preferred help-seeking sources for depression: Comparison of five ethnic groups. *BMC Health Serv. Res.* **2020**, *20*, 648. [CrossRef] [PubMed]
31. Support after Suicide Partnership. Core Standards for Developing and Running a Suicide Bereavement Support Service. 2021. Available online: https://hub.supportaftersuicide.org.uk/resource/core-standards-for-developing-and-running-a-suicide-bereavement-support-service/ (accessed on 3 November 2021).

International Journal of
Environmental Research and Public Health

MDPI

Article

The Reactions of Adolescents, Parents and Clinicians to Participating in Qualitative Research Interviews Regarding Adolescents Bereaved by Suicide and Other Traumatic Death

Karl Andriessen [1,*], Karolina Krysinska [1], Debra Rickwood [2] and Jane Pirkis [1]

1 Centre for Mental Health, Melbourne School of Population and Global Health, The University of Melbourne, Parkville, VIC 3010, Australia; karolina.krysinska@unimelb.edu.au (K.K.); j.pirkis@unimelb.edu.au (J.P.)
2 Faculty of Health, University of Canberra, Canberra, ACT 2617, Australia; Debra.Rickwood@canberra.edu.au
* Correspondence: karl.andriessen@unimelb.edu.au

Abstract: There are concerns that involving adolescents bereaved by suicide and other traumatic death in research may cause distress and harm. However, no study has investigated such bereaved adolescents' research experiences. In addition, no study has looked at the experiences of parents and clinicians as participants in adolescent suicide and traumatic death bereavement research. This study aimed to explore the short-term impact of research participation experienced by adolescents, parents, and clinicians. A total of 61 participants (adolescents, n = 17; parents, n = 12; clinicians, n = 32) filled out a short survey within two weeks of having taken part in a qualitative interview study. Data were analyzed descriptively. Most participants had experienced no distress while participating and no negative effects of participating; rather, participation was experienced as helpful for them and they would highly recommend participating in a study like this to others. A few adolescents and parents reported some distress, related to anxiety about participation and the unpleasantness of grief memories. The study clearly indicates that bereaved adolescents, parents and clinicians can safely participate in research interviews regarding their experiences of grief and help after suicide, generally valuing the opportunity to share their experience. To prevent and mitigate potential distress, training of research staff and implementation of appropriate participant distress protocols are imperative. Future studies could include longitudinal follow-up of participants to assess any longer-term consequences.

Keywords: grief; bereavement; suicide; traumatic death; research participation; ethics; research ethics

Citation: Andriessen, K.; Krysinska, K.; Rickwood, D.; Pirkis, J. The Reactions of Adolescents, Parents and Clinicians to Participating in Qualitative Research Interviews Regarding Adolescents Bereaved by Suicide and Other Traumatic Death. *Int. J. Environ. Res. Public Health* **2022**, *19*, 452. https://doi.org/10.3390/ijerph19010452

Academic Editor: Paul B. Tchounwou

Received: 18 November 2021
Accepted: 24 December 2021
Published: 1 January 2022

1. Introduction

1.1. Rationale

Adolescents who are bereaved by the death of someone close to them, such as a family member or a friend, often experience short-term and long-term impacts regarding their grief, mental health and social functioning [1–5]. Experiencing a death is often an unfamiliar, disruptive and stressful event in their lives, leading to acute grief reactions such as crying, and feelings of numbness, sadness and longing for the deceased person [2–5]. Compared to other types of bereavement, adolescents bereaved by suicide and other traumatic death can experience more pronounced feelings of shock, guilt, anger, and abandonment [3,4,6]. They can struggle more with "why" questions, finding meaning in the loss, and experience less social support [1–3,6]. In addition, they have an increased risk of mental health problems, such as depression, anxiety, posttraumatic stress disorder, and long-term increased risk of suicidal behavior compared to other bereaved and non-bereaved adolescents [7–9].

While negative grief reactions are more prominent, there is also emerging evidence of personal or posttraumatic growth in this population [10,11]. The growth is understood as a positive psychological transformation that occurs as the result of a struggle with a traumatic and highly distressing event [12]. Traumatically bereaved adolescents can experience personal or posttraumatic growth in various domains, including increased appreciation of life and relationships, increased maturity and self-care, and finding new opportunities, for example, regarding school or professional career paths [3,11,12]. Nonetheless, bereavement by suicide and other traumatic death among adolescents can disconnect them from their friends and rupture the family equilibrium [13–15], which in turn may affect their parents' and guardians' capacity to support them and/or refer them to professional help [16].

Given the potential ramifications of bereavement by suicide and other traumatic death in adolescents, conducting research with this population poses important ethical challenges. The Australian National Statement on Ethical Conduct in Human Research (2007) (Updated 2018) [17] places value on principles of research merit and integrity, justice, beneficence, and respect. Researchers are required to minimize and manage potential risks to participants, and risks are only justified when they are outweighed by potential benefits for participants or the community. The National Statement [17] stipulates that research with bereaved minors/adolescents requires specific attention to participants' capacity to understand the research and consent.

Important concerns regarding participant safety and the potential negative impact of research participation have been voiced in various research fields involving vulnerable populations, including suicide [18–21], trauma and violence [22,23], palliative care [24], psychiatry [25,26], and bereavement [27,28]. In studies with adults bereaved by suicide, research ethics committees have expressed concerns about potential harm to research participants, particularly that talking about grief experiences may traumatize them and increase their suicide risk [29–31]. Further, there are concerns about whether research participants who are negatively impacted will receive enough support [31].

Nonetheless, a recent systematic review found that most participants in suicide bereavement studies experience research participation positively [32]. Positive experiences included gaining insight into their grief experience and providing opportunities for helping others. However, a minority of participants reported unpleasant or negative experiences when participating in studies, such as being reminded of painful experiences, e.g., [27,33]. Despite the importance of these findings, the reviewed studies had several limitations [32]. Most were psychological autopsy studies (in which participants provide information about the deceased person rather than about themselves), and only one study included adolescents in the sample [34]. Hence, little is known about the experiences of adolescents of being involved in research regarding their own grief and help-seeking after a loss by suicide or other traumatic death. In addition, no study has looked at the experiences of parents and clinicians as participants in adolescent suicide and traumatic death bereavement research. This study aimed to address this gap by exploring the short-term impact of research participation experienced by adolescents, parents, and clinicians.

1.2. Background: Original Study

1.2.1. Sampling

The original study, about which participants were then asked about their participation experience, was a qualitative study that examined how to best help adolescents bereaved by suicide and other traumatic death. Although details have been published [13,35], we summarize the original study here to provide context for the current study of participant experiences.

The original study adhered to the COREQ criteria [36] and involved a purposive sample of three groups of participants (adolescents, parents and clinicians) recruited in Australia between October 2019 and March 2020. Adolescents could participate if they had lost a family member or friend through suicide or other cause when they were aged between 12 and 18 years, and had experienced the death between six months and 10 years before participating in the study. Parents could participate if they were the parent of an eligible adolescent. Adolescents and parents could participate whether or not their parents or adolescent children participated. Clinicians could participate if they had at least five years of experience with providing professional help to bereaved adolescents.

Study participants (N = 72) included a total of 20 adolescents, 18 parents and 34 clinicians. The adolescent participants (16 girls, 4 boys) were aged 14 to 26 years (M = 19.50, SD = 2.95). They had lost their father (n = 9), brother (n = 3), sister (n = 2), mother (n = 2), other family member (n = 2), or friend (n = 2), by suicide (n = 18) or by accident (n = 2), on average 4 years previously (M = 3.92, SD = 2.49, range 1 to 10 years).

The parents (18 mothers) were aged 43 to 60 years (M = 53.20, SD = 4.35). The deceased person was the child's father (n = 10), brother (n = 4) or sister (n = 4), and the person had died by suicide (n = 13), accident (n = 2), manslaughter (n = 1), illness (n = 1) and undetermined (n = 1), on average 5 years previously (M = 5.31, SD = 2.89, range 1.5 to 10 years).

The clinicians (28 females, 6 males) were aged 26 to 71 years (M = 48.47, SD = 11.35). About one in four clinicians had five to nine years of experience (n = 8, 23.5%), 12 others (35.3%) had 10 to 19 years, and 14 (41.2%) had more than 20 years of experience.

1.2.2. Data Collection and Analyses

Participants could choose between taking part in an individual interview by telephone or an in-person group interview [37–41]. We conducted 28 individual interviews, and 11 group interviews with 44 participants. Individual interviews lasted, on average, 46 min (range 19–76), and group interviews were an average of 77 min (range 40–102).

The interview guide was adaptable for individual and group interviews. It consisted of open-ended questions allowing for probes and follow-up questions. The lead questions addressed different aspects of the help (for example: "In your opinion, what help should be provided to a bereaved adolescent?", "How should the help be provided?", "How long after the loss?", "What is the role of professional versus peer support?", "What are the characteristics that make help helpful?"). Adopting an inductive approach, we analyzed the interview data through a codebook-based thematic analysis [42–44].

2. Materials and Methods

2.1. Survey

We created a short survey with five questions to assess the participants' experiences of taking part in the individual or group interviews. Table 1 lists the survey questions. Participants were asked to answer the first four questions on a 5-point Likert-type scale (1. Not at all; 5. Absolutely). After each question, participants could write a free text comment. Question five was an open-ended question asking the participant if anything important to them was not discussed during the interview. The survey was anonymous, did not collect sociodemographic data, and could be filled out in less than five minutes.

Table 1. Survey questions.

	Questions
1.	At the time of participating, did you feel distressed when you participated in the Focus Group/interview?
2.	Today, do you think that participating helped you in anyway?
3.	Today, do you feel that participating had any negative effects for you?
4.	Would you recommend participating in a study like this to others?
5.	Was there a topic very important to you that you thought we should discuss but did not? If yes, please describe.

2.2. Sampling

Participants who took part in an in-person group interview received a hard copy of the survey at the end of the interview, and/or by email, as requested. We emailed the survey to those who had taken part in a telephone interview. We asked all participants to return the survey within two weeks, and 85% (61 out of 72) did so. This included 85% (17 out of 20) of the adolescents, 67% (12 out of 18) of the parents, and 94% (32 out of 34) of the clinicians. This amounted to 96% (n = 42) of group interview participants and 68% (n = 19) of individual interview participants.

Of those who returned the survey, 54% (n = 33) provided at least one comment in the free text boxes of the four survey questions and the open-ended question. This included 41% (n = 7) of the adolescents, 58% (n = 7) of the parents, and 59% (n = 19) of the clinicians. There was no difference between the three groups (χ^2 (2) = 1.589, p = 0.452). Additionally, an equal proportion of individual (53%, n = 10) and group participants (55%, n = 23) provided comments (χ^2 (1) = 0.024, p = 0.877).

2.3. Analyses

We uploaded all data into SPSS version 26 [45]. We analyzed the quantitative data descriptively and results are presented as frequencies and percentages. Levels 1 and 2 of the 5-point Likert-type scale are considered as low, level 3 is moderate/medium, and levels 4 and 5 are high. We used the Kruskal–Wallis H test to test if there were differences between the three groups of participants. We used Kendall's tau-b correlation coefficient (2-tailed) to investigate the correlations between the data derived from the four Likert-type questions.

As most comments provided in the free text boxes were short (a few words or a short sentence), we opted to summarize the qualitative data allowing for a quantitative and qualitative report of the findings [46]. The summary applied a deductive approach, based on the survey questions. Two researchers (KA and KK) summarized the data independently and compared their report; there were no discrepancies. The research team discussed the progress and results to maximize consistency throughout the study.

2.4. Ethical Approval

The Human Research Ethics Committee of The University of Melbourne approved the study (ID 1955213). All participants provided written informed consent.

3. Results

3.1. Quantitative Findings

3.1.1. At the Time of Participating, Did You Feel Distressed When You Participated in the Focus Group/Interview?

Most participants (75%, n = 46) reported that they had no or hardly any distress (18%, n = 11) while participating in the interview. Four participants (6.6%, three adolescents, one parent) reported moderate levels, and none reported high levels of distress (Figure 1). The Kruskal–Wallis test indicated a significant difference between the three groups (H(2) = 11.772, p = 0.003). Pairwise comparisons showed that adolescent participants scored higher than clinicians ($adj.\ p$ = 0.002).

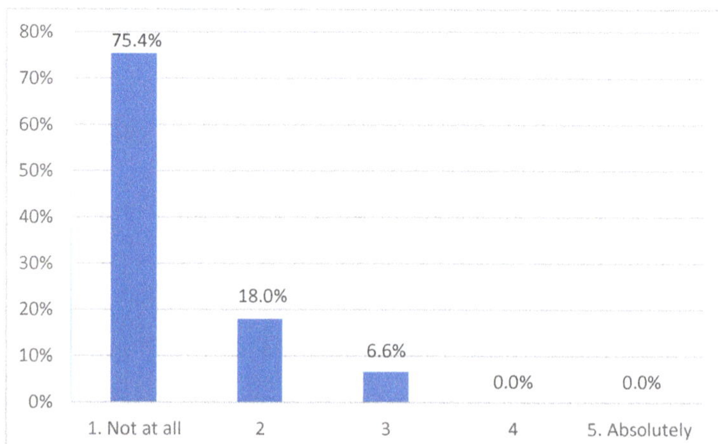

Figure 1. Experienced level of distress.

3.1.2. Today, Do You Think That Participating Helped You in Anyway?

About 75% ($n = 46$) of participants reported they felt that participation was helpful, 16% ($n = 10$) reported a medium level of perceived helpfulness, and 8% (2 adolescents, 1 parent, 2 clinicians) reported low levels (Figure 2). There was no difference between the three groups ($H(2) = 0.210$, $p = 0.900$).

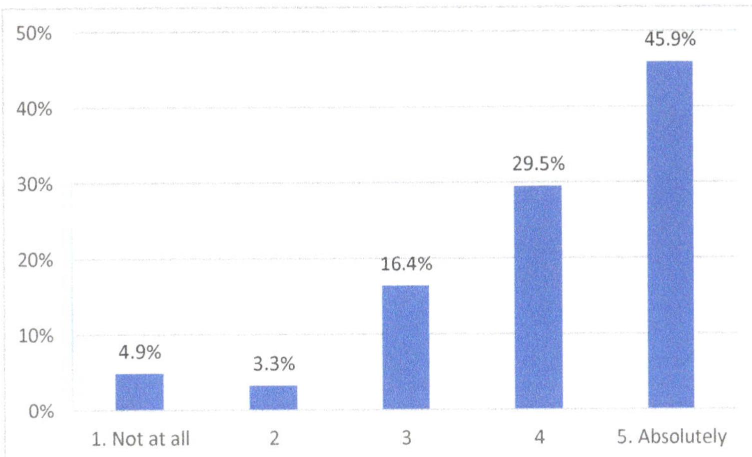

Figure 2. Perceived helpfulness.

3.1.3. Today, Do You Feel That Participating Had Any Negative Effects for You?

About 95% ($n = 58$) of participants reported having experienced no or hardly any negative effects of participating (Figure 3); 1.6% (1 adolescent) reported a moderate level, and 3.2% (1 adolescent, 1 parent) a high level of experienced negative effects. The Kruskal–Wallis test found a significant difference between the three groups ($H(2) = 11.836$, $p = 0.003$). Pairwise comparisons showed that adolescent participants scored higher than clinicians (*adj.* $p = 0.002$).

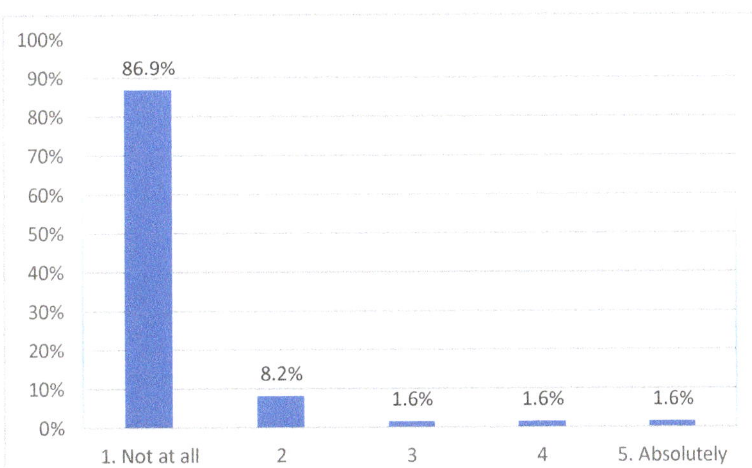

Figure 3. Experienced negative effects.

3.1.4. Would You Recommend Participating in a Study Like This to Others?

Almost all participant (97%, n= 59) said they would absolutely or close to absolutely recommend participating in a study like this to others, with the other 3.3% (2 parents) being somewhat likely to recommend (Figure 4). There was no difference between the three groups ($H(2) = 0.568$, $p = 0.753$).

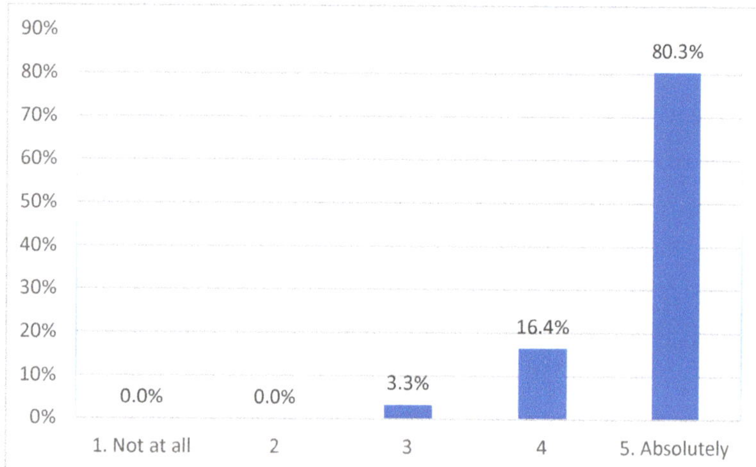

Figure 4. Recommending taking part to others.

3.1.5. Correlation Analysis

Table 2 presents the correlations, showing that there were significant associations between questions 1 and 3 (p = 0.007), and questions 2 and 4 (p = 0.026). This reveals that greater feelings of distress during participation were weakly related to more negative experienced effects of participation, and that greater perceived helpfulness of participation was weakly related to recommending participation to others.

Table 2. Correlations.

	1	2	3	4
1. At the time of participating, did you feel distressed when you participated in the Focus Group/interview?	1			
2. Today, do you think that participating helped you in anyway?	0.056	1		
3. Today, do you feel that participating had any negative effects for you?	0.335 **	−0.071	1	
4. Would you recommend participating in a study like this to others?	0.000	0.264 *	0.077	1

*. Correlation is significant at the 0.05 level (2-tailed). **. Correlation is significant at the 0.01 level (2-tailed).

3.2. *Qualitative Findings*

3.2.1. At the Time of Participating, Did You Feel Distressed When You Participated in the Focus Group/Interview?

Six participants provided a comment: 2 adolescents, 1 parent, and 3 clinicians. Two adolescents reported having felt some anxiety but were otherwise fine, as stated by one: "Have anxiety but it was really okay". One parent reported feeling "distress" after hearing stories of other participants, but the participant continued that this was experienced as a "helpful connection and catharsis", which helped to reflect "how far" they "had come in their own grief". Three clinicians reported having felt safe and supported while participating in the interview, as stated by this clinician: [It was] "Very supportive and informative".

3.2.2. Today, Do You Think That Participating Helped You in Anyway?

Twenty-two participants commented on this question: 5 adolescents, 5 parents, and 12 clinicians. Four adolescents and two parents experienced participating as being helpful for themselves, as stated by this adolescent: "It helped me open up and share my experience". One adolescent and three parents referred to being able to use their experiences to help others in similar situations, for example, one parent wrote: "I appreciate being able to share to help those behind me". Eight clinicians commented that participating in the interview was a learning experience, as stated by this clinician: "It's always beneficial to talk about one's practice and reflect on the strategies used in your daily work". Three other clinicians experienced the interview also as a validation and encouragement, as said by this clinician: "It reminds practitioners to continue doing great work". Still, one clinician commented on the interview as a "one-way conversation".

3.2.3. Today, Do You Feel That Participating Had Any Negative Effects for You?

Two participants noted a comment (1 adolescent, 1 parent). The adolescent stated that: "It brought up unpleasant memories but not overwhelming". The parent reported having felt sad and having cried after the interview "particularly after listening to other participants, their loss of their loved ones".

3.2.4. Would You Recommend Participating in a Study Like This to Others?

Seven participants provided a comment (2 parents, 5 clinicians). The parents emphasized the importance of listening to others "across cultures and genders" to "identify evidence-based approaches that will work". In addition, it may help us "learn how to best equip and cope with a suicide loss". The clinicians would recommend participating because it "gives support and facilitates time to reflect, focus, and share ideas about a neglected cohort". In addition, it can "increase education and awareness" for clinicians, and "support for young people".

3.2.5. Was There a Topic Very Important to You That You Thought We Should Discuss but Did Not?

Eighteen participants (4 adolescents, 3 parents, 11 clinicians) wrote a comment in the last free text box of the survey, although several comments appeared to be more about what participants thought was important regarding grief and bereavement, rather than about topics that were not addressed in the interviews. Three adolescents emphasized what they saw as crucial for helping bereaved adolescents. One wrote: "trust and knowing that there is good information and discussion out there", and another highlighted the "need to let the younger teens know it's not weak to speak and get help". In addition, one parent elaborated on the "secrecy around suicide" and the tendency of blaming someone for a suicide, which may hinder bereaved adolescents. Subsequently, this parent argued for increased literacy around dealing with grief in society. Two clinicians pointed at cultural sensitivity in providing help, and financial impact of the loss, as important topics for further discussion.

One parent commented on the composition of the group in which she participated. Most participants in her group had lost a husband to suicide and only one participant had lost a child to suicide. Hence, the participant recommended that groups in future studies could be more balanced regarding types of relationship.

Twelve participants (1 adolescent, 2 parents, 9 clinicians) confirmed that everything important had been discussed in their interview, as exemplified by one adolescent who noted: "I believe we covered everything vital", and participants expressed gratitude for having been involved, as stated by this clinician: "I'm sure there is more, but right now it feels good".

4. Discussion

This study was a first to investigate the reactions of adolescents, parents, and clinicians regarding their participation in a study on adolescents bereaved by suicide and other traumatic death. Most participants reported that they experienced no distress while participating and no negative effects of participating. Rather, they found participation helpful for them and said they would definitely recommend participating in a study like this to others. These findings reflect results of bereavement studies with parents [47,48], siblings [49], and people bereaved by suicide [30,32], which reported that research participation was mostly a positive experience, with few negative experiences, and participants perceiving participation as being beneficial for themselves and others [30,32,47]. In addition, the correlation analysis showed that there is no contradiction between reporting distress or negative effects of participation and experiencing participation as helpful and recommending it to others. This finding is corroborated by suicide-related research with adolescents and trauma research with adults suggesting that emotional distress can be understood as an indicator of engagement in a data collection process rather than as an indicator of harm [50–52].

Although the overall levels of distress and negative effects reported in our study were low, adolescents reported the highest scores, and a few mentioned having experienced anxiety or unpleasant memories. This has also been reported with regard to adolescents participating in health-related studies [53]. As suggested above, these emotional reactions may be due to participants' engagement with the research project [51], and a study by Hawton and colleagues [34] suggested that this may lead to them benefitting more from participating than adults. However, it may also point to the presence of emotional problems [53,54]. One study in a systematic review [53] examining children's and adolescents' reactions to participating in biomedical and health-related studies found that the presence of emotional problems in children was the only variable associated with short-lived negative research participation experiences [55]. Objective variables such as age, gender, methods of data collection, and topic/health condition examined in the studies, were not associated with participants' appraisals of study participation [53,55]. Another study on pain also reported that age and level of pain did not affect responses regarding experiences of research participation [56]. However, as in our study, young participants still recommended participation to others [56]. Nonetheless, while only a few participants reported negative experiences, the phenomenon needs further investigation in bereaved adolescents, especially since both short-term deterioration and improvement in mood have been reported in adolescent mental health research [54].

Parents in our study were very positive about research participation. This is corroborated by other research with parents who participated in a study concerning the sudden and traumatic death of their children [27]. All parents in that study reported positive experiences and none regretted participating, despite 73% experiencing the interviews as (a little to very) painful [27]. As in our study, having the opportunity to share experiences and being able to help others contributed to a positive experience [27]. Still, one parent in our study reported being emotionally affected, although this parent still perceived participation as helpful. Follow-up data from adults participating in suicide research revealed that participants can be susceptible to short-term deteriorations in mood [57]. However, any negative effects of participation were confined to the days immediately following the study and this temporary deterioration in mood did not increase risk of suicidal thoughts [57].

As with research with bereaved adolescents, research with suicide bereaved adults indicated that objective factors such as gender of participants, their relationship to the deceased, the method of suicide, and time since loss appeared to have little effect on their experiences of participating in a research interview [58]. Moreover, research regarding mental health in adults showed that the presence of mental health problems did not differentiate participants with negative or positive experiences of research participation [59]. Hence, it may be that the presence of emotional problems has a stronger impact on the research experience of children and adolescents compared to adults, though further research is needed to ascertain such differences between children/adolescents and adults.

Clinicians in our study found research participation to be a learning experience. This is supported by findings from studies with clinicians who had lost a patient to suicide, who reported their research participation as a learning and therapeutic experience [60,61]. The finding is also in line with literature on substance abuse research participation [62]. Clinical research participants were more willing to use research findings in practice, especially those with favorable attitudes toward evidence-based practices and whose agencies supported professional growth. The combined findings of our study and others from the literature [60,62] suggest that research participation may reinforce clinicians' willingness to use research findings in practice, thus contributing to quality of services.

Although our participants expressed gratitude for being involved in the research, a phenomenon also noted in the literature [63], our data suggest that from the three groups of participants, adolescents potentially experience the most distress and negative effects of participation in research interviews. Thus, researchers must inform potential participants, especially adolescents, about both the potential benefits and distress of research participation, and implement appropriate participant distress management protocols. As Parkes [64] pointed out, if a participant becomes distressed, "the needs of the respondent should take priority over the needs of the research" (p. 174). According to such protocols, researchers must provide support to a distressed interview participant according to the level of distress. This can range from allowing them to pause or withdraw from participation, providing emotional support to participants, providing or arranging referral to an appropriate support service (which may include a parent or guardian), or calling medical emergency services.

The literature indicates the important roles of narrating and sharing grief experiences in the processes of meaning-making and personal growth in those bereaved by suicide, which may also contribute to a positive experience as a study participant [10,58]. Interactions with a skilled and empathetic interviewer can also contribute to positive experiences for bereaved study participants [48,65]. While researchers must be sensitive to potential distress in participants, and provide emotional support if needed, they must also be aware of the potential methodological and ethical challenges when research and therapy blur [50,66]. For example, Biddle and colleagues [50] cautioned that participants may share information that they do not want to be used for the research, and researchers may not have the skills or capacity to deal with the distress or unintended shared information from the participant [50,64,66]. Hence, our findings and the broader literature imply that research interviews must be conducted by experienced and properly trained interviewers who can deal with participants' emotions and make judgements about pausing or continuing an interview, or referring participants to external support [50,64,66]. Further research is needed to clarify the role of the researcher and their approach to participants regarding balancing data collection and being empathic and supportive for the research experience of bereaved participants [48,65,67,68].

To fully understand the study findings, it is important to note that the study involved participants who volunteered to share their experiences, and study participants may not be representative of the population from which they are recruited. In a bereavement study, Akard and colleagues [69] found that those who are motivated and have the capacity to participate tended to respond to the initial researchers' invitations, and sending more than three invitations hardly increased the response rate [69]. Bereaved people who perceive research participation as too difficult may either decline participation or refuse passively by not responding [69,70]. These findings of the literature indicate the soundness of (potential) participants' judgements about research participation [50] and indicate that participants make appropriate cost–benefit appraisals of their participation [52]. Research is needed to confirm these observations in adolescents bereaved by suicide, parents or other family members of bereaved adolescents, and clinicians. Nonetheless, researchers and research ethics committees may consider these when designing and assessing research studies in this field. In addition, participants in our study had experienced the bereavement at least six months before participating, which may also have contributed to participants reporting little distress.

Limitations

The study involved a modest sample from a qualitative interview study. Despite the high response rate, the findings may not reflect the experiences of those who were invited to participate and chose not to. It is also not known whether findings apply to participants of other interview studies or studies utilizing other methods of data collection. Further, the survey did not include definitions of 'distress' or 'negative effects', and data were collected only at one point in time shortly after research participation. Future studies could include pre- and post-measures and longitudinal follow-up to assess any longer-term consequences.

5. Conclusions

The study clearly indicates that bereaved adolescents, parents and clinicians can safely participate in research interviews regarding their experiences of grief and help after suicide and other traumatic death. Participants reported that they experienced little distress and would recommend participation to others. To prevent and mitigate potential distress, training of research staff and implementation of appropriate participant distress protocols are imperative. Future studies could include longitudinal follow-up of participants.

Author Contributions: Conceptualization, K.A., D.R. and J.P.; methodology, K.A.; software, K.A.; data collection, K.A. and K.K.; formal analysis, K.A. and K.K.; writing—original draft preparation, K.A.; writing—review and editing, K.A., K.K., D.R. and J.P.; supervision, D.R. and J.P.; project administration, K.A.; funding acquisition, K.A. All authors have read and agreed to the published version of the manuscript.

Funding: K.A. is supported by a National Health and Medical Research Council Early Career Fellowship (GNT1157796) and an Early Career Researcher Grant of The University of Melbourne (ECR1202020). J.P. is funded by a National Health and Medical Research Council Investigator Grant (GNT1173126).

Institutional Review Board Statement: The study was conducted according to the guidelines of the Declaration of Helsinki and approved by the Human Research Ethics Committee of The University of Melbourne (ID 1955213, 8 October 2019).

Informed Consent Statement: Informed consent was obtained from all subjects involved in the study.

Data Availability Statement: According to the ethics approval, data can only be accessed by the members of the research team.

Acknowledgments: We are most grateful to the participants for sharing their experiences, and to the numerous individuals and organizations who helped with recruitment and/or hosted the focus groups, especially: The Compassionate Friends Victoria, Support After Suicide Jesuits Social Services, Standby Support After Suicide, headspace National, Anglicare Suicide Prevention and Grief Support South Australia, Sabrina's Reach 4 Life, and the Australian Centre for Grief and Bereavement.

Conflicts of Interest: The authors declare no conflict of interest. The funding bodies had no role in the design of the study, the collection, analysis and interpretation of data, the writing of the manuscript, and the decision to submit it for publication.

References

1. Feigelman, W.; Rosen, Z.; Joiner, T.; Silva, C.; Mueller, A.S. Examining longer-term effects of parental death in adolescents and young adults: Evidence from the national longitudinal survey of adolescent to adult health. *Death Stud.* **2017**, *41*, 133–143. [CrossRef] [PubMed]
2. Balk, D.E. *Dealing with Dying, Death, and Grief during Adolescence*; Routledge: New York, NY, USA, 2014.
3. Andriessen, K.; Mowll, J.; Lobb, E.; Draper, B.; Dudley, M.; Mitchell, P.B. "Don't bother about me". The grief and mental health of bereaved adolescents. *Death Stud.* **2018**, *42*, 607–615. [CrossRef] [PubMed]

4. De Rosbo-Davies, C.; Laletas, S.; Round, P. Daughters' experiences of maternal bereavement during adolescence: A scoping review. *Death Stud.* **2021**, 1–11, Online ahead of print. [CrossRef]
5. Farella Guzzo, M.; Gobbi, G. Parental death during adolescence: A review of the literature. *Omega* **2021**, 1–31, Online ahead of print. [CrossRef]
6. Bartik, W.; Maple, M.; Edwards, H.; Kiernan, M. Adolescent survivors after suicide—Australian young people's bereavement narratives. *Crisis* **2013**, *34*, 211–217. [CrossRef] [PubMed]
7. Brent, D.; Melhem, N.; Donohoe, M.B.; Walker, M. The incidence and course of depression in bereaved youth 21 months after the loss of a parent to suicide, accident, or sudden natural death. *Am. J. Psychiatry* **2009**, *166*, 786–794. [CrossRef]
8. Pham, S.; Porta, G.; Biernesser, C.; Walker Payne, M.; Iyengar, S.; Melhem, N.; Brent, D.A. The burden of bereavement: Early-onset depression and impairment in youths bereaved by sudden parental death in a 7-year prospective study. *Am. J. Psychiatry* **2018**, *175*, 887–896. [CrossRef]
9. Del Carpio, L.; Paul, S.; Paterson, A.; Rasmussen, S. A systematic review of controlled studies of suicidal and self-harming behaviours in adolescents following bereavement by suicide. *PLoS ONE* **2021**, *16*, e0254203. [CrossRef]
10. Levi-Belz, Y.; Krysinska, K.; Andriessen, K. "To turn a personal tragedy into a triumph": A systematic review and meta-analysis of studies on posttraumatic growth among suicide survivors. *Psychol. Trauma* **2021**, *13*, 322–332. [CrossRef]
11. Şimşek Arslan, B.; Özer, Z.; Buldukoğlu, K. Posttraumatic growth in parentally bereaved children and adolescents: A systematic review. *Death Stud.* **2020**, 1–13, *Online ahead of print*. [CrossRef]
12. Tedeschi, R.G.; Shakespeare-Finch, J.; Taku, K.; Calhoun, L.G. *Posttraumatic Growth: Theory, Research, and Application*; Routledge: New York, NY, USA, 2018.
13. Andriessen, K.; Krysinska, K.; Rickwood, D.; Pirkis, J. "It changes your orbit": The impact of suicide and traumatic death on adolescents as experienced by adolescents and parents. *Int. J. Environ. Res. Public Health* **2020**, *17*, 9356. [CrossRef] [PubMed]
14. Hoffmann, W.A.; Myburgh, C.; Poggenpoel, M. The lived experiences of late-adolescent female suicide survivors: 'A part of me died'. *Health SA Gesondheid* **2010**, *15*, 1–9. [CrossRef]
15. Cerel, J.; Jordan, J.R.; Duberstein, P.R. The impact of suicide on the family. *Crisis* **2008**, *29*, 38–44. [CrossRef]
16. Glazer, H.R.; Clark, M.D.; Thomas, R.; Haxton, H. Parenting after the death of a spouse. *Am. J. Hosp. Palliat. Med.* **2010**, *27*, 532–536. [CrossRef]
17. National Statement on Ethical Conduct in Human Research 2007 (Updated 2018). In *The National Health and Medical Research Council, the Australian Research Council and Universities Australia*; Commonwealth of Australia: Canberra, Australia, 2018. Available online: https://www.nhmrc.gov.au/about-us/publications/nationalstatement-ethical-conduct-human-research-2007-updated-2018 (accessed on 11 October 2021).
18. Andriessen, K.; Reifels, L.; Krysinska, K.; Robinson, J.; Dempster, G.; Pirkis, J. Dealing with ethical concerns in suicide research: A survey of Australian researchers. *Int. J. Environ. Res. Public Health* **2019**, *16*, 1094. [CrossRef]
19. Andriessen, K.; Reifels, L.; Krysinska, K.; Robinson, J.; Dempster, G.; Pirkis, J. Ethical concerns in suicide research: Results of an international researcher survey. *J. Empir. Res. Hum. Res. Ethics* **2019**, *14*, 383–394. [CrossRef]
20. Barnard, E.; Dempster, G.; Krysinska, K.; Reifels, L.; Robinson, J.; Pirkis, J.; Andriessen, K. Ethical concerns in suicide research: Thematic analysis of the views of human research ethics committees in Australia. *BMC Med. Ethics* **2021**, *22*, 41. [CrossRef]
21. Hom, M.A.; Podlogar, M.C.; Stanley, I.H.; Joiner, T.E., Jr. Ethical issues and practical challenges in suicide research. *Crisis* **2016**, *38*, 107–114. [CrossRef] [PubMed]
22. McClinton Appollis, T.; Lund, C.; de Vries, P.J.; Mathews, C. Adolescents' and adults' experiences of being surveyed about violence and abuse: A systematic review of harms, benefits, and regrets. *Am. J. Public Health* **2015**, *105*, e31–e45. [CrossRef] [PubMed]
23. Rosenbaum, A.; Langhinrichsen-Rohling, J. Meta-research on violence and victims: The impact of data collection methods on findings and participants. *Violence Vict.* **2006**, *21*, 404–409. [CrossRef]
24. Gysels, M.H.; Evans, C.; Higginson, I.J. Patient, caregiver, health professional and researcher views and experiences of participating in research at the end of life: A critical interpretive synthesis of the literature. *BMC Med. Res. Methodol.* **2012**, *12*, 1–17. [CrossRef] [PubMed]
25. Jorm, A.F.; Kelly, C.M.; Morgan, A.J. Participant distress in psychiatric research: A systematic review. *Psychol. Med.* **2007**, *37*, 917–926. [CrossRef]
26. Hiriscau, E.I.; Stingelin-Giles, N.; Wasserman, D.; Reiter-Theil, S. Identifying ethical issues in mental health research with minors adolescents: Results of a Delphi study. *Int. J. Environ. Res. Public Health* **2016**, *13*, 489. [CrossRef]
27. Dyregrov, K. Bereaved parents' experience of research participation. *Soc. Sci. Med.* **2004**, *58*, 391–400. [CrossRef]
28. Buckle, J.L.; Dwyer, S.C.; Jackson, M. Qualitative bereavement research: Incongruity between the perspectives of participants and research ethics boards. *Int. J. Soc. Res. Methodol.* **2010**, *13*, 111–125. [CrossRef]
29. Feigelman, W.; Jordan, J.R.; McIntosh, J.L.; Feigelman, B. *Devastating Losses: How Parents Cope with the Death of a Child to Suicide or Drugs*; Springer: New York, NY, USA, 2012.
30. Omerov, P.; Steineck, G.; Dyregrov, K.; Runeson, B.; Nyberg, U. The ethics of doing nothing. Suicide-bereavement and research: Ethical and methodological considerations. *Psychol. Med.* **2014**, *44*, 3409–3420. [CrossRef] [PubMed]
31. Moore, M.; Maple, M.; Mitchell, A.M.; Cerel, J. Challenges and opportunities for suicide bereavement research: The experience of ethical board review. *Crisis* **2013**, *34*, 297–304. [CrossRef]

32. Andriessen, K.; Krysinska, K.; Draper, B.; Dudley, M.; Mitchell, P.B. Harmful or helpful? A systematic review of how those bereaved through suicide experience research participation. *Crisis* **2018**, *39*, 364–376. [CrossRef] [PubMed]
33. Cooper, J. Ethical issues and their practical application in a psychological autopsy study of suicide. *J. Clin. Nurs.* **1999**, *8*, 467–475. [CrossRef]
34. Hawton, K.; Houston, K.; Malmbergand, A.; Simkin, S. Psychological autopsy interviews in suicide research: The reactions of informants. *Arch. Suicide Res.* **2003**, *7*, 73–82. [CrossRef]
35. Andriessen, K.; Krysinska, K.; Rickwood, D.; Pirkis, J. "Finding a safe space". What makes help helpful for adolescents bereaved by suicide: A thematic analysis. *Death Stud.* **2021**, 1–11, *Online ahead of print*. [CrossRef] [PubMed]
36. Tong, A.; Sainsbury, P.; Craig, J. Consolidated criteria for reporting qualitative research (COREQ): A 32-item checklist for interviews and focus groups. *Int. J. Qual. Health Care* **2007**, *19*, 349–357. [CrossRef] [PubMed]
37. Heath, J.; Williamson, H.; Williams, L.; Harcourt, D. "It's just more personal": Using multiple methods of qualitative data collection to facilitate participation in research focusing on sensitive subjects. *Appl. Nurs. Res.* **2018**, *43*, 30–35. [CrossRef] [PubMed]
38. Guest, G.; Namey, E.; Taylor, J.; Eley, N.; McKenna, K. Comparing focus groups and individual interviews: Findings from a randomized study. *Int. J. Soc. Res. Methodol.* **2017**, *20*, 693–708. [CrossRef]
39. Guest, G.; Namey, E.; McKenna, K. How many focus groups are enough? Building an evidence base for nonprobability sample sizes. *Field Methods* **2017**, *29*, 3–22. [CrossRef]
40. Malterud, K.; Siersma, V.D.; Guassora, A.D. Sample size in qualitative interview studies: Guided by information power. *Qual. Health. Res.* **2016**, *26*, 1753–1760. [CrossRef]
41. Guest, G.; Bunce, A.; Johnson, L. How many interviews are enough? An experiment with data saturation and variability. *Field Methods* **2006**, *18*, 59–82. [CrossRef]
42. DeCuir-Gunby, J.T.; Marshall, P.L.; McCulloch, A.W. Developing and using a codebook for the analysis of interview data: An example from a professional development research project. *Field Methods* **2011**, *23*, 136–155. [CrossRef]
43. Braun, V.; Clarke, V.; Hayfield, N.; Terry, G. Thematic Analysis. In *Handbook of Research Methods in Health Social Sciences*; Liamputtong, P., Ed.; Springer: Singapore, 2019; pp. 843–860. [CrossRef]
44. Braun, V.; Clarke, V. Using thematic analysis in psychology. *Qual. Res. Psychol.* **2006**, *3*, 77–101. [CrossRef]
45. IBM Corp. *IBM SPSS Statistics for Windows, Version 26.0*; IBM Corp.: Armonk, NY, USA, 2019.
46. Bryman, A. *Social Research Methods*, 4th ed.; Oxford University Press: Oxford, UK, 2012.
47. Butler, A.E.; Hall, H.; Copnell, B. Bereaved parents' experiences of research participation. *BMC Palliat. Care* **2018**, *17*, 1–9. [CrossRef]
48. Hynson, J.L.; Aroni, R.; Bauld, C.; Sawyer, S.M. Research with bereaved parents: A question of how not why. *Palliat. Med.* **2006**, *20*, 805–811. [CrossRef]
49. Eilegård, A.; Steineck, G.; Nyberg, T.; Kreicbergs, U. Bereaved siblings' perception of participating in research—A nationwide study. *Psycho-Oncology* **2013**, *22*, 411–416. [CrossRef] [PubMed]
50. Biddle, L.; Cooper, J.; Owen-Smith, A.; Klineberg, E.; Bennewith, O.; Hawton, K.; Kapur, N.; Donovan, J.; Gunnell, D. Qualitative interviewing with vulnerable populations: Individuals' experiences of participating in suicide and self-harm based research. *J. Affect. Disord.* **2013**, *145*, 356–362. [CrossRef] [PubMed]
51. Dyregrov, K.; Dyregrov, A.; Raundalen, M. Refugee families' experience of research participation. *J Trauma Stress* **2000**, *13*, 413–426. [CrossRef] [PubMed]
52. Newman, E.; Kaloupek, D.G. The risks and benefits of participating in trauma-focused research studies. *J Trauma Stress* **2004**, *17*, 383–394. [CrossRef] [PubMed]
53. Crane, S.; Broome, M.E. Understanding ethical issues of research participation from the perspective of participating children and adolescents: A systematic review. *Worldviews Evid. Based Nurs.* **2017**, *14*, 200–209. [CrossRef]
54. Hasking, P.; Tatnell, R.C.; Martin, G. Adolescents' reactions to participating in ethically sensitive research: A prospective self-report study. *Child Adolesc. Psychiatry Ment. Health* **2015**, *9*, 1–12. [CrossRef]
55. Ellonen, N.; Pösö, T. Children's experiences of completing a computer-based violence survey: Ethical implications. *Child. Soc.* **2011**, *25*, 470–481. [CrossRef]
56. Hawley, K.; Huang, J.S.; Goodwin, M.; Diaz, D.; de Sa, V.R.; Birnie, K.A.; Chambers, C.T.; Craig, K.D. Youth and parent appraisals of participation in a study of spontaneous and induced pediatric clinical pain. *Ethics Behav.* **2019**, *29*, 259–273. [CrossRef]
57. Littlewood, D.L.; Harris, K.; Gooding, P.; Pratt, D.; Haddock, G.; Peters, S. Using my demons to make good: The short-and long-term impact of participating in suicide-related research. *Arch. Suicide Res.* **2021**, *25*, 315–339. [CrossRef]
58. Dyregrov, K.M.; Dieserud, G.; Hjelmeland, H.M.; Straiton, M.; Rasmussen, M.L.; Knizek, B.L.; Leenaars, A.A. Meaning-making through psychological autopsy interviews: The value of participating in qualitative research for those bereaved by suicide. *Death Stud.* **2011**, *35*, 685–710. [CrossRef]
59. Tan, D.P.; Morgan, A.J.; Jorm, A.F.; Reavley, N.J. Emotional impacts of participation in an Australian national survey on mental health-related discrimination. *Ethics Behav.* **2019**, *29*, 438–458. [CrossRef]
60. Hendin, H.; Lipschitz, A.; Maltsberger, J.T.; Haas, A.P.; Wynecoop, S. Therapists' reactions to patients' suicides. *Am. J. Psychiatr.* **2000**, *157*, 2022–2027. [CrossRef]

61. Dransart, D.A.C.; Treven, M.; Grad, O.T.; Andriessen, K. Impact of client suicide on health and mental health professionals. In *Postvention in Action: The International Handbook of Suicide Bereavement Support*; Andriessen, K., Krysinska, K., Grad, O.T., Eds.; Hogrefe: Göttingen, Germany; Boston, MA, USA, 2017; pp. 245–254.
62. Pinto, R.M.; Yu, G.; Spector, A.Y.; Gorroochurn, P.; McCarty, D. Substance abuse treatment providers' involvement in research is associated with willingness to use findings in practice. *J. Subst. Abus. Treat.* **2010**, *39*, 188–194. [CrossRef] [PubMed]
63. Wilson, A. Consumer participation: Ensuring suicide postvention research counts for end users. *Int. J. Nurs. Pr.* **2010**, *16*, 7–13. [CrossRef]
64. Parkes, C.M. Guidelines for conducting ethical bereavement research. *Death Stud.* **1995**, *19*, 171–181. [CrossRef]
65. Caserta, M.; Utz, R.; Lund, D.; De Vries, B. Sampling, recruitment, and retention in a bereavement intervention study: Experiences from the Living After Loss project. *Omega* **2010**, *61*, 181–203. [CrossRef]
66. Rosenblatt, P.C. Ethics of qualitative interviewing with grieving families. *Death Stud.* **1995**, *19*, 139–155. [CrossRef] [PubMed]
67. Kitson, G.C.; Clark, R.D.; Rushforth, N.B.; Brinich, P.M.; Sudak, H.S.; Zyzanski, S.J. Research on difficult family topics: Helping new and experienced researchers cope with research on loss. *Fam. Relat.* **1996**, *45*, 183–188. [CrossRef]
68. Henry, M.; Greenfield, B.J. Therapeutic effects of psychological autopsies: The impact of investigating suicides on interviewees. *Crisis* **2009**, *30*, 20–24. [CrossRef] [PubMed]
69. Akard, T.F.; Gilmer, M.J.; Miller, K.; Steele, A.C.; Hancock, K.; Barrera, M.; Compas, B.; Davies, B.; Dietrich, M.S.; Fairclough, D.L.; et al. Factors affecting recruitment and participation of bereaved parents and siblings in grief research. *Prog. Palliat. Care* **2014**, *22*, 75–79. [CrossRef]
70. Burnell, R.H.; O'Keefe, M. Asking parents unaskable questions. *Lancet* **2004**, *364*, 737–738. [CrossRef]

International Journal of
Environmental Research and Public Health

MDPI

Review

Continuing Bonds after Loss by Suicide: A Systematic Review

Rebecca Goodall [1], Karolina Krysinska [2] and Karl Andriessen [2,*]

1 Melbourne Medical School, The University of Melbourne, Parkville, VIC 3010, Australia; rngoodall@student.unimelb.edu.au
2 Centre for Mental Health, Melbourne School of Population and Global Health, The University of Melbourne, Parkville, VIC 3010, Australia; karolina.krysinska@unimelb.edu.au
* Correspondence: karl.andriessen@unimelb.edu.au

Abstract: The concept of continuing bonds as an alternative to detachment from the deceased person has gained traction in grief literature over the years. Those bereaved by suicide are likely to experience various grief reactions and may be at-risk for adverse grief and mental health outcomes. However, it remains unclear how those bereaved by suicide experience continuing bonds. To address this gap, we conducted a systematic review according to PRISMA guidelines. Searches of peer-reviewed literature in Medline, PsycINFO, Embase, Emcare, EBM Reviews, and Scopus identified 15 studies (2 quantitative and 13 qualitative) reporting on 12 samples, published between 2010 and 2021. The study quality of the quantitative studies was poor, but it was fair amongst the qualitative studies. People bereaved by suicide experienced continuing bonds across a variety of domains and reported mostly positive experiences. Factors that tended to have an impact on the expression of continuing bonds included time since bereavement, relationship to the deceased, social expectations, sex of the bereaved, and the ability of the bereaved to make meaning of the death. The review concludes that most participants reported positive experiences with continuing bonds. However, discrepancies between males and females and between those bereaved by suicide and those bereaved by other causes warrants further investigation. In addition, longitudinal community-based research involving representative samples is needed to understand the evolution and experience of continuing bonds over time in those bereaved by suicide and to inform future efforts in supporting them.

Keywords: continuing bonds; grief; bereavement; suicide; systematic review

Citation: Goodall, R.; Krysinska, K.; Andriessen, K. Continuing Bonds after Loss by Suicide: A Systematic Review. *Int. J. Environ. Res. Public Health* **2022**, *19*, 2963. https://doi.org/10.3390/ijerph19052963

Academic Editor: Paul B. Tchounwou

Received: 29 January 2022
Accepted: 1 March 2022
Published: 3 March 2022

1. Introduction

Suicide claims the lives of over 700,000 people per year globally [1]. A recent meta-analysis of population-based studies indicated that approximately one in twenty people experience a loss by suicide in one given year and one in five do so during their lifetime, although the impact of the death may depend on the closeness of the relationship [2]. Due to the complex nature of grief after suicide, individuals bereaved by suicide have a higher risk of adverse mental health outcomes such as posttraumatic stress disorder, depression, suicidal ideation, and attempted suicide than those bereaved by other causes [3]. People bereaved by suicide also have particular needs for professional help in dealing with their grief (for example, regarding feelings of guilt and struggles with 'why' questions) compared to those bereaved by natural causes [4].

Initially, grief literature suggested that bereaved individuals progress through different stages of grief in order to achieve detachment from the deceased person [5]. However, Klass and colleagues [6] challenged this theory and proposed the concept of continuing bonds as an alternative to detachment. They defined continuing bonds as the presence of an ongoing inner relationship with the deceased person [6]. Still, the concept of continuing bonds has been described in cultural literature and various religions over the centuries [7]. Klass and colleagues drew attention to specific rituals which demonstrated the practice of continuing bonds long before the theory gained traction in grief literature [6,7]. They gave the example of Japanese Buddhism, in which the deceased become part of the spirit family and are accessible to the bereaved, and in Judaism, in which the deceased are remembered through prayer and the physical lighting of a candle [6,7].

Recent studies have aimed to characterise continuing bonds as positive or negative and to specify the ways in which they manifest [7]. The process of meaning-making emerged as an important tool in the formation of positive bonds [8]. Meaning-making refers to the way in which bereaved individuals process the death in a way that holds meaning for them [9]. The concept of continuing bonds has gained traction over the years, as witnessed through the development of designated instruments [10] and studies in various bereaved populations (such as after the death of a parent or a child) [7]. However, it remains unclear how continuing bonds manifest themselves in those bereaved by suicide and how this population experiences continuing bonds. To-date, no review on this topic has been conducted. Still, a better understanding of this aspect of grief in people bereaved by suicide may provide useful information for future efforts in supporting them.

This review will address this gap by synthesising and analysing the research on continuing bonds in individuals bereaved by suicide. It aims to characterise aspects of the continuing bond including how they manifest, and whether those bereaved experience them as positive or negative.

2. Materials and Methods

2.1. Search Strategy

The review adhered to PRISMA guidelines [11], and the protocol was registered in the PROSPERO database (CRD42021271971). The review involved systematic searches of the following databases: Medline, PsycINFO, Embase, Emcare and EBM Reviews (all accessed via Ovid), and Scopus. The search in Medline comprised MeSH and text words: (Continu* bond*.mp OR continu* relationship*.mp OR continu* connection*.mp OR Ongoing bond*.mp OR Ongoing relationship*.mp OR Ongoing connection*.mp OR meaning making.mp OR Memorial*.mp OR Ritual*.mp) AND (Grie*.mp OR Grief/ OR Mourn*.mp OR Bereav*.mp OR Bereavement/ OR Suicide bereave*.mp OR Bereave* by suicide.mp OR loss by suicide.mp OR suicide loss survivor*.mp) AND (suicide.mp OR Suicide/). A similar search string including headings and keywords was used in the other databases.

One researcher (R.G.) conducted the search in August 2021. It was limited to publications in English but not by date of publication. Two researchers (R.G., K.A.) assessed titles and abstracts for eligibility and any discordance was resolved through discussion with the third researcher (K.K.). The same two researchers then assessed the full text of potentially relevant studies using the inclusion/exclusion criteria. Researcher R.G. hand-searched the references of the included studies and conducted a forward-citation search in Google Scholar to identify any further studies. Figure 1 summarises the search strategy.

2.2. Inclusion and Exclusion Criteria

Studies were included if: (1) the study population consisted of people bereaved by suicide; (2) the study provided empirical qualitative and quantitative data on continuing bonds with an individual lost to suicide; (3) the study was published in the English language; and (4) the study was published as a paper in a peer-reviewed journal.

The review excluded: (1) studies not providing data specifically on people bereaved by suicide; (2) studies not providing data on continuing bonds in the context of suicide bereavement; (3) studies based on other methods, such as case studies, reviews and opinion paper; (4) studies not written in English; and (5) studies which were not peer-reviewed. Unclarity on the inclusion of three studies was resolved through discussion with the third researcher (K.K.).

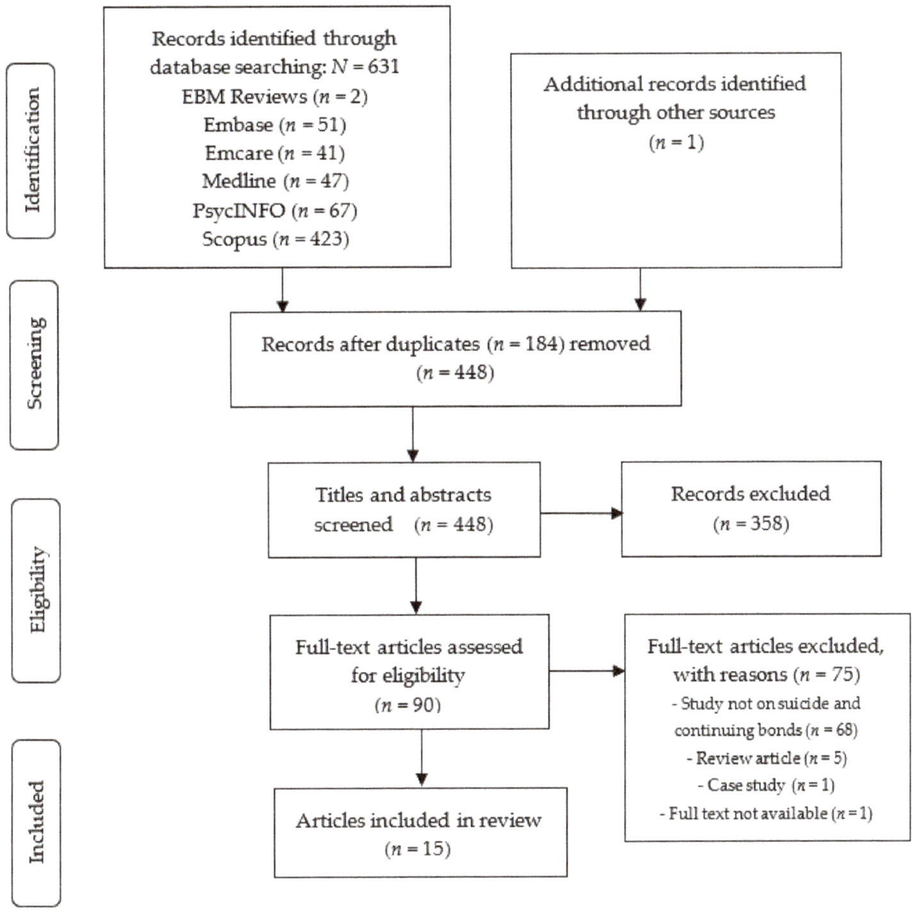

Figure 1. PRISMA Flow Diagram.

2.3. Data Extraction

Two researchers (R.G., K.A.) independently extracted the following data: author, year and location of study, eligibility criteria, sample size, participants' sex, age, time since bereavement and relationship to the deceased, setting, study design, and main findings.

2.4. Quality Assessment

Two researchers (R.G., K.A.) independently conducted the quality assessment and resolved disagreements through discussion. No eligible study was excluded based on its quality. Quantitative studies were assessed using the Newcastle-Ottawa Quality Assessment Form for Cohort Studies [12], comprising eight items across three domains: (1) selection (four items), (2) comparability (one item), and (3) outcome (three items). Scores in each domain were totalled to determine study quality as good, fair, or poor. The interrater reliability was high ($\kappa = 0.82$).

The qualitative studies were assessed using the Consolidated Criteria for Reporting Qualitative Research (COREQ) [13] consisting of thirty-two items across three domains: (1) research team and reflexivity (eight items), (2) study design (fifteen items), and (3) analysis and findings (nine items). For each study, the number and percentage of items satisfied within each domain and across all domains was calculated. The interrater agreement was high ($\kappa = 0.92$).

3. Results

3.1. Study Characteristics

The searches identified fifteen studies reporting on twelve samples. Five studies were conducted in Australia [14–18], three in the USA [9,19,20], three in the UK [21–23], two in Israel [24,25], one in Canada [26], and one in Switzerland [27]. There were two quantitative and thirteen qualitative studies. The quantitative studies collected data via online questionnaires [19,24]. One also utilised the Two-Track Bereavement Questionnaire (TTBQ) [10] to measure the level of functioning of bereaved individuals and their relationship with the deceased person [24]. Eleven of the thirteen qualitative studies involved semi-structured or in-depth interviews either in-person or via telephone, one utilised a survey [20] and one collected data through a series of workshops over twelve weeks [18].

The quantitative studies had sample sizes ranging from $N = 159$ [24] to $N = 1301$ [19], whilst qualitative studies had sample sizes ranging from $N = 7$ [14] to $N = 50$ [27], with the exception of Jahn [19,20] who used the same data set for both a quantitative and qualitative study. Tables 1 and 2 summarise the quantitative and qualitative studies, respectively.

A large percentage (67–89%) of participants in most studies ($n = 9$) were female [16,19–22,24–27]. Three studies had equal numbers of both sexes [15,17,23], two had slightly more male (57–60%) than female participants [9,14], and one study did not report the sex of participants [18]. Across studies, the age range was between 8 and 85 years [19,23].

Whilst most studies included a broad range of relationships between the bereaved individuals and the deceased, six focused on a specific relationship, including bereaved parents ($n = 3$) [15–17], siblings ($n = 2$) [14,25], and children ($n = 1$) [23].

Time since death ranged between two months and over forty-five years [18,24]. Two studies focused on the grief reactions from five months onwards [21,22], whilst others looked at continuing bonds and grief reactions on a longer-term from five years onward [9] or within a ten-year period [14]. Eight studies did not limit participants by time since loss [16,19,20,23–27], and three included longitudinal data [15,17,18].

3.2. Quality Assessment

Appendix A presents the methodological quality of the quantitative studies, and the two included studies received a rating of 'poor' quality. One study [24] scored well in the 'comparability' domain, but both studies [19,24] tended to score poorly in the 'selection' and 'outcome' domains by using selected samples and relying on self-reported outcomes. Appendix B outlines the quality assessment of the 13 qualitative studies. The studies satisfied between 34% [22] and 75% [15,17] of the COREQ criteria [13]. Most studies reported only few items across the 'research team and reflexivity' domain (on average 35% of items were reported). However, most items (on average 63%) in both the 'study design' and 'analysis and findings' domains were reported.

3.3. Study Findings

3.3.1. In What Way Can Continuing Bonds Manifest?

Findings from the included studies showed that continuing bonds manifested or were experienced in various ways. Quantitative data showed that 63% of participants reported having spiritual experiences [19]. The most common experiences included dreams about the deceased (73.4%), feeling the presence of the deceased (53%), and profound coincidences (40.3%) [19]. In qualitative studies, participants reported the use of rituals and memorials (both physical and online) [9,16,21,23], spiritual and religious beliefs [9,26,27], metaphysical experiences [20,26], physical objects [9], and suicide-related thoughts and behaviours, such as a desire to join the deceased and/or understand what they went through [9].

Table 1. Summary of quantitative studies.

Author, Year, Location	Eligibility Criteria	Sample Size	Male/Female	Age	Time since Bereavement	Relationship to Deceased	Setting	Study Design	Outcome Measures	Main Results
Levi-Belz (2017) Israel [24]	>18 y/o, identify as a bereaved family member. Excl.: <15 y/o at time of death, inability to speak or write in Hebrew or English.	*N* = 159 suicide loss survivors = 58, sudden-death bereavers = 48, expected-death bereavers = 53 (F = 81%)	M = 30 F = 129 suicide loss survivors: M = 13, F = 45 sudden-death bereavers: M = 6, F = 42 expected-death bereavers: M = 11, F = 42	18–73 suicide loss survivor M = 40.5, SD = 15.6, sudden-death bereavers M = 35.7, SD = 13.1, expected-death bereavers M = 33.1, SD = 12.3	2 m–45 y (M = 95 m, SD = 105.46 m)	25 parents, 11 children, 26 siblings, 30 spouses, and 44 close family members, 9 unknown	Online questionnaire	Cross sectional	Level of functioning: Two-track bereavement questionnaire (TTBQ), Post-traumatic grief level: Stress-Related Growth Scale (SRGS)	Suicide-loss survivors reported lower levels of close positive continuing bonds with the deceased than did participants from the sudden- and expected-death bereaved groups. Intense grief and preoccupation were associated with less positive personal transformation, particularly among the suicide bereaved. This suggests that continuing bonds in those bereaved by suicide are more likely to be experienced negatively than in those bereaved by other causes.
Jahn et al. (2014) USA [19]	Survivors of suicide loss	*N* = 1301	M = 135 F = 1155 U = 11	40–85	1 y–3 y (28.9%; n = 376), <1 y (25.7%; n = 334), 4 y–10 y (22.0%; n = 286), 11 y–20 y (12.2%; n = 159), and >20 y (8.2%; n = 107).	Parent (n = 362), sibling (n = 235), spouse/partner (n = 204), child (n = 180), friend (n = 112), niece/nephew (n = 21), grandchild (n = 9), another relationship (n = 119).	Two questionnaires—one demographics and one about experience of suicide. Both containing both qualitative and quantitative info	Descriptive statistics used to explore characteristics of loss and chi squared to examine demographical differences between responses	Two questionnaires: (i) demographic questionnaire, (ii) spiritual experiences of survivors of suicide, including questions about type and frequency of spiritual experiences	Most (n = 819, 63%) of those bereaved by suicide reported after-death spiritual experiences including dreams, feeling the presence of the person and profound coincidences. These experiences are often regarded as positive with 74.5% of participants (n = 610) finding them 'helpful' and only 4.8% (n = 39) viewing them as 'harmful' (19.9%, n = 163 saw them as neither helpful nor harmful). Being female and having a closer pre death relationship (family member as opposed to friend or client) was positively associated with spiritual experiences.

Table 2. Summary of qualitative studies.

Author, Year, Location	Eligibility Criteria	Sample Size	Male/Female	Age (Years)	Time Since Bereavement	Relationship to Deceased	Setting	Study Design	Main Results
Adams et al. (2019) AUS [14]	Bereaved by suicide of sibling (sibling <20 y/o) in past 10 yrs	*N* = 7	M = 4 F = 3	20–27 at time of interview (16–23 at time of suicide)	Average time = 3 y 9 m	Sibling	Telephone interview	Interpretive phenomen-ological analysis (IPA)	Identified 4 main themes: (a) the process of grief, (b) grief interactions (within families and outside), (c) continuing bonds, and (d) meaning-making and growth through grief.
Bailey et al. (2015) UK [21]	Family members and friends who own suicide memorial sites	*N* = 11	M = 3 F = 8	20–60	5 m–4 y	Parent, siblings or friends	Face-to-face interviews—semi-structured narrative style	Qualitative interpretative approach, combining constant comparison techniques with thematic analysis	The most common motivating factor for starting a memorial page was to 'keep the deceased alive' and maintain a connection. Participants found that they were able to better construct and refine relationships with the deceased using online memorials. Whilst most people had positive experiences with memorial sites, the dangers of becoming overly attached and experiencing compounding grief or 'double loss' was highlighted.
Bell et al. (2015) UK [22]	Individuals who had set up or were managing memorial sites for those who dies by suicide	*N* = 11	M = 3 F = 8	20–60	5 m–4 y	Parent, siblings or friends	Individual interviews	Qualitative interpretative approach, combining constant comparison techniques with thematic analysis	Provided insight into how online memorialisation allows more flexibility and depth in the exploration of grief than can traditional mourning objects—this allows users to reminisce on positive aspects of deceased life but can elicit negative experiences as users can't control how memories are framed.
Castelli Dransart (2018) Switzerland [27]	Suicide-survivors: A person was considered as a survivor of suicide if: (1) he/she self-qualified as such; (2) he/she felt emotionally close to the deceased; and (3) his/her life had been disrupted by a suicide (self-perception). >18 y/o, able to speak Italian, French or German	*N* = 50	M = 11 F = 39	14–73	<12 m–16 y	18 mothers, 5 fathers, 10 sisters, 3 brothers, 3 daughters, 1 son, 7 partners, 1 aunt, 2 friends	Face-to-face in depth interviews conducted by author or mental health carer, either at home or location chosen by bereaved	Grounded Theory using constant comparison of data and 3 steps of coding: open, axial & selective	Suicide triggered spiritual and religious thoughts and experiences for most participants. Even those who claimed to be atheist or agnostic noted religious rituals and spiritual symbols as being important contributors in forging and maintaining a continuing bond with the deceased and in honouring their memory. Interviewees believed loved ones continued to exist in an alternative dimension or space (regardless of religion).

Table 2. *Cont.*

Author, Year, Location	Eligibility Criteria	Sample Size	Male/Female	Age (Years)	Time Since Bereavement	Relationship to Deceased	Setting	Study Design	Main Results
Entilli et al. (2021) AUS [15]	Parents who had lost a child by suicide less than 6 months prior to starting the study	N = 14 at 6 and 12 months. N = 11 at 24 months	M = 7 F = 7 (6 and 12 months). M = 6 F = 5 (at 24 months)	Female mean = 60.1 years, range = 50–78 years and male mean = 59.9 years, range = 50–68 years	6 m, 12 m and 24 m	Parents who had lost a child (aged 15–51) by suicide. Ten were bereaved of sons and four bereaved of daughters	Semi-structured interviews either phone or face-to-face	Longitudinal study using thematic analysis	Three key themes were identified in an earlier analysis (at 6 and 12 months post loss): searching for answers and sense-making, coping strategies and support, and finding meaning and purpose. Further exploration of these themes at 24 months revealed significant differences between mothers and fathers with the latter adopting more maladaptive coping strategies. Maintaining the relationship with the deceased and paranormal experiences were new themes at 24 months (not present at 6 and 12 months) and a shift from brooding to reflection/sense-making was seen at 24 months. The adaptation process was fluctuating and dynamic.
Gall et al. (2015) Canada [26]	Individuals who had personal experiences of suicide bereavement	N = 15 (11 bereaved and 4 mental health workers)(MHW)	M = 2 F = 9 (bereaved) M = 1 F = 3	Mean age was 49 (bereaved) and 53 (MHW)	Mean = 13 y, minimum of 2 y	The deceased persons were: four sons, two fathers, two close friends, two uncles and one mother.	Semi-structured interviews	Phenomenological approach, thematic analysis	Individuals had difficulty reconciling the suicide death of a loved one with their religious views. This often led to a personally defined spirituality rather than a complete loss of faith. Many individuals (also non-religious) found meaning in the belief of an afterlife and/or felt hopeful that the deceased was in a better place and would someday reconnect with them. Engagement in activities to maintain a bond were common.
Hunt et al. (2019) USA [9]	>18 y/o, self-identified as suicide loss survivor, >5 years since death	N = 10	M = 6 F = 4	30–72 (mean = 47.6)	5 y–30 y (mean = 18.6 y)	5 siblings, 2 partners, 2 parents and one participant who had lost a sibling, grandfather and cousin	Face-to-face semi-structured interviews at participants homes	Thematic analysis informed by grounded theory	Three major themes were identified: - one harmful (feelings of responsibility) - one helpful (making meaning) to the process of suicide bereavement. - one that helped shift from harmful to helpful (social support) Participants did not identify with the Kubler-Ross stages of grief theory.

Table 2. *Cont.*

Author, Year, Location	Eligibility Criteria	Sample Size	Male/Female	Age (Years)	Time Since Bereavement	Relationship to Deceased	Setting	Study Design	Main Results
Jahn et al. (2018) USA [20]	Any person who identified as bereaved by suicide	N = 1301	M = 135 F = 1155 U = 11	40–85	1 y–3 y (28.9%; n = 376), <1 y (25.7%; n = 334), 4 y–10 y (22.0%; n = 286), 11 y–20 y (12.2%; n = 159), and >20 y (8.2%; n = 107).	Anyone bereaved by suicide	Two questionnaires—one demographics and one about spiritual experiences after suicide bereavement. Both containing both qualitative and quantitative info	Inductive thematic analysis	Nine main themes were identified: (1) a helpful sense of comfort; (2) a helpful sense of connection with the deceased; (3) intense sadness evoked by the spiritual experiences; (4) confusion regarding the spiritual experiences; (5) negative reminders of the deceased or negative meanings of spiritual experiences; (6) evidence of an afterlife; (7) general importance of the spiritual experiences' meaning; (8) impact of and on religious beliefs; and (9) others' responses to disclosure of suicide or spiritual experiences. Generally, participants found spiritual experiences aided in healing and transformation and were regarded as positive.
Leichtentritt et al. (2015) Israel [25]	Having experienced the loss of a sibling to suicide and the death having occurred at least five years prior to the interview	N = 9	M = 3 F = 6	29–63	5 y–37 y	Sibling	In-depth interviews	Relational dialect theory and narrative analysis used.	Five characteristics of the post death relationship were identified, each existing along a continuum: (1) concrete-symbolic (2) dynamic-static (3) conscious-unconscious (4) personal-public (5) monologue-dialogue Findings suggest that labelling post death relationships as 'adaptive' or 'maladaptive' is simplistic. Bereavement can be better understood when plotted within the 5 continua.
Maple et al. (2013) AUS [16]	Parents who lost a child by suicide	N = 22	M = 6 F = 16	NA	6 m–>26 y	22 parents (6 fathers and 16 mothers) from 18 families bereaved of 15 sons and 3 daughters. 14 participated individually and 4 as couples	In-depth interviews, mostly face-to-face (one phone)	Narrative Inquiry, recursive technique used to explore in more depth.	Contrary to traditional grief literature, it was found that parents needed to maintain a relationship with their deceased child. Manifestations of continuing bonds varied between parents. Commencing with the funeral, parents began developing rituals ensuring that their child's life, and not the manner of death, was celebrated. Some participants were limited in their expression of grief due to social pressure to resolve grief.

Table 2. *Cont.*

Author, Year, Location	Eligibility Criteria	Sample Size	Male/Female	Age (Years)	Time Since Bereavement	Relationship to Deceased	Setting	Study Design	Main Results
Ross et al. (2018) AUS [17]	Parents bereaved by suicide loss of their child 6 months prior to commencement of study	*N* = 14	M = 7 F = 7	50–78 (female mean = 60.1 years and range = 50–78, male mean = 59.9 years and range = 50–68)	6 m and 12 m	Parents who had lost a child (aged 15–51) by suicide. Ten were bereaved of sons and four bereaved of daughters	Individual, semi-structured interviews either face-to-face or telephone	Longitudinal study with inductive qualitative approach.	Identified three key themes (searching for answers and sense-making, coping strategies and support, and finding meaning and purpose) in parental responses to suicide bereavement. The phases of sense-making and meaning-making experienced by participants and the range of both adaptive and maladaptive coping strategies indicated that adapting to bereavement is a dynamic and fluctuating process.
Sands et al. (2010) AUS [18]	Adults >19 y/o, bereaved through the suicide death of a significant person in their lives	*N* = 16	NA	Aged 19+	>2 m	Family members or spouses: partner grieving a partner, parent grieving a child, sibling grieving a sibling, and adult child grieving a parent	A series of workshops delivered over 12 weeks and 30 h–involved discussion, artwork, grief rituals and journal writing	Generic thematic analysis	Identified 3 core themes that assisted in meaning making in relationships with the themselves, the deceased, and with others. The 3 themes were: (i) Intentionality ('tying on the shoes' or adopting the perspective of the deceased), (ii) Reconstruction ('walking in the shoes'), (iii) Repositioning ('taking off the shoes')
Wood et al. (2012) UK [23]	8–15 y/o (M = 11.80, SD = 2.57), whose parent had died by suicide within the previous 13 to 53 months	*N* = 10	M = 5 F = 5	8–15	13 m–53 m (M = 33.4, SD = 17.44)	Eight children bereaved of a father and two bereaved of a mother	Semi-structured interviews, face-to-face at participants' homes	Interpretative Phenomen-ological Analysis	Found 3 main themes: thinking about the deceased; coping strategies; and connecting to the deceased. Highlighted differences in childhood suicide bereavement as well as factors which may influence adaptiveness.

Suicide bereaved individuals tended to experience continuing bonds across multiple domains both concurrently and over time [15,25]. It was common to experience continuing bonds across a continuum, for example, engaging in both public and private expressions of continuing bonds [25]. A public manifestation may include participation in ceremonies or rituals such as a funeral whilst a private manifestation may include writing to or talking to the deceased [25]. Although the process of developing continuing bonds was never described as linear, time since bereavement did appear to affect how the bonds were experienced. Entilli and colleagues [15] and Ross and colleagues [17] described experiences with continuing bonds as they appeared at 6, 12, and 24 months, observing that memorialisation and intrusive thoughts were present early on whereas paranormal beliefs and the maintenance of the relationship with the deceased were new themes at 24 months. Similarly, Sands and colleagues [18] reported themes as they appeared during workshops spanning over 12 weeks. Participants experienced thoughts around 'why' the person had died by suicide before reconstructing the death story and repositioning the relationship in order to establish positive ongoing bonds [18]. Suicidal ideation with a desire to join the deceased and/or to understand what they went through was another common initial reaction that typically subsided over time [9,14].

Qualitative studies found that most participants wanted to experience continuing bonds and actively pursued them [14,26]. They achieved this through the creation of online memorials [21,22], visiting places that were frequented by the deceased [16], keeping objects that belonged to the deceased [26], actively reminiscing about the deceased [26], and writing to the deceased [15]. However, some participants found that the social expectations of grief and the stigma associated with suicide limited their public expression of continuing bonds, forcing them to express their grief privately [16,21,22].

There were differences in the types of bonds experienced according to sex and type of relationship to the deceased person [15,20,21]. A qualitative study found that female participants and those who had a close pre-death relationship with the deceased family member or partner had more spiritual experiences with the deceased [20]. Females also created more online memorials than males [21]. Conversely, males appeared to engage more in avoidant coping strategies and would express their grief less openly [15]. Though children may experience continuing bonds in similar domains as adults, research suggests they tend to interpret their experiences differently and this varies depending on age [23].

3.3.2. Continuing Bonds as a Positive or Negative Experience

Participants generally perceived continuing bonds as positive experiences [16,17,19–21,27], which they associated with comfort and hope [26]. Although less common, negative experiences were those that were beyond the control of the bereaved individuals and included subconscious thoughts or feelings [25], spiritual or metaphysical experiences [26], or the unexpected discovery of facts relating to the deceased that were not in-line with the perceptions of the bereaved [21]. A quantitative study [19] demonstrated that 74.5% of participants interpreted spiritual experiences with the deceased as helpful whilst only 4.8% viewed them as harmful [19]. However, another quantitative study comparing outcomes of those bereaved by suicide with those bereaved by sudden or expected death found that those bereaved by suicide had lower levels of close positive relationships with the deceased both pre- and post-death, including less expression of continuing bonds [24].

4. Discussion

This review aimed to synthesise the research literature concerning continuing bonds in people bereaved by suicide, including how they manifest and whether the bereaved experienced them as positive or negative. The review identified 15 studies reporting on 12 samples. Factors that affected the way in which continuing bonds manifested included time since death, type of relationship, societal expectations, sex of the bereaved person, and their ability to make meaning of the death. In all but one study [22], participants reported mostly positive thoughts, feelings and experiences regarding continuing bonds.

4.1. Factors That Affect the Manifestation of Continuing Bonds

Aside from two longitudinal studies [15,17], there appears to be little research on the effect of time since bereavement on the manifestation of continuing bonds in those bereaved by suicide. Participants from one study [9] reported that the intensity of the bonds had not lessened up to 10 years following the suicide. This is supported by a quantitative study [24] which found that when compared to those bereaved by sudden or expected deaths, those bereaved by suicide tended to maintain more intense bonds for a longer period of time and consequently took longer to engage in 'meaning-making'. These findings are important due to the strong association between intense grief and less positive personal transformation [24], highlighting the need for more longitudinal, comparative data.

Societal beliefs and expectations may impact on the manifestation of continuing bonds in several ways [16,21,22,27]. Some participants felt they were forced to express their ongoing relationship more privately due to the stigma surrounding suicide [9,21], and the expectation to resolve grief [16]. Our review revealed that suicidal ideation [9,14] in suicide bereaved individuals can be a way to reconnect with the deceased or to understand what they went through, suggesting that suicidal ideation may be a manifestation of continuing bonds in those bereaved by suicide. Interestingly, participants claimed that this process aided their grief work by helping them to make sense of the suicide; however, reported they felt discouraged from sharing these thoughts with others [9]. These findings illustrate the importance of addressing suicidal thoughts in a constructive manner as opposed to inadvertently reinforcing suicide stigma by silencing them [9].

The stigma associated with suicide in the context of religions may be particularly strong, with some bereaved individuals choosing to hold private ceremonies following a suicide death [27,28]. This is supported by a qualitative systematic review that found that religious individuals often isolate themselves due to feelings of shame and suicide-related stigmatisation emanating from religious doctrines [29]. Interestingly, taking part in religious ceremonies was common practice even in those participants who identified as agnostic [27]. A possible explanation for this may be that societal and cultural expectations dictate how we grieve, insofar as rituals such as funerals are expected in western culture [30]. Future studies conducted in different cultures may shed light on the expression of continuing bonds with regards to spiritual and religious themes and the possible stigma in this context.

Referring to the 'Dual Process Model of Coping with Bereavement' [31], studies reported differences between males and females with females engaging in more 'loss-oriented' behaviours, including continuing bonds, and males engaging in more 'restoration-oriented' behaviours, including learning new skills [15]. Whilst it may be the case that males experience continuing bonds to a lesser extent than females and/or in different domains [32], literature suggests that societal perceptions of gender and masculinity may influence the expression of grief, and grief after suicide, in males [33], resulting in males engaging in restoration-oriented activities as a distraction from or expression of their grief [33]. This view is supported by Entilli and colleagues [15] who found that fathers avoided discussing their feelings regarding the loss by suicide. Future studies may further compare the experience of continuing bonds between males and females and inform services to be directed accordingly.

The process of 'meaning-making' was mentioned throughout the reviewed studies. It refers to the ability of the bereaved person to make sense of or find meaning in the death [8,34] and has been widely recognised in grief literature [8,34]. Milman and colleagues described meaning-making as a method of alleviating the cognitive dissonance caused by the death through purposeful reflection [34]. They highlight the importance of differentiating this process from rumination as the latter fails to negotiate this discrepancy and is characterised by passive, repetitive and negative thoughts [34]. Our review indicated that those who were able to make meaning of the suicide experienced more positive continuing bonds whilst those who were unable to make meaning experienced more negative continuing bonds. In addition, high resilience characteristics and a strong social support network tended to predict less intense continuing bonds and higher levels of posttraumatic growth [24].

4.2. Continuing Bonds as a Positive or a Negative Experience

Most participants in the included studies reported positive feelings experienced with continuing bonds [16,18,23], a finding that is mirrored by those of general bereavement studies [35,36]. However, a quantitative study comparing different forms of bereavement indicated that those bereaved by suicide reporting lower levels of close and positive relationships with the deceased both pre-and post-death [24]. The incorporation of multiple factors, including close and positive, and pre-and post-death relationships, make it hard to accurately compare these results with other studies. As demonstrated by Leichtentritt and colleagues [25], a 'close' relationship is not necessarily synonymous with a 'positive' one. Likewise, as suggested throughout this review, the process of meaning-making transforms the relationship so that the pre- and post-death relationships may not be equivalent. Further studies comparing experiences of continuing bonds between those bereaved by different causes may further clarify how to understand these experiences.

Negative experiences occurred when continuing bonds in the form of memories or objects faded or were lost [14,21], when participants were not able to make meaning of the loss [15], or when aspects of continuing bonds were beyond the control of the bereaved [22,25]. Participants experienced feelings of distress at fading memories of the deceased [14], or due to the sudden and unexpected disappearance of online memorials [21], which was described as a 'double loss' [22]. Some expressed apprehension and guilt as contributing to the continuing bonds as they did not want to abandon the deceased person [10]. Additionally, participants experienced cognitive dissonance when their religious beliefs were in opposition to the actions of the deceased [27], or upon the discovery of new information about the deceased that was contradictory to their own internal representation of the deceased person [21,22]. These psychological discrepancies were found to hinder the ability of the bereaved person to make meaning of the death and enhanced negative feelings associated with continuing bonds [9]. Further research may clarify in which circumstances it may be more beneficial for the bereaved person to relinquish than to maintain the bond [35,36].

Participants utilised several tools and behaviours to create or maintain positive continuing bonds. Many studies observed the tendency of participants to omit certain aspects of the deceased personality or behaviour when recalling memories of them [23], or to hold more symbolic or fictitious representations of the deceased [25,27]. Some bereaved individuals favoured online memorials due to them being more interactive than traditional mourning objects [21]. This is supported by literature reporting that this allows the bereaved to explore the relationship in more depth and to discover new things about the deceased, thus enabling the relationship to evolve [37]. Nonetheless, a potential negative aspect of online grief-related activities is the ease with which those bereaved can become preoccupied with the relationship, hindering the meaning-making process [21,38].

Positive and negative experiences with continuing bonds were often intertwined. Wood [23] found that negative thoughts about the deceased's personality or behaviour initially evoked distress but with reflection and perspective, understanding and personal growth could be achieved. This was echoed by Maple [16], who found that parents could initially be distressed at the ongoing 'presence' of their deceased child but in time came to enjoy these experiences. Nonetheless, participants reported a bitter 'aftertaste' associated with positive thoughts about the deceased as they tended to trigger difficult emotions and memories [23]. Remembering the more holistic picture (both good and bad) was beneficial in making sense of the suicide and relieving responsibility and guilt in those bereaved by suicide [23,39].

4.3. Limitations

The studies included in the review and the review itself entailed a few limitations. Most studies were qualitative, or cross-sectional (of relatively poor quality) with primarily female participants from western countries, making the impact of culture, sex and time since bereavement difficult to discern. This highlights the need for international research involving representative samples. Also, further studies involving control groups or adopting community-based longitudinal designs may enable researchers to capture the experiences of continuing bonds over time. While the review involved searches in six databases, future reviews can broaden the scope by including more databases as well as grey literature, which may increase, for example, the likelihood of finding negative experiences in the context of continuing bonds.

4.4. Implications

A better understanding of continuing bonds in suicide bereavement may inform future interventions and enable service providers to deliver more accurate and targeted support. In particular, the review highlights the substantial impact that societal expectations and stigma continue to have on the experience of grief in suicide bereaved individuals [40]. The findings of this review may direct future studies and help to characterise the experiences of continuing bonds in people bereaved by suicide with greater clarity.

5. Conclusions

People bereaved by suicide commonly experience continuing bonds and generally interpret these as positive experiences. Factors such as time since bereavement, social and cultural expectations, sex of the bereaved person, and the ability of the bereaved to make meaning of the death may influence how continuing bonds manifest and whether they are experienced as positive or negative (although further research is needed). Postvention efforts should consider the process of meaning-making in creating the basis for positive continuing bonds and should attempt to address the stigma and societal expectations surrounding suicide bereavement. Future studies should involve representative samples, compare with continuing bonds after other causes of death, and investigate continuing bonds in suicide bereavement longitudinally.

Author Contributions: Conceptualization, K.A., K.K. and R.G.; methodology, R.G., K.K. and K.A.; software, R.G.; validation, K.K. and K.A.; formal analysis, R.G. and K.A.; investigation, R.G.; data curation, R.G. and K.A.; writing—original draft preparation, R.G.; writing—review and editing, R.G., K.K. and K.A.; supervision, K.K. and K.A.; project administration, K.A. All authors have read and agreed to the published version of the manuscript.

Funding: K.A. was supported by a National Health and Medical Research Council Early Career Fellowship (GNT1157796). The funder had no role in the design of the study, in the collection, analyses, or interpretation of data, in the writing of the manuscript, or in the decision to publish the results.

Institutional Review Board Statement: Not applicable.

Conflicts of Interest: The authors declare no conflict of interest.

Appendix A

Table A1. Quality assessment [1] of quantitative studies.

Topic	Jahn & Spencer-Thomas, 2014 [19]	Levi-Belz, 2017 [24]
Selection		
(1) Representativeness of the exposed cohort		
(a) Truly representative (one star)		
(b) Somewhat representative (one star)		
(c) Selected group	X	X
(d) No description		
(2) Selection of the non-exposed cohort		
(a) Drawn from the same community as the exposed cohort (one star)	N/a	X

Table A1. *Cont.*

Topic	Jahn & Spencer-Thomas, 2014 [19]	Levi-Belz, 2017 [24]
(b) Drawn from a different source		
(c) No description		
(3) Ascertainment of exposure		
(a) Secure record (e.g., surgical record) (one star)		
(b) Structured interview (one star)		
(c) Written self-report	X	X
(d) No description		
(e) Other		
(4) Demonstration that outcome of interest was not present at start of study		
(a) Yes (one star)	X	X
(b) No		
Comparability		
(1) Comparability of cohorts on the basis of the design or analysis controlled for confounders		
(a) The study controls for age, sex and marital status (one star)		X
(b) Study controls for other factors (list) (one star)		X
(c) Controls are not comparable		
Outcome		
(1) Assessment of outcome		
(a) Independent blind assessment (one star)		
(b) Record linkage (one star)		
(c) Self-report	X	X
(d) No description		
(e) Other		
(2) Was follow-up long enough for outcomes to occur		
(a) Yes (one star)	X	X
(b) No		
Indicate the mean duration of follow-up and a brief rationale for the assessment above	Range <1–20+ years	Range 2–540 months
(3) Adequacy of follow-up of cohorts		
(a) Complete follow-up, all subjects accounted for (one star)		
(b) Subjects lost to follow-up unlikely to introduce bias, number lost less than or equal to 20% or description of those lost suggested no different from those followed (one star)		
(c) Follow-up rate less than 80% and no description of those lost		
(d) No statement	X	X
Stars		
Selection	1	2
Comparability	0	2
Outcome	1	1
Rating	Poor	Poor

[1] Newcastle-Ottawa Quality Assessment Form for Cohort Studies [12]. Note: A study can be given a maximum of one star for each numbered item within the Selection and Outcome categories. A maximum of two stars can be given for Comparability. Thresholds for converting the Newcastle-Ottawa scales to AHRQ standards (good, fair, and poor): Good quality: 3 or 4 stars in selection domain AND 1 or 2 stars in comparability domain AND 2 or 3 stars in outcome/exposure domain. Fair quality: 2 stars in selection domain AND 1 or 2 stars in comparability domain AND 2 or 3 stars in outcome/exposure domain. Poor quality: 0 or 1 star in selection domain OR 0 stars in comparability domain OR 0 or 1 stars in outcome/exposure domain.

Appendix B

Table A2. Quality assessment [1] of qualitative studies.

	Topic	Adams et al., 2019 [14]	Bailey et al., 2015 [21]	Bell et al., 2015 [22]	Castelli, 2018 [27]	Entilli et al., 2021 [15]	Gall et al., 2015 [26]	Hunt et al., 2019 [9]	Jahn et al., 2018 [20]	Leichtentritt et al., 2015 [25]	Maple et al., 2013 [16]	Ross et al., 2018 [17]	Sands et al., 2010 [18]	Wood et al., 2012 [23]
		Domain 1: Research team and reflexivity												
		Personal characteristics												
1	Interviewer/facilitator	p. [2] 324–325			p. 4			p. 337			p. 59	p. 3	p. 103	
2	Credentials	p. 325				p. 2						p. 2	p. 121	
3	Occupation	p. 325				p. 2				p. 1107	p. 59	p. 3	p. 121	
4	Gender	p. 324				p. 2		p. 337				p. 2	p.105/121	
5	Experience and training	p. 325			p. 4	p. 2				p. 1107	p. 59	p. 2	p. 121	
		Relationship with participants												
6	Relationship established				p. 4									p. 878
7	Participant knowledge of the interviewer							p. 337				p. 3		
8	Interviewer characteristics	p. 324–325						p. 337			p. 59	p. 2		
		Domain 2: Study design												
		Theoretical framework												
9	Methodological orientation and theory	p. 325	p. 75	p. 379	p. 3–4	p. 3	p. 102	p. 336	p. 6	p. 1105–1106	p. 59	p. 2–3	p. 99–102	p. 877
		Participant selection												
10	Sampling	p. 325	p. 74	p. 378	p. 4	p. 2–3	p. 101	p. 336	p. 5	p. 1105	p. 59	p. 2	p. 103	p. 877
11	Method of approach	p. 325	p. 74	p. 378	p. 4	p. 2	p. 101–102	p. 336–337	p. 5–6	p. 1105	p. 59	p. 2	p. 103–104	p. 877–879
12	Sample size	p. 325	p. 74	p. 378	p. 5	p. 2	p. 101	p. 336	p. 5	p. 1105	p. 59	p. 2–3	p. 103	p. 877
13	Non-participation	p. 325				p. 2–3								
		Setting												
14	Setting of data collection	p. 325	p. 75		p. 4	p. 2		p. 336	p. 5		p. 59	p. 2	p. 103	p. 878
15	Presence of non-participants										p. 59			
16	Description of sample	p. 325	p. 74	p. 378	p. 5	p. 2–3	p. 101	p. 336	p. 5	p. 1105	p. 59	p. 2–3	p. 103	p. 877–878
		Data collection												
17	Interview guide	p. 325	p. 74–75	p. 378	p. 3–4	p. 2	p. 102	p. 337	p. 5–6	p. 1106	p. 59	p. 2	p. 103–104	p. 878–879
18	Repeat interviews					p. 2	p. 102					p. 2		
19	Audio/visual recording	p. 325	p. 75	p. 378	p. 4	p. 2	p. 102	p. 337		p. 1106	p. 59	p. 2	p. 103	p. 879

Table A2. *Cont.*

	Topic	Adams et al., 2019 [14]	Bailey et al., 2015 [21]	Bell et al., 2015 [22]	Castelli, 2018 [27]	Entilli et al., 2021 [15]	Gall et al., 2015 [26]	Hunt et al., 2019 [9]	Jahn et al., 2018 [20]	Leichtentritt et al., 2015 [25]	Maple et al., 2013 [16]	Ross et al., 2018 [17]	Sands et al., 2010 [18]	Wood et al., 2012 [23]
20	Field notes				p. 4					p. 1107				
21	Duration	p. 325	p. 75		p. 4	p. 3	p. 101			p. 1106	p. 59	p. 2	p. 103–104	p. 878
22	Data saturation				p. 5	p. 2		p. 338				p. 2–3		
23	Transcripts returned				p. 5									
	Domain 3: Analysis and findings													
	Data analysis													
24	Number of data coders	p. 325				p. 3	p. 102	p. 337	p. 6			p. 3	p. 105	p. 879
25	Description of the coding tree	p. 326				p. 3–6		p. 337–338						
26	Derivation of themes	p. 325	p. 75	p. 378	p. 4	p. 3	p. 102	p. 337	p. 6	p. 1107	p. 59	p. 3	p. 105–106	p. 879
27	Software				p. 4	p. 3			p. 6			p. 3		
28	Participant checking				p. 5			p. 337						
	Reporting													
29	Quotations presented	p. 326–329	p. 76–81	p. 380–385	p. 6–14	p. 3–6	p. 102–108	p. 338–342	p. 6–10	p. 1108–1114	p. 60–64	p. 3–6	p. 107–113	p. 880–888
30	Data and findings consistent	p. 329–331	p. 81–83	p. 383–386	p. 14–17	p. 6–10	p. 108–110	p. 342–343	p. 10–11	p. 1115–1117	p. 65–67	p. 7–8	p. 114–117	p. 888–894
31	Clarity of major themes	p. 326–329	p. 78–81	p. 379–382	p. 5–14	p. 3–6	p. 102–108	p. 338–342	p. 6–10	p. 1107–1115	p. 60–64	p. 3	p. 106–114	p. 880–888
32	Clarity of minor themes					p. 3–6		p. 338–342					p. 105–106	p. 880–888
	Rating													
	Domain 1: Research team and reflexivity	6/8 (75%)	0/8 (0%)	0/8 (0%)	3/8 (38%)	4/8 (50%)	0/8 (0%)	4/8 (50%)	0/8 (0%)	2/8 (25%)	4/8 (50%)	7/8 (88%)	5/8 (63%)	1/8 (13%)
	Domain 2: Study design	10/15 (67%)	9/15 (60%)	7/15 (47%)	12/15 (80%)	12/15 (80%)	9/15 (60%)	9/15 (60%)	7/15 (47%)	9/15 (60%)	10/15 (67%)	11/15 (73%)	9/15 (60%)	9/15 (60%)
	Domain 3: Analysis and findings	6/9 (67%)	4/9 (44%)	4/9 (44%)	6/9 (67%)	8/9 (89%)	5/9 (56%)	8/9 (89%)	6/9 (67%)	4/9 (44%)	4/9 (44%)	6/9 (67%)	6/9 (67%)	6/9 (67%)
	Total	22/32 (69%)	13/32 (41%)	11/32 (34%)	21/32 (66%)	24/32 (75%)	14/32 (44%)	21/32 (66%)	13/32 (41%)	15/32 (67%)	18/32 (56%)	24/32 (75%)	20/32 (63%)	16/32 (50%)

[1] Consolidated Criteria for Reporting Qualitative Research (COREQ) [13]. [2] In this table, "p." refers to page numbers.

References

1. World Health Organisation. *Suicide*; [Updated 17 June 2021]; World Health Organisation: Geneva, Switzerland, 2021. Available online: https://www.who.int/news-room/fact-sheets/detail/suicide (accessed on 6 September 2021).
2. Andriessen, K.; Rahman, B.; Draper, B.; Dudley, M.; Mitchell, P.B. Prevalence of exposure to suicide: A meta-analysis of population-based studies. *J. Psychiatr. Res.* **2017**, *88*, 113–120. [CrossRef] [PubMed]
3. Pitman, A.; Osborn, D.; King, M.; Erlangsen, A. Effects of suicide bereavement on mental health and suicide risk. *Lancet Psychiatry* **2014**, *1*, 86–94. [CrossRef]
4. Jordan, J.R.; McIntosh, J.L. *Grief after Suicide: Understanding the Consequences and Caring for the Survivors*; Routledge: New York, NY, USA, 2011.
5. Boerner, K.; Stroebe, M.; Schut, H.; Wortman, C.B. Theories of Grief and Bereavement. In *Encyclopedia of Geropsychology*; Pachana, N.A., Ed.; Springer: Singapore, 2015; pp. 1–10.
6. Klass, D.; Silverman, P.R.; Nickman, S.; Nickman, S.L. *Continuing Bonds: New Understandings of Grief*; Taylor & Francis: Washington, DC, USA, 1996.
7. Klass, D.; Steffen, E. *Continuing Bonds in Bereavement: New Directions for Research and Practice*; Routledge: New York, NY, USA, 2017.
8. Neimeyer, R.A.; Baldwin, S.A.; Gillies, J. Continuing bonds and reconstructing meaning: Mitigating complications in bereavement. *Death Stud.* **2006**, *30*, 715–738. [CrossRef]
9. Hunt, Q.A.; Young, T.A.; Hertlein, K.M. The process of long-term suicide bereavement: Responsibility, familial support, and meaning making. *Contemp. Fam. Ther.* **2019**, *41*, 335–346. [CrossRef]
10. Rubin, S.S.; Nadav, O.B.; Malkinson, R.; Koren, D.; Goffer-Shnarch, M.; Michaeli, E. The two-track model of bereavement questionnaire (TTBQ): Development and validation of a relational measure. *Death Stud.* **2009**, *33*, 305–333. [CrossRef] [PubMed]
11. Page, M.J.; McKenzie, J.E.; Bossuyt, P.M.; Boutron, I.; Hoffmann, T.C.; Mulrow, C.D.; Shamseer, L.; Tetzlaff, J.M.; Akl, E.A.; Brennan, S.E.; et al. The PRISMA 2020 statement: An updated guideline for reporting systematic reviews. *BMJ* **2021**, *372*, n71. [CrossRef]
12. Wells, G.; Shea, B.; O'Connell, D.; Peterson, J.; Welch, V.; Losos, M.; Tugwell, P. Newcastle-Ottawa Quality Assessment Scale Cohort Studies. University of Ottawa: Ottawa, ON, Canada, n.d. Available online: https://www.ncbi.nlm.nih.gov/books/NBK99082/bin/appb-fm4.pdf (accessed on 6 September 2021).
13. Tong, A.; Sainsbury, P.; Craig, J. Consolidated criteria for reporting qualitative research (COREQ): A 32-item checklist for interviews and focus groups. *Int. J. Qual. Health Care* **2007**, *19*, 349–357. [CrossRef]
14. Adams, E.; Hawgood, J.; Bundock, A.; Kõlves, K. A phenomenological study of siblings bereaved by suicide: A shared experience. *Death Stud.* **2019**, *43*, 324–332. [CrossRef]
15. Entilli, L.; Ross, V.; De Leo, D.; Cipolletta, S.; Kõlves, K. Experiences of parental suicide-bereavement: A longitudinal qualitative analysis over two years. *Int. J. Environ. Res. Public Health* **2021**, *18*, 564. [CrossRef]
16. Maple, M.; Edwards, H.E.; Minichiello, V.; Plummer, D. Still part of the family: The importance of physical, emotional and spiritual memorial places and spaces for parents bereaved through the suicide death of their son or daughter. *Mortality* **2013**, *18*, 54–71. [CrossRef]
17. Ross, V.; Kõlves, K.; Kunde, L.; de Leo, D. Parents' experiences of suicide-bereavement: A qualitative study at 6 and 12 months after loss. *Int. J. Environ. Res. Public Health* **2018**, *15*, 618. [CrossRef] [PubMed]
18. Sands, D.; Tennant, M. Transformative learning in the context of suicide bereavement. *Adult Educ. Q.* **2010**, *60*, 99–121. [CrossRef]
19. Jahn, D.; Spencer-Thomas, S. Continuing bonds through after-death spiritual experiences in individuals bereaved by suicide. *J. Spiritual. Ment. Health* **2014**, *16*, 311–324. [CrossRef]
20. Jahn, D.; Spencer-Thomas, S. A qualitative examination of continuing bonds through spiritual experiences in individuals bereaved by suicide. *Religions* **2018**, *9*, 248. [CrossRef]
21. Bailey, L.; Bell, J.; Kennedy, D. Continuing social presence of the dead: Exploring suicide bereavement through online memorialisation. *New Rev. Hypermedia Multimed.* **2015**, *21*, 72–86. [CrossRef]
22. Bell, J.; Bailey, L.; Kennedy, D. 'We do it to keep him alive': Bereaved individuals' experiences of online suicide memorials and continuing bonds. *Mortality* **2015**, *20*, 375–389. [CrossRef]
23. Wood, L.; Byram, V.; Gosling, A.; Stokes, J. Continuing bonds after suicide bereavement in childhood. *Death Stud.* **2012**, *36*, 873–898. [CrossRef] [PubMed]
24. Levi-Belz, Y. Relationship with the deceased as facilitator of posttraumatic growth among suicide-loss survivors. *Death Stud.* **2017**, *41*, 376–384. [CrossRef]
25. Leichtentritt, R.D.; Yerushalmi, A.; Barak, A. Characteristics of the ongoing bond. *Br. J. Soc. Work* **2015**, *45*, 1102–1118. [CrossRef]
26. Gall, T.L.; Henneberry, J.; Eyre, M. Spiritual beliefs and meaning-making within the context of suicide bereavement. *J. Study Spiritual.* **2015**, *5*, 98–112. [CrossRef]
27. Castelli Dransart, D.A. Spiritual and religious issues in the aftermath of suicide. *Religions* **2018**, *9*, 153. [CrossRef]
28. Krysinska, K.; Andriessen, K.; Corveleyn, J. Religion and spirituality in online suicide bereavement: An analysis of online memorials. *Crisis* **2014**, *35*, 349–356. [CrossRef] [PubMed]
29. Čepulienė, A.A.; Pučinskaitė, B.; Spangelytė, K.; Skruibis, P.; Gailienė, D. Spirituality and religiosity during suicide bereavement: A qualitative systematic review. *Religions* **2021**, *12*, 766. [CrossRef]
30. Parker, C.M.; Laungani, P.; Young, B. *Death and Bereavement across Cultures*; Routledge: New York, NY, USA, 1997.

31. Stroebe, M.; Schut, H. The dual process model of coping with bereavement: A decade on. *Omega* **2010**, *61*, 273–289. [CrossRef] [PubMed]
32. Foster, T.L.; Gilmer, M.J.; Davies, B.; Dietrich, M.S.; Barrera, M.; Fairclough, D.L.; Vannatta, K.; Gerhardt, C.A. Comparison of continuing bonds reported by parents and siblings after a child's death from cancer. *Death Stud.* **2011**, *35*, 420–440. [CrossRef] [PubMed]
33. Grad, O.T.; Treven, M.; Krysinska, K. Suicide Bereavement and Gender. In *Postvention in Action: The International Handbook of Suicide Bereavement*; Andriessen, K., Krysinska, K., Grad, O., Eds.; Hogrefe: Gottingen, Germany, 2017; pp. 39–49.
34. Milman, E.; Neimeyer, R.A.; Fitzpatrick, M.; MacKinnon, C.J.; Muis, K.R.; Cohen, S.R. Rumination moderates the role of meaning in the development of prolonged grief symptomatology. *J. Clin. Psychol.* **2019**, *75*, 1047–1065. [CrossRef]
35. Root, B.L.; Exline, J.J. The role of continuing bonds in coping with grief: Overview and future directions. *Death Stud.* **2014**, *38*, 1–8. [CrossRef]
36. Stroebe, M.; Schut, H.; Boerner, K. Continuing bonds in adaptation to bereavement: Toward theoretical integration. *Clin. Psychol. Rev.* **2010**, *30*, 259–268. [CrossRef]
37. Krysinska, K.; Andriessen, K. Suicide Bereavement Online: Sharing Memories, Seeking Support, and Exchanging Hope. In *Suicide Prevention and New Technologies. Evidence Based Practice*; Mishara, B., Kerkhof, A., Eds.; Palgrave-Macmillan: New York, NY, USA, 2014; pp. 150–165.
38. Krysinska, K.; Andriessen, K. Online memorialization and grief after suicide: An analysis of suicide memorials on the Internet. *Omega* **2015**, *71*, 19–47. [CrossRef]
39. Sands, D. A tripartite model of suicide grief: Meaning-making and the relationship with the deceased. *Grief Matters* **2009**, *12*, 10–17.
40. Evans, A.; Abrahamson, K. The influence of stigma on suicide bereavement: A systematic review. *J. Psychosoc. Nurs. Ment. Health Serv.* **2020**, *58*, 21–27. [CrossRef] [PubMed]

International Journal of
Environmental Research and Public Health

MDPI

Review

Scoping Review of Peer-Led Support for People Bereaved by Suicide

Agnes Higgins [1,*], Lisbeth Hybholt [2,3], Olivia A. Meuser [4], Jessica Eustace Cook [1], Carmel Downes [1] and Jean Morrissey [1]

1 School of Nursing and Midwifery, Trinity College Dublin, D02PN40 Dublin, Ireland; eustacj@tcd.ie (J.E.C.); cadownes@tcd.ie (C.D.); morrisje@tcd.ie (J.M.)
2 Mental Health Services East, Psychiatry Region Zealand, 4200 Slagelse, Denmark; lihy@regionsjaelland.dk
3 Psychiatric Research Unit, Psychiatry Region Zealand, 4200 Slagelse, Denmark
4 College of Arts & Sciences, University of Pennsylvania, Philadelphia, PA 19102, USA; omeuser@sas.upenn.edu
* Correspondence: ahiggins@tcd.ie

Abstract: Suicide bereavement support groups are a widely available format of postvention service. Although other reviews have addressed peer-led bereavement interventions, no review has focused specifically on peer-led support for people bereaved by suicide. Informed by a framework for undertaking scoping reviews, we conducted a systematic review according to PRISMA-ScR guidelines. Searches conducted in May 2021 of peer-reviewed literature in MEDLINE (EBSCO), CINAHL Complete (EBSCO), PsycINFO (EBSCO), EMBASE (Elsevier), AMED (EBSCO), ERIC (EBSCO), Web of Science (Core Collection), ASSIA (Proquest), and Global Index Medicus. The search was not limited by language, and all studies were included to full text screening. The search identified 10 studies conducted between 1994 and 2020 in five countries. The selected papers were subjected to quality assessment. The interventions included face-to-face groups, telephone and online groups/forums and were evaluated using a variety of methodologies, which made comparison and synthesis challenging. Thematic analysis resulted in four themes: motivation, impact, aspects of intervention which hindered/enhanced outcomes, and recommendations for the practice of peer support made by the authors. While there were methodological limitations to most studies included in this review; the studies do indicate the potential benefit of peer-led support to those bereaved through suicide. Future studies should provide a definition of 'peer' and a clear description of the intervention being evaluated. As the field matures there is a need for more rigorous evaluation of peer interventions with representative samples, studies that compare the impact of various types of peer interventions, and studies of the peer group processes.

Keywords: bereavement; suicide; peer interventions; scoping review; postvention

Citation: Higgins, A.; Hybholt, L.; Meuser, O.A.; Eustace Cook, J.; Downes, C.; Morrissey, J. Scoping Review of Peer-Led Support for People Bereaved by Suicide. *Int. J. Environ. Res. Public Health* **2022**, *19*, 3485. https://doi.org/10.3390/ijerph19063485

Academic Editors: Karl Andriessen, Karolina Krysinska and Yossi Levi-Belz

Received: 31 January 2022
Accepted: 10 March 2022
Published: 15 March 2022

1. Introduction

Death by suicide is an extremely complex issue that impacts hundreds of thousands of people every year globally, with estimates suggesting that almost 700,000 people die from suicide every year [1,2]. A suicide death not only impacts the wellbeing of close family members and friends but also affects many people outside of this immediate circle, including neighbours, passers-by, or professionals caring for the person.

It is estimated that 135 individuals are exposed by every suicide death [3]. Cerel et al. [4] provides a nested model of suicide survivorship. The outer circle of the model encompasses all those who have been 'exposed', defined as anyone who knows or identifies with someone who dies by suicide and within this group there are those that are 'affected' by the loss. Within the affected group are two further subgroups comprising those who have an attachment relationship to the deceased and experience 'short term' or 'long-term' distress.

Coping and adapting to a loss by suicide can be particularly challenging owing to feelings of guilt, responsibility, shame, and rejection [5,6] and may have long-lasting impact on physical and mental health, including increased risk of suicidal thoughts and behaviours [7–9]. The bereavement may also have long-lasting consequences for families as well as individuals, altering patterns of communications within the family unit and contributing to the loss of cohesion and relationship breakdown [10]. Hence, one of the key priorities within suicide prevention policy and strategy (for example [1,11–14]) is the provision of a range of supports, both informal and formal, to help those affected by suicide and suicide behaviour to navigate the grieving process and reduce the risk of suicide and other adverse effects [15]. In addition, statement five in the National Institute of Health and Care Excellence's Suicide Prevention Quality Standard focuses on 'supporting people bereaved or affected by suspected suicide' [16].

Suicide bereavement support groups are a widely available postvention service. Frequently initiated by people bereaved by suicide, they are often based on the principles of sharing experiences and offering mutual assistance, with the aim of reducing distress and risk of mental and emotional problems. Despite the increasing use of peer support groups as well as user demand for peer-delivered services, Rawlinson et al. [17], notes that there was scant attention given to peer support for suicide bereavement as an intervention, and no evidence regarding impact or effectiveness. To the authors' knowledge, five systematic reviews of interventions for people bereaved by suicide have been published to date [5,6,18–20]. Four of these reviews focus on the effectiveness of individual and group-based interventions delivered in a school, family, and community context and facilitated by health care professionals, researchers, or health care professionals in conjunction with volunteers. Although the reviews point to some evidence of positive impact of the interventions on mental health and grief outcomes [5,6,18,20], few of these reviews included peer-led interventions. In two of the reviews, only controlled studies were included [5,20] while Linde et al. [6] only included studies with quantifiable outcome measures.

Three reviews were found that addressed peer-led interventions. One scoping review focused on peer support programs (excluding bereavement programs) that aim to reduce suicidality in people deemed at risk [21], and another scoping review focusing on describing the breadth of peer-delivered suicide preventions services and their outcomes, to inform future service delivery and research [22]. Bartone et al.'s [19] systematic review focused on peer support services for bereaved survivors, irrespective of the cause of death. Whilst this review provides evidence of beneficial impacts of peer interventions in terms of reduced grief symptoms, depression and suicidal thinking, as well as enhanced well-being and personal growth, and is helpful in understanding the benefits to those bereaved by suicide, it does not focus exclusively on peer support for suicide bereaved, with only seven of the thirty-two studies included involving those bereaved by suicide, including members of community mental health teams and counsellors bereaved by suicide. Of the seven studies included, the authors state that in six, support was provided by others who were also bereaved by suicide. However, it is unclear how the term peer was conceptualised and defined, or what types of peer intervention were provided. Given the distinctive nature of bereavement by suicide, in terms of stigma, self-blame, guilt, societal reactions [6], the potential for prolonged and complicated grief [23], and the absence of a review in this area, the authors were of the view there was merit in conducting a separate review to examine the extent, range, and nature of research activity in this area. Pooling data and sharing information and learnings from a review is also important for people who are involved in developing peer interventions and preparing peer facilitators.

Aims of the Review

This scoping review was informed by Arskey and O'Malley's [24] paper on scoping reviews and aimed to examine peer-led interventions for people bereaved by suicide. Using a systematic process following PRISMA guidelines the objectives of the review were to: (i) describe how peer is conceptualised and defined; (ii) discuss models of peer-led interventions used; (iii) describe the outcomes of peer-led interventions; (iv) identify elements of peer-led intervention that enhanced or hindered outcomes.

2. Methods

A systematic search of the following electronic databases was undertaken by the librarian (J E-C): MEDLINE (EBSCO), CINAHL Complete (EBSCO), PsycINFO (EBSCO), EMBASE (Elsevier), AMED (EBSCO), ERIC (EBSCO), Web of Science (Core Collection), ASSIA (Proquest), and Global Index Medicus (WHO). These included the main databases used in any health sciences-related systematic review, as well as important databases for educational and social sciences research.

Previous reviews and the authors' knowledge were used to determine keywords, for example, terms denoting suicide (e.g., killing oneself), bereavement (e.g., loss, mourn, grief), as well as peer support (e.g., self-help, social support, peer group). In all cases, these terms were searched for, in titles and abstracts, and, where appropriate, other fields such as the "contributed indexing" field in MEDLINE (EBSCO). These were combined with controlled vocabulary terms such as MeSH, EMTREE, and CINAHL Headings as appropriate (see example MEDLINE search strategy, in Supplementary Table S1).

The search was run from the inception of the database and limited to peer-reviewed papers published before May 2021. These search boundaries resulted in 13,663 papers. A further 227 articles were located through a grey literature search, which resulted in a total of 13,890 papers. Endnote was used to screen the majority of duplicates (6987) and a further 123 duplicates were removed on import into Covidence. After duplicates were removed, the resulting 6780 papers were screened according to the following inclusion and exclusion criteria (see Table 1).

Table 1. Inclusion/exclusion criteria.

Inclusion
i. Empirical studies using any research design
ii. Studies focusing on peer-led interventions
iii. Target population -people bereaved by suicide
iv. Conducted in any country, location, and setting, and using any modes of delivery (online, face to face, phone etc.)
v. Reported on any outcomes (e.g., feasibility, acceptability, effectiveness etc.)
Exclusion
i. Descriptive or theoretical papers focused on a peer intervention without evaluation findings
ii. Studies focused on evaluating peer interventions for bereavement (including bereavement by suicide) where it was not possible to extract information specific to bereavement by suicide
iii. Studies of interventions for bereavement (including bereavement by suicide) where there was a co-facilitation element by a professional
iv. Literature reviews, systematic reviews, discussion papers, opinion articles/editorials, commentaries, book chapters, conference papers, and case studies (n = 1).

Covidence screening software (www.covidence.org (accessed on 30 June 2021)) was used to manage the screening process. Two reviewers independently assessed each title and abstract against the inclusion/exclusion criteria identified in Table 1 to identify potentially relevant papers (LH, AH, OM, JM, each pair assessed 50% or 3390 papers) and any discrepancies were resolved by a third reviewer not involved in screening that paper. For stage two screening, the full texts of 115 papers were obtained and assessed independently by two reviewers, one person assessed all (LH, AH, OM, JM). Any discrepancies at this stage were resolved by discussion with the wider team. This stage resulted in the exclusion of a further 105 papers, primarily due to their not being focused on peer-led intervention, not focused on bereavement because of suicide, not being primary research, or including those not bereaved by suicide. Following this, reference lists in these papers were reviewed, which resulted in no new additions, resulting in 10 studies in the final review. Figure 1 shows the PRISMA diagram.

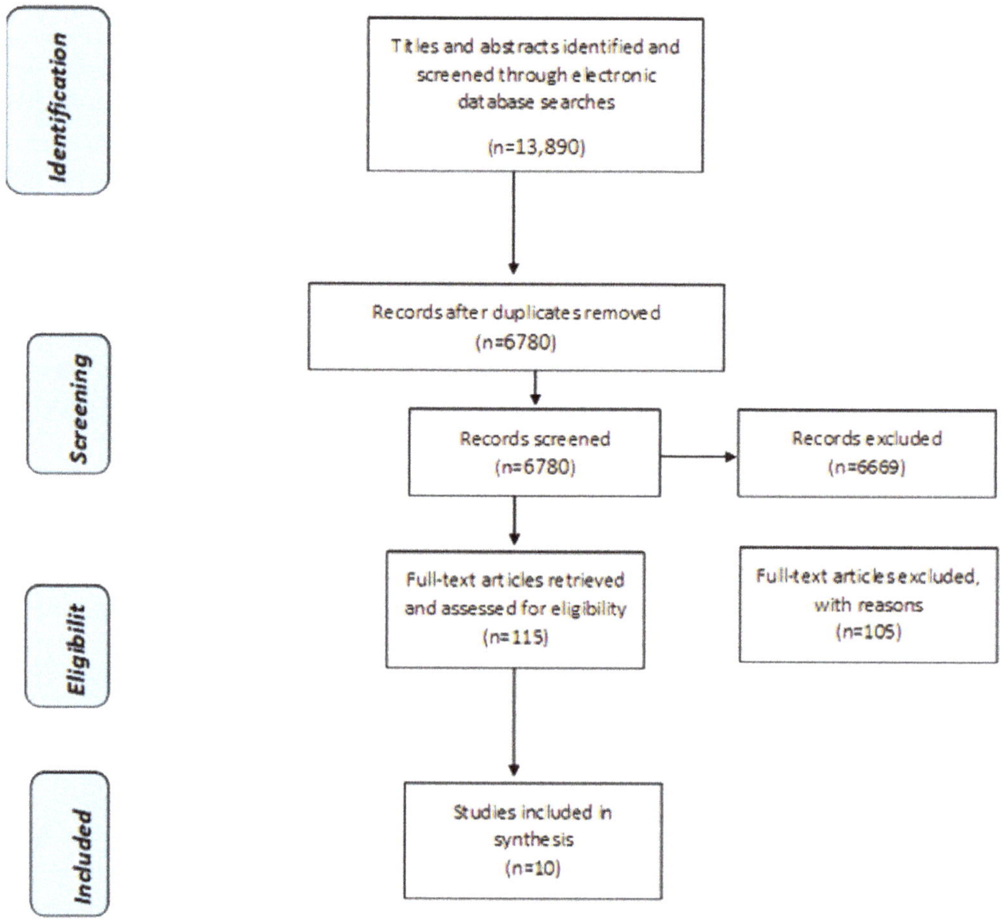

Figure 1. PRISMA Flow Diagram of Selection Process.

3. Data Extraction and Analysis

A Microsoft Excel data extraction form was developed and piloted for extracting information from each study. Information on author, year, country of origin, study aim, sample achieved, population characteristics, and core data on methodology, outcomes of peer support, and factors that enhanced or hindered outcomes and findings were extracted and inputted into the Excel form (see Supplementary Table S2 for overview of studies and Supplementary Table S3 for more information on findings). In line with the aims of the review, information related to how peer support was defined/conceptualised, the nature and type of the peer intervention, as well as recommendations for further study in the area were also extracted. Following this, data were coded inductively into themes in line with the aims of the review. To ensure consistency, data extraction for each paper was completed independently by at least two people (LH, AH, CD, OM).

4. Quality Appraisal and Quality of the Studies

While quality appraisal may or may not be part of a scoping review, given the relative newness of research on peer interventions, we chose to include a quality appraisal element to help inform and improve the quality of future research. Two reviewers independently scored each paper and came together to agree the final score using the categories, weak, moderate, and strong. To support the assessment of quality, quantitative studies were reviewed using the Effective Public Health Practice Project Quality Assessment tool [25] and the Critical Appraisal Skills Programme Qualitative Critical Appraisal Tool (CASP) (https://casp-uk.net/casp-tools-checklists/ (accessed on 9 July 2021)) was completed on studies using qualitative methods (see Supplementary Table S2 for more information on the tools).

Overall, the body of evidence was of mixed quality. The main reasons for the low/weak scoring in the qualitative studies were: insufficient information on issues such as ethics and data analysis, and lack of discussion on relevance/transferability of research to other contexts or discussion on reflexivity and influence of the researcher on the research, and vice-versa. In addition, the quality of the supporting data was sparse in some studies.

For the studies which were quantitative or had a quantitative component, half of them did not report receiving ethical approval or the consent of participants. Despite collection of data using a range of existing survey tools or designed measures to capture data, such as the benefits and limitations of internet forums [26], or helpfulness and comfort of meetings [27], only a few of the studies commented on the reliability of the tools used. The absence on information on demographics, withdrawals, and selection bias were also reasons for weak scores.

5. Findings

5.1. Study Characteristics

The ten studies included were conducted between 1994 and 2020. Three studies were conducted in the USA [28–30], two in Canada [27,31], and one in England [32], Italy [33], and Sweden [34]. Two of the studies, which were online forums, contained participants from different countries. One of them comprised mostly US-based participants with smaller numbers from Canada, the UK, and Australia [26]. The second contained both Dutch and Belgian participants [35]. The study designs included six qualitative studies, three quantitative studies, involving the use of surveys [26,29,31], and one mixed method study, which used both interviews and surveys [27]. The six qualitative studies collected data using participant observation [28,33] and interviews [33]; one study used a focus group and semi structured interviews [32]; one used telephone interviews [30]; two used online forum messages as data [34,35].

The studies that were quantitative in nature or had a quantitative element [26,27,29,31] collected data using a range of existing survey tools or designed measures to capture data, such as the benefits and limitations to internet forums [26], or helpfulness and comfort of meetings [27]. Only a few of the studies commented on the reliability of the tools used [26,27,29]. In addition to the closed questions, two studies used several open-ended questions to elicit information about the helpfulness of the meetings [27] and participants' social networks, their motivations for attending groups, and their experiences of groups [31]. All surveys were administered during the intervention, apart from Barlow et al. [27], who administered the Hogan Grief Reaction Checklist pre- and post-intervention. Analysis was conducted using descriptive statistics [26,29,31], and also inferential statistics [27,29].

5.2. Participant Characteristics

All studies involved people who were bereaved by suicide, with one group including three people who had tried to take their own life [33]. In terms of participants' relationship to the deceased, two studies focused solely on parents [29,34]; two studies listed the relationships as including parents, children, spouses/partners, siblings and others, without specifying the actual number of each [27,28]; one study had parents in the majority of the sample [32], while the remaining two, which stipulated the relationship, had similar numbers of parents and partners [33,35]. In addition to parents and partners/spouses, all samples included at least some siblings and children, while other relatives and non-relatives, including friends, comprised a minority of the samples. In terms of the duration of time since suicide, the range was 6 weeks to 20 years [27,32]. One study gave the mean duration as being 3 years [32]. In most of the studies, the majority of participants had sustained the loss within the past five years [26,27,35]; only in Feigelman & Feigelman [30] were the majority of participants bereaved for more than five years.

It is not possible to report the collective sample number, as Hopmeyer & Werk [31] did not report sample size and or demographics, while the sample size in another study was the number of online messages analysed, rather than the number of participants [34]. In those that reported age, participant age ranged from 17 to 81 years [26,27,32,33]. Two studies gave the mean ages of the sample as 46.9 and 52.3 [26,27]. Age was not reported or there was incomplete reporting of age in several studies [28–31,34,35]. Over 70% of the reported samples were female [27,32,33,35], with as many as 94.6% females in one study [26]. None of the studies reported on the ethnicity, sexual orientation, or education level of participants.

5.3. How Peer and Peer Support Is Conceptualised and Defined

No study specifically defined what they meant by the term peer. Of the studies that briefly alluded to the concepts of 'peer support' or 'peer help' in the introductions to the papers, it is evident that peer support or peer help is regarded as an exchange of support among people who share similar experiences [27,28,32]. Feigelman & Feigelman [28], in their introduction, briefly discuss the perceived benefits and drawbacks of peer-led versus professional-led support groups, without defining either. One study described the groups being researched as "mutual aid" groups [33], while another described them as "self-help" groups [31].

5.4. Type of Peer Interventions Evaluated

The interventions included five face-to-face groups [29–33] and four online groups/forums [26,29,34,35]. One of the studies was a face-to-face or telephone peer support program in which a peer supporter was matched with a 'client' who had experienced the same type of loss [27]. Six studies indicated that the groups/pairings were facilitated/moderated by a peer bereaved by suicide [27,28,30,31,33,34]. The background of the person/s was not stipulated in three studies [29,32,35] while it was unclear if one of the studies involved any facilitation/moderation [26].

Three studies indicated that the groups met monthly for approximately two hours [29,30,32] while one group met weekly for 1.5 h [33] and another held bi-monthly meetings [31]. The 24/7 availability of the online groups/forums was mentioned in two studies [26,29] but presumably all four were always accessible for an indefinite period of time. Only three studies indicated the duration of the group/pairing; in the case of Barlow et al. [27], the pairing met for a period of four months, while two studies indicated that the groups were open-ended (meaning members could join at any time) [28,31].

Few studies make any reference to the format and structure of the groups/forums. One of the groups is described as "open discussion" [31]. Another described how the group opened with a brief period of informal social interaction before the peer-facilitator initiated introductions, encouraged people to contribute in a non-judgemental fashion, and ensured new members had the opportunity to speak if they so wished. The group then closed with a serenity prayer and refreshments [28,30]. One of the internet forum studies described how members were given some instructional guidance about items of interest and how best to contribute to the forum, but otherwise were free to "dialogue" with other members [29].

Whether peer facilitators/moderators were offered education and support for the role was not or poorly described in most studies. One study stipulated that the peer was trained and partook in monthly debriefing and educational sessions [27], while two indicated that the peer facilitator had the support of professionals, one of whom was a social worker, while the other study didn't specify except to say that it was a 'team of professionals' [31,35].

5.5. Outcomes of the Intervention

Four themes were identified: motivation, impact, aspects of intervention which hindered/enhanced outcomes, and recommendations for the practice of peer support made by the authors.

5.5.1. Motivation

In the five studies that reported motivation for accessing peer support, the main reasons included wanting to meet others with the same experiences, to access information and support to understanding, and coping with the suicide loss. Feelings of depression and loneliness as well as stigma from social networks prompted people to seek out a safe, understanding, and non-judgemental environment with peers. Helping and giving support to others was also a motivating factor [27,31,32,34,35]. In one study, accessing online support was linked to being 'turned off' by face-to-face groups or none being available [29].

5.5.2. Impact

The shared understanding, empathy, and the information received from peer support impacted participants positively in terms of a reduction in self-blame, isolation, and stigma, as well as gains in hope, self-worth (by helping others), personal well-being, and a sense of connectedness. Participants reported better coping strategies, problem-solving skills, and empowerment to grieve and change. In relation to the grief process, the peer group helped with acceptance and processing the grief by enabling participants to gain a better understanding of their own and others' experiences, normalise the loss, as well as offering the opportunity to memorialise the deceased, which was important to the bereavement process [26–33]. In addition, Silvén Hagström [34], reported that peers helped participants construct new meanings or narratives around the suicide. Only one study conducted pre- and post-testing of the intervention and reported that some grief reactions (despair, detachment, and disorganisation) were reduced at post-intervention follow-up while peer support was rated highly in terms of comfort and helpfulness [27]. Schotanus-Dijktra et al. [35] found more positive comments about the online experience when compared to negative comments (9 vs. 1%), however, most of their findings related to the nature of online interactions rather than their impact. In the few studies that reported negative impacts, these related to feelings of distress and depression as a result of being involved in the peer intervention [26,28–30].

5.6. Aspects of Intervention Which Enhanced Outcomes

Helpful aspects of interventions fell into three categories: group process, group format, and group composition. The group process was enhanced by good facilitation and leadership skills. These included facilitators being flexible and accommodating regarding time and place of meeting, 'being present', providing additional support, structure, and managing group diversity and dynamics effectively [27,29,30]. In addition, debriefing opportunities and support for peer leaders provided reassurance and confidence in their role [27]. In terms of format, peers bereaved by suicide appreciated the 24/7 availability, anonymity, and 'democratic participatory style' of internet support groups [26,29], with some participants in one study identifying it as preferable to face-to-face support [29]. While members with similar kinship relationships facilitated a connection and shared understanding to form group diversity, [27], in terms of having a mix of individuals with different kinship relationships to the deceased, including individuals at different stages of grief and individuals who had tried to take their own life, this was identified as beneficial for generating a dialogue in which different perspectives challenged ways of thinking [28,33]. It also meant that some peers who were longer bereaved could adopt a more supportive role in which they offered guidance and hope to others [32].

5.7. Aspects of Intervention Which Hindered Outcomes

Unhelpful aspects of interventions fell into three categories: group process, group format/structure, and logistical challenges. In terms of the group process, poor facilitation made the intervention less acceptable to participants, in some cases, causing individuals to leave or change groups. Poor facilitation included insufficient monitoring of online posts, not addressing participants' upset, allowing some members to monopolise the group or form cliques, and spending too much emphasis on some topics and not enough on others [26,28–30]. In addition, two studies identified issues in relation to the management of expectations and boundaries around interactions, including how to terminate relationships and respond to people who took political and social action agendas in relation to suicide into the group [27,30]. Group format/structure issues, which affected the acceptability and effectiveness of interventions included groups being too large, lacking members with the same kinship relationship or experiences, the degree of spirituality/religiosity of the group, and group sharing/disclosure which some members found uncomfortable or upsetting [28–30,32]. Finally, logistical issues such as distance to travel to groups, timing, and available space were identified as challenging in two studies [27,32].

5.8. Recommendations for the Practice of Peer Support Made by the Authors of the Studies Included

Training and support for facilitators was regarded as essential by some authors to enable people to facilitate groups with confidence and address problems which arise in groups, such as monopolisation by some individuals, feelings of distress, how to manage different expectations and agendas of members, and how to set clear guidelines from the outset [27,28,30]. As well as developing group facilitation and leadership skills, knowledge of the bereavement process and referral resources were deemed important parts of the ongoing education of facilitators [30]. One paper recommended that support group members also be given information and tools to enable them to participate effectively, equitably, and non-judgementally in groups [28]. In terms of online forums, Bailey et al. [26] recommended the development of guidelines "governing the conceptualisation, development, and maintenance of Internet forums in order to ensure their safety and clinical utility" (p. 399) while consultation with users was advised to ensure that the forums meet the needs of different groups. Finally, Feigelman & Feigelman [30] recommended that support groups be open-ended; although they acknowledged that there may be conflicts in terms of the needs of newly bereaved people in comparison to longer term survivors, they believed that there was benefit to having both in the mix.

6. Discussion

The involvement of peers and peer intervention are now an acknowledged cornerstone of all mental health policy [36–39] and this review set out to examine peer-led interventions for people bereaved by suicide. Although the aim of the studies included was to evaluate a peer-led intervention, in the majority of cases, peer support was not explicitly defined, hence the authors inferred that it was understood as a form of reciprocal support between individuals who share similar experiences and as being distinct from professional support. While the type of peer-led intervention offered was typically a group format in which there was a moderator/facilitator present, the nature of the peer interventions was poorly described in terms of duration, specification of the intervention (i.e., short-term vs. long-term; open vs. closed membership), or if the interventions followed a certain structure, used ground rules, or addressed certain topics. It was also unclear if training and support was provided to the facilitators/moderators or whether people attending had to disclose their loss or identify how the person died to meet the criteria to join the group. These omissions made comparison and interpretation of findings a challenge, as similarities and differences between groups were not explicit.

Nevertheless, a recurring theme within the data was the positive impact of being able to share narratives of loss in a non-judgemental and supportive environment, wherein people, by virtue of their similar experiences, could help and support each other to process their grief. This support in turn buoyed individuals to the extent that they felt less alone and stigmatised, and more hopeful and empowered. Recent qualitative studies of the support needs of people bereaved by suicide highlight how the feelings of stigma make social interactions difficult, uncomfortable, and painful, which in turn leads to withdrawal and self-isolation [40,41]. While there were differences of opinions in terms of who should lead peer groups, participants in both of these studies iterated the importance of finding a place to talk, without fearing people's reactions and judgement. While talking to peers and sharing experiences within a group may decrease feelings of being alone and is an important element of meaning reconstruction following a loss [23], it can also be burdensome or even retraumatisating for some people. Indeed, findings in the current review indicate that some members found group sharing and disclosure uncomfortable or upsetting, a view that is also supported by a recent study of individuals with mental health problems who reported that listening to others' recovery narratives can be burdening, saddening, and make some people feel inadequate and disconnected [42].

Another important issue highlighted in this review relates to the preparation of peer facilitators. Although the findings suggest that a person's experience of a peer support group is highly influenced by the facilitation of the group, the nature and type of preparation provided to the facilitators was not made explicit. This may be the reason why many of the authors recommended that facilitators be provided with education to help them manage issues related to group dynamics, as well as the distress that some participants will inevitably experience. The preparation and on-going support for facilitators is also in line with many of the guidelines on bereavement support that have been published internationally (see [43–45]). While the authors of the studies included in the review did not question whether people bereaved by suicide should ever facilitate groups, bereaved participants in Ross et al.'s [41] recent study were of the view that people bereaved by suicide may not necessarily be able to lead a group. Hence, they were of the view that trained professionals should facilitate the support groups to ensure a safe and helpful dynamic in the group.

In terms of online support, although a small number of people commented on inadequate moderation and the posting of inaccurate information, online peer support interventions emerged as having advantages over face-to face peer interventions in terms of the accessibility and anonymity offered. Thus, the reported acceptability and benefits from using online support forums highlight this as a type of peer support with potential, however, similar to face-to-face groups, issues around quality and safety need to be addressed. Only one of the studies included in the review compared online peer group support with face-to-face peer group support [29], and although they found that grief symptoms were higher in the online community, they were unable to attribute this to any deficiency in online support but rather identified greater stigmatisation from family and friends as a possible reason for the discrepancy.

In addition to education and preparation, the review also identifies several gaps that need consideration in further research. To enhance future comparison and synthesis of research findings, there is a need for researchers to clearly define what they mean by peer and describe in detail the intervention being evaluated. Without methodologically rigorous studies involving control groups using valid outcomes measures, that not only relate to grief and mental health outcomes, but also outcomes such as hope, empowerment, stigma, coping and impact on life outside the group etc., it is difficult to determine the true impact of peer-led support interventions. The comparative impact of various types of peer interventions (face to face/online support) versus other types of support, such as those offered by professionals, also warrants study. Existing studies do not shed light on what is the optimal length of time since the loss before one may benefit from a peer support intervention, or indeed what the optimal length of time is for support.

Further research is also needed in the form of observational studies that explore group processes in real time, for example, how groups practice and maintain helpful elements such as a non-judgemental approach, generate feelings of connectedness, and how they share stories and thoughts to help and support each other. The potential for distress from being exposed to individuals' narratives of loss also warrants attention, as well as the reasons people leave peer groups. Additionally, the impact of different biographical backgrounds (relationships to the deceased, age, gender, and different stages of grief) on group processes and outcomes also warrants further attention.

There is also a need for research with more representative samples to determine if results can be generalised. The lack of representation of men and older people (those aged over 65) in the samples begs the question of whether the interventions would have demonstrated the same utility for these cohorts, particularly as men are believed to employ different coping strategies in response to bereavement in comparison to women [46]. Indeed, Hopmeyer & Werk's [31] study, albeit dated, indicates that men may be more focused on problem solving than sharing emotions within peer support groups. It is also not known if the findings could be replicated across cultural contexts, given that many of the peer interventions were based in North America and Western Europe. The absence of longitudinal research in this area is a research gap, which also needs to be filled in order to identify causal factors affecting grief experiences overtime. Only one of the studies explored factors contributing to departures from groups [30]; the authors in this paper recognise this as an area which requires further attention. In terms of online forums, the quality of the forums and the impact of this on efficacy, the perceptions of different groups (users, moderators, professionals) about their efficacy, and the potential for distress are also areas for further research.

Although the review has several strengths such as its breadth of questions, the use of a comprehensive multi-database search strategy, and dual-author data extraction and analysis, it needs to be read with the following limitations in mind. First, some relevant papers may have been missed because of the exclusion of non-English literature. Second, as discussed, most of the studies included in the review were of low or moderate quality. Third, the potential for interpretative bias impacting the findings is also an issue, as many papers did not clearly define the meaning of terms, such as peer, or provide detailed information on the intervention being evaluated.

7. Conclusions

While there were clear methodological limitations to many of the studies included in this review, the studies do indicate the potential benefit of peer-led support to those bereaved through suicide. The review revealed an unclear conceptualising of peers and the peer facilitators of the support group. It became clear that the role of the facilitator was very important and could influence the group process. However, it was not clear in each study how the peer facilitators were prepared for the role and how this may influence the outcome. This field of study would benefit from more in-depth description of the interventions provided, including how facilitators are selected and prepared to facilitate groups. In addition, larger studies with more representative samples to allow for comparisons across groups, including professionally facilitated peer groups, is required. Research to explore the long-term impact of peer-led intervention, including people's reasons for leaving peer support groups is also needed.

The findings also suggest that not all participants may benefit from partaking in a group, as some experienced the process of sharing upsetting. This suggests a need for further investigation into this issue, including the impact of facilitator style and training on this outcome. In line with this, it is important to explore how helpful processes arise and are maintained in a peer-led group and how attending a peer-led group influences everyday life, such as feelings of stigma and recovery in the aftermath, as support groups are supposed to enhance life outside the group.

Supplementary Materials: The following supporting information can be downloaded at: https://www.mdpi.com/article/10.3390/ijerph19063485/s1, Table S1: Sample MEDLINE Search; Table S2: Study Characteristics; Table S3: Findings.

Author Contributions: Conceptualisation, A.H., J.M. and L.H.; methodology, A.H., J.M., J.E.C., O.A.M. and L.H., formal analysis, A.H., C.D., J.M., J.E.C., L.H. and O.A.M.; writing—original draft preparation, C.D. and A.H.; writing—review and editi A.H., C.D., J.M., J.E.C., L.H. and O.A.M.; project administration, A.H. and C.D.; funding acquisition L.H., The Health Science Research Foundation, Region Zealand. All authors have read and agreed to the published version of the manuscript.

Funding: Region Zealand Health Scientific Research Foundation: Denmark. Funding number: A575.

Institutional Review Board Statement: Not applicable.

Informed Consent Statement: Not applicable.

Data Availability Statement: Not applicable.

Conflicts of Interest: The authors declare no conflict of interest.

References

1. World Health Organization (WHO). *LIVE LIFE: An Implementation Guide for Suicide Prevention in Countries*; WHO: Geneva, Switzerland, 2021. Available online: https://www.who.int/publications/i/item/9789240026629 (accessed on 24 January 2022).
2. Roth, G.A.; Abate, D.; Abate, K.H.; Abay, S.M.; Abbafati, C.; Abbasi, N.; Abbastabar, H.; Abd-Allah, F.; Abdela, J.; Abdelalim, A.; et al. Global, regional, and national age-sex-specific mortality for 282 causes of death in 195 countries and territories, 1980–2017: A systematic analysis for the Global Burden of Disease Study 2017. *Lancet* **2018**, *392*, 1736–1788. [CrossRef]
3. Cerel, J.; Brown, M.M.; Maple, M.; Singleton, M.; van de Venne, J.; Moore, M.; Flaherty, C. How Many People Are Exposed to Suicide? Not Six. *Suicide Life Threat. Behav.* **2019**, *49*, 529–534. [CrossRef] [PubMed]
4. Cerel, J.; McIntosh, J.L.; Neimeyer, R.A.; Maple, M.; Marshall, D. The continuum of "survivorship": Definitional issues in the aftermath of suicide. *Suicide Life Threat. Behav.* **2014**, *44*, 591–600. [CrossRef] [PubMed]
5. McDaid, C.; Trowman, R.; Golder, S.; Hawton, K.; Sowden, A. Interventions for people bereaved through suicide: Systematic review. *Br. J. Psychiatry J. Ment. Sci.* **2008**, *193*, 438–443. [CrossRef] [PubMed]
6. Linde, K.; Treml, J.; Steinig, J.; Nagl, M.; Kersting, A. Grief interventions for people bereaved by suicide: A systematic review. *PLoS ONE* **2017**, *12*, e0179496. [CrossRef]
7. Pitman, A.; Osborn, D.; King, M.; Erlangsen, A. Effects of suicide bereavement on mental health and suicide risk. *Lancet Psychiatry* **2014**, *1*, 86–94. [CrossRef]
8. Spillane, A.; Matvienko-Sikar, K.; Larkin, C.; Corcoran, P.; Arensman, E. What are the physical and psychological health effects of suicide bereavement on family members? An observational and interview mixed-methods study in Ireland. *BMJ Open* **2018**, *8*, e019472. [CrossRef]
9. Grafiadeli, R.; Glaesmer, H.; Hofmann, L.; Schäfer, T.; Wagner, B. Suicide risk after suicide bereavement: The role of loss-related characteristics, mental health, and hopelessness. *J. Psychiatr. Res.* **2021**, *144*, 184–189. [CrossRef]
10. Jordan, J.R. Postvention is prevention—The case for suicide postvention. *Death Stud.* **2017**, *41*, 614–621. [CrossRef]
11. World Health Organization. Public Health Action for the Prevention of Suicide: A Framework. 2012. Available online: https://apps.who.int/iris/handle/10665/75166 (accessed on 12 October 2021).
12. World Health Organization. Preventing Suicide: A Global Imperative. 2014. Available online: https://www.who.int/publications/i/item/9789241564779 (accessed on 12 October 2021).
13. Department of Health (Irl). *Connecting for Life: Ireland's National Strategy to Reduce Suicide 2015–2020*; Department of Health: Dublin, Ireland, 2015.
14. Department of Health (UK). *2012 Preventing Suicide in England: A Cross-Government Outcomes Strategy to Save Lives*; Department of Health: London, UK, 2012.
15. Aguirre, R.T.P.; Slater, H. Suicide Postvention as Suicide Prevention: Improvement and Expansion in the United States. *Death Stud.* **2010**, *34*, 529–540. [CrossRef]
16. National Institute of Health and Care Excellence. Suicide Prevention Quality Standard [QS189]. 2019. Available online: https://www.nice.org.uk/guidance/qs189(accessed on 24 February 2022).
17. Rawlinson, D.; Schiff, J.W.; Barlow, C.A. A review of peer support for suicide bereavement as a postvention alternative. *Curr. Scholarsh. Hum. Serv.* **2009**, *8*, 1–20.
18. Szumilas, M.; Kutcher, S. Post-suicide intervention programs: A systematic review. *Can. J. Public Health/Revue Canadienne de Santé Publique* **2011**, *102*, 18–29. [CrossRef]
19. Bartone, P.T.; Bartone, J.V.; Violanti, J.M.; Gileno, Z.M. Peer Support Services for Bereaved Survivors: A Systematic Review. *Omega* **2019**, *80*, 137–166. [CrossRef]
20. Andriessen, K.; Krysinska, K.; Hill, N.; Reifels, L.; Robinson, J.; Reavley, N.; Pirkis, J. Effectiveness of interventions for people bereaved through suicide: A systematic review of controlled studies of grief, psychosocial and suicide-related outcomes. *BMC Psychiatry* **2019**, *19*, 49. [CrossRef]
21. Schlichthorst, M.; Ozols, I.; Reifels, L.; Morgan, A. Lived experience peer support programs for suicide prevention: A systematic scoping review. *Int. J. Ment. Health Syst.* **2020**, *14*, 65. [CrossRef]

22. Bowersox, N.W.; Jagusch, J.; Garlick, J.; Chen, J.I.; Pfeiffer, P.N. Peer-based interventions targeting suicide prevention: A scoping review. *Am. J. Community Psychol.* **2021**, *68*, 232–248. [CrossRef]
23. Sanford, R.L.; Cerel, J.; Frey, L.M. Survivor of Suicide Loss Support Group Facilitators: Do Peers and Professionals Differ? *Soc. Work Groups* **2017**, *41*, 306–322. [CrossRef]
24. Arksey, H.; O'Malley, L. Scoping studies: Towards a methodological framework. *Int. J. Soc. Res. Methodol.* **2005**, *8*, 19–32. [CrossRef]
25. Thomas, B.H.; Ciliska, D.; Dobbins, M.; Micucci, S. A process for systematically reviewing the literature: Providing the research evidence for public health nursing interventions. *Worldviews Evid. Based Nurs.* **2004**, *1*, 176–184. [CrossRef]
26. Bailey, E.; Krysinska, K.; O'Dea, B.; Robinson, J. Internet Forums for Suicide Bereavement. *Crisis* **2017**, *38*, 393–402. [CrossRef]
27. Barlow, C.A.; Schiff, J.W.; Chugh, U.; Rawlinson, D.; Hides, E.; Leith, J. An evaluation of a suicide bereavement peer support program. *Death Stud.* **2010**, *34*, 915–930. [CrossRef]
28. Feigelman, B.; Feigelman, W. Surviving After Suicide Loss: The Healing Potential of Suicide Survivor Support Groups. *Illn. Crisis Loss* **2008**, *16*, 285–304. [CrossRef]
29. Feigelman, W.; Gorman, B.S.; Beal, K.C.; Jordan, J.R. Internet support groups for suicide survivors: A new mode for gaining bereavement assistance. *Omega* **2008**, *57*, 217–243. [CrossRef]
30. Feigelman, B.; Feigelman, W. Suicide Survivor Support Groups: Comings and Goings, Part II. *Illn. Crisis Loss* **2011**, *19*, 165–185. [CrossRef]
31. Hopmeyer, E.; Werk, A. A comparative study of family bereavement groups. *Death Stud.* **1994**, *18*, 243–256. [CrossRef]
32. Ali, F.; Lucock, M. It's like getting a group hug and you can cry there and be yourself and they understand'. Family members' experiences of using a suicide bereavement peer support group. *Bereavement* **2020**, *39*, 51–58. [CrossRef]
33. Tosini, D.; Fraccaro, D. "Like climbing a glass wall": Suicide survivors in an Italian province. *Death Stud.* **2020**, 1–9. [CrossRef]
34. Hagström, A.S. 'Suicide stigma' renegotiated: Storytelling, social support and resistance in an Internet-based community for the young suicide-bereaved. *Qual. Soc. Work.* **2016**, *16*, 775–792. [CrossRef]
35. Schotanus-Dijkstra, M.; Havinga, P.; Van Ballegooijen, W.; Delfosse, L.; Mokkenstorm, J.; Boon, B. What do the bereaved by suicide communicate in online support groups? A content analysis. *Crisis* **2014**, *35*, 27–35. [CrossRef]
36. Council of Australian Governments Health Council. The Fifth National Mental Health and Suicide Prevention Plan. 2017. Available online: http://www.coaghealthcouncil.gov.au/Portals/0/Fifth%20National%20Mental%20Health%20and%20Suicide%20Prevention%20Plan.pdf (accessed on 24 January 2022).
37. Health Education England. Stepping Forward to 2020/21: The Mental Health Workforce Plan for England. 2017. Available online: https://www.basw.co.uk/system/files/resources/basw_62959-3_0.pdf (accessed on 24 January 2022).
38. Stratford, A.C.; Halpin, M.; Phillips, K.; Skerritt, F.; Beales, A.; Cheng, V.; Hammond, M.; O'Hagan, M.; Loreto, C.; Tiengtom, K.; et al. The growth of peer support: An international charter. *J. Ment. Health* **2019**, *28*, 627–632. [CrossRef]
39. Department of Health. Sharing the Vision: A Mental Health Policy for Everyone. 2020. Available online: https://www.gov.ie/en/publication/2e46f-sharing-the-vision-a-mental-health-policy-for-everyone/ (accessed on 24 January 2022).
40. Wainwright, V.; Cordingley, L.; Chew-Graham, A.C.; Kapur, N.; Shaw, J.; Smith, S.; McGale, B.; McDonnell, S. Experiences of support from primary care and perceived needs of parents bereaved by suicide: A qualitative study. *Br. J. Gen. Pr.* **2020**, *70*, e102–e110. [CrossRef] [PubMed]
41. Ross, V.; Kõlves, K.; De Leo, D. Exploring the Support Needs of People Bereaved by Suicide: A Qualitative Study. *Omega* **2019**, *82*, 632–645. [CrossRef] [PubMed]
42. Rennick-Egglestone, S.; Ramsay, A.; McGranahan, R.; Llewellyn-Beardsley, J.; Hui, A.; Pollock, K.; Repper, J.; Yeo, C.; Ng, F.; Roe, J.; et al. The impact of mental health recovery narratives on recipients experiencing mental health problems: Qualitative analysis and change model. *PLoS ONE* **2019**, *14*, e0226201. [CrossRef]
43. Public Health England. Support after A Suicide: A Guide to Providing Local Services National Suicide Prevention Alliance Supported by A Practice Resource.Public Health England. 2016. Available online: https://assets.publishing.service.gov.uk/government/uploads/system/uploads/attachment_data/file/590838/support_after_a_suicide.pdf (accessed on 24 February 2022).
44. Scottish Government Health Directorate. Shaping Bereavement Care. A Framework for Action. 2011. Available online: http://www.sehd.scot.nhs.uk/mels/CEL2011_09 (accessed on 12 October 2021).
45. Support after Suicide Partnership and the National Bereavement Alliance. Guidelines for Delivering Bereavement Support Groups 2019. Available online: https://nationalbereavementalliance.org.uk/wp-content/uploads/2019/11/SASP-NBA-Guidelines-booklet.pdf (accessed on 24 February 2022).
46. Stroebe, M.; Stroebe, W.; Schut, H. Gender Differences in Adjustment to Bereavement: An Empirical and Theoretical Review. *Rev. Gen. Psychol.* **2001**, *5*, 62–83. [CrossRef]

International Journal of
Environmental Research and Public Health

MDPI

Article

Psychosocial Outcomes of Individuals Attending a Suicide Bereavement Peer Support Group: A Follow-Up Study

Eve Griffin [1,2,*], Selena O'Connell [1,2], Eimear Ruane-McAteer [1], Paul Corcoran [2] and Ella Arensman [1,2]

[1] School of Public Health, University College Cork, T12 XF62 Cork, Ireland; selena.oconnell@ucc.ie (S.O.); eruanemcateer01@qub.ac.uk (E.R.-M.); ella.arensman@ucc.ie (E.A.)

[2] National Suicide Research Foundation, T12 XF62 Cork, Ireland; pcorcoran@ucc.ie

* Correspondence: evegriffin@ucc.ie

Abstract: Individuals bereaved by suicide represent an important group in terms of postvention. While peer support groups are often accessed by those bereaved, few studies have examined their impact in terms of physical and mental health wellbeing. The aim of this study was to examine psychosocial outcomes of individuals attending suicide bereavement peer support groups in Ireland. Between August 2020 and June 2021, all members were invited to complete a survey, with new members also surveyed at three- and six-month follow-up, to examine changes in wellbeing, depressive symptoms and grief reactions. Results were analyzed using descriptive statistics and mixed linear regression models. The 75 participants were mostly female, with lower levels of overall wellbeing and a higher prevalence of depressive symptoms and suicidal ideation than the general population. Participants also reported high levels of social adjustment difficulties and grief reactions, which were more pronounced for those more recently bereaved. At follow-up (n = 28), a significant improvement in wellbeing and a reduction in grief reactions were found, adjusting for time since bereavement. Participants identified the groups as creating a safe space and providing a sense of belonging and hope. Notwithstanding the small number of participants at follow-up, these findings underline the enduring mental health challenges for those bereaved by suicide and provide further evidence for the role of peer support in postvention.

Keywords: suicide; bereavement; peer support; postvention; suicide prevention

Citation: Griffin, E.; O'Connell, S.; Ruane-McAteer, E.; Corcoran, P.; Arensman, E. Psychosocial Outcomes of Individuals Attending a Suicide Bereavement Peer Support Group: A Follow-Up Study. *Int. J. Environ. Res. Public Health* **2022**, *19*, 4076. https://doi.org/10.3390/ijerph19074076

Academic Editor: Paul B. Tchounwou

Received: 3 March 2022
Accepted: 27 March 2022
Published: 29 March 2022

1. Introduction

Compared with other types of bereavement, including other types of sudden death, suicide bereavement is in general associated with more negative impacts on emotional, mental and physical health [1–3]. Some people may develop long-lasting psychosocial sequalae, including increased risk of suicide and self-harm [2,4]. For every suicide that occurs, 10 people are deeply impacted and up to 135 are affected by the death [5]; therefore, the impacts of suicide can be significant and often wide reaching. Given that grief after suicide tends to be more prolonged and intense, the support and intervention required is likely to be more intensive and specialized than with other types of loss.

Peer support groups specific to suicide bereavement offer compelling appeal to those bereaved by suicide, often over seeking professional assistance. In general, there is growing evidence of the perceived helpfulness of peer support groups for people bereaved by suicide [6,7]. In particular, support groups seem to offer a space where shared experience and understanding among members of the groups provide a unique support [8–10]. In many cases, people bereaved by suicide place more confidence in those with similar bereavements, often above medical professionals, feeling that they can understand their particular needs and challenges [9].

However, there are very few studies examining the outcomes of individuals attending suicide bereavement peer support groups [6,11–14]. To date, only two studies have evaluated such groups. A small study conducted by Barlow and colleagues examined the impact of face-to-face peer support dyads [13]. The findings indicated short-term improvements in aspects of grief reactions among participants measured before and after participation. A more recent study of online support forums found that after 12 months there were significant increases in wellbeing as well as reductions in depressive symptoms [15].

The aim of the current study was to examine the psychosocial wellbeing of individuals attending community-based suicide bereavement peer support groups in Ireland and to determine changes in outcomes at three- and six-month follow-up.

2. Materials and Methods

2.1. Study Design

A prospective longitudinal study design was used to examine outcomes of individuals attending the peer support groups, using an online survey.

2.2. Peer Support Groups

HUGG is a charitable organization that provides community-based peer support groups to adults aged 18 years and older who have been bereaved by suicide (www.hugg.ie (Accessed on 28 March 2022)). The overarching mission of HUGG is to support individuals by reducing isolation and stigma and by promoting resilience and healing. This is achieved by providing evidence-informed peer support groups which promote social connection and coping mechanisms through the lived experience of others.

Each group is led by a trained facilitator and co-facilitator, who have lived experience of suicide bereavement. The meetings have a common format with a structured opening emphasizing the purpose of the meeting and guidelines for participants such as respect, non-judgment and confidentiality to create a safe environment. Following the facilitated group discussion, each meeting is closed in a timely manner with a grounding exercise and a reminder of self-care and other services available. Facilitators may also dedicate some time to sharing information or educational material about grief and bereavement before the meeting is closed. The meeting structure is informed by consultation with guidance from the United Kingdom and Australia [16,17]. At the time this study commenced, there were two operational groups in the wider Dublin area. These groups traditionally met face-to-face on a fortnightly basis, with each session lasting two hours. A maximum number of 12 individuals attended each group. In response to public health restrictions, which were implemented in March 2020 in response to the COVID-19 pandemic, these groups were moved online using video conferencing software. Between August 2020 and June 2021, a further nine groups were established across Ireland.

2.3. Participants

All current group members as of August 2020 were invited to participate in a once-off survey. In addition, all new members joining the groups between August 2020 to June 2021 were asked to complete a baseline survey (T1) before attending their first group session. These individuals were also invited to complete two further surveys at three- and six-month follow-up (T2 and T3). All participants were aged over 18 years of age.

2.4. Data Items

2.4.1. Demographics

Information on the demographic details recorded included age, gender and marital status. The participants were also asked to provide information on other supports accessed as part of their bereavement, as well as the length of time participating in the support groups. Information on the number of suicide bereavements experienced, the participants' relationship(s) to the deceased(s) and the month and year of their bereavement(s) were also included in the survey. A series of open-ended questions asked participants about the most and least beneficial aspects of the groups and suggestions for improvements.

2.4.2. Outcome Measures

Overall wellbeing was measured using the World Health Organization-Five Well-being Index (WHO-5) [18,19]. Raw scores range from 0–25 and are multiplied by four to get a total percentage score. It is generally accepted that a score of <50 is indicative of being clinically significant [18].

Depression and suicidal ideation were measured using the Patient Health Questionnaire Depression Scale (PHQ-9) [20]. The PHQ-9 incorporates DSM diagnostic criteria that is used for screening and monitoring depressive symptoms. Scores range from 0–27, with scores of 10 or more suggesting moderate–severe depressive symptoms. Item 9 of the PHQ-9 ('How often have you been bothered by thoughts that you would be better off dead or of hurting yourself in some way?') was used to assess suicidal ideation based on the proportion of respondents selecting a response of 'several days', 'more than half the days' or 'nearly every day' within the previous two weeks.

Impaired functioning with regards to social and work settings was measured using the Work and Social Adjustment Scale (SAS-SR) [21]. Scores range from 0–40 with a score of 10 or more indicating impairment of clinical significance.

Traumatic grief was measured using the Traumatic Grief Inventory-Self-Report (TGI-SR) [22,23]. Scores can range from 18–90 and it is thought that scores of 53 or more reflect clinically significant levels of grief.

Two subscales of the Grief Experience Questionnaire (GEQ) were used to measure self-reported somatic reactions and perceived stigma to grief [24,25]. Possible scores range from 5–25 and 11–55, respectively, with higher scores indicating more severe perceptions of stigma and/or somatic reactions. There are no accepted clinical cut-offs for the somatic subscale, while the perceived stigma subscale is generally dichotomized.

2.5. Missing Data

Total scores were not computed for the PHQ-9, TGI-SR and GEQ measures where there were three or more items missing or for the SAS-SR and WHO-5 measures where there were two or more missing items. This resulted in data from four participants being excluded at T1. Where fewer items were missing, the mean score of the complete items for that participant was used. There were no data excluded from participants at T2 or T3.

2.6. Data Analysis

Descriptive statistics were used to examine the characteristics of participants. Proportions are reported for categorical variables and the mean and standard deviation or median and interquartile range are reported for continuous variables. Differences in categorical variables between groups were examined using chi-square tests. Differences in outcome measures according to time since most recent bereavement were tested using linear regression models, adjusting for age and gender of respondents. The samples were divided into two groups for this analysis: those bereaved within the previous three years and those bereaved for three years or more. Open-ended questions were analyzed using content analysis.

Data from participants who were followed up were analyzed using multilevel linear mixed-effects regression models, estimating the mean change from baseline (T1) to each follow-up (T2 and T3) for all continuous outcome measures. Mixed-effects models use all available data at each time point. A random intercept for individual participants was included in the model to adjust for random heterogeneity in outcome measures between participants. Statistical significance was determined by the p-values for the model coefficients. A Bonferroni correction was also applied to provide adjusted p-values, which are the original p-values multiplied by the number of outcomes examined. Exact McNemar tests were used to explore changes in suicidal ideation (as a categorical variable) from T1 to T2 and from T1 to T3. Analyses were conducted using SPSS Statistics 27.0 (IBM Corp., Armonk, NY) and Stata IC Version 16 (StataCorp, College Station, TX, USA).

3. Results

3.1. Sample Characteristics

A total of 75 participants completed the baseline surveys; of these, 52 (69.3%) were new group members who completed the baseline survey before attending their first group meeting. The characteristics of these participants are summarized in Table 1. Most were female (*n* = 64; 85.3%) and the median age was 46 years (interquartile range (IQR): 16). Approximately half (*n* = 40; 53.3%) of participants were currently in a relationship or married, with one quarter (19; 25.3%) separated, divorced or widowed.

Table 1. Demographics of survey respondents (*n* = 75).

	N (%)
Gender	
Female	64 (85.3)
Male	11 (14.7)
Age in years (Median, IQR)	46 (16)
Current relationship status (missing *n* = 1)	
In a relationship/married	40 (53.3)
Separated/divorced/widowed	19 (25.3)
Single	15 (20.0)
Experienced multiple bereavements to suicide	15 (20.0)
Time since most recent bereavement in years (median, IQR)	1.9 (4.3)
Bereaved less than three years	45 (60.0)
Bereaved more than three years	30 (40.0)
Relationship to deceased	
Spouse/partner	21 (28.0)
Other direct relative	49 (65.3)
Other relationship	5 (6.7)
First time attending support group	
Yes	64 (85.3)
No	11 (14.7)
Other supports accessed	
Counseling	58 (77.3)
Other peer support	8 (10.7)
Bibliotherapy	9 (12.0)
Mindfulness therapy	15 (20.0)
Writing therapy	12 (16.0)

The median time since bereavement was 1.9 years, ranging from less than 1 month to 51 years. Most of the participants had been bereaved in the previous 3 years (*n* = 45; 60.0%). Approximately one in five had experienced multiple suicide bereavements (*n* = 15; 20.0%). Most participants had lost a spouse or partner to suicide (*n* = 21; 28.0%) or another direct relative (49; 65.3%). All indicated that they had or were currently engaged in other supports for their bereavement, most commonly counseling (*n* = 58; 77.3%), mindfulness therapy (*n* = 15; 20.0%) and writing therapy (12; 16.0%). A small number had attended other peer support groups (*n* = 8; 10.7%). For existing members of the groups (*n* = 23), the median time attending the groups was 9 months and ranged from 1 month to 3 years.

3.2. Psychosocial Wellbeing of Respondents

At baseline, most participants recorded negative scores across outcome measures. For wellbeing, more than three quarters of participants reported negative wellbeing scores as measured by the WHO-5 within the clinical range (n = 58; 77.3%). A similar proportion (n = 59; 78.7%) reported some depressive symptoms as measured by the PHQ-9, with 36 (48.0%) reporting moderate–severe symptoms. Suicidal ideation in the previous two weeks was reported by 18 (24.0%) respondents. More than two thirds (49; 65.3%) of participants reported moderate–severe impairment with regards to social adjustment following their loss and approximately half (n = 39; 52.0%) reported clinically significant levels of traumatic grief. The mean score on the somatic subscale of the GEQ was 10.4 (SD: 3.2), while 26.7% (n = 20) of participants reported high levels of perceived stigma (see Table 2).

Table 2. Baseline outcome measures and differences according to time since bereavement (n = 75).

	All Respondents (n = 75; 100%)	Bereaved Less than Three Years (n = 45; 60.0%)	Bereaved Three Years or More (n = 30; 40.0%)		
	Mean (95% CI)	**Mean (95% CI)**	**Mean (95% CI)**	**Mean Diff (95% CI)**	***p*-Value**
Wellbeing (WHO-5)	32.5 (27.3 to 37.7)	27.1 (21.6 to 32.5)	40.4 (30.8 to 50.0)	−11.8 (−21.3 to −2.2)	0.016
Depressive symptoms (PHQ-9)	10.5 (8.9 to 12.1)	11.9 (9.8 to 14.1)	8.3 (5.9 to 10.5)	3.5 (0.4 to 6.6)	0.027
Social adjustment (WSAS)	15.4 (13.1 to 17.8)	17.9 (15.0 to 20.9)	11.7 (8.1 to 15.4)	5.8 (1.3 to 10.4)	0.013
Traumatic grief (TGI-SR)	53.8 (49.8 to 57.7)	58.7 (54.6 to 62.7)	46.7 (39.4 to 53.9)	11.6 (4.0 to 19.2)	0.003
Somatic reactions (GEQ subscale)	10.4 (9.6 to 11.1)	10.3 (9.5 to 11.0)	9.8 (8.5 to 11.1)	0.6 (−0.9 to 2.1)	0.460
Perceived stigma (GEQ subscale)	27.9 (25.7 to 30.2)	27.7 (24.8 to 30.5)	28.5 (24.6 to 32.3)	−1.4 (−5.7 to 2.9)	0.518

Outcomes varied according to time since most recent bereavement. Compared with those bereaved three or more years, those whose bereavement was within three years had poorer levels of wellbeing (mean diff: −11.8; 95% CI: −21.3 to −2.2; p = 0.016), stronger indications of depressive symptoms (+3.5; 0.4 to 6.6; p = 0.027), poorer social adjustment (+5.8; 1.3 to 10.4; p = 0.013) and higher levels of traumatic grief (+11.6; 4.0 to 19.2; p = 0.003). There were no observed differences in terms of somatic grief reactions or perceived stigma (Table 2).

3.3. Changes in Outcome Measures at Follow-Up

Of the subset of new members who completed a baseline survey (T1) before attending their first group (n = 52), 28 provided at least one follow-up survey (T2 or T3), culminating in 23 completed surveys at both T2 and T3 (44.2%). These participants had attended on average seven sessions after three months (SD: 4.8) and thirteen after six months (SD: 2.8). They did not differ on key demographics (age, time since most recent bereavement, relationship status) or scores on baseline outcome measures. However, males were more likely to participate in follow-up, accounting for 3.4% of new members at T1 but 26.7% of those surveyed at T2 (X^2 (df) = 5.5 (1); p = 0.018).

Adjusting for time since most recent bereavement, a significant improvement in wellbeing was found at T2 (mean difference: +11.8, 95% CI: 4.7 to 18.8), along with a significant reduction in traumatic grief (−6.9, −10.7 to −3.1). All changes held at T3. Changes in somatic reactions to grief, depressive symptoms, social adjustment and perceived stigma were observed, but these did not reach statistical significance (Table 3; Figure S1). No significant changes in the proportion of respondents reporting suicidal ideation at T2 or T3 were observed (Table S1).

Table 3. Change in outcome measures at three-month (T2) and six-month (T3) follow-up.

	T1 M (95% CI)	T2 M (95% CI)	T3 M (95% CI)	Change T1–T2		Change T1–T3	
				Mean Change (95% CI)	*p*-Value (Adjusted)	Mean Change (95% CI)	*p*-Value (Adjusted)
Wellbeing (WHO-5)	36.5 (27.6 to 45.5)	48.3 (38.3 to 58.3)	48.6 (38.6 to 58.6)	+11.8 (4.7 to 18.8)	0.001 (0.006)	+12.1 (4.9 to 19.3)	0.001 (0.006)
Depressive symptoms (PHQ-9)	8.8 (6.1 to 11.5)	7.3 (4.3 to 10.2)	7.3 (4.3 to 10.3)	−1.6 (−3.5 to 0.4)	0.117 (0.702)	−1.5 (−3.5 to 0.5)	0.133 (0.798)
Traumatic grief (TGI-SR)	48.8 (42.4 to 55.2)	41.9 (35.0 to 48.8)	42.3 (35.5 to 49.2)	−6.9 (−10.7 to −3.1)	<0.001 (<0.001)	−6.5 (−10.3 to −2.7)	0.001 (0.006)
Social adjustment (SAS-SR)	12.4 (8.3 to 16.6)	11.1 (6.6 to 15.6)	12.2 (7.7 to 16.7)	−1.4 (−4.0 to 1.3)	0.310 (>1.0)	−0.2 (−2.9 to 2.5)	0.860 (>1.0)
Somatic reactions (GEQ subscale)	9.6 (8.1 to 11.1)	8.3 (6.6 to 10.0)	8.3 (6.6 to 9.9)	−1.3 (−2.5 to −0.1)	0.043 (0.258)	−1.3 (−2.6 to −0.1)	0.037 (0.222)
Perceived stigma (GEQ subscale)	28.0 (23.9 to 32.1)	25.8 (21.3 to 30.3)	25.9 (21.5 to 30.4)	−2.2 (−5.1 to 0.6)	0.127 (0.762)	−2.1 (−5.0 to 0.8)	0.162 (0.972)

Changes in outcome measures were examined separately for individuals bereaved within the previous three years and individuals bereaved three years or more (Table 4). Improvements in wellbeing held only for those bereaved three years or more (mean change T1 to T2: 13.5, 6.6 to 20.3; $p < 0.001$). In addition, improvements in depressive symptoms between T1 and T2 (−2.5, −5.2 to −0.3) were also observed and some indications of improvements in social adjustment at T2 and T3, for those bereaved three years or more.

Table 4. Change in outcome measures at three-month (T2) and six-month (T3) follow-up according to time since bereavement.

	Bereaved within Previous Three Years				Bereaved Three Years or More			
	Change T1–T2		Change T1–T3		Change T1–T2		Change T1–T3	
	Mean Change (95% CI)	*p*-Value	Mean Change (95% CI)	*p*-Value (Adjusted)	Mean Change (95% CI)	*p*-Value (Adjusted)	Mean Change (95% CI)	*p*-Value (Adjusted)
Wellbeing (WHO-5)	9.2 (−4.2 to 22.6)	0.178 (>1.0)	12.1 (−0.8 to 25.0)	0.066 (0.396)	13.5 (6.6 to 20.3)	<0.001 (<0.001)	11.9 (4.5 to 19.2)	0.002 (0.012)
Depressive symptoms (PHQ-9)	−0.0 (−3.0 to 2.9)	0.988 (>1.0)	−1.1 (−3.9 to 1.9)	0.479 (>1.0)	−2.7 (−5.2 to −0.3)	0.030 (0.180)	−1.9 (−4.6 to 0.7)	0.157 (>1.0)
Traumatic grief (TGI-SR)	−8.3 (−13.7 to −2.9)	0.003 (0.018)	−5.6 (−10.8 to −0.4)	0.035 (0.210)	−5.4 (−10.5 to −0.3)	0.039 (0.234)	−7.1 (−12.6 to −1.7)	0.010 (0.06)
Social adjustment (SAS-SR)	0.9 (−3.8 to 5.8)	0.688 (>1.0)	1.62 (−2.9 to 6.2)	0.491 (>1.0)	−3.3 (−5.9 to −0.6)	0.015 (0.090)	−1.8 (−4.7 to 0.9)	0.198 (>1.0)
Somatic reactions (GEQ subscale)	−2.0 (−3.9 to −0.1)	0.039 (0.234)	−1.0 (−2.9 to 0.9)	0.292 (>1.0)	−0.6 (−2.1 to 0.8)	0.396 (>1.0)	−1.7 (−3.2 to −0.1)	0.038 (0.228)
Perceived stigma (GEQ subscale)	−3.9 (−8.1 to 0.4)	0.076 (0.456)	−1.8 (−5.9 to 2.3)	0.384 (>1.0)	−0.9 (−4.8 to 2.8)	0.607 (>1.0)	−2.5 (−6.5 to 1.6)	0.238 (>1.0)

3.4. Participant Feedback on Group Benefits

Most participants who provided open-ended feedback (n = 51) were female (n = 40, 78.4%) and had attended the groups for a median of 5 months (IQR: 6). Participants mainly highlighted positive aspects of the groups, which included shared understanding of group members, the group as a safe place to talk, sense of belonging and sense of hope provided by the group, information and advice gained via the group and flexibility to contact group members outside of meetings times (Table 5). A minority of participants suggested challenges or areas for improvements, the most common being to increase the reach/awareness of the groups (n = 9, 17.6%).

Table 5. Benefits of peer support groups and frequency of participants reporting.

Benefit	N (%)	Description	Supporting Quotation
Shared understanding	35 (68.7)	Participants reported the benefit of speaking to people who had also experienced suicide grief with whom they felt immediately understood and that their experiences were validated.	"The shared experience make the group one of acceptance from the start. The unspoken shared grief through suicide made the group feel like we just all understood."
Safe place to talk	23 (45.1)	Participants reported the unique space of the groups where they could discuss their experiences without judgement or fear of upsetting others.	"It has given me a chance to talk honestly to people who understand but don't know me outside of the group, so I'm not worried about their judgment or making them feel bad like I would be if talking to people in my family or friends who might worry about me or feel sad."
Belonging and connection	16 (31.4)	The sense of belonging to the group and connection to others reduced feelings of isolation.	"I feel part of a group going through the same horrific thing rather than alone."
Hope and strength	12 (23.5)	Participants felt hope in seeing the progression of others who were further in the grief journey and for some the group was described as a lifeline, particularly during the isolation of the pandemic.	"I would never have been able to cope with the grief alone and it gives me a shimmer of hope that my pain will become manageable."
Information and advice	11 (21.6)	Participants reported benefit from practical information and resources discussed within the group.	"We all learn from each other and get useful tips and resources from the facilitators."
Flexibility to contact outside of meeting	11 (21.6)	Participants valued the opportunity to reach out between meetings to facilitators directly or to peers via text messaging group.	"I know at any stage I can reach out for support from the facilitator and members."

4. Discussion

This is one of the few studies that reports on outcomes of individuals attending a suicide bereavement peer support group. Our findings show that in general those who are bereaved by suicide have poorer mental health than the general population, particularly in relation to general wellbeing, symptoms of depression and suicidal ideation. These mental health impacts were more prevalent for those more recently bereaved. This study makes a unique contribution to the literature by examining the wellbeing of group members up to six months after joining a peer support group. Notable improvements among the relatively small number of participants at three- and six-month follow-ups were observed in wellbeing and indications of traumatic grief.

The demographic profile of participants included in this study is similar to other evaluation studies of peer support groups [13,26]. The majority of participants were immediate family members of the deceased and time since bereavement varied considerably in line with previous research [13,27]. It is difficult to directly compare the baseline scores on the psychosocial indicators with other studies of those bereaved by suicide due to significant variation in the definitions and measures used [28]. However, reported levels of impaired functioning in social and work settings, traumatic grief and perceived stigma were similar to other studies conducted in this area [29–31]. The baseline psychosocial measures reported by the respondents of the current study were lower than general population estimates, particularly in relation to overall wellbeing, severity of depressive symptoms and expressions of suicidal ideation [32–34]. Psychosocial wellbeing varied according to time since most recent bereavement. Those bereaved more recently, within the past three years, reported poorer wellbeing scores, more severe depressive and somatic symptoms, along with higher levels of traumatic grief and difficulties with social adjustment. All participants reported similar levels of perceived stigma.

While improvements in wellbeing have also been demonstrated in other studies of suicide bereavement peer support [13,15], there are differences in the outcomes showing improvement. For example, a study of users of online peer support forums reported similar improvements on wellbeing at follow-up in addition to reductions in depressive symptoms, but no significant change in traumatic grief [15]. Our study observed changes in wellbeing, traumatic grief and somatic reactions, though there were no significant changes in depressive symptoms, social adjustment or perceived stigma. The current findings suggest that peer support groups may offer different benefits according to how recent the bereavement was, with those more recently bereaved reporting improvements in symptoms of grief rather than overall wellbeing. To our knowledge, how experiences of peer support vary according to time since bereavement have not been examined in the existing literature and future research should consider the mechanisms by which peer support groups work to provide support to individuals according to the time since their bereavement.

Few studies have explored the effective attributes of peer support for suicide bereavement. Drawing on broader peer support literature and theory, perceived benefits include understanding and empathy between peers with similar experiences, social support (emotional and practical) provided by peers, role modeling by peers via experiential knowledge, as well as meaning making through receiving and giving support [7,35,36]. A qualitative study with managers of bereavement peer support programs identified best practices such as ease of accessibility, confidentiality, a safe environment, training and mentoring of peer supporters and close matching of the peer supporters, particularly concerning the bereavement circumstances [36]. The feedback reported in this study is in line with these findings. Broadly positive in their experiences, participants identified the groups as creating a safe space and providing a sense of belonging and hope, as well as providing important peer support even outside the formal group meetings. An ongoing qualitative study builds on these data and explores the experiences of peer support as provided by the HUGG groups and key benefits of this form of support for people bereaved by suicide.

Despite an overall improvement in psychosocial outcomes, the enduring negative wellbeing of participants underlines the need to consider the longer-term impacts of bereavement. In particular, we identified that all participants reported high levels of perceived stigma regardless of time since bereavement, which did not improve at follow-up. This is supported by research which indicates that a suicide bereavement is often associated with increased isolation and social awkwardness in particular [37,38]. While social contact with peers has been identified as one of the most effective interventions for mental-health-related stigma in the short-term, research has not supported its benefits in the long-term [39]. Further research is needed to understand how stigma can be reduced for people bereaved by suicide given that perceived stigma predicts suicidal thoughts and behaviors in this population [31]. Furthermore, the proportion of participants reporting active suicidal ideation did not reduce at follow-up, similar to other research [15], which highlights the ongoing risk of suicidal behavior in those bereaved by suicide. Given that suicide bereavement is associated with a ten-fold risk of suicide [2], services which provide support should consider this ongoing risk and develop appropriate safeguards and signposting to more specialized services as needed. This may involve complementary psychotherapeutic interventions to address the assessment and treatment of suicidal behavior.

Limitations

There are a number of limitations to this research study. First, we cannot draw firm conclusions on the effects of participation due to the limited sample size at follow-up. Despite the small sample, data completeness at follow-up was high with no missing data on the primary outcome measures. Second, we did not have a control group. To mitigate this limitation, we ensured that baseline surveys were gathered before respondents attended their first group meeting and adjusted for time since most recent bereavement in the analysis. Third, most of the survey respondents were actively engaged with the peer support groups at the time of the research. While the research invitation was circulated to all individuals registered with the peer support groups, we did not have data on rates of disengagement or dropout. Therefore, it is possible that our sample may have more positive attitudes to the peer support groups and indeed may have better coping skills than others who did not engage with the research. Related to this, a fourth limitation is that all participants indicated that they had availed of other supports and treatments, most commonly counseling, which may have contributed to the observed effects. Fifth, the research was undertaken during the COVID-19 pandemic; while usually held in person, the peer support groups moved online in March 2020. The follow-up study involved individuals who had only attended online and any limitations to the online format may have been offset by additional supports such as group text messaging in between meetings.

5. Conclusions

It has been flagged in recent years that there are critical gaps in research in the field of suicide bereavement and postvention [40], particularly in relation to evaluation studies. This study has added to the existing evidence supporting the role of suicide bereavement peer support groups, further highlighting the important role of support groups in postvention, while also underlining the enduring mental health challenges related to suicide bereavement.

Supplementary Materials: The following supporting information can be downloaded at https://www.mdpi.com/article/10.3390/ijerph19074076/s1: Figure S1, Changes in outcome measures at three-month (T2) and six-month (T3) follow-up. Table S1, Change in suicidal ideation at three-month (T2) and six-month (T3) follow-up.

Author Contributions: Conceptualization, E.G., E.A. and P.C.; Methodology, E.G., E.R.-M., S.O., P.C. and E.A.; Formal Analysis, E.G., S.O., E.R.-M. and P.C.; Writing—Original Draft Preparation, E.G. and S.O.; Writing—Review & Editing, E.G., S.O., E.R.-M., P.C. and E.A.; Supervision, E.G. and E.A.; Funding Acquisition, E.G. All authors have read and agreed to the published version of the manuscript.

Funding: This research was funded by the Irish Research Council's New Foundations 2020 scheme (NF/2020/20965640).

Institutional Review Board Statement: The study was conducted according to the guidelines of the Declaration of Helsinki and approved by the Clinical Research Ethics Committee of the Cork Teaching Hospitals (CREC) in July 2020 (ECM 4 (h) 7 July 2020).

Informed Consent Statement: Informed consent was obtained from all participants involved in the study.

Data Availability Statement: The data presented in this study are available on request from the corresponding author. The data are not publicly available due to the sensitive nature of the research topic.

Acknowledgments: The authors would like to thank those who generously participated in the research, along with Fiona Tuomey, Chief Executive Officer HUGG, and Adam Grennan, Chairperson HUGG, for facilitating this research study.

Conflicts of Interest: The authors declare no conflict of interest. The sponsors had no role in the design, execution, interpretation, or writing of the study.

References

1. Maple, M.; Cerel, J.; Sanford, R.; Pearce, T.; Jordan, J. Is exposure to suicide beyond kin associated with risk for suicidal behavior? A systematic review of the evidence. *Suicide Life-Threat. Behav.* **2017**, *47*, 461–474. [PubMed]
2. Pitman, A.; Osborn, D.; King, M.; Erlangsen, A. Effects of suicide bereavement on mental health and suicide risk. *Lancet Psychiatry* **2014**, *1*, 86–94. [PubMed]

3. Spillane, A.; Larkin, C.; Corcoran, P.; Matvienko-Sikar, K.; Riordan, F.; Arensman, E. Physical and psychosomatic health outcomes in people bereaved by suicide compared to people bereaved by other modes of death: A systematic review. *BMC Public Health* **2017**, *17*, 939. [CrossRef]
4. Erlangsen, A.; Runeson, B.; Bolton, J.M.; Wilcox, H.C.; Forman, J.L.; Krogh, J.; Shear, M.K.; Nordentoft, M.; Conwell, Y. Association between spousal suicide and mental, physical, and social health outcomes: A longitudinal and nationwide register-based study. *JAMA Psychiatry* **2017**, *74*, 456–464. [PubMed]
5. Cerel, J.; Brown, M.M.; Maple, M.; Singleton, M.; Van de Venne, J.; Moore, M.; Flaherty, C. How many people are exposed to suicide? Not six. *Suicide Life-Threat. Behav.* **2019**, *49*, 529–534. [PubMed]
6. Schlichthorst, M.; Ozols, I.; Reifels, L.; Morgan, A. Lived experience peer support programs for suicide prevention: A systematic scoping review. *Int. J. Ment. Health Syst.* **2020**, *14*, 65.
7. Bartone, P.T.; Bartone, J.V.; Violanti, J.M.; Gileno, Z.M. Peer support services for bereaved survivors: A systematic review. *Omega J. Death Dying* **2019**, *80*, 137–166.
8. Cerel, J.; Padgett, J.H.; Conwell, Y.; Reed, G.A. A call for research: The need to better understand the impact of support groups for suicide survivors. *Suicide Life-Threat. Behav.* **2009**, *39*, 269–281.
9. Feigelman, B.; Feigelman, W. Surviving after suicide loss: The healing potential of suicide survivor support groups. *Illn. Crisis Loss* **2008**, *16*, 285–304.
10. Begley, M.; Quayle, E.J.C. The lived experience of adults bereaved by suicide: A phenomenological study. *Crisis* **2007**, *28*, 26–34.
11. Linde, K.; Treml, J.; Steinig, J.; Nagl, M.; Kersting, A. Grief interventions for people bereaved by suicide: A systematic review. *PLoS ONE* **2017**, *12*, e0179496.
12. Andriessen, K.; Krysinska, K.; Hill, N.T.M.; Reifels, L.; Robinson, J.; Reavley, N.; Pirkis, J. Effectiveness of interventions for people bereaved through suicide: A systematic review of controlled studies of grief, psychosocial and suicide-related outcomes. *BMC Psychiatry* **2019**, *19*, 49. [CrossRef] [PubMed]
13. Barlow, C.A.; Waegemakers, S.J.; Chugh, U.; Rawlinson, D.; Hides, E.; Leith, J. An evaluation of a suicide bereavement peer support program. *Death Stud.* **2010**, *34*, 915–930. [CrossRef] [PubMed]
14. Griffin, E.; McMahon, E. Suicide Bereavement Support: A Literature Review. 2019. Available online: https://www.hse.ie/eng/services/list/4/mental-health-services/connecting-for-life/publications/suicide-bereavement-support-a-literature-review-april-2019.pdf (accessed on 23 March 2022).
15. Kramer, J.; Boon, B.; Schotanus-Dijkstra, M.; van Ballegooijen, W.; Kerkhof, A.; Van Der Poel, A.J.C. The mental health of visitors of web-based support forums for bereaved by suicide. *Crisis* **2015**, *36*, 38–45. [CrossRef] [PubMed]
16. Lifeline Australia. Towards Good Practice: Standards and Guidelines for Suicide Bereavement Support Groups. 2009. Available online: https://sprc.org/sites/default/files/resource-program/LIFELINE_SBSG_Standards_and_Guidelines.pdf (accessed on 28 February 2022).
17. Support after Suicide Partnership and National Bereavement Alliance. Guidelines for Delivering Bereavement Support Groups. 2011. Available online: https://nationalbereavementalliance.org.uk/wp-content/uploads/2019/11/SASP-NBA-Guidelines-booklet.pdf (accessed on 28 February 2022).
18. Topp, C.; Østergaard, S.D.; Søndergaard, S.; Bech, P. The WHO-5 Well-Being Index: A systematic review of the literature. *Psychother. Psychosom.* **2015**, *4*, 167–176. [CrossRef] [PubMed]
19. World Health Organisation. *Wellbeing measures in Primary Care: The DepCare Project*; WHO, Regional Office for Europe: Copenhagen, Denmark, 1998.
20. Kroenke, K.; Spitzer, R.L.; Williams, J.B. The PHQ-9: Validity of a brief depression severity measure. *J. Intern. Med.* **2001**, *16*, 606–613.
21. Mundt, J.C.; Marks, I.M.; Shear, M.K.; Greist, J.M. The Work and Social Adjustment Scale: A simple measure of impairment in functioning. *Br. J. Psychiatry* **2002**, *180*, 461–464. [CrossRef]
22. Boelen, P.A.; Smid, G.E. The Traumatic Grief Inventory Self-Report version (TGI-SR): Introduction and preliminary psychometric evaluation. *J. Loss Trauma* **2017**, *22*, 196–212. [CrossRef]
23. Boelen, P.A.; Djelantik, A.; de Keijser, J.; Lenferink, L.I.M.; Smid, G.E. Further validation of the Traumatic Grief Inventory-Self Report (TGI-SR): A measure of persistent complex bereavement disorder and prolonged grief disorder. *Death Stud.* **2019**, *43*, 351–364.
24. Barrett, T.W.; Scott, T.B. Development of the Grief Experience Questionnaire. *Suicide Life-Threat. Behav.* **1989**, *19*, 201–215. [CrossRef]
25. Bailley, S.E.; Dunham, K.; Kral, M.J. Factor structure of the Grief Experience Questionnaire (GEQ). *Death Stud.* **2000**, *24*, 721–738. [PubMed]
26. Lestienne, L.; Leaune, E.; Haesebaert, J.; Poulet, E.; Andriessen, K. An integrative systematic review of online resources and interventions for people bereaved by suicide. *Prev. Med.* **2021**, *152*, 106583. [CrossRef] [PubMed]
27. Gehrmann, M.; Dixon, S.D.; Visser, V.S.; Griffin, M. Evaluating the outcomes for bereaved people supported by a community-based suicide bereavement service. *Crisis* **2020**, *41*, 437–444. [CrossRef] [PubMed]
28. Sveen, C.A.; Walby, F.A. Suicide survivors' mental health and grief reactions: A systematic review of controlled studies. *Suicide Life-Threat. Behav.* **2008**, *38*, 13–29. [CrossRef]

29. Tal, I.; Mauro, C.; Reynolds, C.F., 3rd; Shear, M.K.; Simon, N.; Lebowitz, B.; Skritskaya, N.; Wang, Y.; Qiu, X.; Iglewicz, A.; et al. Complicated grief after suicide bereavement and other causes of death. *Death Stud.* **2017**, *41*, 267–275. [CrossRef]
30. Lenferink, L.I.M.; de Keijser, J.; Eisma, M.C.; Smid, G.E.; Boelen, P.A. Treatment gap in bereavement care: (Online) bereavement support needs and use after traumatic loss. *Clin. Psychol. Psychother.* **2021**, *28*, 907–916. [CrossRef]
31. Pitman, A.; Rantell, K.; Marston, L.; King, M.; Osborn, D. Perceived stigma of sudden bereavement as a risk factor for suicidal thoughts and suicide attempt: Analysis of British cross-sectional survey data on 3387 young bereaved adults. *Int. J. Environ. Res. Public Health* **2017**, *14*, 286. [CrossRef]
32. Ellervik, C.; Kvetny, J.; Christensen, K.S.; Vestergaard, M.; Bech, P. Prevalence of depression, quality of life and antidepressant treatment in the Danish General Suburban Population Study. *Nord. J. Psychiatry* **2014**, *68*, 507–512. [CrossRef]
33. Hinz, A.; Mehnert, A.; Kocalevent, R.D.; Brähler, E.; Forkmann, T.; Singer, S.; Schulte, T. Assessment of depression severity with the PHQ-9 in cancer patients and in the general population. *BMC Psychiatry* **2016**, *16*, 22. [CrossRef]
34. Tomitaka, S.; Kawasaki, Y.; Ide, K.; Akutagawa, M.; Yamada, H.; Ono, Y.; Furukawa, T.A. Distributional patterns of item responses and total scores on the PHQ-9 in the general population: Data from the National Health and Nutrition Examination Survey. *BMC Psychiatry* **2018**, *18*, 108. [CrossRef]
35. Harrington-LaMorie, J.; Jordan, J.R.; Ruocco, K.; Cerel, J. Surviving families of military suicide loss: Exploring postvention peer support. *Death Stud.* **2018**, *42*, 143–154. [CrossRef] [PubMed]
36. Bartone, P.T.; Bartone, J.V.; Gileno, Z.; Violanti, J.M. Exploration into best practices in peer support for bereaved survivors. *Death Stud.* **2018**, *42*, 555–568. [CrossRef] [PubMed]
37. Pitman, A.L.; Stevenson, F.; Osborn, D.P.; King, M.B. The stigma associated with bereavement by suicide and other sudden deaths: A qualitative interview study. *Soc. Sci. Med.* **2018**, *198*, 121–129. [CrossRef] [PubMed]
38. Evans, A.; Abrahamson, K. The influence of stigma on suicide bereavement: A systematic review. *J. Psychosoc. Nurs. Ment. Health Serv.* **2020**, *58*, 21–27. [CrossRef] [PubMed]
39. Thornicroft, G.; Mehta, N.; Clement, S.; Evans-Lacko, S.; Doherty, M.; Rose, D.; Koschorke, M.; Shidhaye, R.; O'Reilly, C.; Henderson, C. Evidence for effective interventions to reduce mental-health-related stigma and discrimination. *Lancet* **2016**, *387*, 1123–1132. [CrossRef]
40. Maple, M.; Pearce, T.; Sanford, R.; Cerel, J.; Castelli Dransart, D.A.; Andriessen, K. A systematic mapping of suicide bereavement and postvention research and a proposed strategic research agenda. *Crisis* **2018**, *39*, 275–282. [CrossRef]

International Journal of
Environmental Research and Public Health

MDPI

Article

Attitudes toward Suicide and the Impact of Client Suicide: A Structural Equation Modeling Approach

Irene Pisnoli and Ruth Van der Hallen *

Clinical Psychology, Department of Psychology, Education & Child Studies, Erasmus University Rotterdam, 3062 PA Rotterdam, The Netherlands
* Correspondence: vanderhallen@essb.eur.nl

Abstract: Previous research has revealed that mental health professionals (MHPs) often experience significant short- and long-term impacts in the aftermath of client suicide. Individual differences are significant, yet what factors explain these differences remain unclear. The current study aimed to investigate to what extent MHPs' attitudes toward (client) suicide could predict the short- and long-term impacts of client suicide. A total of 213 MHPs, aged between 18 and 75, reported on a client suicide and their attitudes toward (client) suicide using self-report questionnaires. The results indicate that MHPs who believe it is one's "rightful choice" to die by suicide report less and MHPs who believe "suicide can and should be prevented" report more impact of client suicide. Predictability and preventability of client suicide proved strongly, positively correlated; yet, neither predicted the impact of client suicide. Taken together, these findings highlight the importance of MHPs' attitudes toward (client) suicide with respect to clients and MHPs (self-)care.

Keywords: practitioner; clinician; survivor; patient; PTSS

Citation: Pisnoli, I.; Van der Hallen, R. Attitudes toward Suicide and the Impact of Client Suicide: A Structural Equation Modeling Approach. *Int. J. Environ. Res. Public Health* **2022**, *19*, 5481. https://doi.org/10.3390/ijerph19095481

Academic Editors: Paul B. Tchounwou, Karolina Krysinska, Karl Andriessen and Yossi Levi-Belz

Received: 12 March 2022
Accepted: 29 April 2022
Published: 30 April 2022

1. Introduction

Suicide, defined as an intentional, self-destructive, and self-inflicted act that causes death, is a challenging public health dilemma worldwide [1]. Each year, between 0.5 and 1.2 million people globally die by suicide [2]. For every single loss, it has been estimated that about 135 individuals consider themselves significantly affected [3]. These "suicide survivors", i.e., people that shared an emotional connection with a person who died by suicide, include family and friends as well as mental health practitioners (MHPs), whose grief is often disregarded [4]. Considering that mental illness has been argued to play an important role in about 60–98% of all suicides [5,6], high levels of exposure to suicide (loss) in practitioners are not surprising [7]. In fact, practitioners are at the forefront of supporting individuals at risk of suicide, with 30% to 80% of MHPs in Belgium, the U.S., Ireland, and Australia, as well as approximately 98% of MHPs in Slovenia having lost a client to suicide, commonly referred to as "client suicide" [8–10].

The impact of client suicide on MHPs has been a topic of investigation since the early 1980s. Research suggests short-term consequences of client suicide may include emotions of shock, disbelief, confusion, and denial, as well as feelings of distress, depression, and anger at the client/society, guilt, shame, a profound sense of responsibility, failure, and feelings of incompetence [11,12]. Post-traumatic distress symptoms, such as intrusive thoughts, avoidant behavior toward potential suicidal clients, sleep disturbances, irritability, difficulty managing life events, and emotional burnout, have been suggested to affect about 50% of MHPs following client suicide [13,14]. Long-term consequences of client suicide may involve feelings of self-doubt and inadequacy, sensitivity to signs of suicidal risk, vigilance and caution when dealing with at-risk patients, concern over one's competence to treat patients, as well as feelings of anxiety, depression, or helplessness when doing so [14–16]. Individual differences regarding the impact of client suicide on MHPs have been associated with differences in gender, age, previous exposure to suicide, or coping strategies [10,14,17,18]. Interestingly, however, it remains unclear to what extent MHPs' attitudes toward (client) suicide are associated with the impact of client suicide.

Attitudes toward suicide are defined as multidimensional evaluations of the most critical aspects of suicidal behavior as manifested in emotional, instrumental, and cognitive components and can vary widely between individuals (for a review, see [19]). For instance, suicide attempters and suicide contemplators have been found to be more accepting of suicide than non-attempters or people without a history of suicidal ideation [20,21]. Furthermore, people with more permissive attitudes toward suicide have been associated with greater rates of suicide ideation [22]. More recently, Pitman and colleagues [23] conducted a qualitative study of attitudes toward suicide in 429 young bereaved adults and found that exposure to the suicide of a close friend or relative can influence attitudes to suicide in ways that would influence one's own risk of suicide later in life. The attitudes of medical staff toward suicide have been known to affect the care they provide suicidal patients [24]. Moreover, Samuelsson and colleagues [25] found nurses' willingness to treat and their ability to empathize with suicidal patients depended on their attitudes toward suicide.

MHPs' attitudes toward suicide, such as the attitudes of psychologists, psychotherapists, psychiatrists, or social workers, have not been researched extensively. Werth and Liddle [26] investigated attitudes toward suicide in 186 psychotherapists and found significant individual differences in accepting suicidal ideation as well as actions taken to prevent a suicide depending on why a person had decided to die by suicide. Overall, psychotherapists with more experience were found to be more accepting of suicide and to take less action to prevent suicide than less experienced psychotherapists. Swain and Domino [27] investigated attitudes toward suicide in 1441 mental health professionals. Overall, clergy and general physicians were found to be less accepting of suicide, especially when compared to social workers, who were found to be the most accepting of suicide. Moreover, professionals with personal experience or acquaintance with suicide were found more likely to accept the notion of suicide and better able to recognize signs of suicidal ideation [27–29]. That being said, one can wonder if one's attitude toward suicide might not just dictate how we deal with, treat, assess, or intervene in cases of suicide, but also how we cope or deal when faced with a client's suicide.

Therefore, the current study aims to investigate to what extent MHPs' attitudes toward suicide are associated with the impact of client suicide. In other words, to what extent are MHPs' attitudes toward (client) suicide informative regarding the short- and long-term emotional and professional impacts of client suicide? The results of this study may help broaden our understanding of the effects of a client's suicide as experienced by MHPs, providing insights relevant for training purposes or to reduce professional stigmatization following a client loss.

2. Method

2.1. Participants

This study included data from 213 participants (25% male, 72% female, and 1% non-binary) aged between 18 and 75 years. All participants had experienced at least one client suicide. The majority of the sample originated from Belgium (47%), Germany (18%), or The Netherlands (15%). A total of 46% of the participants were psychologists, 14% were psychiatric nurses, 13% were psychiatrists, 10% were counselors, and 9% were social workers.

2.2. Procedure

The present study is part of a larger research project looking into the impact of client suicide (for more details, see [17]). All study protocols were in accordance with the Declaration of Helsinki and approved by the Ethics Committee of the Erasmus University Rotterdam, The Netherlands (19-007.R1). The study was conducted via an online survey and was aimed at MHPs who had experienced client suicide. Recruitment was set up via social media, professional newsletters, and email. Individual informed consent was obtained from all participants involved in the study prior to participation. Data were collected using a self-administered, online survey available in English, Dutch, and German. All participants completed two questionnaires regarding their attitudes toward (client) suicide as well as three questionnaires related to the impact of client suicide (for more detail, see below). Survey completion took approximately 15–20 min.

2.3. Materials

The ATTS-18 [30] is an abbreviated version of the Questionnaire on Attitudes Toward Suicide [31], a self-report questionnaire developed to assess one's attitudes toward suicide. Example items include: *"people do have the right to take their own lives"* and *"if someone wants to commit suicide it is their business and we should not interfere"*. Each item is rated on a 5-point Likert scale, ranging from 1 *"strongly disagree"* to 5 *"strongly agree"*. Following EFA/CFA of the ATTS-18, construct reliability was evaluated for our subscales (see Results).

To assess participants' attitudes regarding the predictability or preventability of client suicide, inspired by Alexander and colleagues [15], the following two sets of questions were included. In general, "how predictable is client suicide?", and "how preventable is client suicide?" (labeled as Pred1 and Prev1). In reference to one particular client's suicide, "how predictable was that client's suicide?" and "how preventable was that client's suicide?" (labeled as Pred2 and Prev2). Either item is rated on a 5-point Likert scale, ranging from 1 *"very unpredictable"* to 5 *"very predictable"* or 1 *"very unpreventable"* to 5 *"very preventable"*.

The IES-22-R is a revised version of the original IES [32,33], a self-report questionnaire that aims to measure the subjective stress of a particular (traumatic) event in the seven days following. It includes 22 items divided over 3 subscales: (1) intrusion, (2) hyperarousal, and (3) avoidance. Each item is rated on a 5-point Likert scale, ranging from 0 *"not at all"* to 4 *"extremely"*. All 22 items are included in a total sum score. Cronbach's alpha as calculated for the current sample was $\alpha = 0.95$, suggesting excellent scale reliability.

The Long-Term Emotional Impact Scale (LTEIS; [34,35]) is a self-report questionnaire that aims to measure the long-term emotional impact of MHPs who have experienced client suicide. It consists of 10 items focusing on negative emotions that can occur following client suicide. Examples include aspects of therapeutic competence, such as a diminished sense of personal effectiveness, increased anxiety when evaluating suicidal clients, or the evaluation of a greater number of clients as being at risk of suicide. Each item is rated on a 5-point Likert scale, ranging from 1 *"disagree"* to 5 *"agree"*. All 10 items are included in a total average score. Cronbach's alpha as calculated for the current sample was $\alpha = 0.87$, suggesting good scale reliability.

The Professional Practice Impact Scale (PPIS; [34], inspired by [36]) is a self-report questionnaire that aims to measure long-term changes in professional practices in MHPs who have experienced client suicide. It consists of nine items that focus on the changes in professional practice that often follow client suicide, such as the refusal to work with suicidal clients, a greater inclination to consult colleagues, or the consideration of leaving the profession because of client suicide. Each item is rated on a 5-point Likert scale, ranging from 1 *"disagree"* to 5 *"agree"*. All nine items are included in a total average score. Cronbach's alpha as calculated for the current sample was $\alpha = 0.77$, suggesting good scale reliability.

2.4. Data Analysis

Statistical analyses included exploratory factor analysis (EFA) and structural equation modeling (SEM) using IBM SPSS Statistics 27.0 and AMOS 28.0 for Windows. EFA analyses were performed in SPSS using principal axis factoring as an extraction method, with oblimin rotation and Kaiser normalization. To determine the best factor structure, the eigenvalues (>1), factor loadings ($\geq$0.4), scree plot, and conceptual coherence of the individual factors were taken into account [37]. SEM analyses were performed in AMOS using the maximum likelihood estimation method. Global model fit was evaluated using the comparative fit index (CFI; CFI $\geq$ 0.90) and root mean square error of approximation (RMSEA; 0.05 $\geq$ RMSEA $\leq$ 0.08) [38,39].

3. Results

To investigate the extent to which one's attitudes toward suicide, as measured by the ATTS-18, are associated with the short- (IES-R) and long-term (LTEIS and PPIS) impacts of client suicide, EFA and path analysis in SEM were conducted. First, the ATTS-18 was explored using EFA. Factor loadings for the 18 items of the ATTS-18 and their item descriptions are presented in Table 1. EFA analysis identified a two-factor structure accounting for 45.12% of the total variance. Factor 1 was defined as *Rightful Choice* (nine items) and accounted for 32.28% of the variance with an eigenvalue of 5.81. Factor 2 was defined as *Preventability* (six items) and accounted for 12.84% of the variance with an eigenvalue of 2.31. Item 1, Item 8, and Item 17 were removed from the model as they did not load sufficiently on either factor (<0.40). Next, this two-factor structure was confirmed using SEM. To obtain a good model fit, guided by the modification indices and the correlation matrix, Item 12 and Item 13 were removed from the model, and an error correlation between Items 9 and 15 was included. Acceptable model fit, with CFI = 0.91 and RMSEA = 0.08, 90% CI (0.068–0.092), was achieved for a model with two first-order latent variables (i.e., *Rightful Choice*, seven items, and *Preventability*, six items).

Table 1. Factor loadings for the 18 items of the ATTS-18.

		Component	
		1	**2**
14.	People do have the right to take their own lives.	.760	
02.	Suicide can never be justified. (R)	.741	
09.	I would consider the possibility of taking my life if suffering from a severe, incurable disease.	.720	
11.	A person suffering from disease expressing wishes to die should get help to do so.	.693	
13.	I can understand that people suffering from a severe, incurable disease commit suicide.	.688	
07.	There may be situations where the only reasonable resolution is suicide.	.671	
15.	I would like to get help to commit suicide if I were to suffer from a severe, incurable disease.	0.636	
12.	I am prepared to help a person in a suicidal crisis by making contact.	.601	
08.	Although you would prefer to die in a different way, encountering painful life circumstances could make you consider suicide.	.565	
18.	Suicides among young people are particularly puzzling since they have everything to live for.		
17.	Suicide should not always be prevented.		
10.	If someone wants to commit suicide it is their business and we should not interfere. (R)		.774
04.	Once a person has made up their mind about suicide no one can stop them. (R)		0.670
05.	It is a human duty to try to stop someone from committing suicide.		0.665
16.	Suicide can be prevented.		.651
03.	Committing suicide is among the worst things to do to one's relatives.		0.515
06.	Loneliness could for me be a reason to take my life. (R)		0.471
01.	It is always possible to help a person with suicidal thoughts.		

Extraction method: principal axis factoring. Rotation method: oblimin with Kaiser normalization.

Next, a path analysis in SEM was constructed to evaluate the extent to which the two-factor structure of the ATTS-18 was able to predict the short- and long-term impacts of client suicide (see Figure 1 and Table 2). The two-factor model explained 14% of short-term, 7% of long-term emotional, and 12% of long-term professional impact variance. Rightful Choice and Preventability were both significantly related to all three impact variables ($p < 0.05$). Specifically, Rightful Choice had a negative significant relationship with short-term ($\beta = -0.31$, $p < 0.001$), long-term emotional ($\beta = -0.22$, $p = 0.017$), and long-term professional ($\beta = -0.19$, $p = 0.037$), whereas Preventability had a positive significant relationship with short-term ($\beta = 0.42$, $p < 0.001$), long-term emotional ($\beta = 0.29$, $p = 0.002$), and long-term professional ($\beta = 0.40$, $p < 0.001$). In other words, to hold the view that it is one's rightful choice to complete suicide is associated with less impact of client suicide, whereas to hold the view that suicide is (and should be) prevented is associated with more impact of client suicide.

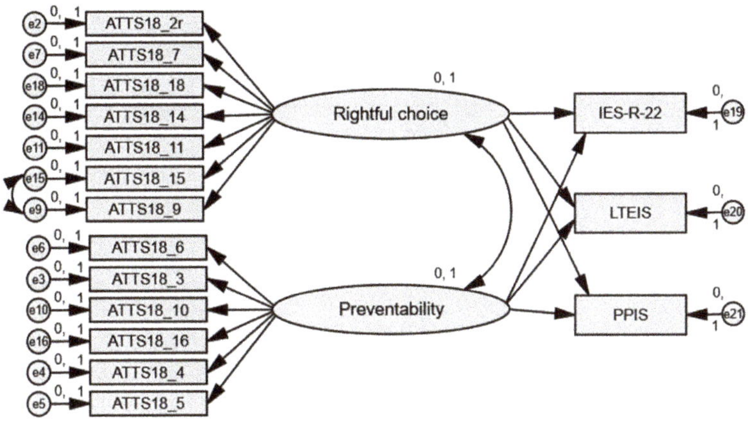

Figure 1. Path analysis for the short-term (IES-R), long-term emotional (LTEIS), and long-term professional (PPIS) impacts of client suicide, as predicted by the ATTS-18.

Table 2. Regression weights for the ATTS-18 predicting short- and long-term outcomes of client suicide.

		Unstandardized Estimate	Standard Error	Standardized Estimate	*p*-Value
Rightful Choice	IES-R	−6.020	1.734	−0.314	<.001
Rightful Choice	LTEIS	−0.199	0.083	−0.217	.017
Rightful Choice	PPIS	−0.135	0.065	−0.187	.037
Preventability	IES-R	8.019	1.778	0.418	<.001
Preventability	LTEIS	0.266	0.085	0.291	.002
Preventability	PPIS	0.290	0.067	0.401	<.001

Note. IES-R: Impact of Event Scale—Revised; LTEIS: Long-Term Emotional Impact Scale; PPIS: Professional Practice Impact Scale.

To investigate the extent to which MHPs' attitudes toward client suicide are associated with the short- (IES-R) and long-term (LTEIS and PPIS) impacts of client suicide, CFA and path analysis were conducted. First, the two-item, two first-order latent variable factor structure (i.e., Predictability and Preventability) was confirmed using SEM. Since both latent variables contain only two indicators, factor loadings were constrained to be equal prior to analysis [40]. Good model fit, with CFI = 0.97 and RMSEA = 0.05, was achieved.

Second, a path analysis in SEM was constructed to evaluate the extent to which the two-factor structure was able to predict short- and long-term impacts of client suicide (see Figure 2 and Table 3). The model explained 44% of short-term, 65% of long-term emotional, and 63% of long-term professional impact variance. Predictability and Preventability were highly positively correlated ($r = 0.97$, $p < 0.001$), yet neither proved significantly related to any of the three impact variables ($p > 0.05$). Predictability was not significantly related to short-term ($\beta = -2.43$, $p = 0.225$), long-term emotional ($\beta = -3.04$, $p = 0.213$), or long-term professional impact ($\beta = -2.94$, $p = 0.220$). Similarly, Preventability was not significantly related to short-term ($\beta = 2.54$, $p = 0.190$), long-term emotional ($\beta = 3.08$, $p = 0.191$), and long-term professional impact ($\beta = 3.04$, $p = 0.189$). In other words, MHPs' attitudes toward (a particular) client suicide were not associated with the impact of said client suicide.

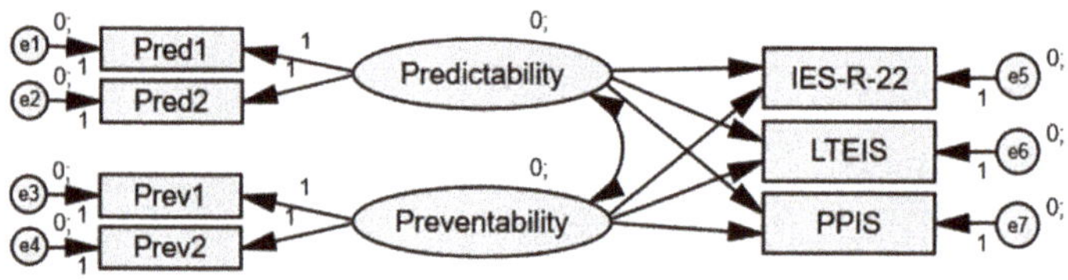

Figure 2. Path analysis for the short-term (IES-R), long-term emotional (LTEIS), and long-term professional (PPIS) impact of client suicide as predicted by Predictability vs. Preventability.

Table 3. Regression weights for Predictability and Preventability predicting short- and long-term outcomes of client suicide.

		Unstandardized Estimate	Standard Error	Standardized Estimate	*p*-Value
Predictability	IES-R	−88.962	73.257	−2.432	.225
Predictability	LTEIS	−5.288	4.242	−3.038	.213
Predictability	PPIS	−4.050	3.301	−2.940	.220
Preventability	IES-R	177.257	135.131	2.540	.190
Preventability	LTEIS	10.217	7.818	3.076	.191
Preventability	PPIS	7.992	6.089	3.040	.189

Note. IES-R: Impact of Event Scale—Revised; LTEIS: Long-Term Emotional Impact Scale; PPIS: Professional Practice Impact Scale.

4. Discussion

Individual differences regarding the impact of client suicide on MHPs have long been a topic of investigation, for instance, with regard to the difference in gender, age, previous exposure to suicide, or coping strategies (e.g., [10,14]). Interestingly, the extent to which one's attitudes toward (client) suicide might be associated with the impact of client suicide on MHPs had not received a lot of attention. Therefore, the current study aimed to investigate to what extent MHPs' attitudes toward (client) suicide are informative regarding the short- and long-term impacts of client suicide. Looking at attitudes toward suicide, our model explained 14% of short-term, 7% of long-term, and 12% of the long-term professional impact variance. Rightful Choice was associated with less short- and long-term impact, whereas Preventability was associated with more short- and long-term impact. Looking at attitudes toward client suicide, our model explained 44% of the short-term, 65% of the long-term emotional, and 63% of the long-term professional impact variance. Yet, neither Predictability nor Preventability predicted impact. Implications for both research and clinical practice are discussed.

Regarding attitudes toward suicide, our results indicate that generally, one's attitudes toward suicide can indeed play an important role in understanding individual differences in impact following client suicide. Rightful Choice was negatively associated with short- and long-term impact, whereas Preventability was positively associated with short- and long-term impact. In other words, participants who hold the belief that "one has the right to take their own life", "would consider the possibility if (...)", or "can understand that people complete suicide" reported less impact of client suicide, whereas participants who hold the belief that "suicide can be prevented", "it is our human duty to prevent (...)", or "(suicide) is among the worst things to do (...)" reported more impact of client suicide. Whilst novel, overall, these findings seem in line with previous research that suggests that our attitudes toward suicide impact how we perceive suicide-related behavior or intentions. As aforementioned, individuals with a history of suicidal ideation or non-fatal suicide attempts have been found to be more accepting [20,21] and individuals with more permissive attitudes toward suicide have been associated with greater rates of suicide ideation [22]. Moreover, exposure to the suicide of a close friend or relative has been found to influence one's attitudes toward suicide [23], and attitudes of medical staff toward suicide have been known to affect the (willingness to and) care provided to suicidal patients [24,25]. Last but not least, the belief that "any and every suicide is preventable" has been associated with increased distress in MHPs, as MHPs and their organizations involved in a client suicide may therefore be more inclined to look for a scapegoat or direct blame to one person [41].

Regarding attitudes toward client suicide, our results reveal that the more one considers client suicide predictable, the more preventable one considers it to be, and the other way around; yet, neither stance was significantly associated with the impact of client suicide. Previous research considering attitudes toward client suicide is limited and mostly descriptive. Rothes and colleagues [10] investigated the impact of client suicide in 107 psychiatrists and revealed that 57% of psychiatrists considered their most distressing case of client suicide to be little or not at all preventable and 39% of them thought the event was little or not at all predictable. As such, the predictability and preventability expectations of client suicide seemed to be associated with subsequent distress. Moreover, while Alexander and colleagues [15] reported that publicity in the media and the prospect of litigation exacerbated or modulated the impact of client suicide, attitudes toward client suicide did not. Interestingly, however, the authors did note the importance of said attitude, concluding that *"psychiatrists have to strike a difficult balance in their attitudes to suicide. If they regard suicide as fundamentally unavoidable (...) such a belief may foster therapeutic nihilism, (...) if suicide is perceived to be largely preventable and predictable, this may foster a culture of blame."* [15] (p. 1573). Last but not least, previous research suggests that if one can recognize that it is the client, not the MHP, who is ultimately responsible for a client's suicide, this ameliorates the impact of client suicide on the mental health professional [35,42].

Important implications for clinical practice (and supporting research) follow from these results. The current results suggest our attitudes toward (client) suicide do not only influence how we think about client suicide, suicidality, or the care we provide, but also to what extent we are affected or impacted by a client's suicide. Currently, however, (post)graduate training programs for MHPs pay little to no attention to one's attitudes toward suicide [43]. If within these programs suicide is discussed, the emphasis is on understanding suicide, its prevention, and care, and rarely are MHPs asked to reflect on their own ideas or attitudes toward suicide, nor are they stimulated to consider the relevance of such beliefs [44]. Helping MHPs become more aware of the (importance) of their attitudes toward suicide may prove valuable with regard to prevention, (self-)care, and MHPs' understanding of what they may (not) experience in the aftermath of client suicide. Individual differences in how MHPs respond to client suicide are significant and often puzzling to all parties involved. Increased awareness of what factors underlie these individual differences may prevent stigma, maladaptive emotional responses, or feelings of loneliness and isolation. This proposition is in line with previous work by Linke and colleagues [45], who have suggested that MHPs' professional training should foster the idea that suicides are not always preventable. Similarly, Sanders and colleagues [46] have argued in favor of exploring feelings of powerlessness that may arise following a client's suicide and of the notion that not all suicides can be prevented. While the goal would not be (and should not be) to change MHPs' attitudes toward suicide, conversations about the relevance of one's attitudes toward suicide among fellow students or colleagues may prove highly valuable for both patient care as well as self-care regarding suicidality. Moreover, suicide-related training programs should educate MHPs on the likelihood or probabilities of (client) suicide, that suicide is not always preventable, and what the personal and professional impact of a client's suicide might involve. The vast majority of MHPs do not typically receive suicide-related training in assessment, treatment, or risk management, while such programs have been found to positively impact professional practices, clinic policy, and clinicians' confidence and beliefs [47,48].

Limitations and Recommendations

The design of the current study was cross-sectional and employed a convenience sample. Moreover, retrospective self-report data were collected and analyzed. An implication of this would be that the events, thoughts, feelings, and behaviors reported by the participants could have taken place at any time, even many years previously, and may be subject to self-report bias. Although self-report questionnaires and convenience samples are frequently used in trauma research (e.g., [49–53]), the generalizability of the results may be limited as a result. Moreover, MHPs' attitudes toward suicide were collected when at least one client suicide had already taken place (see inclusion criteria for the current study), rather than before (and after) such event had taken place. The number of client suicides experienced, or the time passed since the event, were not recorded. Previous research, however, suggests that experiencing a client's suicide can alter a clinician's attitudes toward suicide [26,28,29,54]. As such, the current results pertain only to the relationship between MHPs' attitudes toward (client) suicide and the impact of said client suicide as measured after the fact and may not entirely generalize to attitudes toward (client) suicide measured when no such client suicide has taken place (yet). Finally, the ATTS-18 included in the current study was subject to an EFA, resulting in two distinct factors not identified by others previously, potentially limiting the generalizability of the results. Future research is advised to employ a longitudinal design and/or employ a more qualitative approach, assessing attitudes toward (client) suicide in MHPs at the start of their career, allowing for the (re)evaluation of said attitudes over time and, if the situation occurs, following one or more client suicides. That way, research could also further investigate to what extent the number of client suicides one has experienced impacts both MHPs' attitudes toward suicide as well as the impact of client suicide [34]. Moreover, qualitative approaches would allow for a deeper understanding of the experience the MHP has gone through and of the correlated emotions in the MHPs' own words.

5. Conclusions

To conclude, the current study conducted an in-depth investigation of MHPs' attitudes toward (client suicide) in light of the short- and long-term impacts of client suicide. Overall, the results indicate that MHPs who believe it is one's "rightful choice" to complete suicide tend to report less impact of client suicide, whereas MHPs who believe "suicide in general can and should be prevented at all times" tend to report more impact of client suicide. Moreover, the more MHPs consider client suicide as predictable, the more preventable MHPs consider it to be, and the other way around. As such, the current findings highlight the importance of suicide-related training programs and the extent to which such training programs should discuss MHPs' attitudes toward (client) suicide to improve client care as well as MHPs' self-care and mental well-being.

Author Contributions: Conceptualization and data curation, R.V.d.H.; formal analysis, I.P. and R.V.d.H.; writing—original draft preparation, I.P.; writing—review and editing, R.V.d.H. All authors have read and agreed to the published version of the manuscript.

Funding: This research received no external funding.

Institutional Review Board Statement: The study was conducted in accordance with the Declaration of Helsinki, and approved by the Ethics Committee of Erasmus University Rotterdam (protocol code 19-007.R1, 21 May 2019).

Informed Consent Statement: Informed consent was obtained from all subjects involved in the study.

Data Availability Statement: The data that support the findings of this study are available on request from the corresponding author, Ruth Van der Hallen.

Conflicts of Interest: The authors declare no conflict of interest.

References

1. World Health Organization. *Suicide in the World Global Health Estimates*; World Health Organization: Geneva, Switzerland, 2019.
2. Bachmann, S. Epidemiology of Suicide and the Psychiatric Perspective. *Int. J. Environ. Res. Public Health* **2018**, *15*, 1425. [CrossRef] [PubMed]

3. Cerel, J.; Brown, M.M.; Maple, M.; Singleton, M.; Venne, J.; van de Moore, M.; Flaherty, C. How Many People Are Exposed to Suicide? Not Six. *Suicide Life Threat. Behav.* **2019**, *49*, 529–534. [CrossRef] [PubMed]
4. Gutin, N.; McGann, V.L.; Jordan, J.R. The impact of suicide on professional caregivers. In *Grief after Suicide: Understanding the Consequences and Caring for the Survivors*; Routledge: London, UK; Taylor & Francis Group: Abingdon, UK, 2011; pp. 93–111.
5. Chang, B.; Gitlin, D.; Patel, R. The depressed patient and suicidal patient in the emergency department: Evidence-based management and treatment strategies. *Emerg. Med. Pract.* **2011**, *13*, 1–23. [PubMed]
6. Ferrari, A.J.; Norman, R.E.; Freedman, G.; Baxter, A.J.; Pirkis, J.E.; Harris, M.G.; Page, A.; Carnahan, E.; Degenhardt, L.; Vos, T.; et al. The Burden Attributable to Mental and Substance Use Disorders as Risk Factors for Suicide: Findings from the Global Burden of Disease Study 2010. *PLoS ONE* **2014**, *9*, e91936. [CrossRef]
7. Luoma, J.B.; Martin, C.E.; Pearson, J.L. Contact with mental health and primary care providers before suicide: A review of the evidence. *Am. J. Psychiatry* **2002**, *159*, 909–916. [CrossRef]
8. Finlayson, M.; Simmonds, J.G. Impact of Client Suicide on Psychologists in Australia. *Aust. Psychol.* **2018**, *53*, 23–32. [CrossRef]
9. Landers, A.; O'Brien, S.; Phelan, D. Impact of patient suicide on consultant psychiatrists in Ireland. *Psychiatrist* **2010**, *34*, 136–140. [CrossRef]
10. Rothes, I.A.; Scheerder, G.; Van Audenhove, C.; Henriques, M.R. Patient suicide: The experience of Flemish psychiatrists. *Suicide Life-Threat. Behav.* **2013**, *43*, 379–394. [CrossRef]
11. Kleespies, P.M.; Smith, M.R.; Becker, B.R. Psychology interns as patient suicide survivors: Incidence, impact, and recovery. *Prof. Psychol. Res. Pract.* **1990**, *21*, 257–263. [CrossRef]
12. Ting, L.; Sanders, S.; Jacobson, J.M.; Power, J.R. Dealing with the aftermath: A qualitative analysis of mental health social workers' reactions after a client suicide. *Soc. Work.* **2006**, *51*, 329–341. [CrossRef]
13. Dransart, D.A.C.; Gutjahr, E.; Gulfi, A.; Didisheim, N.K.; Séguin, M. Patient suicide in institutions: Emotional responses and traumatic impact on Swiss mental health professionals. *Death Stud.* **2014**, *38*, 315–321. [CrossRef]
14. Ellis, T.E.; Patel, A.B. Client suicide: What now? *Cogn. Behav. Pract.* **2012**, *19*, 277–287. [CrossRef]
15. Alexander, D.A.; Klein, S.; Gray, N.M.; Dewar, I.G.; Eagles, J.M. Suicide by patients: Questionnaire study of its effect on consultant psychiatrists. *BMJ Clin. Res. Ed.* **2000**, *320*, 1571–1574. [CrossRef] [PubMed]
16. Hendin, H.; Lipschitz, A.; Maltsberger, J.T.; Haas, A.P.; Wynecoop, S. Therapists' reactions to patients' suicides. *Am. J. Psychiatry* **2000**, *157*, 2022–2027. [CrossRef] [PubMed]
17. Van der Hallen, R. Suicide Exposure and the Impact of Client Suicide: A Structural Equation Modeling Approach. *Arch. Suicide Res.* **2021**, 1–13. [CrossRef]
18. Van der Hallen, R.; Godor, B.P. Exploring the Role of Coping Strategies on the Impact of Client Suicide: A Structural Equation Modeling Approach. *OMEGA J. Death Dying* **2022**, 302228211073213. [CrossRef]
19. Ghasemi, P.; Shaghaghi, A.; Allahverdipour, H. Measurement Scales of Suicidal Ideation and Attitudes: A Systematic Review Article. *Health Promot. Perspect.* **2015**, *5*, 156–168. [CrossRef]
20. Limbacher, M.; Domino, G. Attitudes toward Suicide among Attempters, Contemplators, and Nonattempters. *OMEGA J. Death Dying* **1986**, *16*, 325–334. [CrossRef]
21. McAuliffe, C.; Corcoran, P.; Keeley, H.S.; Perry, I.J. Risk of Suicide Ideation Associated with Problem-Solving Ability and Attitudes Toward Suicidal Behavior in University Students. *Crisis J. Crisis Interv. Suicide Prev.* **2003**, *24*, 160–167. [CrossRef]
22. Stein, D.; Witztum, E.; Brom, D.; DeNour, A.K.; Elizur, A. The association between adolescents' attitudes toward suicide and their psychosocial background and suicidal tendencies. *Adolesc. Rosl. Heights* **1992**, *27*, 949–959.
23. Pitman, A.; Nesse, H.; Morant, N.; Azorina, V.; Stevenson, F.; King, M.; Osborn, D. Attitudes to suicide following the suicide of a friend or relative: A qualitative study of the views of 429 young bereaved adults in the UK. *BMC Psychiatry* **2017**, *17*, 400. [CrossRef]
24. Bagley, C.; Ramsay, R.F. Attitudes toward suicide, religious values and suicidal behavior. Evidence from a community survey. In *Suicide and Its Prevention: The Role of Attitude and Imitation*; Diekstra, R.F.W., Ed.; BRILL: Leiden, The Netherlands, 1989; pp. 78–90.
25. Samuelsson, M.; Sunbring, Y.; Winell, I.; Åsberg, M. Nurses' Attitudes to Attempted Suicide Patients. *Scand. J. Caring Sci.* **1997**, *11*, 232–237. [CrossRef] [PubMed]
26. Werth, J.L.; Liddle, B.J. Psychotherapists' attitudes toward suicide. *Psychother. Theory Res. Pract. Train.* **1994**, *31*, 440–448. [CrossRef]
27. Swain, B.J.; Domino, G. Attitudes toward suicide among mental health professionals. *Death Stud.* **1985**, *9*, 455–468. [CrossRef]
28. Boukouvalas, E.; El-Den, S.; Murphy, A.L.; Salvador-Carulla, L.; O'Reilly, C.L. Exploring Health Care Professionals' Knowledge of, Attitudes Towards, and Confidence in Caring for P. *Arch. Suicide Res.* **2020**, *24*, 32. [CrossRef] [PubMed]
29. Kodaka, M.; Inagaki, M.; Poštuvan, V.; Yamada, M. Exploration of factors associated with social worker attitudes toward suicide. *Int. J. Soc. Psychiatry* **2013**, *59*, 452–459. [CrossRef] [PubMed]
30. Stecz, P. Psychometric evaluation of the Questionnaire on Attitudes Towards Suicide (ATTS) in Poland. *Curr. Psychol.* **2021**, *40*, 2528–2542. [CrossRef]
31. Renberg, E.S.; Jacobsson, L. Development of a Questionnaire on Attitudes Towards Suicide (ATTS) and Its Application in a Swedish Population. *Suicide Life Threat. Behav.* **2003**, *33*, 52–64. [CrossRef]
32. Creamer, M.; Bell, R.; Failla, S. Psychometric properties of the Impact of Event Scale—Revised. *Behav. Res. Ther.* **2003**, *41*, 1489–1496. [CrossRef]

33. Weiss, D.S.; Marmar, C.R. The Impact of Event Scale—Revised. In *Assessing Psychological Trauma and PTSD*; The Guilford Press: New York, NY, USA, 1997; pp. 399–411.
34. Gulfi, A.; Castelli Dransart, D.A.; Heeb, J.-L.; Gutjahr, E. The impact of patient suicide on the professional reactions and practices of mental health caregivers and social workers. *Crisis* **2010**, *31*, 202–210. [CrossRef]
35. Horn, P.J. Therapists' psychological adaptation to client suicide. *Psychother. Theory Res. Pract. Train.* **1994**, *31*, 190–195. [CrossRef]
36. Henry, M.; Séguin, M.; Drouin, M.-S. Les réactions des professionnels en snaté mentale au décès par suicide d'un patient. [Mental health professionals' response to the suicide of their patients.]. *Rev. Québécoise De Psychol.* **2004**, *25*, 241–257.
37. Ledesma, R.D.; Valero-Mora, P.; Macbeth, G. The Scree Test and the Number of Factors: A Dynamic Graphics Approach. *Span. J. Psychol.* **2015**, *18*, E11. [CrossRef] [PubMed]
38. Hu, L.; Bentler, P.M. Cutoff criteria for fit indexes in covariance structure analysis: Conventional criteria versus new alternatives. *Struct. Equ. Model.* **1999**, *6*, 1–55. [CrossRef]
39. Wang, S.; Chen, C.-C.; Dai, C.-L.; Richardson, G.B. A call for, and beginner's guide to, measurement invariance testing in evolutionary psychology. *Evol. Psychol. Sci.* **2018**, *4*, 166–178. [CrossRef]
40. Kenny, D.A.; Kashy, D.A.; Bolger, N. Data analysis in social psychology. In *The Handbook of Social Psychology*, 4th ed.; McGraw-Hill: New York, NY, USA, 1998; Volume 1–2, pp. 233–265.
41. Walter, G.; Pridmore, S. Suicide is preventable, sometimes. *Australas. Psychiatry* **2012**, *20*, 271–273. [CrossRef]
42. Trimble, L.; Jackson, K.; Harvey, D. Client suicidal behaviour: Impact, interventions, and implications for psychologists. *Aust. Psychol.* **2000**, *35*, 227–232. [CrossRef]
43. Mackelprang, J.L.; Karle, J.; Reihl, K.M.; Cash, R.E. Suicide intervention skills: Graduate training and exposure to suicide among psychology trainees. *Train. Educ. Prof. Psychol.* **2014**, *8*, 136–142. [CrossRef]
44. Hawgood, J.; Krysinska, K.; Mooney, M.; Ozols, I.; Andriessen, K.; Betterridge, C.; De Leo, D.; Kõlves, K. Suicidology Post Graduate Curriculum: Priority Topics and Delivery Mechanisms for Suicide Prevention Education. *Int. J. Environ. Res. Public Health* **2021**, *18*, 9926. [CrossRef]
45. Linke, S.; Wojciak, J.; Day, S. The impact of suicide on community mental health teams: Findings and recommendations. *Psychiatr. Bull.* **2002**, *26*, 50–52. [CrossRef]
46. Sanders, S.; Jacobson, J.M.; Ting, L. Preparing for the Inevitable: Training Social Workers to Cope with Client Suicide. *J. Teach. Soc. Work.* **2008**, *28*, 1–18. [CrossRef]
47. Berlim, M.T.; Perizzolo, J.; Lejderman, F.; Fleck, M.P.; Joiner, T.E. Does a brief training on suicide prevention among general hospital personnel impact their baseline attitudes towards suicidal behavior? *J. Affect. Disord.* **2007**, *100*, 233–239. [CrossRef] [PubMed]
48. Oordt, M.S.; Jobes, D.A.; Fonseca, V.P.; Schmidt, S.M. Training mental health professionals to assess and manage suicidal behavior: Can provider confidence and practice behaviors be altered? *Suicide Life Threat. Behav.* **2009**, *39*, 21–32. [CrossRef] [PubMed]
49. Blaney, P.H. Affect and memory: A review. *Psychol. Bull.* **1986**, *99*, 229–246. [CrossRef]
50. Frissa, S.; Hatch, S.L.; Fear, N.T.; Dorrington, S.; Goodwin, L.; Hotopf, M. Challenges in the retrospective assessment of trauma: Comparing a checklist approach to a single item trauma experience screening question. *BMC Psychiatry* **2016**, *16*, 20. [CrossRef]
51. Roemer, L.; Litz, B.T.; Orsillo, S.M.; Ehlich, P.J.; Friedman, M.J. Increases in retrospective accounts of war-zone exposure over time: The role of PTSD symptom severity. *J. Trauma. Stress* **1998**, *11*, 597–605. [CrossRef]
52. Southwick, S.M.; Morgan, C.A.; Nicolaou, A.L.; Charney, D.S. Consistency of memory for combat-related traumatic events in veterans of Operation Desert Storm. *Am. J. Psychiatry* **1997**, *154*, 173–177. [CrossRef]
53. Wessely, S.; Unwin, C.; Hotopf, M.; Hull, L.; Ismail, K.; Nicolaou, V.; David, A. Stability of recall of military hazards over time: Evidence from the Persian Gulf War of 1991. *Br. J. Psychiatry* **2003**, *183*, 314–322. [CrossRef]
54. Fairman, N.; Montross Thomas, L.P.; Whitmore, S.; Meier, E.A.; Irwin, S.A. What Did I Miss? A Qualitative Assessment of the Impact of Patient Suicide on Hospice Clinical Staff. *J. Palliat. Med.* **2014**, *17*, 832–836. [CrossRef]

International Journal of
Environmental Research and Public Health

MDPI

Article

"It's a Living Experience": Bereavement by Suicide in Later Life

Trish Hafford-Letchfield [1,*], Jeffrey Hanna [1], Evan Grant [1], Lesley Ryder-Davies [1], Nicola Cogan [2], Jolie Goodman [3], Susan Rasmussen [2] and Sophie Martin [1]

1 School of Social Work and Social Policy, Faculty of Humanities and Social Sciences, University of Strathclyde, Glasgow G1 1XQ, UK; jeffrey.hanna@qub.ac.uk (J.H.); evan@camgrant.org.uk (E.G.); lryderdavies@btinternet.com (L.R.-D.); sophie.martin.2017@uni.strath.ac.uk (S.M.)
2 School of Psychological Sciences, Faculty of Humanities and Social Sciences, University of Strathclyde, Glasgow G1 1XQ, UK; nicola.cogan@strath.ac.uk (N.C.); s.a.rasmussen@strath.ac.uk (S.R.)
3 Mental Health Foundation, London SE1 9QB, UK; jgoodman@mentalhealth.org.uk
* Correspondence: trish.hafford-letchfield@strath.ac.uk

Abstract: Bereavement by suicide for people in later life is significantly under-researched. Research on ageing and suicide has yet to address the experiences of those bereaved by suicide and how such a devastating loss affects the ageing experience. **Objectives**: We explored the substantive issues involved in bereavement by suicide and its impact on later life. **Methods**: This was a co-produced qualitative study. Peer researchers with lived experience conducted in-depth interviews with twenty-four people aged 60–92 years. A phenomenological approach informed the data analysis. **Main Findings:** Themes described included (1) moral injury and trauma; (2) the rippling effect on wider family and networks; (3) transitions and adaptations of bereaved people and how their 'living experience' impacted on ageing. **Conclusions**: It is important to understand how individual experiences of suicide intersect with ageing and the significance of targeted assessment and intervention for those bereaved by suicide in ageing policies and support.

Keywords: bereavement; suicide; ageing; later life; suicide prevention; moral injury; trauma; peer support

Citation: Hafford-Letchfield, T.; Hanna, J.; Grant, E.; Ryder-Davies, L.; Cogan, N.; Goodman, J.; Rasmussen, S.; Martin, S. "It's a Living Experience": Bereavement by Suicide in Later Life. *Int. J. Environ. Res. Public Health* **2022**, *19*, 7217. https://doi.org/10.3390/ijerph19127217

Academic Editors: Karolina Krysinska, Karl Andriessen and Yossi Levi-Belz

Received: 28 April 2022
Accepted: 10 June 2022
Published: 13 June 2022

1. Introduction

Death by suicide is a complex issue of global concern. It is estimated that 700,000 people die from suicide every year [1,2]. In the UK, 8.67% of all deaths are from suicide [3]. This has a significant impact on those bereaved by suicide (commonly defined as someone who has: "lost a significant other (or a loved one) by suicide, and whose life is changed because of the loss" (p. 43) [4]. The interpersonal impact stretches far beyond those closely related to the person [5].

The experiences of suicide bereavement of those aged >60 years old, however, remains a significantly under-researched area. A systematic review of studies found that none fulfilled the inclusion criteria [6]. Hyboldt et al.'s [7] subsequent qualitative empirical study investigated the age-related factors for participants during the post-bereavement restoration process and their re-orientation to life after such a devastating loss. The lack of theoretical and methodological consistency in suicide and ageing research has also been noted [8,9]. Research findings also call for the greater engagement of care professionals [10–12] and consideration of the interpersonal and structural impacts of ageism [13] in order to find answers to the multi-faceted impact of bereavement by suicide. This study sought to explore the experience of being bereaved by suicide on the individual in later life, the implications for help-seeking, support needs and how bereavement by suicide interacts with ageing experiences.

2. Materials and Methods

This study used an in-depth interpretative phenomenological approach (IPA) [14] to explore the substantive issues for people bereaved by suicide in later life. IPA is concerned with the human lived experience, and posits that experience can be understood through exploring the meanings which people impress upon it [15,16]. The research team comprised of academic researchers from social work, psychology, a national mental health charity engaged with ageing empowerment, and two peer researchers (aged 60+ years, with lived experience). Peer research is thought to promote accessibility by grounding data collection in the experiences of those being researched [17,18] and to produce more relevant and practice-oriented knowledge [19,20].

We recruited peer researchers through our charity partner. Peer researchers were remunerated in line with UK guidance for working with experts by experience [20]. This democratisation of the research process required the team to have clear structures to support team members with different expertise and knowledge such as regular briefings and debriefings to mitigate the impact of emotive interviews and practices that more experienced researchers may take for granted [18]. This included providing formal training on qualitative interviewing and data analysis and opportunities for both verbal and written structured dialogue to facilitate mutual and reciprocal learning. The topic guide (see Table 1) was informed by a literature review and scoping of current suicide prevention strategies for potential domains and constructs [21]. While the topic guide had a strong focus on support after loss, it sought to gain broader insights into participants' lived experiences of their loss(es) and their specific relationship to their experiences of ageing.

Table 1. Areas covered in the Interview Topic Guide.

- Individual's experience of support after their loss at different time points.
- Their reflections on who or what supported them and how helpful it was; their own help-seeking behaviour and self-identified needs; What was unhelpful?
- What worked best in managing their lives after the loss? How they feel they experienced their bereavement, any particular crises or transformational moments; the role of family, friends; the role of any services; the pros and cons of being supported by people who knew you and the person you lost and those who didn't know you both.
- What support would they recommend to others? Any tips for people who have are bereaved by suicide; practical things they did to manage grief; advice to family and friends that would help them supporting others; what would they like to tell professionals to do and not do.
- How the experiences have affected their later life and experience of ageing?

The framework underpinning data collection encouraged participants to recount events and the impact of the loss surrounding the person(s) they were talking about by narrating their experience into temporal order and meaning, with a particular emphasis on how this affected their later life. This flexible approach to interviewing encouraged reflective thinking and effort to explain their situation and response to it [22].

The target population were people who were aged 60 years and over, living in the UK, with experience of the loss of a significant other by suicide at least 12 months prior to engaging in the interview. Omerov, Steineck and Dyregrov et al. [23] suggested that meaning-making, recall of experiences and post-traumatic growth are better after this period. The team used purposive and opportunistic sampling to recruit participants using direct mail shot through organisations connected with older people in the UK and via social media. Following screening and informed consent, participants completed a short demographic questionnaire, which captured their individual characteristics, their relationship to the person who died, and the length of time that had passed since the suicide.

One-to-one interviews were conducted virtually on the telephone (n = 10) or Zoom (n = 14) over 3 months in 2021 coinciding with a period of COVID-19 lockdown in the UK. These were audio-recorded with informed consent and professionally transcribed verbatim. Interviews lasted between 39 and 100 min (mAvg = 58 min). Four members of the team conducted twenty-four individual interviews; and the peer researchers conducted sixteen of these interviews.

As a descriptive, cooperative study, data analysis was inductive. Two researchers read and coded every transcript and met to discuss each transcript as well as identify and reflect upon preliminary themes. These meetings were audio recorded and the transcriptions used to verify and report on the main themes. This method drew on constant comparison [24] to help uncover participants' meanings and furthering interpretive understandings [25]. The team observed data saturation after approximately 17 interviews. In the transcripts, we looked for complex ideas, particularly age-related issues, metaphors and critical moments. We also engaged in a critical reflection of how the qualitative data were interpretated in order to capture any biases and misperceptions during the analytical process. Analyses focused on understanding the breadth of experiences and building a picture of bereavement by suicide, and what this meant for later life grounded in the participants' own narratives.

Ethical approval was provided by the University of Strathclyde Ethnics Committee. Participation was voluntary and followed both verbal and written consent. A key ethical consideration was the impact on researchers and participants from talking about bereavement and suicide [26,27]. The protocol drew on established guidance for working with people bereaved by suicide [28]. Participants were given a structured debriefing and signposted towards support. Participants were followed up one week after the interview to remind them about self-care. Researchers kept a critical incident/reflective diary for their own personal use alongside interviewing. The team adopted guidelines on working with vicarious trauma and had regular debriefings and access to a clinical psychologist. In the spirit of cooperative enquiry, we established clear processes for the peer-research members of the team to ensure that their contributions were valued and provided opportunities for their challenge and leadership [29].

A project advisory group comprised members working in suicide prevention, bereavement support, mental health social work, and a lay older person. This group reviewed the research protocol and tools, and commented on the findings from the interim report.

3. Results

Table 2 provides details on the characteristics of the participant sample (n = 24). The participants were predominantly female. Participants were aged 60–94 years old (mAvg = 72.0 years). Their relationship to the person who died by suicide included; being their parent (n = 15), spouse/partner (n = 4), parent in-law (n = 1), grandparent (n = 1), aunt/uncle (n = 1), and sibling (n = 2). The time elapsed between the death was between 1 and 20 (mAvg = 6.8 years).

Table 2. Characteristics of the 24 participants included in the study.

Variables	n	Variables	n
Gender of participant		**Ethnicity of participant**	
Female	21	Black, African	1
Male	3	White, British	1
Age of participant		White, English	13
60–64 years old	6	White, European	2
65–69 years old	4	White, Northern Irish	1
70–74 years old	7	White, Scottish	5
75–79 years old	3	White, Welsh	1
80–84 years old	2	**Disability**	
85–89 years old	1	Yes	3
90–94 years old	1	No	21
Relationship to the deceased		**Religion/belief of participant**	
Aunt/uncle	1	Buddhism	1
Grandparent	1	Christianity	11
Parent	15	Judaism	1
Parent in-law	1	No religion	9
Sibling	2	Prefer not to say	1
Spouse/partner	4	Quaker	1

Table 2. *Cont.*

Variables	*n*	Variables	*n*
Sexual identity of participant		**Location of participant**	
Bisexual	2	England	17
Heterosexual	22	Northern Ireland	1
		Wales	5
		Scotland	1

Table 3 provides a schematic diagram and description of the three themes and sub-themes discussed in this paper. Age-related experiences were integrated across three themes comprising: (1) moral injury; (2) the rippling effect on relationships; and (3) transition and adaptation through a living experience in later life.

Table 3. Schematic diagram of key themes from the qualitative data.

Theme	Description of Theme	Sub-Themes
Moral Injury and Trauma	The overall sense of failing responses and trauma to prevent, bearing witness to, or learning about the suicide and how this transgresses deeply held moral beliefs and expectations linked to the sense of negative judgement and stigma from others. Moral injury was strongly associated with feelings of guilt and shame associated with traumatic loss.	Poor engagement and lack of appropriate care from professionals Critical of own failure to prevent/save Feeling helpless and calls for help unrecognised Being left alone to deal with grief Lack of insight from others including avoidance Being given unsolicited advice/careless thoughtless comments from others Lack of physical/practical support Perception of having failed from others/shame/stigma and guilt Grappling with conflicted feelings towards the person who died Use of metaphors to express dramatic experiences and incongruities in situations that emerged
Rippling effects	Positive and negative The effect on self (beliefs about self), significant others (partners, children, friends, wider family) and wider social networks (acquaintances, work colleagues, neighbours, community) is evident both in the aftermath as well as the longer term impact and consequences.	Igniting of existing or previous traumas Expositing quality of relationships Lack of care from people close to them Taking up care roles and new responsibilities Invisibility as a mature person Own unmet needs/disappointment Providing substitute care Being unable to assert own needs Impact on physical and mental health of own and others Fear/awareness of suicide in self/others Significance of key people reaching out Making sense of disruption to expected natural order
Adaptation and transformation to the living experience in later life	How the bereaved person reflected with time on the impact of suicide on themselves and their lived experiences particularly as they became older. How they learned to adapt following the loss by suicide and connected with peers. This related to the importance of disclosure talking, listening and validation of experiences following loss through suicide and meaning-making about their own lives and life with the person.	Timing of help seeking Quality of responses to help seeking e.g., family doctor Recognising different types of pain Suicidal thoughts and behaviour Radical acceptance of loss Temporal perspectives/time lost vs. time left Marking anniversaries/meaning of significant events Peer support/peer education/activism Role of professionals in recognising bereavement by suicide

3.1. Moral Injury and Trauma

Most participants provided vivid and visceral descriptions of learning about the suicide and its immediate aftermath. These encompassed intense physical and emotional pain with severe shock and numbness. Two people used the metaphor of 'a bomb going off' to convey the immediate and uncontrollable devastation experienced by such a traumatic loss.

A sense of moral injury in the aftermath of experiencing a loss by suicide incorporated an overall sense of failing to prevent, bearing witness to, or learning about the suicide and how this transgressed deeply held moral beliefs and expectations, which compounded the traumatic loss. The distressing psychological, social, behavioural aftermath following the suicide in turn gave rise to moral injury. Negative reactions from people in the bereaved person's network left them feeling isolated and removed from crucial sources of support:

> *"Because it was suicide, I could instantly tell by the person's reaction whether to go on with the conversation. A lot of them, kind of, just back away and wouldn't even respond. I remember walking down the town that I used to live in, this lady that I knew really well was walking towards me, she crossed over when she saw me. I'll never forget that."*(female, 69, parent).

This literal crossing of the street to avoid the bereaved person came up regularly. Moral injury stemmed from the lack of insight and discomfort of other people which one participant described as 'sheer callousness'. Self-stigma, guilt, shame and self-blame inevitably gave rise to feelings that they should have been able to prevent this, to have foreseen it, been a better parent or partner, and awareness of the manifest negative judgement and stigma from others:

> *" ... it's the guilt that this person ... could do something so awful to themselves. To be so desperate that they'd take their own life. You know, ... I think, the guilt just gets to you, just ... and you feel that everybody's sort of, not judging you, but they must think, gosh, you know, what's happened in this family, that this person could do this to themselves? Why did he not come to you and talk to you?"* (female, 64 years, parent).

Despite some knowing that suicide was a risk and that it could happen, it was still a tremendous shock that made people feel responsible or that they had failed in some way:

> *" ... I felt I should have been able to do something to have spotted what was going on ... done something to change the course of events."* (male, 72 years, partner).

Moral injury also occurred where participants were dismissed where they had asked for professional help. They described missed opportunities during the immediate period before the suicide:

> *"he'd been threatening with suicide and that day they had the mental health team out, a crisis team and he told them he was wanting to die and they dismissed it, basically and left him in the community. They had convinced me and my daughter that, oh, we were overreacting ... it was only a few hours later he killed himself."* (female, 62 years, grandparent).

3.1.1. The Rippling Effect on Relationships and Wider Social Networks

> *"I can honestly say it was the most devastating thing that's ever, ever happened to me. I had been bereaved, I'd lost both my parents, I'd lost my friends, I had a miscarriage, I've been divorced. I had gone through major life affecting events but honestly this was ... I just can't tell just how devastating it was."* (female, 72 years, parent).

Participants not only gave testament to the devastating effect on their own lives but this touched significant others (partner, children, friends, wider family) and social networks (acquaintances, work colleagues, neighbours, community) both in the immediate aftermath and longer-term impact. From their later life perspective, some framed these impacts in the context of historical traumatic events and problematic relationships. These affected their coping mechanisms and particularly the family.

The bereaved person's caring role often took precedence over their own immediate needs. One man talked about his mother who deteriorated quickly after the suicide with cognitive decline and died soon after:

> *"she was diagnosed with Alzheimer's in February and I truly believe, it was bought on by the shock of my brother's death. . . . she went down so quickly, it was shocking"* (female, 62 years, sibling).

Earlier traumatic events involving domestic violence, alcohol issues and the ambivalence from particular family members involved the bereaved person moderating challenging relationships. They were often responsible for all the practical arrangements. Roles became complex where there were blended or reconstituted families. Several participants bereaved as parents, articulated challenges associated with a difficult relationship with an ex-partner or the other parent. They felt unable to comfort each other, remained in dispute about the arrangements for their loved ones such as who could attend the funeral. These experiences contributed to the participants' own lack of self-care and, for some, to extreme post-traumatic stress. Combined with blame and shame, post-suicide family interactions became extremely stressful. Such fractured relationships compounded the person's own loss, and for some, led to a deep sense of betrayal. This extended to their wider friendships:

> *"There was one friend actually who I thought was a good friend and she sent flowers and sent a card and then I didn't hear anything from her at all for nine months . . . I was absolutely furious, I thought she has not been in touch with me since he died, not once to say are you okay, is there anything I can do, do you want to talk? . . . and then nine months later when it's my birthday she just gets in touch and asked me if I wanted to go out for lunch. No mention of [name], no mention of how are you feeling . . . And I just said I don't want you to contact me ever again . . . . . . she didn't even come to the funeral, she didn't ask when it was, she didn't come, and I was so livid that after 20 years I just cut off all connection with her."* (female, 62 years, grandparent).

These silences were as injurious as insensitive comments. Participants spoke of awkward silences or countered expectations that they *'should have got over it by now'* or *'it was God's will"* (Participant 22, female, 63 years, partner). They longed to be asked how they were coping, to have the person's name spoken and experience other meaningful exchanges about the things most important to them.

Sources of practical support were, however, highly valued:

> *"The practical things my daughter is absolutely amazing. She took over everything. I mean, I'm absolute . . . I'm at the stage in life, I'm nearly 70, I just couldn't deal with anything anyway, but she is so good . . . she thinks of everything, actually. And she still does."* (female, 62 years, grandparent).

From a later life perspective, participants often reflected an appreciative and empathetic understanding of the impact of the suicide on the family. Losing a child in later life conflicted with the expected 'natural order'. Their social standing or position within the family subsequently changed with new responsibilities and dependencies; taking care of grandchildren, siblings and younger family members. They found themselves compensating for the absence of the deceased person, being tentative about their own grief and holding back:

> *"She needs me . . . . . . and what I did was, I became the . . . I, kind of, absorbed everyone's pain. My mum, my niece, my nephew, my sister, so I didn't actually have time to process me. And my aunt actually rang me and said, [name] what about you?"* (female, 62 years, sibling).

Another participant (male, 78 years, partner) was concerned about their daughter, who at the time of losing her mother by suicide, had four girls all under four including twins of three months. Another commented:

"So, the first few weeks really was me being there for them and cooking and cleaning and doing all the things that she couldn't do. I had to be there and I had to be strong and look after my granddaughter because her mother wasn't capable of doing it at the time, she was in such grief that she couldn't do anything. My daughter couldn't go to work, she was in very, very, deep depression ... " (female, 68, grandparent).

These intense caring responsibilities sandwiched between ageing parents and their own children, found participants caught in the firing line. For example, one 78-year-old experienced abusive phone calls after the funeral from her daughter-in-law's parents, blaming her for the suicide. Another 69-year-old, after losing her father, described being at the mercy of her 'controlling' mother and being at the receiving end of her anger, which was very hurtful.

3.1.2. Transition and Adaptation to Ageing through a Living Experience

The third theme reflected poignant and significant experiences in the personal journey of the bereaved person in later life. This included reflections about their own future, motivation, mortality, and accounts of help seeking. Some described periods of transformation often coinciding with activism and leadership with their peers through shared lived experience. While participants were bereaved at different age-points in their life, they reflected on what their experience meant in terms of ageing:

" ... I'm 74 and she was my only child ... she was the future and how things are going to be is something very, very important at the moment. I'm giving sort of a lot of thought to it and it's causing me a lot of sadness. So, it's something that, yeah that I need to really ... that I've been thinking of. At one point years ago, in terms of a Will, in terms of what I do with my property and my precious possessions and things, is something that is huge" (female, 74 years, parent).

This perception of having no-one to look out for you in later life was evident:

"I think that's the older a person is, when the bereavement happens, the more age does have an impact from isolation point of view, or lack of grand-children, or lack of somebody coming in to do your washing for you, or whatever it might be. The older you are, the less time you've got to sort of get your life back together again in some way or other" (female, 73 years, parent).

One woman living alone (aged 74) was now using psychotherapy. She reflected on the COVID-19 national lockdown and how she had 'always been locked down' since her daughter's death. This was an important time for reparation and she did a 'lot of (positive) sorting and thinking' about her daughter. She observed the potential for a greater understanding of the impact of death following the huge loss of people during the pandemic as positive. She also used a telephone befriender service which she found helpful and comforting and described herself as *"emerging again like a metamorphosis, like a butterfly, but it's a long, long process"*.

Two others commented on the relationship between their grief and the physical and psychological effects of growing older:

"Well, the first one is, I find sometimes that something's bothering me or upsetting me, or I'm feeling down, I think well is this [Name] or is just getting old? ... am I attributing all of this to the bereavement, when in actual fact, I'd be feeling like this anyway? ... I don't think you can rush grief. But, at the same time, I'm conscious of the fact that if I don't try and at least twin track, I'm not going to finish grieving before I die." (female, 73 years, parent).

These health concerns triggered greater awareness of the participant's vulnerability and potential dependencies:

"I had a foot operation, nothing serious, about a year and a half ago and that made me really realise that there's not going to be [name] around to come and be my next of kin. It

really struck home that sort of feeling that as you approach old age and all the rest of it, you're not going to have your nearest and dearest around. It's something that I've got to manage very much on my own." (female, 74 years, parent).

Another man's insight was philosophical:

"We struggle with that somebody has gone, and they're actually gone forever. And again, I put it down in part, to a sort of an arrogance that we feel we're impregnable and immortal, yet we know we're not, and I know now, that as I age more and more" (Participant 15, male, 72 years. partner).

Participants reflected on the timing of the suicide within their own life course, how they learned to cope and adapt to the loss and its association with other (sometimes cumulative) losses. One woman was 'glad' this happened when she was older, as she had more time with her daughter and in anticipation of living a short while longer would have less pain to endure:

"Well, I sometimes feel that I've not got the energy for it anymore. . . . I feel as if one leg of the table's missing, if you know what I mean. That sounds a bit weird, but there's still a limp if you know what I mean. That's what I'm trying to say, I think. I feel at times kind of broken, yes." (female, 78 years, parent).

For those retired, they talked about feeling or being very alone, their lack of plans and described temporal and visceral moments that captured these feelings:

"You feel it, and you'll recognise this I'm sure, [name] yourself. It's mornings and evenings, those early hours, those moments when you put yourself into bed, and there is this, almost deafening silence". (male, 72 years, partner).

Some bereaved parents remised about lost opportunities for grandchildren. This meant loss of practical support and angst about their future:

"It feels as if my chest is being torn up". (female, 63 years, parent).

Participants echoed the importance of disclosure, talking, listening and the validation of experiences following loss through suicide. They described different experiences of seeking help, the type of help offered and taken forward. Some appeared to require initial support that focused on the trauma of the suicide, whilst some accessed therapeutic/counselling services earlier on. They perceived these latter interventions as being more valuable once a significant period had passed. The timing of help seeking and help giving was arbitrary but very important. Those who developed extreme post-traumatic stress were able to connect with appropriate services, whereas many had hit or miss experiences with access and signposting to services:

"She gave me permission to fall. And I fell hard. I became scared of everything, I didn't like the dark, I became paranoid, I thought people were talking about me. It was the most frightening time of my life. There was no energy, I just slept all day and all night. So, one or two weeks since . . . I had to go back to the doctor to renew my prescription and he said, what can I do to help, would you like counselling? And I said, yes please. So, that was my turning point. But those few weeks were the darkest period of my life . . . I'm really lucky that I was able to meet with this counsellor, who was my saviour." (female, 74 years, parent).

Help-seeking was connected to motivation to survive, or having to carry on for others:

"You've got a very simply choice, you either carry on or you don't. And I did have moments, I think they were, what I would call, poetic moments . . . I remember going through a period, I can't remember quite when it was, when [name] had gone, and realising that both my daughters are married, they've both had two children, my mother was still alive, she only died, it's coming up to two years now.. and I remember feeling, nobody needs me anymore. Nobody needs me. My kids don't really need me. They've got their own lives, I'm potentially a complication." (male, 72 years, partner).

There were references to suicidal thoughts and/or wish for the hastening of the end of life that came and went:

> *"I sometimes feel I can drive my car into a wall. I just get fed up with it, I can't take anymore. Aye, I think of suicide a lot. I don't think I'd do it, but I sometimes wish I wasn't here"*. (female, 68 years, parent).

One woman whose daughter died 12 years ago reflected on how older people usually hope for a longer life. As someone who was '60 something' at the time, she was comforted by the thought that she would not have to suffer for too long (female, 78 years, parent). Others directly talked about their own mortality and not having enough time to get their life back together. They anticipated a loss of control related to getting older:

> *"I think what I worry about is that, that when I do get older, and I get, I mean, I kind of, if I do realise, if I get to that chance to realise my mortality, and you know, I'm reaching the end of my existence. That I'll start to become more mentally challenged ... Because my belief is that if you suppress it, it doesn't go away, it just goes deep, and when you get older, it then begins to come out, in all sorts of ways"* (female, 73 years, partner).

Learning to adapt and live with grief was often articulated as being a mind-set adopted to radically accept the loss and continue living, despite the adverse challenges, barriers and reminders. Adapting to bereavement in different ways meant neither looking for closure but accepting that this was a possibility. One emphasised that it was a living experience:

> *"I couldn't put people through what we've all been through basically. Although there have been times and certainly even in lockdown last year, although I do feel most of the time I feel incredibly together, but things ... you do think oh this is a battle. Which is why I think it is a living experience, I don't think it's a lived experience"*. (female, 73 years old, parent).

There was some evidence of ageism as one person commented on the research:

> *"I'm really pleased that this is ... you know, somebody's doing things that are about suicide, especially at our age, because when you get older, you're not important, in general"*.(female, 68 years, parent).

Our participants expressed a strong orientation to the importance of the shared lived experiences with others who had lost a loved one through suicide and learning to adapt to such a significant loss. These comprised of transformational moments through helping others. They described secondary gain from this sense of agency and control in one's own life, through interactions with their peers, actively seeking out others with similar experiences and recognising the wider meaning of their own lives within the context of societal responses to suicide. Key organisations were named as hosting and enabling networking and peer support:

> *"I have to say it's been a real privilege to meet some of the people who've lost somebody and to realise how ... and everybody does it their own way and it's just ... but it is unbelievably painful. I wish I wasn't doing any of this because I wish I didn't know about it, but in some way it's given me some meaning in life. You're not alone. They're not alone. It's not just feeling ... we know what it's like"*. (female, 73 years, parent).

One participant took direct action by campaigning locally and setting up an information point at the station where his son died. Such instances of activism and raising public awareness enabled appropriate support based on direct experience being provided at both the prevention and postvention levels. One with twenty years of experience in the peer support movement expressed matured versions of herself as a compassionate and wise older woman:

> *"I was around in London when there was AIDS, and we belonged to a group way back then, and I said, if there's anything I can do? And in fact, I've sort of become, I don't know what I am really ... I think I'll step down. And they keep saying, no, no. And I think I'm just a wise old woman"*. (female, 73 years, parent).

Another talked about becoming a mental health first aider, which had transformed her life in a positive way. Other turning points were exemplified in finding new relationships and love such as one man had done at the age of 72 yrs.

4. Discussion

This study of the experiences of being bereaved by suicide and how it impacted the bereaved person's later life gave rise to three rich themes from the data collected. The emotional manifestation of moral injury and trauma, negative feelings and cognitions present in those living with the traumatic loss and the wider impact on family and other social networks were emphasised in the narratives of adults in later life. Learning to live with the loss and to navigate multiple transitions and adaptations was central to how people navigated and made sense of their experiences in later life. Given the dearth of research to date, the findings offer a novel contribution to our understanding of the experiences of this population who are less recognised or visible.

Fiegleman, Gordon and Jordan [30] noted the complexity of stigmatisation that older people might face in these circumstances. Internalised ageism and factors associated with ageism, for example, insensitive comments from professionals and other people in their networks were reported by our participants. These manifested at different levels and prevented individuals from accessing support or feeling entitled to ask for support or in prioritising their own health and wellbeing. Participants did not always recognise differences in how the bereavement impacted their physical and mental health and instead attributed these to the natural consequence of ageing. Furthermore, professionals tended not to ask directly about their needs or offer psychosocial support such as counselling, perhaps attributing the persons' problems to ageing. Bereaved parents reported particular strained and harmful consequences of their loss. A lack of recognition of the impacts within their own close networks was complicated where there were blended families or a history of family trauma. Reed [31] found more grief-struck survivors detached from their families than those who were less grief-struck. Grief therapies that use a family-focused approach include family-strengthening skills, particularly for families who show a high level of distress and find social and physical adjustment challenging [30,31]. A conceptual review of ageing and suicide [10] has demonstrated how older people experience the loss of something they had enjoyed doing or feeling, a loss of value, a feeling of tiredness and, in some cases, a feeling that they were in a process of losing themselves. All of these factors that can manifest alongside the physical aspects of caring can pose serious risk factors for self-harm and suicide in later life.

It seems important that professionals actively enquire from bereaved people in later life about the kinds of support they need, given the many examples of people in this study who felt unable to assert their needs or where these were subsumed into a caring role.

The role of the family doctor was commented on by some participants. Foggin et al.'s [32] study of general practitioners (GPs) dealing with parents who were bereaved by suicide, however, revealed an unpreparedness and uncertainty with regard to dealing with suicide and its effects on survivors and recommended that GPs were routinely informed of death by suicide to prepare for such ongoing encounters. In our study, a range of concerns were raised about the lack of skills and confidence that different professionals have in working with suicide and suicide bereavement and linked to the need for a more sensitive and timely approach to people and simply knowing what to offer.

There is much to learn from people bereaved by suicide on what support is needed and when and how to act more helpfully. In light of the intense caring roles that older people had demanded of them to step into, together with the negative feelings and cognition arising from moral injury and trauma, they may need help to navigate and evaluate which relationships they should preserve or even temporarily avoid or discontinue. Feigelman, Gordon and Jordan [30] suggested that professionals could guide bereaved people on how to 'teach' people close to them to overcome their own fears and lack of familiarity with suicide loss. Survivors had to accept that some people close to them or in their social networks had limited capacity to comfort or respond appropriately. Furthermore, interventions that directly involve the person's family or social network such as partners, family and friends may have the potential to ameliorate some of the distress documented in this research. Ongoing attention to suicide awareness that challenges and reduces stigma must continue. It is clear that we need more skilled professionals in this area of work.

There was a paradox in that many bereaved survivors took up a leadership role in guiding their own support network and this promoted being able to live with their experiences at least. A novel finding lies in some of the positives that emerged for individuals despite the devastating impact of loss by suicide. There were accounts of transformative experiences (with which come opportunities such as understanding, awareness, peer support, and charitable work) that were so valuable to others and helped with the ongoing living experience and radical acceptance [33]. Many were driven to participate in communities with their peers, found strong connections and new belongings to a group. These are important anchors for coping with later-life challenges [7]. Groos and Shakespeare-Finch's [33] evaluation of peer support groups for suicide bereavement found that an effortful thought process and the level of pain experienced were temporal and dependent on the individual's own post-trauma trajectory or meaning-making process. Kasahara et al. [34] found differences between younger and older bereaved individuals. Older people with more significant life events found comfort through open dialogue, while younger individuals tended to conceal their emotions and suffering. Understanding these different experiences is a first step towards developing nuances in responding in later life. Barlow and Coleman's [35] evaluation of a peer support program developed for survivors of suicide suggested that an intervention protocol that is collaboratively developed and delivered by peer supporters *and* professionals can offer cost-effective person-centred support.

While our participants had much in common with people who are bereaved by suicide, there may be generational differences in coping styles, with older people employing more stoic and avoidant coping styles in dealing with traumatic events. For some, their chronological age intersected with their expectations of themselves and others. Some of our participants gave up work earlier than they might have done. They also took up active roles and enjoyed being in groups or company where they could be more anonymous.

These are speculative explanations, suggesting that future research could systematically investigate the general population to see how views of suicide and suicide stigmatisation) may be shifting across generational cohorts. The intensification of time pressure in later life reflected by participants had both negative and positive impacts on how the process of living beyond the bereavement played out and heightened suicide thoughts in some. Some studies [36] have supported specific associations between suicide bereavement and suicide-related outcomes, justifying the inclusion of people bereaved by suicide in national suicide prevention strategies. Most of this research has examined this in relation to younger people [36]. Participants in our study demonstrated a greater awareness of their own end of life, associated with later life and possibly with a reduced fear of death or wish to die made more explicit in relation to their loss and potential losses. A scoping review of suicide and suicide-related concepts in older people [21] included a range of "grey area" behaviours (for lack of a better term) that are either less common, or present differently than they are in younger population groups. These include terms and behaviours such as "completed life", "hastening of death" and "self-chosen death" [37,38]. The expression of these grey area behaviours may also be mistakenly viewed as a 'normal' part of ageing [39], creating further complexity to their identification and subsequent intervention.

The clinical implications of these findings are that those assessing older people thought to be at risk of suicide should inquire about a history of suicide bereavement and its impact on functioning and mental health [36]. Suicide bereavement is an indicator that stigma might be a marker for motivational moderators of suicidality after such a traumatic and often negative life event such as reluctance to seek help, thwarted belongingness or perceived burdensomeness [40]. The findings from this study highlight other indicators for help-seeking, where there is excessive burdens in caring and self-neglect accompanied by perceived stigma, which warrant further inquiry and inform the development of interventions that address these different impacts of traumatic losses and specifically to mitigate any risk of suicide and to directly ask about this.

There may be a need to unify research from different disciplines, with policy themes on ageing such as healthy ageing, concepts of promoting person-centredness within service provision and giving greater emphasis to participation which enables peer support. Being able to understand the individual experiences and pathways within suicide research can help inform and enrich assessment and evidence-based interventions [21].

Finally, the design of this study enabled the data collection and data analysis to be enriched by the direct insights and contributions of those peer-researchers with lived experience. These methods can be resource intensive, given the time and pace needed to ensure authenticity in this approach, some of which did not always coincide with the need to make progress in terms of project milestones. There was one occasion where the research team took time out and utilised the skills of one team member, a digital artist, in a session to reflect and visualise imagery emerging from the data. This was a valuable team experience enabling restoration and self-care, something not always prioritised in the academy. (One of the images has been included with this paper's abstract). Furthermore, feedback from research participants and our peer researchers reminded the team to take a strengths approach, which offers a perspective on hope and respect for people with lived experience and this was just as important as our robust procedures on signposting and debriefing required in the ethical approval process.

5. Conclusions

The qualitative and exploratory approach provided rich and salient transferable insights concerning bereavement by suicide in later life from the perspectives of those with lived experience. This undoubtedly helps inform future suicide awareness and prevention research. The findings confirmed existing evidence on the experience of bereavement by suicide such as the persistence of stigma, shame and moral injury associated with suicide. We assert the importance of suicide prevention policies in ageing support and the need to target services better. There is a strong indication for the inclusion of older people bereaved by suicide in national suicide prevention strategies and focusing efforts to reduce harm and the adverse impact on ageing experiences. In later life, bereavement by suicide must be considered alongside the effects of other loss experience(s) and in the context of the interpersonal and structural impacts of ageism in society [13]. These are potential areas for marginalising older people from mainstream support. Identifying these individuals may constitute an interdisciplinary approach and improved surveillance including routine assessment in a range of services that interact with people in later life. Professionals in ageing services could also develop competencies around the assessment of the impact of suicide exposure and interventions, particularly given that bereaved people are at increased risk of suicide themselves. Professionals need the right language, confidence, and skills to discuss issues of suicide with people in later life and to articulate concerns where issues are observed [10–12].

Suicide, personal meaning, trauma and membership of marginalised communities should be elevated in the public health conversation surrounding ageing. Critiques of 'successful ageing' encourage us to recognise the intersection of individual and social factors and to consider the life course perspective in research, policy and practice [41]. We recommend further studies comparing the bereavement experiences of those bereaved by suicide in later life with other traumatic bereavements and losses using participatory mixed methods and longitudinal approaches [42]. Framing these within the context of ageing [43] may involve unifying research from different disciplines, with policy themes on ageing such as healthy ageing, personalised support and being able to understand the individual experiences and pathways within suicide research to help inform and enrich assessments and interventions in ageing care.

6. Strengths and Limitations

This study explored experiences of suicide in a hard-to-reach population. The co-produced nature of this study allowed stakeholders and participants to feel comfortable to share experiences which enriched the data and thus improved the quality of the study. More specifically, we believe that employing a co-produced design enhanced communication during the interviews, which adds to the transferability of the materials. However, the sample was self-selective and attracted some participants active in peer support. The findings may therefore only be partially representative. In addition, there were few men or engagement with people from diverse minority backgrounds in this study.

Author Contributions: T.H.-L. conceptualised and designed the project with input from J.G.; T.H.-L. managed the project and secured funding; J.H. and T.H.-L. obtained ethical approval; T.H.-L. and J.G. recruited peer-researchers; J.H. coordinated the recruitment and data collection process; J.H., E.G., L.R.-D. and J.G. conducted the interviews; T.H.-L., J.H., E.G., J.G. and N.C. were involved in the data analysis; T.H.-L. wrote this paper with editing and contributions from all J.H., N.C., J.G., S.R. and S.M. All authors have read and agreed to the published version of the manuscript.

Funding: This research was funded by a small grant from the University of Strathclyde.

Institutional Review Board Statement: This study was conducted in accordance with the Declaration of Helsinki, and approved by the Ethics Committee of The University of Strathclyde in January 2021. Reference: UEC21/10: Hafford-Letchfield/Cogan/Hanna/Rasmussen: Responding to the complex support needs of people in later life bereaved by suicide: A co-produced exploratory study.

Informed Consent Statement: Informed consent was obtained from all subjects involved in the study.

Data Availability Statement: Information about the data reporting results can be obtained by contacting Professor T.H.-L.

Acknowledgments: The research team wish to thank members of the steering group, Adele Owen, QPM' Ruth Teacher' Naresh Mall, Tim Woodhouse and Sharon McDonnell for her encouragement. We thank the University of Strathclyde for funding this project.

Conflicts of Interest: The authors declare no conflict of interest.

References

1. World Health Organisation. 2019–2020 Suicide Report. Available online: https://www.who.int/teams/mental-health-and-substance-use/suicide-data (accessed on 20 March 2022).
2. World Health Organisation (WHO). *Suicide in the World: Global Health Estimates*; World Health Organisation: Geneva, Switzerland, 2019.
3. Ritchie, H.; Roser, M.; Ortiz-Ospina, E. "Suicide". Published Online. 2015. Available online: https://ourworldindata.org/suicide (accessed on 20 December 2021).
4. Andriessen, K. Can postvention be prevention? *Crisis* **2009**, *30*, 43–47. [CrossRef] [PubMed]
5. O'Connor, R. *When It Is Darkest: Why People Die by Suicide and What We Can Do to Prevent it*; Vermillion: London, UK, 2021.
6. Hybholt, L.; Buus, N.; Erlangsen, A.; Lauge Berring, L. Older Adults Bereaved by Suicide: A Systematic Literature Search Identifying Zero Studies. *Arch. Suicide Res.* **2020**, *24*, 119–124. [CrossRef] [PubMed]
7. Hybholt, L.; Lauge Berring, L.; Erlangsen, A.; Fleischer, E.; Toftegaard, J.; Kristensen, E.; Toftegaard, V.; Havn, J.; Buus, N. Older Adults' Conduct of Everyday Life After Bereavement by Suicide: A Qualitative Study. *Front. Psychol.* **2020**, *11*, e1131. [CrossRef] [PubMed]
8. Cavalcante, F.G.; Minayo, M.C.D.S. Qualitative study on suicide attempts and ideations with 60 elderly in Brazil. *Cienc. Saude Coletiva* **2015**, *20*, 1655–1666. [CrossRef]
9. van Orden, K.A.; Conwell, Y. Issues in research on aging and suicide. *Aging Ment. Health* **2016**, *20*, 240–251. [CrossRef]
10. Hafford-Letchfield, T.; Gleeson, H.; Ryan, P.; Billings, B.; Teacher, R.; Quaife, M.; Vicentini, S. 'He just gave up': An exploratory study into the perspectives of paid carers on supporting older people living in care homes with depression, self-harm, and suicide ideation and behaviours. *Ageing Soc.* **2020**, *40*, 984–1003. [CrossRef]
11. Nilsson, C.; Bremer, A.; Blomberg, K.; Svantesson, M. Responsibility and compassion in prehospital support to survivors of suicide victim—Professionals' experiences. *Int. Emerg. Nurs.* **2017**, *35*, 37–42. [CrossRef]
12. Roush, J.F.; Brown, S.L.; Jahn, D.R.; Mitchell, S.M.; Taylor, N.J.; Quinnett, P.; Ries, R. Mental health professionals' suicide risk assessment and management practices: The impact of fear of suicide-related outcomes and comfort working with suicidal individuals. *Crisis: J. Crisis Interv. Suicide Prev.* **2018**, *39*, 55–64. [CrossRef]

13. World Health Organisation (WHO). Ageism. 2021. Available online: https://www.who.int/westernpacific/news/q-a-detail/ageing-ageism (accessed on 20 March 2022).
14. Eatough, V.; Smith, J.A. Interpretative phenomenological analysis. *Sage Handb. Qual. Res. Psychol.* **2008**, *179*, 194.
15. Miller, R.M.; Chan, C.D.; Farmer, L.B. Interpretative phenomenological analysis: A contemporary qualitative approach. *Couns. Educ. Superv.* **2018**, *57*, 240–254. [CrossRef]
16. Smith, J. Interpretative Phenomenological Analysis. *Existent. Anal.* **2010**, *21*, 186–192.
17. Devota, K.; Woodhall-Melnik, J.; Pedersen, C.; Wendaferew, A.; Dowbor, T.P.; Guilcher, S.J.T.; Hamilton-Writht, S.; Ferentzy, P.; Hwang, S.W.; Matheson, F.I. Enriching qualitative research R by engaging peer interviewers: A case study. *Qual. Res.* **2016**, *16*, 661–680. [CrossRef]
18. Faulkner, A.; Carr, S.; Gould, D.; Khisa, C.; Hafford-Letchfield, T.; Cohen, R.; Megele, C.; Holley, J. 'Dignity and respect': An example of service user leadership and co-production in mental health research. *Health Expect.* **2019**, *24*, 10–19. [CrossRef] [PubMed]
19. Berring, L.L.; Hummelvoll, J.K.; Pedersen, L.; Buus, N. A Co-operative Inquiry Into Generating, Describing, and Transforming Knowledge About De-escalation Practices in Mental Health Settings. *Issues Ment. Health Nurs.* **2016**, *37*, 451–463. [CrossRef] [PubMed]
20. Hickey, G.; Brearley, S.; Coldham, T.; Denegri, S.; Green, G.; Staniszewska, S.; Tembo, D.; Torok, K.; Turner, K. *Guidance on Co-Producing a Research Project*; INVOLVE: Southampton, UK, 2018.
21. Hafford-Letchfield, T.; Jain, B.; Roesch, C.; Ellmers, T. A scoping review exploring the "grey area" of suicide-related expression in later life: Developing a conceptual framework for professional engagement. *Aging Soc.* 2022, *in press*.
22. Sandelowski, M. Telling stories: Narrative approaches in qualitative research. *J. Nurs. Sch.* **1991**, *23*, 161–166. [CrossRef]
23. Omerov, P.; Steineck, G.; Dyregrov, K.; Runeson, B.; Nyberg, U. The ethics of doing nothing. Suicide-bereavement and research: Ethical and methodological considerations. *Psychol. Med.* **2014**, *44*, 3409–3420. [CrossRef]
24. Miles, M.B.; Huberman, A.M. *Qualitative Data Analysis*; Sage: Thousand Oaks, CA, USA, 1994.
25. Charmaz, K. *Constructing Grounded Theory. A Practical Guide to to Qualitative Analysis*; Sage: London, UK, 2006.
26. Runeson, B.; Beskow, J. Reactions of survivors of suicide victims to interviews. *Acta Psychiatr. Scand.* **1991**, *83*, 169–173. [CrossRef]
27. Mckenzie, S.K.; Li, C.; Jenkin, G.; Collings, S. Ethical considerations in sensitive suicide research reliant on non-clinical researchers. *Res. Ethics* **2017**, *13*, 173–183. [CrossRef]
28. Samaritans. Guidance for Working with People Bereaved by Suicide. 2020. Available online: https://www.samaritans.org/about-samaritans/media-guidelines/guidance-working-people-bereaved-suicide/ (accessed on 9 June 2022).
29. Gould, D. *Service Users' Experiences of Recovery Under the 2008 Care Programme Approach*; Reprint; NSUN and the Mental Health Foundation: London, UK, 2015; Available online: https://www.mentalhealth.org.uk/sites/default/files/CPA_research_study.pdf (accessed on 20 December 2021).
30. Feigelman, W.; Gorman, B.S.; Jordan, J.R. Stigmatization and suicide bereavement. *Death Stud.* **2009**, *33*, 591–608. [CrossRef]
31. Reed, M.D. Sudden death and bereavement outcomes: The impact of resources on grief symptomatology and detachment. *Suicide Life Threat. Behav.* **1993**, *23*, 204–220.
32. Foggin, E.; McDonnell, S.; Cordingley, L.; Kapur, N.; Shaw, J.; Chew-Graham, C. How do general practitioners deal with parents bereaved by suicide? A qualitative study. *Br. J. Gen. Pract.* **2016**, *66*, e737–e746. [CrossRef]
33. Groos, A.D.; Shakespeare-Finch, J. Positive Experiences for Participants in Suicide Bereavement Groups: A Grounded Theory Model. *Death Stud.* **2013**, *37*, 1–24. [CrossRef]
34. Kasahara-Kiritani, M.; Ikeda, M.; Yamamoto-Mitani, N.; Kamibeppu, K. Regaining my new life: Daily lives of suicide bereaved individuals. *Death Stud.* **2017**, *41*, 447–454. [CrossRef]
35. Barlow, C.A.; Coleman, H. The healing alliance: How families use social support after suicide. *Omega* **2003**, *47*, 187–201. [CrossRef]
36. Pitman, A.L.; Osborn, D.P.J.; Rantell, K. Bereavement by suicide as a risk factor for suicide attempt: A cross-sectional national UK-wide study of 3432 young bereaved adults. *BMJ Open* **2016**, *6*, e009948. [CrossRef]
37. Monforte-Royo, C.; Villavicencio-Chávez, C.; Tomás-Sábado, J.; Balaguer, A. The wish to hasten death: A review of clinical studies. *Psycho-Oncology* **2011**, *20*, 795–804. [CrossRef]
38. van Wijngaarden, E.; Leget, C.; Goossensen, A. Caught between intending and doing: Older people ideating on a self-chosen death. *BMJ Open* **2016**, *6*, e009895. [CrossRef]
39. Balasubramaniam, M. Rational suicide in elderly adults: A clinician's perspective. *J. Am. Geriatr. Soc.* **2018**, *66*, 998–1001. [CrossRef]
40. O'Connor, R.C.; Nock, M.K. The psychology of suicidal behaviour. *Lancet Psychiatry* **2014**, *1*, 73–85. [CrossRef]
41. Rowe, J.W.; Kahn, R.L. Successful aging 2.0: Conceptual expansions for the 21st century. *J. Gerontol. Psychol. Sci. Soc. Sci.* **2015**, *70*, 593–596. [CrossRef]
42. Farberow, N.L.; Gallagher-Thompson, D.; Gilewski, M.; Thompson, L. Changes in grief and mental health of bereaved spouses of older suicides. *J. Gerontol.* **1992**, *47*, 357–366. [CrossRef]
43. Hansen, R.O.; Stroebe, M.S. *Bereavement in Later Life: Coping, Adaption, and Developmental Influences*; American Psychological Association: Washington, DC, USA, 2007.

International Journal of
Environmental Research and Public Health

MDPI

Article

Tragedies, Fates, Furies and Fuels: Narratives of Individuals Bereaved by Suicide

Diane Macdonald [1,*], Alexandra Nicolopoulos [1,2], Kathryn McLachlan [1], Stephanie Habak [1], Helen Christensen [1,2] and Katherine M. Boydell [1,2]

1 Black Dog Institute, University of New South Wales, Randwick, NSW 2031, Australia; a.nicolopoulos@blackdog.org.au (A.N.); k.mclachlan@blackdog.org.au (K.M.); s.habak@blackdog.org.au (S.H.); h.christensen@blackdog.org.au (H.C.); k.boydell@blackdog.org.au (K.M.B.)
2 School of Psychiatry, Faculty of Medicine, University of New South Wales, Randwick, NSW 2031, Australia
* Correspondence: d.macdonald@blackdog.org.au

Abstract: Suicide is the leading cause of death for Australians aged 15 to 44, with fifty to sixty per cent of individuals who die by suicide 'flying under the radar', dying in this way without receiving formal mental health care or treatment. This paper explores how people bereaved by suicide interpret and narrate the lead-up to, act and aftermath of a male family member who died by suicide. We used qualitative semi-structured interviews to explore how narratives of suicide were articulated by loved ones bereaved by suicide. Analytic findings were conceptualised through Bamberg's four layers of cognitive narrative structure–setting, complication, resolution, coda. We derived three complications conveyed by the group as a whole: that the men felt sentenced by fate, charged with fury and were fueled by alcohol. These narratives by individuals bereaved by suicide draw us into the larger picture of meaning-making, the loss of life and finding closure. They also speak to the need for early interventions, as most of these stories are rooted in childhood tragedy that was not sufficiently addressed or supported.

Keywords: bereavement; suicide; grief; qualitative methods; narrative analysis; lived experience

Citation: Macdonald, D.; Nicolopoulos, A.; McLachlan, K.; Habak, S.; Christensen, H.; Boydell, K.M. Tragedies, Fates, Furies and Fuels: Narratives of Individuals Bereaved by Suicide. *Int. J. Environ. Res. Public Health* **2022**, *19*, 8715. https://doi.org/10.3390/ijerph19148715

Academic Editors: Karl Andriessen, Karolina Krysinska and Yossi Levi-Belz

Received: 1 June 2022
Accepted: 15 July 2022
Published: 18 July 2022

1. Introduction

[E]very good story must have a beginning, a middle and an end, with the end foreshadowed in the beginning. -Miranda Cowley Heller [1] (p. 387)

One ending in this paper is foreshadowed from the start. The tragedy of a loved one's suicide represents a closing chapter for one and the beginning of a new one for another. Listening to the stories of individuals bereaved by suicide can lead to a broader understanding of suicide and the shortcomings of our community care systems in preventing it [2]. This paper explores how people bereaved by suicide interpret and narrate the lead-up to, act and aftermath of a male family member who died by suicide. Suicide is the leading cause of death for Australians aged 15 to 44 [3]. Fifty to sixty per cent of individuals who die from suicide 'fly under the radar', dying in this way without receiving formal mental health care or treatment [4]. Most have been in contact with health services for reasons relating to their physical health in the days or months preceding an attempt but do not receive help for their suicidal thoughts, mental health problems or personal circumstances [5]. The participants in our study identified the men as 'flying under the radar' before dying by suicide.

Despite the prevalence of suicide globally, individuals bereaved by suicide remain a group that has been understudied [6]. Even less is known about the bereaved whose loved ones are at risk of suicide who are not in mental health care. Insight from loved ones who experienced the lead-up to and aftermath of a death by suicide can offer recipes for change to our mental health systems [7]. Their stories of suicide can inform decision-making to develop better care models for individuals at risk of suicide. This paper presents a cognitive narrative approach to interpreting 12 narratives of suicide: how participants remember, make sense of and describe a tragic event like suicide [8,9]. In the following sections, we explore, interpret and analyse storytellers' narratives and story arcs to understand their perspectives on their loved ones' suicides and what we can learn from their lived experiences.

1.1. Context of Our Study

The 12 stories of a loved one's suicide were collected as part of a multi-phase study, Under the Radar (UtR), conducted by Black Dog Institute in 2021. UtR employed a mixed-methods approach to explore the demographic and clinical characteristics, personal circumstances, and preferences for services amongst people at risk of suicide, with the aim of developing a comprehensive pathway to care. At the onset of this larger project, Black Dog conducted a systematic review of the published literature examining predictors of dying by suicide without having received professional help. Key risk factors were identified for being under the radar: male sex, both younger and older age, rural location and the absence of a mental health diagnosis [10]. In the second phase, Black Dog surveyed 415 men and interviewed 37 men experiencing suicidal thoughts and/or behaviours to examine their views toward health services and family members and to understand coping styles and preferences for service provision. These methods, however, do not specifically shed light on those men whose suicidal thoughts and/or behaviours led them to die. This current study represents an approach to understanding these events through the lens of those bereaved by the death of a man who was not in contact with formal mental health services at the time of his death. Our paper focuses on the narratives from the bereaved to understand how the overarching structure of their stories are told to gain insight into their lived experiences of suicide [8].

1.2. Reflexivity

Reflexivity involves exploring one's own situatedness, background and perspectives in relation to the research topic, participants and research processes and practices [11,12]. The authors of this paper are women researchers with lived experience of suicide and expertise in qualitative research, mental health, arts-based methods, knowledge translation, co-design and community health. All interviewers had their own lived experience of suicide. We acknowledge our privileges and gendered subjectivities have influenced our understandings and interpretations of men's suicidality, including our socially constructed ideas of masculinity and men's health risks [13]. Qualitative research explores the nuanced, richly textured and deeply contextual lived experience of people as they lived their lives and does not lend itself to a neutral comparison of data [14]. By involving multiple researchers in this study, we hope to contest and strengthen each other's findings to mitigate our subjectivities in the analysis and report writing [15].

1.3. Research Questions

What are the personal experiences and insights of loved ones bereaved by the loss of male friend or family member to suicide who was not in contact with mental health services?

How do the bereaved describe the lead up to, the act and the aftermath of a loved one's suicide?

What meaning is conferred by the bereaved onto a loved one's suicide?

2. Materials and Methods

This paper investigates how bereaved participants interpret and narrate the lead-up to, act, and aftermath of a loved one who died by suicide. Stories and narratives (used interchangeably here) help us make sense of events [16]. Narratives offer a portal into lived experience of events that incorporate interpretations and subjective meaning onto those events [8]. Events that may be random and chaotic or related and connected are constructed into meaning through the active creation of narrative patterns or order [9].

Narrative analysis aligns people with the stories they tell, offering researchers a rich source of knowledge [17]; and a more in-depth understanding of people and their experiences [18]. Narrators are, therefore, active agents who incorporate a beginning, middle and end, locating their stories in a social context at a specific time and place, adding some evaluative, relational and personal aspects [19].

This study used qualitative methodology to collect data through photo elicitation and semi-structured in-depth interviews. Through its exploration of lived experience in its natural environment, qualitative inquiry can contribute to a broader understanding of knowledge [2]. This study explored how narratives of suicide were articulated by loved ones bereaved by suicide. Semi-structured interviews were conducted online with 11 individuals who had lost a loved one to suicide; one interview was conducted through emailed written responses.

2.1. Photo Elicitation

Prior to the scheduled interview, participants were offered the option of bringing along a photograph that held meaning to them vis-a-vis their experience. All participants chose to do so. At the start of each interview, the participant showed and described a cherished photo of the deceased. Photo elicitation is an arts-based methodology used in qualitative research, whereby photographs encourage conversation about the research topic at hand [20]. It is a method in which photographs produced by the participant are used as a stimulus to guide the interview. Using photographs with personal meaning—whether explicitly taken for this research interview, obtained from an archive of historical photos or a visual representation of an object which holds significant meaning—can evoke deep emotions, memories and ideas [21]. The photo elicitation in our interviews served as both an interview stimulus and an interview guide, allowing the interviewer to obtain insights and rich context which may not otherwise have been obtained. The photos in our study were used as a prompt and were not part of the analysis or data collection.

2.2. Semi-Structured, In-Depth Interviews

A co-design approach with people who have identified lived experience of suicidal thoughts and/or behaviours was utilised to develop the guideline questions that form the semi-structured, in-depth interview. Co-design between the research team and lived experience advisors contributed to developing suitable and relevant prompts throughout the interview, aligned with the research questions and goals. See supplementary for interview questions and prompts.

Questions included:

1. I would like to explore the meaning behind the photos you have taken/provided. Can you please tell me about them?
2. Can you please tell me about the experience/s of your loved one?
3. What kind of support would have been helpful for your loved one?
4. If you could envisage something that would have worked for your loved one in difficult times, what would that look like?
5. In what ways do you feel you have been able to share your loved ones' experience in this interview?

2.3. Data Collection

Participants were recruited through social media advertisements (Facebook, Twitter, Instagram and LinkedIn) and external partners and organisations. Recruitment took place from August 2021 to October 2021. Participants were required to be 18 years of age or older, living in Australia, comfortable with the interview being conducted in English, and to have experienced a male family member or friend who died by suicide and was *not* in contact with mental health services at the time of his death.

Interview participants were given an option to receive a call from a clinical psychologist within two business days, if they required additional support, to mitigate risk. None of the participants required additional support. At the cessation of the interviews, all participants were sent a 'thank you for participating' email, including the contact information for Lifeline, MensLine and/or Suicide Call Back Service. Participants were offered a reimbursement of $170 as an acknowledgement of the time and effort required to prepare for, attend, and complete the interview and the significance of the value their story is bringing to the research.

After one of the first interviews, the participant, who works in suicide postvention and is bereaved by suicide, suggested that the interviews be conducted by an interviewer with experience of being bereaved by suicide. They suggested that those who have been bereaved may be more comfortable with, and open to, sharing their experiences with someone who has also experienced bereavement. This suggestion was taken on board by the interview team, and subsequently, nine of the twelve interviews were undertaken by a team member (KM). Author AN and a team researcher completed one interview each. The email (n = 1) interview took the form of written responses to the same oral questions and prompts as the participant found it too painful to speak about the experience of their loved one but also wanted to contribute and be a part of the project. Digitally recorded interviews were transcribed through artificial intelligence, checked for accuracy, cleaned and de-identified.

2.4. Sample

We highlight that 11 of the 12 interviewees were women and acknowledge that the stories of men's suicides were told through a predominantly female lens. These women were aged 31 years and older and the one male participant was aged 45 (One father joined a mother later in one interview, but no demographics were collected from him.). All (n = 12) self-identified as Caucasian and urban with stable living conditions. Participants were de-identified and assigned a letter and a number (i.e., P1–P15), reflecting the fifteen participants who initially agreed to take part, the three who opted out (P5, P8 and P13) and the twelve who completed the interview. The loved ones of the bereaved were sons, husbands, fathers or brothers, see Table 1.

Table 1. Participant relationship to the decedent.

Participant Reference	Participant's Age	Decedent's Details
P1	45	brother died in 2019, age not stated
P2	31	partner died in 2014 when he was 25 years old
P3	38	relationship unclear, died around 2020
P4	74	husband died in 2013, age not stated
P6	47	father died in 1988, age not stated
P7	63	husband died in 2004 when he was 44 years old
P9	52	son died in 2018, age not stated
P10	48	father died in 2011, age not stated
P11	44	son died in 2018, age early to mid-20 s
P12	51	son died in 2017 when he was 18 years old
P14	58	son died in 2018 when he was 26 years old
P15	44	husband died in 2021 when he was 50 years old

2.5. Analysis

Reflexive thematic analysis offered an organic approach to analysis, as it allowed for a broad and flexible application of the analytic approach [11]. Our team drew upon both semantic and latent theme identification. Semantic themes were descriptive level themes, wherein the content of the data was identified and summarised. The content of the data captured the surface meaning, reflecting what was explicitly said. Latent theme identification at the interpretive level allowed the team to go beyond what was explicitly said, revealing the underlying ideas, assumptions and conceptualisations within the data.

Our team followed the six phases of reflexive thematic analysis, where we engaged in an iterative process of reflexivity; a process of self-examination; revealing ourselves as individuals and as researchers while understanding how our personal world views may impact the research process [11]. This process of acknowledging our positionality was practised throughout the research.

Rigour in team analysis was addressed by applying well-established trustworthiness criteria: through prolonged engagement with the subject matter, persistent observation of experiences and perspectives about suicide and researcher triangulation [22,23]. Team discussions in regular analysis meetings included reflexive, recursive engagement with the data and continual acknowledgement of the research teams' active role in knowledge production and interpretation.

'After a thorough coding process, we identified common storylines occurring in the data. Therefore, we analysed the bereaved accounts of suicide through their cognitive structure: the plots, themes, and coherence expressed by participants [8]. We incorporated a bottom-up, inductive construction process, at first, that later reflected a top-down, deductive structure to analyse the relationship between narrative phrases/words and the broader picture of suicide. From 131 codes and subcodes, we focused on shared descriptions of common (a) pain points (triggers, abuse, burdens, trauma, tragedy and exposure to suicide); (b) feelings (helplessness, hopelessness, powerlessness and anger) and (c) coping mechanisms (actions, substance use and exercise) which guided our interpretive conclusions about bereaved stories of suicide.

3. Results

We constructed our analytic findings through Bamberg's [8] four layers of cognitive narrative structure. We chose this framework as it most closely aligned with the storylines formed by the bereaved and conveyed the substantive part of their narratives. Bamberg's [8] stories are comprised of:

1. An orientation or setting
2. Complication
3. Resolution
4. Coda or closure

We re-coded our analysis of shared descriptions to align with these four layers, see Table 2.

Table 2. Narrative alignment.

Four Layers of Cognitive Narrative Structure	Initial Thematic Analysis Heading	Narrative Analysis Heading
Setting	Pain points	Tragedies
Complications	Feelings and coping mechanisms	Fates, furies and fuels
Resolution	Suicidal thoughts and behaviours	Suicide
Coda	Looking back	Making sense out of chaos and tragedy

In ten out of twelve interviews, we constructed and connected a story arc of tragedy, fates, furies and fuels, see Figure 1. Two participants (P11, P14) told a different story from that of the ten–one of a sudden snap after an argument or event that led to their loved one's suicide. Both men were in their twenties when they died and a parent supplied the narrative. While rich and valuable, their data have not been included in our findings. The following sections examine each layer of the story arc with narrative examples from the interviews.

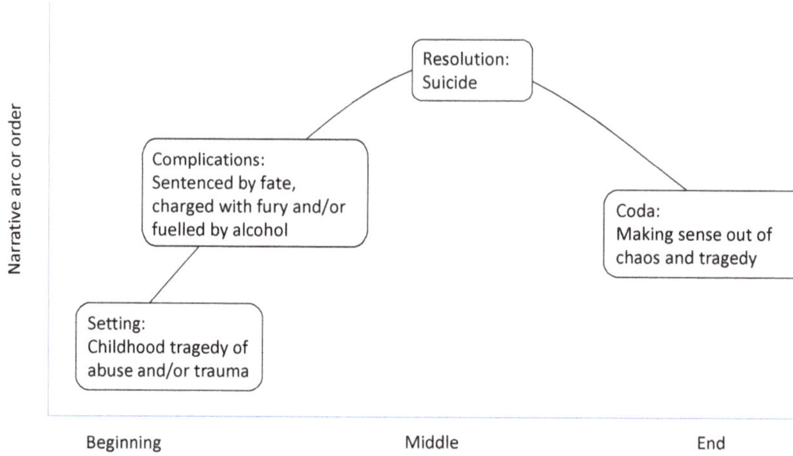

Figure 1. Story arc of suicide.

3.1. Setting: Childhood Tragedy

Participants described their loved one as having experienced abuse and/or trauma in ten of the twelve narratives. This constancy across narratives established a setting of abuse or trauma, mainly in childhood (n = 9), that impacted their loved one.

Seven participants (P2, P4, P7, P9, P10, P12, P15) described some form of abuse, either expressly or implicitly:

> *So his parents were terrible every single day every every day. And I'm not, I'm not like I'm exaggerating, his dad would leave a voicemail on his phone like you're a ******* ****. You're a ******* hacker stole my ******* business. You done this.* (P2)

> *His father was ten years older than his mother, there was, it was a domestic violence relationship with his parents...and his father would rape his mother really while she was in that kind of state, and then send her back to the institution again. His father was abusive. Uh, my, my mother did say that his father sexually abused him, but I've never heard that from my father, and I've never heard that from anyone else.* (P10)

> *[He] was bullied at school . . . He was really chubby. And then as he got older he grew out. You know how they boys do that? There was these kids on the football team and they gave him so much grief, called him nugget and that would upset him.* (P12)

> *[He] had a pet rabbit when he was young and his brother killed it and and and he'd told me about that pet rabbit and told me that a fox killed it and so I think there was some pretty horrific maybe abuse that went on.* (P15)

Eight participants (P1, P3, P4, P6, P7, P9, P12, P15) set scenes of trauma occurring in their stories of suicide:

> *You know, if the same thing happened now, when you know, if a young child saw their sibling die? There would be so much support for them and they would be monitored and they'd be looked after and all that sort of stuff.* (P1)

> *Childhood trauma I think. He had a very, very different, I guess, childhood, where he was often left alone or without support.* (P7)

> *And then my father and mother died three weeks before he did, and he just didn't cope well with it.* (P12)

3.2. Complications

A complication (or complications) is the part of the story where something happens, typically an issue or problem for the main character, that triggers a chain of events [8]. The series of events tells how the characters react to the complication; how rising tension occurs, leading to a high point or major drama and resolution. We derived three complications conveyed by the group as a whole: that the men felt sentenced by fate, charged with fury and were fueled by alcohol. Each complication is explored below.

3.2.1. Sentenced by Fate

Five participants (P3, P4, P7, P10 and P15) constructed a narrative arc that indicated the loved one considered themselves to be doomed or diminished by fate:

> *Some of us are just not meant for this world.* (P3)

> *He really was sort of like resigned to, well this is me; you know this is this is me. This is my lot.* (P4)

> *He believed that no one could help him because that's just the way the world was. This was a fact.* (P7)

3.2.2. Charged with Fury

Eight participants (P2, P3, P4, P6, P7, P9, P12, P15) described their loved one as being charged with fury, signaling emotive, instinctual or irrational behaviours:

> *He used to headbutt walls and get into fights because he was so angry and didn't understand why those thoughts were in his head.* (P3)

> *Stemmed from feelings of powerlessness and then getting so angry.* (P4)

> *He would just be very negative and um, angry. I guess. Um, with ... life and the world. He'd express negativity about everything.* (P7)

3.2.3. Fueled by Alcohol

Seven interviewees (P1, P2, P3, P6, P9, P12, P15) spoke of problematic substance use (drugs and alcohol) by their loved one:

> *He was, he was happy to drive around and doing all that while I was while he was drunk on drugs and drinking. So, I guess in hindsight like yeah he's alcohol and drug use really like increased.* (P2)

> *I think it was the alcohol that perhaps allowed him to express that this is the way that he was feeling. And this is [what] you wanted to do to end that pain.* (P6)

> *[H]e was drinking a lot and I didn't like that and he I'm still finding wine bottles hidden around the house.* (P15)

3.3. *Resolution: Suicide*

Resolution refers to an action or action orientation, in this case, the suicide of a loved one [8].

> *[He's] wrapped some chains around himself and got in the pool or something and she'd gotten home and... she'd kind of found him. He wasn't. It obviously hadn't worked. She'd gotten home, and he was in the process of doing it, or had just tried to do it, or whatever ... It might have been three or four days before he passed away. He was in intensive care in hospital.* (P1)

> *But he always he always had...looked down on people who were, who were, who were who had suicided because, so in that instance, I was like, oh he's fine. Then at the weekend that he killed himself we had been arguing and he had said a few things like I'm gonna go away. I'm gonna go away. But I didn't really think of it as that ... I was telling him to leave me like he was being so intense and he got a knife, but I like I didn't realize the, I didn't realize. But he'd never actually like vocally voiced that he had suicidal intent or suicidal ideations.* (P2)

> *He didn't have his seatbelt on, and he lined his car up with the pole and drove into it at 180 kms an hour. In the video he explained that he had been having thoughts about wanting to end it for years. He said that the last few months, the thoughts had taken over his life and none of his distractions were working anymore.* (P3)

3.4. Coda: Making Sense out of Chaos and Tragedy

A coda underlines how the character has changed and what they learnt as a result of the experience they went through [8]. The coda takes the listener/reader away from the act of suicide and back to the present.

> *Yeah, I think it was going to be hard for him as a 48-year-old [42 years later] decided now just access this, um, these services, having never done it before, I think you know there was obviously, you know, all of those years of resistance and, you know, there's just so much to unpack for him. Yeah, I just feel like, you know, if it had been a process that was, you know, gradual from when he was young all through his life you know it would have been easier.* (P1)

> *You realise that it was their decision and they did it. And if they didn't do it then, they would have done it some other time. That's my thought.* (P7)

> *I think I could have helped him more. I may not have stopped it, but I'm sure that I was dealing with it so wrong. The best you know, and I think that's the only way I can get through this, as I've just had to find peace with it and and light and not going to that dark place and just go. He's found peace and this was obviously [his] journey and for whatever reason this is also my journey.* (P15)

4. Discussion

This paper aims to make meaning from a group of narratives that describe the lead-up to, act, and aftermath of suicide. The participants in our study, mainly women, were family members of the decedent who identified that their loved one died without receiving formal mental health care or treatment. In this context, we explore their unique viewpoint to spark life-saving changes to our mental health and community care systems [2,7]. Their stories of suicide can inform better decision-making to help individuals at risk of suicide. Insight into their collective story of suicide can facilitate the development of services and pathways to better care.

Incorporating photo elicitation at the start of each interview acted as a stimulus to guide conversation [21]. Qualitative inquiry develops a broader understanding of social events in their natural context [2]. Through a rigorous analytical process, we were able to determine a common cognitive pattern and story arc through ten of the twelve interviews [8,9]. The participants in our study established a setting that involved tragedy, including abuse and trauma, mostly in childhood. These tragic encounter(s) had long-lasting effects that were described as diminishing or enraging the decedent. Childhood trauma, including physical, emotional, and sexual abuse and physical neglect, is noted to be a modifiable risk factor for suicide [24]. Problematic substance use added a further complication, echoing research findings of the strong relationship between suicide and substance abuse [25]. The resolution, a final act taken by each of the men, was foreshadowed at the start. Developing this grim story arc leads to important implications for men who 'fly under the radar'.

Tragedies and tragic events will continue to occur. Watching the nightly news, alone, provides evidence of daily death, disaster and destruction. How we as individuals and communities engage, react and learn from these events can be key. The men in our study were not taking part in any formal mental health care, reflecting the experiences of over half of all people who die by suicide in Australia [4]. Trauma and abuse mostly occurred in childhood, with little or no support at the time, suggesting that early intervention through community response will offer an avenue of help. Resilience training, equipping men with skills and knowledge to recognise feelings and learn to develop appropriate responses, can also help and support those at risk. However, the 'under the radar' men are difficult to reach by the very nature of their experiences. Connecting with men in innovative and non-stigmatising ways, through a variety of non-health settings such as workplaces, schools, social welfare agencies, cultural organisations and social media is needed [10]. As participant P1 described earlier in this paper, there is currently a greater community response to the needs of young people impacted by tragedy, abuse and trauma than ever before.

So far in this discussion we have focused on the lead-up to and act of suicide, through the eye of the bereaved. It is equally valuable to explore the codas, the aftermath, and how the bereaved described what they learnt as a result [8]. Participant P15 voiced a need for better skills and knowledge of managing a loved one's mental illness (*I was dealing with it so wrong*). P1 indicated that early intervention may have helped her loved one (*all of those years of resistance* [to seeking help]). P7 was resigned to the inevitability of her loved one's suicide (*if they didn't do it then, they would have done it some other time*). The first two indicate mental health/suicide education and communication can play a positive role in the future. Further investigation into their insights is warranted.

5. Limitations

We acknowledge that the stories told by family members bereaved by suicide may not reflect the reality of the men's experiences or actual events. We also note that the interviewees were largely white urban women, like the authors of this paper. A lack of diversity in participants suggests that further research could focus on a more diverse group of the bereaved. Some work has begun to focus on the experience of bereavement by suicide in ethnic minority groups as in Rivart et al.'s [26] article in this special issue. Our findings were also limited by the gendered lens that the women participants and women researchers overlaid on stories of men's suicide that may help sustain damaging masculinity tropes [13]. Input from men researchers and more men participants would have been a welcomed perspective. In addition, a differing story arc, as told by two of the participants (one of a sudden snap after an argument or event that led to their suicide), is worth exploring to broaden our understanding of suicide and pathways to suicide prevention.

6. Conclusions

A narrative analysis, to be merited on its worth, must be grounded in rigour and a thorough review of the data [18]. Through prolonged engagement with the narratives, persistent observation of experiences and perspectives about suicide, and researcher triangulation, we constructed an overarching storyline from ten stories of suicide. Consolidating ten stories into one cohesive story arc can help us see through the complexity of components that play into a decision as grave as suicide and make sense of events [16]. Expanding our knowledge of their experiences will drive change in our community care systems [2].

These narratives by the bereaved draw us into the larger picture of meaning-making, the loss of life and finding closure. They also speak to the need for early interventions, as most of these stories are rooted in childhood tragedy that was not addressed or supported. Our community care systems have improved over the years, but there is a need to develop greater resources to equip our young people with the skills and knowledge to build resilience. Decision-makers, practitioners and researchers can use this collective story of tragedies, fates, furies and fuels to broaden their understanding of individuals at risk of suicide and develop better models of care.

Supplementary Materials: The following are available online at https://www.mdpi.com/article/10.3390/ijerph19148715/s1, File S1: Interview questions with prompts bereaved.

Author Contributions: Conceptualization, H.C. and K.M.B.; methodology, K.M.B.; software, D.M. and S.H.; validation, all; formal analysis, D.M.; investigation, K.M. and A.N.; writing—original draft preparation, D.M.; writing—review and editing, D.M., A.N., K.M., S.H., H.C. and K.M.B.;

visualization, D.M.; supervision, K.M.B.; project administration, A.N.; funding acquisition, H.C. All authors have read and agreed to the published version of the manuscript.

Funding: Funding for this research was provided by the Medical Research Future Fund, Australia (grant number: 1200195).

Institutional Review Board Statement: Approval for this research was granted by the University of New South Wales' Human Research Ethics Committee, reference HC201582.

Informed Consent Statement: Informed consent was obtained from all participants involved in the study.

Data Availability Statement: The data is not publicly available as per our ethics approval.

Acknowledgments: We thank the participants for their grace and insight and for sharing their stories with us. We acknowledge the larger Under the Radar team for their contribution.

Conflicts of Interest: The authors declare no conflict of interest.

References

1. Cowley Heller, M. The Paper Palace. Riverhead Books: New York, NY, USA, 2021.
2. Malterud, K. The art and science of clinical knowledge: Evidence beyond measures and numbers. *Lancet* **2001**, *358*, 397–400. [CrossRef]
3. ABS. Intentional Self-Harm Deaths (Suicide) in Australia. 2020. Available online: https://www.abs.gov.au/statistics/health/causes-death/causes-death-australia/latest-release#intentional-self-harm-deaths-suicide-in-australia (accessed on 29 April 2022).
4. Johnston, A.K.; Pirkis, J.E.; Burgess, P.M. Suicidal Thoughts and Behaviours Among Australian Adults: Findings from the 2007 National Survey of Mental Health and Wellbeing. *Aust. N. Z. J. Psychiatry* **2009**, *43*, 635–643. [CrossRef] [PubMed]
5. Stene-Larsen, K.; Reneflot, A. Contact with primary and mental health care prior to suicide: A systematic review of the literature from 2000 to 2017. *Scand. J. Public Health* **2017**, *47*, 9–17. [CrossRef]
6. Lavers, G.; Andriessen, K.; Krysinska, K. A Systematic Review of the Experiences and Support Needs of Informal Caregivers for People Who Have Attempted Suicide or Experienced Suicidal Ideation. *Int. J. Environ. Res. Public Health* **2022**, *19*, 5181. [CrossRef] [PubMed]
7. Feldman, M.S.; Sköldberg, K.; Brown, R.N.; Horner, D. Making Sense of Stories: A Rhetorical Approach to Narrative Analysis. *J. Public Adm. Res. Theory* **2004**, *14*, 147–170. [CrossRef]
8. Bamberg, M. Narrative analysis. In *APA Handbook of Research Methods in Psychology*; Cooper, P.M.C.H., Long, D.L., Panter, A.T., Rindskopf, D., Sher, K., Eds.; American Psychological Association: Washington, DC, USA, 2012; Volume 2, pp. 85–102.
9. Gonçalves, Ó.F.; Machado, P.P. Cognitive narrative psychotherapy: Research foundations. *J. Clin. Psychol.* **1999**, *55*, 1179–1191. [CrossRef]
10. Tang, S.; Reily, N.M.; Arena, A.F.; Batterham, P.J.; Calear, A.L.; Carter, G.L.; Mackinnon, A.J.; Christensen, H. People Who Die by Suicide Without Receiving Mental Health Services: A Systematic Review. *Front. Public Health* **2022**, *9*, 12. [CrossRef] [PubMed]
11. Braun, V.; Clarke, V. Reflecting on reflexive thematic analysis. *Qual. Res. Sport Exerc. Health* **2019**, *11*, 589–597. [CrossRef]
12. Dodgson, J.E. Reflexivity in Qualitative Research. *J. Hum. Lact.* **2019**, *35*, 220–222. [CrossRef] [PubMed]
13. Courtenay, W.H. Constructions of masculinity and their influence on men's well-being: A theory of gender and health. *Soc. Sci. Med.* **2000**, *50*, 1385–1401. [CrossRef]
14. Charmaz, K. *Constructing Grounded Theory*; Sage: Thousand Oaks, CA, USA, 2014.
15. Malterud, K. Qualitative research: Standards, challenges, and guidelines. *Lancet* **2001**, *358*, 483–488. [CrossRef]
16. Riessman, C.K. *Narrative Methods for the Human Sciences*; Sage: Thousand Oaks, CA, USA, 2008.
17. Frank, A.W. *The Wounded Storyteller: Body, Illness, and Ethics*; University of Chicago Press: Chicago, IL, USA, 2013.
18. O'Toole, J. Institutional storytelling and personal narratives: Reflecting on the 'value' of narrative inquiry. *Ir. Educ. Stud.* **2018**, *37*, 175–189. [CrossRef]
19. McAlpine, L. Why might you use narrative methodology? A story about narrative. *Eest. Haridusteaduste Ajakiri. Estonian J. Educ.* **2016**, *4*, 32–57. [CrossRef]
20. Oliffe, J.L.; Bottorff, J. Further Than the Eye Can See? Photo Elicitation and Research with Men. *Qual. Health Res.* **2007**, *17*, 850–858. [CrossRef] [PubMed]
21. Glaw, X.; Inder, K.; Kable, A.; Hazelton, M. Visual methodologies in qualitative research: Autophotography and photo elicitation applied to mental health research. *Int. J. Qual. Methods* **2017**, *16*, 1609406917748215. [CrossRef]
22. Korstjens, I.; Moser, A. Series: Practical guidance to qualitative research. Part 4: Trustworthiness and publishing. *Eur. J. Gen. Pract.* **2017**, *24*, 120–124. [CrossRef] [PubMed]
23. Nowell, L.S.; Norris, J.M.; White, D.E.; Moules, N.J. Thematic analysis: Striving to meet the trustworthiness criteria. *Int. J. Qual. Methods* **2017**, *16*, 1609406917733847. [CrossRef]

24. Zatti, C.; Rosa, V.; Barros, A.; Valdivia, L.; Calegaro, V.C.; Freitas, L.H.; Ceresér, K.M.M.; da Rocha, N.S.; Bastos, A.G.; Schuch, F.B. Childhood trauma and suicide attempt: A meta-analysis of longitudinal studies from the last decade. *Psychiatry Res.* **2017**, *256*, 353–358. [CrossRef] [PubMed]
25. Pompili, M.; Serafini, G.; Innamorati, M.; Biondi, M.; Siracusano, A.; Di Giannantonio, M.; Giupponi, G.; Amore, M.; Lester, D.; Girardi, P.; et al. Substance abuse and suicide risk among adolescents. *Eur. Arch. Psychiatry Clin. Neurosci.* **2012**, *262*, 469–485. [CrossRef] [PubMed]
26. Rivart, P.; Wainwright, V.; Flynn, S.; Hunt, I.M.; Shaw, J.; Smith, S.; McGale, B.; McDonnell, S. Ethnic Minority Groups' Experiences of Suicide Bereavement: A Qualitative Exploratory Study. *Int. J. Environ. Res. Public Health* **2021**, *18*, 11860. [CrossRef] [PubMed]

International Journal of
Environmental Research and Public Health

MDPI

Article

The Role of Spirituality during Suicide Bereavement: A Qualitative Study

Austėja Agnietė Čepulienė * and Paulius Skruibis *

Suicidology Research Center, Psychology Institute, Faculty of Philosophy, Vilnius University, 01513 Vilnius, Lithuania
* Correspondence: austeja.cepuliene@fsf.vu.lt (A.A.Č.); paulius.skruibis@fsf.vu.lt (P.S.)

Abstract: Background: A loved one's loss due to suicide can be a traumatic experience and trigger a complex grief process. Although spirituality, defined as a search for the Sacred in a broad sense, can be a resource and an obstacle in coping with the suicide bereavement process, there is a gap in scientific understanding of the role spirituality plays during the process. Methods: To explore the role of spirituality in people bereaved by suicide, we recruited 11 women who lost a life partner due to suicide. We conducted semi-structured interviews and analyzed the data using reflexive thematic analysis. Results: We identified the following three themes: spirituality is a supportive resource that can be reached for or achieved without conscious involvement; spirituality provides helpful ways to cope with grief; spirituality makes the grief process more difficult. Conclusions: Spirituality, if personally meaningful and supported by others, can function as a resource after a loved one's suicide and even add to post-traumatic growth after the loss. On the contrary, spirituality-related issues, such as stigmatization and a lack of personally meaningful traditions, can distress the bereaved. Difficult spiritual experiences and questions can become an intricate part of the grief process.

Keywords: postvention; suicide bereavement; spirituality; religion; religious coping; spiritual coping

Citation: Čepulienė, A.A.; Skruibis, P. The Role of Spirituality during Suicide Bereavement: A Qualitative Study. *Int. J. Environ. Res. Public Health* **2022**, *19*, 8740. https://doi.org/10.3390/ijerph19148740

Academic Editors: Karl Andriessen, Karolina Krysinska and Yossi Levi-Belz

Received: 16 June 2022
Accepted: 15 July 2022
Published: 18 July 2022

1. Introduction

Every year, around 700,000 people die due to suicide [1]. In Lithuania, where the current study was conducted, the suicide rate is around 26.1 per 100,000 [1], which is more than double the average. Each suicide leaves approximately ten times more people bereaved by suicide [2]. Such loss is a painful experience that can negatively influence different aspects of life, such as psychological [3] and physical health [4] and relationships [5]. As another potentially important dimension of life, spirituality can also be affected by loss due to suicide [6,7]. However, spirituality-related experiences and beliefs, if not too shattered by the loss, might also function as a resource during suicide bereavement [6,8].

Spirituality is a complex phenomenon which is difficult to define accurately. The ongoing discussion of spirituality's relationship with religiosity and religion makes the definition even more complicated. Earlier viewed as a deep religiosity [9], today spirituality can be seen as not connected to religiosity [10,11] or connected to religiosity by being a part of it [12,13]. Spirituality, separated from religiosity, can be defined as a personal need, experience, and by ways to connect to transcendence, e.g., [14], including concepts of Higher Power and supernatural or not including these [14]. Personal spirituality can be experienced and practised in various ways, such as through music [13,15], relationships or nature [13]. Religiosity can be seen as an affiliation to a religious organization consisting of internalized beliefs and values, performing religious rituals and practices [16]. The spiritual part of religiosity would be a personal inner connection to the Higher power [13,17]. Some authors suggest that because of the broadness of the definitions of spirituality, it is essential to what spirituality is for a particular group of people or to choose one of the definitions for the specific research [18].

In the current study, we chose to see spirituality as a search for the domain of the Sacred [13]. To delve deeper into understanding the phenomenon, we also made use of analytical psychology's ideas. Analytical psychology, created by C. G. Jung, offers extended explanations of psychology, religion and spirituality. According to analytical psychology, spirituality is a human need to connect with something bigger, a subjective and live experience [11]. It can differ from connecting to God or Higher power, to nature or virtues [13,17]. In a way, spirituality can be seen as a process of connecting to the archetype of the Self—a hidden guiding part of the psyche, which gives the potential to connect consciousness with unconsciousness [19], which can be defined as part of the psyche, which contains personal material that has been repressed or simply forgotten and the collective material of the inherited experiences of all humankind that guides the conscious mind [19]. According to this definition, religiosity in the current study was seen as a method of searching for the Sacred, therefore, as a part of spirituality chosen by a person [11,13].

A loved one's death, in general, but also due to suicide, can evoke spiritual questions. Therefore, facing the death of a loved one can be a turning point for the search for the Sacred [6,7,20]. The loved one's death reminds the bereaved of the temporality of life, which raises questions about the purpose of life, beliefs in the afterlife, or the existence of the soul [6–8]. Spiritual experiences, which can strike the bereaved person, evoke questions about the nature of those experiences [8,21–23]. If a person is highly religious, the answers might be easier to find [24]. However, the questions and experiences also visit non-religious people [8], which adds the interdisciplinary phenomenon of spirituality to the psychological issues of suicide bereavement.

When the cause of death is suicide, the search for the Sacred can become even more complicated. Since suicide is not a religiously appropriate death [6,25], the bereavement process can be influenced by stigmatizing or self-stigmatizing attitudes [6,7,25]. Suicide is hard to comprehend and leaves a person with a haunting question of why [26,27], which can cause the unsatisfied need for spiritual explanations, why the tragedy happened, or where God was when the loved one died [6,8]. The feelings of disappointment and distrust in Higher powers can cause a spiritual crisis [6–8] and the need to re-estimate one's beliefs and virtues. All those experiences related to spiritual issues add to the challenging grief process.

Despite the complications related to spirituality during grief, some aspects of spirituality seem helpful during suicide bereavement. Spirituality and religiosity can be potential resources during bereavement after a loved one's death [21,28,29]. The religious community can support the bereaved [24,25] if it withstands stigmatizing attitudes and behaviors [8]. The issues related to belief in the afterlife can be eased if a person has higher religiosity [30] or if the bereaved person perceives spiritual experiences as proof of the hereafter [21,22]. Beliefs in the afterlife can satisfy the need to continue the bond with the deceased as a further existing figure [8].

The positive and negative religious coping models might be applied in the context of suicide bereavement [31]. Positive coping refers to using religious and spiritual methods, such as religious forgiveness, seeking spiritual support, and coping in a community, which can help with better health and adjustment outcomes after difficult life events [31,32]. Negative religious coping refers to discontent in religious and spiritual matters or, for example, feeling as if one is being punished by God, which has negative correlations with adjustment after difficult life events [31,32]. Spirituality and positive spiritual coping could function as a resource during suicide bereavement. Nevertheless, it depends on at least several specific aspects of how the person understands spirituality if they belong to a religious community or what their beliefs in the afterlife are.

A few scientific studies and reviews about suicide bereavement and spirituality indicate the topic's complexity and importance. The research about spirituality during suicide bereavement is limited by several quantitative studies, which reveal that the bereaved by suicide often have spiritual experiences, which are helpful with adjustment [22]. Belief in the afterlife can help with adjustment to bereavement if the bereaved has the hope to meet the deceased again [30]; the bereaved tend to seek spiritual support and advice [22,33]; and 61 percent of parents bereaved by a child's suicide struggle to find meaning in the loss [34]. Qualitative studies reveal that a loved one's loss due to suicide can strengthen spirituality regardless of the person's previous beliefs [6]. Religiosity can help answer questions regarding the afterlife [25] and solve questions about responsibility [35]. Spiritual experiences are essential for transforming the continuing bond with the deceased [6,23]. Spiritual rituals help to sooth oneself after the loss [7]. Religious social support is vital in practical, emotional, and spiritual ways [25]. A loved one's suicide can also induce a spiritual crisis [6,7,25] and perceived or real stigmatization from the religious community [6,25,35]. The mentioned studies focused only partially on spirituality, religiosity or suicide bereavement processes. They indicated the need to conduct a focused qualitative study on the broad phenomenon of spirituality during suicide bereavement [6–8,25]. A better scientific understanding of spirituality and suicide bereavement could help reach a more profound knowledge about suicide bereavement in general and formulate guidelines for practitioners who help people who suffer after a loved one's suicide. Therefore, the current study aimed to qualitatively explore the role of spirituality during suicide bereavement.

To explore the phenomenon, we decided to ensure the homogeneity of the research participant's group [36] by conducting interviews only with women who lost their life partners (husbands, fiancées or romantic partners with whom they lived before the loss). The group of women were chosen because, in Lithuania, where the study was conducted, there is a huge gap between male (36 per 100,000) and female (6 per 100,000) suicide rates [1]. Masculinity is also considered a risk factor for suicide in different countries [37]. Since more than 90 percent of people see themselves as heterosexual [38], the people who suffer a life partner's suicide are primarily women. The suicide bereaved life partners can have even more expressed complicated grief than friends, parents, or colleagues [39] and children or siblings [40]. This can be explained by challenges related to financial or housing issues, difficulties of suddenly becoming a single parent, and loneliness related to the loss of a partner such as the loss of the intimacy and ability to share the feeling of grief and feelings [40]. Additionally, people bereaved by a partner's suicide can experience more anger toward the deceased than parents would feel for a deceased child [41]. Nevertheless, partners receive less emotional support than those bereaved by other causes of death [42,43]. The partner's suicide increases the bereaved's suicide risk [44] and worsens general mental and psychological health [4]. Therefore, the wellbeing of this specific group of bereaved people is an essential focus for scientific studies of experiences and help strategies [45].

2. Materials and Methods

2.1. Materials

For data collection, we chose to conduct semi-structured face-to-face interviews consisting of the following 3 main questions: "Tell me, please, about your loss"; "What is the role of spirituality during your suicide bereavement?"; "How did spirituality-related topics reveal themselves concerning relationship to others (religious community, other people, the deceased)?". After the interviews, we asked the participants about their primary demographic information.

2.2. Participants

We interviewed 11 women aged 28 to 62 (see Table 1 for more details). Ten interviewed women were Lithuanian, and one was Lithuanian Russian. Nine lost their husbands, one her fiancé and one her romantic partner, due to suicide. Time elapsed since suicide ranged from 2 to 5 years. The women were in a relationship with the deceased men from 1.5 to 39 years (17.7 years on average). All of them lived with the deceased men at their death. Eight research participants had one or more children with the deceased. Nine women had higher education and two professional education. Eight women at the time of the interview lived in a city, two in a town, and one in a rural area. Five of the participants ascribed themselves to Catholicism, one to the Eastern Orthodox Church, one described her affiliation as "Catholic, but with a question mark", one participant described herself as Catholic but not practicing the faith, two participants had no religious affiliation, and one described herself as having no affiliation or belonging to all religions. Nine of the deceased men died by hanging, one by overdose and hanging, and one by cutting his veins. The average age of the deceased was 41, ranging from 30 to 57.

Table 1. Characteristics of the interviewees and interviews.

Nickname	Age	Deceased Was Her	The Method of Suicide	Age of the Deceased	Time Elapsed After Suicide	Years Spent Together with the Deceased	The Number of Children	Education	Religious Affiliation	Place of Living	How Was the Interview Conducted?	Interview Duration	How Was the Participant Reached?
Rasa	41	Husband	Hanging	44	2.2	20	3	Higher	Catholic	Rural area	Videocall	1:49	Filled the questionnaire
Nida	35	Husband	Overdose and hanging	32	4.9	8	0	Higher	Not affiliated	City	Videocall	1:58	Filled the questionnaire
Liepa	49	Husband	Hanging	44	5	26	2	Professional	Catholic with a question mark	Town	Videocall	1:36	Filled the questionnaire
Laima	28	Fiancée	Hanging	30	4.5	6	0	Higher	Catholic	City	In person	1:58	Filled the questionnaire
Karolina	46	Husband	Hanging	55	2	26	2	Higher	Catholic	City	Videocall	1:01	Proactively called by researchers
Eglė	31	Romantic partner	Hanging	34	2.4	1.5	0	Professional	No affiliation	City	In person	1:43	Proactively called by researchers
Elena	34	Husband	Hanging	32	2.4	17	2	Higher	No affiliation or all religions	City	In person	1:13	Proactively called by researchers
Jurga	49	Husband	Hanging	47	2.1	26	2	Higher	Not practicing catholic	City	In person	1:35	Filled the questionnaire
Agnė	36	Husband	Cutting veins	44	5	8	2	Higher	Catholic	Town	Videocall	1:28	Filled the questionnaire
Dalia	62	Husband	Hanging	57	5	39	2	Higher	Catholic	City	Videocall	2:03	Proactively called by researchers
Asta	36	Husband	Hanging	32	4	17	1	Higher	Eastern orthodox	City	Videocall	2:09	Proactively called by researchers
Average	40.64			41	3.59	17.89						1:41	
SD	9.98			9.63	1.35	11.2							

2.3. Procedure

We used purposeful and snowball sampling to reach participants who fit our research aims. We spread the invitation through emails and social media posts to members of the Lithuanian psychologist alliance, practicing psychologists, social media followers, and friends to reach research participants. We also invited potential participants through educational articles in online and printed newspapers and an educational talk on the radio. Lastly, we searched for participants proactively, calling on the participants (who earlier consented to be invited for other studies) of another research project conducted in the suicide research center. We asked the participants to contact the first author through email or phone by themselves or to fill out a short questionnaire and be contacted by the researcher later. Eight people filled out the questionnaire, and eight of them participated. We called fourteen people proactively, and five agreed to participate (see Table 1).

We collected the interviews between January 2021 and November 2021. Because of the COVID-19 situation and nationwide lock-down, we provided the participants with a choice to provide the interview through a video call with the program "Zoom" or in person. Although we were aware that in-person and video call interviews might differ because of differences in creating contact with the participant and the participant's sense of privacy, studies suggest that the differences might not be significant for the duration of the interview, the number of codes, and the interview analysis [46,47] or sharing deeply personal experiences [48]. We conducted 7 interviews through video calls and 4 in person in the first author's consulting room. The interviews lasted 1–2.5 h (see Table 1). The first author carried out eight interviews. The other three interviews were carried out by master's degree students who were members of the project and were trained by the first author to reach consistency.

Before the interview, all participants provided written or scanned informed consent. Each participant received an identification code, so they could withdraw from the study at any time (even after the interview) and maintain anonymity. After the interviews, we provided the participants with written information about emotional and psychological help resources and contact details of researchers in case they needed to talk about their feelings and thoughts after the interviews.

2.4. Data Analysis

We audio-recorded, transcribed and coded each interview. To reflect on the potential researchers' influence on the data analysis, from the beginning of collecting interviews until the final themes were created, the researchers who analyzed the data kept a research diary in which they reflected on their feelings, thoughts, insights, memories, and interpretations of the data. The personal involvement of the first author was exhaustively described in a separate article [49].

We chose the phenomenological approach to analyze the data, which explains that the lived experience of the research participants allows the researchers to explore the chosen phenomenon from their subjective reality. The approach insists that, as limited human beings, we cannot capture the whole of objective reality (if it exists). We can only come as close as possible to the subjective realities of other people. Qualitative methods, such as thematic analyses, combine these subjective realities and find meaningful patterns in the experiences [50]. We used a reflexive thematic analysis [51–54] to identify the main themes in the data. We chose this method and an inductive data-driven analysis of the data [51] because they were deemed a good match for the current study question, which is oriented to the previously not researched exploration of experiences related to spirituality during suicide bereavement.

We conducted a reflexive thematic analysis following the steps provided by Braun and Clarke [51–54]. The coders listened to the interviews and read the transcripts to familiarize themselves with the data. For initial coding, we used Atlas.ti Web [55]. The first author coded six interviews. Codes were reviewed by master's and bachelor's degree students who were members of the current research project. Members of the research project coded five other interviews, and the first author reviewed the codes. The first author then organized the codes to the potential themes and sub-themes. The second author reviewed the initial thematic map, and the disagreements were solved by discussion. Afterwards, the final thematic map was created.

2.5. Ethical Approval

The Psychology Research Ethics Committee of Vilnius University approved the study (22 January 2021, Number 56).

3. Results

From the data, we identified the following three main themes followed by subthemes (see Figure 1): spirituality is a supportive resource that can be reached for or achieved without conscious involvement; spirituality provides helpful ways to cope with grief; spirituality makes the grief process more difficult. We discuss the themes below.

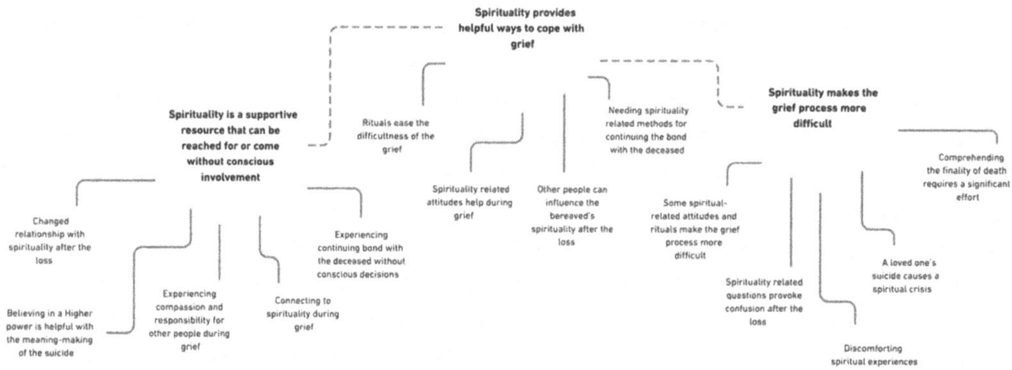

Figure 1. The thematic map.

3.1. *Spirituality Is a Supportive Resource That Can Be Reached for or Come without Conscious Involvement*

All the participants spoke about spirituality as a supportive resource. The resource sometimes was activated through active involvement, while at other times it functioned without one's conscious efforts.

3.1.1. Changed Relationship with Spirituality after the Loss

Eight participants noticed a changed relationship with spirituality after the loved one's suicide.

Participants felt new abilities to connect with a Higher power after the loss:

> *My service is like this, prayer service, during glorification, when I have to pray with my community, and ask the spirit, what the spirit says not just to me personally, but to the community, then the prayers too are strong and they just come and you don't need to translate the scripture, words from the scripture just come to consciousness and then I say them, translate them to people who are near me and for me ... I make sure that God is talking to me, I don't remember anything by heart, but I just read, and God gives me strength to remember exact things that he wants me to say.* (Agnė, 36)

Several noticed the intuitive understanding that the loved one had died and where to find the body:

> *I don't know, I just turned, and some force pushed me into the child's room. And I go into the room, turn to the left and he was just there on the wardrobe.* (Asta, 36)

Many participants noticed that their spirituality strengthened after the loss. This manifested through a clearer understanding and holding onto one's virtues:

> *To have those base virtues and comply with them. Like I said, I never blamed anyone for this situation (for husband's death), didn't blame. hh the one everyone attacked (blamed for the husband's suicide).* (Elena, 34)

Participants also felt strengthened trust in people and relationships:

> *But like I said, we concentrate on the negative things and can't see anything else. And here is where Lithuanians seem genuine. Some of course I met horribly. I am also saying this as a Russian and it doesn't depend on nationality, it's just about the person ... So now I understand that all of us, we are all the same, absolutely the same. And I felt amazing, even if I say that there are humanely humans, that it still exists.* (Asta, 36)

Several participants talked about strengthened self-worth and emotional endurance after the loss:

> *But you know, when a year passed, then I felt that I am strong. And I stopped getting mad about their comments. I felt that no matter how hard it is, I manage the kids well.* (Rasa, 41)

Some noticed the ability to accept the relative insignificance of temporal human life:

> *When you start to become aware, create a better world, to do something, then it doesn't have any meaning. And somehow like I said that understanding, it came, and there is no point to it, you just must experience it and spirituality is part of the experience—to not harm another, not harm nature, to create, to leave something better when your gone, it doesn't have to be visible, and people forget really fast, really fast. It's an existential, like you're nothing.* (Nida, 35)

Others spoke of strengthened religiosity after the loss:

> *I feel like a giant comparing my spirituality five years back. Because there is a different quality, a completely different level of faith, communication with God and the work with community, worship. It's like God says, I will give you an abundant life, and now I have that abundance. Abundance, the fulfillment, in any way, I have everything.* (Agnė, 36)

Some of the participants felt support from a Higher power after the loss:

> *And throughout the mourning, during the funeral, I felt as if I was being carried on arms, I don't know how to say it, I actually felt, that I was being carried by God, and I couldn't by myself, I saw his mom, and his mom was hysterical, going crazy, and she suffered terribly, and there was a lot of guilt there, childhood did its own thing, i understand, that feeling of guilt, but I also saw what kind of pain one can feel if they don't believe in God, when the person is alone in that pain, he is alone and he doesn't have anyone to call upon, he doesn't have anyone to rely on, like it says in the psalms, if thousands fall from the right and thousands from the left, you will be untouched and I felt like the world had fallen, it was falling, and I was left with two small kids, I didn't have a job, but I felt, that I am in God's hands, in his embrace and I never felt guilt, I was just sad, really sad, and I understood his pain.* (Agnė, 36)

3.1.2. Believing in a Higher Power Is Helpful with the Meaning-Making of the Suicide

Believing in a Higher power and its function in a person's life helped participants make meaning of the suicide. Six participants spoke of thinking that the Higher power was preparing them for the suicide of the loved one, which would be proof that the suicide was in some ways supervised by the Higher power:

> *And another thing that supported me, well supported, I unconsciously knew that someday it will happen. Even though you don't think about it. Because like I said, since I'm interest in esotericism, I was in regression some time ago. In a regression seminar. That you can go back, go to the future. It's a conscious dream. And that was seventeen years ago. A long time ago. And then I dreamed about a different country, where my future husband works, town, all their buildings, I remember how I explored it. I dreamed about myself with kids in mourning clothes. I was wearing a black dress and the three of us with kids, the husband wasn't with us. And then I cried, o God, how I cried. I've never cried as much as I did then.* (Jurga, 49)

Participants also used ideas related to spirituality to understand the reasons for suicide. This included religious explanations about human suffering, the importance of accepting the decisions of others, trust in God's will or believing in fate. For example:

> *There was suicide in his family, his grandfather ended up under the tracks, or something, it looks like that, whoever believes in those things. I think it's of the same matter and maybe he finished it in his family.* (Laima, 28)

One participant believed that the deceased was obsessed with demonic powers:

> *I absolutely saw I mean that we have a situation and now looking back, we had a situation with the ghost of the dead and when the exorcist prayed for him and asked him, where do you feel in the body, some sort of sensation right, they make conclusion according to that, diagnosis and he said in the spine.* (Agnė, 36)

Some participants viewed the loss as a test sent by God. The bereaved felt the need to prove to God the integrity of their faith:

> *It looks like maybe he (God) wanted to make me stronger and that I would be ready for my current life.* (Asta, 36)

Some of the participants believed that the deceased was preparing himself spiritually for the suicide, which helped with the relief that the loved one is happier in the afterlife:

> *In the end he talked more about God and believed in him, and he talked about the last judgement day or something, about a refinery. That's why he also encouraged me and somehow, he was slowly taking control, I mean, to not do anything bad. Because I thought maybe that he was sorry or not sorry, but I just think: "well yeah, however much it hurts me, but he doesn't have any problems there (in the afterlife)."* (Rasa, 41)

3.1.3. Experiencing Compassion and Responsibility for Other People during Grief

Seven participants spoke of the strengthened compassion and responsibility for other people. Participants revealed that experiencing compassion and responsibility for their children or other people was a way to find the strength to live on:

> *It was really difficult at first, but it's like I said two little kids and it's not okay. You have someone to take them, you can't just put them aside, you must stand up, stand tall and move forward. So in this case my focus is on the first days.* (Elena, 34)

The wish to help others who suffered after similar losses helped regain some of the control over one participant's life:

> *The journey continues even now slowly, like the muscles, the spiritual ones, they are stronger now, the first step shows this, that I want to do that group (self-help group) so I believe that this is a sign that if I can help others, that it's a sort of healing process. If that energy, when I start to move and I'm ready to share with others, the balance is being restored.* (Liepa, 49)

The wish to participate in the current study was also perceived to help others who suffer:

> *Right after the loss, I received one questionnaire, then another, and my mom said stop, let it go, why do you need this, to reopen the wound, she said, don't you understand, I rethink the event over and over and over again, and a thousand times more, and I said it's not getting any better, and … if I'm doing a good job by sharing my thoughts, if they are worthy or not, but I say, maybe it'll help someone, maybe someone will see that moment, when it happens.* (Dalia, 62)

3.1.4. Connecting to Spirituality during Grief

Five participants spoke of the need and active ways by which to connect to spirituality during grief. For example, the ways to connect with spirituality during grief involved active praying:

> *I never knew how to pray, because it always seemed, that there are some kind of rules, how you should address … If it's God, or the earth, or what you believe and somehow I thought I'm not doing it right and then I asked my grandmother, so how should I pray now, in your own words, how you want to, that's how you should pray, you'll be heard anyway, or so I would say a worldly prayer, the one for the dead of course, because I thought, that it is necessary. And then in my own words I'd just pray, I actually would just ask, not pray, that I wouldn't go crazy, that I'd be given strength, to be here, but I*

prayed to him. Yeah. For an easy path, I prayed for his forgiveness, somehow my prayer was related to his easy departure. (Laima, 28)

As well as spending time in a sacral place:

And that is why, why I say that it would happened in church. I would want to kneel, to lean on those wooden things, to lay my head and cry. And somehow that atmosphere would provoke that reaction, those organs, when they play. And the priests' sermons, it always seemed that it was talking about me, or about him, or about our family. Somehow everything seems to be happening at the right time and place. (Rasa, 41)

Or listening to music, which started to have spiritual meaning after the loss:

It has a special effect on me even now, mass and the sacral music, singing, it's unbelievable, maybe it's even painful, the music. I always, it tears me up. (Laima, 28)

3.1.5. Experiencing Continuing Bond with the Deceased without Conscious Decisions

Six participants experienced continuing bonds with the deceased, which they comprehend as occurring without a conscious choice being made. They felt that the dead initiate communication and help the bereaved:

Later I was going to work, a few years after his death, I was sleeping, and with his knee to my side boom boom near the bed, get up, boom boom, get up, I look aaaa it's 8, I overslept, that means before I opened the store, at that moment and my subconscious connected my alarm, that I need to go to sleep, but I thought that I felt him, that he is waking me up, that honey, wake up, go to work, was him, and I don't know how to say it, I just felt that substance. It seems that the air is denser and if you turned on the light you'd see that it's him in layers, like turning the light on in a fog, this way and that way, and when you catch this fog with a flashlight, from one corner it is clear, but from another you see the layers, it's an impression, or it's my experience talking, if it's real, I want to believe it, that it can actually happen. (Dalia, 62)

The communication from the deceased mainly was perceived as comforting and provided relief:

And I dreamed that he ... As if there was a party and he came a bit drunk, but he was in a good mood, happy. The only thing is that he didn't come near me. His brother was there. And he went up to his brother to talk and I hear what he is speaking. And he was interacting with him in a brotherly way, in a manly way. And he tells him: "you know why I love my life? Because, however much money I spend, there will always be more. Whenever I come back home, nobody is mad at me and (starts crying) whatever sins I commit, He always forgives me. And "he" as I understand, was Jesus, I knew that very clearly for some reason, that he was in His care, in that other life. And there is eternal joy, and he doesn't have any problems there ... It affected me deeply, it was very strong, because ... You know some dreams are very vivid, others not so much ... but that dream, it's like I said, it seems I see it clearly, word for word. And somehow, I felt that ... you know this was after, wait after, after five months, or four months after his death, that type of dream. So I don't know, it seems to me, that was the first, clearly some connection from him. (Rasa, 41)

To provide an overview, spirituality and spiritual experiences during suicide bereavement can function as a supportive resource, which helps to explain why the suicide happened and provides spiritual strength to cope with grief. Spirituality can be experienced as coming from outside without consciously thinking about it or asking for it. This involves noticing changed and strengthened spirituality or religiosity, feelings of more profound compassion and responsibility to others, and experiential manifestations of continuing bonds. Active praying or travelling to sacral spaces activated the connection to a Higher power and provided comfort after the loss.

3.2. Spirituality Provides Helpful Ways to Cope with Grief

All research participants spoke of how spirituality and religiosity provided ways to cope with grief. We discuss them one by one below.

3.2.1. Rituals to Ease the Difficulty of the Grief

If having personal meaning, for nine participants, rituals seemed to ease the difficulty of the grief. The funeral ritual was perceived as an essential part of the bereavement process. For some, organizing the funeral provided a short break from the loneliness of grief:

> *People were lost after a sudden death. They experience it the same, they are in a period of shock. Then they, if they continue the burial service, all those things and have the energy to do all of that. But usually, they don't want to be alone, they want to take care of everything.* (Karolina, 46)

For others, funeral and fare-well rituals were a way to express the last respects for the deceased:

> *But I said right away (giggles) … find me the best hall, the best place. I will pay whatever you want, but I want the best … There were no questions because he was also always the one to choose the best. Or choosing closest to the best. Money was spent so that it'd be nice. I knew that people would come, and you need to, so that the funeral would be, how to say so that he would truly be respected.* (Jurga, 49)

The ritual of a funeral also helped to comprehend that the loved one died:

> *What I understood, when his casket was being buried, I actually understood that he is not here, that this is a body, I thought of this often.* (Agnė, 36)

Participants spoke of the many different forms personal rituals can take such as travelling and being in nature:

> *So those journeys and world knowledge and new knowledge of nature, that you climb the mountain, it means those special paths right, and you get to the top and there is this huge wind, and you can't think of anything else and it's a new place for you and a place you can't find in Lithuania, you start to think about the world differently, new colors appear. You understand that … there is more of everything and it's different from what you're used to. Or when you stand up, on salt, the lake of salt right where it is white and there is no horizon, and you are in the middle of nowhere. You just hang in the middle and you understand that there is something … Something magical.* (Nida, 35);

creating something which could be related to emotional expressions:

> *My nature is creative, and I am creative, so I searched through drawing and my hobby allowed me to find that, what I did in my childhood, I drew a lot, was picky, sewed and still I came back to that after the funeral, I found wool, I found wool and looked at the process in a more creative way.* (Liepa, 49)

meditating and doing yoga:

> *In that hour and a half when you do yoga, you just, translate stress, anxiety, tension, thoughts through the body, because when you do it, you don't think about other things, you just think how to do yoga. How to bend your legs, how to bend your body and other stuff. And in the end, there is shavasana, where you just lay ten minutes, it's called the dead pose. You must disconnect and not think of anything. So, this is the best thing, when you lay down, open your body, and not see or hear anything anymore. That is equal to meditation actually. And yeah. This thing was taught by the teacher and told us that when you come to yoga it's like a new page, you forget everything that is around you, and start from scratch. Actually, that helps a lot.* (Jurga, 49)

Even self-analyzing was considered a spiritual experienced in a psychologist's room or a helpful evening ritual:

Just after my husband's death I had space, usually during my talks with my psychologist. And you know that once a week you will complete that exercise either way . . . I tried to and each evening, right before going to sleep to think about the day . . . with completed facts, put into drawers and not worry about things, that are out of your control. (Elena, 34)

Several participants perceived gratitude as a meditation or a prayer as an antidote for suffering:

There are people, I started to move from household stuff to people, God and those people exist, and I have a job and friends and my relatives don't turn from me and then everything expands, I have so much and to be grateful, and then joy comes from gratitude and then I understood, I concentrate on what I don't have. And that is a huge problem. And when I started to focus on what I do have, how much there is and health, and that my kids are healthy and that is amazing. (Agnė, 36)

Personal rituals related to fire as having a cleansing, easing, and finishing power, were necessary for some of the participants:

And when we talked about fire, then I just wanted to burn something. Because Rimas (the deceased) wanted to be cremated. So, fire, even to him, seemed to cleanse and that it will somehow show all those bad things and fire is powerful, that it just burns (whispers) just burns. (Eglė, 31)

Lastly, religious rituals such as attending mass every week for several participants were found to be helpful after the loss:

This is about being religious, or how to say it, but I know now how much it snowed, how much it winded . . . but I walk there . . . and my knee joint is week, I have a hard time walking, fifty meters is a lot . . . I must go to church . . . so I had to walk a kilometer and three hundred meters. (Dalia, 62)

3.2.2. Spirituality Related Attitudes Help during Grief

Nine participants spoke of helpful attitudes related to spirituality. This involved beliefs about death not being the end:

How to say . . . I'm a believer in energy and energetic bodies. I'm not sorry when someone dies and I usually don't cry, because I know that around our body . . . I can feel other bodies and that consciousness is not in the body, but it's . . . you can expand your consciousness to eternity. (Eglė, 31)

Other spirituality or religiosity related beliefs were also helpful, such as accepting the uncontrollability:

As for spirituality, in the sense of religion, I discovered specific philosophical points in Buddhism. Through literature, I started to read more books that helped me . . . I found that the whole theory of mindfulness came from Buddhist philosophy . . . The simplicity of philosophy and the simplicity of being has helped me restore that spiritual balance . . . I am suffering because I wanted everything. It is that desire to have a person, the desire to be attached . . . the desire to control that situation . . . Well, it does not happen that way. This understanding of mind through mindfulness . . . and all these fundamental truths and points of reference in Buddhism may have helped restore that spiritual balance little by little . . . some kind of mantra, as some kind of reminder that no one has promised you anything. (Nida, 35)

Similarly, the idea of not being able to control many aspects of life, and trusting in a Higher power or God's will was helpful:

What more to hang on to? Some kind of will of God that God knows what he is doing. To trust Him and His plan. Maybe it is awful for me now, it is hard, but apparently, for some reason, it must be that way. (Rasa, 41)

3.2.3. Other People Can Influence the Bereaved's Spirituality after Loss

For eight participants, communicating with other people in a spiritual context provided another spiritual way to cope. Participants spoke firstly about the need for psychological or emotional support and spiritual help after the loss. For some, it was hard to find the service:

> *The possibility of getting some information to reach or go on that kind of spiritual path … we do not have such very easily accessible information … like could you help me here now, if not for some kind of psychological help, but let's say something like that.* (Karolina, 46)

For some participants, spiritual help seemed more helpful than psychological help:

> *Like even psychologists cannot share advice. They must force a person to choose some solution. I received honest, real help (from the clergy) when I was told to thank the Lord. I was angry at first for such advice … However, I tried to practice what he told me, what was being advised to me, and it worked, and it actually worked.* (Agnė, 36)

Several participants said that psychological help was related to spiritual support. For example, a psychologist helped to understand the meaning of a funeral:

> *The cremation itself and saying goodbye before an essential aspect I talked about to my psychologist … That here is the fact of death. Well, that is why … the funerals usually are for the comprehending that it will not be like that anymore, that the husband will not be here anymore.* (Elena, 34)

Many participants spoke of a very beneficial relationship with a religious person after the loss. Some of them befriended a priest, who helped with reducing guilt after a loved one's suicide:

> *We have been with him so far. We have become like a family. We do not … discuss all those religious issues and so on. He is so humanly, so secular. Without those, you know, those constant sermons … He says: why are you torturing yourself … he (the husband) has chosen such a path, an easy path because it is much harder to fix problems than to die … he left you with the child, with your problems … You would be guilty if, say, you would hold him by the hands … and put his head in a loop, tighten it and push the chair … to the side, then you might be guilty of his death. And he did it himself, he decided so, he got into the loop, he was still so romantic, he says: with the music, he went away … And I would think so, but seriously, I did not throw him in that loop.* (Asta, 36)

In one case, the priest was the person who noticed that the bereaved required psychological and psychiatric help:

> *He noticed me, and he said … you must worry about yourself. There has been where people just from that high tension are getting problems … He apparently saw that already … I am already disappearing because my weight and everything … I was talking there, I did not even see anything, but I already had those somatic problems … And the priest drove me to the Crisis Centre. Nobody would help, only him.* (Liepa, 49)

It was important that the priest was friendly and understanding. For example, that he would reassure the bereaved that the suicide is no longer condemned in the Catholic church, at least when it happens in a not wholly conscious and healthy state:

> *This bishop goes … And he talks to parishioners … I say I do not know how to approach you, but my husband hanged himself … So, he will never get forgiveness? … He took my hand, held it, and said, we are all invited to this earth … No religion appreciates suicide … it can be a condemnation for seven generations, like a cross, a sin … However, if at that moment when you do this … I even cannot say the word 'suicide' … When you do this, some button is on, I believe, that at that moment there is like a trance, darkness, you are not able to think anything else.* (Dalia, 62)

Several participants spoke of other people who helped in rituals or spiritual ways after the loss. Emotional as well as financial support during the funeral were perceived as very important:

> *I do not know what I would do if not for my friends. Four friends of him came to the funeral and three hundred friends of mine, who supported me ... I do not remember, but there were rows. Moreover, they gathered for me 10,000 euros during the funeral.* (Asta, 36)

One participant met a Muslim friend, who helped to cope and was, from her point of view, less critical than Catholic people:

> *I see that he (the Muslim friend) understands that this is terrible and hurtful, but he believes in the afterlife ... , and he thinks that everything is in God's hands, nothing happens without reason, we met not without reason ... He never criticized my views, he is interested in how I see the world, and I am interested in how he sees the world.* (Nida, 35)

In some cases, other people shared dreams as a message from the deceased, showing their involvement in the grief process:

> *I met this nurse ... believe it or not, she says, "I do not know, to say or not to say" ... She says, I dreamt (the deceased husband) ... I knew him ... I stand there, and he sees me and goes to me, goes goes goes, says, how great is this, that I met you ... You can pass over to (the bereaved woman), that the reason, why it happened ... is that I killed a person in a car accident, I hid it, and I could not live with it ... The first thought to me, because he hid so much from me ... This could have been true.* (Liepa, 49)

3.2.4. Needing Spirituality-Related Methods to Continue the Bond with the Deceased

For six participants, spirituality-related methods were also crucial to managing the continuing bond with the deceased. For some, the ritual of visiting the grave was a method to remind oneself of the fact of death:

> *I need some kind of process, some kind of ritual, which would help me understand and accept. So, I drove to his grave. Traditionally, I lit a candle.* (Eglė, 31)

For others, rituals helped to connect to the deceased in different ways. For example, to ease the deceased's soul's way to heaven:

> *When I am in a city, I always go to the church, light a candle, because the candle is somehow cleansing ... lifting his soul ... it was always important to me that it would be easier for him, I lit the candles ... so he would travel somewhere through the more straightforward path than it was for him here.* (Laima, 28)

Adjusting the funeral to the personality of the deceased seemed for many participants an essential part of the farewell ritual, potentially to maintain aspects of the dead visibly:

> *And his grave ... I did not want a common grave. He was a wild person, and I made the grave like this. I planted perennial flowers, which can grow by themselves how they want.* (Agnė, 36)

The funeral was also a place to talk with the deceased:

> *During the funeral I said to everyone, go out and give me half an hour to be with him alone ... I lay near him, on the coffin and talked to him ... Why did you do that, and for what?* (Asta, 36)

The other spirituality-related way to communicate with the deceased was, in one case, active praying for him and seeing him as an angel:

> *At first, the conversations with him were casual ... Now they are ... when it is hard for me, for example, I talk to him, ask for help ... I feel that he sees me all the time, my good and bad behaviors, he does not judge me, but he understands me ... he is my angel, and when I pray, I always pray for him that he would care for my child and me.* (Laima, 28)

In brief, spirituality provides tools which can help during grief. These tools vary from similar to personal and religious rituals to holding onto some spiritual or religious attitudes. The tools help the individuals cope, as well as to continue the bond with the deceased. Priests, psychologists, and friends helped the participants provide these spiritual tools to manage and discuss helpful attitudes.

3.3. *Spirituality Makes the Grief Process More Difficult*

The role of spirituality during suicide bereavement is not only positive and helpful. Spirituality, for nine participants, made the grieving process more difficult in different ways.

3.3.1. Some Spiritual-Related Attitudes and Rituals Make the Grief Process More Difficult

For eight participants, some spirituality-related attitudes and traditions were experienced as disturbing by the bereaved. This was closely related to the reactions and expectations from other people and internalized attitudes and potential projections on other people. For example, the attitude that suicide is a mortal sin, which meant the condemnation of the deceased, caused fear, and prevented individuals from talking to the priest about other spiritual matters:

> *I do not know if I could talk to the priest, it would be hard for me . . . Although, it would be interesting to find out his views towards people who died by suicide . . . what do they think, is it a big sin . . . My father said that for a priest, it is a sin not to live, to go away voluntarily . . . That is why I was afraid that he would talk badly about my fiancé . . . I did not want that.* (Laima, 28)

Several participants experienced prohibition from priests and religious people to cry during their grieving process:

> *Strangely, everyone would say, "do not cry because you are holding him here. You are not allowing him to go away . . . Nevertheless, I still cry. It's cleansing for me . . . It eases me, but I am holding him here because of my tears . . . If you cry, his soul is drowning.* (Laima, 28)

The religious idea of suicide being a test or a punishment angered the participants:

> *There were many opinions from the women, who are standardly religious . . . That God sends for people that much that they can carry . . . Yeah . . . I say, ok, what else can I carry? (Laughing ironically).* (Elena, 34)

The attitude that it required spiritual strongness to withstand suicide provoked tension, and feelings of being not understood:

> *I heard from everybody on my first birthday without my husband . . . Many of them said that "not everybody is that strong" and congratulated me that they wanted to be as strong as me . . . I thought about it later, how people see the strength . . . that you don't cry, smile, care for the children and move further . . . But a lot can happen. You just find the space for your emotions . . . It doesn't mean that you don't have them.* (Elena, 34)

Participants noticed that some people who pretended to want to help after the loss concentrated mainly on spiritual issues and did not notice the psychological pain of the bereaved:

> *There were many attacks . . . for example, somebody brought the book of angels . . . I sat through this session and thought, what a moment . . . She (the spiritual leader) told me to do a break, pause, and use something . . . And then she went, and I sent here the sign of a pause in music . . . My healthy mind turned on . . . And I sent it (laughing) and didn't talk to her anymore . . . It's strange that she would want to include me into something and then powder everything, that I am not hurting, because . . . I AM HURTING . . . Why should I deny it?* (Liepa, 49)

Several participants perceived some religious rituals and traditions as focusing too much on death:

When I started to walk a spiritual path, I understood that any connection to the deceased is idolatry and witchcraft. I don't understand our festivities, vėlinės (a traditional Lithuanian celebration for the souls of the dead). I don't go to his grave, don't light the candles. (Agnė, 36)

For some, a loved one's funeral provoked disgust even years after the loss:

You know how the season has its perfume. Autumn, the scent of autumn and flowers, lilies. It seemed to me that the death happened again somewhere ... My new husband gave me flowers as a gift and those lilies, I went inside my home and ... the smell of death, the associations ... death and corps, disgusting, even candles, you know, when they stand around the body, and the heat causes the smell of the dead body. (Laima, 28)

The funeral for several participants was a problematic, even torturing experience:

That sitting and watching the dead body is torturing for me, I don't know, it is like, let's torture ourselves now and watch the deceased person. To say goodbye is ok, but you need 15 min for that. (Liepa, 49)

Some experienced pressure to keep in line with the trends of funerals and organizing funerals because of other people:

I am determined to follow the trends (of the funeral) because it's unnecessary for me. It is meaningless to me. On another side, we did it all for the parents. Because they are from an older generation, it was, wow, how important for them. (Jurga, 49)

or the pressure to keep in line with cherishing the grave:

And all those stories about graves and tombstones, and this comparison with other monuments, which are more interesting ... Maybe if it would ... not be Catholicism, but Protestantism ... maybe there would be fewer problems, they like simplicity. (Nida, 35)

Overall, funerals caused different problems for many participants. This included financial and organizational issues:

It was a problem for me where to leave my child with disabilities because nobody knew how to feed him ... Children should not be near the coffin ... But not everybody has people who could watch them. (Asta, 36)

It also included problems related to interactions with other people, who sometimes behaved aggressively and unsupportively:

Nobody listened to his wish to be cremated because the family was furious and blamed me ... The funeral was tragic ... It was very hard for me, and his relatives didn't allow me to his coffin, said terrible things to me ... (Eglė, 31)

Some participants met insensitive priests, which caused disappointment and anger:

The unpreparedness of the priest, inability to sympathize, comfort, comment about stuff that we all go through the same stages of life, everybody dies, and it's a challenge ... During the funeral or a month after ... , he chooses the text from the Bible about how Jesus heals sick people and raises the dead. He accentuates the text several times, especially the point about blindness. But he should know that the blindness in the Bible is not actual blindness ... So, what he wanted to say about my husband was that he had this physical disability, but it doesn't mean that he was spiritually blind ... You must search for metaphors in the Bible and not only cite the text and talk about it that the community member had a visual disability. I didn't understand what he wanted to say. (Nida, 35)

The personal rituals or wanting to adjust the funeral to one's needs, in some cases, were met with criticism:

You light a candle–they shout at you: "why did you light that candle?". But it's nice for me, it helps me. I wanted to light the candle at this place ... It's my spirituality and faith. (Eglė, 31)

3.3.2. Spirituality Related Questions Provoke Confusion after the Loss

Eight participants spoke of spirituality related questions after the loss provoking confusion and doubts. Some contemplated existential or spiritual questions. For example, what do I have to live for?

> *It's sad–you don't want to eat, to get up ... I don't want to do anything, I don't have what to give to others, and my energy level is too low. I am on a line of exhaustion. And then the questions came: if I don't have what to give and no energy to live, is it worth it to torment myself and live ... ? It is the most challenging moment.* (Eglė, 31)

Some questioned why this had happened to them:

> *Why, what, why for me, not for someone else? I didn't do anything wrong in life. And you start to reconsider your whole life, how, how, how. Maybe you did something to somebody. And of course, people come who "help" you find it.* (Asta, 36)

The haunting question of responsibility and guilt about suicide was contemplated by each participant. For example:

> *And I was sorry before that was guilt because I was angry about many things, mad about him when he was still alive, that these letters from the bank, his debts ... I am still mad ... And others ask, why did it happen? And I say to them, just because, I don't know why.* (Liepa, 49)

The experience of searching for spirituality after loss was perceived as dynamic and emotional:

> *You know how you go from one extreme to another ... you start to blame God, that he is terrible and how could he let it ... you start to pray ... then start to hate everybody, God doesn't exist, every human is awful ... Then you begin to love everybody. Then you start to hate everybody because you need help but don't know what helps, and you are mad at people who can't help you.* (Asta, 36)

3.3.3. A Loved One's Suicide Causes a Spiritual Crisis

For five participants, a loved one's suicide caused a spiritual crisis. Participants described the spiritual state after the loss as cancer of the soul:

> *This cancer of the soul eats you from inside. It spiritually kills you ... You don't want anything; you don't believe in anything ... I called myself a mass then. The mass, which doesn't think, is languid. And to gather this mass inside, you need a lot of effort ... A lot of self-reflection.* (Asta, 36)

In some cases, the spiritual crisis was primarily related to seeing suicide as treason or abandonment of the bereaved; therefore, their trust in people and love was shattered:

> *And you know, we agreed nicely to each other, cherished one another, and then you feel abandoned, betrayed ... that he left me.* (Asta, 36)

Suicide seemed, for some of the participants, as a breaking of spiritual rules:

> *I would not want that my daughter would know what suicide is. That there would not be such a concept–to kill. Who tells the people that they can kill themselves? ... I disagree with that.* (Eglė, 31)

A couple of participants said that they were not spiritually prepared for such a disaster; therefore, the effects of the loss were strong:

> *There was one more sign before ... I wanted to volunteer at a suicide helpline ... I wanted to go to the courses ... I went through. And in the end, there is like an exam ... And I didn't pass this exam ... Later I understood that I would not be able to withstand this topic. All the depression, children. These hurtful topics, only during the courses do I comprehend that it is seriously hard ... Later I thought that ... the life led me to this*

> *helpline, that I would know more about depression, but I gave up. I didn't understand that I needed this.* (Jurga, 49)

Participants spoke of disappointment in previous beliefs. For example, disappointment in the Catholic community:

> *In the church, there is a mass paid for. And the priest doesn't hesitate to take the money for the mention of the deceased . . . , and he also decides to congratulate a birthday person. On the same mass . . . And when you stand in the first row, there is a candle in front of you . . . And the choir sings "happy birthday" I just want to take the candle holder and throw it into that priest . . . Because it is a complete disrespect to people, their grief . . . I started not to believe in religion, especially in Christian people.* (Nida, 35);

in good God and His helpfulness:

> *There is this anger if God exists, why is he doing that. Why do others live without any losses? Everything is good for them . . . And for me, punch after punch . . . When will it end? Or why? I say to God, why do you do that? Do you want to kill me? I don't have the strength anymore.* (Asta, 36);

in existential psychology, which previously was important and fulfilled spiritual needs:

> *We soaked in existentialism together (with the deceased husband). Heidegger and all other saints, I used to say to him . . . And I started to think that it was too narrow for me . . . I said to him, there are many other thinkers, other thoughts, and perspectives on life, not only existentialism . . . It is too narrow . . . It can't save me.* (Agnė, 36)

3.3.4. Comprehending the Finality of Death Requires Significant Effort

Seven participants revealed difficulties comprehending or contemplating the finality of death. Some participants spoke of their doubts and wished to believe in the afterlife:

> *I don't have the answer about the afterlife. I would like to believe that it exists, but I have doubts about it.* (Rasa, 41)

Several participants could not stop thinking or dreaming about the look of the decaying body of the deceased:

> *I dreamt of the decaying body . . . I think about it, how that body looks now under this clayey earth?* (Nida, 35)

Participants searched for ways to comprehend the fact of the death:

> *There were moments when you spend time with children and catch yourself thinking, how nice it would be if he would be here . . . If I start to notice myself in these illusions, dreams, where is the person . . . I would go to the grave. To put it into my head, this is the reality, not what you are thinking about.* (Elena, 34)

Some tried to hold onto the attitude that death is the end of the relationship with the deceased and that life is for the living:

> *The bond is through memories . . . What we did, how we communicated, talked, but I don't believe that he . . . watches me from Heaven . . . I don't know his state if he is sleeping, how the Jews say, Sheol, the afterlife, where they wait for resurrection . . . I don't raise these questions for myself. I live my life with the living.* (Agnė, 36)

Others had to actively block the continuing bond with the deceased:

> *When he appears in dreams, it unnerves me . . . We were harmonized when we lived together. I just would comply, not listen . . . But now I see that two years went by . . . And I don't want to comply with him anymore, even in the dream. It's better that I would take him and push him aside . . . I don't need it. I will manage by myself . . . If you went away, live your life on your own.* (Jurga, 49)

Some participants expressed beliefs that holding onto the deceased is harmful:

If you are nearby ... you will constantly be with various emotions ... His mother goes to his grave every day. I think she harms herself. She takes her energy away from herself ... Why fall together? (Eglė, 31)

3.3.5. Discomforting Spiritual Experiences

Five participants spoke of experiencing discomforting feelings regarding the deceased, activated through other people, spaces, things, visuals, memories, and sounds:

It was an all-surrounding, the death ... I tried to explain it to my doctor, the paralyzing fear of dark powers, which is very terrifying ... It seemed that I was going out of my mind, nobody could understand me, and I couldn't explain what I feared. I saw something when I walked the dog ... I worked at the time and before work at 7.30 a.m. In the morning, I had to walk my dog before work in winter. It was cruel, I went only on the streets, near the cars, but if I looked at the forest, it seemed that somebody was in the woods. I saw the hanging men in the woods. (Laima, 28)

Some participants experienced the sense of the presence of the deceased as discomforting and as provoking fear:

One thing was tricky ... the earth was frozen ... I cremated him ... And they say, we can't dig, to bury the urn. So, it stood at my home for a couple days ... It preyed on me cruelly. And my parents, grandma ... they felt that he is nearby ... They are not believers in ghosts or else ... But they felt that he had walked in the house, only in the corridor, not the rooms ... It was a hard feeling inside that he was not away. I didn't comprehend that feeling. (Asta, 36)

Some participants needed to send the deceased away actively and interpreted this sense of presence as related to suicide's unnaturally:

And I dream about him, and he is angry. He is gloomy, he is a grim person, and he comes angry in my dreams. I scream at him, go away, and don't disturb my life anymore ... Several weeks ago. He annoyed me, slipping into my nights and days. And I say in my thoughts, go away ... Help us, don't annoy us. Why do you need to come here and be grim, regulate something ... Give us peace. And then the spirit goes away ... When the person dies his own death, it is not the same. When he raises his hand against himself, it is cruel. The soul flies around, I don't know, for hundred years. (Jurga, 49)

Overall, spirituality can make the grief process difficult because of interactions with other people who express unhelpful and stigmatizing attitudes related to suicide and grief. The rituals become disturbing if they do not meet the personal needs of the bereaved. Suicide can provoke confusing existential and unanswerable questions that must be explored and contemplated. Suicide can also cause a spiritual crisis and lead a person to reconsider their beliefs. Lastly, loss due to suicide can provoke scary and disturbing spiritual experiences, including the feeling that the death was felt nearby.

4. Discussion

This study aimed to explore the role of spirituality during suicide bereavement. The findings implicate that spirituality's role during grief depends on spirituality's subjective experiences and beliefs. Spirituality can become a supportive resource that helps cope with various challenges after the loved one's suicide. It can be perceived as coming without conscious involvement, potentially coming from Higher powers or something more significant than a human being. The bereaved person can also reach for a connection to spirituality by making a specific effort, which also helps during suicide bereavement. Spirituality can provide helpful ways to cope with grief and manifest as active actions, such as rituals, or as beliefs and attitudes a person holds onto. Spirituality also provides methods to form a continuing bond with the deceased and inspires interactions with other spiritual or religious people or discussing spiritual matters even with not necessarily religious people. Lastly, spirituality can make the grief process more difficult through discordant traditions and rituals, interactions with unsupportive religious people, experiences of spiritual crisis or frustration about existential questions. We discuss the main findings below.

4.1. Spirituality Is a Supportive Resource That Can Be Reached for or Come without Conscious Involvement

The strengthened spirituality, intuition, a feeling of support from a Higher power and experiencing a continuing bond with the deceased helped the participants cope with complicated feelings of grief. Studies reveal that higher religiosity and positive spiritual/religious coping are related to better bereavement outcomes [28,29,56,57]. The sense of presence and continuing the bond with the deceased as an outer figure can be helpful during bereavement to assure the existence of the afterlife with a hope to meet again and not lose the connection to the loved one [6,8,23]. Our study revealed an additional aspect of spiritual resources during bereavement being perceived as activated without one's wish. From an analytical psychology point of view, we interpreted this finding as an example of the psyche's tendency to self-regulate even in the most challenging situations, such as grief [20]. The more the psychological damage, the more definite an answer is given by the unconscious mechanisms to heal the psyche.

In some cases, the bereaved person feels the need and ability to actively invite spiritual resources into the grief process through praying, spending time in sacral places or listening to music. Conscious involvement might be necessary as an active connection with a sense of control and may be a symbolic invitation to start a dialogue with the conscious parts of the psyche [58]. According to the religious coping model, a person can use behaviors, cognitions, emotions, relationships, and virtues related to the sacred domain to cope with complex life events [31,32]. Our study findings show that a person can consciously choose to lean on positive coping strategies related to religion or spiritual domains and find comfort.

Spiritual growth, together with strengthened compassion and responsibility for other people after the suicide loss can be seen as a manifestation of post-traumatic growth [33,59,60], which aligns with the previous findings [6]. Positive religious and spiritual coping can induce post-traumatic growth in different life situations [31,32,61]. In the Jungian approach, encounters with the reality of death can be seen as an unwilling encounter with the personal and collective shadow [20], defined as an unconscious part of the psyche which accommodates everything and that the conscious ego refuses to acknowledge [62]. Since death is culturally and personally repressed [63], facing such a loss, mainly because of an even more socially repressed reason such as suicide [6,24], causes the disturbing experience of meeting one's own and even a collective shadow. Although renewing the conscious connection with the shadow is complicated and challenging, the positive outcome can manifest as being brave and open to other people's pain and shadowy experiences. The loved one's suicide can be seen as a provocation of the whole established system of a person's conscious–unconscious connection. This can lead to dangerous consequences. Therefore, the concept of post-traumatic growth should not be seen without acknowledging the distress of the loss [64]. However, in some cases, the provocation can translate into personal growth.

Beliefs in a Higher power helped the bereaved with meaning-making of the loss. The theory that grief can be processed through meaning-making in the practical, personal, existential, and spiritual sense is related to the idea that the loss shatters the whole person and their belief system [65]. Religious coping is seen as a helpful way to make meaning of difficult life events [31,32]. Our study revealed that different spiritual and religious beliefs provide ways to make meaning and find some relief during suicide bereavement. Religious and spiritual perspectives offer many insights and traditions about grief, death, the afterlife and how to cope [56,66], which helps the bereaved explain the tragedy and find some sense of meaning in it. Suicide usually leaves the bereaved person with a haunting question of "why" [26,27]. Therefore, if a person believes in religious or spiritual explanations, it can be helpful [6,8,34]. The meaning-making of suicide through explaining its reasons and God's involvement in the process seem to structure a chaotic and emotional experience of grief after suicide. This could be made from the conscious position but should be congruent with one's inner beliefs. Our study revealed that constantly reviewing this congruency and adjusting the ideas and explanations is a part of coping with grief.

4.2. Spirituality Provides Helpful Ways to Cope with Grief

Our findings revealed and expanded the understanding of the role of spiritual activities, such as rituals, during suicide bereavement. Personally meaningful rituals were the most helpful for the participants to live day by day after the loss. This is a conscious choice to take a specific action [8] which has a personal meaning for the bereaved. The rituals vary from connecting to the deceased or relating to God, lighting candles to calming oneself down before sleep with gratitude, meditation, yoga, or an analysis of the day. Rituals can be helpful because they assure a person of not being condemned by society, as certain rituals, such as funerals, are performed with others [6].

Nevertheless, the effect of the ritual might be related to how much control or personal involvement a person has in creating, organizing or performing the ritual [67]. It could be most important when grief reactions are stronger [68] or, we argue, when grief reactions are provoked by traumatic losses such as suicide. Personal religious or secularized rituals allow for the relief of difficult emotions [69]. They are experiential, culturally ancient [70] methods by which to regain control and act constructively. Rituals as spiritual practices are embodied ways to relate to the deceased, other people, or Higher powers [71]. They can be interpreted as a tribute to the unconscious for more fluent communication [58]. Since suicide loss and grief provoke the experiences of destructive powers of the unconscious [20], rituals as a tribute might function as a regulator.

Symbolic actions can be supplied by spirituality-related attitudes, which help during grief. This includes beliefs in the afterlife, acceptance of uncontrollability and the unknown or trusting God's will. Holding onto spiritual beliefs and values can be a positive coping strategy during bereavement [28,29,56]. The impact of facing death and experiencing challenging feelings of grief after the suicide of a loved one seem to require more than rational thoughts and understanding of feelings. Searching and holding onto one's belief system might be helpful after losing a loved one.

Other people, such as those who surround the bereaved, play an essential role in influencing the bereaved's spirituality after the loss. This is congruent with the general research on religious social support (a kind of support which comes from the religious community) being related to better adjustment to bereavement if the religious support is positive [56] and that bereaved people tend to search for comfort in religious activities and communities [72]. Connecting to other people and receiving spiritual support is another spiritual method by which to cope. The spiritual explanations of suicide and grief from spiritual leaders or spiritual people can function as support. Being together with the bereaved during the funeral can help the person to feel less lonely. The helpfulness of religious communities during grief was revealed in other studies [6,7,25]. Our study demonstrated that the importance of spiritual help can be actualized even if the bereaved is not religious and does not belong to a religious community. In hard times, other people can function as carriers of a part of the bereaved's feelings, questions, and fears. However, for this interaction to happen, other people must be ready to take on the burden [73].

4.3. Spirituality Makes the Grief Process More Difficult

In line with other studies [6,7], our findings reveal the 'other' side of spirituality's role during suicide bereavement. Spirituality-related attitudes, rituals, traditions, questions, and experiences can burden the bereaved. The stigma associated with attitudes toward suicide reach the bereaved through the destructive behaviors of religious people and priests. Stigma might be supported by different religions' harmful views of suicide as a mortal sin [74]. The funerals and other farewell traditions are not comfortable for everybody but are usually pushed on the suffering. This could be explained by our research participants' cultural and religious contexts. Suicide, from a Catholic point of view, was looked at as a mortal sin for hundreds of years [75]. Specifically, Lithuania's Catholicism can be seen as very conservative. During the Soviet occupation, which lasted from 1945 to 1990, the church did not have opportunities to connect freely with the Vatican and develop together but worked as resistance to the Soviet occupation [76]. There are speculations that the church became more political than spiritual [77], which sometimes leaves the religious community as only providing religious beliefs and tools, but with little empathic human contact.

Another aspect of understanding what happens in these problematic interactions is related to caring about other people's opinions and being unable to confront them. The loss due to suicide and grief is an exhausting, emotionally draining experience [26,27]. Therefore, the bereaved person might not have enough inner resources to express and fight for their opinions and needs. Thus, the need for proactive help to access at least one friendly face after the loss [27] is crucial.

Existential questions, difficulties in comprehending the death, discomforting spiritual experiences, and spiritual crisis affect the bereavement process. On one side, it makes the bereavement process more difficult; on the other side, it can also be seen as a naturally occurring task, which must be in some ways resolved after the loss to make meaning [65], to reach the integration of the loss [27] and to be able to live further. The loss due to suicide can shatter the whole belief system of the bereaved, which causes distress, hopelessness, and distrust in Higher powers [6,7]. From an analytical point of view, the constant inner contemplation of the spiritual experiences, questions, and reconsideration of one's beliefs might be a component of the grief process [20], which requires time, effort, support, and sometimes help from spiritual leaders and clinicians.

4.4. Practical Implications

Our study provided critical practical implications. Practitioners who work with people bereaved by suicide should consider the role of spirituality during suicide bereavement. If necessary for the bereaved, spirituality should be viewed as an additional resource after the loss [6,25]. Acknowledging the importance and discussing rituals, spiritual methods, and helpful beliefs can help with meaning-making after the loss and provide ways to reach emotional relief. Informing the bereaved about the possibility of meeting with a spiritual leader to talk about spiritual crisis and existential questions might also be a productive way to activate the spiritual resources during grief. The practitioners could also receive specific training on how to deal with spiritual issues. They should also be aware of strong emotional reactions to spiritual experiences, help understand these feelings and find constructive expressions for those emotions.

Spiritual leaders should reach for better preparedness and knowledge about bereavement after suicide. Their support and help in spiritual and emotional contexts are required by people who are bereaved by suicide [6,7,25]. Spiritual leaders could normalize the spiritual experiences and issues the bereaved is confronted with. The spiritual explanations for death, suicide, and grief can provide the bereaved with new perspectives about loss and bereavement. Patiently accepting that the suffering might not hold onto specific beliefs and that beliefs and virtues can change during grief is essential. Lastly, spiritual leaders should be responsible for educating their communities about healthy attitudes toward suicide and inspiring compassion in the spiritual members. Otherwise, insensitive comments to the bereaved by suicide or the ignorance toward the psychological state of the bereaved can hurt and challenge the bereaved during the already uncertain time after a loved one's suicide.

Together with other authors [78], we emphasize the importance of spirituality in postvention strategies, which should involve spiritual support as a potential helping strategy for people bereaved by suicide.

4.5. Limitations and Future Research

The current study suffers from several limitations. With its purposive sampling, the explorative qualitative study does not allow for generalizing the findings. The women who participated in the study were volunteers who wanted to tell their stories, which could mean that they had more positive experiences of the spirituality manifestations during grief than those women who did not want to participate. Although homogenous, the sample was only composed of women who lost their life partners, which allowed us to focus on the phenomenon of spirituality but did not allow us to make conclusions about spirituality during suicide bereavement in other groups of bereaved people. The relationship with the deceased differed by the duration and status of the relationship, which might have affected the loss differently. The participants also discussed spiritual and religious beliefs, which provided a broader view of spirituality although this may have made the results more wide-ranging but not as in-depth. Since spirituality might change during a lifetime, the differences in participants' age might have also biased the study results.

Despite these limitations, our study contributes to the existing literature on spirituality during suicide bereavement. It provides exceptional insights into spirituality as a resource, as a method and as a disturbance during the process of grief after suicide. These findings also raise questions for further research.

Future studies should explore the role of spirituality during suicide bereavement in broader groups of bereaved people due to suicide. They could also expand the research topic to comparisons between the groups based on the person lost due to suicide or based on gender with a deeper exploration of the differences between gender, sex and spirituality during suicide bereavement. For the sake of postvention, research should also focus on spiritual help, spiritual leaders' preparedness to support the bereaved and the manifestations and integrations of spiritual service in psychological or psychotherapeutic use. With a quantitative approach, future studies should investigate the risk and protective factors related to spirituality during suicide bereavement; more importantly, the positive/negative religious coping strategies and suicide bereavement outcomes should be explored to expand our findings on the different forms that spirituality that can take during suicide bereavement.

5. Conclusions

The current study explored the role of spirituality during suicide bereavement and found that the role varies from helpful and providing methods to cope to disturbing and making the grief process more difficult. Findings reveal the helpfulness of personal adjusted rituals, practices, beliefs, and qualitative relationships with spiritual leaders and other people during grief. However, stigmatizing religious attitudes and not personally meaningful traditions provoke distress, anger, and disappointment. Difficult spiritual experiences and spiritual crises might be an intricate part of the bereavement process. Practitioners, spiritual leaders and postvention creators are invited to address the role of spirituality while working with people bereaved by suicide.

Author Contributions: Conceptualization, methodology, data analysis, A.A.Č. and P.S.; writing—original draft preparation, A.A.Č.; writing—review and editing, A.A.Č. and P.S.; supervision, P.S. All authors have read and agreed to the published version of the manuscript.

Funding: This research received no external funding.

Institutional Review Board Statement: The study was conducted in accordance with the Declaration of Helsinki, and approved by the Psychology Research Ethics Committee of Vilnius University (22 January 2021, Number 56).

Informed Consent Statement: Informed consent was obtained from all subjects involved in the study.

Data Availability Statement: Not applicable.

Conflicts of Interest: The authors declare no conflict of interest.

References

1. WHO (World Health Organization). *Suicide*; World Health Organization Media Centre: Geneva, Switzerland, 2022. Available online: https://www.who.int/data/gho/publications/world-health-statistics (accessed on 12 July 2022).
2. Cerel, J.; Brown, M.M.; Maple, M.; Singleton, M.; Van de Venne, J.; Moore, M.; Flaherty, C. How Many People Are Exposed to Suicide? Not Six. *Suicide Life Threat. Behav.* **2018**, *49*, 529–534. [CrossRef] [PubMed]
3. Bellini, S.; Erbuto, D.; Andriessen, K.; Milelli, M.; Innamorati, M.; Lester, D.; Sampogna, G.; Fiorillo, A.; Pompili, M. Depression, hopelessness, and complicated grief in survivors of suicide. *Front. Psychol.* **2018**, *9*, 198. [CrossRef] [PubMed]
4. Erlangsen, A.; Runeson, B.; Bolton, J.M.; Wilcox, H.C.; Forman, J.L.; Krogh, J.; Shear, K.; Nordentoft, M.; Conwell, Y. Association between spousal suicide and mental, physical, and social health outcomes: A longitudinal and nationwide register-based study. *JAMA Psychiatry* **2017**, *74*, 456–464. [CrossRef]
5. Andriessen, K.; Krysinska, K.; Hill, N.T.M.; Reifels, L.; Robinson, J.; Reavley, N.; Pirkis, J. Effectiveness of interventions for people bereaved through suicide: A systematic review of controlled studies of grief, psychosocial and suicide-related outcomes. *BMC Psychiatry* **2019**, *19*, 49. [CrossRef] [PubMed]
6. Castelli Dransart, D.A. Spiritual and religious issues in the aftermath of suicide. *Religions* **2018**, *9*, 153. [CrossRef]
7. Gall, T.L.; Henneberry, J.; Eyre, M. Spiritual beliefs and meaning-making within the context of suicide bereavement. *J. Study Spiritual.* **2015**, *5*, 98–112. [CrossRef]
8. Čepulienė, A.A.; Pučinskaitė, B.; Spangelytė, K.; Skruibis, P.; Gailienė, D. Spirituality and religiosity during suicide bereavement: A qualitative systematic review. *Religions* **2021**, *12*, 766. [CrossRef]
9. Koenig, H.G. Research on religion, spirituality, and mental health: A review. *Can. J. Psychiatry* **2009**, *54*, 283–291. [CrossRef]
10. Hornborg, A.C. Are We All Spiritual? A Comparative Perspective on the Appropriation of a New Concept of Spirituality. *J. Study Spiritual.* **2011**, *1*, 249–268. [CrossRef]
11. Tacey, D. *The Spirituality Revolution: The Emergence of Contemporary Spirituality*; Brunner-Routledge/Tailor & Francis Group: New York, NY, USA, 2004.
12. Zinnbauer, B.J.; Pargament, K.I.; Scott, A.B. The emerging meanings of religiousness and spirituality: Problems and prospects. *J. Pers.* **1999**, *67*, 889–919. [CrossRef]
13. Pargament, K.I. *Spiritually Integrated Psychotherapy: Understanding and Addressing the Sacred*; Guilford Press: New York, NY, USA, 2007.
14. Schnell, T. Spirituality with and without religion—Differential relationships with personality. *Arch. Psychol. Relig.* **2012**, *34*, 33–61. [CrossRef]
15. Atkins, P.; Schubert, E. Are spiritual experiences through music seen as intrinsic or extrinsic? *Religions* **2014**, *5*, 76–89. [CrossRef]
16. Koenig, H.G. Religion, spirituality, and health: The research and clinical implications. *ISRN Psychiatry* **2012**, *2012*, 278730. [CrossRef] [PubMed]
17. Pargament, K.I.; Lomax, J.W. Understanding and addressing religion among people with mental illness. *World J. Psychiatry* **2013**, *12*, 26–32. [CrossRef] [PubMed]
18. Jastrzębski, A.K. The challenging task of defining spirituality. *J. Spiritual. Ment. Health* **2022**, *24*, 113–131. [CrossRef]
19. Von Franz, M.L. The Process of Individuation. In *Man and His Symbols*; Jung, C.G., Ed.; Ancor Press: New York, NY, USA, 1988; pp. 158–229.
20. Kast, V. *Time to Mourn: Growing through the Grief Process*; Daimon Verlag: Einsiedeln, Switzerland, 1993.
21. Krysinska, K.; Jahn, D.R.; Spencer-Thomas, S.; Andriessen, K. The Roles of Religion and Spirituality in Suicide Bereavement and Postvention. In *Postvention in Action: The International Handbook of Suicide Bereavement Support*, 1st ed.; Andriessen, K., Krysinska, K., Onja, T.G., Eds.; Hogrefe: Boston, MA, USA, 2017; pp. 186–197.
22. Jahn, D.; Spencer-Thomas, S. Continuing bonds through after-death spiritual experiences in individuals bereaved by suicide. *J. Spiritual. Ment. Health* **2014**, *16*, 311–324. [CrossRef]
23. Jahn, D.; Spencer-Thomas, S. A qualitative examination of continuing bonds through spiritual experiences in individuals bereaved by suicide. *Religions* **2018**, *9*, 248. [CrossRef]
24. Stelzer, E.M.; Palitsky, R.; Hernandez, E.N.; Ramirez, E.G.; O'Connor, M.F. The role of personal and communal religiosity in the context of bereavement. *J. Prev. Interv. Community* **2020**, *48*, 64–80. [CrossRef]
25. Vandecreek, L.; Mottram, K. The Religious Life during Suicide Bereavement: A Description. *Death Stud.* **2009**, *33*, 741–761. [CrossRef]
26. Jordan, J.R. Is Suicide Bereavement Different? A Reassessment of the Literature. *Suicide Life Threat. Behav.* **2001**, *31*, 91–102. Available online: https://onlinelibrary.wiley.com/doi/pdf/10.1521/suli.31.1.91.21310?casa_token=mCuuR7SbKIAAAAA:wVS8peEcnM_hGIqSL1J2wA21tGlQEluDR083Tku6DCpDZt8sZ4youqpu9qYWqH9GzSJcnMy6LsG (accessed on 17 May 2022).
27. Jordan, J.R. Postvention is prevention—The case for suicide postvention. *Death Stud.* **2017**, *41*, 614–621. [CrossRef]
28. Becker, G.; Xander, C.J.; Blum, H.E.; Lutterbach, J.; Momm, F.; Gysels, M.; Higginson, I.J. Do religious or spiritual beliefs influence bereavement? A systematic review. *Palliat. Med.* **2007**, *21*, 207–217. [CrossRef] [PubMed]
29. Hai, A.H.; Currin-McCulloch, J.; Franklin, C.; Cole, A.H., Jr. Spirituality/religiosity's influence on college students' adjustment to bereavement: A systematic review. *Death Stud.* **2018**, *42*, 513–520. [CrossRef] [PubMed]
30. Lichtenthal, W.G.; Neimeyer, R.A.; Currier, J.M.; Roberts, K.; Jordan, N. Cause of Death and the Quest for Meaning after the Loss of a Child. *Death Stud.* **2013**, *37*, 311–342. [CrossRef] [PubMed]

31. Pargament, K.I.; Smith, B.W.; Koenig, H.G.; Perez, L. Patterns of positive and negative religious coping with major life stressors. *J. Sci. Study Relig.* **1998**, *37*, 710–724. [CrossRef]
32. Pargament, K.; Feuille, M.; Burdzy, D. The Brief RCOPE: Current psychometric status of a short measure of religious coping. *Religions* **2011**, *2*, 51–76. [CrossRef]
33. Feigelman, W.; Jordan, J.R.; Gorman, B.S. Personal growth after a suicide loss: Cross-sectional findings suggest growth after loss may be associated with better mental health among survivors. *OMEGA* **2009**, *59*, 181–202. [CrossRef]
34. Murphy, S.A.; Johnson, L.C. Finding Meaning in a Child's Violent Death: A Five-Year Prospective Analysis of Parents' Personal Narratives and Empirical Data. *Death Stud.* **2003**, *27*, 381–404. [CrossRef]
35. Mastrocinque, J.M.; Hartwell, T.; Metzger, J.W.; Carapella-Johnson, R.; Navratil, P.K.; Cerulli, C. Spirituality and religion after homicide and suicide: Families and friends tell their stories. *Homicide Stud.* **2020**, *24*, 107–126. [CrossRef]
36. Robinson, O.C. Sampling in Interview-Based Qualitative Research: A Theoretical and Practical Guide. *Qual. Res. Psychol.* **2014**, *11*, 25–41. [CrossRef]
37. Liddon, L.; Barry, J. *Perspectives in Male Psychology: An Introduction*; John Wiley and Sons: Hoboken, NJ, USA, 2021.
38. Bailey, J.M.; Vasey, P.L.; Diamond, L.M.; Breedlove, S.M.; Vilain, E.; Epprecht, M. Sexual orientation, controversy, and science. *Psychol. Sci.* **2016**, *17*, 45–101. [CrossRef]
39. Mitchell, A.M.; Kim, Y.; Prigerson, H.G.; Mortimer-Stephens, M. Complicated grief in survivors of suicide. *Crisis* **2004**, *25*, 12–18. [CrossRef] [PubMed]
40. de Groot, M.; Kollen, B.J. Course of bereavement over 8–10 years in first degree relatives and spouses of people who committed suicide: Longitudinal community based cohort study. *BMJ* **2013**, *347*, f5519. [CrossRef] [PubMed]
41. McIntosh, J.L.; Wrobleski, A. Grief reactions among suicide survivors: An exploratory comparison of relationships. *Death Stud.* **1988**, *12*, 21–39. [CrossRef]
42. Farberow, N.L.; Gallagher-Thompson, D.; Gilewski, M.; Thompson, L. Changes in grief and mental health of bereaved spouses of older suicides. *J. Gerontol.* **1992**, *47*, 357–366. [CrossRef]
43. Ferlatte, O.; Oliffe, J.L.; Salway, T.; Knight, R. Stigma in the bereavement experiences of gay men who have lost a partner to suicide. *Cult. Health Sex.* **2019**, *21*, 1273–1289. [CrossRef] [PubMed]
44. Agerbo, E. Midlife suicide risk, partner's psychiatric illness, spouse and child bereavement by suicide or other modes of death: A gender specific study. *J. Epidemiol. Community Health* **2005**, *59*, 407–412. [CrossRef]
45. Caine, E.D. Does spousal suicide have a measurable adverse effect on the surviving partner? *JAMA Psychiatry* **2017**, *74*, 443–444. [CrossRef]
46. Gray, L.M.; Wong-Wylie, G.; Rempel, G.R.; Cook, K. Expanding Qualitative Research Interviewing Strategies: Zoom Video Communications. *Quality* **2020**, *25*, 1292–1301. Available online: https://www.proquest.com/scholarly-journals/expanding-qualitative-research-interviewing/docview/2405672296/se-2 (accessed on 16. June 2022). [CrossRef]
47. Krouwel, M.; Jolly, K.; Greenfield, S. Comparing Skype (video calling) and in-person qualitative interview modes in a study of people with irritable bowel syndrome—An exploratory comparative analysis. *BMC Med. Res. Methodol.* **2019**, *19*, 219. [CrossRef]
48. Jenner, B.M.; Myers, K.C. Intimacy, rapport, and exceptional disclosure: A comparison of in-person and mediated interview contexts. *Int. J. Soc. Res. Methodol.* **2019**, *22*, 165–177. [CrossRef]
49. Čepulienė, A.A. Silence and sounds: An autoethnography of searching for spirituality during suicide bereavement in life and research. *Religions* **2022**, *13*, 500. [CrossRef]
50. Neubauer, B.E.; Witkop, C.T.; Varpio, L. How phenomenology can help us learn from the experiences of others. *Perspect. Med. Educ.* **2019**, *8*, 90–97. [CrossRef]
51. Braun, V.; Clarke, V. Using thematic analysis in psychology. *Qual. Res. Psychol.* **2006**, *3*, 77–101. [CrossRef]
52. Braun, V.; Clarke, V. Teaching Thematic Analysis: Overcoming Challenges and Developing Strategies for Effective Learning. *Psychologist* **2013**, *26*, 2. Available online: https://uwe-repository.worktribe.com/preview/937606/Teaching%20 (accessed on 9 May 2022).
53. Braun, V.; Clarke, V. Reflecting on reflexive thematic analysis. *Qual. Res. Sport Exerc. Health* **2019**, *11*, 589–597. [CrossRef]
54. Braun, V.; Clarke, V. Can I use TA? Should I use TA? Should I not use TA? Comparing reflexive thematic analysis and other pattern-based qualitative analytic approaches. *Couns. Psychother. Res.* **2021**, *21*, 37–47. [CrossRef]
55. ATLAS.ti. *Qualitative Data Analysis*; Web. ATLAS.ti Gmbh: Berlin, Germany, 2022.
56. Wortmann, J.H.; Park, C.L. Religion and spirituality in adjustment following bereavement: An integrative review. *Death Stud.* **2008**, *32*, 703–736. [CrossRef]
57. Parente, N.T.; Ramos, D.G. The influence of spiritual-religious coping on the quality of life of Brazilian parents who have lost a child by homicide, suicide, or accident. *J. Spiritual. Ment. Health* **2020**, *22*, 216–239. [CrossRef]
58. Johnson, R.A. *Inner Work*; Harper San Francisco: San Francisco, CA, USA, 1986.
59. Tedeschi, R.G.; Calhoun, L. Posttraumatic Growth: A New Perspective on Psychotraumatology. *Psychiatr. Times* **2004**, *21*, 58–60. Available online: https://www.bu.edu/wheelock/files/2018/05/Article-Tedeschi-and-Lawrence-Calhoun-Posttraumatic-Growth-2014.pdf (accessed on 17 May 2022).
60. Moore, M.M.; Cerel, J.; Jobes, D.A. Fruits of trauma? Posttraumatic growth among suicide-bereaved parents. *Crisis* **2005**, *36*, 241. [CrossRef] [PubMed]

61. Lee, J.R.S.; Hunter, A.G.; Priolli, F.; Thornton, V.J. "Pray that I live to see another day": Religious and spiritual coping with vulnerability to violent injury, violent death, and homicide bereavement among young Black men. *J. Appl. Dev. Psychol.* **2020**, *70*, 101180. [CrossRef]
62. Jung, C.G. *The Archetypes and the Collective Unconscious*, 2nd ed.; Routledge: London, UK, 1996.
63. Darrell, A.; Pyszczynski, T. Terror management theory: Exploring the role of death in life. In *Denying Death: An Interdisciplinary Approach to Terror Management Theory*; Harvell, L.A., Nisbett, G.S., Eds.; Routledge: New York, NY, USA; London, UK, 2016; pp. 1–15.
64. Smith, A.; Joseph, S.; Nair, R.D. An interpretative phenomenological analysis of posttraumatic growth in adults bereaved by suicide. *J. Loss Trauma* **2011**, *16*, 413–430. [CrossRef]
65. Neimeyer, R.A.; Baldwin, S.A.; Gillies, J. Continuing bonds and reconstructing meaning: Mitigating complications in bereavement. *Death Stud.* **2006**, *30*, 715–738. [CrossRef]
66. Park, C.L.; Halifax, R.J. Religion and spirituality in adjusting to bereavement: Grief as a burden, grief as a gift. In *Grief and Bereavement in Contemporary Society*; Neimeyer, R.A., Harris, D.L., Winokuer, H.R., Thornton, G., Eds.; Routledge: New York, NY, USA; London, UK, 2021; pp. 355–363.
67. Aksoz-Efe, I.; Erdur-Baker, O.; Servaty-Seib, H. Death rituals, religious beliefs, and grief of Turkish women. *Death Stud.* **2018**, *42*, 579–592. [CrossRef]
68. Mitima-Verloop, H.B.; Mooren, T.T.M.; Boelen, B.A. Facilitating grief: An exploration of the function of funerals and rituals about grief reactions. *Death Stud.* **2021**, *45*, 735–745. [CrossRef]
69. Possick, C.; Buchbinder, E.; Etzion, L.; Yehoshua-Halevi, A.; Fishbein, S.; Nissim-Frankel, M. Reconstructing the loss: Hantzacha commemoration following the death of a spouse in a terror attack. *J. Loss Trauma* **2007**, *12*, 111–126. [CrossRef]
70. Scrutton, A.P. Grief, ritual and experiential knowledge: A philosophical perspective. In *Continuing Bonds in Bereavement*; Klass, D., Steffen, E.M., Eds.; Routledge/Taylor and Francis Group: New York, NY, USA, 2017; pp. 214–226.
71. Doehring, C. Searching for wholeness amidst traumatic grief: The role of spiritual practices that reveal compassion in embodied, relational, and transcendent ways. *Pastor. Psychol.* **2019**, *68*, 241–259. [CrossRef]
72. Balaswamy, S.; Richardson, V.; Price, C.A. Investigating patterns of social support used by widowers during bereavement. *JMS* **2004**, *13*, 67–84. [CrossRef]
73. Sedgwick, D. *The Wounded Healer: Counter-Transference from a Jungian Perspective*; Routledge: New York, NY, USA; London, UK, 1994.
74. Colucci, E.; Martin, G. Religion and spirituality along the suicidal path. *Suicide Life-Threat. Behav.* **2008**, *38*, 229–244. [CrossRef]
75. Solano, P.; Pizzorno, E.; Pompili, M.; Serafini, G.; Amore, M. Conceptualizations of suicide through time and socio-economic factors: A historical mini-review. *Ir. J. Psychol. Med.* **2018**, *35*, 75–86. [CrossRef] [PubMed]
76. Gailienė, D. Why are suicides so widespread in Catholic Lithuania? *Religions* **2018**, *9*, 71. [CrossRef]
77. Ališauskienė, M.; Samuilova, I. Modernizacija ir Religija Sovietinėje ir Posovietinėje Lietuvoje. (Modernization and Religion in Soviet and Post-Soviet Lithuania). *Cult. Soc. J. Social. Res.* **2011**, *2*, 67–81. Available online: https://etalpykla.lituanistikadb.lt/object/LT-LDB-0001:J.04~{}2011~{}1367180257082/J.04~{}2011~{}1367180257082.pdf (accessed on 17 May 2022).
78. Kopacz, M.S.; Silver, E.; Bossarte, R.M. A Position Article for Applying Spirituality to Suicide Prevention. *J. Spiritual. Ment. Health* **2014**, *16*, 133–146. [CrossRef]

International Journal of
Environmental Research and Public Health

MDPI

Article

The Spaces of Peer-Led Support Groups for Suicide Bereaved in Denmark and the Republic of Ireland: A Focus Group Study

Lisbeth Hybholt [1,2,*], Agnes Higgins [3], Niels Buus [4,5], Lene Lauge Berring [1,5], Terry Connolly [6], Annette Erlangsen [7,8,9,10] and Jean Morrissey [3]

1 Psychiatric Research Unit, Psychiatry Region Zealand, 4200 Slagelse, Denmark
2 Mental Health Services East, Psychiatry Region Zealand, 4000 Roskilde, Denmark
3 School of Nursing and Midwifery, Trinity College Dublin, D02 PN40 Dublin, Ireland
4 School of Nursing and Midwifery, Faculty of Medicine, Nursing and Health Sciences, Monash University, Clayton, VIC 3800, Australia
5 Department of Regional Health Research, University of Southern Denmark, 5000 Odense, Denmark
6 Friends of Suicide Loss (FOSL), D06 T685 Dublin, Ireland
7 Danish Research Institute for Suicide Prevention, Mental Health Centre Copenhagen, 2900 Hellerup, Denmark
8 Copenhagen Research Centre for Mental Health, 2900 Hellerup, Denmark
9 Department of Mental Health, Johns Hopkins Bloomberg School of Public Health, Baltimore, MD 21205, USA
10 Center of Mental Health Research, Australian National University, Canberra, ACT 0200, Australia
* Correspondence: lihy@regionsjaelland.dk

Abstract: Research has shown that people bereaved by suicide have an increased risk of mental health problems, suicidality and associated stigma, as well as higher rates of sick leave and increased rates of receiving disability pensions. Peer-led suicide bereavement support groups are perceived to enhance people's recovery by enabling shared experiences with others who are bereaved in similar circumstances. The aim of the research was to explore the viewpoints of participants living in Denmark and the Republic of Ireland on these peer-led support groups. This study focused on how the participants experienced being part of the peer-led support and how the participation affected them. We conducted four focus groups, two in Denmark and two in the Republic of Ireland, and two individual interviews, involving a total of 27 people bereaved by suicide. Data were analyzed thematically. The participants' experiences in the peer-led support groups were in contrast to what they had experienced in their daily lives. They felt alienated in daily living, as they believed that people could not comprehend their situation, which in turn led participants to search for people with similar experiences and join the peer-led support groups. While peer-led support groups may not be helpful for everyone, they created 'supportive spaces' that potentially affected the participants' recovery processes, from which we generated three key themes: (i) 'A transformative space', describing how the peer-led support group created a place to embrace change, learning and knowledge about suicide and suicide bereavement and the making of new connections; (ii) 'An alternative space for belonging and grieving', describing how the participants felt allowed to and could give themselves permission to grieve; and (iii) 'A conflicted space' describing how it was troublesome to belong to and participate in the peer-led support groups. In conclusion, despite the two cultural settings and different organizational approaches, the experiences were comparable. Peer-led support groups can, despite being a conflicted space for some, provide supportive spaces aiding the participants' recovery process.

Keywords: peer-support; postvention; suicide bereavement; qualitative research

Citation: Hybholt, L.; Higgins, A.; Buus, N.; Berring, L.L.; Connolly, T.; Erlangsen, A.; Morrissey, J. The Spaces of Peer-Led Support Groups for Suicide Bereaved in Denmark and the Republic of Ireland: A Focus Group Study. *Int. J. Environ. Res. Public Health* **2022**, *19*, 9898. https://doi.org/10.3390/ijerph19169898

Academic Editors: Karl Andriessen, Karolina Krysinska and Yossi Levi-Belz

Received: 19 July 2022
Accepted: 9 August 2022
Published: 11 August 2022

1. Introduction

The impact of death by suicide is extensive, and it has been described as a death like no other [1]. Many people struggle in the aftermath of suicide and are at an increased risk of prolonged grief [2]. Death by suicide is associated with troublesome emotions and feelings such as blame, guilt, emptiness and shame [3,4]. Grief after suicide can be considered a 'disenfranchised grief' [5], as the grieving person is often unable to publicly mourn the loss because of a societal reluctance to discuss death by suicide, which can increase people's feeling of isolation.

The World Health Organization [6] estimates that worldwide approximately 700,000 people die by suicide annually, with Andriessen et al.'s [7] meta-analysis suggesting that 1 in 20 people are affected by suicide in any given year and that 1 in 5 are affected during their lifetime. An American survey found that 51% of 1432 participants had experienced one or more suicides by someone they knew during their lifetime, out of which 35% indicated having suffered from moderate to severe emotional distress after the loss [8]. Being bereaved by suicide has been linked to social withdrawal, reduced psychological and somatic functioning, and an increased prevalence of mental health morbidities such as depression, anxiety disorders and psychiatric hospitalization [9–11]. In addition, bereaved relatives also have an elevated risk of suicide themselves when compared to those bereaved by homicide or other types of sudden death [12]. Prevalence rates of 38% and 8% have been reported for suicidal ideation and suicide attempt, respectively, among people bereaved by suicide [13]. Higher rates of sick leave and becoming the recipient of a disability pension have also been shown among those bereaved by suicide [14].

According to the dual-process model of coping with bereavement [15], navigating the bereavement process is a combination of an inner psychological experience and a social and cultural event. Bereavement may change a person's identity as they work on their new roles, relationships and circumstances, which may include a continuing bond with the deceased [15]. A Japanese study found that people bereaved by suicide conceptualize the aftermath as a process that moves from experiencing life as out of their control to living a redefined life. Two types of people were identified in the study: (i) 'dialoguers', who receive comfort through open dialogue, and (ii) 'mood changers', who tended to conceal their emotions and suffering [16]. Thus, it seems that the needs for support are likely to depend on the individual's way of dealing with the added challenges associated with suicide bereavement. Andriessen [17] (p. 43) defined postvention as 'activities that have been developed to facilitate recovery after suicide, and to prevent adverse outcomes including suicidal behavior'. One such activity is peer support groups, which are sometimes called mutual-support groups. Although definitions of peer support vary, peer support usually refers to support that is reciprocal in nature and occurs between people who share similar life experiences [18]. In addition to providing support, empathy, compassion, validation and a sense of belonging and community, peer groups are perceived to provide social spaces, which enables people to negotiate new understandings and meanings of their distress, allowing them to become active participants in their own recovery [19,20].

Mental health policies increasingly dictate that support services should engage with and involve people with lived experience in the design and delivery of services and interventions [18]. Studies that focus on peer-led suicide bereavement interventions are scarce. In a systematic review of peer-led postvention, Higgins et al. [21] identified 10 papers of low to moderate quality. Findings from this review suggested that peer-led suicide bereavement interventions potentially might improve participants' well-being, sense of connectedness, hope and grief by normalizing the loss, reducing self-blame, isolation and stigma. Nevertheless, some participants expressed dissatisfaction with the intervention or reported distress from listening to others' grief. Suicide bereavement support groups initiated by people with lived experiences are likely to be the primary resource for many bereaved people, and considering the limited evidence in this area, there is a need for more research [22,23]. Qualitative research can contribute towards important findings regarding participants' experiences of postvention, for instance, what is perceived as helpful or not [24]. In this study, we focused on the perceived usefulness of those peer-led groups in two countries, i.e., the Republic of Ireland and Denmark. The analogue assessment allowed for a comparison of similarities and differences across cultural settings, thus potentially being able to induce some universal features related to the experiences of participating in a peer-led support group.

Aim of This Study

The aim of this study was to explore participants' perspectives on peer-led support groups for people bereaved by suicide. In this paper, we focused on how the participants experienced being part of a peer-led support group in Denmark and the Republic of Ireland and how the peer-led support affected them.

2. Method

2.1. Study Design

We applied a qualitative descriptive design where focus groups and individual interviews were conducted to collect data for a reflexive thematic analysis. A qualitative descriptive design was selected to address first-person perspectives of people with lived experiences and provide rich descriptions of their experiences [25]. Focus groups were chosen as they were considered the preferred method to facilitate the participants to share their experiences of being a member of a peer-led support group, and to provide insight into the participants' experiences and processes as a group member [26]. To enhance participation, individual interviews were offered to those who wished to participate but could not attend the focus group. A growing body of literature points towards the importance of patient and public involvement in the design and conduct of research [27]. The chairperson of the Irish organization 'Friends of Suicide Loss' initiated this research project, and representatives from the two organizations involved in the study provided feedback on the design and the formulation of the interview schedule.

2.2. Setting for the Postvention Services

Both the 'National Association for the Bereaved by Suicide' (NABS) in Denmark and the Irish organization 'Friends of Suicide Loss' (FOSL) were initiated by people bereaved by suicide, in Denmark in 2002 [28] and in the Republic of Ireland in 2015 [29]. The philosophy behind both organizations is underpinned by the belief that if people bereaved by suicide engage in dialogue with peers, it can support their grieving process. At the same time, those bereaved by suicide gain inspiration to move forward in their lives in a constructive way. Both organizations are underpinned by ground rules centering on confidentiality, respect and a non-judgmental approach. As both groups are not-for-profit organizations, they are supported economically through donations, fundraising and, in Denmark, by a small membership fee.

NABS provides a range of activities such as café evenings (open groups), where people meet, talk and share their experiences, peer-support via the telephone, walk and talk, access to books on relevant topics and weekend seminars/workshops with a focus on sharing experiences and learning how to help oneself. While people bereaved by suicide lead the work, professionals are invited to contribute to seminars/workshops. All activities are advertised in newsletters, on social media platforms such as Facebook, and on their website. Everybody can join in all activities without invitation or prior appointment, except for the seminars that need registration and a small payment.

FOSL provides a similar range of activities, such as coffee mornings, walk and talk, workshops, symposiums, conferences, hosting of 'International Survivors of Suicide Loss Day', access to a library on suicide bereavement for members, support via telephone, email and online platforms, outreach support to families, if needed, in their own homes and peer-led support group meetings. The core group, mainly long-term members, meets twice monthly for a period of two hours, and people are free to join, leave and re-join the group on an ongoing basis. The newly bereaved groups meet weekly and participate in a 6–10-week program. To join an FOSL group, the individual first contacts the named group 'organizer/facilitator', who meets with the person to discuss their expectations, provides information about the group format and ground rules, and jointly decides if the peer group is suitable for the person at that time.

2.3. Recruitment

Participant recruitment was based on purposive sampling focused on recruiting 'information-rich' participants [30], rather than a statistically representative sample. Inclusion criteria specified that participants had to (i) be over the age of 18, (ii) be bereaved by suicide within more than one year and (iii) have participated in peer-led support groups conducted by NABS in Demark or the Irish organization FOSL. Both organizations were involved in advertising the study through posts on social media. Potential participants contacted the research team directly or gave permission to the respective organizations to pass on their contact details. Following this, a member of the research team provided detailed written and oral information and subsequently answered any questions. Once all participants had their queries addressed, a date and time for the focus group was set.

2.4. Participants

In total, 27 people participated, 14 in Denmark and 13 in Ireland, with a gender mix of 8 men and 19 women. The participants' kinship to the deceased person varied and included children, siblings, partners and spouses (See Table 1). Five participants reported experiencing multiple losses by suicides. The duration of time since the bereavement varied from 1 to 44 years, with the majority being bereaved within the previous 10 years. Some participants had met through the activities in the organizations and thus knew each other before the focus groups. Members of the same family were allocated to separate focus groups. The participants had typically attended several of the activities described above, including support groups and self-help seminars/workshops. The Danish participants had attended NABS for a period ranging from 1 to 19 years and the Irish participants for a period from 1 to 5 years.

Table 1. The participants.

Participant	Male	Female	Loss of Child	Loss of Spouse/Partner	Loss of Sibling	Multiple Loss *
Denmark (n = 14)	4	10	7	5	2	4
Ireland (n = 13)	4	9	7	3	3	1
In all (n = 27)	8	19	14	8	5	5

* Multiple loss is in addition to the primary loss.

2.5. Focus Groups

In Denmark, two focus groups [26] were conducted face to face in hotel facilities. Due to COVID-19 restrictions in the Republic of Ireland at the time, two focus groups were conducted online on Microsoft Teams. The length of the focus groups was between 120 and 150 min. During the focus group, one of the facilitators made field notes of the interactions in the group. In Ireland, individual interviews were conducted via telephone (approx. 60 min each) with two people who were unable to participate in the online focus groups.

In Denmark, a senior researcher in psychiatric nursing (L.H.) and a research assistant facilitated the focus groups. In the Republic of Ireland, an assistant professor (J.M.) and a professor in mental health nursing (A.H.) conducted the focus groups. With the exception of the research assistant, all were Ph.D.-educated female researchers and from disciplinary backgrounds of mental health nursing, counselling and with extensive experience in qualitative research. Only the participants and facilitators were present. The researchers did not know the participants personally. All (both face to face and online) focus groups were audio-recorded, as well as the interviews. Data were collected in 2021.

The focus groups were guided by a schedule (see Supplementary Materials) developed by the researchers in consultation with representative members from the two organizations, NABS and FOSL. The goal was to stimulate dialogue and group interaction [26], and the interview schedule was mainly used as a reminder of relevant topics to address rather than as a protocol to be followed. The focus groups were opened with a brief round of introductions and a short input by the moderators on the format, including information on how data were stored, analyzed and published to protect confidentiality. All focus groups ended with a thank you and a reminder of the available support, including a follow-up telephone call from a research team member. The focus groups in Denmark were conducted in Danish, and professional translators were used to translate the interview schedule and the selected quotations used in this article. A Danish-speaking researcher (L.H.) reviewed all translations.

Overall, the conversation in the focus groups flowed freely, with the moderators only occasionally needing to engage to seek clarification. The way in which the participants described their experiences of participating in the peer-led support group was reflected in the focus groups, with people listening attentively to each other and ensuring everyone had space to speak uninterrupted. Participants sometimes assisted one another, finding words, and gently reminded each other if someone was going off track. Further, they mainly spoke from a personal or 'I-position', i.e., saying 'this is how it is for me', while being mindful that it may not be the same for others. When differences in opinion or experience were expressed, they did not judge others but used it as an opportunity to reflect on their own views and experiences.

2.6. Data Analysis

The focus groups and interviews were transcribed verbatim and analyzed using a reflexive thematic approach inspired by Braun and Clarke [31–33]. Reflexive thematic analysis was used to generate patterns of shared meaning across a qualitative dataset through a reflective and thoughtful engagement with the data [33]. The process of analysis was iterative, moving back and forth between reading and coding of the data, comparing codes across groups and countries, combined with dialogue among the research team to agree on generated themes. Over time, this emphasis changed as researchers explored their understanding of the data corpus and compared data across groups and countries. At the outset, the focus was on how participation in the peer-led support groups influenced recovery in the aftermath of the suicide loss. Later, the analytical emphasis was on the parts of the data corpus that focused on how the participants described the peer-led support groups as different spaces compared to other settings in their everyday life and how peer-led support affected them and their daily living.

Braun and Clarke's 6 phases [31] of analysis were merged into 4 phases according to the needs of our study, as detailed below.

2.6.1. Phase 1: Familiarizing Yourself with Your Data

The first phase involved letting members of the research team listen to the audio recordings, reading and re-reading the transcripts from their own country. LH, NB and LLB focused on the Danish transcriptions, and JM and AH revisited the Irish transcriptions. The emphasis was on sharing initial impressions and identifying potential meanings, patterns and codes. Once this was completed, both groups connected to discuss their developing ideas.

2.6.2. Phase 2: Generating Initial Coding

Data were coded in the temporal order of events, commencing with the experiences of suicide bereavement through to their experiences of the peer-led support groups. This was followed by the exploration of the participants' thinking and emotions in relation to the peer-led support groups and their impact. First, each group summarized its country's findings; then the groups came together to combine their findings and discuss differences and similarities across the two countries.

2.6.3. Phase 3: Focused Coding

In this phase, the focus was on the individual and collective activities/processes that had taken place in the peer-led support groups. Emphasis was placed on how people described and interpreted the activities, as well as what flowed from the activities within and outside the group. The coded data from each country were compared and summarized and formed the basis for the next dialogue in the research group.

2.6.4. Phase 4: Theme Identification

As an outcome of the dialogue, potential themes were discussed. At this stage, it was agreed to write memos on each theme and include selected quotations to illustrate the themes. Once completed, the research team once again scrutinized and discussed the similarities and differences emerging from the two cultural contexts and agreed on the final title of themes, including the representative quotations that exemplified them.

2.7. Ethical Considerations

In accordance with Danish legislation, the Danish Data Protection Agency (Reg-117-2020) and the regional research ethics committee (J.nr. 20-000013) were notified about the Danish arm of the study. The Irish arm of the study received ethical approval from the Faculty of Health Science Research Ethics Committee (FHSREC), Trinity College Dublin. The study adhered to the ethical principles of the Declaration of Helsinki [34]. Participation was informed and voluntary. Written consent was obtained from all participants. To ensure participants' well-being, a follow-up telephone call was made after the interviews. There were no reports of any negative effects. Due to data protection issues, the sharing of raw data across national borders was not permitted. The data are not publicly available due to the rules of the ethical committee. To protect the participants' confidentiality, we use pseudonyms in the quotations.

3. Results

Participants from both cultural settings, i.e., Denmark and the Republic of Ireland, described how their motivation for seeking peer-led support came from their encounters with people in their network and with professionals. They described how their social network had focused on the deceased person and on comforting them in the first period after the suicide. However, as time passed, they felt that being bereaved by suicide limited their sense of social connectedness and alienated them from others. They perceived a lack of understanding for their loss, emotions, reactions, situation and grief. They experienced a difference between 'us', who were bereaved by suicide, and 'others', who were not able to comprehend the depth of their pain. This affected their regular social interactions and resulted in different social sanctions, such as people avoiding them and trying to close down any conversation about grief or trying to find simple solutions. In essence, they perceived that people expected them to get over their grief and move on with their lives, which made them feel uncomfortable expressing their emotions.

Most of the participants sought support from different health professionals, professional-led support groups or religious groups. There were mixed views about the support from these sources. While some acknowledged how the professionals' theoretical insight helped them understand their own and their relatives' grief processes, others did not find the professional support helpful. For example, Amine stated *'I went to see a counsellor, I only went twice because she just didn't understand what I was going through'* (Irish focus group 1). They all longed for community and a sense of togetherness, which they did not find in encounters with laypeople or professionals; hence, they searched for peers to help them address their grief and to handle the aftermath of suicide. The following three themes were generated from the thematic analysis, which described the experiences of the bereaved in the peer-led support group and how it affected them: (i) 'A transformative space', (ii) 'An alternative space for belonging and grieving' and (iii) 'A conflicted space'. The themes were identified in both cultural settings. We use the term space, as it was a term used by the participants, which not only represented the physical reality that existed in the support group, but it also captured the interpersonal space that participants created and held for each other. We found that this space existed equally via Zoom meetings as well as face-to-face and as such became a prominent concept in our analysis.

3.1. A Transformative Space

The peer-led support group was perceived as a transformative space because it enabled participants to process the change and find new ways to come to terms with their grief. It also helped them handle the expectations and reactions of people in their social network 'outside' the support group. For example, Alexis describes how she often had to take on a role in daily living, pretending she was doing fine, but felt devastated inside:

> *Alexis: I think I would be able to get an Oscar statuette for best acting performance. Because you go on and live and manage your life. You manage your life and you play some character, but in the peer group the masks drop completely. They are not needed at all among peers (Danish focus group 2).*

The peer-support group was described as an empowering space where participants could disclose and display their grief, which helped them handle societal expectations in their daily lives. They learned to understand their grief by listening to and comparing themselves with the narratives of peers, for example, how they dealt with needs and challenges in the aftermath of suicide. They learnt not only how to process their grief by re-telling their own stories, reading books and listening to podcasts recommended by the group, but also how to keep the memory of the deceased alive without being overwhelmed by it. The peer-led support group enabled the participants to learn about themselves, their situation and how they could regain a meaningful life with the bereavement as a lifelong companion. In the following quotation, Mary described how she recognized her own feelings when listening to the stories of peers who enabled her to believe and see recovery as a possibility:

> *Mary: The main thing I found was that here were other people who were at different stages, some were further down the road, and they were surviving. Because I couldn't figure out how to survive I didn't know how long this freaking out was going to last. So, when I went to the group, other people were managing it, they were back in their jobs doing various things, and as I listened and heard their stories, I realized that they were feeling the same things I was feeling. And they were managing and it kind of gave me courage and hope (Irish focus group 1).*

The mutual sharing activated new reflections and insights, which broadened their understanding of themselves and others. By comparing themselves with their peers, they identified similarities and differences in situations, reactions, feelings and actions. Those who told their story processed their grief by narrating their own situation and by listening to the narration of others; this initiated reflections that influenced how they handled and understood their reactions and situation in daily living. The participants described how every time they shared experiences in the group, it became a little easier to bear the grief in general. For example, in this dialogue, the participants talk about how being in the support group prompted reflection and action:

> *Kimberly: [...] Participation in activities affects you.*
>
> *Clare: Yes, it affects in the sense that it starts things in yourself in terms of what you are going through. You hearing others describe how they deal with matters or have read something or the like, which may be just one small sentence that starts something in you. Then you begin contemplating 'Well, yeah, that is one way to deal with it—perhaps I should try and find out something'.*
>
> *Taylor: Some people are better at wording their feelings. I mean something has been obscure to me, and then I listen to someone who just states it so clearly.*
>
> *Clare: Like they hold the missing piece of the puzzle. (Danish focus group 2)*

Listening to others telling and re-telling their stories of their loss validated their own experiences. In addition, telling and retelling of their own story taught them to be more empathetic to themselves and others and gave them a sense of hope and strength to live with the loss. The support and learning from the peer-led support group empowered participants to share with people outside the group, thus reducing the feeling of alienation, even though they would not be able to fully understand the bereavement process:

> *Helen: I was so devastated, but then coming back 2 or 3 years later I am so much stronger. I have told my story over and over again in the group and then one day where I was, I was able to talk openly and I didn't mind if I cried. I was able to. And because the way I could handle it they appreciated as well. You know they had compassion with me as well. But it was the group that, it was like a family behind you, you had the strength, do you understand? (Irish focus group 2)*

The retelling over and over of their story gave them the opportunity and ability to find the language to express their inner world; as the story was retold over and over, it began to change, and they were able to find the words and the strength to express themselves. The support group community also had the potential to reach outside the group setting, as peers from the support group offered support and comfort, for example, by sending a text message on anniversaries or an open invitation to make a phone call or take a walk when needed. Some participants described how, as a result, they had established a network of peers who became part of their private daily lives. The nature and impact of the support provided is captured in Rowan's narrative:

> *Rowan: I have received a lot of help besides the group. Several peers said I could always call or suggested we can do this and that, which I have used a lot. For example, my husband jumped from a bridge, and I did not ever, never want to get near it, but then a peer said let's go for a walk to see the bridge. She literarily held my hand when we went to look at what turned out to be a complete harmless bridge ... and it was such a relief. I do not know what I had imagined; that there would be a huge sign, but it was just a bridge. I have received a lot of help from the members outside the group sessions. (Danish focus group 1)*

The community in the support group had the potential to transform the participants' understanding of themselves, of others and their social conditions supporting them in regaining life in the aftermath of the suicide loss.

3.2. An Alternative Space for Belonging and Grieving

The peer-led support group as an alternative space for belonging and grieving described how the participants felt, whereby they could give themselves permission to grieve and mourn within the group. The feeling of belonging was based on the bereavement by suicide as a common denominator, making them feel a mutual understanding, as opposed to their experiences from other settings. Gale described this in his first meeting with peers:

> *Gale: I picked myself up and decided I had to go to the next 'walk and talk', and all of a sudden, it made a real difference because they (peers) were someone who I could talk to; they understood. It did not sound out there at all—like others had thought prior to this. 'You just need to hit the restart button' and 'get back on the horse' and whatever else people say. I even have a perfectly pleasant elderly woman for a neighbor who decided she would help me sign up for dance classes. This way I would have some positive experiences and maybe even meet a new girlfriend.*
>
> *Ingrid: Oh no. [Sympathetic laughter in the group].*
>
> *Gale: After a couple of months, right. [laughs himself].*
>
> *Taylor: You simply needed to take a dance class and then everything would magically be okay again. [Sympathetic laughter in the group].*
>
> *Ingrid: That is just how things are.*

Gale: Exactly.

Ingrid: However, they do mean well.

Gale: And I know that. (Danish focus group 2)

The participants in the above interaction, by their sympathetic laughter and supportive statements, also reveal how they recognized Gale's experience of being advised to get over the grief; while well-intended, it was out of place from an inside perspective. Participants described how they experienced an instant mutual understanding and a shared language by being with peers. In contrast to other settings, they did not have to explain or defend how they felt on a given day:

> *Mary: When I came across the group, it was such an overwhelming thing to be with people. I didn't have to explain [to them] if I was doing well or having a good day. And on another day, I didn't have to explain that I still missed my daughter or that I am still heartbroken. And if I wanted to talk about her or not, they knew. It was like they did away with the word 'should', so it was complete acceptance [of members within the group]. (Irish focus group 1)*

The alternative space for belonging and grieving was created and sustained by group actions and rituals, for example, lighting a candle of confidentiality, mentioning group ground rules, cozy gatherings and a round of introductions where all participants presented themselves as bereaved by suicide. They experienced the group as a non-judgmental space, which confirmed that everything could be shared; no feelings, reactions or thoughts were wrong or unacceptable. Further, it was also a space that provided the opportunity to openly deal with the grief, which they often had to conceal in their daily lives. This ability to speak freely within the group and discuss the 'undiscussable' made it possible to strengthen their identity as bereaved by suicide in their ordinary lives, even though the pain of the loss was continuously present:

> *Ashley: When you are in that space [the support group] where you have the opportunity to deal with your grief, where you can have your grief and you enter this space of grief. Not that you put on a facade, but you simply do not have room for your grief in a working life—or at least I do not in mine [...] To me, what has been important is that you are active with the organization, and then you sort of withdraw and go back to your 'normal' life where your grief is a bit of a taboo. Here you need to live life the way you always have and then kind of be allowed to return to your grief. It is a way to bring ... to allow myself to grieve and mourn and process my grief in this space [...] (Danish focus group 1).*

The group provided a space where people could share thoughts, feelings and challenges without fear of judgment or stigmatization, as the conventional expectations around grief in other contexts were suspended. As a result, participants felt safe to tell and re-tell their stories to strangers with different backgrounds, genders, ages, etc., without feeling the need to explain or censor themselves for fear of burdening others:

> *Kate: You could cry if you wanted to, it was such a relief that you could cry and that it didn't make other people uncomfortable. I couldn't grieve in front of my husband, not because he isn't wonderful, he is, but if he was having a better day, no way was I going to tell him I am having a rough day and drag him down (Irish focus group 2).*

They inherently trusted their thoughts, reactions and feelings to be bearable for their peers, but our findings also contained rare examples of the opposite. For example, a participant mentioned she also was grateful for the death of her beloved one, because she had learned some profound lessons about life. Another participant reacted to this statement, as perceiving the loss as something 'appreciative' was not something she could understand. The first participant tried to repair the conflict by saying that it was her personal experience and perhaps verbalizing or mentioning to the group may have been inappropriate:

Max: [...] I thank [name of deceased] for starting a process for me. I think there is a gift for us in what happens, regardless of what comes. It is my conviction, with reservations for all the losses and all the grief.

Vinnie: I haven't exactly figured out what I should learn.

Ashley: It can take time to find it. [Laughs in disbelief].

Max: Well I don't think of it as something to rush and there is also a difference in exactly what you lose.

[Silence]

Vinnie: Well, no matter what, it was still something they decided ... I guess the relationship is a bit subordinate in my eyes, still, I don't understand ... What am I to learn from this?

Max: It may not have been appropriately said by me.

Vinnie: Well, I don't know.

Max: It is just what I experience in relation to myself.

Vinnie: Yes, and I am not saying that it is wrong. I'm just saying I haven't found that common thread.

Max: No no.

Vinnie: I don't know if I ever will. (Danish focus group 1).

Later, group members acknowledged they also thought they had acquired new perspectives, but highlighted that it had come at a high price.

The peer-led support group was described as a unique space where the participants not only had the possibility to focus on themselves as bereaved by suicide but were also allowed to disclose how they felt. This was an invaluable alternative to other contexts in their daily living.

3.3. A Conflicted Space

Some participants experienced participating and belonging to the group as troublesome. They deeply appreciated and needed the connectedness and shared experience, but at the same time felt discomfort in the encounter with peers, which was also a hardship. For example, the participants had never desired to be a part of the bereavement group. It was not their choice to become bereaved by suicide. The experience created a feeling of being distant from people in their usual social network, which led them to seek connections with peers. Meeting peers was described as both pleasant and unpleasant. On the one hand, the peer community was perceived as a valuable and helpful space where they felt comforted and could express their true feelings about the tragedy. On the other hand, it was a space that they did not want to belong to:

Paul: I think for me the main thing of the group is there's a sort of, it's a difficult thing to say because it is a group, you don't really, you wish you weren't in, but there's a comfort in it, when you meet people and you're talking to people. There's a comfort in it because you feel you can sort of relax and you can say you know what you want. (Irish focus group 1)

However, being confronted with other people's grief could also be discomforting, as this activated reflections on their own grief. They felt it was necessary to enter the space of the support group, but they were occasionally tempted to avoid coming to meetings, as described by Ashley:

Ashley: Leading up to a meeting, I could ask myself if maybe I was coming down with something [laugh] or the like. Because you need to walk in and out of that room of grief, and sometimes it is simply easier just not to walk in in the first place. Coming up with reasons not to go is easy, but you ... you need to be able to take part in it [...

> *]. Otherwise, I might stay on the surface and make sure everything else runs smoothly, without actually noticing myself all that much. So, it is good to have a space where I have to take stock of . . . of me (Danish focus group 1)*

Indeed, some participants spoke of how they had to take a break from the group for shorter or longer periods because the stories from peers at times could be too hard to take in:

> *Clare: That was actually one of the reasons I stopped joining the group's sessions; it began to take up too much and my cup ran over almost. Both with other people's grief . . . and it was . . . it was not that I did not gain anything from hearing about how others deal with matters and such, but it also started things in me that was hard to handle (Danish focus group, 2).*

The fact that group membership was not time-limited and that people had the freedom to step out for periods of time, helped participants feel they were in control. It was also good to know that the other participants fully understood if one was unable to participate because of obligations in their daily living or lack of energy. This freedom also ensured that participants actively chose to step into the grief when they were present in the peer-led support group. In addition, knowing that they could always return to a welcoming group without explanation or justification was viewed as an important lifeline.

The determination to participate despite the discomfort and hardship was driven by the valuable contribution the peer group made. Participating in the peer-led support group can be understood as a strong driving force towards making room for and learning to live with the new conditions of life and reclaiming viability in daily living, despite the conflicts embedded in the space.

4. Discussion

In this study, those bereaved by suicide described their experiences of being part of a peer-led support group and how it affected them, mostly in contrast to encounters with non-bereaved individuals, both laypeople and professionals. The findings do not imply that all professionals were unhelpful; however, they do emphasize the particularity and strength of being with peers. Despite being a conflicted space for some, the peer-led support group provided a distinct and legitimate space for grieving and belonging and a transformative space supporting learning, change and finding ways to process their grief and handle the expectations of people in social interactions in everyday life. Although the themes were presented separately, in reality, they are interconnected, as the experience of the group as 'an alternative space for belonging and grieving' was essential for the experience of the peer-led group as 'a transformative space'. The experience of gaining and learning through the group also made it worth overcoming feelings that it was a conflictual space to participate in.

Participants not only had to deal with the loss of a loved one; being bereaved by suicide created a rupture in their sense of belonging with their social network within their community. They felt alienated, as their grief did not fit with the expectations of their surroundings. As summarized in a systematic review [4], those bereaved by suicide often report feelings of shame and guilt, which complicates the process of grieving and affects their ability to grieve openly. In order to avoid negative reactions, some bereaved resorted to isolation and concealed their thoughts and emotions. The awkwardness, discomfort and embarrassment experienced in social settings resulted in inadequate social support, and the bereaved found themselves alone in their grief [4]. In this study, participants reported a strong consensus about the 'us' and 'others' as they perceived especially non-bereaved laypeople and some professionals as being unable to understand their profound grief as a new condition of life. According to the theory of belonging, human beings have a universal basic need to form and maintain at least a minimum quantity of interpersonal relationships and that people are naturally driven toward establishing and sustaining a state of belonging [35]. We found that participants perceived a special connectedness, sense of belonging and mutual understanding in the non-judgmental environment of the peer-led support group. This aligns with previous findings that loneliness and stigma from social networks and community encouraged those bereaved by suicide to search for a safe, understanding and non-judgmental environment with peers [21]. The participants' search for a peer community may be viewed as a means to compensate for the lack of support in their social network. This is in line with the study by Griffin et al. [36] that linked improved wellbeing and a reduction in somatic grief reactions after community-based peer support to the participant's descriptions of the group as a safe space to talk and that provides a sense of belonging and connection.

Concealable stigmatized identities are aspects of the self or characteristics that are socially devalued with negative stereotypes, which can be hidden for others, such as bereavement by suicide. People with stigmatized identities often use concealment in order to increase social belonging and reduce personal experiences of discrimination. However, active concealment can also hinder their feeling of connectedness and well-being [37]. Levi-Belz and Lev-Ari [38,39] found that self-disclosure among suicide-bereaved individuals increased feelings of belonging and perceived social support, which in turn reduced complicated grief and facilitated post-traumatic growth and recovery. The findings of the current study indicated that it was important for the participants to be allowed to grieve in their own way when in the peer-led support group. People with concealable stigmatized identities have to determine in which contexts they conceal or disclose, both having benefits and disadvantages, as it is likely to impact the social interactions, sense of belonging and physical and psychological well-being [37]. Our findings indicated that the participants often preferred to withhold disclosure as it helped them focus on usual activities in daily living and live up to the expectations of their social network. However, being in the support group also empowered them to share their grief with relatives or non-bereaved outside the group, thus reducing the feeling of alienation. This is in line with previous findings linking peer-led suicide bereavement interventions to reduced feelings of stigma [21]. However, the participants in our study described daily living wherein they often concealed their true state of mind from people in their surroundings, due to adverse reactions. Disclosing personal and emotional information can benefit the grieving process [40]. The participants primarily used the peer-led support group to disclose their grief and described it as helpful, as they felt they became better at handling and adjusting to the expectations of their wider community. Thus, they did not necessarily explore opportunities for support in their social network; some participants resigned to the fact that non-bereaved people would not understand and only revealed their true state of mind when in the peer support group. Concealment may protect from occasions of prejudice and discrimination, but it can also limit social support. Disclosure can increase social support, but disclosing to unsupportive others may also lead to psychological distress [37]. Our findings indicate that although the participants found social support inside the group, some participants found the group had enabled them to talk more openly to others outside, but they still longed for more attention and support in their social network.

Limitations and Strengths

This study has some limitations: the two organizations differed in the kind of activities they offered and had different organizational structures. FOSL is governed by a central board, whereas NABS consists of a nationwide umbrella organization for many local organizations that are governed by local volunteers. Although this complicated our comparisons, the analysis revealed similarities in the associations' core principles and in the experiences from the participants.

In addition to recall bias, social desirability bias may have also been an issue, as data were collected by focus groups. Given the sensitive nature of the research topic area, participants may have consciously or unconsciously concealed some of their impressions. Further, the focus groups were conducted online and face to face, respectively, in the Republic of Ireland and Denmark. In FOSL, the participants were already using online support groups as they had adjusted to the COVID-19 situation. Therefore, representatives from FOSL deemed it possible to carry out the focus groups online as well. In the Danish setting, the representatives from NABS stressed that the focus groups should be face to face, as their members had no experience in online meetings. The different formats might have influenced the findings. Further, the relatively small sample size and the fact that participants were self-selecting may also have biased the findings. All participants were positive and grateful users of a peer-led organization, implying that experiences of those who chose to leave the group were not represented. Thus, negative or challenging aspects of participating in a peer-support group, such as the pain of listening to people's stories, feelings of being burdensome or re-traumatized, and the lack of a group facilitator [41,42], may be under-represented. Still, the findings revealed that participating in a peer-led support group could evoke conflicts, suggesting a need for further research into people who do not engage with or have left the peer support group would be useful for both organizations. There is also a need for further research investigating how stigma can be reduced outside the peer-led support groups. The overall findings reflected the experiences of people within two specific communities and may not apply to or fit other settings. However, the cross-cultural similarities related to participation and experienced effects of the peer-led support group were underlined, as the findings correlated with the findings from a scoping review including studies from five additional countries (USA, Canada, England, Italy and Sweden) [21].

It was a strength that the participants were purposefully sampled to represent people who engaged in peer-led support groups, and thus they had experiences with the subject under investigation and could therefore share how they perceived participating in peer-led support groups and how it affected them. Another strength was that the trustworthiness of the qualitative, descriptive research's version of rigor addresses credibility, confirmability, dependability, transferability and reflexivity applied [25,43]. Table 2 provides a summary of the provisions made by the researchers in this study to address these issues.

Table 2. Trustworthiness of data.

Quality Criterion	Provisions Made by Research Team
Credibility is the confidence in the findings	• The focus group schedule was developed in collaboration between researchers and experts by experience • Participants were heterogeneous (gender, duration of contact with the groups, different kinship to the deceased, diverse cultures and backgrounds) • The moderator had contact with each of the participants before the focus groups and initiated a trusting relationship • Data were systematically compared across groups and countries
Confirmability is the extent to which the findings of a study are shaped by the respondents and not researcher bias, motivation or interest	• Analysis was completed by more than one person and interpretations were agreed upon collectively • Codes and themes were discussed between researchers to minimize interpretative bias • Presented data extracts included examples of exceptions/variations of the themes • Lengthy quotes were used to demonstrate and support interpretations
Dependability is the description of the conduct of the study, including changes to make procedures and processes clear	• The description of the study's methods to enable replication • Detailed descriptions of the coding process included the changing perspectives in the interpretive process
Transferability is about the degree to which findings have applicability in other contexts by making the context explicit and descriptive	• Purposive sampling included people bereaved by suicide that had participated in peer-led support groups • Descriptions of research setting, peer-led interventions and participant profiles were provided • Data extracts included rich descriptions of the themes with direct quotes
Reflexivity is critical self-reflection of how the researchers' social background, assumptions, positioning and behavior may have affected the research process	• Care was taken to work reflexively by continually questioning interpretations, assumptions and positions • The analytical process was based on an ongoing dialogue between members of the research team who had different background and expertise

5. Conclusions

Despite being placed in two different cultural settings, i.e., Denmark and the Republic of Ireland, and different organizational approaches, comparable experiences were reported by people bereaved by suicide in the peer-led support groups. Although peer-led support groups may not be helpful for all bereaved by suicide, they can provide supportive spaces that aid the participants' recovery process. In terms of facilitating recovery, peer-led support groups may aid people bereaved by suicide process the grief and cope with societal expectations and act as a vehicle to help circumvent the problem of stigma surrounding suicide.

Supplementary Materials: The following supporting information can be downloaded at: https://www.mdpi.com/article/10.3390/ijerph19169898/s1, File S1: The schedule for the focus groups.

Author Contributions: Conceptualization, L.H., A.H., N.B., L.L.B., T.C., A.E. and J.M.; Formal analysis, L.H., A.H., N.B., L.L.B. and J.M.; Funding acquisition, L.H.; Investigation, L.H., A.H. and J.M.; Methodology, L.H., A.H., N.B., L.L.B., T.C. and J.M.; Project administration, L.H. and J.M.; Writing—Original draft, L.H., A.H., N.B., L.L.B. and J.M.; Writing—Review and editing, L.H., A.H., N.B., L.L.B., T.C., A.E. and J.M. All authors have read and agreed to the published version of the manuscript.

Funding: Region Zealand Health Scientific Research Foundation: Denmark. Funding number: A575.

Institutional Review Board Statement: The study was conducted according to the guidelines of the Declaration of Helsinki. In accordance with Danish legislation, the Danish Data Protection Agency (Reg-117-2020) and the regional research ethics committee (J.nr. 20-000013) were notified about the Danish arm of the study. The Irish arm of the study was approved by the Faculty of Health Science Research Ethics Committee (FHSREC), Trinity College Dublin.

Informed Consent Statement: Informed consent was obtained from all the participants involved in the study.

Data Availability Statement: The data are not publicly available due to the rules of the ethical committee.

Conflicts of Interest: The authors declare no conflict of interest.

References

1. Feigelman, B.; Feigelman, W. Surviving After Suicide Loss: The Healing Potential of Suicide Survivor Support Groups. *Illn. Crisis Loss* **2008**, *16*, 285–304. [CrossRef]
2. Young, I.T.; Iglewicz, A.; Glorioso, D.; Lanouette, N.; Seay, K.; Ilapakurti, M.; Zisook, S. Suicide bereavement and complicated grief. *Dialogues Clin. Neurosci.* **2012**, *14*, 177–186. [CrossRef]
3. Shields, C.; Kavanagh, M.; Russo, K. A Qualitative Systematic Review of the Bereavement Process Following Suicide. *Omega J. Death Dying* **2017**, *74*, 426–454. [CrossRef] [PubMed]
4. Evans, A.; Abrahamson, K. The Influence of Stigma on Suicide Bereavement: A Systematic Review. *J. Psychosoc. Nurs. Ment. Health Serv.* **2020**, *58*, 21–27. [CrossRef]
5. Corr, C.A. Enhancing the Concept of Disenfranchised Grief. *OMEGA-J. Death Dying* **1999**, *38*, 1–20. [CrossRef]
6. World Health Organisation. *Suicide Worldwide in 2019: Global Health Estimates*; World Health Organization: Geneva, Switzerland, 2021.
7. Andriessen, K.; Rahman, B.; Draper, B.; Dudley, M.; Mitchell, P.B. Prevalence of exposure to suicide: A meta-analysis of population-based studies. *J. Psychiatr. Res.* **2017**, *88*, 113–120. [CrossRef]
8. Feigelman, W.; Cerel, J.; McIntosh, J.L.; Brent, D.; Gutin, N. Suicide exposures and bereavement among American adults: Evidence from the 2016 General Social Survey. *J. Affect. Disord.* **2018**, *227*, 1–6. [CrossRef]
9. Hanschmidt, F.; Lehnig, F.; Riedel-Heller, S.G.; Kersting, A. The stigma of suicide survivorship and related consequences-A systematic review. *PLoS ONE* **2016**, *11*, e0162688. [CrossRef] [PubMed]
10. Maple, M.; Cerel, J.; Sanford, R.; Pearce, T.; Jordan, J. Is Exposure to Suicide Beyond Kin Associated with Risk for Suicidal Behavior? A Systematic Review of the Evidence. *Suicide Life Threat. Behav.* **2017**, *47*, 461–474. [CrossRef]
11. Pitman, A.; Osborn, D.; King, M.; Erlangsen, A. Effects of suicide bereavement on mental health and suicide risk. *Lancet Psychiatry* **2014**, *1*, 86–94. [CrossRef]
12. Hamdan, S.; Berkman, N.; Lavi, N.; Levy, S.; Brent, D. The Effect of Sudden Death Bereavement on the Risk for Suicide. *Crisis* **2020**, *41*, 214–224. [CrossRef] [PubMed]
13. McDonnell, S.; Flynn, S.; Shaw, J.; Smith, S.; McGale, B.; Hunt, I.M. Suicide bereavement in the UK: Descriptive findings from a national survey. *Suicide Life-Threat. Behav.* **2022**. [CrossRef] [PubMed]

14. Erlangsen, A.; Runeson, B.; Bolton, J.W.; Wilcox, H.C.; Forman, J.; Krogh, J.; Shear, M.K.; Nordentoft, M.; Conwell, Y. Association between spousal suicide and mental, physical, and social health outcomes: A longitudinal and nationwide register-based study. *JAMA Psychiatry* **2017**, *74*, 456–464. [CrossRef] [PubMed]
15. Stroebe, M.; Schut, H. The dual process model of coping with bereavement: Rationale and description. *Death Stud.* **1999**, *23*, 197–224. [CrossRef]
16. Kasahara-Kiritani, M.; Ikeda, M.; Yamamoto-Mitani, N.; Kamibeppu, K. Regaining my new life: Daily lives of suicide-bereaved individuals. *Death Stud.* **2017**, *41*, 447–454. [CrossRef]
17. Andriessen, K. Can postvention be prevention? *Crisis* **2009**, *30*, 43–47. [CrossRef]
18. World Health Organization. *Guidance on Community Mental Health Services: Promoting Person-Centred and Rights-Based Approaches*; World Health Organization: Geneva, Switzerland, 2021.
19. Mcintosh, J.L.; Bolton, I.; Andriessen, K.; Campbell, F. History of survivor support. In *Postvention in Action: The International Handbook of Suicide Bereavement Support*; Andreissen, K., Krysinska, K., Grad, O.T., Eds.; Hogrefe Publishing: Göttingen, Germany, 2017; pp. 101–116.
20. Murphy, R.; Higgins, A. The complex terrain of peer support in mental health: What does it all mean? *J. Psychiatr. Ment. Health Nurs.* **2018**, *25*, 441–448. [CrossRef]
21. Higgins, A.; Hybholt, L.; Meuser, O.A.; Cook, J.E.; Downes, C.; Morrissey, J. Scoping Review of Peer-Led Support for People Bereaved by Suicide. *Int. J. Environ. Res. Public Health* **2022**, *19*, 3485. [CrossRef]
22. Maple, M.; Poštuvan, V.; McDonnell, S. Editorial. Progress in Postvention. A Call to a Focused Future to Support Those Exposed to Suicide. *Cris. J. Cris. Interv. Suicide Prev.* **2019**, *40*, 379–382. [CrossRef]
23. Andriessen, K.; Krysinska, K.; Kõlves, K.; Reavley, N. Suicide Postvention Service Models and Guidelines 2014–2019: A Systematic Review. *Front Psychol.* **2019**, *10*, 2677. [CrossRef]
24. Andriessen, K.; Krysinska, K.; Hill, N.T.M.; Reifels, L.; Robinson, J.; Reavley, N.; Pirkis, J. Effectiveness of interventions for people bereaved through suicide: A systematic review of controlled studies of grief, psychosocial and suicide-related outcomes. *BMC Psychiatry* **2019**, *19*, 49. [CrossRef]
25. Bradshaw, C.; Atkinson, S.; Doody, O. Employing a Qualitative Description Approach in Health Care Research. *Glob. Qual. Nurs. Res.* **2017**, *4*. [CrossRef]
26. Bloor, M.; Frankland, J.; Thomas, M.; Robson, K. *Focus Groups in Social Research*; SAGE Publications Ltd.: Thousand Oaks, CA, USA, 2001.
27. Andriessen, K.; Castelli Dransart, D.A.; Cerel, J.; Maple, M. Current Postvention Research and Priorities for the Future. *Crisis* **2017**, *38*, 202–206. [CrossRef]
28. Erlangsen, A.; Fleischer, E. Denmark–Support for the Bereaved by Suicide. In *Postvention in Action: The International Handbook of Suicide Bereavement Support*; Andriessen, K., Krysinska, K., Grad, O.T., Eds.; Hogrefe Verlag: Göttingen, Germany, 2017; Chapter 32; pp. 320–324.
29. Friends of Suicide Loss. Available online: https://friendsofsuicideloss.ie (accessed on 7 July 2022).
30. Patton, M.Q. *Qualitative Research & Evaluation Methods: Integrating Theory and Practice*, 4th ed.; SAGE Publications, Inc.: Thousand Oaks, CA, USA, 2015.
31. Braun, V.; Clarke, V. Using thematic analysis in psychology. *Qual. Res. Psychol.* **2006**, *3*, 77–101. [CrossRef]
32. Braun, V.; Clarke, V. Reflecting on reflexive thematic analysis. *Qual. Res. Sport. Exerc. Health* **2019**, *11*, 589–597. [CrossRef]
33. Braun, V.; Clarke, V. One size fits all? What counts as quality practice in (reflexive) thematic analysis? *Qual. Res. Psychol.* **2021**, *18*, 328–352. [CrossRef]
34. World Medical Association. World Medical Association Declaration of Helsinki: Ethical Principles for Medical Research Involving Human Subjects. *JAMA* **2013**, *310*, 2191–2194. [CrossRef]
35. Baumeister, R.F.; Leary, M.R. The need to belong: Desire for interpersonal attachments as a fundamental human motivation. *Psychol. Bull.* **1995**, *117*, 497–529. [CrossRef]
36. Griffin, E.; O'Connell, S.; Ruane-McAteer, E.; Corcoran, P.; Arensman, E. Psychosocial Outcomes of Individuals Attending a Suicide Bereavement Peer Support Group: A Follow-Up Study. *Int. J. Environ. Res. Public Health* **2022**, *19*, 4076. [CrossRef]
37. Camacho, G.; Reinka, M.A.; Quinn, D.M. Disclosure and concealment of stigmatized identities. *Curr. Opin. Psychol.* **2020**, *31*, 28–32. [CrossRef]
38. Levi-Belz, Y. Stress-Related Growth among Suicide Survivors: The Role of Interpersonal and Cognitive Factors. *Arch. Suicide Res.* **2015**, *19*, 305–320. [CrossRef] [PubMed]
39. Levi-Belz, Y.; Lev-Ari, L. Attachment Styles and Posttraumatic Growth Among Suicide-Loss Survivors. *Crisis* **2018**, *40*, 186–195. [CrossRef] [PubMed]
40. Levi-Belz, Y.; Lev-Ari, L. "Let's Talk About It": The Moderating Role of Self-Disclosure on Complicated Grief over Time among Suicide Survivors. *Int. J. Environ. Res. Public Health.* **2019**, *16*, 3740. [CrossRef]
41. Sanford, R.L.; Cerel, J.; Frey, L.M. Survivor of Suicide Loss Support Group Facilitators: Do Peers and Professionals Differ? *Soc. Work Groups.* **2018**, *41*, 306–322. [CrossRef]
42. Feigelman, B.; Feigelman, W. Suicide survivor support groups: Comings and goings, Part II. *Illn. Cris Loss.* **2011**, *19*, 165–185. [CrossRef]
43. Guba, E.G.; Lincoln, Y.S. *Fourth Generation Evaluation*; Sage: Newbury Park, CA, USA, 2003.

International Journal of
Environmental Research and Public Health

MDPI

Article

Loss-Related Characteristics and Symptoms of Depression, Prolonged Grief, and Posttraumatic Stress Following Suicide Bereavement

Raphaela Grafiadeli [1,*], Heide Glaesmer [2] and Birgit Wagner [1]

[1] Department of Psychology, Medical School Berlin, Rüdesheimerstraße 50, 14197 Berlin, Germany
[2] Department of Medical Psychology and Medical Sociology, Medical Faculty, University of Leipzig, Philipp-Rosenthal-Str. 55, 04103 Leipzig, Germany
* Correspondence: raphaela.grafiadeli@medicalschool-berlin.de

Abstract: (1) Background: The aim of the present study was to examine symptom classes of major depressive disorder (MDD), prolonged grief disorder (PGD), and posttraumatic stress disorder (PTSD) in a sample of suicide-bereaved individuals, while accounting for loss-related characteristics. (2) Methods: A latent class analysis was conducted to identify classes of the suicide bereaved, sharing symptom profiles, in a German suicide-bereaved sample (N = 159). (3) Results: Our analyses revealed three main classes: a resilient class (16%), a class with high endorsement probability for PGD symptoms (50%), and a class with high endorsement probability for combined PGD/PTSD symptoms (34%). Prolonged grief and intrusive symptoms emerged across all classes, while MDD showed low endorsement probability. Our results indicate an association between class membership and time passed since the loss; however, this applies only to the comparison between the PGD and the resilient class, and not for the PGD/PTSD class. (4) Conclusions: Our results may provide information about the predictability of symptom clusters following suicide bereavement. The findings also represent a significant step towards tailoring treatments based on the needs of relevant suicide-bereaved subgroups through a symptom-level approach. Time passed since loss might explain differences between symptom clusters.

Keywords: suicide bereavement; latent class; depression; prolonged grief; posttraumatic stress; loss-related characteristics

Citation: Grafiadeli, R.; Glaesmer, H.; Wagner, B. Loss-Related Characteristics and Symptoms of Depression, Prolonged Grief, and Posttraumatic Stress Following Suicide Bereavement. *Int. J. Environ. Res. Public Health* **2022**, *19*, 10277. https://doi.org/10.3390/ijerph191610277

Academic Editors: Karl Andriessen, Karolina Krysinska and Yossi Levi-Belz

Received: 13 July 2022
Accepted: 14 August 2022
Published: 18 August 2022

1. Introduction

Suicide bereavement represents a widely recognized stressor conferring risk for mental disorders and negative social outcomes. The increasing attention on the vulnerability of this population to forming maladaptive emotional reactions has led to the development of several psychological interventions over the past decade [1]. Despite the variety of existing interventions for suicide-bereaved individuals, results from existing efficacy studies indicate only small to medium effect sizes, while the superiority of psychological interventions over unspecific interventions has not been consistently shown [1,2]. The lack of robustness of these effects might be an indication of a not-yet-fully developed understanding of the specific needs of this high-risk population.

According to a population-based study in Canada, nearly half of suicide-bereaved parents develop at least one mental health disorder within two years after the bereavement (Bolton et al., 2013 [3]). A register-based cohort study from Denmark revealed an increased risk for the development of mental disorders in suicide-bereaved spouses when compared to the general population, or spouses bereaved through other means [4]. Research has shown that suicide bereavement is associated with a high risk for the development of emotional disorders such as major depressive disorder (MDD), anxiety disorders, and specifically posttraumatic stress disorder (PTSD) [3,5,6]. Additionally, a high proportion of those bereaved show persisting grief reactions, with increased probability for the development of a prolonged grief disorder (PGD), with prevalence rates ranging between 7% and 10% [7–11]. Additionally, a co-occurrence of these disorders following bereavement is commonly observed [3,12]. Recent estimates on post-loss symptomatology indicate that 63% of bereaved individuals with PGD show co-occurring depression, while 49% show a PTSD comorbidity [13].

The examination of this co-occurrence following bereavement has received increased attention over the past decade. PGD has been included in the ICD-11 [14] and was only recently introduced as a distinct disorder in the text revision of the DSM-5 (DSM-5-TR; APA 2020 [15]). PGD is characterized by elevated and persistent grief following the loss of a significant person while causing functional impairment to the individual. PGD is mainly characterized by a persistent yearning or longing for the deceased individual. Research notes the high relatedness of emotional disorders, especially between PGD, MDD, and PTSD. Despite the close similarities of these disorders, several main differences exist. For example, while PGD and PTSD share symptoms of intrusion and avoidance, the expressions of these symptoms differentiate. While trauma-related avoidance is associated with fear, bereavement-related avoidance is often associated with loss-related aspects such as (positive) memories of the deceased and separation distress. Sufficient insight into the overlap of emotional disorders exists, as well as with regard to their distinctiveness [16,17].

Following a person-centered approach using latent class analysis (LCA) research on psychological sequelae following bereavement, researchers examined classes of patients presenting similar symptom profiles. LCA represents a powerful method of cluster analysis that can be used to identify patterns of similar responses for categorical indicator variables (e.g., symptom present or symptom absent). The goal is to create a set of exclusive latent classes; that is, to split respondents into groups with homogeneous symptom profiles. This approach has been previously used in bereavement literature to examine symptom profiles of the three most commonly prevalent syndromes in bereaved individuals: MDD, PGD, and PTSD. For instance, Djelantik and colleagues (2017) [18] used this approach to investigate symptom clusters of MDD, PGD, and PTSD in a bereaved community sample, revealing three classes of symptoms: a PGD class (48%), a PGD and PTSD symptom profile class (27%), and a resilient class (25%). Another study applying LCA to a trauma-exposed bereaved sample revealed four classes: a resilient class (13%), a class with prominent PGD and MDD symptoms (23%), a class with PGD and PTSD symptoms (20%), and a class with MDD, PGD, and PTSD symptoms (45%) [19]. A study including a disaster-bereaved sample again revealed three classes as the best fit: a resilient class with low probability of MDD, PGD, and PTSD symptoms (20%), a class characterized only by PGD symptoms (41.8%), and a combined class with a moderate to high probability for the presence of all three symptom clusters (38.2%) [20]. One recent study focusing on a recently bereaved sample examined symptoms of MDD, PGD, and PTSD within the first 6 months of bereavement and revealed again a three-class symptom profile: a low-symptom class (35.4%), a predominantly PGD class (29.8%), and a high-symptom profile class (34.8%) including symptoms of all symptom clusters [21]. For a summary of the main findings of previous latent class research following bereavement, see Figure 1.

While existing research highlights the predominant role of PGD symptoms in bereaved populations, the examination of these symptom clusters in suicide-bereaved individuals remains unclear. The aim of the present study was to identify classes regarding symptoms of MDD, PGD, and PTSD in a German sample of suicide-bereaved individuals by examining patterns of symptom co-occurrence. We additionally aimed to examine possible differences in symptom severity based on loss-related characteristics such as kinship and the period of time since the loss. The examination of symptom clusters may offer important insights for the refinement of psychological treatments for the suicide bereaved.

Figure 1. Summary of research findings on symptom profile classes following bereavement. Boelen & Lenferink, 2020 [21], Djelantik et al., 2017, 2019 [18,19], Lenferink et al., 2017 [20].

2. Materials and Methods

2.1. Participants and Procedure

Participant data were derived from a help-seeking sample, which completed the assessment for participation in a randomized controlled trial assessing the effectiveness of an online group intervention for suicide-bereaved adults [22]. The study protocol was approved by the review board of the Medical School Hamburg. Participant recruitment took place primarily through support organizations for bereaved individuals in Germany, as well as through online advertisements. After signing the informed consent form, participants aged between 18 and 75 years were invited to complete the online screening assessment, followed by a telephone interview conducted by the study coordinators. Participants with acute suicidality, self-harm, current psychosis, alcohol or substance abuse, severe depression (BDI > 35), bipolar disorder, or borderline personality disorder were not eligible for participation in the trial. This resulted in a total number of N = 159 participants who completed the screening assessment.

2.2. Variables and Measures

Sociodemographic variables included in our analysis were gender, age of the bereaved, education, and marital status. Loss-related variables comprised the age of the bereaved since the day of loss, and relationship to the deceased.

Due to the limitation of the number of item inclusions in the LCA analysis, a subset of core symptoms for each disorder in correspondence with the diagnostic criteria of the ICD-11 and/or DSM-5 was included. In case of overlap of items between two disorders, items were included in the category which we considered more representative. The items of each questionnaire were dichotomized in 0 (=symptom absent for lower item ratings) and 1 (=symptom present for higher item ratings), based on prior research examining latent class symptom profiles of bereaved individuals [19,23].

Symptoms of depression were assessed with the revised German version of the Beck Depression Inventory (BDI-II; Beck, Steer, & Brown., 1996 [24]; Hautzinger, Keller, Kühner, & Beck, 2009 [25]), assessing depressive symptom severity. Each symptom is formulated as four statements with increasing levels of severity (e.g., sadness/depressed mood:

0 = "I do feel sad"–3 = "I am so sad and unhappy I cannot stand it"). We selected 7 out of 21 BDI-II items in accordance with depressive disorder symptoms in the ICD-11. We included both "worthlessness" and "guilt", as these symptoms were especially relevant for the suicide-bereaved sample. Furthermore, we excluded the item "concentration difficulty", as there was an overlap with the scale for posttraumatic stress symptoms, as well as "suicide ideation", as acute suicidality represented one of the exclusion criteria for participation in the study (for an overview of the included items and the corresponding symptom description, see Table 1). Based on a previously set cut-off from previous research conducting LCA analyses with the BDI-II, each item was considered absent (=0) if rated with 0 or 1, while it was considered present (=1) if rated with 2 or 3 [18].

Table 1. Description of included symptoms of each questionnaire.

	BDI-II Items for MDD Symptoms	ICG-D Items for PGD Symptoms	IES-R Items for PTSD Symptoms	
1	Sadness	Longing/Yearning	Intrusion	Thoughts
2	Loss of interest	Preoccupation		Images
3	Loss of energy	Upsetting memories		Dreams
4	Worthlessness	Difficulty accepting the loss	Avoidance	Avoid reminders
5	Guilt	Disbelief		Avoid thoughts
6	Changes in sleep	Feeling stunned/numb since loss		Numbness
7	Changes in appetite	Disconnection from others	Hypervigilance	Startled
8		Feeling life is empty		Anger
9				Concentration difficulty

Symptoms of prolonged grief were assessed with the German version of the Inventory of Complicated Grief (ICG; Prigerson et al., 1995 [26]; ICG-D; Lumbeck, Brandstaetter, & Geissner, 2012 [27]). We selected 8 out of 19 items of the ICG corresponding closely to the diagnostic criteria proposed by Prigerson et al. (2009) [28], allowing a reliable distinction from other mental health disorders (Bellini et al., 2018; Boelen, 2013; Stroebe, Schut, & Van den Bout, 2013 [10,16,29,30]). According to previous studies conducting LCA research using the ICG, we created dichotomized indicator variables for each included item (Djelantik et al., 2017; Lenferink et al., 2017; Zhou et al., 2018 [18,20,31]). Each item was defined as symptom absent (=0) for ratings between 1 = "never" to 2 = "rarely" and was considered as symptom present (=1) for ratings between 3 = "sometimes" to 5 = "always".

Symptoms of posttraumatic stress were measured with the use of the adapted version of the Impact of Event Scale-Revised (IES-R; Horowitz et al., 1979 [32]; Maercker & Schützwohl, 1998 [33]), which assesses symptoms of PTSD. Items were selected as corresponding to the DSM-5 categories for intrusion symptoms (thoughts, images, dreams), avoidance of thoughts and behavior (reminders, thoughts, numbness), and changes in arousal and reactivity (irritability/anger, concentration difficulties). Aiming for consistency of dichotomization, we set a similar cut-off as described for the measures above. A symptom rating between 0 = "not at all" and 1 = "minimal" was defined as symptom absent (=0) while ratings between 2 = "moderately" and 4 = "extremely" were considered as symptom present (=1).

2.3. Data Analysis

The first part of the statistical analysis was conducted in RStudio, version 4.0.0 (RStudio Team, Boston, MA, USA 2020 [34]). No examination of missing data was necessary, as a full adherence at the screening assessment was a prerequisite for participation in the trial. To identify classes of suicide-bereaved individuals with comparable MDD, PGD, and PTSD symptom profiles, the poLCA package was used [35]. The estimation process began with two latent class profiles, while increasing the number of profiles in order to find the optimal number of classes. For the identification of model fit, the following indices were examined: Akaike's Information Criterion (AIC), Bayesian Information Criterion (BIC), and entropy (classification quality). As indicated in previous research, lower AIC and BIC values and higher entropy values indicate better fit [36]. Furthermore, an additional LCA was conducted, adding important covariates in our model.

3. Results

3.1. Sociodemograhic Characteristics

The sample consisted of 159 adults (n = 142, 89.3% female) with a mean age of 40.62 (SD = 12.67) years. The majority of the sample was in a relationship (n = 31, 19.5%) or married (n= 45, 28.3%), and had received a degree from vocational school, university or higher (69.8%). The sample included first-degree bereaved relatives (n = 102; 64.2%), bereaved spouses or partners (n = 36, 22.6%), and bereaved friends, colleagues, or others (n = 21, 13.2%). The mean age of the bereaved individual at the time of loss was 41.45 (SD = 17.02) years. The mean time since the loss was 28.18 (SD = 55.77) months. For an overview of all sociodemographic and loss-related characteristics, see Table 2.

Table 2. Sociodemographic and loss-related characteristics of the sample.

	n (%)	M (SD)	Range
Gender (female)	142 (89.3%)		
Age		40.62 (12.67)	19.0–69.0
Marital status			
in a relationship	31(19.5%)		
married	45 (28.3%)		
single	51 (32.1%)		
divorced	10 (6.3%)		
widowed	22 (13.8%)		
Education			
low	7 (4.4%)		
middle	41 (25.8%)		
high	111 (69.8%)		
Age of bereaved at time of loss		41.45 (17.02)	3.0–68.0
Kinship to deceased			
child	40 (25.2%)		
parent	27 (17.0%)		
sibling	35 (22.0%)		
spouse/partner	36 (22.6%)		
friend/colleague/other	21 (13.2%)		
Time passed since loss (months)		28.18 (55.77)	0.0–312.0
<6 months	62 (39.0%)		
6–12 months	39 (24.5%)		
13–24 months	28 (17.6%)		
>24 months	30 (18.9%)		

3.2. Latent Class Analysis

The fit indices for the latent class profiles are listed in Table 3. Based on the goodness-of-fit indices, three class solutions appeared adequate with a better fit and interpretability, and were therefore retained. We considered a value of >0.60 as a high probability of symptom endorsement [19,37]. The three-class model revealed one resilient class (class 1; 16% of the sample), one class with a higher probability for some symptoms of PGD and intrusion symptoms of PTSD (class 2; 50% sample), and one class with prominent symptoms of PGD and PTSD (class 3; 34% of the sample). The distinct symptom occurrences are presented in Figure 2.

In class one (resilient class), only the PGD items "longing for the deceased" and "upsetting memories", as well as the PTSD item "intrusive thoughts", had a high probability of endorsement. In class two (PGD class), all PGD items except "disconnection" and "life is empty" showed a high endorsement probability, while this was again observed for the intrusion items of PTSD "intrusive thoughts" and "intrusive images". In class three (combined PGD and PTSD class), all PGD items and PTSD items except "intrusive dreams" and "numbness" had a high endorsement probability. This is the only class in which a symptom of depression showed higher endorsement, though this only applied to the item "sadness". In general, symptoms of PGD and especially "longing" and "upsetting memories", similar to the PTSD item "intrusive thoughts", had a high endorsement probability in all classes, while the probability for endorsement of all depressive symptoms, besides "sadness", was low.

Table 3. Goodness-of-fit criteria.

	2 Classes	3 Classes	4 Classes	5 Classes
Number of estimated parameters	49	74	99	124
Residual degrees of freedom	110	85	60	35
AIC	3870.78	3782.93	3774.32	3761.15
BIC	4021.15	4010.03	4078.14	4141.70
Likelihood ratio	2171.95	2034.11	1975.49	1912.33
Entropy	0.87	0.90	0.93	0.89

Note. AIC = Akaike information criterion; BIC = Bayesian information criterion.

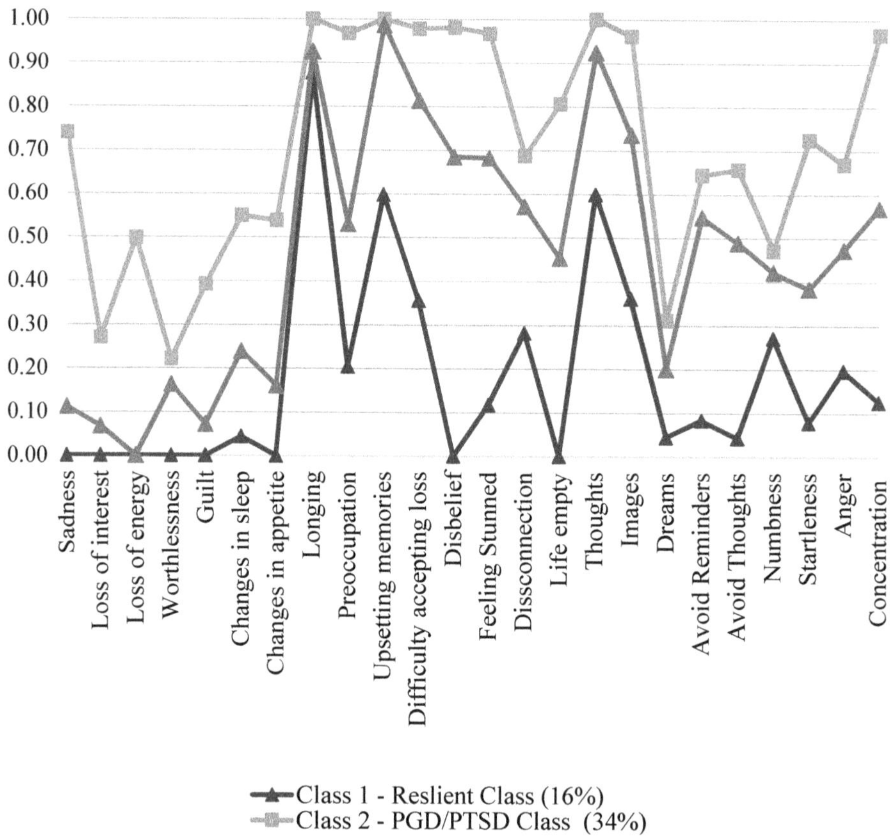

Figure 2. Estimated symptom endorsement profiles for the 3-class model of the latent class analysis ($N = 159$).

We extended our analysis by adding important covariates to our LCA analysis. Table 4 depicts differences between the classes regarding sociodemographic (age, gender) and loss-related (kinship, time passed since day of loss) variables between the classes. The first (resilient) class was used as the class of reference. No statistically significant differences between the classes for age, gender, or kinship were found. Time passed since the day of loss was the only variable significantly associated with the class membership. However, this significance only applied to differences between the PGD and the resilient class. Time since loss appeared lower for individuals in the PGD class compared to the resilient class.

Table 4. Latent class model with analysis of covariance.

	B	SE	*t*-Value	*p*-Value
PGD/PTSD vs. resilient class				
Age	−0.01	0.04	−0.39	0.70
Gender	1.32	0.97	1.36	0.18
Kinship	0.05	0.25	0.19	0.85
Time since the loss	−0.40	0.50	−0.80	0.42
PGD vs. resilient class				
Age	−0.01	0.04	−0.25	0.81
Gender	1.53	1.42	1.07	0.29
Kinship	0.49	0.31	1.60	0.12
Time since the loss	−1.34	0.54	−2.50	0.01

Note. B = Beta; SE = Standard Error; PGD = Prolonged Grief Disorder; PTSD = Posttraumatic Stress Disorder.

4. Discussion

To our knowledge, this is the first study employing LCA to explore classes of MDD, PGD, and PTSD symptoms in a suicide-bereaved sample. Half of the examined population showed mainly elevated PGD symptom endorsement, while one-third of the included sample showed high PGD and PTSD symptom endorsement. PGD symptoms had a high endorsement probability for all classes, while no pattern of increased MDD symptom endorsement was revealed. A tendency towards higher endorsement probability for one MDD item appeared, but only in the class characterized by increased combined PGD and PTSD endorsement.

Our findings are in line with previous research focusing on community or trauma-exposed samples showing classes of patients with increased PGD and with combined PGD and PTSD symptom endorsement [18,19]. Based on the findings of this symptom approach, it becomes clear that the targeted treatment of PGD reactions might be especially valuable for the highest proportion of the population. "Longing/ yearning" appears to be the most predominant symptom across all classes, independent of the time passed since the loss [18,23]. Additionally, our findings are in line with research stressing the need to pay attention to treatment options targeting comorbid PGD and PTSD symptoms [18,19,38]. Again, intrusive posttraumatic stress symptoms and in particular "intrusive thoughts" showed high endorsement in all classes. Our findings offer an indication that time since the loss might play a role in PGD symptom reduction, while there is no similar indication for comorbid PGD/PTSD symptoms.

5. Conclusions

In conclusion, the assessment for comorbid treatment of PTSD appears crucial for those bereaved through suicide. Similarly, the finding that a subgroup of participants appeared to be affected by combined symptoms of PGD, PTSD, and only to a lesser extent by MDD symptoms, agrees with previous research focusing on bereaved individuals [18,23,39]. Thus, one partial explanation for our findings could be the exclusion of more severe depression. Including severely depressed bereaved individuals might have led to differential findings.

Several limitations should be noted. First, our data are based on self-report questionnaires, leading to strengthened associations between variables. Second, our sample consisted mainly of female, highly educated adults. Future studies should aim to examine larger and more heterogeneous suicide-bereaved samples. Third, there was a wide range regarding the time since bereavement, ranging from less than one month to more than 20 years. A high percentage of participants were bereaved for more than 6 months, which is the prerequisite for a PGD diagnosis [28]. Furthermore, there was not a full correspondence with the diagnostic criteria, in contrast to the ICD-11 and DSM-5 criteria. In our approach, which aimed at minimizing the number of items for the analysis and including only the most characteristic symptoms of each disorder, we intentionally excluded doubled items (e.g., "anger", "concentration difficulties") which simultaneously resemble symptoms of more than one clinical diagnosis category. Through including all items, it appears likely that symptom endorsement would increase as the interrelatedness of symptoms would increase [16,17]. Thus, assessing formal diagnoses was beyond the scope of the present study. A replication of our findings on a larger population, while also examining the full spectrum of ICD-11 and DSM-5 criteria, is needed.

Notwithstanding the above-mentioned limitations, this study offers an important first insight into subgroups of those bereaved through suicide, based on a symptom-level approach. This was examined in a sample with a wide range of time elapsed since the loss, and with different levels of kinship or relationship to the deceased. We found three distinct classes of suicide bereavement, with participants appearing to be especially affected by PGD symptoms, commonly combined with the presence of PTSD symptoms, and especially with symptoms of intrusion. In line with previous findings on bereavement, our findings highlight the necessity for concurrent treatment for PGD and PTSD for the suicide bereaved [18]. Taking the traumatic circumstances following a violent death and the exposure when discovering the deceased into account, it is not surprising that this population shows an increased risk for developing PTSD [40]. Moreover, previous research underlines the relatedness of PGD and PTSD, suggesting that the likelihood of yearning for the deceased is higher for individuals who experience death-related intrusive thoughts and memories related to the circumstances of death [41]. This attempt to avoid painful experiences appears to mediate the relationship between the traumatic distress and yearning. Trauma-focused, exposure-based treatments targeting PGD and PTSD symptoms simultaneously, while promoting the development of a comprehensive narrative, could represent effective treatment options for those bereaved through suicide [42,43]. It appears likely that a targeted treatment for PGD and PTSD could lead to simultaneous MDD symptom relief.

Author Contributions: Formal analysis, R.G.; Funding acquisition, B.W.; Supervision, B.W.; Writing—original draft, R.G.; Writing—review & editing, H.G. and B.W. All authors have read and agreed to the published version of the manuscript.

Funding: This work was supported by the German Federal Ministry of Health under grant number ZMVI1-517FSB126.

Institutional Review Board Statement: The study was conducted in accordance with the Declaration of Helsinki, and approved by the Institutional Review Board of Medical School Hamburg Ethical Committee (Reference Number MSB-2018-11, 3 March 2018).

Informed Consent Statement: Informed consent was obtained from all subjects involved in the study.

Data Availability Statement: Data available on request due to privacy/ethical restrictions.

Conflicts of Interest: The authors declare that there is no conflict of interest.

References

1. Andriessen, K.; Krysinska, K.; Hill, N.T.M.; Reifels, L.; Robinson, J.; Reavley, N.; Pirkis, J. Effectiveness of interventions for people bereaved through suicide: A systematic review of controlled studies of grief, psychosocial and suicide-related outcomes. *BMC Psychiatry* **2019**, *19*, 49. [CrossRef] [PubMed]
2. Wagner, B.; Hofmann, L.; Grafiadeli, R. Wirksamkeit von Interventionen für Hinterbliebene nach einem Suizid: Ein Systematischer Review. *Psychiatr. Prax.* **2020**, *48*, 9–18. [CrossRef]

3. Bolton, J.M.; Au, W.; Leslie, W.D.; Martens, P.J.; Enns, M.W.; Roos, L.L.; Katz, L.Y.; Wilcox, H.C.; Erlangsen, A.; Chateau, D.; et al. Parents Bereaved by Offspring Suicide. *JAMA Psychiatry* **2013**, *70*, 158–167. [CrossRef] [PubMed]
4. Erlangsen, A.; Runeson, B.; Bolton, J.M.; Wilcox, H.C.; Forman, J.; Krogh, J.; Shear, M.K.; Nordentoft, M.; Conwell, Y. Association Between Spousal Suicide and Mental, Physical, and Social Health Outcomes. *JAMA Psychiatry* **2017**, *74*, 456–464. [CrossRef]
5. Young, I.T.; Iglewicz, A.; Glorioso, D.; Lanouette, N.; Seay, K.; Ilapakurti, M.; Zisook, S. Suicide bereavement and complicated grief. *Dialog-Clin. Neurosci.* **2012**, *14*, 177–186. [CrossRef]
6. Zisook, S.; Chentsova-Dutton, Y.; Shuchter, S. PTSD Following Bereavement. *Ann. Clin. Psychiatry* **1998**, *10*, 157–163. [CrossRef]
7. De Groot, M.; Kollen, B.J. Course of bereavement over 8-10 years in first degree relatives and spouses of people who committed suicide: Longitudinal community based cohort study. *BMJ* **2013**, *347*, f5519. [CrossRef]
8. Mitchell, A.M.; Kim, Y.; Prigerson, H.G.; Mortimer-Stephens, M. Complicated Grief in Survivors of Suicide. *Crisis* **2004**, *25*, 12–18. [CrossRef]
9. Shear, M.K. Complicated Grief. *N. Engl. J. Med.* **2015**, *372*, 153–160. [CrossRef]
10. Stroebe, M.; Schut, H.; Van den Bout, J. *Complicated Grief: Scientific Foundations for Health Care Professionals*; Routledge: London, UK, 2013.
11. Zisook, S.; Iglewicz, A.; Avanzino, J.; Maglione, J.; Glorioso, D.; Zetumer, S.; Seay, K.; Vahia, I.; Young, I.; Lebowitz, B.; et al. Bereavement: Course, Consequences, and Care. *Curr. Psychiatry Rep.* **2014**, *16*, 482. [CrossRef]
12. Boelen, P.A.; Prigerson, H.G. The influence of symptoms of prolonged grief disorder, depression, and anxiety on quality of life among bereaved adults. *Eur. Arch. Psychiatry Clin. Neurosci.* **2007**, *257*, 444–452. [CrossRef] [PubMed]
13. Komischke-Konnerup, K.B.; Zachariae, R.; Johannsen, M.; Nielsen, L.D.; O'Connor, M. Co-occurrence of prolonged grief symptoms and symptoms of depression, anxiety, and posttraumatic stress in bereaved adults: A systematic review and meta-analysis. *J. Affect. Disord. Rep.* **2021**, *4*, 100140. [CrossRef]
14. Maercker, A.; Brewin, C.R.; Bryant, R.A.; Cloitre, M.; Reed, G.M.; van Ommeren, M.; Humayun, A.; Jones, L.M.; Kagee, A.; Llosa, A.E.; et al. Proposals for mental disorders specifically associated with stress in the International Classification of Diseases-11. *Lancet* **2013**, *381*, 1683–1685. [CrossRef]
15. American Psychiatric Association (APA). Board approves new pro-longed grief disorder for DSM. In *Psychiatric News*; American Psychiatric Association: Washington, DC, USA, 2020. [CrossRef]
16. Bellini, S.; Erbuto, D.; Andriessen, K.; Milelli, M.; Innamorati, M.; Lester, D.; Sampogna, G.; Fiorillo, A.; Pompili, M. Depression, Hopelessness, and Complicated Grief in Survivors of Suicide. *Front. Psychol.* **2018**, *9*, 198. [CrossRef] [PubMed]
17. Lenferink, L.I.M.; Munckhof, M.J.A.V.D.; de Keijser, J.; Boelen, P.A. DSM-5-TR prolonged grief disorder and DSM-5 posttraumatic stress disorder are related, yet distinct: Confirmatory factor analyses in traumatically bereaved people. *Eur. J. Psychotraumatology* **2021**, *12*, 2000131. [CrossRef]
18. Djelantik, A.M.J.; Smid, G.E.; Kleber, R.J.; Boelen, P.A. Symptoms of prolonged grief, post-traumatic stress, and depression after loss in a Dutch community sample: A latent class analysis. *Psychiatry Res.* **2017**, *247*, 276–281. [CrossRef]
19. Djelantik, A.A.A.M.J.; Robinaugh, D.J.; Kleber, R.J.; Smid, G.E.; Boelen, P.A. Symptomatology following loss and trauma: Latent class and network analyses of prolonged grief disorder, posttraumatic stress disorder, and depression in a treatment-seeking trauma-exposed sample. *Depress. Anxiety* **2019**, *37*, 26–34. [CrossRef]
20. Lenferink, L.I.M.; de Keijser, J.; Smid, G.E.; Djelantik, A.A.A.M.J.; Boelen, P.A. Prolonged grief, depression, and posttraumatic stress in disaster-bereaved individuals: Latent class analysis. *Eur. J. Psychotraumatology* **2017**, *8*, 1298311. [CrossRef]
21. Boelen, P.A.; Lenferink, L.I. Symptoms of prolonged grief, posttraumatic stress, and depression in recently bereaved people: Symptom profiles, predictive value, and cognitive behavioural correlates. *Soc. Psychiatry* **2019**, *55*, 765–777. [CrossRef]
22. Wagner, B.; Grafiadeli, R.; Schäfer, T.; Hofmann, L. Efficacy of an online-group intervention after suicide bereavement: A randomized controlled trial. *Internet Interv.* **2022**, *28*, 100542. [CrossRef]
23. Boelen, P.A.; Reijntjes, A.; Djelantik, M.; Smid, G.E. Prolonged grief and depression after unnatural loss: Latent class analyses and cognitive correlates. *Psychiatry Res.* **2016**, *240*, 358–363. [CrossRef]
24. Beck, A.T.; Steer, R.A.; Ball, R.; Ranieri, W.F. Comparison of Beck Depression Inventories-IA and-II in Psychiatric Outpatients. *J. Pers. Assess.* **1996**, *67*, 588–597. [CrossRef]
25. Hautzinger, M.; Keller, F.; Kühner, C.; Beck, A.T. Beck depressions-Inventar: BDI II. In *Manual: Pearson Assessment*; Pearson: London, UK, 2009.
26. Prigerson, H.G.; Maciejewski, P.K.; Reynolds, C.F., III; Bierhals, A.J.; Newsom, J.T.; Fasiczka, A.; Frank, E.; Doman, J.; Miller, M. Inventory of complicated grief: A scale to measure maladaptive symptoms of loss. *Psychiatry Res.* **1995**, *59*, 65–79. [CrossRef]
27. Lumbeck, G.; Brandstaetter, M.; Geissner, E. Preliminary validation of the German version of the Inventory of Complicated Grief (ICG-D). *Z. Klin. Psychol. Psychother.* **2012**, *41*, 243–248. [CrossRef]
28. Prigerson, H.G.; Horowitz, M.J.; Jacobs, S.C.; Parkes, C.M.; Aslan, M.; Goodkin, K.; Raphael, B.; Marwit, S.J.; Wortman, C.; Neimeyer, R.A.; et al. Prolonged Grief Disorder: Psychometric Validation of Criteria Proposed for DSM-V and ICD-11. *PLoS Med.* **2009**, *6*, e1000121. [CrossRef] [PubMed]
29. Boelen, P.A. Symptoms of prolonged grief, depression, and adult separation anxiety: Distinctiveness and correlates. *Psychiatry Res.* **2013**, *207*, 68–72. [CrossRef]
30. Boelen, P.A.; van de Schoot, R.; Hout, M.A.V.D.; de Keijser, J.; Bout, J.V.D. Prolonged Grief Disorder, depression, and posttraumatic stress disorder are distinguishable syndromes. *J. Affect. Disord.* **2010**, *125*, 374–378. [CrossRef]

31. Zhou, N.; Yu, W.; Tang, S.; Wang, J.; Killikelly, C. Prolonged grief and post-traumatic growth after loss: Latent class analysis. *Psychiatry Res.* **2018**, *267*, 221–227. [CrossRef]
32. Horowitz, M.; Wilner, N.; Alvarez, W. Impact of Event Scale: A Measure of Subjective Stress. *Psychosom. Med.* **1979**, *41*, 209–218. [CrossRef]
33. Maercker, A.; Schützwohl, M. *Erfassung von Psychischen Belastungsfolgen: Die Impact of Event Skala-Revidierte Version (IES-R)*; Diagnostica; American Psychological Association: Washington, DC, USA, 1998. [CrossRef]
34. RStudio Team. *RStudio: Integrated Development for R. RStudio, PBC*; RStudio Team: Boston, MA, USA, 2020.
35. Linzer, D.A.; Lewis, J.B. poLCA: An R package for polytomous variable latent class analysis. *J. Stat. Softw.* **2011**, *42*, 1–29. [CrossRef]
36. Nylund, K.L.; Asparouhov, T.; Muthén, B.O. Deciding on the Number of Classes in Latent Class Analysis and Growth Mixture Modeling: A Monte Carlo Simulation Study. *Struct. Equ. Model. A Multidiscip. J.* **2007**, *14*, 535–569. [CrossRef]
37. Maccallum, F.; Bryant, R.A. Symptoms of prolonged grief and posttraumatic stress following loss: A latent class analysis. *Aust. N. Zeal. J. Psychiatry* **2018**, *53*, 59–67. [CrossRef] [PubMed]
38. de Heus, A.; Hengst, S.M.C.; De La Rie, S.M.; Djelantik, A.A.A.M.J.; Boelen, P.A.; Smid, G.E. Day patient treatment for traumatic grief: Preliminary evaluation of a one-year treatment programme for patients with multiple and traumatic losses. *Eur. J. Psychotraumatology* **2017**, *8*, 1375335. [CrossRef] [PubMed]
39. Nickerson, A.; Liddell, B.J.; Maccallum, F.; Steel, Z.; Silove, D.; Bryant, R.A. Posttraumatic stress disorder and prolonged grief in refugees exposed to trauma and loss. *BMC Psychiatry* **2014**, *14*, 106. [CrossRef] [PubMed]
40. Murphy, S.A.; Johnson, L.C.; Chung, I.-J.; Beaton, R.D. The prevalence of PTSD following the violent death of a child and predictors of change 5 years later. *J. Trauma. Stress* **2003**, *16*, 17–25. [CrossRef]
41. Hardt, M.M.; Williams, J.L.; Jobe-Shields, L. The role of experiential avoidance in the relationship between traumatic distress and yearning in sudden and unexpected bereavement. *J. Clin. Psychol.* **2021**, *78*, 559–569. [CrossRef]
42. Eddinger, J.R.; Hardt, M.M.; Williams, J.L. Concurrent Treatment for PTSD and Prolonged Grief Disorder: Review of Outcomes for Exposure- and Nonexposure-Based Treatments. *Omega-J. Death Dying* **2019**, *83*, 446–469. [CrossRef]
43. Larsen, L.H. Letter Writing as a Clinical Tool in Grief Psychotherapy. *Omega-J. Death Dying* **2022**, 00302228211070155. [CrossRef]

International Journal of
Environmental Research and Public Health

Article

Prolonged Grief Symptoms among Suicide-Loss Survivors: The Contribution of Intrapersonal and Interpersonal Characteristics

Yossi Levi-Belz [1,*] and Tamir Ben-Yaish [1,2]

1 The Lior Tsfaty Center for Suicide and Mental Pain Studies, Ruppin Academic Center, Emek Hefer 40250, Israel
2 Clinical Psychology of Adulthood and Aging M.A. Program, Ruppin Academic Center, Emek Hefer 40250, Israel
* Correspondence: yossil@ruppin.ac.il; Tel.: +972-9-8983028; Fax: +972-9-8983022

Abstract: Background: Suicide-loss survivors (SLSs) are a population with unique characteristics that place them at increased risk for developing grief complications and painful feelings of guilt that may impact their supportive social environment. However, no studies to date have examined the role of intrapersonal and interpersonal variables that may contribute to prolonged grief symptoms (PGS) as outlined by the new DSM-5 criteria. The present study aimed to extend knowledge regarding the role of interpersonal variables, such as perceived burdensomeness, thwarted belongingness, and self-disclosure, in determining the impact of guilt on the development of PGS among SLSs. Method: This study is part of a longitudinal study, though, in this study, we used a cross-sectional examination of the recently completed fourth measurement. Study participants included 152 SLSs aged 22 to 76 who completed questionnaires measuring guilt, depression, perceived burdensomeness, thwarted belongingness, self-disclosure, and PGS using the Prolonged Grief–Revised Inventory. Participants' demographics and loss-related characteristics, such as time since suicide and participant's age at the time of suicide, were examined. Results: Confirming the hypotheses, intrapersonal variables (i.e., guilt and depression), as well as interpersonal variables (i.e., perceived burdensomeness, thwarted belongingness, and self-disclosure), contributed significantly to PGS beyond sociodemographic and loss-related factors. Perceived burdensomeness significantly moderated the contribution of guilt to PGS: for participants with high burdensomeness levels, guilt contributed to PGS more strongly than for participants with low burdensomeness. Conclusion: Guilt is an important contributor to PGS among SLSs, and perceived burdensomeness plays a critical role in moderating this contribution. In light of these findings, it can be suggested that SLSs with high levels of guilt should receive special attention and may benefit from therapeutic interventions focusing on reducing maladaptive cognitions that elicit intense guilt or perceived burden.

Keywords: suicide; bereavement; prolonged grief; guilt; self-disclosure; belongingness

Citation: Levi-Belz, Y.; Ben-Yaish, T. Prolonged Grief Symptoms among Suicide-Loss Survivors: The Contribution of Intrapersonal and Interpersonal Characteristics. *Int. J. Environ. Res. Public Health* **2022**, *19*, 10545. https://doi.org/10.3390/ijerph191710545

Academic Editor: Paul B. Tchounwou

Received: 8 August 2022
Accepted: 20 August 2022
Published: 24 August 2022

Publisher's Note: MDPI stays neutral with regard to jurisdictional claims in published maps and institutional affiliations.

1. Introduction

1.1. Prolonged Grief Disorder (PGD)

Grief is a universal, inevitable, painful part of life that has its origins in the severing of close relationships [1]. The psychological response to the loss of a loved one is usually accompanied by grief and emotional distress. Most bereaved individuals go through a natural grieving process in which the intensity of symptoms decreases over time as the bereaved gradually acclimates to the impact of the loss [1]. However, a significant minority of these individuals experience abnormally intense and persistent grief symptoms, resulting in significant functional impairment [2]. For decades, these and other symptoms following loss were equated with symptoms of depression. Recently, cumulative evidence has indicated that prolonged grief symptoms (PGS) represent a bereavement-specific diagnosis [3] that comprises part of the clinical syndrome of prolonged grief disorder, a condition recently supplemented to the International Classification of Diseases, 11th Revision (ICD-11; [4]). Prolonged grief disorder is now included for the first time in the Diagnostic and Statistical Manual of Mental Disorders, Fifth Edition, Text Revision (DSM-5-TR) in the chapter on trauma and stressor-related disorders [3,5].

Although PGD is an identifiable and distinct disorder [6], research suggests it should be viewed as a continuum of normal to prolonged and severe grief reactions rather than a qualitative category [6,7]. Therefore, clinically relevant levels of prolonged grief symptoms (PGS) are commonly used as a proxy to identify prolonged grief disorder [8].

The core element of PGD is intense longing or craving for the deceased or engaging in thoughts or memories of them [3]. Other symptoms include intense emotional pain related to the death, feeling that a part of oneself has been lost, difficulty accepting the death, avoiding cues that might trigger thoughts of the deceased, and difficulty engaging in social or other activities following the loss [3]. According to DSM-5 criteria, symptoms should persist for at least 12 months after the loss [9], whereas ICD diagnostic criteria anticipate symptoms persisting for more than six months after the loss [5].

Until the criteria for PGD were established and recognized, researchers and clinicians used other related concepts, such as complicated grief, pathological grief, persistent complex bereavement disorder, and traumatic grief [10]. These constructs were assessed in recent decades by various standards, instruments, and cutoff scores for disordered grief, such as PG-13, ICD-11 criteria, and ICG-R [11]. These PG-related structures have been associated with various adverse health outcomes [1], substance abuse [12], increased suicide risk [13], and decreased psychological quality of life [14]. However, in the absence of valid self-report measures that met the DSM-5-TR criteria of PGD [3], these findings could not be generalized to enable a fuller understanding of the prevalence of PGD and its correlates. A population that should be assessed using the new DSM-5-TR criteria is suicide-loss survivors, who have recently been classified among those at highest risk for developing PGS [15].

1.2. Suicide-Loss Survivors

Suicide is a significant public health problem, causing an estimated 700,000 deaths annually, making it the seventeenth leading cause of death worldwide [9]. Each death caused by suicide can affect approximately 135 people [16]; these are referred to as suicide-loss survivors (SLSs). Many SLSs are at high risk of experiencing severe emotional, physiological, or social distress over an extended period following the suicide of a significant other [17–19]. Moreover, SLSs are particularly at risk for developing PGS [15], which the particular nature of suicide grief can explain. Most SLSs have difficulty understanding the cause of death and why their loved one chose to end their life [20]. They may be dominated by the grieving process, resulting in higher levels of PGS [21,22]. Therefore, it is essential to understand the psychological contributors and moderators of PGS among SLSs.

1.3. Intrapersonal and Interpersonal Factors

It is well-established in the literature that SLSs often suffer from feelings of shame, rejection, and social stigma [17,23]. However, one factor that has been repeatedly highlighted, and is perhaps the most common reaction in suicide grief, is guilt [24–26]. Guilt is a remorseful emotional reaction, a sense of failure in one's relationship with the deceased and of not living up to one's standards and expectations [27]. Guilt following a suicide loss often emerges from the belief that the suicide could have been avoided had the bereaved behaved differently, such as being more attentive [1]. As a result, many SLSs are disinclined to share their thoughts and feelings with others [28,29]. This aversion to sharing can undermine the foundation of SLSs' interpersonal relationships [18], promote loneliness and withdrawal, and exacerbate adverse psychological outcomes such as depression, anxiety [1], and hopelessness [30]. Recently, Feigelman and Cerel [25] showed that feelings of blameworthiness (a factor closely related to guilt) are associated with grief difficulties among bereaved parents of children who died by suicide. However, despite this widespread understanding of the importance of guilt in the suicide grieving process, few studies have focused on examining the factors that may facilitate or exacerbate its contribution to the development of PGS. Depression also characterizes SLSs, as it reflects the high mental burden that SLSs may carry in the aftermath of suicide loss [17]. Several studies have found that suicide bereavement is related to higher levels of depression than among other bereaved individuals [31]. Considering that depression is closely related to PGS in general and among SLSs in particular, it is crucial to investigate depression's role alongside the guilt experience.

Several studies have suggested that interpersonal factors are among the main contributors to distress, depression, and complicated grief reactions among SLSs (e.g., [29,32,33]). The widely recognized interpersonal theory of suicide (ITS; [34]) posits that two interpersonal constructs—perceived burdensomeness and thwarted belongingness—are the primary causal interactional risk factors for distress and suicidality [35]. Each dimension represents a particular perception of the interpersonal environment, viewed as a dynamic cognitive–affective state. Perceived burdensomeness (PB) refers to an individual's sense that their existence is a burden to friends, family members, or society and consists of two facets: 1. the belief that oneself is so flawed that one is a burden to others and 2. affectively charged cognitions of self-hatred [36]. Thwarted belongingness (TB) is the experience of loneliness and the lack of relationships based on reciprocity [36]. The sense of not belonging highlights the painful feeling of being external to the family, friends, and other social groups [36].

Both TB and PB were found to be related to several adverse outcomes in the aftermath of suicide loss. For example, recent research found that TB and PB predicted the extent of complicated grief over time in a sample of SLSs [22], while the experience of high belongingness promoted the development of higher levels of adaptive functioning after suicide loss [37]. We can thus assume that higher levels of PB and TB could contribute to higher levels of PGS among SLSs. Guilt is one of the painful feelings reported in post-suicide grief [25], and it may have intrapersonal and interpersonal ramifications that can undermine SLSs' interpersonal relationships [28]. Indeed, it is likely that interpersonal perceptions such as TB and PB play a critical role in PGS among SLSs who suffer from guilt.

Recent studies have shown that self-disclosure (SD)—a process by which people communicate themselves to others [38]—can help reduce distress and suicidal ideation [39] during the adjustment of SLSs [29] and even lead to posttraumatic growth [32]. SD promotes the healing process and reduces emotional distress by providing new perspectives on the self and the suicide event and helping to create constructive narratives about the changes that have occurred [40,41]. SD also provides intimacy, a sense of being with others, and an experience of social support [42] that allows one to overcome the walls of stigma and distance [43]. As SLSs tend to experience painful guilt [25], disclosing intimate feelings and thoughts is likely to be difficult for them, evoking feelings of ambivalence and psychological pain they may prefer to avoid [28]. A limited level of SD is liable to comprise a buffer between the individual and their social environment, leading to loneliness and social isolation and exacerbating the difficulties of bereavement [43,44]. Interestingly, no studies to date have examined the interpersonal contributors to PGS following suicide loss.

1.4. The Present Study

Considering the formal recognition of prolonged grief disorder as a new diagnostic entity and the evidence that it is associated with various health problems and impairments in quality of life, there is an increasing need to identify the factors contributing to the severity of PGS. However, few studies have examined such predictors of PGS among SLSs. To address this gap, this study aimed to examine the role of intrapersonal characteristics (i.e., guilt and depression) and interpersonal characteristics (i.e., TB, PB, and SD) and the impact of their co-occurrence as potential factors contributing to PGS after a suicide loss, using the revised DSM-TR diagnosis of PGD. In light of the linkage between depression and PGS, we also aimed to examine the contribution of guilt to PGS beyond the contribution of depression. Overall, identifying factors contributing to the development of PGS will facilitate the design of preventive interventions for individuals at increased risk and establish therapeutic measures targeting elements contributing to the onset and severity of PGS.

Three hypotheses were at the core of this study:

Hypothesis 1. *Higher levels of guilt will contribute to higher levels of PGS among SLSs, beyond sociodemographic and loss-related factors (i.e., the time elapsed since the loss, participant's age at the time of suicide, and fear of a future suicide of a family member) and beyond depression levels.*

Hypothesis 2. *Lower levels of self-disclosure and higher levels of perceived burdensomeness and thwarted belongingness will contribute to higher levels of PGS among SLSs, beyond sociodemographic, loss-related, and intrapersonal factors (guilt and depression).*

Hypothesis 3. *Interpersonal factors (TB, PB, and SD) will moderate the relationship between guilt and PGS among SLSs. As SD scores decrease and TB and PB increase, the relationships between guilt and PGS will become stronger.*

2. Method

2.1. Participants

The present study is part of a longitudinal study with four measurement points (see [22]). The present study used the fourth measurement point, conducted in 2020–2021. A total of 189 SLSs participated in the first measurement point of the study, conducted in 2015–2016. Of these, 152 (80.4%) participated in the fourth measurement. Thus, the final sample of the current study comprised 152 suicide survivors (80.4% women), ranging in age from 22 to 76.

Participants were recruited in two main ways. Most participants were recruited through a nonprofit organization, The Path to Life, the national agency for suicide survivors in Israel. The remaining participants were recruited through the official Facebook group of Israeli suicide survivors and other social media groups of suicide survivors in Israel. Inclusion criteria for suicide survivors were individuals who had lost a family member or other close friend due to suicide. Exclusion criteria were age less than 15 years at the time of suicide and inability to read and write Hebrew.

2.2. Measures

2.2.1. Guilt

Guilt levels were measured with Trauma-related guilt (TRG; [45]), an abbreviated form of the Trauma-Related Guilt Inventory (TRGI; [46]). The inventory assesses guilt characteristics following a traumatic event with five items representing the severity of guilt related to the experienced trauma (e.g., "I did something I should not have done", reflecting a negative evaluation of the self). All items were measured on a Likert-type scale, ranging from 0 (Does not match at all) to 10 (Matches completely), resulting in a mean score of 0–10. Øktedalen et al. [45] reported the scale's high reliability and content validity. For the present sample, Cronbach's alpha was $\alpha = 0.87$.

2.2.2. Depression

Depression symptoms were assessed using the 9-item Patient Health Questionnaire Depression Scale (PHQ-9; [47]). Participants were asked, "Over the last two weeks, how often have you been disturbed by any of the following problems?" They then rated the frequency of each of the symptoms (e.g., Poor appetite or overeating? Little interest or pleasure in doing things?) using the following four anchors: 0 (not at all), 1 (several days), 2 (more than half of the days), and 3 (nearly every day). For this study, the mean of the scale scores was used, ranging from 0 to 27. Higher scores indicated more severe depressive symptoms. High PHQ-9 scores have been associated with increased physician visits, physical disability, risk of psychiatric comorbidity, and overall severity of the syndrome [47]. Cronbach's alpha for the present sample was $\alpha = 0.90$.

2.2.3. Thwarted Belongingness and Perceived Burdensomeness

Thwarted belongingness and perceived burdensomeness were assessed using the 10-statement Interpersonal Needs Questionnaire (INQ; [35]). Five items evaluated each of the two subscales: thwarted belongingness (e.g., "These days, other people care about me" [reversed scored]) and perceived burdensomeness (e.g., "These days, I feel like a burden on the people in my life"). Respondents indicated the extent to which the statements applied to them on a 7-point Likert-type scale, with higher scores reflecting more severe levels of thwarted belongingness and perceived burdensomeness. In this study, we used the Hebrew translation of the INQ, which has been employed in several studies (e.g., [22]). Cronbach's alpha for the present sample was $\alpha = 0.85$ for thwarted belongingness and $\alpha = 0.90$ for perceived burdensomeness.

2.2.4. Self-Disclosure

The Distress Disclosure Index (DDI; [48]) was used to measure the individual's inclination to disclose personally distressing information (e.g., "I usually don't share issues that bother me" [reverse scored]; "I try to find people to talk to about my problems"). The 12-item DDI is presented on a 5-point Likert-type scale, ranging from 1 (strongly disagree) to 5 (strongly agree). Higher scores represent a greater inclination to disclose. Confirmatory factor analysis of the DDI yielded a single construct with high reliability and validity [48]. Cronbach's alpha for the present sample was $\alpha = 0.94$.

2.2.5. Prolonged Grief Disorder (PGD) Symptoms

PGD symptoms were assessed using the Prolonged Grief-13-Revised (PG-13-R) scale [3]. This 10-item questionnaire is presented on a 5-point Likert-type scale, ranging from 1 (not at all) to 5 (overwhelmingly). The sum of the scale is used for the assessment of grief intensity on a dimensional scale for diagnosing PGD according to the new DSM-5-TR criteria (yearning, preoccupation, identity disruption, disbelief, avoidance, intense emotional pain, difficulty with reintegration, emotional numbness, feeling that life is meaningless, and intense loneliness). Higher scores reflect higher levels of PGS, with a PG-13-R symptom score of 30 or above indicative of syndrome-level PGD symptomatology [3].

The PG-13-R scale also presents three items, responded to dichotomously ("yes" or "no"), that are not included in the total score. They assess three diagnostic criteria: whether the respondent has lost a significant other, how long ago the death occurred, and the impairment associated with the symptoms. The PG-13-R scale has been shown to be reliable for measuring grief symptoms on a dimensional scale in three different community-based populations [3,49]. Cronbach's alpha for the present sample was $\alpha = 0.87$.

2.2.6. Demographic and Loss-Related Characteristics

Demographic and diagnostic data on suicide loss were collected for each participant. These data included the age of the survivor and the deceased at the time of the suicide, the time elapsed since the suicide, the participant's relationship to the person who died by suicide (e.g., child, spouse, parent, friend), the extent to which the suicide was expected or unexpected, and the extent of the fear of a future suicide of a family member.

2.3. Procedure

The study was approved by the ethics committee of the Ruppin Academic Center. Potential participants were informed of the risks and compensation procedures. They were assured of anonymity, confidentiality, and the right to withdraw from the study at any time. Participants were required to confirm their willingness to participate by signing an informed consent form and completing the questionnaire online (using Qualtrics online survey software). After completing the questionnaire, participants were asked if they consented to being contacted for a follow-up in the future. Consenting participants were invited to subsequent measurements (T2, T3, and T4) and were requested to complete a brief questionnaire that included the main study variables. After completing the online questionnaire, participants were compensated with vouchers at each measurement point (approximate value at each measurement: USD 25).

2.4. Statistical Analysis

Pearson correlation tests were calculated to examine the relationships among the study variables, followed by a hierarchical multiple regression with PGS as the dependent variable. As Aiken, West, and Reno [50] recommended, all continuous predictor variables were standardized, as were the cross-product interaction terms. To examine the nature of the interaction within a regression framework, moderation analysis was performed using the PROCESS macro (Model 1; [51]). The Statistical Package for the Social Sciences (SPSS, v26.0 for Windows, Armonk, NY, USA) was used for all analyses. A Bonferroni correction was applied to all analyses. The level of statistical significance was set at $p = 0.05$.

3. Results

3.1. The Sample's Demographics

The mean age of the sample was 47.5 ($SD = 14.7$). Regarding participants' marital status, 69 (45.4%) reported being married, 49 (32.2%) single, 20 (13.1%) divorced, and 14 (9.2%) widowed. Regarding religiosity, most of the participants (112, 73.7%) reported being secular, 29 (19.1%) reported being moderately religious, and the others (11, 7.3%) reported being religious Jewish. Regarding socioeconomic status (SES), 35 (23%) participants reported a very low SES, 38 (25%) low SES, and the remaining 79 (52%) medium and high SES. Regarding schooling, almost all participants ($n = 132$, 86.9%) reported completing at least 12 years of education, and 96 (63.2%) reported having a university degree.

3.2. Suicide-Related Demographic Information

The time elapsed since suicide varied, with a mean of 166 months ($SD = 105.5$). The mean age of participants at the time of suicide was 30.7 ($SD = 10.1$). Similarly, the mean age of the deceased at the time of suicide was 30.8 ($SD = 13.9$). Regarding the expectation of the suicide, only 9 (5.9%) participants indicated that the suicide was expected to a high degree, whereas 47 (30.9%) participants indicated that suicide was wholly unexpected. Regarding the nature of the participant's relationship with the person who died by suicide, 26 (17.1%) participants reported losing a parent, 43 (28.3%) lost a sibling, 29 (19.1%) lost a child, 16 (10.5%) lost a spouse, 9 (5.9%) lost a relative (uncle, aunt, cousin), and 29 (19.1%) lost a close friend.

3.3. Intercorrelations of Study Variables

Pearson correlations between the study variables were calculated for preliminary data analysis. The means, standard deviations, and intercorrelations are presented in Table 1. The matrix shows that PGS were significantly and positively correlated with the TB and PB dimensions of the interpersonal theory of suicide and negatively correlated with SD. In addition, a relatively strong positive correlation was found between PGS and depression and between PGS and guilt. Furthermore, scores for PGS were positively associated with participants' age at the time of suicide and the fear of a future suicide by a family member. However, the time elapsed since the suicide was not significantly associated with PGS.

Table 1. Means, standard deviations, and intercorrelations between main study measures (n = 152).

	Measures	1	2	3	4	5	6	7	8	9
1	Time since suicide [1]	1								
2	Participant's age at the time of suicide	−0.41 **	1							
3	Fear of a future suicide of a family member	−0.17	−0.12	1						
4	Depression	−0.08	0.13	0.42 ***	1					
5	Guilt	−0.09	0.13	0.34 ***	0.59 ***	1				
6	PB	−0.09	−0.09	0.47 ***	0.55 ***	0.42 ***	1			
7	TB	−0.18	0.14	0.25 ***	0.42 ***	0.33 ***	0.71 ***	1		
8	Self-disclosure	0.12	−0.31 ***	−0.07	−0.18 *	−0.22 **	−0.24 **	−43 **	1	
9	PGS	−0.18	0.32 ***	0.35 ***	0.71 ***	0.57 ***	0.37 ***	0.19 *	−0.30 ***	1
	Mean	166.03	30.68	4.84	6.41	3.53	12.90	20.35	3.66	2.08
	Standard Deviation	105.52	10.13	1.14	3.61	1.03	3.82	5.39	0.73	0.50
	Range: Min-max	24–672	9–60	1–7	0–25	1–10	8–33	9–42	1–7	1–4

* $p < 0.05$, ** $p < 0.01$, *** $p < 0.001$. PB = perceived burdensomeness; TB = thwarted belongingness; PGS = prolonged grief symptoms according to the PG-13-R scale. [1] In months.

3.4. Hierarchical Regression Analyses

A four-step hierarchical multiple regression was performed to determine if interpersonal variables (PB, TB, and SD) predict the level of PGS among SLSs, beyond demographics, depression, and guilt variables [52] and with PGS as the dependent variable. In Step 1, three variables (time elapsed since the suicide, the age of the participant at the time of the suicide, and the level of fear of a future suicide of a family member) were entered into the equation. In Step 2, the intrapersonal factors (depression and guilt) were entered into the equation. In Step 3, the interpersonal characteristics (PB, TB, and SD) were entered into the equation to examine their contribution beyond the intrapersonal factors. In the final step, the Guilt X PB and the TB X SD interactions were added to the model.

Overall, the model was significant and explained 60% of the variance in PGS ($F(11, 140) = 18.95$, $p < 0.001$). Table 2 presents the contribution of each variable when entered into the regression. In Step 1, suicide-related demographic variables explained 24.6% of the variance ($F(3, 148) = 16.09$, $p < 0.001$). Specifically, we found that the participant's age at the time of suicide had a significant positive contribution to PGS ($\beta = 0.34$, t (148) = 4.98, p <.001). Fear of future suicide by a family member also had a significant positive contribution to PGS ($\beta = 0.32$, t (148) = 5.30, $p < 0.001$). However, time since suicide did not significantly contribute to PGS. In Step 2, depression and guilt contributed by 24.4% to the explained variance beyond suicide-related demographic variables ($F(2, 146) = 34.94$, $p < 0.001$). Specifically, both depression ($\beta = 0.45$, t (146) = 6.10, $p < 0.001$) and guilt ($\beta = 0.19$, t (146) = 2.67, $p < 0.01$) had a significant positive contribution to PGS. In Step 3, PB, TB, and SD contributed an additional 6% of the variance beyond the intrapersonal and suicide-related demographic variables ($F(3, 143) = 5.79$, $p < 0.001$). Specifically, TB had a significant positive contribution to PGS ($\beta = 0.32$, t (143) = 3.80, $p < 0.001$). In addition, SD had a significant negative contribution to PGS ($\beta = -0.21$, t (143) = −3.07, $p < 0.01$). However, PB yielded only a marginally significant positive contribution to PGS. At the final step, the three interactions between guilt and PB, TB, and SD significantly contributed to PGS beyond all other variables, accounting for an additional 5.3% of the total variance ($F(3, 140) = 6.15$, $p < 0.001$). Specifically, the interaction of guilt and PB had a significant contribution to PGS ($\beta = 0.46$, t (140) = 3.87, $p < 0.001$). Additionally, the interaction of guilt and TB had a significant negative contribution to PGS ($\beta = -0.30$, t (140) = −2.42, $p < 0.05$). The Guilt X SD interaction did not significantly contribute to PGS.

Table 2. Summary of hierarchical multiple regression analysis for predicting PGS (n = 152).

Predictors	B	SE B	β	ΔR^2	R^2/Adj. R^2	F_{change}
Step 1				0.25 ***	0.25/0.23	16.08 ***
Time since suicide [1]	0.00	0.01	−0.02			
Participant's age at the time of suicide.	0.34	0.07	0.37 ***			
Fear of a future suicide of a family member	0.34	0.06	0.38 ***			
Step 2				0.24 ***	0.49/0.47	34.95 ***
Depression	0.17	0.07	0.45 ***			
Guilt	0.44	0.06	0.19 **			
Step 3				0.06 ***	0.55/0.52	5.79 ***
PB	0.16	0.08	0.16			
TB	0.29	0.08	0.32 ***			
Self-disclosure	−0.19	0.06	−0.21 **			
Step 4				0.05 ***	0.60/0.57	6.15 ***
Guilt X PB	0.21	0.05	0.46 ***			
Guilt X TB	0.12	0.05	0.30 *			
Guilt X SD	−0.05	0.06	−0.06			

Degrees of freedom for Step 1, $F(3, 148)$; for Step 2, $F(5, 146)$; for Step 3, $F(8, 143)$; and for Step 4, $F(11, 140)$. * $p < 0.05$. ** $p < 0.01$. *** $p < 0.001$. PB = perceived burdensomeness; TB = thwarted belongingness; SD = self-disclosure; PGS = prolonged grief symptoms as measured by the PG-13-R scale. [1] no. months.

Moderation Analyses

To understand the nature of the significant interactions, two moderation analyses were conducted using the PROCESS macro (Model 1; [51]). Two moderation analyses were performed with standard scores (Z) of PGS as the dependent variable and guilt as the independent variable. The moderators were PB and TB levels.

As presented in Figure 1, a significant interaction was found between guilt and PB in predicting PGS (b = 0.11, SE = 0.04, 95% CI [0.03, 0.17], t (172) = 2.83, $p < 0.01$). Examining the interaction revealed that for SLSs with higher levels of PB, guilt had a positive and stronger contribution to PGS (for low PB: b = 0.34, SE = 0.09, 95% CI [0.16, 0.52], t (172) = 3.81, $p < 0.001$; for moderate PB: b = 0.44, SE = 0.07, 95% CI [0.31, 0.58], t (172) = 6.38, $p < 0.001$; for high PB: b = 0.55, SE = 0.07, 95% CI [0.42, 0.68], t (172) = 8.12, $p < 0.001$). The interaction between guilt and TB in predicting PGS was not found to be significant in the moderation analysis (b = 0.03, SE = 0.03, 95% CI [−0.03, 0.09], t (172) = 0.98, p = 0.328).

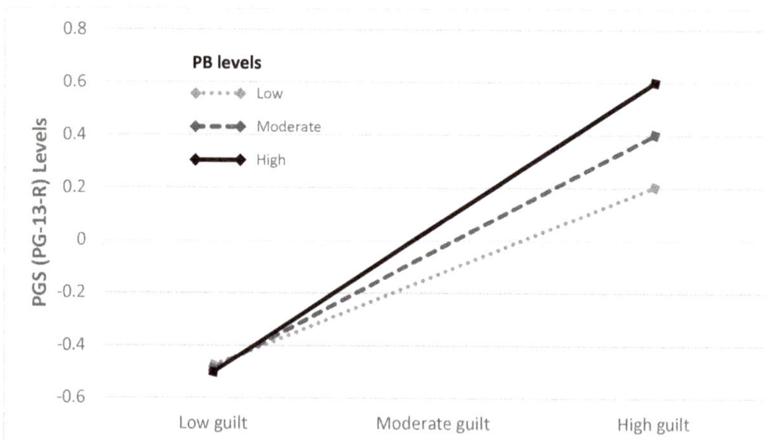

Figure 1. The association between guilt and PGS as moderated by PB levels (n = 152). PB = perceived burdensomeness. PGS = prolonged grief symptoms.

4. Discussion

To our knowledge, this study is the first to demonstrate the critical contribution of interpersonal variables to the relationship between guilt and PGS in the aftermath of suicide loss by using the revised DSM−TR diagnosis of PGD. As SLSs are at increased risk of experiencing guilt, shame, and stigma [25], it is critical to understand the mechanisms that facilitate (or buffer) the contribution of such feelings to the development of PGS.

Our results indicated that guilt and depression are critical contributors to the level of PGS beyond sociodemographic and loss-related factors. These findings align with several studies that have highlighted the importance of guilt as a significant predictor of the development or progression of psychopathological symptoms in grief following suicide loss [19,30] and grief in general [53–55]. Other studies have suggested that feelings of guilt are longer lasting and more intense in suicide grief than in other forms of grief [56,57].

Furthermore, we found that interpersonal variables (i.e., perceived burdensomeness, thwarted belongingness, and self-disclosure) contributed to PGS beyond intrapersonal, sociodemographic, and loss-related factors. Given the strong association between depression and PGS, any contributions beyond depression can be considered highly noteworthy. Thus, our results suggest that the SLSs' devastating feelings of lack of belonging, isolation, being a burden to their surroundings, and difficulty disclosing intimate feelings and thoughts may contribute to PGS. This finding aligns with several cross-sectional and longitudinal studies that highlight the critical role of these variables in maladaptive grief response [22,30,58,59].

This study's main finding was that PB levels significantly moderated the contribution of guilt to PGS. Thus, it can be inferred from these results that perceived burdensomeness plays a significant role in facilitating PGS among SLSs, especially those experiencing guilt.

4.1. The Contribution of Interpersonal Characteristics to PGD among Suicide-Loss Survivors

Our findings offer evidence that interpersonal factors can have a positive and protective effect on the development of PGS among SLSs. We suggest that sense of belonging, considered one of the basic psychological needs of humankind [60], may provide a significant protective barrier to these grief reactions and may thus help SLSs to better cope with different psychological difficulties [61], even with suicidal ideation and behavior [36,62]. Moreover, our results suggest that self-disclosure may play an essential role in coping with grief after the suicide of a loved one. Previous studies [33] found that encouraging survivors to self-disclose promotes the exchange of social support and the experience of belonging, connectedness, and togetherness, which may inhibit complications in grief [33]. Self-disclosure may help organize intrapsychic grief and process the emotional aspects of the traumatic suicide event [61,63], especially for individuals who have difficulty accepting and regulating their emotions [64,65]. When SLSs conceal the suicidal event or avoid talking about it (for example, because they perceive themselves as a burden to those around them), they risk shutting themselves off from people who are a potential source of help, comfort, and support [41]. Similarly, Oexle et al. [66] showed that the tendency to maintain a veil of secrecy regarding suicide loss is associated with more severe grief difficulties among SLSs.

These findings are not surprising considering that coping with loss after a suicide has been shown to have severe effects on relationships in the social support systems of SLSs [41,43]. Many SLSs feel that their relationships with those around them become more distant after the suicidal event [67], and they are less confident in and less reliant on their social networks [68]. Moreover, these findings are consistent with the new DSM-5-TR criteria, which indicate intense loneliness and a sense of detachment from others as symptoms (listed in Criterion C) for the diagnosis of PGD [5]. In addition, we may speculate that damage to the supportive interpersonal network of a SLS may exacerbate other grief reactions listed as symptoms in the DSM-5-TR. For example, SLSs may experience significant disruption in their social relationships due to a desire to stave off reminders of the deceased. These unwanted reminders and cues may include people, places, or situations that could trigger their sense of loss and other painful feelings related to the deceased and the suicide event (listed as a symptom in Criterion C for the diagnosis of PGD according to the DSM-5-TR criteria) [5]. The resultant profound loneliness may even intensify their longing for and preoccupation with the deceased person (listed as a symptom in Criterion B for the diagnosis of PGD according to the DSM-5-TR criteria) [5]. We recommend that these issues be investigated in future longitudinal studies to demonstrate clear causality.

Thus, experiences of belongingness and solidarity may help SLSs cope with painful feelings of grief, including social isolation which could lead to PGD, as formulated in the DSM-TR-5 [5]. Knowing that one can rely on the support of friends and family and not face a lonely future can help soften the blow of loss and possibly ward off its harmful effects. These benefits can be achieved, among others, through religious affiliation, which may provide a sense of belonging [69]. Religious affiliation is thought to help cope with grief; it has been shown to protect against painful emotions associated with grief [70].

4.2. The Moderating Role of Perceived Burdensomeness in the Association between Guilt and PGD among Suicide-Loss Survivors

Our results suggest that PB levels significantly moderate the contribution of guilt to PGS. PB is interactively related to interpersonal variables such as social belonging, social support, and self-disclosure [37]. Therefore, we suggest that SLSs who experience intense feelings of guilt following the suicide of a loved one but also feel justified remaining within their immediate social environment may incur significant benefits. These SLSs will then likely benefit from the healing qualities of a sense of belonging and togetherness and the opportunity to share the distressing guilt they carry in their hearts with those around them. Conversely, when SLSs who experience guilt are confronted with the belief that they are a burden to those around them, the emotional pain they carry can intensify and interfere with their grieving process in several ways.

Guilt may reinforce survivors' perceptions that they are burdensome to those around them during the grieving process [22,57]. After the loss, many SLSs ruminate intensely about the conceivable reasons for the suicidal event and their role in it [56,71,72] and often exaggerate their responsibility [20,73]. In addition, the internal guilt that many SLSs feel regardless of their environment [67] may be met with society's negative stereotypes and prejudices [43,74], which has recently been associated with higher levels of perceived burden [75]. Thus, guilt may reinforce SLSs' perception that they are so defective that their presence could harm and burden their loved ones or society in general [75].

SLSs may also feel that the expression of guilt, loneliness, and grief burdens their social environment, particularly if their acquaintances are grieving for the same person who died of suicide [59]. Thus, they may be reluctant to share their feelings of guilt with others, preferring to remain alone with them [76]. This perception may even lead SLSs to avoid entering new relationships for fear of further loss because they believe they are "cursed" [67]. Therefore, it is likely that this interactive relationship may increase feelings of loneliness and disconnection from their environment. In addition, we suggest that SLSs' deeply held belief that their loved ones would be better off without them exacerbates their feelings of guilt. For example, when SLSs experience themselves as a burden, they inevitably feel dependent on others to some degree and may experience frustration and guilt for the resulting difficulties [77]. Finally, PB and guilt contain a strong emotional component associated with self-loathing [36,78], and their coexistence could dramatically exacerbate their inner turmoil, self-accusation, and emotional distress following the loss. This perspective would be interesting to explore in future studies.

Thus, we suggest that the destructive relationship between guilt and feelings of burdensomeness may interfere with normative grief processes and increase the likelihood of PGD among SLSs. This process may be driven by severely limiting the individual's capacity to seek help in their immediate environment, deepening feelings of isolation, being cut off from others, and increasing self-hatred and emotional distress. In addition, this interactive relationship can interfere with the ability of the SLS to experience hope and vitality, making their future seem bleak, empty, and meaningless. These perceptions and feelings correspond to the symptoms listed in Criterion C for the diagnosis of PGD, as articulated in the DSM-TR-5 [5].

4.3. Limitations and Future Directions

This study has several methodological limitations. The first limitation concerns the voluntary nature of the sample. Most participants were members of organizations and forums concerned with loss in the wake of suicide. Therefore, individuals with some potential for enduring pain may be overrepresented in the current sample. In addition, the recruitment process likely yielded an overrepresentation of people active on the Internet and social media. Consequently, our sample may comprise fewer individuals with high levels of distress who do not have Internet access or are not active on social media platforms.

Furthermore, our sample consisted mainly of participants with a high education level and a high proportion were women (80.4%), limiting the generalizability of the current results to other populations. However, even in representative samples of SLSs, women are typically overrepresented to some degree, given that men are three times more likely than women to die of suicide [58]. However, as women are often more prone to higher levels of guilt [79], gender should be considered in future studies. In addition, the overrepresentation of secular individuals in our sample (73.7%) may bias the study findings due to the protective effects of religion and spirituality on grief [70] and guilt [80]. Finally, using an Israeli sample with specific cultural scenarios regarding grief and sharing [81] may limit the generalizability of our findings to other cultures. Therefore, a broader and more representative sample of SLSs will facilitate a more comprehensive and representative understanding of PGS among suicide survivors.

Another limitation relates to the type of questionnaires used in our study. The use of self-report questionnaires may introduce various biases in participants' reports (e.g., social desirability), a factor particularly relevant when addressing the sensitive topic of PGD and guilt following a suicide. Furthermore, PGD identification was derived from self-report questionnaires derived from cross-sectional samples. Future studies should therefore consider collecting data from multiple sources of information and incorporate more objective measures. For example, a more rigorous method for identifying PGD could include systematic clinical interviews where trained mental health professionals would make the diagnosis.

Finally, the study's cross-sectional nature and the lack of an assessment of interpersonal functioning before the suicidal event limit our ability to determine the order of the phenomena and thus the causality of these relationships. The effects of guilt, PB, TB, and SD on PGS may be interactive and circular. Moreover, some participants may have had a history of mental disorders (e.g., depression) and may have been prone to guilt prior to the suicidal event [82]. Therefore, we cannot rule out the possibility that a participant's current report of guilt and depression reflects circumstances that preceded the suicidal event and contributed to its affect while not being directly related to the suicide. Thus, we recommend that future studies consider the psychiatric history of participants and conduct a longitudinal study that might reveal the approximate causal relationship between intrapersonal and interpersonal characteristics and PGS.

4.4. Theoretical and Practical Implications

Despite the noted limitations, the present study has theoretical and practical implications. Concerning theoretical implications, the study's findings highlight PB's crucial and moderating role in the relationship between guilt and PGD among SLSs. Thus, our findings suggest that the recovery process relies upon SLSs' interpersonal experiences and perceptions when dealing with the suicide of a loved one, especially for those with high levels of guilt.

Feelings of guilt and other painful emotions associated with death may impact SLSs' social networks by creating the harsh perception that they are a burden to those around them. These sensations and perceptions interfere with normative grieving processes, impede receiving support and sharing their pain, and increase the likelihood that they will suffer from PGD. Thus, the study findings highlight the importance of the resilience factors of sense of belonging and self-disclosure, which can be served as barriers to PGS among SLSs. It is noteworthy that the contribution of guilt and perceived burdensomeness on PGS is likely interactive and circular, as high levels of PGS also contribute to increases in guilt and PB which, in turn, increase the severity of PGS. Therefore, it would be essential to investigate this complex relationship in future longitudinal studies, which could contribute to designing targeted interventions for SLSs.

Concerning practical implications, our findings suggest that interpersonal variables may serve as buffers against grief complications, particularly among SLSs who suffer from painful guilt. Therefore, health care professionals and the general environment surrounding the SLS should monitor the social involvement of the SLS and the extent of social support they receive. Furthermore, disclosing intimate feelings and thoughts may protect against PGD by enhancing a sense of belonging, relieving harmful cognitions (e.g., perceived burdensomeness), and reducing guilt [23,83].

It is noteworthy that PB and TB typically reflect distorted perceptions and are not based on facts [84]. Therefore, primary psychoeducational interventions could help SLSs gain support and a new perspective on themselves and the suicide event [85]. In addition, psychotherapy protocols aiming to help people understand their relationships with others may benefit individuals with high TB and PB levels. For example, interpersonal psychotherapy (IPT), which aims to improve interpersonal skills, especially self-disclosure, may prove effective for SLSs [86]. Moreover, psychosocial therapies focusing on activating social support (to reduce feelings of thwarted belongingness) and reducing maladaptive cognitions (i.e., helping survivors find ways to contemplate death that do not evoke strong feelings of guilt or perceived burdensomeness) may benefit SLSs [1].

Another possible treatment avenue may be group therapy, which can facilitate SLSs sharing and disclosing their feelings of guilt, modifying the meaning of the suicide event, normalizing the grief experience of suicide, and, most importantly, providing them with a sense of belonging [87]. However, peer support programs may provide similar benefits [88], where SLSs can share their feelings and personal stories with each other, validate their grief experience, and exchange psychosocial support that strengthens their sense of belonging and "togetherness" [88]. Furthermore, our findings point to the potential of mindfulness-based interventions to promote self-compassion, which has been shown to positively impact feelings such as TB and PB [32,65], as well as coping with unpleasant emotions such as guilt [89]. These approaches could help the bereaved overcome the painful loss of a loved one and even exhibit growth in the wake of these painful circumstances [32].

5. Conclusions

In conclusion, this study has expanded the current knowledge of the factors and mechanisms contributing to PGD according to the criteria proposed in the DSM-5-TR [3] after a suicide loss. Moreover, the study's findings indicate the crucial and moderating role of perceived burdensomeness in the relationship between guilt and PGD among SLSs. It can be suggested that guilt and perceived burdensomeness may have a detrimental interaction on a person's connection to their social network, thus interfering with normative grief processes and increasing the risk of PGD among SLSs. In addition, the study's findings highlight the importance of social and community factors in preventing PGD among suicide-loss survivors and suggest that the resilience factors of sense of belonging and self-disclosure may help SLSs to effectively cope with PGS.

Author Contributions: Conceptualization, Y.L.-B.; formal analysis, Y.L.-B. and T.B.-Y.; methodology, Y.L.-B.; supervision, Y.L.-B.; validation, T.B.-Y.; writing—original draft, T.B.-Y. All authors have read and agreed to the published version of the manuscript.

Funding: This research was funded by the American Foundation for Suicide Prevention (PRG-2-083-14).

Institutional Review Board Statement: The study was conducted in accordance with the Declaration of Helsinki and approved by the Institutional Review Board of the Ruppin Academic Center (protocol code 122, 5 January 2015).

Informed Consent Statement: Informed consent was obtained from all subjects involved in the study.

Data Availability Statement: Due to ethical concerns, supporting data cannot be made openly available. Further information about the data and conditions for access can be received by approaching the corresponding author.

Conflicts of Interest: The authors declare no conflict of interest.

References

1. Shear, M.K. Complicated grief. *N. Engl. J. Med.* **2015**, *372*, 153–160. [CrossRef] [PubMed]
2. Boelen, P.A.; Prigerson, H.G. The influence of symptoms of prolonged grief disorder, depression, and anxiety on quality of life among bereaved adults. *Eur. Arch. Psychiatry Clin. Neurosci.* **2007**, *257*, 442–452. [CrossRef] [PubMed]
3. Prigerson, H.G.; Boelen, P.; Xu, J.; Smith, K.V.; Maciejewski, P.K. Validation of the new DSM-5-TR criteria for prolonged grief disorder and the PG-13-Revised (PG-13-R) scale. *World Psychiatry* **2021**, *20*, 96–106. [CrossRef]
4. Maercker, A.; Brewin, C.R.; Bryant, R.A.; Cloitre, M.; Van-Ommeren, M.; Jones, L.M.; Humayan, A.; Kagee, A.; Liosa, A.; Rousseau, C.; et al. Diagnosis and classification of disorders specifically associated with stress: Proposals for ICD-11. *World Psychiatry* **2013**, *12*, 198–206. [CrossRef] [PubMed]
5. American Psychiatric Association (APA). *Diagnostic and Statistical Manual of Mental Disorders, Fifth Edition, Text Revision (DSM-5-TR)*; American Psychiatric Association Publishing: Washington, DC, USA, 2022.
6. Prigerson, H.G.; Kakarala, S.; Gang, J.; Maciejewski, P.K. History and status of prolonged grief disorder as a psychiatric diagnosis. *Annu. Rev. Clin. Psychol.* **2021**, *17*, 109–126. [CrossRef] [PubMed]
7. Holland, J.M.; Neimeyer, R.A.; Boelen, P.A.; Prigerson, H.G. The underlying structure of grief: A taxometric investigation of prolonged and normal reactions to loss. *J. Psychopathol. Behav. Assess.* **2009**, *31*, 190–201. [CrossRef]
8. Komischke-Konnerup, K.B.; Zachariae, R.; Johannsen, M.; Nielsen, L.D.; O'Connor, M. Co-occurrence of prolonged grief symptoms and symptoms of depression, anxiety, and posttraumatic stress in bereaved adults: A systematic review and meta-analysis. *J. Affect. Disord. Rep.* **2021**, *4*, 100140. [CrossRef]
9. World Health Organization. *Suicide Worldwide in 2019: Global Health Estimates*; World Health Organization: Geneva, Switzerland, 2021.
10. Jordan, A.H.; Litz, B.T. Prolonged grief disorder: Diagnostic, assessment, and treatment considerations. *Prof. Psychol. Res. Pract.* **2014**, *45*, 180–187. [CrossRef]
11. Boelen, P.A.; Lenferink, L.I.M. Comparison of six proposed diagnostic criteria sets for disturbed grief. *Psychiatry Res.* **2020**, *285*, 112786. [CrossRef]
12. Parisi, A.; Sharma, A.; Howard, M.O.; Wilson, A.M. The relationship between substance misuse and complicated grief: A systematic review. *J. Subst. Abuse Treat.* **2019**, *103*, 43–57. [CrossRef]
13. Maciejewski, P.K.; Maercker, A.; Boelen, P.A.; Prigerson, H.G. "Prolonged grief disorder" and "persistent complex bereavement disorder," but not "complicated grief," are one and the same diagnostic entity: An analysis of data from the Yale Bereavement Study. *World Psychiatry* **2016**, *15*, 266–275. [CrossRef] [PubMed]
14. Maccallum, F.; Bryant, R.A. A network approach to understanding quality of life impairments in prolonged grief disorder. *J. Trauma. Stress* **2020**, *33*, 106–115. [CrossRef] [PubMed]
15. Djelantik, M.J.; Smid, G.E.; Mroz, A.; Kleber, R.J.; Boelen, P.A. The prevalence of prolonged grief disorder in bereaved individuals following unnatural losses: Systematic review and meta regression analysis. *J. Affect. Disord.* **2020**, *265*, 146–156. [CrossRef] [PubMed]
16. Cerel, J.; Brown, M.M.; Maple, M.; Singleton, M.; van de Venne, J.; Moore, M.; Flaherty, C. How many people are exposed to suicide? Not six. *Suicide Life Threat. Behav.* **2019**, *49*, 529–534. [CrossRef]
17. Pitman, A.; Osborn, D.; King, M.; Erlangsen, A. Effects of suicide bereavement on mental health and suicide risk. *Lancet Psychiatry* **2014**, *1*, 86–94. [CrossRef]
18. Sveen, C.A.; Walby, F.A. Suicide Survivors' Mental Health and Grief Reactions: A Systematic Review of Controlled Studies. *Suicide Life Threat. Behav.* **2008**, *38*, 13–29. [CrossRef]
19. Tal, I.; Mauro, C.; Reynolds, C.F.; Shear, M.K.; Simon, N.; Lebowitz, B.; Skritskaya, N.; Wang, Y.; Qiu, X.; Iglewicz, A.; et al. Complicated grief after suicide bereavement and other causes of death. *Death Stud.* **2017**, *41*, 267–275. [CrossRef]
20. Young, I.L.; Iglewicz, A.; Glorioso, D.; Lanouette, N.; Seay, K.; Ilapkurti, M.; Zisook, S. Suicide bereavement and complicated grief. *Dialogues Clin. Neurosci.* **2012**, *14*, 177–186. [CrossRef]
21. Nam, I. Suicide bereavement and complicated grief: Experiential avoidance as a mediating mechanism. *J. Loss Trauma.* **2016**, *21*, 325–334. [CrossRef]
22. Levi-Belz, Y.; Aisenberg, D. Interpersonal predictors of suicide ideation and complicated-grief trajectories among suicide bereaved individuals: A four-year longitudinal study. *J. Affect. Disord.* **2021**, *1*, 1030–1035. [CrossRef]

23. Jordan, J.R. Is suicide bereavement different? A reassessment of the literature. *Suicide Life Threat. Behav.* **2001**, *31*, 91–102. [CrossRef] [PubMed]
24. Begley, M.; Quayle, E. The lived experience of adults bereaved by suicide: A phenomenological study. *Crisis* **2007**, *28*, 26–34. [CrossRef] [PubMed]
25. Feigelman, W.; Cerel, J. Feelings of blameworthiness and their associations with the grieving process in suicide mourning. *Front. Psychol.* **2020**, *11*, 610. [CrossRef]
26. McMenamy, J.M.; Jordan, J.R.; Mitchell, A.M. What do suicide survivors tell us they need? Results of a pilot study. *Suicide Life Threat. Behav.* **2008**, *38*, 375–389. [CrossRef] [PubMed]
27. Li, J.; Stroebe, M.; Chan, C.; Chow, A. Guilt in bereavement: A review and conceptual framework. *Death Stud.* **2014**, *38*, 165–171. [CrossRef] [PubMed]
28. Bruno, S.; Lutwak, N.; Agin, M.A. Conceptualizations of guilt and the corresponding relationships to emotional ambivalence, self-disclosure, loneliness, and alienation. *Personal. Individ. Differ.* **2009**, *47*, 487–491. [CrossRef]
29. Levi-Belz, Y.; Lev-Ari, L. "Let's Talk About It": The moderating role of self-disclosure on complicated grief over time among suicide survivors. *Int. J. Environ. Res. Public Health* **2019**, *16*, 3740. [CrossRef]
30. Wagner, B.; Hofmann, L.; Grafiadeli, R. The relationship between guilt, depression, prolonged grief, and posttraumatic stress symptoms after suicide bereavement. *J. Clin. Psychol.* **2021**, *77*, 2545–2558. [CrossRef]
31. Levi-Belz, Y.; Feigelman, W. Pulling together—The protective role of belongingness for depression, suicidal ideation and behavior among suicide-bereaved individuals. *Crisis* **2022**, *43*, 278. [CrossRef]
32. Levi-Belz, Y.; Krysinska, K.; Andriessen, K. "Turning personal tragedy into triumph": A systematic review and meta-analysis of studies on posttraumatic growth among suicide-loss survivors. *Psychol. Trauma* **2021**, *13*, 322–332. [CrossRef]
33. Levi-Belz, Y.; Lev-Ari, L. Is there anybody out there? Attachment style and interpersonal facilitators as protective factors against complicated grief among suicide-loss survivors. *J. Nerv. Ment. Dis.* **2019**, *207*, 131–136. [CrossRef] [PubMed]
34. Joiner, T. *Why People Die by Suicide*; Harvard University Press: Cambridge, MA, USA, 2005.
35. Joiner, T.E.; Van Orden, K.A.; Witte, T.K.; Selby, E.A.; Ribeiro, J.D.; Lewis, R.; Rudd, M.D. Main predictions of the interpersonal-psychological theory of suicidal behavior: Empirical tests in two samples of young adults. *J. Abnorm. Psychol.* **2009**, *118*, 634–646. [CrossRef]
36. Van Orden, K.A.; Witte, T.K.; Cukrowicz, K.C.; Braithwaite, S.R.; Selby, E.A.; Joiner, T.E. The interpersonal theory of suicide. *Psychol. Rev.* **2010**, *117*, 575–600. [CrossRef] [PubMed]
37. Levi-Belz, Y. With a little help from my friends: A follow-up study on the contribution of interpersonal characteristics to posttraumatic growth among suicide-loss survivors. *Psychol. Trauma* **2019**, *11*, 895–904. [CrossRef] [PubMed]
38. Jourard, S.M. *Self-Disclosure: An Experimental Analysis of the Transparent Self*; John Wiley: New York, NY, USA, 1971.
39. Apter, A.; Horesh, N.; Gothelf, D.; Graffi, H.; Lepkifker, E. Relationship between self-disclosure and serious suicidal behavior. *Compr. Psychiat.* **2001**, *42*, 70–75. [CrossRef]
40. Brown, E.J.; Heimberg, R.G. Effects of writing about rape: Evaluating Pennebaker's paradigm with a severe trauma. *J. Trauma. Stress* **2001**, *14*, 781–790. [CrossRef]
41. Jordan, J.R. Bereavement after suicide. *Psychiatr. Ann.* **2008**, *38*, 679–685. [CrossRef]
42. Hemenover, S.H. The good, the bad, and the healthy: Impacts of emotional disclosure of trauma on resilient self-concept and psychological distress. *Pers. Soc. Psychol. Bull.* **2003**, *29*, 1236–1244. [CrossRef]
43. Cvinar, J.G. Do suicide survivors suffer social stigma: A review of the literature. *Perspect. Psychiatr. Care* **2005**, *41*, 14–21. [CrossRef]
44. Solano, C.H.; Batten, P.G.; Parish, E.A. Loneliness and patterns of self-disclosure. *J. Pers. Soc. Psychol.* **1982**, *43*, 524–531. [CrossRef]
45. Øktedalen, T.; Hoffart, A.; Langkaas, T.F. Trauma-related shame and guilt as time-varying predictors of posttraumatic stress disorder symptoms during imagery exposure and imagery rescripting—A randomized controlled trial. *Psychother. Res.* **2015**, *25*, 518–532. [CrossRef] [PubMed]
46. Kubany, E.S.; Haynes, S.N.; Abueg, F.R.; Manke, F.P.; Brennan, J.M.; Stahura, C. Development and validation of the Trauma-Related Guilt Inventory (TRGI). *Psychol. Assess.* **1996**, *8*, 428–444. [CrossRef]
47. Kroenke, K.; Spitzer, R.L.; Williams, J.B. The PHQ-9: Validity of a brief depression severity measure. *J. Gen. Intern. Med.* **2001**, *16*, 606–613. [CrossRef] [PubMed]
48. Kahn, J.H.; Hessling, R.M. Measuring the tendency to conceal versus disclose psychological distress. *J. Soc. Clin. Psychol.* **2001**, *20*, 41–65. [CrossRef]
49. Hwang, Y.; Lee, D.H.; Prigerson, H.G. Psychometric properties, stability, and predictive validity of the Korean version of the Prolonged Grief Disorder Scale (PG-13-K): A longitudinal study among bereaved Koreans. *Death Stud.* **2022**, 1–11. [CrossRef]
50. Aiken, L.S.; West, S.G.; Reno, R.R. *Multiple Regression: Testing and Interpreting Interactions*; Sage: New York, NY, USA, 1991.
51. Hayes, F.H. *Introduction to Mediation, Moderation, and Conditional Process Analysis: A Regression-Based Approach*, 3rd ed.; The Guilford Press: New York, NY, USA, 2017.
52. Cohen, J.; Cohen, P.; West, S.G.; Aiken, L.S. *Applied Multiple Regression/Correlation Analysis for the Behavioral Sciences*, 3rd ed.; Lawrence Erlbaum: Mahwah, NJ, USA, 2003.
53. Kokou-Kpolou, C.K.; Park, S.; Lenferink, L.; Iorfa, S.K.; Fernández-Alcántara, M.; Derivois, D.; Cénat, J.M. Prolonged grief and depression: A latent class analysis. *Psychiatry Res.* **2021**, *299*, 113864. [CrossRef]

54. LeBlanc, N.J.; Toner, E.R.; O'Day, E.B.; Moore, C.W.; Marques, L.; Robinaugh, D.J.; McNally, R.J. Shame, guilt, and pride after loss: Exploring the relationship between moral emotions and psychopathology in bereaved adults. *J. Affect. Disord.* **2020**, *263*, 405–412. [CrossRef]
55. Li, J.; Tendeiro, J.N.; Stroebe, M. Guilt in bereavement: Its relationship with complicated grief and depression. *Int. J. Psychol.* **2019**, *54*, 454–461. [CrossRef]
56. Camacho, D.; Pérez-Nieto, M.Á.; Gordillo, F. The role of rumination in the guilt associated with bereavement according to cause of death. *Psychiatry Res.* **2018**, *270*, 1053–1058. [CrossRef]
57. Pitman, A.; Osborn, D.; Rantell, K.; King, M. The stigma perceived by people bereaved by suicide and other sudden deaths: A cross-sectional UK study of 3432 bereaved adults. *J. Psychosom. Res.* **2016**, *87*, 22–29. [CrossRef]
58. Feigelman, W.; Cerel, J.; Sanford, R. Disclosure in traumatic deaths as correlates of differential mental health outcomes. *Death Stud.* **2018**, *42*, 456–462. [CrossRef] [PubMed]
59. Hill, R.M.; Penner, F.; Vanwoerden, S.; Mellick, W.; Kazimi, I.; Sharp, C. Interpersonal trust and suicide ideation among adolescent psychiatric inpatients: An indirect effect via perceived burdensomeness. *Suicide Life Threat. Behav.* **2019**, *49*, 240–252. [CrossRef]
60. Baumeister, R.F.; Leary, M.R. The need to belong: Desire for interpersonal attachments as a fundamental human motivation. *Psychol. Bull.* **1995**, *117*, 497–529. [CrossRef] [PubMed]
61. Choenarom, C.; Williams, R.A.; Hagerty, B.M. The role of sense of belonging and social support on stress and depression in individuals with depression. *Arch. Psychiatr. Nurs.* **2005**, *19*, 18–29. [CrossRef] [PubMed]
62. Gvion, Y.; Levi-Belz, Y. Serious suicide attempts: Systematic review of psychological risk factors. *Front. Psychiatry* **2018**, *9*, 1–17. [CrossRef]
63. Stroebe, W.; Schut, H.; Stroebe, M.S. Grief work, disclosure and counseling: Do they help the bereaved? *Clin. Psychol. Rev.* **2005**, *25*, 395–414. [CrossRef]
64. Lacour, O.; Morina, N.; Spaaij, J.; Nickerson, A.; Schnyder, U.; von Känel, R.; Bryant, R.A.; Schick, M. Prolonged grief disorder among refugees in psychological treatment: Association with self-efficacy and emotion regulation. *Front. Psychiatry* **2020**, *11*, 256. [CrossRef]
65. Umphrey, L.R.; Sherblom, J.C.; Swiatkowski, P. Relationship of self-compassion, hope, and emotional control to perceived burdensomeness, thwarted belongingness, and suicidal ideation. *Crisis* **2021**, *42*, 121–127. [CrossRef]
66. Oexle, N.; Feigelman, W.; Sheehan, L. Perceived suicide stigma, secrecy about suicide loss and mental health outcomes. *Death Stud.* **2020**, *44*, 248–255. [CrossRef]
67. Dunn, R.G.; Morrish-Vidners, D. The psychological and social experience of suicide survivors. *OMEGA J. Death Dying* **1988**, *18*, 175–215. [CrossRef]
68. Farberow, N.L.; Gallagher-Thompson, D.; Gilewski, M.; Thompson, L. Changes in grief and mental health of bereaved spouses of older suicides. *J. Gerontol.* **1992**, *47*, 357–366. [CrossRef] [PubMed]
69. Zhang, H.; Hook, J.N.; Farrell, J.E.; Mosher, D.K.; Captari, L.E.; Coomes, S.P.; Van Tongeren, D.R.; Davis, D.E. Exploring social belonging and meaning in religious groups. *J. Psychol. Theol.* **2019**, *47*, 3–19. [CrossRef]
70. Wortmann, J.H.; Park, C.L. Religion and spirituality in adjustment following bereavement: An integrative review. *Death Stud.* **2008**, *32*, 703–736. [CrossRef] [PubMed]
71. Eisma, M.C.; de Lang, T.A.; Boelen, P.A. How thinking hurts: Rumination, worry, and avoidance processes in adjustment to bereavement. *Clin. Psychol. Psychother.* **2020**, *27*, 548–558. [CrossRef]
72. Morina, N. Rumination and avoidance as predictors of prolonged grief, depression, and posttraumatic stress in female widowed survivors of war. *J. Nerv. Ment. Dis.* **2011**, *199*, 921–927. [CrossRef]
73. Dyregrov, K.M.; Dieserud, G.; Hjelmeland, H.M.; Straiton, M.; Rasmussen, M.L.; Knizek, B.L.; Leenaars, A.A. Meaning-making through psychological autopsy interviews: The value of participating in qualitative research for those bereaved by suicide. *Death Stud.* **2011**, *35*, 685–710. [CrossRef]
74. Hanschmidt, F.; Lehnig, F.; Riedel-Heller, S.; Kersting, A. The stigma of suicide survivorship and related consequences: A systematic review. *PLoS ONE* **2016**, *11*, 1–16. [CrossRef]
75. Douglas, V.J.; Kwan, M.Y.; Gordon, K.H. The roles of weight stigma, emotion dysregulation, and eating pathology in suicide risk. *Body Image* **2021**, *38*, 162–170. [CrossRef]
76. Barr, P. Guilt and shame-proneness and the grief of perinatal bereavement. *Psychol. Psychother.* **2004**, *77*, 493–510. [CrossRef]
77. Wilson, K.G.; Kowal, J.; Caird, S.M.; Castillo, D.; McWilliams, L.A.; Heenan, A. Self-perceived burden, perceived burdensomeness, and suicidal ideation in patients with chronic pain. *Can. J. Pain* **2017**, *1*, 127–136. [CrossRef] [PubMed]
78. Bowlby, J. Pathological mourning and childhood mourning. *J. Am. Psychoanal. Assoc.* **1963**, *11*, 500–541. [CrossRef] [PubMed]
79. Ferguson, T.J.; Crowley, S.L. Gender differences in the organization of guilt and shame. *Sex Roles* **1997**, *37*, 19–44. [CrossRef]
80. Bohannon, J.R. Grief responses of spouses following the death of a child: A longitudinal study. *OMEGA J. Death Dying* **1991**, *22*, 109–121. [CrossRef]
81. Rubin, S.S. Loss and mourning in the Jewish tradition. *OMEGA J. Death Dying* **2014**, *70*, 79–98. [CrossRef]
82. Van Dongen, C.J. Experiences of family members after a suicide. *J. Fam. Pract.* **1991**, *33*, 375–380. [PubMed]
83. Levi-Belz, Y. To share or not to share? The contribution of self-disclosure to stress-related growth among suicide survivors. *Death Stud.* **2016**, *40*, 405–413. [CrossRef]

84. Joiner, T.E.; Van Orden, K.A. The interpersonal-psychological theory of suicidal behavior indicates specific and crucial psychotherapeutic targets. *Int. J. Cogn. Ther.* **2008**, *1*, 80–89. [CrossRef]
85. Wittouck, C.; Van Autreve, S.; Portzky, G.; van Heeringen, K. A CBT-based psychoeducational intervention for suicide survivors: A cluster randomized controlled study. *Crisis* **2014**, *35*, 193–201. [CrossRef]
86. Markowitz, J.C.; Weissman, M.M. Interpersonal psychotherapy: Principles and applications. *World Psychiatry* **2004**, *3*, 136–139.
87. Groos, A.D.; Shakespeare-Finch, J. Positive experiences for participants in suicide bereavement groups: A grounded theory model. *Death Stud.* **2013**, *37*, 1–24. [CrossRef]
88. Harrington-LaMorie, J.; Jordan, J.R.; Ruocco, K.; Cerel, J. Surviving families of military suicide loss: Exploring postvention peer support. *Death Stud.* **2019**, *42*, 143–154. [CrossRef] [PubMed]
89. Hall, J.H.; Fincham, F.D. Self-forgiveness: The stepchild of forgiveness research. *J. Soc. Clin. Psychol.* **2005**, *24*, 621–637. [CrossRef]

International Journal of
Environmental Research and Public Health

MDPI

Review

The Impact of Colleague Suicide and the Current State of Postvention Guidance for Affected Co-Workers: A Critical Integrative Review

Hilary Causer [1,*], Johanna Spiers [1], Nikolaos Efstathiou [2], Stephanie Aston [3], Carolyn A. Chew-Graham [4], Anya Gopfert [5], Kathryn Grayling [6], Jill Maben [1], Maria van Hove [7] and Ruth Riley [1]

1 School of Health Sciences, University of Surrey, Kate Granger Building, 30 Priestly Road, Surrey Research Park, Guildford GU2 7YH, UK
2 School of Nursing and Midwifery, Institute of Clinical Sciences, College of Medical and Dental Sciences, University of Birmingham, Birmingham B15 2TT, UK
3 Samaritans, The Upper Mill, Kingston Road, Ewell, Surrey KT17 2AF, UK
4 School of Medicine, Keele University, Newcastle ST5 5BG, UK
5 Department of Health and Community Sciences, University of Exeter Medical School, Exeter EX4 4PY, UK
6 NHS Employers', 2 Brewery Wharf, Leeds LS10 1JR, UK
7 University of Exeter Medical School, Exeter EX4 4PY, UK
* Correspondence: h.causer@surrey.ac.uk

Citation: Causer, H.; Spiers, J.; Efstathiou, N.; Aston, S.; Chew-Graham, C.A.; Gopfert, A.; Grayling, K.; Maben, J.; van Hove, M.; Riley, R. The Impact of Colleague Suicide and the Current State of Postvention Guidance for Affected Co-Workers: A Critical Integrative Review. *Int. J. Environ. Res. Public Health* **2022**, *19*, 11565. https://doi.org/10.3390/ijerph191811565

Academic Editors: Karolina Krysinska, Karl Andriessen and Yossi Levi-Belz

Received: 27 July 2022
Accepted: 8 September 2022
Published: 14 September 2022

Publisher's Note: MDPI stays neutral with regard to jurisdictional claims in published maps and institutional affiliations.

Abstract: People bereaved by suicide are affected psychologically and physically and may be at greater risk of taking their own lives. Whilst researchers have explored the impact of suicide on family members and friends, the area of colleague suicide has been neglected and postvention guidance for supporting surviving colleagues is often poorly developed. This critical integrative review explored the impact of colleague suicide on surviving co-workers and reviewed postvention guidance for workplaces. Systematic searches found 17 articles that met the inclusion criteria. Articles were appraised for quality and extracted data were analysed using a thematic network method. Article quality was moderate. Two global themes were developed: impact of a colleague suicide comprised themes of 'suicide loss in the workplace'; 'professional identities and workplace roles'; 'perceptions of professional uniqueness'; and 'professional abandonment and silencing'. Postvention following a colleague suicide comprised 'individualised responses'; 'the dual function of stigma'; and 'complex pressure on managers'. A unifying global network 'after a colleague suicide' describes the relationships between all themes. A series of disconnects between existing postvention guidance and the needs of impacted workers are discussed. This review demonstrates the need for robust, systemic postvention for colleagues impacted by the complex issue of colleague suicide.

Keywords: suicide; postvention; impact; loss; grief; bereavement; colleague; co-worker; guidance; review

1. Introduction

Suicide is one of the leading causes of death around the world, with more than 700,000 people dying by suicide every year [1]. This means that 1% of all global deaths are due to suicide [2]. Suicide affects the physical and psychological health of the bereaved [3] and, compared to other causes of sudden death, those bereaved by suicide report higher levels of rejection, shame, stigma, and a need to conceal the method of death [4,5]. Every suicide impacts approximately 80 [6] to 135 [7] people, of which 1 in 30 may be deeply impacted and so can be considered bereaved [8]. Suicide bereavement has also been identified as a risk factor for attempted suicide [9–11]; approximately 7–9% of people bereaved by suicide subsequently attempt suicide [11,12]. There is also an association with occupational dropout [13].

Previous studies have measured and explored the impact of suicide on family members [14–17], friends [18], teachers [19], university staff [20,21], therapists, and other healthcare workers [22–24]. A recent UK-wide survey on the impact of suicide [4] found that 2% of participants reported being bereaved by a colleague's death. However, the impact of colleague suicide has not been widely investigated, even though the suicide rate in the UK is higher for certain professions; approximately 12 deaths per 100,000 were suicides between 2011 and 2015 while the risk of suicide for female healthcare professionals was 24% higher than this national average [25].

The support offered to those impacted by suicide is known as postvention [26–29]. Effective postvention has been shown to improve mental health and grief-related outcomes [30], help bereaved people seek and share support and information, and memorialise their loved ones [31]. While there is some postvention guidance for workers impacted by colleague suicide, see e.g., [28,32,33], existing guidance is limited and is not always evidence based.

Additionally, we argue that suicide research often focuses on the individual rather than the context in which suicide happens [34,35] or on preventing more deaths rather than improving quality of life [36,37]. Critical suicidology, an approach which considers the context and cultures in which suicides happen, such as the occupational factors or antecedents [35,37–39], provides a useful lens through which to explore the impact of suicide and support needs of those bereaved. We used this to inform our analysis.

Our review has drawn together empirical research and current guidance on colleague suicide, highlighting what we already know and what the gaps in the research are, signposting the next steps for researchers and support.

Review Aims

Three questions guided the review:

1. What is the impact on staff of a colleague death by suicide?
2. What is the current guidance for providing postvention support to staff following a colleague suicide and has this guidance been evaluated?
3. What kinds of postvention have been offered, or ought to be offered, to staff affected by a colleague suicide and what are staff experiences of that postvention?

2. Methods

An integrative review is a robust methodology [40] that allows a comprehensive understanding of a topic via the synthesis of all available evidence [41]. It is suited to reviewing a combination of diverse methodologies, including experimental and non-experimental research [42], and allows a broad sampling frame [43]. We followed the five steps set out by Whittemore and Knafl [42]: problem identification, through which we developed our review questions; literature search; data evaluation; data analysis; and presentation of conclusions.

2.1. Eligibility Criteria

We were interested in reports of the impact of colleague suicide, postvention guidance for workers, and evaluations of that guidance. The eligibility criteria are shown in Table 1.

2.2. Search Strategy

The databases listed in Table 2 were searched for the below terms between October and November 2021. The selection process ended in May 2022.

Table 1. Inclusion and exclusion criteria.

Inclusion Criteria	Exclusion Criteria
Reported on the experiences of people following a colleague suicide	Reported experiences following the suicide of a client, patient, service-user, student, family member, or anyone outside of work
Reported responses to an incident of, or set out guidance or policy in response to, the suicide of an employee or colleague	Reported only on prevention or intervention of colleague or employee suicide or on causes of suicidal ideation or behaviour
Qualitative, quantitative, or mixed methods research studies, reviewed original data, reported a first-person account, case study, or opinion piece	
Reported or evaluated the implementation of postvention guidance or support programmes for staff	
Published in the English language	
Contributed usefully to addressing the review problem	

Table 2. Databases and search terms.

Databases	Grey Literature Databases	Search Terms
Medline PsycINFO CINAHL	BASE Google Scholar British Library	suicide AND [colleague* OR co-worker* OR staff OR personnel OR employee OR workplace]
Embase Web of Science	Ethos ZETOC	AND [postvention OR guidance OR guidelines OR support* OR therap* OR response OR policy OR evaluat*]
ProQuest PubMed Scopus	AMC Digital Library Cochrane Library IEEE Xplore NHS Evidence Social Care Online Social Science Research Network United Kingdom Department of Health GreyLit.org	

The reference lists of chosen papers were hand-searched for further relevant articles. We did not apply any search limiters in terms of dates or country as we wished to scope the literature as widely as possible.

2.3. Article Screening

HC and JS independently screened all article titles, rejecting those that did not fit the criteria. We used the Rayyan.ai platform to support article screening. Duplicates were deleted. HC and JS accepted or rejected articles based on their abstracts. Disagreements were discussed until consensus was reached; had we not reached a consensus, a third reviewer (NE) was available to make a final decision. The full articles were read and any which did not fit the inclusion criteria were rejected. Seventeen articles were included in the review. The screening process is summarized in the PRISMA diagram in Figure 1.

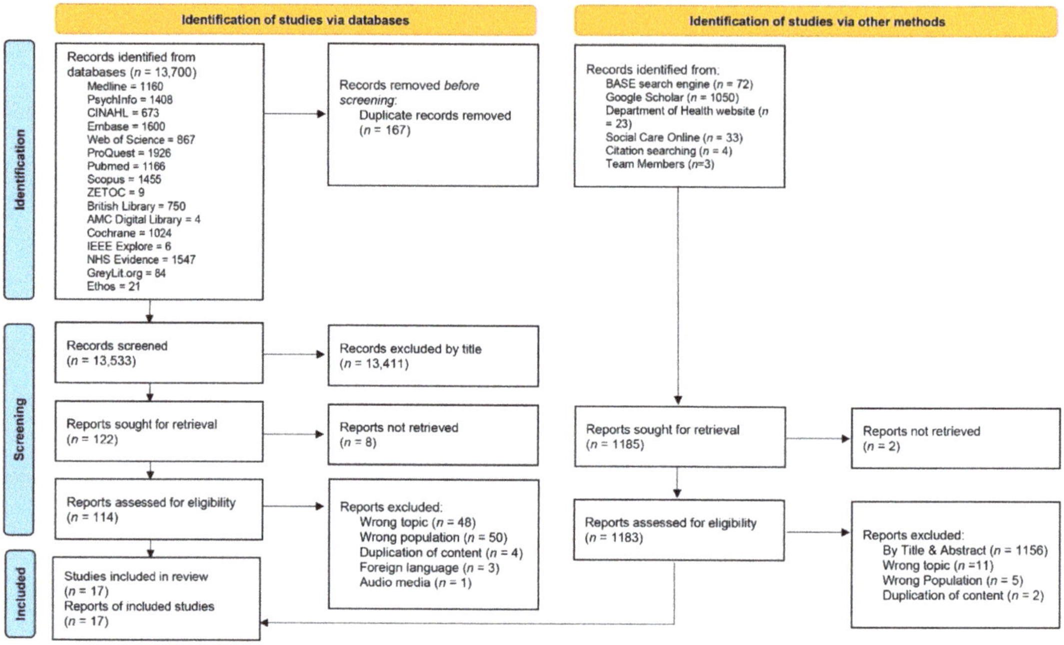

Figure 1. PRISMA flow diagram of the selection process. Adapted from the preferred reporting items for systematic review and meta-analyses (PRISMA) flow diagram [44].

2.4. Quality Appraisal

Our purpose in appraising the quality of the included articles was not to exclude any articles that could usefully contribute to answering the review questions [45,46] but instead to be aware of the overall quality of the papers.

HC and JS appraised the 17 included articles using a range of tools, including the AGREE-II tool [47], Joanna Briggs Institute (JBI) qualitative appraisal tools [48], the Mixed Methods Appraisal Tool (MMAT) [49], and the Quality of Survey Studies in Psychology (QSSP) tool [50].

HC and JS conducted independent assessments of the quality of all papers, providing inter-rater reliability to check each other's assessments. Any disagreements were discussed and resolved.

2.5. Data Extraction

Data were extracted to meet two aims. Firstly, HC extracted data from all articles to inform an overview of the article attributes. These data are reported in Tables 3 and 4.

Table 3. Attributes of the included empirical studies, survey studies, case studies, and opinion pieces.

Author & Date	Location	Type of Study	Study Aim/Research Question	Setting and Participant Details	Data Collection	Data Analysis	Results/Findings
Bogle, C.L. (2018) [51]	US	Qualitative study	Exploring the lived experiences of law enforcement officers concerning colleague suicide and the impact a suicide has on a law enforcement agency/department.	Police Department Law enforcement officers $n = 11$ Male = 7 African American = 10 Caucasian = 1	Semi-structured interviews	Thematic analysis	Four major themes: (1) Uniqueness of the law enforcement community (2) Lack of available resources regarding mental health services (3) Reactive response to the suicide event and (4) The necessity for consistent mental health services.
Carr, R.B. (2011) [52]	Iraq	First-person account	Reporting the author's first-hand experience of supporting a US army unit in Iraq after a soldier suicide.	US Army Psychiatrist in support role. $n = 1$ Male	N/A	N/A	Acute effects of suicide and effects over the subsequent four months.
Deheeger, J. (2008) [53]	Belgium	Report	Reporting the incidence, impact and postvention response following a colleague suicide in the Belgian Defence.	Belgian Armed Forces No Participants	N/A	N/A	Grief, guilt, and feelings of blame Fear of social stigma The service member's need for help Postvention trajectory of care: Pre-incident education Post-incident procedure of psychosocial care for victims Structure of the postvention crisis intervention procedure.
Gulliver et al. (2016) [36]	US	Evaluation	To subject the New York City Fire Department (FDNY) standard operating procedure (SOP) to an iterative process to develop a national guideline for suicide postvention.	US Fire Department Initial Expert Review Group: $n = 5$ Female = 1 All = at least two years exp in fire service Six focus groups: $n = 61$ 75% male Mean age = 47 years 22.9% Hispanic 9.8% African American 72/1% Caucasian	Expert review group and 90-min focus groups, video recorded. Six focus groups in three test cities reviewed the SOP manual and provided feedback on barriers to implementation	Data were taken at face value and used to inform the development of the guidance.	The expert review group discussed the need for more depth in the FDNY SOP as well as adding more information and procedures around responding to family and department members. Focus groups suggested making the SOP more operational and directive and breaking it up into two documents: (1) educational material (to be shortened into a pamphlet) and (2) the SOP. They also suggested calling it a guideline rather than an SOP. Feedback was incorporated into the final version of the SOP guidelines.

Table 3. *Cont.*

Author & Date	Location	Type of Study	Study Aim/Research Question	Setting and Participant Details	Data Collection	Data Analysis	Results/Findings
Kleespies et al. (2011) [54]	US	Literature review, interviews, and review of case reports	To investigate the incidence of psychologist suicide and its impact on colleagues, students or interns, patients or clients and the profession.	US Psychologists. Reports that 14 cases of suicide were identified but does not clarify the number of participants interviewed nor participant details.	Interviews	Not reported	Postvention efforts to address the needs of all survivors are needed. Professionals can help colleagues by clarifying the wishes of the deceased for closing their practice. The extent to which colleagues may experience a complicated bereavement and need support is undetermined.
Lynn, C.W. (2008) [55]	US	Case study	To explore the role of the occupational health nurse in supporting staff following the death co-worker suicide.	US Hospital Health workers	Case Study	N/A	Occupational health nurses can be the guiding force for first-line nurses after a suicide. Preparation begins with recognising that suicide is a genuine health emergency and requires the same planning as any other safety-related issue. Education and resources through EAP can prevent suicide and facilitate postvention.
Malecka, K.A. (2020) [56]	Poland	Qualitative multiple case study	Exploring how four Polish universities managed suicides. Presenting the lived experiences of participants holistically.	Higher Education Institutions Colleagues of deceased HE workers. $n = 7$ Academic staff = 5 Administrative staff = 2 Polish = 5 'Of foreign descent' = 2	Semi-structured interviews	Thematic data explication	Eight thematic areas: Notification of the deaths Personal responses to the deaths Institutional & managerial responses Professional help Formal and informal acknowledgements Administrative matters The reality of organisationally sponsored loss of education Mortality (mis)management: additional loss stories
Pak et al. (2019) [57]	US	Literature review	Providing a summary of the postvention literature with special emphasis placed on the military organisation; proposing a conceptual model for understanding Military-Unit Suicide Survivorship; and highlighting postvention strategies within the DoD.	US Army No participants	Qualitative, narrative, and evaluative review. Methods of data collection and analysis are not reported.		Proposes a conceptual model for military unit suicide survivorship based on the literature. Proposes postvention strategies and recommendations. Makes research, clinical, and policy recommendations.

Table 3. *Cont.*

Author & Date	Location	Type of Study	Study Aim/Research Question	Setting and Participant Details	Data Collection	Data Analysis	Results/Findings
Sever & Ozdemir (2019) [58]	Turkey	Qualitative study	Exploring the impact of a staff member's suicide on the organisation, faculty, and administration in a Turkish academic institution. Highlighting the influence of culture and belief in responses to suicide, where many people are Sunni Muslims, a belief system that strongly disapproves of suicide.	Higher Education Institution $n = 7$ Male = 4 Colleagues $n = 5$ Administrators $n = 2$	Open questions provided by email	Interpretative phenomeno-logical design	Two categories, seven themes Personal: Shock Questioning and feeling responsible Stigmatisation or asking for forgiveness Personal lessons Regrets Organisational: Solidarity and administrative support What needs to be changed
Yentis, Shinde, Plunkett & Morti-more (2019) [59]	UK	Survey	A working party to review anaesthetist suicide and provide guidance for anaesthetists, departments, and employers.	Survey sent to anaesthetists working in the UK. $n = 3638$	Anonymous online survey	Descriptive statistics	Most respondents were unaware of the existence of policies on mental illness, addiction, or suicide. 1916 cases of suicide were reported by 1397 respondents. A third of respondents who reported a suicide had experienced more than one case. Most reported suicide in the last 10 years involving anaesthetic drugs. Deficiencies were noted in support and how deaths were handled, although examples of good support were also described.

Table 4. Attributes of included guidance.

Authors, Date & Title	Location	Type of Article	Setting	Aims	Evidence Base	Guidance/ Recommendations
Vanderpol & Beyer (2019) [60] Leading a company in the aftermath of a suicide loss	US	Guidance	Construction industry	To share perspectives, strategies, resources, and tools to help contractors respond appropriately to a colleague suicide.	Draws on existing knowledge and guidance. No reference list or evidence base cited.	Defines postvention. Presents key points for critical incident management and strategies to support colleagues following a suicide. Q&A with the authors. Signposts to support websites and articles.

Table 4. *Cont.*

Authors, Date & Title	Location	Type of Article	Setting	Aims	Evidence Base	Guidance/ Recommendations
Berkowitz et al. (2014) [33] Organizational postvention after suicide death	US	Guidance (book chapter)	Organisations	Not stated	Draws on existing literature.	Concludes: Organisational postvention is recommended, but guidance is sparse. Various factors complicate the work. Postvention should be an evolving process that attends to the guidelines and principles in this chapter. Longitudinal and comparative studies are needed. Qualitative studies are needed to understand need and inform postvention interventions.
Austin & McGuinness (2012) [32] Console & The Irish Hospice Foundation Breaking the silence in the workplace: A guide for employers on responding to suicide in the workplace	Ireland	Guidance	The workplace	To help organisations increase their understanding and confidence in responding to workplace suicide.	Presents case studies but does not cite sources, so they could be fictionalised. Cites three references.	Provides guidance for employee suicide on-site and off-site, when an employee is affected by the suicide of someone close and when a former employee dies by suicide. Guidance also provided for developing a bereavement policy for dealing with suicide. Signposts to suicide support organisations.
The workplace postvention taskforce of the American Association of Suicidology & the workplace taskforce of the national alliance for suicide prevention. In partnership with the Carson J Spenser Foundation & Crisis Care Network. (2013) [61] A manager's guide to suicide postvention in the workplace: Ten action steps for dealing with the aftermath of a suicide.	US	Guidance	The workplace	Not stated	Cites a source for their definition of postvention. Cites the Individual Differences Models (Mancini & Bonanna, 2009), the ACT Model (VandePol, 2003) and the CDC definitions of 'suicide' 'suicide attempt' and 'suicidal ideation'. However, no evidence base cited to underpin the guidance.	Defines postvention. Presents a three-phase (acute, recovery, reconstructing) approach to delivery. Provides sample comms memos; signposts to resources; provides a decision-making flow-chart.

Table 4. *Cont.*

Authors, Date & Title	Location	Type of Article	Setting	Aims	Evidence Base	Guidance/ Recommendations
Kinman & Torry (2020) [28] Supporting Occupational Health and Wellbeing Professionals & The Louise Tebboth Foundation. Responding to the death by suicide of a colleague in primary healthcare: A postvention framework	UK	Guidance	Primary healthcare	Guidelines intended to inform a flexible crisis management strategy that provides information and support to primary care practices at different stages following a colleague suicide. May also be useful to similar small organisations.	In-depth interviews with GPs who have experienced a co-worker suicide, as well as contributions from other stakeholders. Interviews analysed by two researchers independently. A grounded theory approach was used where themes were identified and expanded until saturation. Full list of references included.	Presents postvention guidance for the first day, first week, first month, and longer term. Guidance is presented alongside participant quotes. Presents an Actions Needed summary table. Signposts to other resources.
Business in the Community; The Prince's Responsible Business Network; Public Health England; Samaritans (2017). [62] Crisis management in the event of a suicide: A postvention toolkit for employers.	UK	Guidance	The workplace	Toolkit to help organisations consider the issues that arise from workplace suicide; mitigate the impact of suicide; design a relevant postvention protocol.	Includes case studies from named organisations but does not cite these as underpinning evidence. No evidence base or references included.	Presents chronological guidance: Be prepared When suicide happens Grieving, post-traumatic phase Legacy phase Reflection time Includes signposts to resources and case studies.
Samaritans & Association of Ambulance Chief Executives (2021). [63] Ambulance service employee suicide: A postvention toolkit to help manage the impact and provide support.	UK	Guidance	Ambulance service	To help ambulance services, particularly leaders in HR and frontline managers, manage the impact of an employee suicide or attempted suicide on colleagues.	Cites six references that explore: mental health problems among UK ambulance workers; paramedic perceptions of distress, stigma, and utilisation of support services; mental health in the ambulance service; effects of exposure to self-harm on social media study; effects of educative suicide prevention websites; contagion.	Presents chronological guidance: Be prepared Communicating after a suicide When suicide happens Grieving, post-traumatic phase Legacy phase Reflection time Further information and resources.

Secondly, HC and JS extracted relevant primary data, author opinion or interpretation, and any other major findings, such as links to existing theory, into a matrix for analysis. Data were organised under the headings impact of colleague suicide on staff members; postvention guidance; and evaluation of postvention guidance. We then uploaded extracted data into NVivo for coding.

2.6. Data Analysis

Data were analysed following the thematic network method [64]. Thematic networks are 'web-like illustrations' that summarise themes and relationships between themes. We took the following steps as set out by Attride-Stirling [64]:

2.6.1. Coding the Material

HC and JS devised a coding framework based on the research questions and the critical suicidology literature [37,39]. Using NVivo, meaningful sections of the data were coded into that framework [64], which was discussed and refined as analysis continued.

2.6.2. Identifying the Themes

Codes were refined and grouped into similar themes. This resulted in the final table of basic, organising, and global themes (see Table 5).

Table 5. Relationships and connections between the organising, global, and unifying global themes.

Organising Themes	Global Themes	Unifying Global Theme
Suicide loss in the workplace Professional identities and workplace roles Perceptions of professional uniqueness in bereavement	Impact of the loss of a colleague to suicide	After a colleague suicide
Professional unpreparedness, abandonment, and silencing Individualised responses The dual function of stigma Complex pressure on managers	Postvention following a colleague suicide	

2.6.3. Constructing the Networks

HC and JS constructed two thematic networks ('impact of colleague suicide' and 'postvention following a colleague suicide'), which can also be considered as a single network under the unifying global theme 'after a colleague dies by suicide'. Networks were constructed by considering relationships between the three levels of theme.

2.6.4. Describe and Explore the Thematic Networks

HC and JS used the networks as a springboard to fully explore the concepts, connections, and findings arising from the analysis. The upshot of this discussion can be seen in the results section of this paper.

2.6.5. Summarize the Thematic Network

A summary of the thematic networks can be seen in the following section.

2.6.6. Interpret Patterns

Patterns across the two networks were identified and developed during the writing of the results section.

3. Results

3.1. Quality Appraisal of Included Articles

Despite some high and medium scores, we found that many of the papers had important methodological flaws. Regarding the guidance articles, which were assessed using the AGREE-II tool [47], authors [33,60,61] did not always consult with the target population. Austin and McGuinness [32] drew on case studies but did not report their sources. Only Kinman and Torry [28] and Samaritans [63] reported systematic methods of searching for evidence while no authors reported criteria for selecting evidence or described the strengths and limitations of their evidence. It was not always clear how recommendations were reached [32,33,60,61], recommendations were sometimes not evidenced [60,61], and work was not always peer-reviewed [33,60,61]. Only Berkowitz [33] and Kinman and Torry [28] considered facilitators and barriers to carrying out recommendations. Only Samaritans [63] provided any information about funders.

Regarding the empirical and other articles, six [36,51,54,56–58] were appraised using the JBI checklist for qualitative research [48]. All demonstrated congruity between the research methodology and question, although only three [51,56,58] stated the authors' philosophical perspective. Kleespies et al. [54] were unclear in reporting their methodology and offered little interpretation of their results; Pak [57] presented a 'conceptual model' but with no clarity on whether the model was constructed in response to review findings; and Sever and Ozdemir [58] reported their findings in a descriptive rather than interpretative style. Only two papers [51,58] addressed researcher influence on the research. Participants' voices were well represented by all authors except Gulliver et al. [36], who did not include any verbatim quotes and Kleespies et al. [54], who reflected on rather than reported their findings. Kleespsies et al. [54] were the only authors not to make any ethical statement while Gulliver et al. [36] and Małecka [56] offered no evidence of ethical approval for their research. Conclusions were clearly drawn from the analysis or interpretation of the data in all articles.

Two articles [53,55] were appraised using the JBI checklist for text and opinion [48]. They both met all criteria, although it was unclear whether the stated position of either article was the result of an analytical process. Carr [52] was appraised using the JBI checklist for a case study [48]. All criteria were met at least in part, although it is worth noting that this appraisal checklist assumes that the case study is a medical one, so criteria had to be interpreted broadly to accommodate the nature of the article. Overall, the literature appraised using JBI checklists was of mixed quality, but all met our requirement of making a useful contribution toward answering our review questions.

3.2. Thematic Network Analysis

Our analysis resulted in the development of seven organising themes that sit within two global themes, as illustrated in Table 5. We identified several connections between and across the two global themes, which led to the development of a unifying global theme, 'After a colleague suicide'. The relationships and connections between the organising, global, and unifying global themes are illustrated in Figure 2.

3.2.1. Global Theme 1: Impact of the Loss of a Colleague to Suicide

Suicide Loss in the Workplace

The suicide of a colleague impacts individuals in a variety of ways and brings the usually private process of bereavement into a professional realm. Intense, complex emotions, such as sadness, anger, shame, and guilt [63], may be experienced and heightened by the manner of death:

Bereavement after suicide is often called 'grief with the volume turned up'. [63]

The most frequently reported emotions following colleague suicide are shock [28,32,52,53,55,56,58,62,63] and anger [28,52,55,57,63]. Anger may lead to further feelings such as 'confusion, anxiety and shame' that arise from perceptions of anger as an inappropriate response [28].

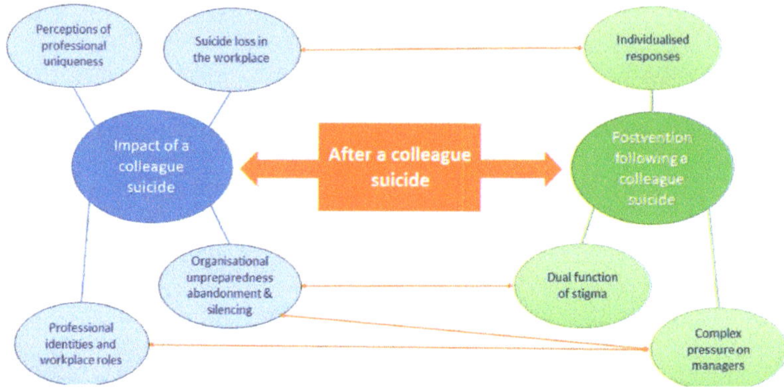

Figure 2. Thematic network.

Additionally, several authors [28,60–62] report behavioural responses, including altered eating and sleeping habits and a need to talk about the event [28]. Some behaviours may be visible and impactful within the workplace, such as absenteeism, presenteeism, or problem drinking [28].

This combination of responses may contribute to the challenging work of grief [32]. Managers must understand that staff are not only experiencing the loss of a colleague by suicide but are also working through the multiple elements of that experience and will require space, support, and empathy. Workers in a 1993 study cited by Lynn [55] (p. 462) expressed the intensity of their experience:

> *as the same emotional burden experienced after the death of a family member.* [65]

Colleagues may feel they must 'carry on' after the suicide. This may be a positive way of getting 'back to normal' [61] or may present tension between the need to keep working and the need to grieve. For instance, Kinman and Torry (p. 6) note that the performative 'effort' of meeting workplace expectations and behaviours 'can be exhausting and compound grief reactions' [28]. A colleague's suicide may give rise to suicidal thoughts or behaviours:

> *Sometimes the rationale for this increase in suicide or suicidal behavior occurs out of guilt, a distorted sense of loyalty, or a perceived false "permission" to do so.* [60] (p. 3)

This is a particularly serious outcome. Leaders and managers ought to be aware of, and alert to, this potential risk. There is a danger that the 'carry on' narrative may detract from and indeed hide the real pain and suffering that some staff members may experience.

Professional Identities and Workplace Roles

Dilemmas arise when staff come face to face with loss, trauma, and grief whilst inhabiting their professional identities. Specific characteristics of job roles might bring colleagues into contact with dying or recently deceased colleagues, such as deployed military personnel [52] or ambulance staff who may have been called to an incident involving their colleague:

> *the ambulance staff that attend the scene could have additional needs in relation to their efforts to help their colleague. There may have been a resuscitation attempt, for example. This places an increased burden on the clinicians present.* [63]

Professionals may feel they are attempting to navigate dual roles following a suicide. For example, doctors 'may experience dissonance' [28] (p. 6) between the roles of 'healer' and colleague of the deceased. These dual roles may be especially challenging for team leaders or managers:

> *As the line manager, when a colleague dies suddenly you have a responsibility to all team members to assist them in coming to terms with the sudden death, whilst dealing with your own emotions.* [62]

A sense of impossibility is evident, as leaders report that no matter which approach they take, it is impossible to meet all needs, especially given the challenges of information containment in the social media age:

> *It was already on social media, but the senior manager said it wasn't our place to tell colleagues, as the family may not know yet, so then you're chastised by staff for not letting people know. [. . .] It all got very messy. And all that was on me. It was a lonely place that day.* [63] (p. 22)

Further, leaders' responsibility to safely contain teams is highlighted by Pak [57], who discusses the broad roles that army captains play in nurturing commitment, trust, and good morale within military units.

Questions may be raised here around responsibility, not only for looking after staff following a colleague suicide but also for the colleague who took their life. The suggestion that a colleague suicide may be seen as a failure of leadership [57], potentially triggering mistrust, is a stark reminder that leadership is about creating and nurturing the cultures within which staff work.

Perceptions of Professional Uniqueness in Bereavement

Many authors [28,32,52,56–58,63] report on the experiences of certain professional populations or participants with specific traits, beliefs, or cultural values. Throughout these reports are perceptions of being 'unique' amongst the wider population of those impacted by suicide, making the experience of colleague suicide somehow harder to bear. Pak [57] describes a combination of setting and relationships to explain perceptions of heightened impact:

> *military suicide may have an even greater impact than bereavement experienced in most collegial relationships due to the proximity and intimacy required for a unit to function in a combat environment . . . It is not uncommon for service members to refer to one another as "brother", "sister", "brother-in-arms".* (p. 189)

Interestingly, Lynn [55] also cites 'proximity' and shared experiences as 'unique' characteristics of healthcare workers' roles. Kinman and Torry [28] focus on the nature of small cohesive teams that nurture friendships for GPs. Finally, the shared professional identity and sense of 'family' is suggested as the reason for a 'deeper' impact on paramedics than others [63].

Perhaps this sense of kinship and shared identities explains professional groups' notion that their experience of colleague suicide is unique. Colleagues may struggle to articulate who it is they have lost; the deceased is more than a colleague but not a family member. There are challenges here for organisations and leaders in understanding the nature of the loss they are supporting staff to come to terms with. Again, the complexity of loss and need sits uncomfortably within the 'carrying on' narrative.

Personal beliefs and cultural norms can also shape a colleague's ideas about and responses to a death by suicide; diverse belief systems may be held by colleagues who work closely together [55]. Dominant discourses within belief systems may present colleagues with additional challenges:

> *"You feel the closeness of death, as in every funeral. However, as a Muslim, I do not find this right. According to our religion, it (suicide) is a rebellion against God."* [58]

As Sever and Ozdemir [58] note, it is complex for individuals and leaders to understand and accommodate a range of belief systems. This poses the question of how diverse belief systems might be accommodated within teams who are impacted by a colleague suicide.

Professional Unpreparedness, Abandonment, and Silencing

Organisational unpreparedness for responding to a colleague suicide due to skill and knowledge gaps shapes staff members' experiences, leading to perceptions of unmet needs:

> *"It was very surreal–I had to deal with all of this, and I just acted on instinct. There was no help or guidance given to me. Suddenly I was in charge of everybody else's feelings and just expected to carry on as normal."* [28] (p. 7)

Unpreparedness may take the form of skill and knowledge gaps or lack of guidance:

> *In the absence of any guidance, our interviewees were obliged to 'ring round' desperately hoping to receive help which was not forthcoming. This clearly intensified their distress and the difficulties that practices, especially small practices, experienced.* [28] (p. 17)

Placing the onus on individuals to seek support to meet their individual needs assumes that people experiencing shock, anger, guilt, and grief can identify and articulate what those needs may be. Whether these staff members knew what they needed, they knew they needed something, and the lack of resources within their organisation led to a wider search.

Małecka [56] reports that similar deficits were experienced in a Higher Education setting, where a colleague's suicide went unacknowledged, leaving staff members feeling abandoned, confused, and angry. Kinman and Torry [28] also report a 'reluctance' toward responding to need. It is unclear what drives this reluctance; perhaps not knowing how to respond or fear of doing it 'wrong'.

Yentis et al. [59] demonstrate the stark difference between the numbers of bereaved anaesthetists who felt supported (n = 22) and those who did not (n = 179):

> *[participants] described absent or poor support and in some cases, deliberate attempts to prevent or stifle discussion and/or debriefing, although in some cases the issue of protecting the deceased's confidentiality and/or sparing the family further anguish was mentioned.* [59]

There is evidence here of a process of silencing, where no platform for acknowledging or discussing needs is provided. Bogle [51] reports the perception of US law enforcement officers who describe the administrative response to their colleague's suicide as 'avoidant':

> *As long as you're doing your job, doing what you need to do and say, administration would acknowledge if you lost your life in the line of duty. You'd be a hero. But the moment [an officer] loses their life because of suicide, it's unspoken.* [51] (p. 97)

A similar response is reported by Belgian military service members [53], whose perceptions of social stigma act to silence them, thus further perpetuating the cycle of stigma. Silencing stigma is also noted by Małecka [56] in a Polish Catholic university; note that in Catholicism, suicide is considered a mortal sin. The conspiracy of silence experienced by these police officers, service members, and academics across organisational, social, and cultural contexts denies them opportunities to honour their deceased colleagues and process the impact of the suicide and risks psychological wellbeing [53]. Ultimately, silencing and stigma leave impacted staff alone with their need to find meaning and answers following their colleague's suicide.

3.2.2. Global Theme 2: Postvention Following a Colleague Suicide

Individualised Responses

Currently, postvention guidance tends to focus on individuals and individual change rather than contexts and systemic change. Attempts to consider the context within which suicidal behaviours occur are often lacking. We see this as a flaw in existing guidance.

A common claim was that personal vulnerabilities and mental health challenges increased the risk of contagion, whereby one death by suicide increases the risk of subsequent deaths by suicide among those who are affected [28,53,56,61,63], with no consideration of context. The following quote from a police officer [51] demonstrates a deep-seated belief that suicidal feelings are solely located within the individual:

> *'We're all adults. You have entrusted us with the authority to take people's freedom and the authority to take lives, if necessary. [...] So aside from offering programs, there's nothing anybody can do to stop them'.* [51] (p. 106)

While this participant describes the culture in which the suicidal behaviour is occurring, they still feel the only available option, on which they place little worth, is individual support.

Strategies for communication about the reasons for suicide were also individualised:

> *the important information is that the person mistakenly felt that they could not get help for his or her problems, when in fact help was possible.* [33] (p. 163)

Since suicide happens within a context, changes to culture (in addition to individual support) may also be beneficial for postvention.

Checklists of postvention tasks [28,32,33,53,61–63] or the utilisation of psychological or organisational models of support [28,32,33,53,57,61] similarly tended to focus on individual needs rather than culture.

Training was mentioned as a potential tool for effective postvention. Most proposed education focused on individual needs or signs of mental ill-health [32,33,51,63]. In contrast, Pak et al. [57] suggested training as a way for leaders to positively influence work culture:

> *Military leaders can be encouraged and taught to recognize that to compartmentalize the unit suicide and to ignore it in the short-term, may also place their units at risk.*

We endorse positive cultural changes as part of postvention [37] whilst cautioning against putting unrealistic pressure on managers, who may also be grieving or operating within an under-resourced system.

Dual Function of Stigma

Stigma both leads to inadequate postvention and arises from it. It leads to inadequate postvention since, if an organisation cannot talk about suicide, it cannot properly support those impacted by it. It arises following poor postvention because, if postvention is steeped in stigma, it perpetuates stigma at individual and organisational levels.

Authors reported that suicide was not properly acknowledged in the workplace [33,53,56,60–62]. However, it was widely agreed that this increased risk [28,32,33,57,60,63]. Discussion of suicide helps address stigma and so could aid postvention. However, one could question whether acknowledgement of suicide is enough without also acknowledging any difficulties with the context in which the suicide occurred.

Workers of various professions reported a culture of invulnerability [52,53,56], where mental ill-health was unacceptable. This could prevent education around suicide, impacting postvention:

> *'To have training on officer suicide would mean that [suicide] would have to be talked about. And that's not going to happen.'* [51] (p. 96)

This culture may further challenge postvention by preventing workers from being open about emotions or asking for help [51,53].

Organisations operating from a culture of invulnerability could also perpetuate stigma:

> *Personnel allowed to attend the service were limited [...]. Restricting access to the memorial service created a sense of shame about the death.* [52]

Additionally, it could be suggested that the term contagion, which was commonly used in reference to the statistic that one suicide may result in more [61–63], may perpetuate stigma and so hamper discussion and healthy postvention. Perhaps non-pejorative language such as 'further suicides' may be more useful. Given the prevalence of this narrative, it is perhaps unsurprising that contagion continues, and has:

> *... sometimes led to misguided efforts to maintain secrecy after a suicide death, including blaming or stigmatizing the deceased.* [33] (p. 168)

More helpfully, several authors made suggestions for how stigma could be combatted. These include the use of more sensitive terminology [63] and group counselling [58]. Several reported workplace cultures that were already supportive [53,58,63].

Complex Pressure on Managers

Complex pressure is placed on managers of workplaces in which a colleague dies by suicide, as the delivery of postvention support becomes their responsibility. Specific tasks that managers might be expected to undertake included regularly checking in with staff, looking out for affected colleagues [28], and being visible to workers [61]. Additionally, leaders may be expected to undergo training to deliver postvention [33,51,61,63].

Managers must also provide practical support such as accompanying employees during inquests [32], offering meals and transport [33], or arranging alternative duties for staff [63]. Some authors provided detailed explanations of ways for employers to emotionally support grieving workers [28,32,53,62,63], such as engaging in empathic listening and sharing stories. Several agreed that leaders must guide employees through the grieving process [55,61,63]. Further pressure on leaders is added by the suggestion that they should be "a role model for healthy grieving" [32,61].

Various authors acknowledged that managers, who are also grieving, must also be supported [28]. Suggestions included covering time off [28,63], regular check-ins with HR [63], and reassurance that it is OK to express emotion [63]. We feel that these are worthy suggestions that may help combat that toxic culture of invulnerability. Working with teams within [52,61] and outside of [28,32,33,53,62,63] the organisation to deliver postvention may also relieve pressure. Such support for managers, who are uniquely pressured following the suicide of an employee, is sorely needed.

3.2.3. Unifying Global Theme

Thus far, we have described two thematic networks: Impact of a colleague suicide and Postvention following a colleague suicide. Both networks are illustrated in Figure 2 in blue and green, respectively. In line with the thematic network methodology [64] (p. 393), this figure is intended to explore and illustrate the deep meaning and relationships behind the reviewed texts rather than to demonstrate causal relationships. We found that both networks describe events that occur simultaneously following a colleague suicide, and that these networks feed into and inform each other. Thus, they can be illustrated as being connected by a unifying global theme: After a colleague suicide, represented in Figure 2 in orange. The orange arrows indicate how individual experiences and needs following a colleague suicide are shaped by the availability and content of postvention support. Likewise, the design and delivery of postvention impact how workers respond to and heal from the suicide of a colleague as illustrated in Figure 2.

Specifically, the impact of suicide loss in the workplace can be heightened or ameliorated by the response of the organisation. Our findings evidence that staff experiences occur within the contexts and cultures of workplace settings, identities, and roles. Guidance, however, promotes individualised approaches to responses that fail to acknowledge these factors. A holistic approach, looking at the context and systems within which the suicide occurred and support for teams and whole organisations, in addition to any necessary individual responses, may reduce overall distress. Further, stigma is linked to organisational unpreparedness, abandonment, and silencing. Teams who are delivering postvention that is marred by stigma will, as our findings demonstrate, find it harder to acknowledge and respond to suicide, leading to a silencing, which, in turn, perpetuates stigma. Solving organisational unpreparedness may fall to managers, adding to their complex pressure; equally, if managers cannot fulfil the unrealistic battery of tasks assigned to them following an employee suicide, the organisation may continue to be unprepared and silence grieving workers. Finally, the organising themes of complex pressure on managers and professional identities and workplace roles are intertwined, as the dual roles that managers must inhabit whilst simultaneously grieving and caring for bereaved employees further add to their complex pressure.

4. Discussion

We reviewed and synthesised 17 articles, including empirical studies ($n = 7$), case studies ($n = 1$), opinion pieces ($n = 2$), and guidance ($n = 7$). We explored the impact of a colleague death by suicide across a range of workplace settings; reviewed the current guidance for workplace postvention support following a colleague suicide; and developed an understanding of what kinds of postvention support have been offered, or authors think should be offered to staff affected by a colleague suicide. We found that the workplace impact of colleague suicide and associated postvention has been sparsely explored, and published articles are of an overall moderate quality. Published guidance is rarely underpinned by empirical evidence while the guidance included in this review cite each other (with and without full acknowledgement and referencing). Some guidance appears comprehensive, but it is not always clear where the underpinning knowledge has come from. Experiences of loss and bereavement by suicide were shaped by workplace contexts, cultures, and job-role identities. Further, organisational responses, or lack thereof, created additional struggles for staff.

In this discussion, we explore three (dis)connections between staff experiences of impact following a colleague suicide and the postvention guidance currently available to managers and organisations, as illustrated in our thematic network (Figure 2).

4.1. Workplace Cultures, Professional Contexts, and Individualised Responses

Suicide loss is shaped by perceptions of professional identity and workplace settings. However, this is unacknowledged in postvention guidance, which takes an individualised view of cause and impact. Whilst the emotional impact reported by staff following a colleague suicide reflects the wider literature [66–69], experiencing this impact within professional identities and workplace settings complicates individual responses.

For instance, perceptions of professional identity and uniqueness shape staff experiences of grief. We reviewed the experiences of police officers, firefighters, military personnel, and primary care health professionals. Such professionals may be working within a culture of invulnerability [70], whereby perceptions of being impervious to work-related stresses become part of a professional identity. Staff who perceive themselves as invulnerable are less likely to find psychological safety following a colleague suicide. Researchers have concluded that talking about vulnerability and illness reduces perceptions of isolation and promotes coping mechanisms for GPs [71]. It is likely that such openness may also promote healthy coping in other professions. Furthermore, we found that staff across a range of professions believed that their experience of suicide loss was more impactful due to their perceptions of the unique traits of their job role or professional identity. While several professions perceived themselves as unique for similar reasons, this indicates that these 'unique' attributes and their impact on professionals' experience of a colleague suicide ought to be understood, acknowledged, and incorporated into support to meet staff needs for all groups.

Currently, workplaces do not provide the time and support required by employees to undertake the emotional work that arises following a colleague suicide. We found that a 'carry on' narrative dominates, prioritising work tasks and productivity over emotional needs. Similarly, when exploring the experiences of bereaved staff on their return to work, Bento [72] used the phrase 'the show must go on' to describe employees' perceptions of silence or pressure to catch up with work tasks. It may be that leaders working in '24/7' professions such as medicine or the military are expected to keep working to prevent the fallout from a depleted workforce, meaning they must put work ahead of their wellbeing.

Hochschild [73,74] utilises the concept of 'feeling rules' to describe the processes of emotion management that occur in workplace settings. Similarly, Doka [75] talks about 'grieving rules' that describe societal norms around loss and grief behaviours. Together, these concepts may provide a framework for better understanding how staff are expected to manage grief in the workplace and how organisations operate to direct grieving processes away from the workplace. Within the social model of individualisation, we are expected to do our emotional work in the privacy of our homes [76]. However, when grief occurs at work, this expectation generates further stress and an understandable disconnect for staff. We found that staff must work to navigate these complex expectations surrounding grief after a colleague's suicide. Similarly, Grandey [77] identified that employees suppress or regulate emotions following a stressful event to deliver an appropriate emotional presentation for the workplace. Such emotional management has been conceptualised as emotional labour [73]. When expressed emotions differ from those that are felt, emotional dissonance and internal tension may result [78]. As such, emotional labour is stressful and may lead to burnout [79].

As Pitimson [80] points out, UK legislation regarding compassionate leave does not recognise the death of a colleague, meaning any leave is at the discretion of the employer. In response to this point and the findings of our review, we argue that time must be offered in workplaces to accommodate the emotional work that may follow a colleague suicide and avoid the risk of emotional burnout.

It would be beneficial for authors of postvention guidance to offer strategies for addressing these specific staff experiences and needs following a colleague suicide. Overall, the guidance we reviewed did not take an organisational perspective, nor did it address professional identity and working spaces as the contexts within which loss and grief must be navigated and postvention support delivered. As previously noted, current guidance has drawn only sparsely on empirical evidence, which may explain this disconnect between need and delivery. We argue that postvention guidance must draw on the lived experiences of the people it aims to support. The reviewed guidance largely misses an opportunity to support organisations and staff by meeting them at the point of their experience.

4.2. Unpreparedness, Abandonment, Silencing, and the Perpetuation of Stigma

We found that organisational unpreparedness for suicide loss generates feelings of abandonment and perceptions of silencing that further complicate experiences of grief and perpetuate perceptions of stigma. Managerial or organisational failure to acknowledge colleague suicide and its impact leaves staff feeling abandoned in navigating their path to recovery. Pitimson [80] reports that a lack of workplace acknowledgement leaves bereaved staff with fears of being judged and a need to find safe places at work for privately expressing grief. As Lattanzi-Licht [81] states, the workplace requires the bereaved to be silent, hiding their feelings. Disenfranchised grief [82] refers to instances of dismissal when either the relationship with the deceased, the nature of the loss, or the griever themselves are not recognised. Doka [82] proposes that acknowledgement of grief is necessary for bereavement to be completed. The silence and silencing found in our review leave staff unable to talk about or process their experiences. Thus, the idea of suicide as a taboo [83] topic is perpetuated, staff are unsupported in their grief, and their trauma remains unacknowledged and unaddressed. Our findings illustrate that, alongside the absence of organisational response, the event of a colleague suicide and attempts by staff to mourn and remember their colleague were actively silenced. Staff grief in the workplace is not just disenfranchised; it is actively stifled [84].

This active silencing has an impact. As our findings demonstrated, stigma both leads to and arises following inadequate postvention. When organisations do not deliver postvention, they perpetuate stigma around suicide by failing to provide forums for conversation, acknowledgement, understanding, and healing. Paradoxically, it is the stigma surrounding suicide, and associated fears, that may contribute to organisations failing in this way. There is a fear of acknowledging suicide due to misunderstandings around risk of 'contagion' and the likelihood of further deaths by suicide [11]. We argue that it is the role of guidance to address these naïvetés. However, if guidance is not underpinned by evidence, it may be difficult to convey these messages robustly.

4.3. Managers: Identities, Roles, and Complex Pressures

Colleague suicide generates complex challenges for managers. This is exacerbated by perceptions of professional identity, whereby managers are perceived as strong and knowledgeable, and further, by postvention guidance, which situates managers as supporters of other staff. Balancing the needs of their team alongside managers' own needs, expectations that the workplace should continue to function as usual alongside staff grief, and the need to communicate clearly to staff whilst balancing the preferences of the deceased's family and the need to protect the deceased's privacy are all factors that generated this complexity. The wider literature also identifies the manager as a key provider of support and comfort when a staff member is bereaved [85–87].

Several authors highlight that, with proactive support and compassion, the workplace can facilitate healing following bereavement [85] and that bereaved staff may feel safe in the familiarity of the workplace [80]. Compassion is defined as 'an active orientation towards the well-being of others who are in pain' [88] (p. 168). Kanov [89] suggests that managers are well placed to offer compassion by noticing the suffering of others, feeling empathic concern, and acting to alleviate suffering. The manager must be alert, empathically in tune with others, and knowledgeable about appropriate proactive responses. It is often assumed that managers will provide this support and compassion whilst managers' struggles are not acknowledged [80,85,89].

The agency of bereaved staff within the supportive relationship is recognised by Dutton et al. [90], who posit that compassion requires both parties to interpret and understand each other's circumstances to make sense of the situation. Even here, however, there is no acknowledgement that the manager may be experiencing their own grief. We propose that, importantly, postvention guidelines provide guidance for the support of managers whilst they, in turn, support their teams. Additionally, guidance can identify external sources of postvention support (the availability of which, we acknowledge, varies), so that the weight of being the expert and supporting staff can be lifted from the potentially grieving manager.

Considering the broader contexts that underpin the complexity faced by managers allows for insights into the competing pressures of meeting staffs' emotional needs alongside the demand for the business to function. Pitimson [80] notes that individualism and capitalism can shape the experiences of grief in the workplace. Peticca-Harris [86] highlights this in her first-person account of restaurant managers' responses to the sudden death of a staff member. She describes how the need to keep the restaurant open blinded managers' ability to see, or relate to, the distress staff were experiencing [86]. Granek [91] suggests that control of grief in workplaces is political in terms of the expectation that staff will continue to contribute within capitalist societies. Peticca-Harris [86] (p. 608) concludes that 'managers did not know what to do and how to do it, and that brought about shame and embarrassment because it was at odds with the archetypes of leadership that dictate that leaders should just know [92]'.

These multiple juggling acts are addressed in part in postvention guidance, which often suggests the formation of a postvention committee or group, meaning postvention tasks are planned for and shared (see e.g., [62,63]). This may be feasible in a larger organisation. However, it is likely that one team manager would still need to provide information, identify staff who need support, and facilitate the implementation of support resources. In smaller organisations, or those that have not implemented a postvention team, individual managers are likely to have to implement postvention support to team members whilst also having to deal with their own responses to the loss. Effective, evidence-based training may help lessen managers' load. Attendees of postvention training for clinicians who support parents following the suicide of a child reported increased knowledge, skills, and confidence following the session [9]. We propose that similar outcomes might be achieved if training was provided to managers and leaders following colleague suicide. However, it must be considered whether such training is available before recommending it as a solution. As Tehan and Thompson [87] acknowledge, managers need to feel knowledgeable, skilled, and equipped.

This is the first review to specifically explore the impact of colleague suicide and related postvention guidance. The robust methodology utilised in this review allowed us to bring together a wide range of source literature and first-person experiences alongside associated guidance. This has enabled us to identify areas of disconnect between experience and response, and make recommendations for improving the guidance and, therefore, the care of staff bereaved or affected by a colleague suicide. A limitation of this review is that we were unable to include papers written in languages other than English, due to time and budget constraints. Additionally, although a comprehensive search strategy was used, we may have missed literature not storied in the searched databases.

We recommend the following steps for practice, policy, and research:

- Physical and emotional time and space for processing and grieving ought to be provided in workplaces to accommodate the emotional work that may follow a colleague suicide.
- Postvention guidance must be developed for specific professional groups, drawing on the lived experiences of that group, so that the specific needs of professional cultures and traits are understood.
- Guidance ought to include education around the dangers of stigma, the misunderstanding or misuse of 'contagion', and the protective factors of acknowledging and talking openly about suicide.
- Postvention guidance should acknowledge the competing pressures that managers experience following a colleague suicide and provide guidance for the support of managers whilst they, in turn, support their teams.
- Guidance could offer alternative models to the 'postvention team' to accommodate the limited resources of smaller or less resource-rich organisations. This may include accessing external expertise and support, if such a service is available.
- Postvention team members, managers, and team leaders should be offered training around topics such as suicide stigma, risk, and 'contagion'. This should include strategies for supporting teams and individuals.
- Future researchers may wish to explore the impact of colleague suicide on those with pre-existing mental health conditions (such as military personnel with PTSD).
- Development and evaluation of postvention guidance that is informed by empirical evidence for specific professional groups is needed

5. Conclusions

We suggest that colleague suicide can impact workers in healthcare and other settings and that perceptions of grief are complicated by professional identities and workplace cultures. A burden is placed on managers to be knowledgeable, skilled, and available to support staff. Current postvention guidance, and the postvention offered to colleagues, whilst well-meaning, is not evidence-based, takes an overly individualistic view and may perpetuate stigma, and has not often been evaluated. As such, we call for more evidence-based, systemic postvention guidance for workers and managers.

Author Contributions: Conceptualization, H.C., J.S., N.E., S.A., C.A.C.-G., A.G., K.G., J.M., M.v.H. and R.R.; Methodology, H.C., J.S., N.E., S.A., C.A.C.-G., A.G., K.G., J.M., M.v.H. and R.R.; Validation, H.C., J.S., N.E. and R.R.; Formal Analysis, H.C., J.S., N.E. and R.R.; Investigation, H.C., J.S., N.E. and R.R.; Data Curation, H.C., J.S. and R.R.; Writing–Original Draft Preparation, H.C., J.S., N.E. and R.R.; Writing–Review and Editing, H.C., J.S., N.E., S.A., C.A.C.-G., A.G., K.G., J.M., M.v.H. and R.R.; Visualisation, H.C., J.S. and R.R.; Supervision, R.R.; Project Administration, H.C., J.S. and R.R.; Funding Acquisition, R.R. All authors have read and agreed to the published version of the manuscript.

Funding: This research was funded by NIHR HS&DR grant number 129341. Carolyn Chew-Graham is part funded by West Midlands ARC (Applied Research Collaboration).

Institutional Review Board Statement: Not applicable.

Informed Consent Statement: Not applicable.

Data Availability Statement: No new data were created or analyzed in this study. Data sharing is not applicable to this article.

Acknowledgments: The authors are grateful for the support of James Barnett at the University of Birmingham library for his assistance in designing the search strategy.

Conflicts of Interest: The authors declare no conflict of interest. The views and opinions expressed therein are those of the authors and do not necessarily reflect those of the NIHR, NHS or the Department of Health.

References

1. World Health Organisation. Suicide. Available online: https://www.who.int/news-room/fact-sheets/detail/suicide (accessed on 30 August 2022).
2. World Health Organisation. One in 100 Deaths Is by Suicide. Available online: https://www.who.int/news/item/17-06-2021-one-in-100-deaths-is-by-suicide (accessed on 30 August 2022).
3. Spillane, A.; Matvienko-Sikar, K.; Larkin, C.; Corcoran, P.; Arensman, E. What are the physical and psychological health effects of suicide bereavement on family members? An observational and interview mixed-methods study in Ireland. *BMJ Open* **2018**, *8*, e019472. [CrossRef]
4. Suicide Berveament UK. PABBS: Evidence-Based Suicide Bereavement Training 2019. Available online: https://suicidebereavementuk.com/ (accessed on 31 August 2022).
5. Sveen, C.-A.; Walby, F.A. Suicide survivors' mental health and grief reactions: A systematic review of controlled studies. *Suicide Life-Threat. Behav.* **2008**, *38*, 13–29. [CrossRef] [PubMed]
6. Berman, A.L. Estimating the population of survivors of suicide: Seeking an evidence base. *Suicide Life-Threat. Behav.* **2011**, *41*, 110–116. [CrossRef] [PubMed]
7. Cerel, J.; Brown, M.M.; Maple, M.; Singleton, M.; Van de Venne, J.; Moore, M.; Flaherty, C. How many people are exposed to suicide? Not six. *Suicide Life-Threat. Behav.* **2019**, *49*, 529–534. [CrossRef] [PubMed]
8. McDonnell, S.; Flynn, S.; Shaw, J.; Smith, S.; McGale, B.; Hunt, I.M. Suicide bereavement in the UK: Descriptive findings from a national survey. *Suicide Life-Threat. Behav.* 2022, *ahead of print*. [CrossRef]
9. McDonnell, S.; Nelson, P.A.; Leonard, S.; McGale, B.; Chew-Graham, C.A.; Kapur, N.; Shaw, J.; Smith, S.; Cordingley, L. Evaluation of the impact of the PABBS suicide bereavement training on clinicians' knowledge and skills. *Crisis* **2020**, *41*, 351–358. [CrossRef]
10. Pitman, A.; Osborn, D.; King, M.; Erlangsen, A. Effects of suicide bereavement on mental health and suicide risk. *Lancet Psychiatr.* **2014**, *1*, 86–94. [CrossRef]
11. Pitman, A.L.; Osborn, D.P.; King, M.B.; Rantell, K. The stigma perceived by people bereaved by suicide and other sudden deaths: A cross-sectional UK study of 3432 bereaved adults. *J. Psychosom. Res.* **2016**, *87*, 22–29. [CrossRef]
12. Swanson, S.A.; Colman, I. Association between exposure to suicide and suicidality outcomes in youth. *Can. Med. Assoc. J.* **2013**, *185*, 870–877. [CrossRef]
13. Pitman, A.; Putri, A.K.; De Souza, T.; Stevenson, F.; King, M.; Osborn, D.; Morant, N. The impact of suicide bereavement on educational and occupational functioning: A qualitative study of 460 bereaved adults. *Int. J. Environ. Res. Public Health* **2018**, *15*, 643. [CrossRef]
14. Hunt, Q.A.; Young, T.A.; Hertlein, K.M. The process of long-term suicide bereavement: Responsibility, familial support, and meaning making. *Contemp. Fam. Ther.* **2019**, *41*, 335–346. [CrossRef]
15. Oexle, N.; Sheehan, L. Perceived social support and mental health after suicide loss. *Crisis* **2019**, *41*, 65–69. [CrossRef] [PubMed]
16. Owens, C.; Lambert, H.; Lloyd, K.; Donovan, J. Tales of biographical disintegration: How parents make sense of their sons' suicides. *Sociol. Health Illn.* **2008**, *30*, 237–254. [CrossRef] [PubMed]
17. Spillane, A.; Larkin, C.; Corcoran, P.; Matvienko-Sikar, K.; Riordan, F.; Arensman, E. Physical and psychosomatic health outcomes in people bereaved by suicide compared to people bereaved by other modes of death: A systematic review. *BMC Public Health* **2017**, *17*, 939. [CrossRef]
18. Bartik, W.; Maple, M.; Edwards, H.; Kiernan, M. The psychological impact of losing a friend to suicide. *Australas. Psychiatr.* **2013**, *21*, 545–549. [CrossRef]
19. Kim, J.E. Korean teachers' bereavement experience following student suicide. *Crisis* **2019**, *40*, 287–293. [CrossRef]
20. Causer, H. A Critical Exploration of Staff Experiences and Roles Following a Student Death by Suicide within Two United Kingdom Higher Education Institutions. Ph.D. Thesis, Worcester University, Worcester, UK, 2020. Available online: https://eprints.worc.ac.uk/10637/1/PhD%20Thesis%20-%20Hilary%20Causer.pdf (accessed on 26 July 2022).

21. Causer, H.; Bradley, E.; Muse, K.; Smith, J. Bearing witness: A grounded theory of the experiences of staff at two United Kingdom Higher Education Institutions following a student death by suicide. *PLoS ONE* **2021**, *16*, e0251369. [CrossRef]
22. Causer, H.; Muse, K.; Smith, J.; Bradley, E. What is the experience of practitioners in health, education or social care roles following a death by suicide? A qualitative research synthesis. *Int. J. Environ. Res. Public Health* **2019**, *16*, 3293. [CrossRef]
23. Christianson, C.L.; Everall, R.D. Constructing bridges of support: School counsellors' experiences of student suicide. *Can. J. Couns. Psychother.* **2008**, *42*, 209–221.
24. Saini, P.; Chantler, K.; While, D.; Kapur, N. Do GPs want or need formal support following a patient suicide?: A mixed methods study. *Fam. Pract.* **2016**, *33*, 414–420. [CrossRef]
25. ONS. Suicide by Occupation, England: 2011 to 2015 Analysis of Deaths from Suicide in Different Occupational Groups for People Aged 20 to 64 Years, Based on Deaths Registered in England between 2011 and 2015. Available online: https://www.ons.gov.uk/peoplepopulationandcommunity/birthsdeathsandmarriages/deaths/articles/suicidebyoccupation/england2011to2015/pdf (accessed on 16 October 2021).
26. Andriessen, K. Can postvention be prevention? *Crisis* **2009**, *30*, 43–47. [CrossRef] [PubMed]
27. Becker, K.; Manthey, T.; Kaess, M.; Brockmann, E.; Zimmermann, F.; Plener, P.L. Suicide postvention: What mental health professionals need to know. *Z. Kinder Jugendpsychiatrie Psychother.* **2017**, *45*, 475–482. [CrossRef] [PubMed]
28. Kinman, G.; Torry, R. Developing a suicide postvention framework for staff in primary healthcare. *Occup. Med.* **2021**, *71*, 171–173. [CrossRef] [PubMed]
29. Leaune, E.; Cuvillier, B.; Vieux, M.; Pacaut-Troncin, M.; Chalancon, B.; Perez, A.-F.; Haesebaert, J.; Chauliac, N.; Poulet, E.; Durif-Bruckert, C. The SUPPORT-S protocol study: A postvention program for professionals after patient or user suicide. *Front. Psychol.* **2020**, *11*, 805–816. [CrossRef]
30. Hill, N. *Evaluation of the Primary Care Navigator (PCN) Model for People Bereaved by Suicide in the Peel and Rockingham, Kwinana (PaRK) Region in WA.*; Telethon Kids Institute: Nedlands, Australia, 2021.
31. Lestienne, L.; Leaune, E.; Haesebaert, J.; Poulet, E.; Andriessen, K. An integrative systematic review of online resources and interventions for people bereaved by suicide. *Prev. Med.* **2021**, *152*, 106583. [CrossRef]
32. Austin, C.; McGuinness, B. *Breaking the Silence in the Workplace: A Guide for Employers on Responding to Suicide in the Workplace*; Irish Hospice Foundation: Dublin, Ireland, 2012.
33. Berkowitz, L.; McCauley, J.; Schuurman, D.L.; Jordan, J.R. Organizational postvention after suicide death. In *Grief after Suicide: Understanding the Consequences and Caring for the Survivors*; Jordan, J.R., McIntosh, J.L., Eds.; Routledge: New York, NY, USA, 2011; pp. 157–178.
34. Marsh, I. Critiquing contemporary suicidology. In *Critical Suicidology: Transforming Suicide Research and Prevention for the 21st Century*; White, J., Marsh, I., Kral, M.J., Morris, J., Eds.; UBC Press: Vancouver, BC, Canada, 2016; pp. 15–30.
35. White, J. What can critical suicidology do? *Death Stud.* **2017**, *41*, 472–480. [CrossRef]
36. Gulliver, S.B.; Pennington, M.L.; Leto, F.; Cammarata, C.; Ostiguy, W.; Zavodny, C.; Kimbrel, N.A.; Flynn, E.J. In the wake of suicide: Developing guidelines for suicide postvention in fire service. *Death Stud.* **2016**, *40*, 121–128. [CrossRef]
37. Marzetti, H.; Oaten, A.; Chandler, A.; Jordan, A. Self-inflicted. Deliberate. Death-intentioned. A critical policy analysis of UK suicide prevention policies 2009–2019. *J. Public Ment. Health* **2022**, *21*, 4–14. [CrossRef]
38. Bantjes, J.; Swartz, L. The cultural turn in critical suicidology: What can we claim and what do we know? *Death Stud.* **2017**, *41*, 512–520. [CrossRef]
39. Marsh, I. 'Critical suicidology': Toward an inclusive, inventive and collaborative (post) suicidology. *Soc. Epis. Rev. Reply Collect.* **2015**, *4*, 6–9.
40. Dhollande, S.; Taylor, A.; Meyer, S.; Scott, M. Conducting integrative reviews: A guide for novice nursing researchers. *J. Res. Nurs.* **2021**, *26*, 427–438. [CrossRef] [PubMed]
41. Torraco, R.J. Writing integrative reviews of the literature: Methods and purposes. *Int. J. Adult Vocat. Educ. Technol.* **2016**, *7*, 62–70. [CrossRef]
42. Whittemore, R.; Knafl, K. The integrative review: Updated methodology. *J. Adv. Nurs.* **2005**, *52*, 546–553. [CrossRef] [PubMed]
43. Whittemore, R.; Chao, A.; Jang, M.; Minges, K.E.; Park, C. Methods for knowledge synthesis: An overview. *Heart Lung* **2014**, *43*, 453–461. [CrossRef]
44. Moher, D.; Liberati, A.; Tetzlaff, J.; Altman, D.G.; PRISMA Group. Preferred reporting items for systematic reviews and meta-analyses: The PRISMA statement. *Ann. Intern. Med.* **2009**, *151*, 264–269. [CrossRef] [PubMed]
45. Noblit, G.; Hare, R. A meta-ethnographic approach. In *Meta-Ethnography*; SAGE: Newbury Park, CA, USA, 1988; Volume 11. [CrossRef]
46. Thomas, J.; Harden, A. Methods for the thematic synthesis of qualitative research in systematic reviews. *BMC Med. Res. Methodol.* **2008**, *8*, 45. [CrossRef]
47. AGREE Next Steps Consortium. The AGREE II Instrument [Electronic Version]. Available online: http://www.agreetrust.org (accessed on 30 November 2021).
48. Joanna BrIggs Institute. Critical Appraisal Tools. Available online: https://jbi.global/critical-appraisal-tools (accessed on 30 November 2021).

49. Hong, Q.; Pluye, P.; F'abregues, S.; Bartlett, G.; Boardman, F.; Cargo, M.; Dagenais, P.; Gagnon, M.-P.; Griffiths, F.; Nicolau, B.; et al. Mixed Methods Appraisal Tool (MMAT), Version 2018. Available online: http://mixedmethodsappraisaltoolpublic.pbworks.com/w/file/fetch/127916259/MMAT_2018_criteria-manual_2018-08-01_ENG.pdf (accessed on 10 February 2022).
50. Protogerou, C.; Hagger, M.S. A checklist to assess the quality of survey studies in psychology. *Method. Psychol.* **2020**, *3*, 100031. [CrossRef]
51. Bogle, C.L. The Impact of a Law Enforcement Suicide on Colleagues. Ph.D. Thesis, The George Washington University, Ann Arbor, MI, USA, 2018. Available online: https://www.proquest.com/dissertations-theses/impact-law-enforcement-suicide-on-colleagues/docview/2029929333/se-2?accountid=8630 (accessed on 2 November 2021).
52. Carr, R.B. When a soldier commits suicide in Iraq: Impact on unit and caregivers. *Psychiatry* **2011**, *74*, 95–106. [CrossRef]
53. Deheegher, J. Suicide of a Service Member: How to Organize Support for the Bereaved Service Members in the Emotional Aftermath. In *Lowering Suicide Risk in Returning Troops: Wounds of War*; Wiederhold, B.K., Ed.; Ios Press: Amsterdam, The Netherlands, 2008; pp. 149–161.
54. Kleespies, P.M.; Van Orden, K.A.; Bongar, B.; Bridgeman, D.; Bufka, L.F.; Galper, D.I.; Hillbrand, M.; Yufit, R.I. Psychologist Suicide: Incidence, Impact, and Suggestions for Prevention, Intervention, and Postvention. *Prof. Psychol. Res. Pract.* **2011**, *42*, 244. [CrossRef]
55. Lynn, C.W. When a coworker completes suicide. *AAOHN J.* **2008**, *56*, 459–469. [CrossRef]
56. Małecka, K.A. "Have you heard about X?": (Mis) management of mortality in academia. *Death Stud.* **2022**, *46*, 1678–1688. [CrossRef] [PubMed]
57. Pak, K.; Ferreira, K.E.; Ghahramanlou-Holloway, M. Suicide postvention for the United States military: Literature review, conceptual model, and recommendations. *Arch. Suicide Res.* **2019**, *23*, 179–202. [CrossRef] [PubMed]
58. Sever, M.; Ozdemir, S. How an academic's death by suicide impacts coworkers and an organization. *Death Stud.* **2019**, *46*, 323–328. [CrossRef] [PubMed]
59. Yentis, S.M.; Shinde, S.; Plunkett, E.; Mortimore, A. Suicide amongst anaesthetists—An Association of Anaesthetists survey. *Anaesthesia* **2019**, *74*, 1365–1373. [CrossRef]
60. VandePol, B.; Beyer, C. *Leading a Company in the Aftermath of a Suicide Loss*; CMFA Building Profits: Princeton, NJ, USA, 2019.
61. Carson J Spencer Foundation; National Action Alliance for Suicide Prevention; American Association of Suicidology. *A Manager's Guide to Suicide Postvention in the Workplace: 10 Action Steps for Dealing with the Aftermath of Suicide*; Carson J Spencer Foundation: Denver, CO, USA, 2013.
62. Business in the Community. *Crisis Management in the Event of a Suicide: A Postvention Toolkit for Employers*; Samaritans: London, UK, 2017.
63. Samaritans. *Ambulance Service Employee Suicide: A Postvention Toolkit to Help Manage the Impact and Provide Support*; Samaritans: Surrey, UK, 2021.
64. Attride-Stirling, J. Thematic networks: An analytic tool for qualitative research. *Qual. Res.* **2001**, *1*, 385–405. [CrossRef]
65. Mericle, B.P. When a colleague commits suicide. *J. Psychosoc. Nurs.* **1993**, *31*, 11–13. [CrossRef]
66. Cerel, J.; Maple, M.; Van De Venne, J.; Brown, M.; Moore, M.; Flaherty, C. Suicide exposure in the population: Perceptions of impact and closeness. *Suicide Life-Threat. Behav.* **2017**, *47*, 696–708. [CrossRef] [PubMed]
67. Shields, C.; Kavanagh, M.; Russo, K. A qualitative systematic review of the bereavement process following suicide. *OMEGA-J. Death Dying* **2017**, *74*, 426–454. [CrossRef]
68. Törnblom, A.W.; Werbart, A.; Rydelius, P.-A. Shame behind the masks: The parents' perspective on their sons' suicide. *Arch. Suicide Res.* **2013**, *17*, 242–261. [CrossRef]
69. Zisook, S.; Iglewicz, A.; Avanzino, J.; Maglione, J.; Glorioso, D.; Zetumer, S.; Seay, K.; Vahia, I.; Young, I.; Lebowitz, B.; et al. Bereavement: Course, consequences, and care. *Curr. Psychiatr. Rep.* **2014**, *16*, 482. [CrossRef]
70. Spiers, J.; Buszewicz, M.; Chew-Graham, C.; Gerada, C.; Kessler, D.; Leggett, N.; Manning, C.; Taylor, A.K.; Thornton, G.; Riley, R. Who cares for the clinicians? The mental health crisis in the GP workforce. *Br. J. Gen. Pract.* **2016**, *66*, 344–345. [CrossRef] [PubMed]
71. Riley, R.; Spiers, J.; Buszewicz, M.; Taylor, A.K.; Thornton, G.; Chew-Graham, C. What are the Sources of Stress and Distress for General Practitioners Working in England? A Qualitative Study. *BMJ Open* **2018**, *8*, e017361. [CrossRef] [PubMed]
72. Bento, R.F. When the show must go on: Disenfranchised grief in organisations. *J. Manag. Psychol.* **1994**, *9*, 35–44. [CrossRef]
73. Hochschild, A.R. *The Managed Heart: Commercialization of Human Feeling*; University California Press: Berkeley, CA, USA, 1983.
74. Hochschild, A.R. *The Managed Heart: Commercialization of Human Feeling*; University California Press: Berkeley, CA, USA, 2010.
75. Doka, K.J. Introduction. In *Disenfranchised Grief: New Directions, Challenges, and Strategies for Practice*; Doka, K.J., Ed.; Research Press: Champaign, IL, USA, 2002.
76. Jacobsen, M.H.; Petersen, A. Introduction: Towards a sociology of grief—Historical, cultural and social explorations of grief as an emotion. In *Exploring Grief: Toward a Sociology of Sorrow*; Jacobsen, M.H., Petersen, A., Eds.; Routledge: London, UK, 2019.
77. Grandey, A.A. Emotional regulation in the workplace: A new way to conceptualize emotional labor. *J. Occup. Health Psychol.* **2000**, *5*, 95–110. [CrossRef]
78. Morris, J.A.; Feldman, D.C. The dimensions, antecedents, and consequences of emotional labor. *Acad. Manag. Rev.* **1996**, *21*, 986–1010. [CrossRef]

79. Zapf, D.; Holz, M. On the positive and negative effects of emotion work in organizations. *Eur. J. Work Organ. Psychol.* **2006**, *15*, 1–28. [CrossRef]
80. Pitimson, N. Work after death: An examination of the relationship between grief, emotional labour, and the lived experience of returning to work after bereavement. *Sociol. Res. Online* **2021**, *26*, 469–484. [CrossRef]
81. Lattanzi-Licht, M. Grief and the workplace: Positive approaches. In *Disenfranchised Grief: New Directions, Challenges, and Strategies for Practice*; Doka, K.J., Ed.; Research Press: Champaign, IL, USA, 2002.
82. Doka, K.J. Disenfranchised Grief. In *Disenfranchised Grief: Recognizing Hidden Sorrow*; Doka, K.J., Ed.; Lexington Books: Lanham, MD, USA, 1989.
83. Chapple, A.; Ziebland, S.; Hawton, K. Taboo and the different death? Perceptions of those bereaved by suicide or other traumatic death. *Sociol. Health Illn.* **2015**, *37*, 610–625. [CrossRef]
84. Eyetsemitan, F. Stifled grief in the workplace. *Death Stud.* **1998**, *22*, 469–479. [CrossRef]
85. Hazen, M.A. Grief and the workplace. *Acad. Manag. Perspect.* **2008**, *22*, 78–86. [CrossRef]
86. Peticca-Harris, A. Managing compassionately? Managerial narratives about grief and compassion. *Hum. Relat.* **2019**, *72*, 588–612. [CrossRef]
87. Tehan, M.; Thompson, N. Loss and grief in the workplace: The challenge of leadership. *OMEGA-J. Death Dying* **2013**, *66*, 265–280. [CrossRef] [PubMed]
88. Tsui, A.S. Presidential address—On compassion in scholarship: Why should we care? *Acad. Manag. Rev.* **2013**, *38*, 176–180. [CrossRef]
89. Kanov, J.M.; Maitlis, S.; Worline, M.C.; Dutton, J.E.; Forst, P.J.; Lilius, J.M. Compassion in organizational life. *Am. Behav. Sci.* **2004**, *47*, 808–827. [CrossRef]
90. Dutton, J.E.; Workman, K.M.; Hardin, A.E. Compassion at work. *Ann. Rev. Organ. Psychol.* **2014**, *1*, 277–304. [CrossRef]
91. Granek, L. Mourning sickness: The politicizations of grief. *Rev. Gen. Psychol.* **2014**, *18*, 61–68. [CrossRef]
92. Gabriel, Y. The caring leader: What followers expect of their leaders and why? *Leadership* **2015**, *11*, 316–334. [CrossRef]

International Journal of
Environmental Research and Public Health

MDPI

Article

Postvention as Prevention: Coping with Loss at School

Nikita Khalid [1,*], Nicole Zapparrata [1], Kevin Loughlin [2] and Glenn Albright [3]

1 The Graduate Center, City University of New York, New York, NY 10016, USA
2 Innovative Learning Sciences, Ascend Learning, Leawood, KS 66211, USA
3 Baruch College, City University of New York, New York, NY 10010, USA
* Correspondence: nkhalid@gradcenter.cuny.edu

Abstract: Many Pre-K through grade 12 (PK-12) students have experienced traumatic events throughout the pandemic in a myriad of ways including the death of family members and peers, loss of social interaction and increased violence at home. The consequences can be traumatic and manifest themselves in fear, anxiety, anger, isolation, and loneliness. Too often this leads to depression, anxiety, grief, substance use disorders, post-traumatic stress disorder, suicidal ideation and even suicides. This study assesses the impact of an innovative virtual human role-play simulation that prepares PK-12 educators, administrators, and school staff to respond to a student death in the school community by creating communities of support to help manage traumatic loss. The simulation addresses crisis response planning, postvention plans, and provides learners with role-play practice in using evidence-based motivational interviewing communication strategies in conversations with students and colleagues after the occurrence of a death. The sample consisted of educators and staff who were recruited from geographically dispersed areas across the US between January 2021 through December 2021. Matched sample t-tests and ANOVAs were used to assess quantitative data, and a qualitative analysis software, MAXQDA, was used to assess open-ended response data. Results show statistically significant increases in school personnel's preparedness and self-efficacy to recognize signs of trauma in their students and colleagues, and to approach them to talk about concerns and, if necessary, make a referral to support services. Simulations such as this hold tremendous potential in teaching educators how address trauma due to a student death.

Keywords: postvention; trauma; mental health; simulation; professional development

Citation: Khalid, N.; Zapparrata, N.; Loughlin, K.; Albright, G. Postvention as Prevention: Coping with Loss at School. *Int. J. Environ. Res. Public Health* **2022**, *19*, 11795. https://doi.org/10.3390/ijerph191811795

Academic Editors: Karolina Krysinska, Karl Andriessen and Yossi Levi-Belz

Received: 28 July 2022
Accepted: 15 September 2022
Published: 19 September 2022

1. Introduction

1.1. COVID-19 and Traumatic Loss

Throughout the COVID-19 pandemic, globally, individuals have been impacted by traumatic loss with increased exposure to grief, loss of social connectivity due to mandated quarantines and lockdowns and increases in suicidal ideation and suicides. COVID-19 has widened the gaps already existing in physical health disparities and contributed to declining mental health. Worldwide, approximately five million deaths occurred from the start of the pandemic, and 5.2 million children lost either a parent or a caregiver [1]. These estimates are based on global reports of COVID-related deaths, some of which come from countries unable to accurately report death rates; thus, the loss of life and corresponding impact on children and adolescents could be even greater. In the United States, COVID-19-related orphanhood resulting from caregiver death impacted over 140,000 children, with the rate of experiencing loss 4.5 times higher among children of racial and ethnic minority groups when compared with non-Hispanic white children [2]. Dependent on geographic region, COVID-19-related death of parents and caregivers is highest for Hispanic children, Black children, and for American Indian/Alaskan Native populations. Children who are orphaned by COVID-19 face adverse consequences such as poverty, abuse, and institutionalization [1].

According to the Centers for Disease Control and Prevention [3], experiencing loss during COVID-19 is similar to experiencing loss in other types of disasters or traumatic events. Grief occurs when there are disruptions to daily routines, loss of life, and any other way in which individuals feel that their stability has been compromised. Grief can include experiencing feelings of shock, anger, sadness or denial, heightened anxiety and distress, and changes in sleeping and eating patterns. Due to the heightened number of bereaved individuals associated with COVID-19, prolonged grief disorder is also a major concern [4]. Specifically, individuals experience more intense acute grief when deaths are associated with COVID-19 than when they are related to other natural illnesses not related to the pandemic [5,6]. The consequences of COVID-19 materialize in heightened rates of trauma, loss and grief for children and have long term impact [7]. In addition, because of higher bereavement rates, individuals are at a higher risk of psychological impairment, especially when experiencing separation distress, grief, and posttraumatic stress [8].

Multiple studies conducted globally demonstrate the negative outcomes of tragic loss, prolonged grief exposure, and heightened anxiety as a result of the pandemic. For example, a qualitative study conducted in Italy, one of the first COVID-19 hotspots with a dramatic rise in mortality, demonstrated that abandonment, anger, guilt, dehumanization, and rumination about the pandemic were key themes that emerged when participants were interviewed regarding their experiences losing family members during lockdown [9]. Participants indicated that online social support and connectivity were extremely valuable in helping them to process grief during this time.

1.2. The Mental Health Impact of Suicide and Bereavement during COVID-19

The pandemic has clearly affected youth mental health as evidenced by elevated levels of depression, stress, anxiety, and suicidal ideation. Prior to the pandemic, the rate of suicide for youth ages 10–24 was already high. This rate increased almost 60% from 2007 to 2018 and is the third leading cause of adolescent death for ages 15–19 [10]. In addition, youth suicide attempts and visits to the emergency department for self-harm have increased since the start of the pandemic [11]. Suicide risk increased when accounting for COVID-19-related post-traumatic stress [12], and for individuals with lower perceived social support [13]. Bereaved individuals who have experienced loss due to suicide and other pandemic-related deaths are at risk of developing complicated grief, or prolonged grief disorder, which is characterized by experiencing major difficulties in accepting the death of a significant other, family member, or close friend [14–16]. Studies have also linked COVID-19 bereavement to intensified psychological distress, especially for those individuals who had previous psychiatric diagnoses [17]. Altogether, COVID-19-related deaths, including those by suicide, have resulted in heightened instances of poor mental health, lack of social connectivity, increased presence of environmental stressors such as financial burden, and lack of access to support services. Thus, the pandemic has put us at the forefront of a mental health crisis where evidence-based approaches to address trauma, loss, grief, and suicide are important to implement in school communities.

1.3. Educator and Student Mental Health

Educators, being on the front lines, were impacted by the pandemic both personally and professionally. School closures have resulted in fewer student resources such as access to school counseling centers, afterschool activities, and tutoring services [18]. Educators experienced disruptions to their jobs with one of the biggest hurdles for many being learning how to teach and engage students through distance learning. This is a difficult transition due to student learning loss and the impact on social and emotional learning and the mental health needs of both students and educators. Due to quarantine, lockdowns, and restrictions on social gatherings during the pandemic, students and educators both experienced social isolation and lack of connection [19]. The only way in which people were able to interact was virtually, which was challenging the viability of technology.

Throughout the pandemic, many children reported increased levels of depression, anxiety, fatigue, and distress [20–22]. Some factors related to poor mental health outcomes in children included living in rural areas, having friends or family members in the healthcare field, knowing someone infected with the virus, and belonging to lower socioeconomic status households. In addition, trauma associated with the pandemic may have a lifelong impact on student learning, behavior, and student social, emotional, and psychological functioning [23]. Additionally, the impact of trauma required many children and adolescents to focus on basic needs such as safety and a sense of security rather than social and academic needs. This can lead to a higher likelihood of attention issues, lower cognitive functioning, behavioral problems, decreased school attendance and difficulty in social relationships [23–26].

1.4. Need for Postvention

Based on the amount of loss that society has experienced in the last several years due to the pandemic, it is important that researchers continue to examine the impact of crisis-response and other preventative programs on children and adolescents, especially those at risk for suicide. According to a survey conducted by the American Federation of Teachers and the New York Life Foundation [27], educators indicate that they would benefit from having more resources to support students' social and emotional needs and that insufficient training is by far the top barrier to supporting grieving students. In total, 91% of educators stated that if there were bereavement training provided in their school or district, they would be interested in participating in it, while 92% stated that there should be a greater focus on supporting grieving students [27]. There is a clear desire from educators to be trained in grief and bereavement support for students, which underscores a critical need for postvention.

When responding to a death in the school community, whether it's by suicide or related to COVID-19, we must address the social, emotional, and mental health consequences that includes creating a community of support amongst students, educators, and parents. This support is vital among bereaved individuals for loneliness is significantly associated with the probability of a post-bereavement suicide attempt and suicidal ideation [28]. This extends into social networks of support which are critical to promoting mental well-being and help students and educators in coping with traumatic loss. In addition, it is crucial to integrate evidence-based coping skills into prevention and postvention programs to promote protective factors and resilience. Evidence exists supporting postvention programs in augmenting mental health outcomes for those impacted by suicide, sudden death, and tragic loss [29]; however, there are gaps in the literature for postvention, as well as for the general use of trauma-informed approaches in schools not specific to suicide postvention [30]. Teaching educators postvention strategies through easily accessible online training where they can engage in active learning in applying motivational interviewing (MI) skills through role-play with virtual students holds great promise in augmenting postvention protocols and ultimately, supporting the student health and wellness.

1.5. Hypotheses

The objectives of this study were to examine the effectiveness of an online virtual role-play simulation designed to teach educators and staff to respond to a death in the school community. Specifically, we hypothesized that as a result of the simulation, as indicated by perceived preparedness and self-efficacy Likert-scales, participants would be better prepared and confident to (1) identify students in psychological distress, (2) talk to students about their concerns and allow them to open up about their feelings of loss, (3) make a referral to support services if necessary, and (4) motivate students and colleagues to engage in self-care. We also hypothesized, based upon Likert-scale measures, that the training would result in (1) high satisfaction ratings; (2) a decrease in stigma related to discussing suicide with others, and (3) an increase in self-reported gatekeeper behaviors two months following completion of the training that include identifying students in psychological distress, helping them to open up to talk about their feelings of loss, and connecting them to support services.

2. Materials and Methods

2.1. Design and Measures

The study followed a repeated measures design with pre-, post, and two-month follow-up surveys and was based on Kirkpatrick's training evaluation model [31,32]. Kirkpatrick's model comprises four levels: (1) satisfaction, (2) learning, impact on attitudes, knowledge, and/or skills (3) behavior changes, and (4) results including the long-term benefits derived from the program or intervention such as shifts in school mental health culture. Level two and level three are interconnected for improvements in skills, knowledge and especially changes in attitudes influence changes in behaviors. This study includes assessing the first three levels and not the fourth due to limitations in implementation and lack of accessibility of more global metrics such as school climate.

Level one satisfaction measures were assessed in the post survey and included:

1. Overall, how would you rate the training? (4-point Likert scale ranging from "poor" to "excellent").
2. Would you recommend the training to your colleagues? (2-point Likert scale ranging from "Yes" to "No").
3. Is the training based on scenarios relevant to you? (2-point Likert scale ranging from "Yes" to "No").

Level one items also included school climate measures collected at post survey and were based on a 5-point Likert scale ranging from "Strongly Disagree" to "Strongly Agree". They included items where participants were asked how much they disagree/agree with the following statements that began with:

If I apply the skills taught in the training:

a. Student attendance will increase.
b. Student academic success will improve.
c. The school learning environment will become more supportive.
d. Classroom safety will improve.
e. My relationship with students will improve.

Level two measures were in the pre-, post, and follow-up surveys and included modified items from the validated Gatekeeper Behavior Scale (see Tables 2 and 3 for items) [33]. The Gatekeeper Behavior Scale (GBS) measures attitudes and intentions that have been shown to be related to changes in gatekeeper behaviors. This survey included two dimensions or subscales that were part of the original validity study: participant preparedness and self-efficacy to engage in gatekeeping behaviors. Lastly, three items measured perceived stigma assessing beliefs about suicide (see Table 4 for items).

Level three measures of behavior were measured at the two-month follow-up where participants were asked whether they believed that as a result of the training there were increases in the number of students: (1) identified as showing signs of psychological distress, (2) helped to open up about their feelings of loss, and (3) connected to support services. In addition, participants were also asked if as a result of the training, there were increases in the number of colleagues: (1) identified as showing signs of psychological distress, (2) helped to open up about their feelings of loss, and (3) connected to support services. Lastly, participants were asked if as a result of the training, there were increases in the number of conversations they have had with other teachers, staff and/or administrators (1) regarding students they were concerned about, and (2) about overall mental health in their school. Lastly, participants were asked to respond to the open-ended question "Now that you have completed the training, can you recall a situation where you used the skills learned in the training? Please describe what happened and be sure not to include any identifiable information."

All participants agreed to an informed consent and then completed a pre-survey, then the 40 min simulation which was followed by the post and two-month follow-up surveys.

2.2. Methods

2.2.1. Simulation Overview

Resilient Together: Coping with Loss at School is a virtual role-play simulation developed by Kognito (www.kognito.com). This simulation follows a similar learning methodology to other virtual role-play simulations that have demonstrated to be effective in training educators and staff in communication techniques that produce attitudinal and behavioral changes. For example, elementary school educators who were trained via simulated role-play reported an average increase of 25% in feelings of preparedness to recognize students in psychological distress and approach their parents to discuss referrals to support [34]. In this same study, educators reported a 36% increase in the number of students recognized as being in distress, a 54% in number of students with whom they had discussions about concerns, and a 72% increase in the number of parents with whom they had discussions about referrals to support for their children. Additional studies demonstrate similar findings for training via virtual role-play simulators [35–37]. In the *Resilient Together: Coping with Loss at School* simulation, participants enter an online environment where they practice role-playing with emotionally responsive intelligent virtual students coded with memory, personality, and will respond like real students who have experienced a loss. The 40 min simulation involves participants practicing role-playing one of two conversations, dependent on their students' grade levels, one is with a virtual student and the other with a virtual teacher. These virtual humans model behaviors that school personnel often see during a highly sensitive time such as after a student suicide in the school community. A virtual coach provides ongoing feedback on effective and ineffective communication strategies and though practicing the role-plays, participants learn how to support students impacted by a death and support their colleagues experiencing compassion fatigue. Several studies have demonstrated the efficacious impact of role-play simulations that have implemented similar learning models as the one examined in this study [34–37]. A more detailed description of simulation design and learning methodology can be found in Albright et al. [38] as well as an overview on simulations in PK-12 [39]. Figure 1 shows a screenshot of the simulated role-play.

Figure 1. Screenshot from Resilient Together: Coping with Loss at School program.

2.2.2. Sampling and Sample Demographics

The sample initially consisted of 4500 educators and staff who were recruited from geographically dispersed areas across the US between January 2021 through December 2021 from district superintendent offices, principals, and by word-of-mouth. Participants gained free access to the simulation via institutional licenses purchased directly from the vendor by school districts or by state departments of education, health or public health, and mental health organizations, and could take the simulation at a time of their choosing and in a convenient location such as their home or office. Participants first completed the pre-survey followed by the simulation, then a post survey and two months later, a follow-up survey. Overall, the final sample size was 383 participants who completed all three surveys. Participants were able to opt out of any survey question they did not want to complete, including demographic information; therefore, demographic information is listed for only those participants who chose to fill out the information. Participants were primarily white female teachers. Table 1 provides complete demographic information. The average age of the sample was 51 years, with 62% being teachers, 12% staff members, 10% administrators, and the remainder of the sample consisting of mental health specialists (3.1%) and paraprofessionals (3.4%).

Table 1. Demographics.

Demographic Item	*n*	Percentage (%)
Female	331	86.4
Male	34	8.9
Non-binary	1	0.3
I prefer not to answer	15	3.9
I prefer to self-describe	0	0
American Indian/Alaska Native	13	3.4
Asian	12	3.1
Black/African American	28	7.3
Hispanic/Latinx	64	16.7
Native Hawaiian/other Pacific Islander	1	<0.1
White	240	62.7
I prefer not to answer	96	25.1
Teaching	238	62.1
Administrator	38	9.9
Mental Health Specialist	12	3.1
Staff Member	47	12.3
Paraprofessional	13	3.4
School resource officer	0	0
Other	33	8.6
Pre-K	97	25.3
Elementary School	156	40.7
Middle/Junior High/Intermediate School	62	16.2
High School	29	7.6
Other	2	0.5

2.2.3. Analyses

To determine whether preparedness and self-efficacy increased overtime as a result of the intervention, a series of one-way repeated measures ANOVAs were run on each item. Post hoc tests using a Bonferroni correction were used to make pairwise comparisons between pre-test and post-test means, pre-test and follow-up means, and post-test and follow-up means. Partial eta squared was calculated for each repeated measures ANOVA as a measure of effect size for each item to determine the magnitude of the effect of the training over time. Frequencies were calculated for satisfaction measures, level two measures regarding application of the skills learned in the training, and behavioral measures.

To incorporate qualitative data, MAXQDA 2020 software was used. This software combines quantitative processing with manual coding. We were able to thematically code the qualitative data and produce frequency tables to directly illustrate the research findings. The qualitative analysis involved coding for reoccurring themes using a joint inductive-deductive coding process. This process involved two independent coders, with each coder reading through responses individually and identifying common themes with the MAXQDA 2020 software. Once a final coding template was established by both coders independently, both coders coded the responses into the full set of thematic categories, refining themes based on overlapping categories. The coders resolved any discrepancies through discussion with one another and reported all thematic categories and the frequency of responses for those categories. Some statements could fit into multiple themes, thus percentages reported do not add to 100%. Statements have been copied directly as reported, without correcting for typos.

3. Results

3.1. Level One Satisfaction Measures

Overall, participants found the simulation to be very effective with 98% stating it was good (37.9%), very good (41.3%), or excellent (18.8%) and 92% indicating that they would recommend the simulation to colleagues. A total of 82% of participants indicated that the training is based on relevant scenarios.

3.2. Level Two Measures

There were significant mean Likert-scale increases (see Tables 2–4 for means and *p*-values)) from pre- to post-survey and pre- to follow-up survey in preparedness and self-efficacy to (1) recognize when a student is showing signs of psychological distress (such as being anxious, depressed or disengaged), (2) recognize changes in behavior in response to a loss (such as losing interest in activities, declines in grades or social isolation), (3) help a student open up to talk about their feelings of loss, (4) motivate a student to connect with support services, (4) motivate a colleague to connect with support services, and (5) engage in self-care (such as supporting a healthy mindset, acknowledging your emotions or maintaining close relationships), (6) motivate a colleague to engage in self-care, and (7) motivate a colleague to connect with support services. Partial eta squared (η_p^2; effect size measure) is reported in Tables 2–4 for each item to demonstrate the magnitude of the effect of the training over time. This effect size scale indicates 0.01 as a small effect, 0.06 as a medium effect, and 0.14 as a large effect.

Table 2. In response to a real or possible death in your school or community, please indicate your preparedness to.

Measure	Pre-Test Mean (SD)	Post-Test Mean (SD)	Follow-Up Mean (SD)	*n*	Repeated Measures ANOVA (η_p^2 in Parenthesis)	Significant Time Points
Recognize when a student is showing signs of psychological distress	3.57 (0.767)	4.03 (0.648)	3.81 (0.686)	381	72.8 *** (0.161)	All
Recognize changes in behavior in response to the loss	3.68 (0.749)	4.08 (0.623)	3.90 (0.663)	381	61.8 *** (0.140)	All
Help a student open up to talk about their feelings of loss	3.53 (0.751)	4.02 (0.669)	3.73 (0.693)	376	80.4 *** (0.177)	All
Motivate a student to connect with support services	3.55 (0.797)	4.06 (0.661)	3.79 (0.716)	378	87.4 *** (0.188)	All
Engage in self-care	3.57 (0.771)	4.05 (0.657)	3.83 (0.709)	379	79.2 *** (0.173)	All
Motivate a colleague to engage in self-care	3.63 (0.778)	4.04 (0.687)	3.83 (0.717)	379	56.4 *** (0.130)	All
Motivate a colleague to connect with support services	3.59 (0.811)	4.02 (0.708)	3.77 (0.730)	376	55.9 *** (0.130)	All

Note. This note is relevant for the table above. Items were on a 5-point scale. *** $p < 0.001$, ** $p < 0.01$, * $p < 0.05$, ns = not significant. Items were scored using a scale from "Very Low = 1" to "Very High = 5".

Table 3. In response to a real or possible death in your school or community, please indicate how much you disagree/agree with the following statements that begin with "I feel confident in my ability to".

Measure	Pre-Test Mean (SD)	Post-Test Mean (SD)	Follow-Up Mean (SD)	*n*	Repeated Measures ANOVA (η_p^2 in Parenthesis)	Significant Time Points
Recognize when a student is showing signs of psychological distress	3.93 (0.630)	4.20 (0.555)	4.08 (0.613)	362	28.4 *** (0.073)	All
Recognize changes in behavior in response to the loss	3.97 (0.604)	4.21 (0.545)	4.11 (0.576)	359	25.5 *** (0.067)	All
Help a student open up to talk about their feelings of loss	3.85 (0.667)	4.18 (0.562)	3.99 (0.623)	357	39.8 *** (0.101)	All
Motivate a student to connect with support services	3.84 (0.701)	4.18 (0.585)	3.98 (0.636)	361	44.9 *** (0.111)	All
Engage in self-care	3.86 (0.663)	4.17 (0.599)	3.99 (0.666)	362	34.2 *** (0.086)	All
Motivate a colleague to engage in self-care	3.88 (0.674)	4.18 (0.608)	4.02 (0.637)	361	36.3 *** (0.177)	All
Motivate a colleague to connect with support services	3.86 (0.676)	4.17 (0.613)	3.99 (0.673)	356	33.0 *** (0.085)	All

Note. This note is relevant for the table above. Items were on a 5-point scale. *** $p < 0.001$, ** $p < 0.01$, * $p < 0.05$, ns = not significant. Items were scored using a scale from "Strongly Disagree = 1" to "Strongly Agree = 5".

Table 4. Please indicate if you disagree/agree with the following statements.

Measure	Pre-Test Mean (SD)	Post-Test Mean (SD)	Follow-Up Mean (SD)	*n*	Repeated Measures ANOVA (η_p^2 in Parenthesis)	Significant Time Points
Talking to a student about suicide will increase the risk that the student will contemplate suicide	2.28 (0.844)	1.97 (0.968)	2.06 (0.831)	354	18.5 *** (0.050)	Pre-Post Pre-FU
When a person dies by suicide, most people feel that it is better not to talk about it with that person's family or friends	2.67 (1.01)	2.73 (1.04)	2.75 (1.01)	347	NS (0.003)	None
I would personally avoid talking about suicide with someone who has lost a family member or friend by suicide	2.55 (0.950)	2.36 (0.886)	2.36 (0.863)	347	25.5 *** (0.069)	All

Note. This note is relevant for the table above. Items were on a 5-point scale. *** $p < 0.001$, ** $p < 0.01$, * $p < 0.05$, ns = not significant. Items were scored using a scale from "Strongly Disagree = 1" to "Strongly Agree = 5".

There were also significant decreases from pre- to post-survey, and pre-to follow-up survey ($p < 0.01$) in the beliefs that (1) talking about suicide will increase the risk of suicide, and significant decreases from pre-test to post-test in the idea that (2) talking about suicide with someone who has lost a family member or friend by suicide should be avoided ($p < 0.01$). These measures had medium effect sizes. Tables 2–4 present the quantitative results.

Participants also either agreed or strongly agreed in the post-survey that if they apply the skills taught in the simulation, there would be increases in (1) student academic success = 72%), (2) student attendance = 64%, (3) classroom safety = 82%, (4) the school learning environment will become more supportive = 91%, and (5) relationships with students will improve = 90%.

3.3. Level Three Behavior Measures

Participants self-reported reported in the two-month follow-up survey that as a result of applying the skills they had learned in the training, they either agreed or strongly agreed that: (1) student attendance increased = 32%, (2) student academic success improved = 36%, (3) the school learning environment became more supportive = 61%, (4) classroom safety improved = 57%, and (5) their relationship with students improved = 61%. Additionally, respondents reported that as a result of taking the training, there has been an increase in the number of students and colleagues that they identified as showing signs of psychological stress (students = 24%; colleagues = 21%), helped open up to talk about their feelings of loss (students = 32%; colleagues = 28%), and connected to support services (students = 27%; colleagues = 17%).

3.4. Qualitative Measures

At the two-month follow-up, participants were also asked to respond to the question "Now that you have completed the training, can you recall a situation where you used the skills learned in the training? Please describe what happened and be sure not to include any identifiable information."

A total of 348 open response comments were examined for this analysis. Respondents may have provided multiple themes if they discussed utilizing more than one skill during the incident they wrote about. Qualitative analysis was conducted via MAXQDA 2020, a software designed to streamline the process of coding qualitative data into useful themes. The coding process was primarily manual; however, the MAXQDA 2020 software assisted the qualitative coding process through key word lexical search capabilities and color coding after themes were identified by researchers. Frequency counts and proportions of responses that were related to each theme were created.

First, the manual iterative coding process was completed by two researchers separately, after which results were combined to reflect the themes which emerged. Results from both researchers were compared using reliability analysis in a two-way mixed model. Intraclass Correlation Coefficient (ICC) was used to determine the level of agreement between the two researchers. The ICC for this qualitative analysis was 0.996, indicating a high level of agreement between the researchers.

Results of the qualitative analysis revealed that a large portion of respondents had not had a chance to utilize the skills learned in the training or virtual instruction prevented them from doing so. However, of those who did, the most mentioned themes included recognition of distress in students, discussing concerns with distressed students, ability to implement open communication, knowing when to refer counseling, recognition of distress in colleagues, dealing with students who lost a family member, and discussing student mental health concerns with parents. The full results of this analysis are displayed in Table 5 below.

Table 5. Now that you have completed the training, can you recall a situation where you used the skills learned in the training? Please describe what happened and be sure not to include any identifiable information.

Theme	Frequency (Researcher 1)	Frequency (Researcher 2)	Delta
No situation occurred	156	156	0
Recognition of distress in students	45	39	6
Discussing concerns with distressed students	38	35	3
Ability to implement open communication	34	34	0
Referral to counseling	33	27	6
Recognition of distress in colleagues	27	33	6

Table 5. *Cont.*

Theme	Frequency (Researcher 1)	Frequency (Researcher 2)	Delta
Unable to implement skills due to COVID/virtual instruction	23	25	2
Student loss of a family member	21	21	0
Discussions with parents/caregivers for students in distress	17	14	3
Implementation of mental health discussions with colleagues	13	11	2
Implementation of mental health support communities	11	5	6
Ability to help to cope with COVID-related hardships	11	12	1
Loss of a student	8	8	0
Did not find training useful	7	7	0
Feel better prepared to help	7	7	0
Not applicable due to role	5	3	2
Ability to help to cope with ailing/ill family members	4	2	2
Already learned prior to the training due to role	4	0	4
Loss of a staff member/colleague	3	3	0
Does not want to disclose information	3	3	0
Recognition of distress in a parent/caregiver	3	0	3
Recognition of family members in psychological distress	2	5	3
Student suicide	1	0	1
Used the skills learned for self-help	1	1	0
Intervention and stopping violent student behavior	1	1	0

4. Discussion

The main objective of this study was to examine the effectiveness of an online virtual role-play simulation designed to teach educators and staff to respond to a death in the school community. We hypothesized that as a result of the simulation, participants would be better prepared and confident to respond to death in the school community.

Quantitative results demonstrated that *Resilient Together: Coping with Loss at School* was an effective tool for teaching learners how to recognize signs of psychological distress, and improved learners' preparedness and self-confidence in their ability to engage in conversations with students and colleagues regarding support services. These findings align with findings from similar studies that assess the efficacy of simulated virtual role-play programs, specifically in significantly increasing attitudes regarding recognition, approach, and referral behaviors [34–39]. However, this study differs in that it also incorporates the importance of identifying the impact of loss and grief on school communities, differing from typical interventions that aim to improve mental health awareness. An important finding to note is that not only did the program assist learners in helping others, but it also increased their preparedness and confidence in their own self-care. The self-care component provides additional support for simulated role-play that previous papers do not. Coping with loss is difficult in any context, especially the death of loved ones. Our school communities have been heavily impacted by loss due to COVID-19 and are experiencing prolonged effects of stress and loss in students' and educators' reintegration into the academic environment. In addition, because the program resulted in significant mental health and suicide stigma reduction, this could help lead to potential changes in institutional climate toward greater acceptance of having conversations about mental health and suicide, thus creating a safer and more trusting educational environment.

When asked about using the skills learned in the simulation, participants reported instances of recognizing distress in students, colleagues, and other school community members. Additionally, they reported increases in approaching and referring students in distress to support services. Lastly, participants mentioned how helpful the program was specifically in helping others deal with the loss of family members or other members of the school community. For specific frequency of the occurrence of these behaviors, please see the qualitative data reported in Table 5. The qualitative data show that participants were able to better understand the impact of simulated role-plays in training school community members how to recognize those in distress and how to engage them in conversations to augment their behavioral health as well as create communities of support within their schools. The benefits of building rapport between students and teachers, and between teachers and administrators themselves cannot be overstated due to potential impact of fostering a positive and safe school climate.

Lastly, many respondents, nearly half in the qualitative data, mentioned that they have not had a chance to utilize the skills learned in the training due to needing to take necessary precautions because of the pandemic as well as virtual classroom instruction. At the same time, a substantial number of respondents reported that they utilized the skills practiced. This observation is important as many school settings are still taking measures to protect students from COVID-19 and ensuing co-variants. This study provides evidence that the use of virtual role-play simulations such as *Resilient Together: Coping with Loss at School* are an effective approach to augmenting prevention and postvention programs within school districts that are vital in supporting student and faculty mental health and well-being.

5. Limitations

As in many field studies, recruitment of subjects for experimental and control groups through random assignment was not possible. Thus, one limitation is that we implemented an experimental design that examined within-group differences that did not include a control group. Another limitation is that behavioral data were self-reported. Ideally, we would have preferred access to school records on classroom attendance, student academic performance, and incidences of school safety, etc. Additionally, the data collected in this study are specific to educator and staff perceptions of student mental well-being; thus, incorporating student data would have allowed us to further assess the efficacy of the intervention. Another limitation was that although the items used to assess attitudinal change were based on the validated Gatekeeper Behavior Scale, the scale used in this study was not previously validated. Thus, although convergent validity has been established for the Gatekeeper Behavior Scale [33], since the scale used in this study was modified, future studies should examine the convergent validity of the modified scale. Lastly, to increase interrater reliability in the qualitative analysis, ideally, we would have liked more researchers to code responses to ensure accuracy. Given these limitations, the results reported in this paper are assumed to represent the population of those who participated in the *Resilient Together: Coping with Loss at School* program.

6. Conclusions

As evidenced in the postvention literature, there is an overwhelming need for school-based interventions. Adolescent and young adult populations are at the highest risk for suicide clusters and contagion effects. Without proper postvention protocol, it is difficult to address a death in a school community, particularly a death by suicide, which can increase the occurrence of suicide clusters and directly impact already at-risk students by amplifying negative emotions (e.g., feelings of hopelessness, anxiety, loneliness). The data from this study provide encouraging evidence that simulations such as *Resilient Together: Coping with Loss at School* can augment postvention efforts. The current use of online virtual role-plays to manage postvention conversations had a positive impact on the perceived preparedness and self-efficacy of educators and staff on their postvention efforts. Overall, the impact of death and the loss of loved ones effects the entire school community, and postvention techniques are essential in coping with the loss. The results from this study provide support that postvention efforts are strengthened through the use of virtual interventions that promote recognition, approach and referral behaviors and can be effective when helping school communities to cope with loss, which has been especially prominent during the COVID-19 pandemic.

Author Contributions: N.K. authored the initial draft and was involved in conducting the qualitative analysis, writing the results of this analysis, survey creation, and coordinating the research activity. N.Z. conducted the quantitative analysis which included data cleaning, conducting the statistical analysis, producing the visualization/data presentation, and writing up the results of this analysis. K.L. was involved in conducting the qualitative analysis and writing the results of this analysis. G.A. was involved in survey creation and the critical review and revision of the manuscript. All authors have read and agreed to the published version of the manuscript.

Funding: This research received no external funding.

Institutional Review Board Statement: Ethical review and approval were waived for this study due to the reason that it was not considered human subject's research.

Informed Consent Statement: Not applicable for study involved archived deidentified data.

Data Availability Statement: Restrictions apply to the availability of these data. Data were obtained from Ascend Learning and are available from glenn.albright@baruch.cuny.edu with the permission of Ascend Learning.

Conflicts of Interest: We are reporting that the authors have employment agreements with Ascend Learning, the company that developed the simulation used in this study. Ascend Learning had no role in the design of the study; in the collection, analyses, or interpretation of data; in the writing of the manuscript; or in the decision to publish the results.

References

1. Unwin, H.J.T.; Hillis, S.; Cluver, L.; Flaxman, S.; Goldman, P.S.; Butchart, A.; Sherr, L. Global, regional, and national minimum estimates of children affected by COVID-19-associated orphanhood and caregiver death, by age and family circumstance up to Oct 31, 2021: An updated modelling study. *Lancet Child Adolesc. Health* **2022**, *6*, 249–259. [CrossRef]
2. Hillis, S.D.; Blenkinsop, A.; Villaveces, A.; Annor, F.B.; Liburd, L.; Massetti, G.M.; Unwin, H.J.T. COVID-19–associated orphanhood and caregiver death in the United States. *Pediatrics* **2021**, *148*, e2021053760. [CrossRef] [PubMed]
3. Centers for Disease Control and Prevention. Grief and Loss. Available online: https://www.cdc.gov/mentalhealth/stress-coping/grief-loss/index.html (accessed on 15 July 2022).
4. Djelantik, A.M.J.; Bui, E.; O'Connor, M.; Rosner, R.; Robinaugh, D.J.; Simon, N.M.; Boelen, P.A. Traumatic grief research and care in the aftermath of the COVID-19 pandemic. *Eur. J. Psychotraumatol.* **2021**, *12*, 1957272. [CrossRef]
5. Eisma, M.C.; Tamminga, A.; Smid, G.E.; Boelen, P.A. Acute grief after deaths due to COVID-19, natural causes and unnatural causes: An empirical comparison. *J. Affect Disord.* **2021**, *278*, 54–56. [CrossRef]
6. Boelen, P.A.; Olff, M.; Smid, G.E. Traumatic loss: Mental health consequences and implications for treatment and prevention. *Eur. J. Psychotraumatol.* **2019**, *10*, 1591331. [CrossRef]
7. Fitzgerald, D.A.; Nunn, K.; Isaacs, D. What we have learnt about trauma, loss and grief for children in response to COVID-19. *Paediatr. Respir. Rev.* **2021**, *39*, 16–21. [CrossRef]
8. Breen, L.J.; Lee, S.A.; Neimeyer, R.A. Psychological risk factors of functional impairment after COVID-19 deaths. *J. Pain Symptom. Manag.* **2021**, *61*, e1–e4. [CrossRef]
9. Testoni, I.; Azzola, C.; Tribbia, N.; Biancalani, G.; Iacona, E.; Orkibi, H.; Azoulay, B. The COVID-19 Disappeared: From Traumatic to Ambiguous Loss and the Role of the Internet for the Bereaved in Italy. *Front. Psychiatry* **2021**, *12*, 564. [CrossRef]
10. Centers for Disease Control and Prevention; National Center for Injury Prevention and Control. Disparities in Suicide. Available online: https://www.cdc.gov/suicide/facts/disparities-in-suicide.html (accessed on 15 July 2022).
11. Yard, E.; Radhakrishnan, L.; Ballesteros, M.F.; Sheppard, M.; Gates, A.; Stein, Z.; Hartnett, K.; Kite-Powell, A.; Rodgers, L.; Adjemian, J.; et al. Emergency Department Visits for Suspected Suicide Attempts Among Persons Aged 12–25 Years Before and During the COVID-19 Pandemic—United States, January 2019–May 2021. *MMWR Morb. Mortal. Wkly. Rep.* **2021**, *70*, 888–894. [CrossRef]
12. Hong, S.; Kim, H.; Park, M.K. Impact of COVID-19 on post-traumatic stress symptoms in the general population: An integrative review. *Int. J. Ment. Health Nurs.* **2021**, *30*, 834–846. [CrossRef]
13. Hamdan, S.; Berkman, N.; Lavi, N.; Levy, S.; Brent, D. The effect of sudden death bereavement on the risk for suicide: The role of suicide bereavement. *Crisis* **2020**, *41*, 214–224. [CrossRef] [PubMed]
14. Bellini, S.; Erbuto, D.; Andriessen, K.; Milelli, M.; Innamorati, M.; Lester, D.; Pompili, M. Depression, hopelessness, and complicated grief in survivors of suicide. *Front. Psychol.* **2018**, *9*, 198. [CrossRef] [PubMed]
15. Robinaugh, D.J.; LeBlanc, N.J.; Vuletich, H.A.; McNally, R.J. Network analysis of persistent complex bereavement disorder in conjugally bereaved adults. *J. Abnorm. Psychol.* **2014**, *123*, 510–522. [CrossRef] [PubMed]

16. Shear, M.K. Complicated grief. *N. Engl. J. Med.* **2015**, *372*, 153–160. [CrossRef]
17. Joaquim, R.M.; Pinto, A.L.; Guatimosim, R.F.; de Paula, J.J.; Costa, D.S.; Diaz, A.P.; Malloy-Diniz, L.F. Bereavement and psychological distress during COVID-19 pandemics: The impact of death experience on mental health. *Curr. Res. Behav. Sci.* **2021**, *2*, 100019. [CrossRef]
18. Lee, J. Mental health effects of school closures during COVID-19. *Lancet Child Adolesc. Health* **2020**, *4*, 421. [CrossRef]
19. Baker, C.N.; Peele, H.; Daniels, M.; Saybe, M.; Whalen, K.; Overstreet, S.; Trauma-Informed Schools Learning Collaborative The New Orleans. View further author information. The experience of COVID-19 and its impact on teachers' mental Health, coping, and teaching. *Sch. Psychol. Rev.* **2021**, *50*, 491–504. [CrossRef]
20. Elharake, J.A.; Akbar, F.; Malik, A.A.; Gilliam, W.; Omer, S.B. Mental Health Impact of COVID-19 among Children and College Students: A Systematic Review. *Child Psychiatry Hum. Dev.* **2022**, 1–13. [CrossRef]
21. Guessoum, S.B.; Lachal, J.; Radjack, R.; Carretier, E.; Minassian, S.; Benoit, L.; Moro, M.R. Adolescent psychiatric disorders during the COVID-19 pandemic and lockdown. *Psychiatry Res.* **2020**, *291*, 113264. [CrossRef]
22. Schwartz, K.D.; Exner-Cortens, D.; McMorris, C.A.; Makarenko, E.; Arnold, P.; Van Bavel, M.; Canfield, R. COVID-19 and student well-being: Stress and mental health during return-to-school. *Can. J. Sch. Psychol.* **2021**, *36*, 166–185. [CrossRef]
23. Kuban, C.; Steele, W. Restoring safety and hope: From victim to survivor. *Reclaiming Child. Youth* **2011**, *20*, 41–44.
24. Frieze, S. How Trauma Affects Student Learning and Behaviour. *BU J. Grad. Stud. Educ.* **2015**, *7*, 27–34.
25. Larson, S.; Chapman, S.; Spetz, J.; Brindis, C.D. Chronic childhood trauma, mental health, academic achievement, and school-based health center mental health services. *J. Sch. Health* **2017**, *87*, 675–686. [CrossRef]
26. Schultz, J.H.; Skarstein, D. I'm not as bright as I used to be–pupils' meaning-making of reduced academic performance after trauma. *Int. J. Sch. Educ. Psychol.* **2021**, *9*, 265–279. [CrossRef]
27. New York Life Foundation: Grief in School Survey Key Findings. Available online: https://www.newyorklife.com/assets/foundation/docs/pdfs/key-findings-and-topline.pdf (accessed on 15 July 2022).
28. Pitman, A.L.; King, M.B.; Marston, L.; Osborn, D.P. The association of loneliness after sudden bereavement with risk of suicide attempt: A nationwide survey of bereaved adults. *Soc. Psychiatry Psychiatr. Epidemiol.* **2020**, *55*, 1081–1092. [CrossRef]
29. Andriessen, K.; Krysinska, K.; Hill, N.; Reifels, L.; Robinson, J.; Reavley, N.; Pirkis, J. Effectiveness of interventions for people bereaved through suicide: A systematic review of controlled studies of grief, psychosocial and suicide-related outcomes. *BMC Psychiatry* **2019**, *19*, 49. [CrossRef]
30. Maynard, B.R.; Farina, A.; Dell, N.A.; Kelly, M.S. Effects of trauma-informed approaches in schools: A systematic review. *Campbell Syst. Rev.* **2019**, *15*, e1018. [CrossRef]
31. Kirkpatrick, D. Great ideas revisited. *Train. Dev. J.* **1996**, *50*, 54–60.
32. Kirkpatrick, D.L.; Kirkpatrick, J.D. *Evaluating Training Programs: The Four Levels*, 3rd ed.; Berrett-Koehler: San Francisco, CA, USA, 2006; ISBN 978-1-57675-348-4.
33. Albright, G.L.; Davidson, J.; Goldman, R.; Shockley, K.M.; Timmons-Mitchell, J. Development and validation of the gatekeeper behavior scale. *Crisis* **2016**, *37*, 271–280. [CrossRef]
34. Long, M.W.; Albright, G.; McMillan, J.; Shockley, K.M.; Price, O.A. Enhancing Educator Engagement in School Mental Health Care Through Digital Simulation Professional Development. *J. Sch. Health* **2018**, *88*, 651–659. [CrossRef]
35. Albright, G.; Fazel, M.; Khalid, N.; Hilty, D.; McMillan, J.; Shockley, K.; Joshi, S. High School Educator Training by Simulation to Address Emotional and Behavioral Concerns in School Settings: A Randomized Study. *J. Technol. Behav. Sci.* **2022**, *7*, 277–289. [CrossRef]
36. Bradley, E.; Albright, G.; McMillan, J.; Shockley, K. Impact of a simulation on educator support of LGBTQ youth. *J. LGBT Youth* **2019**, *16*, 317–339. [CrossRef]
37. Timmons-Mitchell, J.; Albright, G.; McMillan, J.; Shockley, K.; Cho, S. Virtual Role-play: Middle School Educators Addressing Student Mental Health. *Health Behav. Policy Rev.* **2019**, *6*, 546–557. [CrossRef]
38. Albright, G.; Adam, C.; Serri, D.; Bleeker, S.; Goldman, R. Harnessing the power of conversations with virtual humans to change health behaviors. *Mhealth* **2016**, *2*, 44. [CrossRef] [PubMed]
39. Khalid, N.; Albright, G. Trauma-Informed Practices for K12 Schools. In *Advances in Game-Based Learning: Games and Simulations in Teacher Education*; Bradley, E., Ed.; Springer: Cham, Switzerland, 2020; pp. 127–140, ISBN 978-3-030-44525-6.

International Journal of
Environmental Research and Public Health

MDPI

Brief Report

The "Forgotten Grievers": The Impact of Pupil Suicide on Post-Trauma and Grief Symptoms in School Staff

Noa Tiech Fire [1,†], Yari Gvion [2,*,†], Sarit Alkalay [3] and Gil Zalsman [4,5,6]

1 Ministry of Education, Jerusalem 9510557, Israel
2 Department of Psychology, Bar Ilan University, Ramat Gan 5290002, Israel
3 Department of Psychology, Yezreel Valley Academic College, Yezreel Valley 1930600, Israel
4 Geha Mental Health Center, Petah Tikwa 49100, Israel
5 Sackler Faculty of Medicine, Tel Aviv University, Tel Aviv 6997801, Israel
6 Division of Molecular Imaging and Neuropathology, Department of Psychiatry, New York State Psychiatric Institute, Columbia University, New York, NY 10032, USA
* Correspondence: yari@kadi.co.il
† These authors contributed equally to this work.

Highlights:

- Following a suicide of a pupil principals and home-room teachers suffer more from complicated grief and PTSD compared to psychologists and counsellors.
- Principals and home-room teachers should receive more preparatory training.

Abstract: Background: The suicide of a pupil impacts survivors greatly, but most studies on the subject do not consider school staff, and do not differentiate between the various professional domains. Our aim was to investigate the existence of differences in symptoms of complicated grief as well as post-trauma symptoms after a pupil's suicide, among school staff in four domains: counsellors, psychologists, principals and home-room teachers. Method: Eighty-four staff members from schools that lost pupils to suicide within the past five years were assessed for symptoms of complicated grief and trauma. All reported their symptoms using self-report scales. Results: Principals and home-room teachers had significantly higher complicated grief and post-trauma symptoms. The main limitations of this study are that the data were collected via self-report questionnaires, which can introduce bias. Additionally, the sample is relatively small and comprises mainly women. Conclusions: School professionals in domains receiving less coping and crisis training, and those with supervisory responsibilities (principals and home-room teachers) show more symptoms of trauma and complicated grief after a pupil's suicide, and require special attention. More preparatory training would surely benefit them and assist them in coping with such crises.

Keywords: suicide; school staff; grief; trauma

Citation: Tiech Fire, N.; Gvion, Y.; Alkalay, S.; Zalsman, G. The "Forgotten Grievers": The Impact of Pupil Suicide on Post-Trauma and Grief Symptoms in School Staff. *Int. J. Environ. Res. Public Health* **2022**, *19*, 12160. https://doi.org/10.3390/ijerph191912160

Academic Editors: Karolina Krysinska, Karl Andriessen and Yossi Levi-Belz

Received: 20 July 2022
Accepted: 19 September 2022
Published: 26 September 2022

1. Introduction

A pupil's suicide creates extensive circles of vulnerability, not only among the pupil's family members, but also among their classmates, guides, teachers and other acquaintances [1]. Following the death of a pupil, school staff are at the frontline, having to manage the acute crisis. Still, they are often forgotten and not considered among those impacted by the death and needing support [2]. Only in recent years has it been recognized that this subject must be investigated and talked about in order to prevent more such occurrences [3].

Every suicide leaves behind approximately 25 people who were close to the person who died by suicide and are at greater risk of developing psychopathologies after the event [1,4,5], including complicated grief, depression, suicide and post-trauma symptoms [6]. Most studies so far have investigated families and friends of the person who died by suicide. Other studies investigated psychiatrists and therapists. Among other things they found that women reported a greater effect on their clinical confidence [7], and that younger, less-experienced clinicians were more affected by a patient's suicide than older clinicians with more experience [8]. Many studies emphasize the need for social and professional support, which includes opportunities to talk about the suicide experience with others—especially with senior professionals and with those who have also experienced suicide in their family or work. This support is common among mental health practitioners [9]. However, little attention has been paid in the literature to the impact of a pupil's suicide on school staff, and to their need for support and training to cope with a pupil's suicide [1].

It seems reasonable that staff members who have been trained for coping with crises would react differently from staff members who have had no such training. Indeed, it was found that staff members who were trained to cope with emergencies, stress and crises reported less emotional overload, avoidance and detachment in times of school crises than un-trained staff [10]. Moreover, trained personnel demonstrated more competence and reported more satisfaction and a sense of emotional growth after offering support to other grievers [10].

The aim of the current study was to investigate the existence of differences in complicated grief and post-trauma symptoms after a pupil's suicide, among school staff in four domains: counsellors, psychologists, principals and home-room teachers. Given the nature of their professions, school counsellors and psychologists undergo training to cope with crises and loss—their patients' as well as their own. They are also trained and prepared to cope with the impact a patient's crisis has on themselves. Meanwhile, principals and home-room teachers often do not receive such training, and even when they do, it is not as thorough [11]. We hypothesized that psychologists and counsellors will report less symptoms of complicated grief and PTSD compared to principles and home teachers. The research hypotheses were tested in relation to background variables of gender and seniority.

To the best of our knowledge, this is the first study to examine these four domains in the context of pupil suicide.

2. Materials and Methods

2.1. Subjects

We located all the schools in Israel at which a pupil had died by suicide during the previous five years ($n = 29$). All schools were middle schools or high schools. At each school the school counsellor, the school psychologist, the principal and the home-room teacher of the pupil who died by suicide were prospective participants ($n = 116$). In this way we identified the entire population of potential participants and attempted to speak with all of them. Six potential participants (5.2%) refused to participate, claiming that the subject was too emotionally difficult. Twenty-six potential participants (22.4%) could not be located. They no longer worked at the school where the incident occurred, and were not found in the Ministry of Education database, implying that after the incident they had left the profession altogether. Eighty-four (72.4%) agreed to participate, of whom sixty-one (73%) were women. This gender distribution is similar to the general distribution of educational staff in Israel (80% females) [12]. Within the four domains, out of 14 principals, 8 were men; out of 17 home-room teachers, 4 were men, out of 27 counsellors, 3 were men; and out of 26 psychologists, 8 were men. The participants' average age was 47.3 (S.D. 8.8), and their average seniority was 18.8 years (S.D. 8.6). These demographic characteristics are compatible with data for Israeli school staff: sixty percent are aged 30–49, and sixty percent have more than ten years of seniority [12]. With regard to the different professions, we interviewed school counsellors ($n = 27$, 32%), school psychologists ($n = 26$, 31%), principals ($n = 14$, 17%) and home-room teachers ($n = 17$, 20%), all having encountered cases of pupils who died from suicide.

2.2. Procedure

Upon receiving approval from the Israel Ministry of Education's institutional review board, we searched the Ministry of Education's database for schools at which a student had died by suicide during the previous five years (n = 29). After participants signed an informed consent form, they received a link to a set of computerized rating scales. Participants were asked to answer the questionnaires regarding the student's suicide event. Scales were administered in Hebrew. Researchers were blind to the individual rating scale responders.

2.3. Tools

Post-traumatic Diagnostic Scale (PDS) [13]—This is a widely used self-report scale for symptoms of post-traumatic stress disorder (PTSD) based on the DSM IV. The scale includes 49 items (Cronbach α = 0.92).

Inventory of Traumatic Grief (ITG) [14]—The short self-report version that includes 14 items (Cronbach α = 0.95) was used in this study. It covers each of the symptoms of traumatic grief as well as other potentially maladaptive symptoms of grief.

2.4. Statistical Methods

SPSS software (IBM Corp. Version 23.0) was used for statistical analyses. As for the normal distribution of the measures, inter-group differences were analyzed using ANOVA. Post hoc Bonferroni analysis was used to control for multiple testing. The significance level was set at 0.01, and all analyses were two-tailed.

Note that our research design is suitable for a multi-level analysis, whereby one variable is nested within another broader variable (group-level variable) [15]. Specifically, all participants from a particular school were considered part of the same group and might have been affected by the same context variable. However, we could not use multilevel model (HLM) analysis to explore this nesting effect for two reasons. The first relates to the anonymity requirement of the ethics board. We could not match the participants to a specific school (see the ethical consideration section). The second reason relates to the small number of participants from each school. Our research design imposed that a maximum of four potential participants from each school would be approached—the home-room teacher, the school principal, the school counsellor and the school psychologist. It is suggested that "the most commonly offered rule of thumb with regard to sample size for multilevel models is at least 20 groups and at least 30 observations per group" [16] (p. 272). Thus, although 29 schools were located, which satisfies the requirement for the number of groups, each school (i.e., group) consisted of less than 30 observations as required.

3. Results

Following a pupil's suicide, significant differences in symptoms of PTSD ($F_{(3,83)}$ = 5.90, p = 0.001) and complicated grief ($F_{(3,79)}$ = 14.53, p = 0.001) were demonstrated across the four school staff domains. Both complicated grief and PTSD measurements of school principals (M = 2.69, SD = 1.11; M = 11.14, SD = 10.61) and home-room teachers (M = 2.65, SD = 1.03; M = 10.32, SD = 9.02) were found to be significantly higher than those of counsellors (M = 1.89, SD = 0.60; M = 6.26, SD = 8.54) and psychologists (M = 1.94, SD = 0.63; M = 5.16, SD = 7.5) (Figure 1). No differences were found between the groups regarding gender or seniority, (p > 0.01), but more PTSD symptoms were found among males than among females ($t_{(2,54)}$ = 3.08, p = 0.002). Male participants reported higher symptoms of PTSD compared to females (M = 2.11, SD = 1.55 vs. M = 1.50, SD = 1.24). Unfortunately, due to the small sample size we could not test the interaction of profession and gender with regard to PTSD.

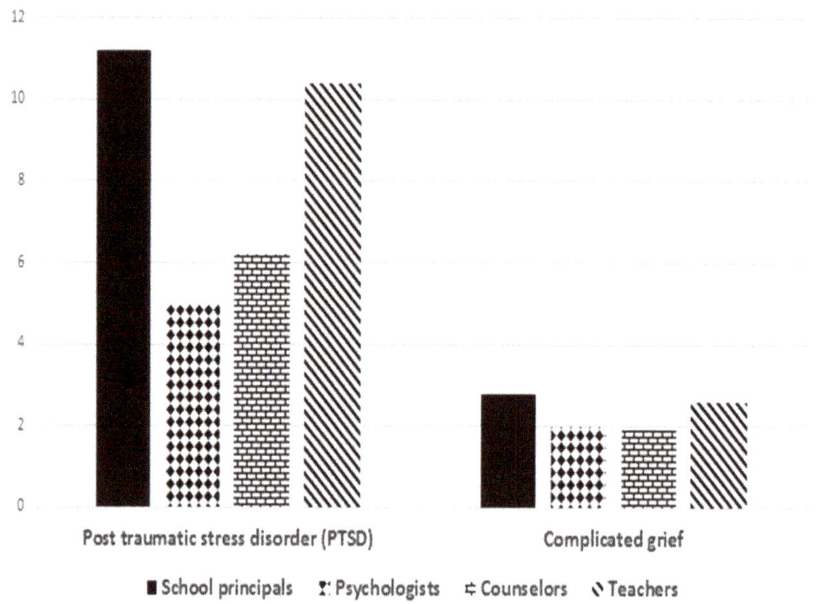

Figure 1. Differences between the domains regarding the intensity of complicated grief and post-traumatic stress disorder (PTSD). The scales of the measures were adjusted so that it would be possible to put them on the same graph in relation to each other. $p < 0.01$.

4. Discussion

This study demonstrated significant differences in symptoms of PTSD and complicated grief among four domains of school staff: principals, counsellors, psychologists and home-room teachers. Principals and home-room teachers reported higher levels of complicated grief and PTSD symptoms than psychologists and counsellors.

Previous studies found a pupil's death to negatively influence the mood of other students and of school staff [17,18]. However, these studies did not focus specifically on suicide, while studies that investigated pupils' suicides did not focus on the specific staff domains discussed in the current study. To the best of our knowledge, this is the first study to assess the coping of these four school staff domains and their emotional parameters after a pupil's suicide.

The literature considers school staff to be "forgotten grievers" [19] since they feel deep loneliness after the loss of a student but are not treated as parties impacted by the death. According to the studies, these people are at high risk for PTSD and complicated grief [6,19].

The findings of the current study support these reports and add a hierarchical structure of symptoms on which the four school staff domains can be placed. Principals and home-room teachers focus on pedagogical and educational skills as well as procedures and organization [20]. They are less involved in situations that require emotional support, and receive less training on the subject. Therefore, they are more likely to be in greater distress when dealing with an event such as the suicide of a pupil.

The confidence of home-room teachers in assisting students with mental health problems is associated with the home-room teachers' subjective psychological well-being, their knowledge and capability to comprehend children's mental health issues and with their satisfaction with the overall school climate [21]. In times of crisis, they are concerned with organization strategy, control and returning to routine [11]. Since they do not feel qualified to treat mental health problems, and because they are engaged in organization strategy and helping pupils return to routine, when a suicidal event occurs in their classroom, their emotional response to the situation is more severe. For example, in the current study, a theme that arose on the part of the subjects was the lack of support from the education system and the feeling that they had been "abandoned" to such a difficult situation; one educator stated: "No support was given to the counselor or the teaching staff who knew the student". "We were left to cope alone". A school principal reported: "The ministry (of education) must provide a solution for educators and caregivers who have experienced the loss of a student, this is a work accident in every respect. On the day of the event, I felt wrapped and so did in the first week. After that, I was left in great solitude and with the feeling that everyone expects us to return to normal as if it never happened. However, this was not the case". A counselor reported: "Unfortunately, I did not feel emotional support for my work as a counselor and no additional professional help was provided for the incident. The feeling is 'alone in the battle'".

Another possible explanation for our findings is that, during a crisis such as the death of a pupil, home-room teachers tend to be closer to the students and to the family and friends of the pupil who died by suicide compared to other staff members [22]. The degree of closeness to the person who died by suicide has been shown to have an impact on PTSD symptoms [23]; thus, the greater the proximity to the students, the higher the symptoms of the trauma.

According to the rules of the Israeli Ministry of Education, psychologists and counsellors are responsible for the well-being and mental health of pupils [24]. They are trained to cope with crises and distress, and are also under ongoing professional supervision throughout the school year.

Interestingly, male participants of our study reported higher levels of PTSD compared to female participants. Due to the small sample of men we could not test the interaction of gender and profession. A plausible explanation for our findings is that, in a country where military service is compulsory and men are commonly assigned to combat roles, men more than women are exposed to traumatic events. Research shows that repeated trauma impedes teachers' and counselors' adaptive coping following a student's suicide [5]. This is in line with findings from another of our projects [25] suggesting that school staff members who previously experienced the suicide or attempted suicide of someone close should be considered a risk group for lower levels of coping strategies.

5. Limitations

The retrospective approach of this study, evaluating the impact of past events and the subjective nature of the measurements used (self-reporting) may introduce recall biases. In addition, the relatively small size of the study population did not allow consideration of the impact of time elapsed since the suicide. There is no doubt that the current impact of a recent loss differs significantly from the current impact of a loss that occurred years earlier. Other limitations concern the study's sample. Our sample consists mostly of women (73%), reflecting the fact that most school employees in Israel are women [12]. Thus, further research should be conducted with a larger sample of men to examine the replicability of our results and their generalizability to the entire population. The small number of men did not allow us to test for interaction with regard to PTSD; it is recommended that this interaction is tested in future studies.

Additionally, 27% of the potential participants did not participate. Most of these potential participants who did not participate could not be located because they no longer worked at the school at which the incident occurred, and we were unable locate them in other ways. Some potential participants refused to participate, claiming the topic was too painful for them. The low rate of this explicit refusal (5%) is lower than in other social science studies [26]. Yet, those who refused to participate or who were not located may have exhibited a different pattern of responses than the pattern exhibited by our participants, and their absence may have influenced the outcomes of our study. Lastly, our study did not examine additional background variables that have the potential to interfere, such as a previous psychopathological situation. Nor did we measure the duration of contact or emotional proximity of study participants to the pupils who died from suicide. However, it is worth mentioning that in the Israeli education system, the home-room teacher is the staff member the student meets most often. The counselor, psychologist and principle are usually background figures.

6. Conclusions

The policy of the Stress Unit in the Ministry of Education emphasizes the need to provide intensive counseling and accompaniment for staff. However, its focus is on the staff being able to provide these responses to the students, and there is no accompaniment and support for the staff themselves. Decision makers must give special consideration to the severe impact of a pupil's suicide on principals and home-room teachers, who are more vulnerable to mental health symptomatology following such an occurrence. Improving coping skills and establishing prevention and support programs for school staff may assist them in better coping with these difficult situations. Thus, similar to psychologists and counselors who undergo training to cope with crises and loss, it is suggested that home-room teachers and principals receive training focused on coping with the crisis of a pupil's death by suicide and the impact this crisis has on themselves.

Author Contributions: Conceptualization, N.T.F., Y.G. and G.Z; validation, N.T.F., Y.G. and G.Z.; Investigation, N.T.F.; formal analysis, N.T.F., Y.G. and S.A.; writing-original draft preparation, N.T.F., Y.G. and G.Z.; writing-review and editing, S.A. and Y.G.; supervision, G.Z. and Y.G. All authors have read and agreed to the published version of the manuscript.

Funding: This research received no external funding.

Institutional Review Board Statement: The study was conducted in accordance with the Declaration of Helsinki, and approved by the Institutional Review Board—Chief Scientist, Ministry of Educationf (protocol code 8089/420 March 2014).

Informed Consent Statement: Informed consent was obtained from all subjects involved in the study.

Data Availability Statement: Upon request.

Conflicts of Interest: The authors declare no conflict of interest.

References

1. Levi-Belz, Y. Stress-related growth among suicide survivors: The role of interpersonal and cognitive factors. *Arch. Suicide Res.* **2015**, *19*, 305. [CrossRef] [PubMed]
2. Swihart, J.; Silliman, B.; McNeil, J. Death of a student: Implications for secondary school counselors. *Sch. Couns.* **1992**, *40*, 55–60.
3. Wasserman, D.; Hoven, C.W.; Wasserman, C.; Wall, M.; Eisenberg, R.; Hadlaczky, G.; Kelleher, I.; Sarchiapone, M.; Apter, A.; Balazs, J.; et al. School-based suicide prevention programmes: The SEYLE cluster-randomised, controlled trial. *Lancet* **2015**, *385*, 1536–1544. [CrossRef]
4. McLoughlin, A.B.; Gould, M.S.; Malone, K.M. Global trends in teenage suicide: 2003–2014. *QJM* **2015**, *108*, 765–780. [CrossRef] [PubMed]
5. Cerel, J.; Maple, M.; van de Venne, J.; Moore, M.; Flaherty, C.; Brown, M. Exposure to Suicide in the Community: Prevalence and Correlates in One, U.S. State. *Public Health Rep.* **2016**, *131*, 100–107. [CrossRef] [PubMed]
6. Cerel, J.; Padgett, J.H.; Conwell, Y.; Reed, G.A. A call for research: The need to better understand the impact of support groups for suicide survivors. *Suicide Life Threat. Behav.* **2009**, *39*, 269–281. [CrossRef] [PubMed]
7. Gibbons, R.; Brand, A.; Carbonnier, A.; Croft, A.; Lascelles, K.; Wolfart, G.; Hawton, K. Effects of patient suicide on psychiatrists: Survey of experiences and support required. *BJPsych Bull.* **2019**, *43*, 236–241. [CrossRef]
8. Chemtob, C.M.; Hamada, R.S.; Bauer, G.; Kinney, B.; Torigoe, R.Y. Patients' suicides: Frequency and impact on psychiatrists. *Am. J. Psychiatry* **1988**, *145*, 224–228. [PubMed]
9. Sandford, D.M.; Kirtley, O.J.; Thaites, R.; O'Connor, R.C. The impact on mental health practitioners of the death of apatient by suicide: A systematic review. *Clin. Psychol. Psychother.* **2021**, *28*, 261–294.
10. Christianson, C.L.; Everall, R.D. Constructing bridges of support: School counsellors' experiences of student suicide. *Can. J. Coun. Psychother.* **2009**, *42*, 209–221.
11. Avney Rosha Institute. Expected Outcomes from School Principals at the Start of Their Career. Available online: http://www.avneyrosha.org.il/eng/Documents/Expected_outcomes.pdf.2010 (accessed on 19 July 2022).

12. Zarad, E. Knesset Report on Teachers in the Israeli Educational System. 25 June 2019. Available online: https://fs.knesset.gov.il/globaldocs/MMM/fa83866a-6e5b-e911-80e9-00155d0aeebb/2_fa83866a-6e5b-e911-80e9-00155d0aeebb_11_13503.pdf (accessed on 19 July 2022).
13. Foa, E.B. *Posttraumatic Diagnostic Scale Manual*; National Computer Systems: Minneapolis, MN, USA, 1996.
14. Prigerson, H.G.; Bierhals, A.J.; Kasl, S.V.; Reynolds, C.F., 3rd; Shear, M.K.; Newsom, J.T.; Jacobs, S. Complicated grief as a disorder distinct from bereavement-related depression and anxiety: A replication study. *Am. J. Psychiatry* **1996**, *153*, 1484–1486. [CrossRef] [PubMed]
15. Cooksey, R.W. *Illustrating Statistical Procedures: Finding Meaning in Quantitative Data*; Springer: Singapore, 2020. [CrossRef]
16. Bickel, R. *Multilevel Analysis for Applied Research*; The Guilford Press: New York, NY, USA, 2007; p. 272.
17. Lazenby, R.B. Teachers Dealing with the Death of Students: A Qualitative Analysis. *J. Hosp. Palliat. Nurs.* **2006**, *8*, 50–56. [CrossRef]
18. Munson, L.J.; Hunt, N. Teachers grieve! What can we do for our colleagues and ourselves when a student dies? *Teach. Except. Child.* **2005**, *37*, 48–51. [CrossRef]
19. Rowling, L. The disenfranchised grief of teachers. *OMEGA-J. Death Dying* **1995**, *31*, 317–329. [CrossRef]
20. Oplatka, I. Learning the principal's future internal career experiences: An assessment of a unique principal preparation programme in Israel. *Int J. Educ. Manag.* **2009**, *23*, 129–144. [CrossRef]
21. Sisask, M.; Värnik, P.; Värnik, A.; Apter, A.; Balazs, J.; Balint, M.; Bobes, J.; Brunner, R.; Corcoran, P.; Cozman, D.; et al. Teacher satisfaction with school and psychological well-being affects their readiness to help children with mental health problems. *Health Educ. J.* **2013**, *74*, 382–393. [CrossRef]
22. Liora, F. *School Management Under Conditions of Terror and Ongoing Trauma*; Ahva College of Education: Beer-Tuvia, Israel, 2008. (In Hebrew)
23. Bonanno, G.A.; Kaltman, S. The varieties of grief experience. *Clin. Psychol. Rev.* **2001**, *21*, 705–734. [CrossRef]
24. Israel Ministry of Education Director General Directive, Educational Counselor. Outline of Educational Psychology Services (Hebrew). Available online: https://cms.education.gov.il/EducationCMS/Units/Sherut/Takanon/Perek5/Yoetz/ (accessed on 16 July 2022).
25. Tiech-Fire, N.; Alkalay, S.; Gvion, Y.; Zalsman, G. The association between school staff's coping strategies following a student's suicide, school climate, and previous experience with suicide. *Br. Educ. Psychol.* 2022. *under review*.
26. Anastasi, A. *Psychological Testing*, 6th ed.; The Open University: Tel Aviv, Israel, 1990. (In Hebrew)

International Journal of
Environmental Research and Public Health

MDPI

Article

Investigating Whether Bereavement by Suicide and Other Unnatural Causes Has a Deterrent Effect on Alcohol or Drug Use in Young Adults

Alexandra Pitman [1,2,*], Fiona Stevenson [3] and David Osborn [1,2]

1 Division of Psychiatry, University College London (UCL), London W1T 7NF, UK
2 Camden and Islington NHS Foundation Trust, London NW1 0PE, UK
3 Department of Primary Care and Population Health, University College London (UCL), London NW3 2PF, UK
* Correspondence: a.pitman@ucl.ac.uk

Abstract: Bereavement by suicide and other unnatural causes is associated with suicide but evidence regarding risk of substance misuse is inconsistent. This may be due to heterogeneity in patterns of alcohol or drug use after traumatic bereavement; some increasing use to cope with the loss and others reducing use. To highlight the problems of focussing on diagnostic thresholds when investigating substance use after traumatic loss, we aimed to test whether people bereaved by suicide or other unnatural causes are more likely to reduce or stop their substance use than people bereaved by sudden natural causes. Using multivariable logistic regression and data from an online survey of 1854 UK-based bereaved adults, we tested the association between bereavement by suicide and other unnatural causes and post-bereavement reduction/cessation in (i) alcohol and (ii) drug use. There were no group differences in the proportions who reduced/stopped alcohol use, but a significantly greater proportion of people bereaved by sudden unnatural causes reduced/stopped drug use post-bereavement than people bereaved by sudden natural causes (AOR = 2.61; 95% CI = 1.44–4.71; $p = 0.001$; 4.1% versus 1.7%). In sub-group analyses this applied separately to people bereaved by suicide and non-suicide unnatural causes. Research into post-bereavement substance use should accommodate apparent divergent sub-diagnostic patterns.

Keywords: bereavement; grief; alcohol; drugs; suicide; cause of death; mixed methods

Citation: Pitman, A.; Stevenson, F.; Osborn, D. Investigating Whether Bereavement by Suicide and Other Unnatural Causes Has a Deterrent Effect on Alcohol or Drug Use in Young Adults. *Int. J. Environ. Res. Public Health* **2022**, *19*, 13245. https://doi.org/10.3390/ijerph192013245

Academic Editors: Karolina Krysinska, Karl Andriessen and Yossi Levi-Belz

Received: 21 September 2022
Accepted: 12 October 2022
Published: 14 October 2022

1. Background

Although bereavement is a near universal experience, and grieving is the natural process by which people adapt to a loss, for some individuals adjustment can be more difficult, with substantial variation in psychological health between individuals and across cultures [1]. Bereavement by any cause is associated with an excess risk of physical and mental health problems [1], suicide [2] and premature all-cause mortality [1]. However, people who experience bereavement due to unnatural causes (such as suicide, homicide or accidental death) are at greater risk of psychiatric illness and suicide than those bereaved by other causes [3]. These types of deaths are also more stigmatised than deaths by natural causes [3]. In attempting to understand mechanisms of suicide risk after bereavement by unnatural causes, researchers have investigated substance use, identifying this as a likely mediator because it is a common means of processing bereavement [4] and a potent risk factor for suicide [5]. This work has tended to rely on recorded diagnoses of substance use disorder or diagnostic interviews as outcomes, finding elevated risks of substance misuse after bereavement by suicide and other unnatural causes when compared with non-bereaved controls [6–8], but no differences when comparing suicide bereavement to bereavement by other unnatural causes [7,9]. However, such work ignores patterns of substance misuse at a sub-diagnostic level, hampering a more nuanced understanding of whether individuals respond differently in their use of substances after a traumatic loss. In the current study, prompted by qualitative findings of varied and divergent patterns of substance misuse after traumatic loss [10–14], we aimed to test a contrary hypothesis using more fine-grained measures of substance use. We hypothesised that people bereaved by unnatural causes (including suicide) are more likely than those bereaved by natural causes to reduce or stop their use of alcohol and drugs after bereavement. This has not yet been investigated, and was intended to complement findings that these groups are also more likely to increase their use of substances (alcohol or drugs) after a bereavement [12], improving our clinical understanding of potentially differing patterns within this population and making a methodological point about factors to consider when investigating substance use after bereavement.

2. Materials and Methods

2.1. Sample

We analysed cross-sectional data from adults who had participated in the 2010 UCL Bereavement Study; a closed online survey of adults aged 18 to 40 working or studying at 37 British higher education institutions (HEIs) who were invited to take part in a survey of *"the impact of sudden bereavement on young adults"*(see Supplementary Material) [15]. All 164 HEIs in the UK at that time had been invited to participate, and 37 had agreed. Each staff and student member of the 37 HEIs (an estimated sample of 659,572 in a sampling frame of 20% of all 164 UK HEIs) received an individual email inviting them to participate in a survey investigating the impact of sudden bereavement on young adults and defining sudden bereavement as *"a death that could not have been predicted at that time and which occurred suddenly or within a matter of days"*. This allowed identification of bereaved individuals without using a help-seeking sample, and was judged to be the optimal means of recruiting a hard-to-reach population of young adults with broad socio-economic and geographic representation [15].

Respondents self-identified type of bereavement as: bereavement by suicide, bereavement by sudden natural causes (for example cardiac arrest), and bereavement by sudden unnatural causes (for example accidental death). In the case of exposure to more than one mode of sudden bereavement, all those bereaved by suicide were asked to relate their responses to their bereavement by suicide (and in the case of more than one suicide bereavement, to the person they had felt closest to). Those bereaved by deaths due to sudden natural causes and to sudden unnatural causes were asked to relate their responses to whichever person they had felt closest to, identifying exposure status accordingly.

2.2. Procedures

Participants completed an online survey that had been designed and piloted in consultation with a group of young, bereaved adults and bereavement counsellors, capturing quantitative and qualitative data on important domains in relation to the impact of bereavement. As well as eliciting quantitative data on socio-demographic and clinical characteristics [15], open questions elicited free-text qualitative data on issues such as the impact of the bereavement on relationships [16], occupational functioning [17], and support needs [18]. Respondents were invited to give as much or little detail as they wished, with no upper word limit, or to skip the question if it did not apply. The question relating to use of drugs and alcohol was worded as follows: *"In what way, if any, has the bereavement affected your drinking habits or your use of unprescribed drugs? (Unprescribed drugs include illicit drugs as well as medications used above their prescribed limits)"*. The wording of this question was designed to be non-leading, neutral (avoiding assuming solely negative outcomes of bereavement), and unambiguous in using the term unprescribed drugs to cover use of illegal drugs, legal highs, over-the-counter drugs, or prescribed drugs used above advised limits.

2.3. Ethical Approval

The UCL Bereavement Study was approved by the UCL Research Ethics Committee (ref: 1975/002). All participants provided online informed consent by ticking a box to indicate they had read the participant information leaflet and consent form and agreed that the anonymised results would be used for research purposes.

2.4. Measures

2.4.1. Outcomes

As reported in our previous mixed methods study describing substance use after sudden bereavement [12], we used the approach of content analysis to analyse large volumes of brief free-text responses to the question on drug and alcohol use to capture perceptions of any increases, decreases, or no changes. This broad approach to categorisation avoided attempting diagnostic categorisation or estimates of the quantity of substances used. Text was analysed with the researchers blinded to the cause of death, except for unblinding in 15 cases where the text mentioned cause.

Two authors (AP; FS) conducted content analysis collaboratively with team discussions providing opportunities to check the validity of codes against data, clarify where meaning was uncertain, and encourage reflexivity. Our cross-disciplinary team comprised clinical and non-clinical perspectives to challenge differences in interpretation.

Our initial content analysis identified 11 mutually exclusive categories capturing the impact of the bereavement on substance use: (i) no change (including those who were abstinent pre-and post-bereavement); (ii) stopped; (iii) reduced; (iv) brief temporary increase (within the week of the death) but then resumed pre-loss pattern of use; (v) increased (unclear if perceived as helpful or harmful); (vi) increased (perceived as helpful); (vii) increased (perceived as harmful); (viii) increased (unclear if perceived as helpful or harmful) but then resumed pre-loss pattern of use; (ix) increased (perceived as helpful) but then resumed pre-loss pattern of use; (x) increased (unclear if perceived as helpful or harmful) but then stopped; and (xi) unable to classify.

We used these categories to create two binary variables: reduction/cessation in alcohol use post-bereavement, and reduction/cessation in drug use post-bereavement. Each used the categories *stopped* and *reduced* above to define a positive outcome specific to alcohol or drugs, and the other nine categories to define a negative outcome.

2.4.2. Exposure

We derived a binary exposure variable to compare all those who related their survey responses to (a) bereavement by suicide or by other sudden unnatural causes and (b) bereavement by sudden natural causes.

2.4.3. Covariates

We chose six variables *a priori* as potential confounders based on previous literature [3] and clinical judgement. Survey data captured these variables as follows:

- Age: continuous measure, defined by participant (options from 18–40 years)
- Gender: binary variable, defined by participant (male; female)
- Time since bereavement: continuous measure, defined by participant (years/months)
- Socio-economic status: categorical measure, derived from a question capturing own occupation (for HEI staff) or parental occupation (for students), using the 5 categories used by the Office for National Statistics (ONS)
- Pre-bereavemen: depression: binary measure, using the Composite International Diagnostic Interview (CIDI) screen for lifetime depression, qualified by whether this was before or after the sudden bereavement, to derive a pre-exposure measure
- Family history of psychiatric problems (including drug and alcohol problems): binary measure derived from responses to the question "Has anyone in your family suffered from an anxiety disorder, a depressive disorder (including postnatal depression), had drug or alcohol problems, or other psychological or emotional difficulties?"

2.5. Statistical Analysis

We described the socio-demographic and clinical characteristics of our sample using χ^2 tests (categorical variables) and one-way analysis of variance (continuous variables) to compare people bereaved by sudden unnatural causes and sudden natural causes.

We used multivariable logistic regression to test the association between bereavement by unnatural causes and our two outcomes (post-bereavement reduction/cessation in alcohol use; post-bereavement reduction/cessation in drug use) adjusted for six potential confounders as listed above. We fitted binary models using *xtlogit* commands in Stata, taking into account any clustering effect at institutional level by estimating random effects for each cluster (n = 37 HEIs).

To identify whether findings differed by whether an individual was bereaved by suicide or non-suicide unnatural causes, we conducted sub-group analyses in which we ran the above models comparing each of these groups separately to the control group of people bereaved by sudden natural causes.

We conducted all analyses in Stata version 16 and used a 2-sided *p*-value threshold of <0.05 for all models.

3. Results

3.1. Response

Of the 5085 bereaved by the sudden death of a close contact who responded to the UCL Bereavement Study questionnaire, 91% eligible adults (n = 4630) consented to participate, and 1854 (40%) responded to the open question on substance use and were therefore included in the current analysis. There was no accurate way of measuring overall response to the survey, as the denominator of bereaved people could not be ascertained.

Of the 1854 adults who provided free-text data on substance use, 353 were bereaved by suicide, 395 by sudden unnatural causes and 1106 by sudden natural causes. We therefore compared the 748 adults bereaved by unnatural causes (353 by suicide; 395 by sudden unnatural causes) to 1106 people bereaved by sudden natural causes.

3.2. Sample Characteristics

The overall gender balance of the sample was 19% male and 81% female, with a mean age of 25.6 years (SD = 6.3). People bereaved by sudden natural causes were significantly more likely than those bereaved by unnatural causes to have been under 21 years when responding, to have been bereaved more recently, and to have been related to the deceased (Table 1).

In the full sample 7.7% reduced/stopped their use of alcohol post-bereavement and 2.7% reduced/stopped their use of drugs, whilst alcohol use was unchanged for 58% and drug use was unchanged for 85% (including those who had never used alcohol/drugs).

3.3. Association of Bereavement Status with Reduction/Cessation in Substance Use

There were no significant group differences in the proportions who had reduced or stopped their alcohol use (Table 2). A significantly greater proportion of people bereaved by sudden unnatural causes reduced/stopped their use of drugs after the bereavement (AOR = 2.61; 95% CI = 1.44–4.71; p = 0.001; 4.1% versus 1.7%) than people bereaved by sudden natural causes.

In sub-group analyses (Table 3), compared with people bereaved by sudden natural causes, significantly greater proportions of people bereaved by suicide (AOR = 3.13; 95% CI = 1.60–6.13; p = 0.001; 5.1% versus 1.7%) and of people bereaved by non-suicide unnatural causes (AOR = 2.19; 95% CI = 1.06–4.53; p = 0.035; 3.3% versus 1.7%) had reduced/stopped their use of drugs post-bereavement, but with no group differences for alcohol use (7.1% versus 8.5% versus 8.6%, respectively).

Table 1. Sociodemographic and clinical characteristics of bereaved sample.

Bereavement Exposure	Sudden Natural Causes (n = 1106)	Sudden Unnatural Causes (Suicide and Non-Suicide Unnatural Deaths) (n = 748)	Sub-Groups of the n = 748 Bereaved by Sudden Unnatural Causes		Total (n = 1854)	*p*-Value †
			Suicide (n = 353)	Sudden (Non-Suicide) Unnatural Causes (n = 395)		
Socio-demographic characteristics	n (%)	n (%)	n (%)	n (%)	n (%)	
Gender ††						0.397
male	217 (19.6)	135 (18.1)	67 (19)	68 (17.2)	352 (19.0)	
female	889 (80.4)	613 (82.0)	286 (81)	286 (81.0)	1502 (81.0)	
missing	0 (0)	0 (0)	0 (0)	0 (0)	0 (0)	
Age of participant (binary variable) [a]						**0.047**
aged 18–21	412 (37.3)	245 (32.3)	112 (31.7)	133 (33.7)	657 (35.4)	
aged 22–40	694 (62.8)	503 (67.3)	241 (68.3)	262 (66.3)	1197 (64.6)	
missing	0 (0)	0 (0)	0 (0)	0 (0)	0 (0)	
Age of participant (years) ††						0.986
mean (SD)	25.5 (6.4)	25.7 (6.2)	25.8 (6.3)	25.6 (6.0)	25.6 (6.3)	
Age participant was bereaved						0.761
between age 10 and 17	440 (39.8)	303 (40.5)	143 (40.5)	160 (40.5)	743 (40.1)	
between age 18 and 40	664 (60.0)	444 (59.4)	209 (59.2)	235 (59.5)	1108 (59.8)	
missing	2 (0.2)	1 (0.1)	1 (0.3)	0 (0)	3 (0.2)	
Self-defined ethnicity						0.186
white	994 (89.9)	685 (91.6)	323 (91.6)	362 (91.7)	1679 (90.6)	
non-white	112 (10.1)	62 (8.3)	30 (8.5)	32 (8.1)	174 (9.4)	
missing	0 (0)	1 (0.1)	0 (0)	1 (0.3)	1 (0.1)	
Socio-economic status ††,b						0.365
social classes 1.1 & 1.2	680 (61.5)	474 (63.4)	222 (62.9)	252 (63.8)	1154 (62.2)	
social classes 3–7 & 9	402 (36.4)	256 (34.2)	124 (35.1)	132 (33.4)	658 (35.5)	
missing	24 (2.2)	18 (2.4)	7 (2.0)	11 (2.8)	42 (2.3)	
Clinical characteristics						
Pre-bereavement depression ††,c						0.540
Yes	230 (20.8)	164 (21.9)	92 (26.1)	72 (18.2)	394 (21.3)	
No	876 (79.2)	582 (77.8)	260 (81.5)	322 (81.5)	1458 (78.6)	
missing	0 (<0.1)	2 (0.3)	1 (0.3)	1 (0.3)	2 (0.1)	
Family history of any psychiatric problems (including drug and alcohol problems) ††						0.104
Yes	737 (66.6)	525 (70.2)	255 (72.2)	270 (68.3)	1262 (68.1)	
No	368 (33.3)	222 (29.7)	98 (27.8)	124 (31.1)	590 (31.8)	
missing	1 (0.1)	1 (0.1)	0 (0)	1 (0.3)	2 (0.1)	
Characteristics of the bereavement						
Years since bereavement ††,a						**0.002**
less than two years	376 (34.0)	204 (27.3)	98 (27.8)	106 (26.8)	580 (31.2)	
two years or more	730 (66.0)	544 (72.7)	255 (72.2)	289 (73.2)	1274 (68.7)	
missing	0 (0)	0 (0)	0 (0)	0 (0)	0 (0)	
Kinship to the deceased						**<0.001**
blood-related	934 (84.5)	376 (50.3)	183 (51.8)	193 (48.9)	1310 (70.7)	
non-blood-related	168 (15.2)	369 (49.3)	170 (48.1)	199 (50.4)	537 (29.0)	
missing	4 (0.4)	3 (0.4)	0 (0)	3 (0.8)	7 (0.4)	

† *p*-values for bivariate associations in relation to main comparison (bereavement by sudden natural causes versus bereavement by any sudden unnatural causes), with those in bold below the threshold for significance (<0.05). †† covariates included in adjusted model. [a] age and time since bereavement were used as continuous variables in our multivariable models but are presented here as binary variables for ease of interpretation. [b] socio-economic status using the five categories from UK Office for National Statistics. [c] measured using CIDI screen for depression.

Table 2. Associations between bereavement by unnatural causes and perceived reduction/cessation in substance use.

Exposure to Bereavement by:	Sudden Natural Causes (n = 1106)		Sudden Unnatural Causes, Including Suicide (n = 748)					Total (n = 1854)
Outcome	**Prevalence n (%)**	**Odds Ratio**	**Prevalence n (%)**	**Unadjusted Odds Ratio (95% CI)**	***p*-Value †**	**Adjusted [a] Odds Ratio (95% CI)**	***p*-Value †**	**Prevalence n (%)**
Perceived reduction or cessation in alcohol use post-bereavement	78 (7.1)	1	64 (8.6)	1.21 (0.85–1.71)	0.287	1.24 (0.87–1.77)	0.239	142 (7.7)
Perceived reduction or cessation in drug use post-bereavement	19 (1.7)	1	31 (4.1)	2.63 (1.45–4.73)	**0.001**	2.61 (1.44–4.71)	**0.001**	50 (2.7)

[a] adjusted for age, gender, socio-economic status, time since bereavement, pre-bereavement depression, and family history of psychiatric problems (including drug and alcohol problems). † *p*-values in bold are below the threshold for significance (<0.05).

Table 3. Sensitivity analyses showing the associations between bereavement exposure sub-type and perceived reduction/cessation in substance use.

Exposure to Bereavement by:	Sudden Natural Causes (n = 1106)		Suicide (n = 353)					Total Sample for Sub-Analysis (n = 1501)
Outcomes	**Prevalence n (%)**	**Odds Ratio**	**Prevalence n (%)**	**Unadjusted Odds Ratio (95% CI)**	***p*-Value**	**Adjusted [a] Odds Ratio (95% CI)**	***p*-Value**	**Prevalence n (%)**
Perceived reduction or cessation in alcohol use post-bereavement	78 (7.1)	1	30 (8.5)	1.20 (0.77–1.87)	0.431	1.25 (0.80–1.97)	0.328	108 (7.4)
Perceived reduction or cessation in drug use post-bereavement	19 (1.7)	1	18 (5.1)	3.25 (1.76–6.32)	**0.001**	3.13 (1.60–6.13)	**0.001**	37 (2.5)
Exposure to Bereavement by:	**Sudden Natural Causes (n = 1106)**		**Sudden (Non-Suicide) Unnatural Causes (n = 395)**					**Total Sample for Sub-Analysis (n = 1459)**
Outcomes	**Prevalence n (%)**	**Odds Ratio**	**Prevalence n (%)**	**Unadjusted Odds Ratio (95% CI)**	***p*-Value †**	**Adjusted[a] Odds Ratio (95% CI)**	***p*-Value †**	**Prevalence n (%)**
Perceived reduction or cessation in alcohol use post-bereavement	78 (7.1)	1	34 (8.6)	1.21 (0.79–1.86)	0.375	1.24 (0.80–1.92)	0.328	112 (7.5)
Perceived reduction or cessation in drug use post-bereavement	19 (1.7)	1	13 (3.3)	2.07 (1.01–4.28)	**0.048**	2.19 (1.06–4.53)	**0.035**	32 (2.1)

[a] adjusted for age, gender, socio-economic status, time since bereavement, pre-bereavement depression, and family history of psychiatric problems (including drug and alcohol problems). † *p*-values in bold are below the threshold for significance (<0.05).

4. Discussion

4.1. Main Findings

We found that it was more common for people bereaved by sudden unnatural causes (including suicide) to reduce or stop their use of illicit drugs after the loss than people bereaved by sudden natural causes. However, we found no differences in the proportions reducing or stopping their alcohol use. Our sub-group analyses showed that the greater tendency to reduce or stop illicit drug use applied individually to people bereaved by suicide and people bereaved by sudden unnatural causes excluding suicide, whilst acknowledging small numbers and limited power. These findings were in the context of the small minority of people in the overall bereaved sample who reduced or stopped their use of alcohol (8%) or drugs (3%) after the loss.

Our differing findings for drugs and for alcohol could reflect a perception that drugs pose a greater risk to health than alcohol. Alcohol is regarded as a socially acceptable way to cope with adversity in many Western societies, with social and cultural influences promoting the practice of self-medicating with alcohol when coping with life stressors such as bereavement [4]. Such influences may be particularly pronounced among young British people [19]. Given the predominance of females in our sample, our findings for drug use may reflect the impact of losing a drug-using partner as well as their facilitative influence on drug use at home or in leisure spaces [20,21].

Another explanation for these findings is that social support is protective against substance misuse [4], and that people bereaved by unnatural causes receive a level of social support that reduces their reliance on drugs. However, this is contradicted by evidence describing the higher levels of stigma perceived by people bereaved by unnatural causes [3] and their lower levels of support [22], particularly for those bereaved by suicide [22,23]. Individuals who reduce their use of drugs after a traumatic bereavement warrant close study to understand how they achieve this in the context of poor social support, and whether their beliefs about the potential harms of drug use are rooted in heightened health anxiety.

4.2. Findings in the Context of Other Studies

No other studies have tested this hypothesis, and our findings complement those of our previous study showing that people bereaved by suicide and people bereaved by non-suicide unnatural causes are both more likely to increase their use of substances after bereavement than people bereaved by natural causes (when considering alcohol or drugs together) [12]. However, when considering alcohol and drugs separately, only the group bereaved by non-suicide unnatural causes are more likely to increase their use of alcohol compared with those bereaved by natural causes [12]. Together, this suggests that people bereaved by non-suicide unnatural causes are more likely to reduce or stop their drug use and also more likely to increase their alcohol use. Our findings regarding no group differences in alcohol reduction/cessation are consistent with quantitative work using Danish registers, which found an elevated risk of alcohol or drug use disorder in suicide-bereaved partners compared with non-bereaved partners, but no differences between suicide-bereaved partners and other-bereaved controls [7]. However, our findings of no differences in alcohol reduction/cessation are inconsistent with findings from a Danish analysis showing that suicide-bereaved partners have a reduced risk of liver cirrhosis (an alcohol misuse marker) when compared to non-bereaved partners and to partners bereaved by other causes [7]. It is possible that such varied findings are interpretable in the context of divergent patterns within the bereaved population, such that patterns differ for those with a formal diagnosis of substance misuse and for those consuming at sub-diagnostic levels. Our study did not investigate sex or age differences due to limited statistical power, but previous work shows that after suicide loss women may be more likely to report using prescription drugs, men may be more likely to report illicit drug use and alcohol use, and younger people may be more likely to report substance misuse [24].

Whilst the more common narrative is that of using alcohol after bereavement to dull the pain and purge sadness [25] the findings of the current study identify a group who find alternative ways of coping. Our findings are consistent with the qualitative accounts of people bereaved by suicide [11] and non-suicide unnatural causes [10] who describe conscious efforts to restrain their use, in order to help them cope. Reasons given include an awareness that alcohol or drugs lower mood, hamper control of emotions, or increase fears that they could become like the person who died [10–12]. People bereaved by alcohol-related deaths describe being confronted by their own mortality and realising that their own substance misuse may pose a risk to their health [26]. They also describe wanting to learn more about substance misuse to better understand the deceased and their problems [27]. Such accounts do not distinguish clearly between attitudes towards drugs and attitudes towards alcohol, and therefore how this might apply differentially to consumption of each.

More work is needed to understand the cognitions of those who change their use of alcohol or drugs after traumatic loss, or order to help design interventions that promote coping and recovery.

4.3. Strengths and Limitations

We analysed data from what we believe to be the largest-scale study collecting qualitative data on self-reported use of alcohol and unprescribed drugs after different modes of sudden bereavement. Nevertheless, low event rates in our sample of 1854 bereaved adults meant we had limited power for statistical models. Recruitment avoided use of a help-seeking sample, and outcomes did not rely on narrow diagnostic criteria. Collection of fine-grained data on consumption of drugs and alcohol in the day-to-day lives of respondents captured more nuanced changes in patterns of drinking and drug use after a negative life event. Registry-based studies using recorded diagnoses of substance misuse or dependence do not permit such a detailed investigation of reduced intake or of reported harmful use. The anonymous format of data collection also promoted disclosure, although did not allow for further probing. Our cross-disciplinary team approach encouraged personal reflexivity when analysing free-text data by challenging differences in interpretation, reducing the influence of theoretical or personal conceptions [28]. However, we acknowledge that subjectivity in coding, social desirability bias, and recall bias may have over-ascertained (particularly in the context of social desirability bias) or under-ascertained our outcomes, biasing our quantitative findings. Our multi-level models were adjusted for covariates agreed *a priori*, although we acknowledge the possibility of residual confounding. Comparison to sudden natural bereavement rather than any bereavement by natural causes took into account the sudden or unexpected nature of the death, which might also be a factor in promoting use of alcohol or drugs. As females of all ages have a greater risk of bereavement [29] we would expect an excess of bereaved females aged 40 and below, particularly given the much higher suicide and accidental death rate in males than females in this age group [30]. However, our findings from a predominantly female (81%), white (90%), high socio-economic status (60%) sample may not be generalisable to all young bereaved adults in the UK or internationally. Given that drug-related deaths of peers and partners are likely to be over-represented in this younger sample, our findings may not be generalisable to other age groups.

4.4. Clinical and Research Implications

Our findings demonstrate that clinicians cannot assume uniform responses to a traumatic bereavement and that a small minority of bereaved people make positive changes to lifestyle factors. The extent that this is driven by health anxiety remains unclear. Whilst other work (analysing the same dataset) shows that a significantly greater proportion of suicide-bereaved individuals increase their use of drug or alcohol use after a sudden loss [12], the current study shows that another sub-group appear motivated to reduce their risk of misusing unprescribed drugs. How these two groups differ in their adjustment to the loss is unclear and requires longitudinal investigation. Those who reduce their use of alcohol or drugs are of interest for their coping strategies. Those who increase their use are concerning because they may be those in most distress and those at greatest risk of suicide attempt. Further longitudinal work is needed to understand the socio-demographic and cognitive characteristics and health outcomes of each group. This will help understand the role of alcohol and drug use in the association between suicide bereavement and suicide.

Patterns of use tend to change over the course of grief. Cohort studies should pay particular attention to the reported tendency for some people bereaved by suicide to increase their use of alcohol or drugs in the early stages of the loss [13] but to reduce this over the next two years [14], as also observed in samples of people bereaved by sudden natural and unnatural causes [12]. Clinicians should be aware of the potential for bereaved individuals to react in a range of ways after a loss, and for these patterns to change over the course of grief. A sensitive discussion about the perceived benefits and risks of drug and alcohol use is important given that some bereaved individuals report finding alcohol helpful in coping with grief over the short-term [10,11,25]. Where an individual is identified as being at risk, educational resources and motivational approaches may be helpful in considering appropriate responses, building on the reported awareness of the potential for negative effects in longer-term use [25]. Future research should explore the predictors of increased and reduced alcohol and drug use after a traumatic life event, and use these to screen sensitively for hazardous use.

5. Conclusions

A small minority of people bereaved by sudden unnatural causes report a reduction in their use of drugs or alcohol after the bereavement, but for drug use this proportion is significantly greater than that for people bereaved by sudden natural causes. This applies both to people bereaved by suicide and to people bereaved by non-suicide unnatural causes when compared to people bereaved by sudden natural causes. It is possible that experiencing the death of a close contact by unnatural causes can influence drug use attitudes and behaviour of some individuals who seek to protect their own health. Further work is needed to understand the cognitions associated with this behaviour, and whether this has a buffering influence on the adverse health outcomes of bereavement by sudden unnatural causes.

Supplementary Materials: The following are available online at https://www.mdpi.com/article/10.3390/ijerph192013245/s1, File S1: UCL Bereavement Study survey instrument.

Author Contributions: Conceptualization, D.O., F.S. and A.P.; Data curation, A.P. Formal quantitative analysis, A.P. Funding acquisition, A.P. Investigation, A.P. Methodology, D.O., F.S. and A.P. Project administration, A.P. Writing—original draft, A.P. Writing—review and editing, D.O., F.S. and A.P. A.P. had full access to all the data in the study and takes responsibility for the integrity of the data. A.P. is the guarantor. All authors have read and agreed to the published version of the manuscript.

Funding: This work was funded by a Medical Research Council Population Health Scientist Fellowship Award to A.P. (G0802441), and a Guarantors of Brain Fellowship award to A.P. Additionally, A.P. and D.O. are supported by the University College London Hospitals (UCLH) National Institute of Health Research (NIHR) Biomedical Research Centre (BRC). D.O. was also part-supported by the NIHR Collaboration for Leadership in Applied Health Research and Care (CLAHRC) North Thames at Bart's Health NHS Trust.

Institutional Review Board Statement: The UCL Bereavement Study was approved by the UCL Research Ethics Committee (ref: 1975/002).

Informed Consent Statement: All participants provided online informed consent by ticking a box to indicate they had read the participant information leaflet and consent form and agreed that the anonymised results would be used for research purposes.

Data Availability Statement: Data are made available to researchers on formal application to the research team, subject to approval of an honorary contract at UCL.

Acknowledgments: We would like to thank all UK higher education institutions (HEIs) that consented to take part in the study, and all of the bereaved individuals who took time to participate in the on-line survey. Participating HEIs were: Bishop Grosseteste University; Bournemouth University; Central School of Speech and Drama; City University; Cranfield University; Courtauld Institute; De Montfort University; University of Greenwich; King's College London; Liverpool Institute for Performing Arts; Liverpool John Moores University; London Metropolitan University; Norwich University of the Arts; Royal Veterinary College; School of Oriental and African Studies; St George's, University of London; Staffordshire University; Trinity Laban Conservatoire of Music and Dance; UCL; University of Suffolk; University of Bedfordshire; University of Chester; University of Cumbria; University of Leeds; University of Liverpool; University of Oxford; University of Southampton; University of Worcester; University of Westminster; Queen Margaret University; Heriot-Watt University; Scottish Agricultural College (now part of Scotland's Rural University College); University of Dundee; Cardiff University; Cardiff Metropolitan University (formerly University of Wales Institute Cardiff); Queen's University Belfast; University of Ulster. We would like to acknowledge the contribution of

Michael King, who made a key contribution to the questionnaire design and the content analysis from which the current quantitative analysis derives, but who died in 2021.

Conflicts of Interest: All authors state that they have no conflict of interest. The funders had no role in the design of the study; in the collection, analyses, or interpretation of data; in the writing of the manuscript, or in the decision to publish the results.

References

1. Stroebe, M.; Schut, H.; Stroebe, W. Health outcomes of bereavement. *Lancet* **2007**, *370*, 1960–1973. [CrossRef]
2. Guldin, M.-B.; Ina Siegismund Kjaersgaard, M.; Fenger-Grøn, M.; Thorlund Parner, E.; Li, J.; Prior, A.; Vestergaard, M. Risk of suicide, deliberate self-harm and psychiatric illness after the loss of a close relative: A nationwide cohort study. *World Psychiatry* **2017**, *16*, 193–199. [CrossRef] [PubMed]
3. Pitman, A.; Osborn, D.; King, M.; Erlangsen, A. Effects of suicide bereavement on mental health and suicide risk. *Lancet Psychiatry* **2014**, *1*, 86–94. [CrossRef]
4. Sudhinaraset, M.; Wigglesworth, C.; Takeuchi, D.T. Social and cultural contexts of alcohol use: Influences in a social–ecological framework. *Alcohol Res. Curr. Rev.* **2016**, *38*, 35–45.
5. Fazel, S.; Runeson, B. Suicide. *N. Engl. J. Med.* **2020**, *382*, 266–274. [CrossRef]
6. Brent, D.; Melhem, N.; Donohoe, M.B.; Walker, M. The incidence and course of depression in bereaved youth 21 months after the loss of a parent to suicide, accident, or sudden natural death. *Am. J. Psychiatry* **2009**, *166*, 786–794. [CrossRef] [PubMed]
7. Erlangsen, A.; Runeson, B.; Bolton, J.M.; Wilcox, H.C.; Forman, J.; Krogh, J.; Shear, M.K.; Nordentoft, M.; Conwell, Y. Association between spousal suicide and mental, physical, and social health outcomes a longitudinal and nationwide register-based study. *JAMA Psychiatry* **2017**, *74*, 456–464. [CrossRef] [PubMed]
8. Spiwak, R.; Elias, B.; Sareen, J.; Chartier, M.; Katz, L.Y.; Bolton, J.M. Spouses bereaved by suicide: A population-based longitudinal cohort comparison of physician-diagnosed mental disorders and hospitalized suicide attempts. *J. Psychiatr. Res.* **2020**, *130*, 347–354. [CrossRef] [PubMed]
9. Bolton, J.M.; Au, W.; Leslie, W.D.; Martens, P.J.; Enns, M.W.; Roos, L.L.; Katz, L.Y.; Wilcox, H.C.; Erlangsen, A.; Chateau, D.; et al. Parents bereaved by offspring suicide: A population-based longitudinal case-control study. *JAMA Psychiatry* **2013**, *70*, 158–167. [CrossRef] [PubMed]
10. Drabwell, L.; Eng, J.; Stevenson, F.; King, M.; Osborn, D.; Pitman, A. Perceptions of the use of alcohol and drugs after sudden bereavement by unnatural causes: Analysis of online qualitative data. *Int. J. Environ. Res. Public Health* **2020**, *17*, 677. [CrossRef]
11. Eng, J.; Drabwell, L.; Stevenson, F.; King, M.; Osborn, D.; Pitman, A. Use of alcohol and unprescribed drugs after suicide bereavement: Qualitative study. *Int. J. Environ. Res. Public Health* **2019**, *16*, 4093. [CrossRef] [PubMed]
12. Pitman, A.; Stevenson, F.; King, M.; Osborn, D. Self-reported patterns of use of alcohol and drugs after suicide bereavement and other sudden losses: A mixed methods study of 1,854 young bereaved adults in the UK. *Front. Psychol.* **2020**, *11*, 1024. [CrossRef] [PubMed]
13. Ross, V.; Kõlves, K.; Kunde, L.; de Leo, D. Parents' experiences of suicide-bereavement: A qualitative study at 6 and 12 months after loss. *Int. J. Environ. Res. Public Health* **2018**, *15*, 618. [CrossRef] [PubMed]
14. Entilli, L.; Ross, V.; de Leo, D.; Cipolletta, S.; Kõlves, K. Experiences of parental suicide-bereavement: A longitudinal qualitative analysis over two years. *Int. J. Environ. Res. Public Health* **2021**, *18*, 564. [CrossRef]
15. Pitman, A.L.; Osborn, D.P.J.; Rantell, K.; King, M.B. Bereavement by suicide as a risk factor for suicide attempt: A cross-sectional national UK-wide study of 3432 young bereaved adults. *BMJ Open* **2016**, *6*, e009948. [CrossRef] [PubMed]
16. Azorina, V.; Morant, N.; Nesse, H.; Stevenson, F.; Osborn, D.; King, M.; Pitman, A. The perceived impact of suicide bereavement on specific interpersonal relationships: A qualitative study of survey data. *Int. J. Environ. Res. Public Health* **2019**, *16*, 1801. [CrossRef] [PubMed]
17. Pitman, A.; Putri, A.K.; De Souza, T.; Stevenson, F.; King, M.; Osborn, D.; Morant, N. The impact of suicide bereavement on educational and occupational functioning: A qualitative study of 460 bereaved adults. *Int. J. Environ. Res. Public Health* **2018**, *15*, 643. [CrossRef] [PubMed]
18. Pitman, A.; De Souza, T.; Putri, A.K.; Stevenson, F.; King, M.; Osborn, D.; Morant, N. Support needs and experiences of people bereaved by suicide: Qualitative findings from a cross-sectional British study of bereaved young adults. *Int. J. Environ. Res. Public Health* **2018**, *15*, 666. [CrossRef] [PubMed]
19. Cooke, R.; Beccaria, F.; Demant, J.; Fernandes-Jesus, M.; Fleig, L.; Negreiros, J.; Scholz, U.; De Visser, R. Patterns of alcohol consumption and alcohol-related harm among European university students. *Eur. J. Public Health* **2019**, *29*, 1125–1129. [CrossRef] [PubMed]
20. Moore, K.; Meastram, F. Exploring Emerging Perspectives on Gender and Drug Use. In *Emerging Perspectives on Substance Misuse*; Mistral, W., Ed.; Wiley: Malden, MA, USA, 2013; pp. 80–97.
21. Arpa, S. Women Who Use Drugs: Issues, Needs, Responses, Challenges and Implications for Policy and Practice. 2017. Available online: https://www.emcdda.europa.eu/system/files/attachments/6235/EuropeanResponsesGuide2017_BackgroundPaper-Women-who-use-drugs.pdf (accessed on 7 October 2022).

22. Pitman, A.L.; Rantell, K.; Moran, P.; Sireling, L.; Marston, L.; King, M.B.; Osborn, D. Support received after bereavement by suicide and other sudden deaths: A cross-sectional UK study of 3432 young bereaved adults. *BMJ Open* **2017**, *7*, e014487. [CrossRef] [PubMed]
23. Pitman, A.L.; Osborn, D.P.J.; Rantell, K.; King, M.B. The stigma perceived by people bereaved by suicide and other sudden deaths: A cross-sectional UK study of 3432 bereaved adults. *J. Psychosom. Res.* **2016**, *87*, 22–29. [CrossRef] [PubMed]
24. McDonnell, S.; Hunt, I.; Flynn, S.; Smith, S.; McGale, B.; Shaw, J. From Grief to Hope: The Collective Voice of Those Bereaved or Affected by Suicide in the UK, Manchester. 2020. Available online: http://research.bmh.manchester.ac.uk/cmhs/research/centreforsuicideprevention/fromgrieftohope/ (accessed on 7 October 2022).
25. Creighton, G.; Oliffe, J.; Matthews, J.; Saewyc, E. "Dulling the Edges": Young men's use of alcohol to deal with grief following the death of a male friend. *Health Educ. Behav.* **2016**, *43*, 54–60. [CrossRef] [PubMed]
26. Valentine, C.; Bauld, L.; Walter, T. Bereavement following substance misuse: A disenfranchised grief. *Omega* **2016**, *72*, 283–301. [CrossRef]
27. Templeton, L.; Ford, A.; McKell, J.; Valentine, C.; Walter, T.; Velleman, R.; Bauld, L.; Hay, G.; Hollywood, J. Bereavement through substance use: Findings from an interview study with adults in England and Scotland. *Addict. Res. Theory* **2016**, *24*, 341–354. [CrossRef]
28. Barry, C.A.; Britten, N.; Barber, N.; Bradley, C.; Stevenson, F. Using reflexivity to optimize teamwork in qualitative research. *Qual. Health Res.* **1999**, *9*, 26–44. [CrossRef]
29. Pitman, A.; McDonald, K.; Logeswaran, Y.; Lewis, G.; Cerel, J.; Erlangsen, A. Proportion of suicides in Denmark attributable to bereavement by the suicide of a first-degree relative or partner: Nested case–control study. *Acta Psychiatr. Scand.* 2022. [CrossRef]
30. Pitman, A.; Krysinska, K.; Osborn, D.; King, M. Suicide in young men. *Lancet* **2012**, *379*, 2383–2392. [CrossRef]

International Journal of
Environmental Research and Public Health

MDPI

Article

Psychiatrists' Experience of a Peer Support Group for Reflecting on Patient Suicide and Homicide: A Qualitative Study

Millie Tamworth [1,*], Helen Killaspy [1,2], Jo Billings [1] and Rachel Gibbons [3]

1 Division of Psychiatry, University College London, London W1T 7NF, UK
2 Camden & Islington NHS Foundation Trust, London NW1 0PE, UK
3 Royal College of Psychiatrists, London E1 8BB, UK
* Correspondence: millie.tamworth.20@ucl.ac.uk

Abstract: There is a lack of support for mental health professionals who experience a patient suicide or homicide. This is despite a high likelihood of such an occurrence and the heavy professional and personal toll the experience can take. We conducted 15 interviews with members of a facilitated peer support group run for consultant psychiatrists who have experienced a patient homicide or suicide. Our interviews explored the trauma of the experience as well as the effectiveness of the group in helping the clinician heal. Our results echoed previous research that the experience can be profoundly traumatic. A professionally facilitated, consultant-only peer group specifically dedicated to suicide and homicide were the key components helping participants to process their grief. Mental health trusts should consider setting up facilitated peer support groups for clinicians who experience patient suicide or homicide.

Keywords: psychiatrists; mental health practitioners; peer-support; postvention; suicide bereavement; qualitative research

Citation: Tamworth, M.; Killaspy, H.; Billings, J.; Gibbons, R. Psychiatrists' Experience of a Peer Support Group for Reflecting on Patient Suicide and Homicide: A Qualitative Study. *Int. J. Environ. Res. Public Health* **2022**, *19*, 14507. https://doi.org/10.3390/ijerph192114507

Academic Editors: Karl Andriessen, Karolina Krysinska and Yossi Levi-Belz

Received: 18 August 2022
Accepted: 4 November 2022
Published: 4 November 2022

1. Introduction

There is limited understanding of what kind of support is helpful for clinicians after a patient suicide or homicide. This is despite the fact that the impact of losing a patient in this way can be prolonged and profound [1]. In the field of suicidology, it has been suggested that coping with bereavement after a suicide can be complicated by higher levels of stigma and associations of blame [2]. In an effort to deepen our understanding of what support is needed, we conducted a qualitative evaluation of a peer support group for consultant psychiatrists who had experienced a suicide or homicide by a patient under their care.

In England, between 2008 and 2018, 1/3 of suicides were carried out by people under the care of mental health services, equating to 1271 suicides per year [3]. Typically, these patients were under the care of a multi-disciplinary team including a consultant psychiatrist, a psychologist, nursing staff, trainees and allied health professionals [4]. The total number of consultant psychiatrists in England as of September 2020 was 4452 [5]. Based on the yearly average of 1271 suicides, each psychiatrist has a one in three chance of losing a patient in this way every year. Put differently, over a 15-year career, the average consultant psychiatrist will experience five patient suicides although that number will vary depending on the area of specialty. Rates of homicide carried out by patients are lower, averaging 54 a year [3], but the personal and professional repercussions of such an event appear both more common and more severe. In a survey assessing the impact of patient homicide on forensic psychiatrists, 81% of respondents said the experience had impacted their mental health, 25% of which described it as 'very significant' [6].

The impact of patient suicide is more widely covered than homicide, due in part to its higher frequency. A recent systematic review outlined the different ways that psychiatrists are affected by patient suicide, whilst Mezey et al. carried out a survey looking at the impact of homicide on the care team [6,7]. Both papers highlight the emotional effect on the individual (such as guilt, shame, blame and anger) and the impact on their professional practice (such as taking on lower-risk patients, prescribing more antidepressants). The severity and duration of these impacts depends on several factors, including the psychiatrist's personality traits, the nature of the therapeutic relationship they had with the patient and the manner of their death [7]. Sandford et al. found that the most significant risk factor for a negative impact was fear of blame or self-blame [7]. Previous research has also found feelings of stigma and persecution to be prevalent [6,8]. To that end, the psychiatrist's experience echoes the wider literature on experiences of suicide and homicide bereavement.

To date there is little evidence as to what organisational and cultural factors may moderate the impact of a patient suicide or homicide on professionals. Sandford et al.'s study noted that informal support was deemed most helpful, but it was unclear whether formal support was considered inadequate or required more individualisation [7]. It has also been noted that the evidence base for what types of interventions are useful for those impacted by suicide more widely is underdeveloped [9].

Research on specific occupational groups exposed to suicide found that, in the case of ambulance workers, a combination of time pressures and a macho culture prevented people seeking support [10]. The study also found that there was limited opportunity for staff to process their own distress but when afforded the means to do so, staff supported one another. For psychiatrists, the likelihood of seeking support needs to be framed in the context of clinical responsibility. The death of their patient by suicide may implicate and stigmatise them in a way that is less the case for doctors working in other specialties [8].

Campaigns and initiatives such as the 'zero-suicide policy' differ in their capacity to motivate workforces, depending in part on implementation. Zero-suicide can be construed positively, as an aspirational goal underlying concrete objectives of delivering reliable and consistent healthcare [11]. Conversely, the same policy can be presented as an absolute target or key performance indicator. Such policies can be unhelpful in exaggerating the degree to which health professionals can prevent these kinds of tragic incidents and risks implying that a 'failure to prevent' a suicide equates to it being the healthcare professional's fault [2,12]. In the wake of a traumatic death, the difficult emotions that arise and the fact that the patient is not there to speak for themselves, means clinical responsibility and blame can conflate [6]. In this context, seeking support can be challenging [12].

The group is run out of an NHS Trust in London and operates an open membership, meaning any consultant psychiatrist is welcome to attend regularly, intermittently or as a one-off. The group was founded 12 years ago by two consultant psychiatrists. Today it is facilitated by one of the group founders who is also a trained psychotherapist. Group membership has grown, and a typical session is now eight to ten people. Five to seven of these are 'core' (regular) members, one of whom is the group facilitator; the remaining, non-core participants might attend following a relevant experience. The group meets every three months face to face for two hours.

Group sessions are loosely based on the Balint model [13] and use a psychoanalytical framework. Consultants share their experience of the event and their reaction-described by the group facilitator as a "stereotyped pattern of response"-with the rest of the group. They then listen to other members discussing what they have shared. This 'stepping back' gives the presenter space to observe their case from an objective viewpoint, uncoloured by their own interpretations and judgements.

A facilitated conversation is then held by the group who consider and reflect on what they have heard. The intention is to bring together multiple perspectives, provide emotional understanding, containment, and an alternative narrative to self-recrimination. Through a combination of the group's collective memory and members' own experiences, the presenter's experience is 'metabolised' within the group and 'handed back' in a manageable form.

Our research had three research objectives:

- To investigate the experiences of psychiatrists after a patient suicide or homicide.

- To investigate the ways in which the group may be helpful to its members and ways in which it may be improved.
- To understand key elements of the group structure and the role of the facilitator.

2. Methods

2.1. Study Design, Participants and Procedures

The study procedures were approved by the University College London Research Ethics Committee (Ref. 20423/001). Consultant psychiatrists who were attending or had previously attended the group were asked if they were happy to be contacted by the research team. Willing participants were sent the Participant Information Sheet and Consent Form. They returned an electronically signed consent form to the principal researcher (MT) before the interview. The topic guide (Supplementary Materials) for the interview was drafted by the research team in consultation with the Royal College of Psychiatrists' working group on patient suicide and homicide, which comprises psychologists, psychiatrists, academics, psychotherapists, and family members with lived experience of losing someone to suicide. MT conducted all the interviews, most of which took place remotely via Microsoft Teams. All the interviews were audio recorded and transcribed verbatim.

2.2. Analysis

Our study adopted a reflexive thematic analysis approach, whereby researcher subjectivity is regarded as an analytic resource [14]. Three members of the research team (MT, JB, HK) conducted the coding and reflexive analysis. HK is a member of the peer support group and subsequently, we ensured the transcript excerpts selected for her input guaranteed the anonymity of the participating member. Participants had been made aware that HK was part of the research team and would have access to participant data and consent was given on this basis. HK did not partake in the interview process. The fourth research team member, RG, is a founder of this peer support group. RG participated in the interview process and therefore did not partake in the analysis. Transcripts were imported into NVivo Pro V12 and a preliminary coding frame was developed. MT conducted initial coding before allocating two transcripts each to HK and JB, who coded these independently. The team then met for further refinement into a coding framework. Coding was done collaboratively, consisting of an interactive process between data, interviewer, and research team. Our purpose was to develop a rich and nuanced reading of the data rather than seek consensus on meaning.

Reflexive thematic analysis is an ongoing and iterative process that does not lend itself well to the concept of data saturation [15]. Our decision about how many people to interview was a function of the finite nature and specificity of the sampling pool rather than a need to reach data saturation. Our results take into consideration and give the reader an indication of when perspectives were unanimous and when opinions varied. Consistent with the principles of reflexive thematic analysis [15], it would be nonsensical to cite frequencies of responses. The interview process in reflexive thematic analysis is necessarily open and evolving, and not every participant is asked the exact same question at the same point in the interview. Certain participants may choose to give certain examples, but this decision could be as much a function of the stage of the conversation as it is an indicator of the relative importance of the topic in question. Our intention in using reflexive thematic analysis was to capture the breadth of experiences and responses, a single point of view is as valid as one which is shared by many [14].

2.3. Reflexivity

Reflexivity is the process of actively recognising your own personal situation as the researcher and the impact this may have on data interpretation [16]. It enables the reader to consider the researcher's perspective as a factor in how the research was constructed, and hence the validity of the analysis [17]. The research team had four authors, MT, JB, HK and RG. Each encompassed different career stages, clinical specialties and academic areas of interest.

MT is a mature student studying an MSc in Clinical Mental Health Sciences. She has research interests in experiences of vicarious trauma across different occupational settings. This subject matter was interesting to MT who sought to better understand society's coping mechanisms for dealing with the pain of suicide-seemingly through silence or by turning away- and how this contributes to the trauma, isolation and experience of stigma for those left behind [10].

JB is a Consultant Clinical Psychologist with over 20 years of experience working in the NHS. An associate professor, she is an experienced academic in all areas of trauma and in the writing of qualitative research. HK is a consultant psychiatrist with expertise in psychosis. A professor with a background in quantitative and qualitative research, her areas of academic interest are services and interventions for people with complex mental health problems. She is also a member of the support group studied in this research. RG is a consultant psychiatrist, psychotherapist and Chair of the Patient Safety Group and Working Group on the Effect of Suicide and Homicide on Psychiatrists at the Royal College of Psychiatrists. She was one of the three founding members of the peer support group following early career experiences of losing patients to suicide. JB, HK and RG all have lived experience of patient suicide and/or homicide.

2.4. Quality and Validity

The quality of this research was based on the Standards for Reporting Qualitative Research Framework (SRQR) [17]; conceptual and design thinking for thematic analysis which formed the foundation of our methodological approach [16]; and the Oxford Handbook of Qualitative Research [18].

Subjectivity lies at the heart of reflexive thematic analysis. Our aim was less to control bias than to explore the complexity of human experience and allow the reader to reflect on researcher perspective as part of their own conclusions [16]. Nevertheless, we have sought to be rigorous, transparent and trustworthy in the reporting of our findings [17], routinely reflecting on our assumptions, expectations and choices throughout the research process [19].

We contacted 19 past and present members out of a total of 50, 15 of whom agreed to be interviewed. Whilst results are not necessarily generalisable beyond the sample, the participants were sufficiently diverse in ethnic diversity, clinical specialty and experience for us to capture a range of views. Those interviewed included male and female members, the group founders, regular and infrequent attenders, former regular attendees and those who had attended only once.

3. Results

Eight females and seven males took part. Areas of specialty and membership status are presented in Table 1. Interviews took place between June and September 2021 with each lasting 45–60 min. Findings were organised into separate domains based on the research objectives. Within each domain, inductive themes were identified (Table 2). Our results use pseudonyms to ensure anonymity.

Table 1. Demographic Information of participants.

Participant	Membership Status	Specialist Area
001	Present	Eating Disorders
002	Present	Rehabilitation Psychiatry
003	Present	Old Age Psychiatry
004	Present	Assessment
005	Present	General Adult Psychiatry
006	Present	Acute Care
007	Present	General Adult Psychiatry
008	Present	Acute Care
009	Present	Personality Disorder Unit
010	Past	Acute Care
011	Past	Acute Care
012	Past	Perinatal
013	Past	General Adult Psychiatry
013	Past	Psychiatric Intensive Care
015	Past	Early Intervention Services

Table 2. Themes and sub-themes by research objectives.

1. The Experience of Psychiatrists After a Patient Suicide or Homicide
1.1 Responsibility
1.1.1 Uniqueness of consultant's role
1.1.2 Types of responsibility
1.1.2.1 Team
1.1.2.2 Clinical
1.1.2.3 Formal
1.2 Support
1.2.1 Attitudes towards seeking support
1.2.2 The support available
2. The value of the group to its members
2.1 Different uses for different people
2.1.1 An alternative perspective
2.1.2 Leaving it behind
2.2 A three-stage journey
2.2.1 Shedding
2.2.2 Safety
2.2.3 Post-traumatic growth
2.2.3.1 Regaining the capacity to think
2.2.3.2 Changes in work behaviour
2.2.3.3 Changes in clinical practice
3. Group structure and the role of the facilitator
3.1 Membership structure
3.1.1 Core members
3.1.2 Non-core members
3.2 Facilitation: what's important?

3.1. The Experience of Psychiatrists after a Patient Suicide or Homicide

3.1.1. Responsibility

Uniqueness of the Consultant's Role

The amount of responsibility held by consultants on behalf of the rest of the team is felt particularly acutely after a suicide or homicide. Consultants described feeling.

> *" ... isolated. You're working very closely in a team; you feel very supported on the one hand, but you are the only consultant."* (Michael)

with an overwhelming sense of responsibility from being

> *" ... the only consultant psychiatrist in a team. [You] have unique experiences in having to be the certain decision-maker ... Ultimately in these sorts of situations, if you go to Coroner's Court, you'll be the person that's there. There are different expectations of you–of what you should know."* (Patricia)

Types of Responsibility

Participants described three different responsibilities after a patient suicide or homicide. These related to the team, clinical decision-making and the formal responsibilities following a serious incident.

Team responsibility. Most participants agreed that, after a serious incident, they felt inhibited by their position of responsibility within the team when it came to processing their own emotions. Participants often used the word 'containment' to describe a process of actively managing other team members' anxiety and uncertainty through listening and facilitating or leading on decision making.

> *"The role of the consultant is to contain a team that is under stress so that the team is functional at times of very high workload. I try to contain the distress of junior doctors and nurses when I can."* (Nina)

Peter described the challenge of having to healthily process his own emotions but in a safe and contained way.

> *"Imagine going into a debrief and the consultant breaking down in front of everyone. It would make the whole team even more unsettled. You are expected, by virtue of your senior role, to keep things going ... but there is a balance between this and showing your vulnerable side."*

Clinical responsibility. Participants described how decisions around patient safety are often taken in a culture of unrealistic expectations about what is controllable. They described their role as that of a 'super-hero', a belief held sometimes by themselves and often by those around them, that they should always be able to save patients.

Comparing a severely unwell psychiatric patient to someone with terminal cancer, one participant pointed out that the idea that the psychiatric patient might die would be unthinkable to most people whereas this would be an accepted reality for the cancer patient. Another compared psychiatrists to ICU doctors:

> *"I don't think society expects them to save everyone. The approach to psychiatry is very different. We should have predicted everything."* (Nina)

Many found these expectations particularly challenging after a serious incident and described a process whereby clinical responsibility could easily be conflated with self-blame.

> *"It's very difficult to differentiate how much of it is your blame and how much of it is professional. Initially, my professional integrity felt threatened. Then personal things come in as well. And this is when things start to merge."* (Adam)

These feelings were rarely alleviated by the knowledge that, clinically, reasonable decisions had been taken.

"On an intellectual level I know these things can happen. But some part of you, somewhere, believes that if we do all the right things, it won't. I thought, 'There must be something wrong with me.'" (Anne)

Formal responsibilities. As part of the investigation, psychiatrists are usually required to attend the Coroner's Court. Generally, this experience was described as extremely challenging. The fact of being a witness rather than the accused rarely tallied with the experience, and the presence of a jury added to feelings of culpability.

"It really feels like you are in court and someone will determine whether you are guilty or not guilty. Well, I mean, who else will have a jury unless you are accused of something?" (Jenny)

Many described the experience of being cross-examined by representatives of the deceased's family, sometimes with no mediation from the judge, as very exposing.

"The relatives, the solicitor of the relatives, they come and don't always see you as the witness for information. Their attitude can be quite hostile." (Peter)

3.1.2. Support

Following a homicide or patient suicide, the support psychiatrists were offered depended on the organisation they were part of as well as factors such as resource constraints.

Attitudes towards Seeking Support

All interviewees valued receiving support after the incident, with informal support (such as from peers) being the most common. Regarding the acceptability of seeking support, the consensus was that, whilst it was getting easier to do so, this remained difficult.

"It might not necessarily be a conscious 'you're weak if you get help' because that goes against what we would be telling anybody else, but yeah, you should be fine and just manage these things." (Michael)

Some participants described a 'stiff upper lip' culture in their NHS Trust where these kinds of incidents were considered part of the job and having a forum to discuss their impact was seen as "sitting around talking about it". Conversely, the Trust affiliated with this group was seen as more open and progressive regarding consultant support by virtue of its hosting of the peer group. More recent consultants explained this had been helpful in overcoming any perceived 'wrongness' in needing support.

"It was an utter relief to see people who have been consultants for 15 to 20 years and who are still so deeply affected by the loss of a patient … Pain is a human response and there's nothing wrong with me." (Anne)

The Support Available

Most psychiatrists had attended some kind of team debrief following an incident, though the form this took varied widely. Team debriefs were considered helpful in terms of feeling collegiate with the team who had experienced the tragedy, but many participants felt constrained in processing their own emotions at these meetings because of their role as emotional containers for the team, as detailed earlier in Section 3.1.1.

Other forms of support that participants mentioned included reflective practice groups, peer groups and Balint groups, again with variation in availability between employing organisations. Often policies about the support that was available contrasted with reality:

"On paper you're supposed to have a peer group, a supervisor, someone you can go to clinically … But the reality of the situation is you are so clinically inundated there's no time to be accessing those sorts of support, and the people we are getting support from are themselves inundated and overspent. … personally, I felt trapped in the deep end." (Anne)

One consultant explained how shortages of skilled facilitators meant sessions were often cancelled, whilst others remarked it could impact how they were run. One described a Balint group they had attended as "a 15 min presentation and discussion, nothing more than that", whilst clinicians using support structures to meet CPD requirements was mentioned by several consultants. Asked whether they could have brought the subject of patient suicide to these other forums, it was thought theoretically possible but practically unwise. Many support structures that were described tended to focus on clinical decision-making but were not considered safe or appropriate places to discuss the consultant's emotional response and experience of a patient suicide or homicide.

> *"The support was there but it was ... very procedural. It's all very business-like and there's no emotional connection ... no sharing of that kind of level of emotional response to the work that we do."* (Michael)

3.2. *The Value of the Group to Its Members*

3.2.1. Different Uses for Different People

Participants used the group in two key ways.

An Alternative Perspective

Participants with an interest or training in psychotherapy tended to show a particular curiosity about the acts of suicide and homicide and the human response to it. This was discussed in different ways but underlying each was a belief that, to truly process the experience and accompanying emotions, one must go beyond medical discourse and instead query human decision-making behind the taking of a life, be it one's own or another's. One member spoke of the common tendency to try to comprehend the act within the Western-medicine framework of 'illness. They felt that, while removing the suicidal act from our understanding of 'normal' human behaviour may feel less painful, it prevents true understanding and healing.

> *"Helping professions want to be seen as dealing with illness, not people acting out in a very destructive manner. So [the group] was about legitimising thinking negatively about suicide."* (Ben)

Many, not all, considered this psychoanalytical lens an important input to the wider grieving process.

The factor valued by all members was a separate and safe space where it is permitted to question *'What if no one did anything wrong and this still happened?'* and consider an alternative narrative to self-blame. Consultants described how, by stepping away from their everyday environment, they could distance themselves from artificial constructs such as omnipotence or the superhero narrative. In the context of a patient suicide or homicide, these constructs were contributing to the sense of self-blame and were prohibiting grief.

> *"You don't see the madness because you are part of it. And then you start to reflect ... but you cannot reflect and question until you get space."* (Jane)

It was felt to be important that the space was dedicated solely to processing suicide and homicide experiences, enabling members to discuss subjects that might be too uncomfortable to raise in mainstream support environments.

> *"Our natural tendency is to not want to go near it because it's too distressing. People will, unless the group is about this and only this, talk about other things."* (Elizabeth)

Leaving It Behind

Some participants attended the group only a few times. These participants described how they used the group as a place to share the ownership of an experience, before depositing the pain as a form of closure.

> *"Once I had processed it and thought about it a bit, I didn't really want to keep talking and I just wanted to forget about it, to the extent that I could."* (Nick)

Those with less interest in psychotherapy still found value in the interpretative framework. Jane, a core member, described members' different purposes in attending as a contributing dynamic to its workings:

"I think some come because they just need to leave it with us. Putting it down and leaving it there and going away."

Interviewer: "And that's enough?"

"That's enough. I think that's a very common and even helpful, reasonable thing to do. It's a gift to us and provides material to work with. It's a gift to them because they can come in green and go out pink. They can just go and get on with things."

3.2.2. A Three-Stage Journey: Shedding, Safety and Growth

Participants described a three-step process of healing encompassing the temporary shedding of their professional responsibilities, containment by group members and the opportunity for personal growth.

Shedding

The group invites its members to step outside the hierarchy of the medical profession and, in doing so, deconstruct their beliefs about responsibility. Core member Sally explained:

"In being a consultant, a superhero is the role you have to enact even if you don't feel it. When you come into this group, you don't have to do that, it's safe to take your hat off."

All participants agreed that shedding responsibilities was possible because the group is only open to peers (fellow consultants).

"I try to contain the distress of junior doctors and nurses when I can. But I need to be contained as well ... We cannot have the people I am supposed to contain in the same room as people tasked with containing me." (Nina)

Participants highlighted two tensions to the group structure. First, other team members apart from the psychiatrist need support too. Second, the consultant-only aspect was described by the group facilitator as a " ... a difficult balance, there's something about the omnipotence of us trying to be omnipotent." In other words, restricting the group to senior clinicians gives it an implied superiority that risks endorsing the superhero narrative they are trying to escape.

Safety

Participants described the confidential exchange of personal experience as key to feeling safe in the group. In the act of presenting, a consultant shares ownership of their experience and its accompanying grief.

"The loneliness of the experience is shared. It is validated, it is acknowledged. The loneliness is not just yours, somebody else is owning it as well." (Adam)

Having shared their account, the presenter listens to others discuss it. Members bring personal experiences as well as reflections from past group discussions, and newer participants begin to see a commonality of experience and feelings. Unanimously, members spoke of how important the sense of sameness was to feeling validated and contained.

"There's something quite shameful for clinicians in a death by suicide. So, I think that the most helpful thing was hearing from others, recognising feelings and normalising them." (Laura)

Post-Traumatic Growth

All participants felt that attending the peer group sessions had enabled self-growth. Three main areas of self-growth were described.

Regaining the capacity to think: Participants reflected on how the opportunity for growth came once they felt safe in the group setting. With their emotions validated, they now had at their disposal a new framework for interpreting what happened, in which they were not cast as playing a central role.

> *"The blame narrative does not disappear. However, you can reflect better on what your role is and not what you fantasise your role to be."* (George)

Within this safe space, there is a renewed ability to adopt a thinking mind. This was felt to be as much a function of the sense of separateness, safety and sameness as it is of the actual exchange with other members explored in the previous section.

> *"We could only move when this absolute terror about suicide-hat we were to blame for it-could reduce. It was only through having the space to think about it that gradually curiosity emerged."* (Jenny)

Changes in work behaviour: Participants described a greater awareness of their daily environment. For some core members, the ability to continue working effectively in acute areas rests on regularly attending the group.

> *"Without the group I don't think I would be continuing, certainly not as healthily."* (Patricia)

One non-core member who worked in an inpatient ward described a new readiness to take time off and to work from home more regularly to help manage their tendency to overwork. The most consistent change outlined was in team communication, specifically breaking down hierarchies that impeded communication.

> *"It certainly has changed how I function in terms of openness ... and how we check in with each other on an ongoing basis. I was keen to break down this whole, you know, consultant superhero narrative. I don't think it does anyone any good."* (Anne)

Changes in clinical practice. Regarding changes to clinical practice, seemingly diverse responses centred on an underlying intention that clinical decisions should not be influenced by fear of recrimination and blame.

> *" ... to not be scared to listen to your intuition. To practice in a way that feels right rather than in a way that's guided by concerns that something awful is going to happen which will end your career."* (Patricia)

Many other consultants talked about prioritising instinct over 'the training manual' and allowing more nuanced risk formulation. Peter described this as.

> *" ... a case of how you think about the risks with the patient, which isn't reflected on the medical notes, on the risk assessment tool, on what the expectation is from the Trust."*

3.3. Group Structure and Facilitator

3.3.1. Membership Structure

The group operates with open membership and has different types of members. Core members are those who attend regularly; non-core members attend episodically or as a one-off.

Core Members

At the time of writing, there are five to six core members who attend the group regularly, many of whom have a background in psychotherapy. Core members described their role as upholding an alternative framework of thought to the one brought by the consultant who is sharing. George, a core member, explained his purpose as

> *" ... bringing a different perspective to suicide, which steps away from something purely psychiatric—where we can get a little bit stuck in thinking ... 'What was the diagnosis? Was the medication the right thing?'-and towards ... 'What is [an] event like suicide like? What are the energies harnessed?"*

This sense of stepping outside the medical formulation and into questioning underlying responses to the experience was a consistent theme.

> *"A key role of a core member is to provide the emotional containment so the other person can process; to investigate what the hooks are in that case that make the pain so unbearable and the loss so profound ... It's not a clinical learning, it's something much more ... [It's] about the emotional structure of how we deal with this very difficult professional issue."* (Nina)

Another role was described as holding the collective memory of the group. By sharing the similarities of past cases, core members could show that the emotional experience is not unique.

> *"You find yourself having similar sort [s] of explorations. The themes about responsibility and roles etc come up again and again."* (George)

As noted in Section 3.2.2., a sense of 'sameness' is critical to feeling validated and safe. Core members described experiencing ongoing reassurance from regularly attending the group and hearing other people's cases. One explained how seeing reactions in other people helped them understand their own weak points better, which amounted to an iterative learning process.

> *"You have the opportunity to digest your own episodes, again and again through new perspectives. Even if you don't present, your own experience is still being re-evaluated."* (Adam)

Non-Core Members

At the time of writing, the group hosts two to three visiting members. Generally, we found that core members had stronger psychoanalytical interests than members who came less regularly. These differences were commented on by non-core members.

> *"The people that attend regularly have been going for longest, [they] are more attuned to the implicit rules of the group [and] the styles of interpretation that are likely to land well."* (Nick)

A sense of "us and them", particularly when first attending, was mentioned. One participant (now a core member) described his first visit as

> *"... not easy. Relationships were already established. The way they were talking about things, the jargon, the facial expressions, the exchange of ideas ... I thought, "Well, if I had to present a case, how would I feel?"* (Adam)

However, this did not seem to impact the effectiveness of the group.

> *"... there's two subgroups within the group. It's probably a little bit of an awkward mix but it doesn't preclude it from being useful."* (Nick)

Whilst some visiting members described feeling safe reasonably quickly, it was rare that people had felt comfortable presenting their experience without having first attended as a listener.

3.3.2. Facilitation: What's Important

Participants were asked whether the group facilitator should be from outside the Trust and whether it was important they had psychoanalytical training. The current facilitator has knowledge of the Trust but does not currently work in it. All participants knew the facilitator in a professional capacity outside the group. This familiarity appeared more important than either of the above questions.

> *"I have never thought about it their position within [the Trust], it feels so natural they are there."* (Adam)

> *"Inside is better. The support you need is also about trust and understanding the institutional dynamics at play."* (Jenny)

Regarding psychoanalytical training, many of those personally inclined to that way of thinking answered in relation to the importance of employing a psychoanalytical lens.

> *"Absolutely critical [a psychoanalytical lens]. It creates the framework in which difficult things can come to the surface, things that you know were not visible before."* (Peter)

> *"It allows the group to be held and to keep the group going in a way that progresses and furthers that kind of psychoanalytic stream of conversation."* (Anne)

The skill and experience of the facilitator was recognised by all participants and was an important factor in their decision to attend. It was described by many participants as paramount to feeling safe:

> *"I wouldn't feel comfortable and contained if it was just a Joe Bloggs psychiatrist facilitator. I wouldn't feel safe in that space."* (Michael)

> *"I think [they] are very skilled in facilitating. I think without them it might feel different."* (Laura)

4. Discussion

4.1. Summary of Research Objective and Results

Our study had three research objectives:

- To investigate the experience of psychiatrists after a patient suicide or homicide
- To investigate the ways in which the consultant peer group may help its members and ways in which it may be improved
- To understand key elements of the group structure and the role of the facilitator

Our data revealed that a sense of fellowship is critical to allowing psychiatrists to first grieve and then grow after experiencing a patient suicide or homicide. It showed the impact of these events depends on several factors including the circumstances surrounding the suicide or homicide, the psychiatrist's sense of their therapeutic alliance with the patient, the manner of the death and the approach taken in the subsequent investigation and coroner's inquest. Our findings in this regard were broadly consistent with research conducted previously [7] although we note that research on the investigative and inquest experience is lacking. Despite the range of potential factors associated with our participants' experiences, we identified common emotional responses of psychiatrists including feelings of acute guilt or shame. Within the peer group setting, this commonality becomes evident through the intimate act of sharing one's own experience and through the collective history of the group shared by core members.

4.2. The Experiences of Psychiatrists after a Patient Suicide or Homicide

The important difference between this support group and other support structures was in providing separation from the conventional clinical framework of thought which, in the context of a suicide, can trap the consultant in a narrative of self-blame. Therefore, this support group was described as helping consultants in a way that other forms of support do not. It does so by being a space dedicated to the processing of the experience of suicide or homicide and by offering a different lens through which to view the experience.

Our participants described the difficulty presented by the superhero narrative that can be held by themselves and society. Whilst the superhero narrative is not confined to psychiatry; its falsity can be accentuated by the experience of a patient suicide or homicide. Gorkin has written about how the extent of a clinician's belief in their omnipotence can shape their trauma after a suicide [20]. Expectations of clinical omnipotence was also reported in a recent meta-synthesis of 10 papers exploring the impact of patient suicide across doctors and nurses [21]. This paper noted differences in blame attribution between doctors and nurses. Doctors reported looking inwardly whereas nurses looked to external factors. Other research is less clear-cut about the personal impact of patient suicide on clinicians [22]. The varied findings alert us the individual nature of the experience and the multitude of factors that can determine how a suicide or homicide impacts a clinician [23]. This goes beyond personality to include contextual and environmental factors [7].

Plakun and Tillman describe a twin bereavement of personal and professional identity for psychiatrists after a patient suicide [24]. In our interviews, we explored the differences between a psychiatrists' personal, professional and organisational self to gauge the different types of blame felt by participants. We found that many psychiatrists experienced a blurring of these domains that added to the challenge of grieving. One such context is the relationship between the psychiatrist and the patient's family after a suicide or homicide. This can be very strained with families often needing to assign blame [25] at precisely the time when the psychiatrist's personal self is seeking absolution. Currently there is no communication protocol for the family and medical team in the aftermath. More could be done to protect both the psychiatrist and family in these circumstances.

4.3. The Support Available

Previous research has shown that psychiatrists can be reluctant to seek support after a patient suicide or homicide [6,26]. Brooks et al. [27] have identified multiple barriers to doctors seeking help for mental health including anticipated negative career implications from either taking time off work or in disclosing their condition. The paper discusses doctors feeling shame, embarrassment, and a sense of weakness in the role reversal implied of becoming 'the patient'.

The feedback from our participants echoed these findings but working in psychiatry introduces another layer of complexity, and the experience of a serious incident, yet another. Participants described psychiatry as having an unspoken cultural resistance toward professionals getting support for themselves, though the extent of this resistance depends on the specific trust and area of specialism. The silence over the issue of support captures the contradictory position of being in a profession which upholds the value of managing one's mental health but not feeling able to seek it out for themselves. The sense of 'not feeling entitled' (to support) may become more prevalent when a psychiatrist graduates to a consultant role and their responsibilities-team and clinical-grow. We have discussed how in the case of a patient suicide or homicide it is common for psychiatrists to feel that they are to blame personally. A further issue then may be that the clinician fears that admitting the need for support is tantamount to an admission of professional guilt. More needs to be done to understand this tension. What our research does make clear is that there is no other situation where the responsibility of containment is so crucial to the wellbeing of your team yet currently, many psychiatrists do not feel able to access the tools that will enable them to do so.

Our study suggests that many other existing forms of support inadvertently magnify rather than challenge the collective silence around suicide. Our participants identified the group being only open to consultants as an important contributor to its effectiveness. This structure was described as enabling clinicians to escape the burden of the superhero narrative and find sanity by doing so. That said, not opening the group to a wider range of clinicians also risks endorsing the 'superhero' narrative they are trying to escape as well as perpetuating the myth of clinical omnipotence. Research on the potential pitfalls of peer groups should be noted [28] and degree of choice in support is important. Future research should compare peer groups to other interventions [29].

4.4. Opportunities for Growth

Post-traumatic growth refers to positive psychological change that may co-exist with significant psychological distress after a shattering of fundamental assumptions [30]. Many participants pointed to examples of growth, including more realistic appraisal of what they could impact and what they could not, and passing on these insights to clinicians moving into a consultant role. Changes to clinical practice was a complex topic in our interviews, but any such changes reported seemed to be the result of growth and entailed a subtle alteration of perspective in relation to responsibility and team interaction. However, growth only became possible once the consultant was released from feelings of blame and could reflect analytically on what had happened. Past research has described how experiencing patient suicide without getting the right support can lead to inhibited clinical decision-making and more defensive practice [7,31].

The need to be more accepting of the possibility of patient suicide has been discussed in past research [7,22]. This issue can be explored in relation to risk assessment-an area of change reported by many of our consultants who spoke of allowing greater intuition and focusing on the clinical encounter. The predictive value of suicide risk assessments is far from clear. One study of suicide risk assessment tools looked at 156 different types used in 85 NHS organisations. Of these, 85% were tick-box checklists which have been shown to be ineffective in predicting suicide [32,33]. Another study [34] looked at the effectiveness of risk assessment in discerning the odds of suicide across low-risk and high-risk inpatient populations. This meta-analysis found that over a 20-year period, the pooled odds ratio of suicide in the high-risk group compared with low-risk group was 7.1 but with an extreme level of between-study heterogeneity. The authors argued the heterogeneity limited any certainty that a similar result would be found across other inpatient populations. Our study gives warning that that distilling the complexity of suicide risk in this way can reinforce false notions about the ability of clinicians to be able to control and prevent such incidents. It also risks shutting down genuine communication between mental health professionals and the patient [35].

4.5. Strengths and Limitations

Little is known about what the most effective interventions are for supporting individuals who experience the death of a patient by suicide or a homicide by a patient under their care. This study adds to the research in the field and enriches overall understanding. Most group members were interviewed, enabling the accumulation of a wide range of perspectives from clinicians of different career stages, areas of psychiatry and genders. The qualitative approach taken enabled us to explore the "phenomenological complexity" of the experience [12]. We examined individual experiences of trauma and the effectiveness of this intervention in helping clinicians recover. Our conversations also explored other forms of support offered, and their respective merits and shortcomings.

However, this was a small-scale, qualitative study, and findings may not be transferrable to other settings. Additionally, whilst good understanding into why the group is only open to consultants was gained, more research is needed on the experiences of other team members and alternative support mechanisms that could be helpful. Finally, the study only interviewed participants of the peer group, which introduces self-selection bias. Whilst participating consultants were asked their views on the limitations of the group, the perspectives of those who chose not to attend the group are essential to fully understanding pitfalls.

4.6. Clinical Implications

Our findings demonstrate the potential benefits of providing a facilitated peer support group for consultant psychiatrists. Whilst this study focused on consultant psychiatrists there is no reason to consider that such groups would not be useful to other professional groups as well. Further research is needed to understand whether support groups that include a range of different professionals would be feasible or as well attended and effective as the group studied in this project.

Clearly this is not the only potential staff intervention needed following these kinds of serious incidents and other structures, such as receiving specific support and guidance to navigate the subsequent formal process that follow a patient suicide or patient perpetrated homicide are likely to be needed. Further research is needed to clarify the kinds of assistance and guidance staff may benefit from.

5. Conclusions

This study builds on previous research showing that the experience of a patient homicide or suicide can be profoundly distressing to psychiatrists and confirms the complexity of the grieving process in tragic situations such as these. Ensuring that clinicians have access to appropriate support is crucial and this study identified many benefits of a facilitated consultant psychiatrist peer support group. Our study has helped to expand the understanding of the underlying causes of this distress and how the structure and facilitation of a peer support group can address them. Further research is needed to investigate the effectiveness of this and other forms of support for clinicians and what kind of support works for whom and why. What we do know at this juncture is that actively supporting psychiatrists, by addressing the stigma they face and the sense of blame they feel, is extremely important for their mental health and well-being, and ultimately their capacity as professionals.

Supplementary Materials: The following supporting information can be downloaded at: https://www.mdpi.com/article/10.3390/ijerph192114507/s1, Interview Transcript.

Author Contributions: Formal analysis, M.T., H.K. and J.B.; Investigation, M.T., H.K. and J.B.; Methodology, M.T. and J.B.; Supervision, H.K., J.B. and R.G.; Writing—Original draft, M.T.; Writing—Review and editing, H.K., J.B. and R.G. All authors have read and agreed to the published version of the manuscript.

Funding: This research received no external funding.

Institutional Review Board Statement: The study was conducted in accordance with the Declaration of Helsinki, and approved by the UCL RESEARCH ETHICS COMMITTEE (protocol 20423/001 date of approval 10 June 2021).

Informed Consent Statement: Informed consent was obtained from all subjects involved in the study.

Acknowledgments: We would like to thank all the members of the peer support group who gave up their time to take part in this research. We would also like to thank the Suicide Working Group for providing invaluable guidance on the design of this study.

Conflicts of Interest: The authors declare no conflict of interest.

References

1. Foley, S.R.; Kelly, B.D. When a patient dies by suicide: Incidence, implications and coping strategies. *Adv. Psychiatr. Treat.* **2007**, *13*, 134–138. [CrossRef]
2. Pitman, A.; Khrisna Putri, A.; Kennedy, N.; De Souza, T.; King, M.; Osborn, D. Priorities for the development and evaluation of support after suicide bereavement in the UK: Results of a discussion group. *Bereave. Care* **2016**, *35*, 109–116. [CrossRef]
3. Appleby, L.; Kapur, N.; Shaw, J.; Hunt, I.M.; Ibrahim, S.; Turnbull, P.; Bojanic, L.; Baird, A.; Rodway, C.; Tham, S.-G.; et al. *The National Confidential Inquiry into Suicide and Safety in Mental Health. Annual Report: England, Northern Ireland, Scotland and Wales 2021*; University of Manchester: Manchester, UK, 2021.
4. Kelleher, E.; Kelleher, M.F.; Grad, O. Effects of patient suicide on the multidisciplinary care team. *Lancet Psychiatry* **2014**, *1*, 174–175. [CrossRef]
5. Workforce Team, N.D. NHS Workforce Statistics: NHS Digital. 2020. Available online: https://digital.nhs.uk/data-and-information/publications/statistical/nhs-workforce-statistics/september-2020 (accessed on 3 March 2021).
6. Mezey, G.; Rowe, R.; Adshead, G. Impact of homicide by a psychiatric patient on forensic psychiatrists: National survey. *BJPsych Bull.* **2021**, *45*, 183–189. [CrossRef]
7. Sandford, D.M.; Kirtley, O.J.; Thwaites, R.; O'Connor, R.C. The impact on mental health practitioners of the death of a patient by suicide: A systematic review. *Clin. Psychol. Psychother.* **2021**, *28*, 261–294. [CrossRef] [PubMed]
8. Gutin, N.J. Losing a patient to suicide: What we know: Suicide loss can impact clinicians' professional identities, relationships with colleagues, and clinical work. *Curr. Psychiatry* **2019**, *18*, 15.
9. Pitman, A.L.; Osborn, D.P.J.; Rantell, K.; King, M.B. The stigma perceived by people bereaved by suicide and other sudden deaths: A cross-sectional UK study of 3432 bereaved adults. *J. Psychosom. Res.* **2016**, *87*, 22–29. [CrossRef]
10. Nelson, P.A.; Cordingley, L.; Kapur, N.; Chew-Graham, C.A.; Shaw, J.; Smith, S.; McGale, B.; McDonnell, S. 'We're the First Port of Call'—Perspectives of Ambulance Staff on Responding to Deaths by Suicide: A Qualitative Study. *Front. Psychol.* **2020**, *11*, 722. [CrossRef]

11. Kathryn, T.; Stapelberg, N.J.; Sveticic, J.; Dekker, S.W. Inconvenient Truths in Suicide Prevention: Why a Restorative Just Culture Should Be Implemented Alongside a Zero Suicide Framework. *Aust. Amp N. Z. J. Psychiatry* **2020**, *54*, 571–581. [CrossRef]
12. Darden, A.J.; Rutter, P.A. Psychologists' Experiences of Grief after Client Suicide: A Qualitative Study. *OMEGA J. Death Dying* **2011**, *63*, 317–342. [CrossRef]
13. Van Roy, K.; Vanheule, S.; Inslegers, R. Research on Balint groups: A literature review. *Patient Educ. Couns.* **2015**, *98*, 685–694. [CrossRef] [PubMed]
14. Braun, V.; Clarke, V. One size fits all? What counts as quality practice in (reflexive) thematic analysis? *Qual. Res. Psychol.* **2021**, *18*, 328–352. [CrossRef]
15. Braun, V.; Clarke, V. To saturate or not to saturate? Questioning data saturation as a useful concept for thematic analysis and sample-size rationales. *Qual. Res. Sport Exerc. Health* **2021**, *13*, 201–216. [CrossRef]
16. Braun, V.; Clarke, V. Conceptual and design thinking for thematic analysis. *Qual. Psychol.* **2022**, *9*, 3–26. [CrossRef]
17. O'Brien, B.C.; Harris, I.B.; Beckman, T.J.; Reed, D.A.; Cook, D.A. Standards for reporting qualitative research: A synthesis of recommendations. *Acad. Med.* **2014**, *89*, 1245–1251. [CrossRef]
18. *The Oxford Handbook of Qualitative Research*; Leavy, P. (Ed.) Oxford University Press: New York, NY, USA, 2014; pp. xxiii, 756-xxiii.
19. Nowell, L.S.; Norris, J.M.; White, D.E.; Moules, N.J. Thematic Analysis:Striving to Meet the Trustworthiness Criteria. *Int. J. Qual. Methods* **2017**, *16*, 1609406917733847. [CrossRef]
20. Gorkin, M. On the suicide of one's patient. *Bull. Menn. Clin.* **1985**, *49*, 1–9.
21. Sameen, M.; Gunn, S.; Robertson, N. The Impact of Patient Suicide on Doctors and Nurses: A Critical Interpretive Meta-Synthesis. *Arch. Suicide Res.* **2022**, *26*, 1266–1285. [CrossRef]
22. Séguin, M.; Bordeleau, V.; Drouin, M.-S.; Castelli-Dransart, D.A.; Giasson, F. Professionals' Reactions Following a Patient's Suicide: Review and Future Investigation. *Arch. Suicide Res.* **2014**, *18*, 340–362. [CrossRef]
23. Campbell, D.; Hale, R. *Working in the Dark*; Routledge: London, UK, 2017.
24. Plakun, E.M.; Tillman, J.G. Responding to clinicians after loss of a patient to suicide. *Dir. Psychiatry* **2005**, *25*, 301–310.
25. Hawton, K.; Brand, F.; Croft, A.; Gibbons, R.; Carbonnier, A.; Lascelles, K.; Makaza, M.; Stegen, G.; Wolfart, G. *If a Patient Dies by Suicide: A Resource for Psychiatrists*; University of Oxford Centre for Suicide Research: Oxford, UK, 2020.
26. Kelleher, E.; Campbell, A. A study of consultant psychiatrists' response to patients' suicide. *Ir. J. Psychol. Med.* **2011**, *28*, 35–37. [CrossRef] [PubMed]
27. Brooks, S.K.; Gerada, C.; Chalder, T. Review of literature on the mental health of doctors: Are specialist services needed? *J. Ment. Health* **2011**, *20*, 146–156. [CrossRef]
28. Seif, N.A.; Bastien, R.J.-B.; Wang, B.; Davies, J.; Isaken, M.; Ball, E.; Pitman, A.; Rowe, S. Effectiveness, acceptability and potential harms of peer support for self-harm in non-clinical settings: A systematic review. *BJPsych Open* **2022**, *8*, e28. [CrossRef] [PubMed]
29. Pitman, A.; De Souza, T.; Khrisna Putri, A.; Stevenson, F.; King, M.; Osborn, D.; Morant, N. Support Needs and Experiences of People Bereaved by Suicide: Qualitative Findings from a Cross-Sectional British Study of Bereaved Young Adults. *Int. J. Environ. Res. Public Health* **2018**, *15*, 666. [CrossRef] [PubMed]
30. Tedeschi, R.G.; Calhoun, L.G. Target Article: Posttraumatic Growth: Conceptual Foundations and Empirical Evidence. *Psychol. Inq.* **2004**, *15*, 1–18. [CrossRef]
31. Gitlin, M.J. A Psychiatrist's Reaction to a Patient's Suicide. *Am. J. Psychiatry* **1999**, *156*, 1630–1634. [CrossRef]
32. Graney, J.; Hunt, I.M.; Quinlivan, L.; Rodway, C.; Turnbull, P.; Gianatsi, M.; Appleby, L.; Kapur, N. Suicide risk assessment in UK mental health services: A national mixed-methods study. *Lancet Psychiatry* **2020**, *7*, 1046–1053. [CrossRef]
33. Carter, G.; Milner, A.; McGill, K.; Pirkis, J.; Kapur, N.; Spittal, M.J. Predicting suicidal behaviours using clinical instruments: Systematic review and meta-analysis of positive predictive values for risk scales. *Br. J. Psychiatry* **2017**, *210*, 387–395. [CrossRef]
34. Large, M.N.; Myles, H.; Myles, A.; Corderoy, M.; Weiser, M.; Davidson, M.; Ryan, C.J. Suicide Risk Assessment among Psychiatric Inpatients: A Systematic Review and Meta-Analysis of High-Risk Categories. *Psychol. Med.* **2018**, *48*, 1119–1127. [CrossRef]
35. Beale, C. Magical thinking and moral injury: Exclusion culture in psychiatry. *BJPsych Bull.* **2021**, *46*, 16–19. [CrossRef]

International Journal of
Environmental Research and Public Health

MDPI

Article

Coping Styles Utilized during Suicide and Sudden Death Bereavement in the First Six Months

Sharna Mathieu [1], Racquel Todor [1], Diego De Leo [1,2,3] and Kairi Kõlves [1,*]

1 Australian Institute for Suicide Research and Prevention, WHO Collaborating Centre for Suicide Research and Training, School of Applied Psychology, Griffith University, Brisbane, QLD 4122, Australia
2 Slovene Centre for Suicide Research, Primorska University, 6000 Koper, Slovenia
3 De Leo Fund, 35137 Padua, Italy
* Correspondence: k.kolves@griffith.edu.au

Abstract: Individuals bereaved by suicide experience substantial emotional distress and are at risk for poorer mental health, substance use concerns, and suicidal behaviors. This study aimed to explore whether those bereaved by suicide reported different coping styles compared to those bereaved by sudden death in the first six months. It also aimed to determine whether a previous mental health diagnosis (PMHD) and experiencing stigma and/or shame impacted the utilization of adaptive and maladaptive coping. The sample was constituted by individuals bereaved by suicide (n = 142) compared to those bereaved by sudden death (n = 63), six months after loss. The study included immediate family members who were 18 years or older and understood the English language. After controlling for demographics there were no significant differences in coping styles between bereavement types. Regardless of bereavement type, having a PMHD was associated with increased avoidant and problem-focused coping, and stigma and shame were each associated with increased avoidant coping. Women were also more likely to report using adaptive coping. Findings demonstrate no difference by bereavement type and have implications for the tailoring of grief/postvention supports that are sensitive to perceived stigma/shame to better facilitate utilization of adaptive emotion-focused coping, particularly for men and those with pre-existing mental health problems.

Keywords: grief; bereavement; coping; suicide; sudden death; stigma; shame; postvention

Citation: Mathieu, S.; Todor, R.; De Leo, D.; Kõlves, K. Coping Styles Utilized during Suicide and Sudden Death Bereavement in the First Six Months. *Int. J. Environ. Res. Public Health* **2022**, *19*, 14709. https://doi.org/10.3390/ijerph192214709

Academic Editor: Paul B. Tchounwou

Received: 7 October 2022
Accepted: 7 November 2022
Published: 9 November 2022

1. Introduction

According to estimates from the World Health Organization, approximately 703,000 individuals died by suicide around the world in 2019 [1]. While each death is a preventable tragedy, the full magnitude of this public health issue is only fully realized when the far-reaching impact on family, friends, colleagues, and communities is also accounted for. Although difficult to determine, recent literature estimates that each suicide results in 135 exposed individuals [2], a third of which (e.g., family members, close relatives) are likely to experience ongoing moderate-to-severe emotional distress [3,4]. Furthermore, being bereaved by suicide, but also by other types of sudden death, can contribute to subsequent mental health problems and suicidal behavior [5–7]. Understanding the grief experiences and adaptive and/or maladaptive coping strategies used in the bereavement process is essential to inform and enhance adequate postvention interventions.

1.1. Bereavement

Traditionally, the grief process has been viewed as linear stages or phases that an individual progresses through before grief can be resolved; however, more recent theories have favored a fluid bereavement journey. The dual-process model of coping with bereavement by Stroebe and Schut [8,9] suggests there are two categories of stressors associated with bereavement: loss-oriented stressors (e.g., focus on the relationship with the deceased, circumstances of death), and restoration-oriented stressors (e.g., legal and financial issues resulting from the loss, new role/identity). Bereaved persons oscillate between loss- (e.g., relocating bonds) or restoration-oriented coping strategies (e.g., attending to life changes) depending on which stressors they are confronted with, where they are in their grief journey, as well as personal and cultural influences [9]. These coping strategies can be emotion- or problem-focused and be adaptive or maladaptive, depending on their appropriateness to the type of stressor and whether they serve to approach or avoid [9]. Regardless of theoretical conceptualizations, the process of bereavement is undoubtedly complex. Normative resolution takes time and relies upon adaptive coping [10], aided by sense-making and interpersonal connections [11] and managing the changing feelings, responsibilities and roles related to the loss [9]. Importantly, how someone initially copes with their grief may play a salient role in the trajectories of their bereavement [12].

1.2. Coping Strategies

Coping strategies can be categorized into three overarching styles: avoidant, active-emotion-focused and problem-focused coping [13]. Avoidant coping styles are typically viewed as maladaptive strategies used to avoid intolerable feelings and can include refusal to accept the loss and deep feelings of grief, alcohol or other substance abuse, blaming others, avoiding/denial of life and identity changes, or distraction [9,14,15]. A reliance on avoidant coping strategies is often linked with complicated grief and increased levels of depression and mental health problems [14]. Emotion-focused coping seeks to actively regulate one's emotions, and can include talking about grief-related stressors, disclosing feelings, and interacting with others [13]. It has been suggested that grief focused interventions that directly target facing one's intrusive thoughts and feelings can help to facilitate the grieving process in those with complicated grief symptoms [16]. Problem-focused coping can be described as active solution-making, such as creating a strategy for how to cope and taking action to improve the situation through planning [13,17]. It may help with certain practical stressors experienced during bereavement [9]. However, an over-reliance on problem-focused coping has been described as unhelpful, as bereavement is typically a situation outside one's control [17].

1.3. Experiences of Shame and Stigma

There may be grief experiences unique to suicide bereavement that further impede the normative resolution of grief and promote the use of maladaptive avoidant coping strategies. For instance, while universal grief experiences (e.g., sadness) may be common to all bereavement, the experience of stigma and shame may be more likely in those who are bereaved by suicide and other forms of violent death [6]. Frequently, those bereaved by suicide report themselves as feeling judged, rejected, and misunderstood by their friends, families and community supports [18,19], and experience guilt, conflictual relationships, and concealment as a consequence of (perceived) stigma and shame [20,21]. The experience of stigma and shame may elicit maladaptive coping and may further isolate individuals from social support [22]. Indeed, individuals bereaved by suicide have reported that social support was often ill-timed and insufficient due to the stigma they experienced, and individuals therefore disengaged from their social networks [18,21,22]. For example, one large cross-sectional study found that around a third of relatives received no formal contact regarding the suicide of a family member who had been in touch with psychiatric facilities in the year prior to their death, and this was associated with potentially stigmatizing characteristics of the decedent such as criminal history, substance abuse, etc. [23]. This represents a considerable missed opportunity for assertive postvention support. Instead, individuals are often required to utilize alternative (solitary) ways to cope, including remaining silent and denying the cause of death [18,24]. This may contribute to disenfranchised grief: a grief that occurs when one cannot openly acknowledge or publicly mourn [25]. However, the distinction between suicide and other forms of bereavement is not clear-cut [26–28], with many studies conflicting in their findings regarding unique outcomes of suicide bereavement [6]. One explanation may be that differences may vary depending on which mode of death it is being compared to, such as expected versus other forms of sudden or violent death [6]. There are still relatively few studies which compare experiences of stigma and shame in those bereaved by suicide as compared to other forms of sudden death. However, it appears that while all forms of sudden death are associated with stigmatizing experiences, this may be heightened in those bereaved by suicide where additional impacts of self-stigma, shame and guilt are also experienced [29,30].

1.4. Aims

The use of adaptive coping strategies for regulating grief-related emotions throughout the bereavement process is important and may be influenced by underlying factors such as pre-existing mental health concerns [12]. However, it is unclear whether individuals recently bereaved by suicide engage in certain coping strategies over others as compared to those bereaved by other causes of sudden death, and whether the presence of underlying mental health conditions may impact the use of these strategies. Furthermore, unique grief experiences such as shame or stigma may adversely influence the use of coping strategies and ultimately grief trajectories for those bereaved by suicide. Therefore, the aims of the current study are to:

- investigate the coping styles of individuals bereaved by suicide as compared to sudden death in the first six months after the loss of their close relative;
- explore the impact of a previous mental health diagnosis (PMHD) on coping styles during early bereavement; and
- investigate how the experience of stigma and shame contribute to the coping styles of people bereaved by suicide.

2. Materials and Methods

2.1. Research Design

The current study forms part of a larger longitudinal investigation of suicide bereavement conducted over two years in Queensland, Australia [28,31,32]. A longitudinal prospective design was used to compare suicide bereavement to bereavement from other types of sudden deaths across three different time points: 6, 12 and 24 months after the death. The rationale to include sudden deaths as a comparison group was the similarity of the sudden and often unexpected nature of the death as opposed to long-term illnesses or other expected causes. To examine these associations in the early stages of bereavement, the current study utilizes data from the six-month time-point. Six months as an indicator of 'early bereavement' was deemed most appropriate by the research team and ethical approval committee in striking an important balance between recency to the highly distressing sudden loss (by suicide or other causes) and the burden of participation in an in-depth research study comprised of both qualitative and quantitative components.

2.2. Data Collection

The current study was approved by the Institution's Human Research Ethics Committee (CSR/04/11/HREC). Inclusion criteria were: being close relatives and family members bereaved by a suicide or sudden death, aged 18 years old or older, able to speak and understand English, and, given that the larger longitudinal study from which the current study information was collected was centered on suicide and sudden death bereavement experiences in Queensland, the death had to have occurred in Queensland, Australia [28,31]. Participants were contacted 6 ± 1 months after the loss. Family members were defined as a spouse, de facto partner, adult child, parent, grandparent, grandchild, sibling, aunt, uncle, niece and nephew, and immediate in-laws. It should be noted that 'children' and 'grandchildren' refers to their kinship relationship type (not age) and were the adult offspring or family member of the decedents.

Those bereaved by suicide were identified through the Queensland Suicide Register, a real-time surveillance system. Clinical interviewers sent letters introducing the study, along with research information and consent forms to the identified individuals. Two weeks after the letters were dispatched, individuals were contacted by telephone to further introduce the study, obtain consent, and arrange a time and place for a six-month time-point interview. Of the participants that were interviewed (response rate 39.9%), 78.2% were interviewed via phone, and the remaining interviewed face-to-face either in their home or at the university.

Participants for the sudden death group were recruited through Queensland Office of State Coroners police forms. Only closed cases of "reportable deaths" of a sudden, violent, or suspicious nature as recorded by the Queensland Coroners Acts 2003 [33] were approached (i.e., not expected deaths due to long-term illness or age-related causes). Letters introducing the study, along with research information and consent forms, were sent to the reported next-of-kin of the deceased. All participants provided written informed consent to participate (response rate 16.1%). No phone calls were made for the sudden death group to collect consent. Half of the sudden death participants lost their loved one suddenly to diseases of the circulatory system (52.4%), followed by other external causes of death (25.4%; mainly transport accidents), sudden death by other medical causes (e.g., epilepsy, asthma; 9.4%), injury, poisoning, and other consequences of external causes (6.3%), and ill-defined and unknown cause of mortality (6.3%). The sudden death group only received responses from immediate family (partners, parents, adult children, and siblings). Therefore, for comparability of the two groups, all responses from non-immediate family members such as uncles, aunts, grandparents/children, and cousins were excluded from the suicide bereaved group.

Semi-structured interviews (~2.5 h duration) were conducted with participants by trained clinical interviewers with postgraduate health qualifications. A short introduction to the research was conducted at the beginning of the interview, and a debrief was conducted at the end of the interview to allow for participant's concerns and questions. The interviews adhered to the following template: (1) a qualitative component—open-ended questions about the events leading to the death [34,35]; and (2) a quantitative component—sociodemographic information, medical and psychiatric history, including suicidal behavior of the deceased and bereaved, and post-event experiences measured with different validated scales [28,32]. A pilot study demonstrated the acceptability of the questionnaire and adequate procedures for recruitment [31] which are further described in more detail elsewhere [28]. The current study used quantitative information only.

2.3. Measures

In addition to basic demographic information for the bereaved participants (e.g., age, gender, type of kinship to the deceased person) and their deceased family member (e.g., age, gender, type of death—suicide or sudden), the participants also provided self-reported information on any previous mental health disorder diagnoses (PMHD) or treatment for they had received before the loss of their relative. The bereaved individuals also completed the following validated surveys:

The Grief Experience Questionnaire (GEQ) [36] is designed to measure typical and unique grief experiences. The version used for the current study was comprised of 40 items assessing the following grief experiences: somatic reactions, search for explanation, loss of social support, guilt, responsibility, rejection, stigmatization, and shame [31]. The subscales of stigmatization (e.g., "I feel uncomfortable revealing the cause of the death"; $\alpha = 0.81$), and shame (e.g., "I feel embarrassed about the death"; $\alpha = 0.73$) were used for the current study.

The BRIEFCope [37] is a 28-item survey which uses a 4-point Likert scale to assess different coping styles. Based on the conceptual and empirical literature [38,39], the items are grouped into the three coping styles: avoidant coping ($\alpha = 0.69$), problem-focused coping ($\alpha = 0.82$) and emotion-focused coping ($\alpha = 0.66$).

2.4. Statistical Analyses

Analyses were conducted using the IBM SPSS, version 27 (IBM Corp, Armonk, NY, USA). Descriptive statistics, including means, standard deviations and frequencies were calculated. Dummy variables were computed for kinship type (partner, parent, adult child, and sibling). The Chi^2 test and Fisher's exact test were used to compare differences between suicide and sudden death bereaved using demographic variables. T-test and one-way ANOVA were utilized for preliminary comparison of coping styles across different groups. Hierarchical multiple regression analyses were conducted to identify factors associated with copying styles: avoidant coping, problem-focused coping, and emotion-focused coping. Age, gender of the deceased and of the bereaved, as well as kinship type, were entered in the first model as control variables. The independent variables, type of bereavement (suicide vs. sudden death), PMHD (yes vs. no), stigma (continuous), and shame (continuous) were entered step-by-step into regression models, respectively.

3. Results

3.1. Participants

The final sample included 142 suicide bereaved (average age: 52.7; SD: 11.6; female: 73.2%) and 63 sudden death bereaved (average age: 53.2; SD: 15.5; female: 69.8%) participants. For the suicide bereaved, the average age of the deceased person was 41.2 years (SD: 18.0; female: 19%) and in the sudden death group, 51.4 years old (SD: 17.1; female: 30.2%). Table 1 provides additional demographic characteristics. There were significant differences between bereavement types for kinship relationships and these were controlled for in the regression models.

Table 1. Demographic characteristics of the sample, including gender of the deceased.

	Bereavement Type					
	Suicide (*n* = 142)		**Sudden Death (*n* = 63)**		**$Chi^2_{(df)}$**	***p***
	n	%	*n*	%		
Gender of the bereaved					$0.25_{(1)}$	0.616
Male	38	26.8	19	30.2		
Female	104	73.2	44	69.8		
Gender of the deceased					$3.11_{(1)}$	0.078
Male	115	81.0	44	69.8		
Female	27	19.0	19	30.2		
Kinship to the deceased					$13.19_{(3)}$	0.004
Spouse/partner	41	28.9	31	49.2		
Parent	72	50.7	17	27.0		
Adult child	16	11.3	11	17.5		
Sibling	13	9.2	4	6.3		
PMHD [1]					$0.14_{(1)}$	0.713
No diagnosis	104	73.2	48	76.2		
One or more	38	26.8	15	23.8		
Depression	24	16.9	13	20.6		
Anxiety	11	7.7	5	7.9		
Bipolar	4	2.8	1	1.6		
Other	10	7.0	2	3.2		
Ethnicity						
Caucasian/White	134	94.4	60	95.2		1.000 [2]
Aboriginal	3	2.1	1	1.6		1.000 [2]
Non-Caucasian	5	3.5	2	3.2		1.000 [2]
Interview type						
Face-to-face	31	21.8	7	11.1	$3.32_{(1)}$	0.068
Over the phone	111	78.2	56	88.9		

[1] People could self-report more than one PMHD; for later analyses this was recoded into 'yes, any PMHD' or 'no diagnosis'. [2] Fisher's exact test was performed.

Group differences by coping style are presented in Table 2. For bereavement type, there were no significant differences between avoidant and problem-focused coping; however, those bereaved by suicide reported significantly more emotion-focused coping than those bereaved by other sudden death. Men recently bereaved reported significantly less avoidant, problem-focused, and emotion-focused coping than women. Those with a PMHD reported significantly more avoidant, problem-focused, and emotion-focused coping than those without a PMHD. Finally, there were significant differences in problem-focused coping between different kinship groups. Spouses/partners reported the most problem-focused coping and offspring of the deceased reported the least. A previous study on the same sample found that after adjusting for kinship, gender, age, PMHD, self-harm (deceased, bereaved), current mental health symptoms and current suicidal ideation that those in the suicide bereavement group reported experiencing significantly more stigma and shame than the sudden death bereavement group at six months [32].

Table 2. Group differences by coping styles.

	Coping Style								
	Avoidant			Problem-Focused			Emotion-Focused		
	M (SD)	*t/F*	*p*	*M (SD)*	*t/F*	*p*	*M (SD)*	*t/F*	*p*
Bereavement		1.09	0.279		0.87	0.384		2.22	0.027
Suicide	13.82 (3.91)			21.01 (5.69)			27.46 (5.21)		
Sudden Death	13.17 (4.05)			20.25 (5.90)			25.67 (5.59)		
Gender of bereaved		−2.54	0.012		−3.55	<0.001		−3.66	<0.001
Male	12.51 (3.86)			18.54 (5.69)			24.75 (5.42)		
Female	14.05 (3.92)			21.64 (5.55)			27.74 (5.14)		
Kinship		1.17	0.324		4.79	0.003		0.88	0.453
Spouse/partner	14.30 (4.10)			22.63 (5.36)			27.08 (5.55)		
Parent	13.41 (3.77)			20.26 (5.73)			27.29 (5.15)		
Adult child	13.00 (3.61)			18.33 (5.72)			25.44 (5.83)		
Sibling	12.94 (4.70)			19.71 (5.59)			26.47 (5.16)		
PMHD		2.96	0.003		2.74	0.007		2.14	0.033
Yes	15.02 (3.91)			22.62 (5.00)			28.25 (3.78)		
No	13.17 (3.87)			20.13 (5.87)			26.41 (5.76)		

3.2. Avoidant Coping

Model 1 was significant, with the age and gender of the bereaved contributing significantly to the prediction of avoidant coping ($F(6,197) = 2.64$, $p = 0.017$; Table 3). Bereavement type was entered into model 2 with no significant change ($F(1,196) = 1.05$, $p = 0.306$), meaning there was no significant difference between people bereaved by suicide and those bereaved by other sudden death. The addition of PMHD accounted for 2.8% additional variance in avoidant coping ($F(1,195) = 6.19$, $p = 0.014$); individuals with a PMHD reported significantly higher levels of avoidant coping. Stigma significantly accounted for 7.9% of unique variance in model 4 ($F(1,194) = 18.75$, $p < 0.001$); greater experience of stigma was associated with increased use of avoidant coping. Shame was added into the final model ($F(1,193) = 5.70$, $p = 0.018$), accounting for 2.3% of unique variance, where an increased experience of shame related to an increase in avoidant coping. In addition, having a PMHD and increased experience of stigma remained significant in the final model.

Table 3. Regression models for each coping style.

	Avoidant				Problem-Focused				Emotion-Focused			
	β	sr^2	ΔR^2	R^2	B	sr^2	ΔR^2	R^2	B	sr^2	ΔR^2	R^2
Model 1				0.074 *				0.160 ***				0.097 **
Age (Bereaved)	−0.20 *	0.03			−0.24 **	0.05			−0.17 *	0.02		
Gender (Deceased)	<0.01	<0.01			0.03	<0.01			−0.02	<0.01		
Gender (Bereaved)	0.14 *	0.02			0.20 **	0.03			0.22 **	0.04		
Kinship (Parent)	−0.03	<0.01			−0.11	0.01			0.09	0.01		
Kinship (Adult child)	−0.15	0.02			−0.30 **	0.07			−0.12	0.01		
Kinship (Sibling)	−0.06	<0.01			−0.09	0.01			0.02	<0.01		
Model 2			0.005	0.079 *			0.003	0.163 ***			0.012	0.109 **
Age (Bereaved)	−0.19 *	0.03			−0.24 **	0.04			−0.16 *	0.02		
Gender (Deceased)	0.01	<0.01			0.04	<0.01			−0.01	<0.01		
Gender (Bereaved)	0.14	0.02			0.19 **	0.03			0.22 **	0.04		
Kinship (Parent)	−0.05	<0.01			−0.13	0.01			0.06	<0.01		
Kinship (Adult child)	−0.15	0.02			−0.30 **	0.07			−0.12	0.01		
Kinship (Sibling)	−0.07	<0.01			−0.10	0.01			<0.01	<0.01		
Bereavement type	0.07	<0.01			0.06	<0.01			0.12	0.01		
Model 3			0.028 *	0.108 **			0.020 *	0.183 ***			0.011	0.120 **
Age (Bereaved)	−0.19 *	0.03			−0.23 **	0.04			−0.15 *	0.02		
Gender (Deceased)	0.02	<0.01			0.04	<0.01			−0.01	<0.01		
Gender (Bereaved)	0.12	0.01			0.18 *	0.03			0.21 **	0.04		
Kinship (Parent)	−0.04	<0.01			−0.12	0.01			0.06	<0.01		
Kinship (Adult child)	−0.15	0.02			−0.30 **	0.07			−0.12	0.01		
Kinship (Sibling)	−0.06	<0.01			−0.09	0.01			0.01	<0.01		
Bereavement type	0.07	<0.01			0.06	<0.01			0.11	0.01		
PMHD	0.17 *	0.03			0.14 *	0.02			0.11	0.01		
Model 4			0.079 ***	0.186 ***			0.010	0.193 ***			0.023 *	0.144 ***
Age (Bereaved)	−0.08	<0.01			−0.20 *	0.03			−0.10	0.01		
Gender (Deceased)	0.05	<0.01			0.05	<0.01			0.01	<0.01		
Gender (Bereaved)	0.10	0.01			0.17 *	0.02			0.20 **	0.03		
Kinship (Parent)	−0.03	<0.01			−0.12	0.01			0.07	<0.01		
Kinship (Adult child)	−0.08	<0.01			−0.28 **	0.06			−0.09	0.01		
Kinship (Sibling)	−0.02	<0.01			−0.08	<0.01			0.03	<0.01		
Bereavement type	−0.01	<0.01			0.03	<0.01			0.07	<0.01		
PMHD	0.15 *	0.02			0.13 *	0.02			0.09	0.01		
Stigma	0.33 ***	0.08			0.11	0.01			0.17 *	0.02		
Model 5			0.023 *	0.210 ***			0.002	0.195 ***			0.014	0.157 ***
Age (Bereaved)	−0.07	<0.01			−0.20 *	0.03			−0.10	0.01		
Gender (Deceased)	0.04	<0.01			0.06	<0.01			0.01	<0.01		
Gender (Bereaved)	0.08	0.01			0.18 *	0.03			0.21 **	0.04		
Kinship (Parent)	−0.03	<0.01			−0.12	0.01			0.06	<0.01		
Kinship (Adult child)	−0.11	0.01			−0.27 **	0.05			−0.06	<0.01		
Kinship (Sibling)	−0.04	<0.01			−0.07	<0.01			0.04	<0.01		
Bereavement type	−0.02	<0.01			0.03	<0.01			0.08	0.01		
PMHD	0.14 *	0.02			0.14 *	0.02			0.10	0.01		
Stigma	0.23 **	0.03			0.14	0.01			0.24 **	0.04		
Shame	0.18 *	0.02			−0.06	<0.01			−0.14	0.01		

* $p < 0.05$, ** $p < 0.01$, *** $p < 0.001$; NB: For kinship, the reference group is 'spouse/partner'.

3.3. Problem-Focused Coping

Model 1 predicting problem-focused coping during bereavement was significant ($F(6,197) = 6.25$, $p < 0.001$; Table 3), with gender and age of the bereaved, and being an adult child of the deceased, significantly contributing to problem-focused coping. Bereavement type did not significantly account for any additional variance in model 2 ($F(1,196) = 0.77$, $p = 0.381$). PMHD significantly accounted for 2% unique variance in model 3 ($F(1,195) = 4.71$, $p = 0.031$). Stigma did not account for any significant variance in model 4 ($F(1,194) = 2.365$, $p = 0.127$) and neither did shame in model 5 ($F(1,193) = 0.50$, $p = 0.479$). However, PMHD, gender and age of the bereaved and being an adult child of the deceased (compared to partners/spouses) remained significant predictors of problem-focused coping in the final model. More specifically, being female, younger-aged, and having a PMHD increased the probability of problem-focused coping, and being an adult child of the deceased was associated with decreased problem-focused coping.

3.4. Emotion-Focused Coping

Model 1 was significant in predicting emotion-focused coping ($F(6,197) = 3.52$, $p = 0.002$; Table 3), where gender and age of the bereaved was significantly associated with emotion-focused coping. Bereavement type did not account for any significant variance in model 2 ($F(1,196) = 2.69$, $p = 0.103$); neither did PMHD in model 3 ($F(1,195) = 2.45$, $p = 0.119$). Stigma significantly accounted for 2.3% of unique variance towards emotion-focused coping in model 4 ($F(1,194) = 5.32$, $p = 0.022$). Shame did not significantly predict any unique variance in the final model ($F(1,193) = 3.11$, $p = 0.08$). Higher levels of stigma and female gender of the bereaved significantly predicted more emotion-focused coping in the final model.

4. Discussion

The current study focused on coping style differences among individuals bereaved by suicide and by other sudden death six months after the loss of a close relative. In addition, the impact of a previous mental health diagnosis, stigma, and shame on coping styles were analyzed. The literature has shown mixed results regarding the experiences and outcomes of suicide bereavement as compared to other types of loss [26,40]. In the current study, there were no significant differences between the two bereavement types and their use of avoidant, problem-focused or emotion-focused coping styles, suggesting similar coping styles in the early stages of bereavement after adjusting for age, kinship type and gender (of the bereaved and deceased). A recent study found that those bereaved by suicide reported significantly higher avoidant coping than those bereaved by combat loss, yet there were no significant differences when compared to those bereaved by accidents, nor were there any differences for self-reported active/problem or emotion/supportive coping in either of the bereaved groups [41]. However, time since the loss varied from one to twelve years [41], whereas the current study analyzed coping and grief experiences only in the first six months, which provides a timely insight into this critical initial bereavement period.

There was no significant difference in the prevalence of a PMHD between the two bereavement groups. Nevertheless, individuals with a PMHD (regardless of bereavement type) reported significantly higher levels of avoidant and problem-focused coping, while there was no significant difference for active emotion-focused coping. This is consistent with the literature, whereby avoidance of emotions and internal sensations (i.e., experiential avoidance) has been linked to several mental health conditions, including depression and anxiety [42]. It is less clear why a PMHD may relate to increased problem-focused coping. One explanation could be that those with a self-reported PMHD onset before the loss of their loved one may have previously sought help for their mental health concerns (hence receiving a diagnosis) and are thus already more active/experienced in help-seeking and more able to draw upon problem-focused coping strategies during the early stages of their bereavement. Another explanation could be that previous experience of mental health concerns makes bereavement more complicated and therefore a reliance on a greater number of coping strategies that are arguably easier to apply are employed in an effort to manage. That is, focusing on practical matters or avoiding facing painful feelings may be 'easier' in more complex or highly painful situations of bereavement (e.g., [15]). In the current study the problem-focused coping subscale included items related to active coping (i.e., trying to actively remove a source of stress), planning (i.e., considering practical steps to take), instrumental support (i.e., seeking practical advice), and religion (i.e., turning to religion/religious activities). While problem-focused coping is generally considered more adaptive than avoidant strategies, an overreliance on problem-focused coping may be less desirable in coping with bereavement whereby many situational elements are outside one's control [17]. Instead, according to the dual-process model of grief, adaptive grief resolution over time relies upon the appropriate use of both emotion-focused and problem-focused coping to manage the fluctuation of loss-oriented and restoration-oriented stressors, and that flexible oscillation between healthy coping strategies is required [9]. That is, the coping strategies of the bereaved can be both adaptive and maladaptive depending on how rigidly one is relied upon above others and whether they are appropriate for the source of stress [9].

In our study, in the final models after accounting for all variables of interest and demographics, bereaved women were more likely to use problem- and emotion-focused adaptive coping than bereaved men, but there were no differences for avoidant coping.

Gender differences in coping with grief have long been discussed [43], and recent research implies that gender may influence the trajectory of 'prolonged grief' over time, with men experiencing more pronounced grief initially which decreased and vice versa for women (there were no differences between genders for more stable and resilient grief profiles [44]). However, there may be few differences regarding actual self-reported symptoms of prolonged grief experienced between genders [45]. The current preliminary findings have implications for the tailored provision of postvention and grief support. For example, while men and women demonstrated similar levels of avoidant coping strategies (after accounting for all variables of interest and demographics), the tendency for men in this study to report less utilization of adaptive emotion- and problem-focused coping strategies in the initial six-month period following loss may correspond to patterns observed in previous studies (e.g., [44]) and it may be particularly useful for practitioners to focus on enhancing adaptive coping strategies in men during this earlier period, which may serve to facilitate grief resolution and contribute to the prevention of suicidal behaviors and other adverse outcomes [6]. Naturally, this relies upon people getting access to timely and appropriate postvention supports which may be impeded by (real or perceived) experiences of stigma and shame [23,46,47]. However, further research is required to determine gender differences in perceived experiences of stigma and shame during bereavement from suicide and sudden death, and to develop and evaluate effective postvention supports that are sensitive to gender differences in coping [48].

4.1. Stigma and Shame

Irrespective of bereavement type, greater self-reported experiences of stigma and shame were each associated with increased avoidant coping in the initial six months of bereavement. This is consistent with the literature, as stigma and shame have been associated with behaviors of withdrawal and secrecy in both suicide and sudden death bereaved populations [19]. More recently, stigma has been described in relation to increased self-reported thwarted belongingness (i.e., alienation from others) in those bereaved by suicide, which, consistent with the interpersonal theory of suicidal behavior, would be associated with suicidal ideation over time [49]. Interestingly, in our study, those who reported greater experience of stigma also reported increased emotion-focused coping (this association was non-significant for shame). Neither shame nor stigma were associated with problem-focused coping.

To date, there is limited research on how coping strategies interact with experiences of stigma and shame during early bereavement. Future research is required to replicate these findings. Nevertheless, these results challenge the notion that stigmatization after suicide or sudden bereavement may hinder one's ability to utilize adaptive coping due to isolation, avoidance, rejection, and fear of discussing the death. One explanation could be that when informal support systems of the bereaved fail to provide adequate assistance, bereaved individuals may seek support elsewhere (e.g., counsellors or support groups). In a recent Lithuanian study, those bereaved by suicide and who sought professional support reported higher levels of stigmatization and guilt than those who did not seek professional support [50]. On the one hand, mental health professionals may provide a more appealing environment to express vulnerable emotions and share personal grief stories to process their loss than informal supports who may be perceived as judgmental or unhelpful (e.g., [18]). On the other hand, by engaging with professional supports, individuals may gain insight into the impacts of societal stigma through the psychoeducation and interaction provided by a supportive professional. A second explanation may relate to the use of the Internet as an alternative source for social support. Studies have shown that individuals bereaved by suicide make social media posts and email friends and family about the loss [51], and they are increasingly accessing blogs, websites, and social networking platforms to interact with other bereaved individuals and memorialize their loved ones [52]. When individuals utilize the Internet in this manor, it has been demonstrated that not only did it remove some fear of stigmatization, but it also helped heal their sorrow [51]. A final explanation could be that the experience of stigma makes grief more complicated, and thus, a greater number of coping strategies are relied upon (adaptive or maladaptive).

4.2. Limitations

The current study was cross-sectional and had more than double suicide bereaved individuals (n = 142) compared to sudden death bereaved individuals (n = 63). Therefore, the sudden death group may not accurately represent full unique variance, resulting in possible missing effects. There were also group differences in the (low) response rates, with those bereaved by suicide having a higher response rate (39.9%) than other causes of sudden death (16.1%). The low response rates likely introduce some bias into the current findings and restrict generalizability. It is understandable that in the early stages of bereavement there may be a general lack of interest in participating in research, hence the low response rates. Reasons for non-participation were available only for the suicide bereaved group and included inability to contact the individual, the individuals not wishing to discuss their bereavement, or the individual being too busy. Differences in recruitment procedure may explain why those bereaved by suicide were more likely to respond to the study invitation. Other possible reasons could be that the research team were from a suicide prevention research institute, which may have unintentionally influenced responses. Furthermore, given the additional layers of shock and challenges with sense-making that may be experienced or perceived following a suicide (as opposed to a shocking sudden death that can be 'explained' by a medical reason), there may have been more motivation to engage with research aimed at furthering our understanding and informing postvention supports. Additionally, the sudden death group was comprised of deaths of heterogenous causes, with the majority comprised of sudden deaths of the circulatory system (e.g., heart attacks) and accidental deaths (e.g., car accident). There may be differences in how experiences of stigma and shame are associated with different coping styles across these subgroups; for example, sudden death causes where a sense of guilt or blame can be assigned (subjectively or objectively through the legal system) as opposed to medical causes. Unfortunately, due to small numbers it was not possible to analyze differences by subgroups and this remains an important area for future research.

Although the larger longitudinal study did include measurements assessing concurrent distress and mental health outcomes [28], the current analysis did not include them, as it was outside of the scope of the study aims. However, by demonstrating that a PMHD was significantly associated with increased avoidant coping, it posits the question as to whether the increased use of avoidant strategies due to a PMHD contributes to negative or positive mental health outcomes in individuals bereaved by suicide and sudden death in the early bereavement period or over time. The current analysis did not include information about individuals' current treatment for their PMHD. Therefore, the current study cannot definitively suggest that having a PMHD promotes an effect on coping styles, or whether it is the type of treatment that may have been received (either previously and/or during the initial bereavement period). These questions should be investigated in future research.

Finally, there are always challenges in selecting survey measures that are valid, robust, and sensitive to change over time. For the current study, the use of a coping style survey designed for use in response to stressful life events may not comprehensively capture all facets of coping during the complex period of bereavement. Nevertheless, the survey measure has been used in previous bereavement studies (e.g., [38,39]). Furthermore, the shame and stigma subscales of the grief experiences questionnaire may have also minimized complexities in relation to self-directed versus external stigma, as well as internal versus external shame. The items in the current study mostly reflect external experiences of grief-related stigma, and the grief-related shame items arguably have some conceptual overlap with avoidant coping strategies.

4.3. Implications

Current findings provide new information regarding the early bereavement experiences of those bereaved by suicide and other sudden death and have important implications for promoting adaptive coping for grief resolution over time. Postvention service delivery frameworks should be tailored to the various levels and needs of support [53]. Postvention workers, therapists, and grief counsellors working with those recently bereaved by suicide or sudden death should be mindful of underlying mental health conditions and what impact these may have on the grief experience and coping strategies utilized. While the current study included different previous diagnoses, the majority of existing PMHD in the current sample were anxiety disorders and depression. The finding that experiences of stigma and shame were each associated with increased avoidant coping is also important for mental health practitioners to note. Not only are real or perceived experiences of stigma and shame distressing and isolating, but avoidant coping has also been implicated in disenfranchised and complicated grief [25]. Clinicians should be mindful of a client's overreliance on maladaptive avoidant coping strategies in the early stages of bereavement, particularly in those with previous experiences of mental health concerns, and in situations of suicide or sudden death where stigma and shame are present. One promising avenue that requires further research is interventions for bereaved individuals focused on mindful self-compassion, which directly targets feelings of shame, stigma, or guilt as well as mental health and wellbeing, and adaptive emotion regulation and coping [54,55]. Regardless of content and delivery, postvention and grief supports should be developed and guided by the involvement of those with lived experience of suicide loss so as to be maximally sensitive to their needs, such as practical support in the early period, perceived experiences, as well as the impact of features such as gender and kinship [21,26,27,56]. It is also crucial that services are assertive, and people bereaved by suicide or sudden death are identified and followed up with quickly to minimize the potential interference of stigma and shame on help-seeking behaviors and other coping strategies.

5. Conclusions

The current study demonstrated that both bereavement groups reported similar coping styles six months after the loss of a close family member. The results indicated that having a PMHD increased both avoidant and problem-focused coping in both the suicide and sudden death bereaved. Grief-related experiences of both stigma and shame were associated with increased use of avoidant coping strategies. Men were less likely to utilize adaptive coping strategies such as active emotion-focused and problem-focused coping. The utilization of adaptive coping strategies is amenable [57], and there is a need for timely and appropriate postvention and grief supports that are effective and tailored to the needs and experiences of those with lived experience of suicide [53] and sudden loss.

Author Contributions: Conceptualization, K.K., R.T. and S.M.; methodology, K.K. and D.D.L.; formal analysis, K.K. and R.T.; resources, K.K.; data curation, K.K.; writing—original draft preparation, S.M. and R.T.; writing—review and editing, K.K., S.M., R.T. and D.D.L.; visualization, S.M.; supervision, K.K.; project administration, K.K.; funding acquisition, K.K. and D.D.L. All authors have read and agreed to the published version of the manuscript.

Funding: This research was supported by a Griffith University Encouragement Grant and the Australian Research Council Discovery Grant 'Bereavement of suicide and sudden death' (No. ARC DP140102567). The funding body had no involvement in the study design, data collection, or manuscript preparation.

Institutional Review Board Statement: The study was conducted in accordance with the Declaration of Helsinki, and approved by the Human Research Ethics Committee of Griffith University (CSR/04/11/HREC).

Informed Consent Statement: Informed consent was obtained from all subjects involved in the study.

Data Availability Statement: De-identified study data can be made available upon reasonable request.

Acknowledgments: The authors acknowledge the role of the clinical interviewers and study participants. We also acknowledge the assistance of the Queensland Department of Justice, Office of State Coroner (OSC) for their role in recruitment.

Conflicts of Interest: The authors declare no conflict of interest.

References

1. World Health Organization. *Suicide Worldwide in 2019: Global Health Estimates*; World Health Organization: Geneva, Switzerland, 2021.
2. Cerel, J.; Brown, M.M.; Maple, M.; Singleton, M.; Venne, J.; Moore, M.; Flaherty, C. How many people are exposed to suicide? Not six. *Suicide Life-Threat. Behav.* **2019**, *49*, 529–534. [CrossRef] [PubMed]
3. Cerel, J.; McIntosh, J.L.; Neimeyer, R.A.; Maple, M.; Marshall, D. The continuum of "survivorship": Definitional issues in the aftermath of suicide. *Suicide Life-Threat. Behav.* **2014**, *44*, 591–600. [CrossRef]
4. Feigelman, W.; Cerel, J.; McIntosh, J.L.; Brent, D.; Gutin, N. Suicide exposures and bereavement among American adults: Evidence from the 2016 General Social Survey. *J. Affect. Disord.* **2018**, *227*, 1–6. [CrossRef]
5. Erlangsen, A.; Runeson, B.; Bolton, J.M.; Wilcox, H.C.; Forman, J.L.; Krogh, J.; Shear, M.K.; Nordentoft, M.; Conwell, Y. Association between spousal suicide and mental, physical, and social health outcomes: A longitudinal and nationwide register-based study. *JAMA Psychiatry* **2017**, *74*, 456–464. [CrossRef]
6. Pitman, A.; Osborn, D.; King, M.; Erlangsen, A. Effects of suicide bereavement on mental health and suicide risk. *Lancet Psychiatry* **2014**, *1*, 86–94. [CrossRef]
7. Hill, N.T.; Robinson, J.; Pirkis, J.; Andriessen, K.; Krysinska, K.; Payne, A.; Boland, A.; Clarke, A.; Milner, A.; Witt, K.; et al. Association of suicidal behaviour with exposure to suicide and suicide attempt: A systematic review and multi-level meta-analysis. *PLoS Med.* **2020**, *17*, e1003074. [CrossRef]
8. Stroebe, M.; Schut, H. The dual process model of coping with bereavement: Rationale and description. *Death Stud.* **1999**, *23*, 197–224. [CrossRef] [PubMed]
9. Stroebe, M.; Schut, H. The dual process model of coping with bereavement: A decade on. *OMEGA-J. Death Dying* **2010**, *61*, 273–289. [CrossRef]
10. Meichenbaum, D.; Myers, J. Strategies for coping with grief. In *Techniques of Grief Therapy: Assessment and Intervention*; Neimeyer, A.R., Ed.; Routledge: New York, NY, USA, 2016; pp. 117–123.
11. Neimeyer, R.A.; Klass, D.; Dennis, M.R. A social constructionist account of grief: Loss and the narration of meaning. *Death Stud.* **2014**, *38*, 485–498. [CrossRef]
12. Stroebe, M.S.; Folkman, S.; Hansson, R.O.; Schut, H. The prediction of bereavement outcome: Development of an integrative risk factor framework. *Soc. Sci. Med.* **2006**, *63*, 2440–2451. [CrossRef] [PubMed]
13. Carver, C.S.; Scheier, M.F.; Weintraub, J.K. Assessing coping strategies: A theoretically based approach. *J. Personality Soc. Psychol.* **1989**, *56*, 267–283. [CrossRef]
14. Lipp, N.S.; O'Brien, K.M. Bereaved college students: Social support, coping style, continuing bonds, and social media use as predictors of complicated grief and posttraumatic growth. *Omega J. Death Dying* **2022**, *85*, 178–203. [CrossRef] [PubMed]
15. Ryckebosch-Dayez, A.S.; Zech, E.; Mac Cord, J.; Taverne, C. Daily life stressors and coping strategies during widowhood: A diary study after one year of bereavement. *Death Stud.* **2016**, *40*, 461–478. [CrossRef]
16. Wagner, B.; Knaevelsrud, C.; Maercker, A. Internet-based cognitive-behavioral therapy for complicated grief: A randomized controlled trial. *Death Stud* **2006**, *30*, 429–453. [CrossRef]
17. Carroll, L. Problem-focused coping. In *Encyclopedia of Behavioral Medicine*; Springer International Publishing: Cham, Switzerland, 2020; pp. 1747–1748.
18. Peters, K.; Cunningham, C.; Murphy, G.; Jackson, D. "People look down on you when you tell them how he died": Qualitative insights into stigma as experienced by suicide survivors. *Int. J. Ment. Health Nurs.* **2016**, *25*, 251–257. [CrossRef] [PubMed]
19. Evans, A.; Abrahamson, K. The influence of stigma on suicide bereavement: A systematic review. *J. Psychosoc. Nurs. Ment. Health Serv.* **2020**, *58*, 21–27. [CrossRef]
20. Sudak, H.; Maxim, K.; Carpenter, M. Suicide and stigma: A review of the literature and personal reflections. *Acad. Psychiatry* **2008**, *32*, 136–142. [CrossRef]
21. Ross, V.; Kõlves, K.; De Leo, D. Exploring the support needs of people bereaved by suicide: A qualitative study. *Omega J. Death Dying* **2021**, *82*, 632–645. [CrossRef]
22. Chapple, A.; Ziebland, S.; Hawton, K. Taboo and the different death? Perceptions of those bereaved by suicide or other traumatic death. *Sociol. Health Illn.* **2015**, *37*, 610–625. [CrossRef]
23. Pitman, A.L.; Hunt, I.M.; McDonnell, S.J.; Appleby, L.; Kapur, N. Support for relatives bereaved by psychiatric patient suicide: National confidential inquiry into suicide and homicide Findings. *Psychiatr. Serv.* **2017**, *68*, 337–344. [CrossRef]
24. Sheehan, L.; Corrigan, P.W.; Al-Khouja, M.A.; Lewy, S.A.; Major, D.R.; Mead, J.; Redmon, M.; Rubey, C.T.; Weber, S. Behind closed doors: The stigma of suicide loss survivors. *J. Death Dying* **2018**, *77*, 330–349. [CrossRef] [PubMed]

25. Doka, K.J. Disenfranchised grief in historical and cultural perspective. In *Handbook of Bereavement Research and Practice: Advances in Theory and Intervention*; Stroebe, M.S., Hansson, R.O., Schut, H., Stroebe, W., Eds.; American Psychological Association: Washington, DC, USA, 2008; pp. 223–240. [CrossRef]
26. Andriessen, K. Suicide bereavement and postvention in major suicidology journals: Lessons learned for the future of postvention. *Crisis* **2014**, *35*, 338–348. [CrossRef]
27. Andriessen, K.; Krysinska, K. Essential questions on suicide bereavement and postvention. *Int. J. Environ. Res. Public Health* **2012**, *9*, 24–32. [CrossRef] [PubMed]
28. Kõlves, K.; Zhao, Q.; Ross, V.; Hawgood, J.; Spence, S.H.; De Leo, D. Suicide and sudden death bereavement in Australia: A longitudinal study of family members over 2 years after death. *Aust. N. Z. J. Psychiatry* **2020**, *54*, 89–98. [CrossRef] [PubMed]
29. Pitman, A.L.; Stevenson, F.; Osborn, D.P.; King, M.B. The stigma associated with bereavement by suicide and other sudden deaths: A qualitative interview study. *Soc. Sci. Med.* **2018**, *1*, 121–129. [CrossRef] [PubMed]
30. Pitman, A.L.; Osborn, D.P.; Rantell, K.; King, M.B. The stigma perceived by people bereaved by suicide and other sudden deaths: A cross-sectional UK study of 3432 bereaved adults. *J. Psychosom. Res.* **2016**, *1*, 22–29. [CrossRef] [PubMed]
31. Kõlves, K.; de Leo, D. Suicide bereavement: Piloting a longitudinal study in Australia. *BMJ Open* **2018**, *8*, e019504. [CrossRef]
32. Kõlves, K.; Zhao, Q.; Ross, V.; Hawgood, J.; Spence, S.H.; De Leo, D. Suicide and other sudden death bereavement of immediate family members: An analysis of grief reactions six-months after death. *J. Affect. Disord.* **2019**, *243*, 96–102. [CrossRef] [PubMed]
33. Queensland Government Coroners Act 2003. Available online: www.legislation.qld.gov.au/view/pdf/inforce/current/act-2003-013 (accessed on 30 September 2022).
34. Entilli, L.; Ross, V.; De Leo, D.; Cipolletta, S.; Kõlves, K. Experiences of parental suicide-bereavement: A longitudinal qualitative analysis over two years. *Int. J. Environ. Res. Public Health* **2021**, *18*, 564. [CrossRef]
35. Ross, V.; Kõlves, K.; Kunde, L.; De Leo, D. Parents' experiences of suicide-bereavement: A qualitative study at 6 and 12 months after loss. *Int. J. Environ. Res. Public Health* **2018**, *15*, 618. [CrossRef] [PubMed]
36. Barrett, T.W.; Scott, T.B. Suicide bereavement and recovery patterns compared with non-suicide bereavement patterns. *Suicide Life-Threat. Behav.* **1990**, *20*, 1–15. [CrossRef] [PubMed]
37. Carver, C.S. You want to measure coping but your protocol's too long: Consider the brief cope. *Int. J. Behav. Med.* **1997**, *4*, 92–100. [CrossRef] [PubMed]
38. Drapeau, C.W.; Cerel, J.; Moore, M. How personality, coping styles, and perceived closeness influence help-seeking attitudes in suicide-bereaved adults. *Death Stud.* **2016**, *40*, 165–171. [CrossRef] [PubMed]
39. Schnider, K.R.; Elhai, J.D.; Gray, M.J. Coping style use predicts posttraumatic stress and complicated grief symptom severity among college students reporting a traumatic loss. *J. Couns. Psychol.* **2007**, *54*, 344. [CrossRef]
40. Jordan, J.R.; McIntosh, J.L. Is suicide bereavement different? Perspectives from research and practice. In *Grief and Bereavement in Contemporary Society*; Neimeyer, R.A., Harris, D.L., Winokuer, H.R., Thornton, G.F., Eds.; Routledge: New York, NY, USA, 2011; pp. 223–234. [CrossRef]
41. Fisher, J.E.; Zhou, J.; Zuleta, R.F.; Fullerton, C.S.; Ursano, R.J.; Cozza, S.J. Coping strategies and considering the possibility of death in those bereaved by sudden and violent deaths: Grief severity, depression, and posttraumatic growth. *Front. Psychiatry* **2020**, *11*, 749. [CrossRef]
42. Akbari, M.; Seydavi, M.; Hosseini, Z.S.; Krafft, J.; Levin, M.E. Experiential avoidance in depression, anxiety, obsessive-compulsive related, and posttraumatic stress disorders: A comprehensive systematic review and meta-analysis. *J. Contextual Behav. Sci.* **2022**, *24*, 65–78. [CrossRef]
43. Stroebe, M.; Stroebe, W.; Schut, H. Gender differences in adjustment to bereavement: An empirical and theoretical review. *Rev. Gen. Psychol.* **2001**, *5*, 62–83. [CrossRef]
44. Lundorff, M.; Bonanno, G.A.; Johannsen, M.; O'Connor, M. Are there gender differences in prolonged grief trajectories? A registry-sampled cohort study. *J. Psychiatr. Res.* **2020**, *129*, 168–175. [CrossRef]
45. Maccallum, F.; Lundorff, M.; Johannsen, M.; Farver-Vestergaard, I.; O'Connor, M. An exploration of gender and prolonged grief symptoms using network analysis. *Psychol. Med.* **2021**, 1–8. [CrossRef]
46. Pitman, A. Addressing suicide risk in partners and relatives bereaved by suicide. *Br. J. Psychiatry* **2018**, *212*, 197–198. [CrossRef]
47. Pitman, A.L.; Rantell, K.; Moran, P.; Sireling, L.; Marston, L.; King, M.; Osborn, D. Support received after bereavement by suicide and other sudden deaths: A cross-sectional UK study of 3432 young bereaved adults. *BMJ Open* **2017**, *7*, e014487. [CrossRef] [PubMed]
48. Andriessen, K. Can postvention be prevention? *Crisis* **2009**, *30*, 43–47. [CrossRef] [PubMed]
49. Levi-Belz, Y.; Aisenberg, D. Interpersonal predictors of suicide ideation and complicated-grief trajectories among suicide bereaved individuals: A four-year longitudinal study. *J. Affect. Disord.* **2021**, *282*, 1030–1035. [CrossRef] [PubMed]
50. Geležėlytė, O.; Gailienė, D.; Latakienė, J.; Mažulytė-Rašytinė, E.; Skruibis, P.; Dadašev, S.; Grigienė, D. Factors of seeking professional psychological help by the bereaved by suicide. *Front. Psychol.* **2020**, *11*, 592. [CrossRef] [PubMed]
51. Chapple, A.; Ziebland, S. How the Internet is changing the experience of bereavement by suicide: A qualitative study in the UK. *Health* **2011**, *15*, 173–187. [CrossRef] [PubMed]
52. Frost, M. The grief grapevine: Facebook memorial pages and adolescent bereavement. *Aust. J. Guid. Couns.* **2014**, *24*, 256–265. [CrossRef]

53. Andriessen, K.; Krysinska, K.; Kõlves, K.; Reavley, N. Suicide postvention service models and guidelines 2014–2019: A systematic review. *Front. Psychol.* **2019**, *10*, 2677. [CrossRef]
54. Scocco, P.; Arbien, M.; Totaro, S.; Guadagnini, M.; Nucci, M. Panta Rhei: A Non-randomized Intervention Trial on the Effectiveness of Mindfulness-Self-compassion Weekend Retreats for People Bereaved by Suicide. *Mindfulness* **2022**, *14*, 1307–1319. [CrossRef]
55. Scocco, P.; Zerbinati, L.; Preti, A.; Ferrari, A.; Totaro, S. Mindfulness-based weekend retreats for people bereaved by suicide (Panta Rhei): A pilot feasibility study. *Psychol. Psychother. Theory Res. Pract.* **2019**, *92*, 39–56. [CrossRef]
56. McGill, K.; Bhullar, N.; Batterham, P.J.; Carrandi, A.; Wayland, S.; Maple, M. Key issues, challenges, and preferred supports for those bereaved by suicide: Insights from postvention experts. *Death Stud.* **2022**, *17*, 1–6. [CrossRef]
57. Stroebe, M.; Schut, H.; Stroebe, W. Health outcomes of bereavement. *Lancet* **2007**, *370*, 1960–1973. [CrossRef]

International Journal of
Environmental Research and Public Health

MDPI

Article

Depression and Suicide Ideation among Suicide-Loss Survivors: A Six-Year Longitudinal Study

Yossi Levi-Belz [1,*] and Shai Birnbaum [1,2]

[1] The Lior Tsfaty Center for Suicide and Mental Pain Studies, Ruppin Academic Center, Emek Hefer 4025000, Israel
[2] Clinical Psychology M.A. Program, Ruppin Academic Center, Emek Hefer 4025000, Israel
* Correspondence: yossil@ruppin.ac.il

Abstract: Suicide is not only a tragic end of life but also may be the beginning of a very challenging life for those left behind. Suicide-loss survivors (SLSs) are individuals who were exposed to the suicide of a close family member or a friend and endure highly emotional distress. The psychological stance and reactions of SLS are deeply colored by painful, intense emotions that are expressed through different psychiatric symptoms, including depression and suicide ideation (SI). The present study investigated the long-term effects of interpersonal factors such as social support, self-disclosure, thwarted belongingness, and perceived burdensomeness on depression and suicidal ideation among SLS. One hundred fifty-two Israeli SLS, aged 20–72, participated in this longitudinal study, during which their suicide ideation and depression levels were assessed at four points over six years (T1-baseline, and two (T2), four (T3), and six (T4) years after baseline). At the last time point, interpersonal factors were also assessed. SLSs' interpersonal variables significantly predicted depression and SI levels beyond their usual trajectories over the years. Significant correlations were found between both perceived burdensomeness and thwarted belongingness and depression levels at all measurement points. Moreover, thwarted belongingness was found to be a significant moderator of the relationship between former and current depression levels, as the contribution of depression-T3 to depression-T4 was lower among SLSs with low thwarted belongingness ($b = 0.14$, CI = 0.05–0.34) compared with SLSs with high thwarted belongingness ($b = 0.25$, CI = 0.22–0.45). These findings emphasize the vital healing role of interpersonal factors such as belongingness, as they may attenuate depression and SI symptoms over time. Hence, clinicians should focus on therapies that boost interpersonal interactions and belongingness, as they seem to be crucial stepping stones on the way to recovery. Moreover, national programs should be implemented to offer SLSs targeted interventions to reduce distress and depression in the aftermath of suicide loss.

Keywords: suicide; depression; suicidal ideation; belongingness; bereavement

Citation: Levi-Belz, Y.; Birnbaum, S. Depression and Suicide Ideation among Suicide-Loss Survivors: A Six-Year Longitudinal Study. *Int. J. Environ. Res. Public Health* **2022**, *19*, 16561. https://doi.org/10.3390/ijerph192416561

Academic Editor: Paul B. Tchounwou

Received: 16 October 2022
Accepted: 7 December 2022
Published: 9 December 2022

1. Introduction

Suicide is not only a tragic end of life but may also be the beginning of a very challenging life for those left behind. Contemporary estimates highlight the profound impact of each suicide on about 60 suicide-loss survivors (SLSs), referring to individuals exposed to the suicide, including family members, friends, co-workers, classmates, or therapists [1–4]. Thus, between 48 million to 500 million people could be considered SLSs annually [5]. The psychological stance and reactions to suicide loss are deeply colored by painfully intense emotions like shame and guilt, which differ at least partly from other bereaved individuals [6–8]. Accordingly, research has highlighted that SLSs are characterized by acute mental pain expressed through highly significant psychiatric symptoms [9]. Serious adverse health, such as higher levels of grief complications and, importantly, higher levels of depression [2] and suicidal ideation [10,11], has been found to be associated with SLSs. These deleterious emotional effects of suicide highlight the importance of studying the influence of suicide on family and friends, as well as ways we can ease the pain and agony that accompany suicide loss.

Only few studies have examined trajectories of depression and SI among SLSs over time. Kõlves et al. [12] examined mental health reactions among SLSs and individuals bereaved by other sudden death events six, 12, and 24 months after their loss, finding that depression levels were significantly reduced over time. In a recent longitudinal study, Levi-Belz and Aisenberg [10] found SI and complicated grief to accompany SLSs, directly and indirectly, over a period of almost 4 years. Another study established a connection between SLSs and subsequent long-term depression 8–10 years following the suicide, finding that the risk of depression and SI decreased over time [13]. While these findings are meaningful, many more studies are needed to explain the contribution of psychological factors to SLSs' depression and SI over time [11]. This study aimed to examine the possible moderators in depression and SI trajectories among SLSs in a six-year longitudinal study.

Several studies have already highlighted factors that might moderate depression and SI consequences among SLSs. For example, De Groot et al. [13] found that children who have lost a parent and individuals with a mental health history were at increased risk 8–10 years after the suicide loss. Other studies found that religious beliefs contribute to psychological adjustment following bereavement [14]. Some self-traits, such as a low sense of control in life, low self-efficacy, and high neuroticism, accounted for elevated depression levels [13]. More recently, another self-attribute, self-forgiveness, was found to exhibit a unique protective effect for SLSs. Self-forgiveness was found to be related to both lower depression and SI for SLSs and had a greater ameliorating effect in this population than in other bereaved individuals [15]. Guilt was also associated with depression and moderated the association between time since the suicide and depressive symptoms [16].

Interestingly, interpersonal factors have gained considerable attention as moderators of depression and SI among SLSs. Much of the spotlight has been centered on perceived social support levels, defined as "an exchange of resources between at least two individuals perceived by the provider or recipient to be intended to enhance the well-being of the recipient" [17]. Investigations have indicated that for SLSs, perceived social support manifests a reverse relationship with depression and SI symptoms [18,19]. In a cross-sectional study [20] relying on the data of 195 convenience-sample SLSs, higher levels of perceived social support were significantly related to lower levels of both depression symptoms and SI. As the study concluded, social support may play an important role in suicide postvention and should be further investigated to better understand the mechanism of its effect [20].

A construct related to perceived social support is self-disclosure, referring to the process by which individuals let themselves be known by others [21]. Self-disclosure was found to be an important protective factor against different psychopathologies among various samples [22,23]. For SLSs, self-disclosure was found to lead to reduced levels of complicated grief, even beyond the natural trajectory of complicated grief over time [24]. In another study, self-disclosure was found to be a protective factor against grief difficulties [25] among a sample of mostly SLSs (131 out of 147 bereaved). However, the protective role of social support and self-disclosure in SLSs' depression and SI remains unclear since longitudinal studies on the moderating role of social support on mental health characteristics among SLSs are scarce.

Interestingly, the relationships between interpersonal factors and mental difficulties such as SI have primarily been examined through Thomas Joiner's interpersonal theory of suicide [26]. This theory emphasizes two main dimensions that may influence depression and SI: perceived burdensomeness (PB) and thwarted belongingness (TB; [27]). PB reflects an affective-cognitive state reflecting the view that one's existence is a burden to friends, family members, or society. It comprises self-hate (e.g., "I hate myself") and feelings of liability (e.g., "I make things worse for people in my life"). TB describes a distinguished cognitive-affective state portrayed by the painful feeling of being alienated or external to one's family, friends, and other valued groups [27]. Since these dimensions have been recognized as comprising the heart of interpersonal interaction [26], it can be suggested that they may contribute an important aspect of interpersonal qualities, thus moderating SLSs' depression and SI.

Recent studies have noted that lower TB levels may serve as a protective factor against SLSs' complicated grief and depression [28]. Levi-Belz and Aisenberg [10] conducted a four-year longitudinal design study and found that TB, but not PB, increases SI for SLSs. On the other hand, PB was found to increase depression levels in various populations [29,30]. However, important information concerning the possible moderation of PB and TB on the evolvement of depressive symptoms over time since suicide loss has yet to be examined.

The Present Study

In the present study, we aimed to explore to what extent interpersonal variables may help SLSs cope more effectively with the deleterious consequences of suicide loss, using 6 years of longitudinal data with four measurement points (T1-index measurement, T2-two years after T1, T3-four years after T1, T4-six years after T1). Specifically, we intended to broaden knowledge regarding depression and SI levels of SLSs over time and examine the moderating effect of interpersonal variables (i.e., perceived social support, self-disclosure, TB, and PB) on SLSs' depression and SI trajectories over time. To date, only a few studies have investigated the contribution of interpersonal factors to the longitudinal course of depression and SI levels among SLSs.

We posited the following hypotheses:

1. Interpersonal variables of social support, self-disclosure, TB, and PB at T4 will contribute to depression and SI symptoms beyond the effect of previous depression and SI levels at T1–T3.
2. Interpersonal variables will moderate the relationship between previous depression and SI levels and current depression and SI levels (T4).

2. Method

2.1. Participants

Participants were 189 Israeli SLSs who were assessed at the T1 measurement point. Of these, 156 (82.5%) were assessed at T2 (1.5 years after T1), and 152 (80.4%) were assessed at T3 and T4 (3.5 years and 5.5 years after T1, respectively). The participants were recruited through social media groups of SLSs in Israel, primarily through the national agency for SLSs in Israel ("The Path to Life").

Of the 37 participants who dropped out from the measurement after T1, 23 could not be located, 13 did not respond to the T2 invitation letter, and one died (due to cancer). We found no significant demographic or psychological differences between participants who completed all four measurements and those who completed only T1. Thus, the current study comprises 152 SLSs (130 females) aged 20–72 at T1. Participants eligible for the study included those who had lost a family member or another close friend due to suicide [2]. Exclusion criteria were the inability to read and write in Hebrew and being under 15 at the time of the suicide (thus including only SLSs whose suicide loss occurred when they were adolescents or older).

2.2. Procedure

Potential participants were required to affirm their willingness to participate by signing an informed consent form. They were also informed of the risks and compensation procedures and were assured anonymity, confidentiality, and their right to withdraw from the study at any time. Those eligible for the study then completed the online questionnaire in Hebrew (using Qualtrics online survey software). At the end of the T1 measurement point, participants were asked if they would agree to be approached again. Those who agreed were invited again at subsequent measurement points (with a gap of approximately two years between measurements). All participants were compensated for their participation (gift vouchers of US $50 were granted for each measurement). The study was approved by the ethics committee at the Ruppin Academic Center.

2.3. Measures

We used perceived burdensomeness, thwarted belongingness, social support, and self-disclosure as independent variables in this study. We used depression and suicide ideation levels as dependent variables. The following section describes each variable and its measurement.

2.3.1. Perceived Burdensomeness (PB) and Thwarted Belongingness (TB)

PB and TB were assessed by the Interpersonal Needs Questionnaire (INQ; Ref. [31]), a 10-statement inventory used to assess either TB (e.g., "These days, other people care about me" [reverse-scored]) and PB (e.g., "These days, I feel like a burden on the people in my life"), with five items presented for each subscale. Each item is presented on a 7-point Likert scale ranging from 1 (*Not at all true for me*) to 7 (*Very true for me*). Higher scores reflected greater TB and PB. TB and PB were measured only at T4. In this study, we used the Hebrew translation of the INQ, which was used in various studies (e.g., Ref. [32]). The internal consistency for the current sample for PB was $\alpha = 0.90$, and for TB, $\alpha = 0.85$.

2.3.2. Social Support

The Multidimensional Scale of Perceived Social Support (MSPPS) was used to assess social support ([33]). The MSPPS is a 12-item questionnaire measuring the perceived adequacy of social support from three sources: family members, friends, and significant others. The 12 items were rated on a 7-point Likert-type scale, ranging from 1 (*disagree very strongly*) to 7 (*agree very strongly*). Higher summed scores indicate greater levels of perceived social support. The MSPSS has good internal and test–retest reliability and a fairly stable factorial structure [34]. It has been used widely in many languages, including Hebrew [35,36]. Social support was measured at T4. The internal consistency for the current sample was $\alpha = 0.92$.

2.3.3. Self-Disclosure

The Distress Disclosure Index (DDI; Ref. [37]) was used to assess the distress disclosure and negative emotions levels. The DDI measures the inclination to disclose distressing information, thoughts, personal problems, and unpleasant emotions across time and situations. The 12 items of the DDI were presented on a 5-point Likert scale, ranging from 1 (*strongly disagree*) to 5 (*strongly agree*). Higher DDI scores reflect a higher degree of disclosing distress to others. The DDI is a highly reliable and valid measure, introducing high coefficients across different samples [38]. Self-disclosure was measured at T4. The internal consistency for the current sample was $\alpha = 0.94$.

2.3.4. Depression

PHQ-9 is a widely used self-administered measure of depression, comprising nine items that reflect the nine DSM-V diagnostic criteria for major depression [39]. Each item assesses the frequency of that symptom over the past two weeks, rated on a 4-point ordinal scale: (0) *Not at all*, (1) *Several days*, (2) *More than half the days*, (3) *Nearly every day*. The PHQ-9 is a valid and reliable measure of depression [39]. The PHQ-9 was validated against professional diagnoses of MDD, resulting in 88% sensitivity and 88% specificity. Depression was measured at three time points (it was not measured at T1) and was found to have adequate to high reliability at T2 ($\alpha = 0.89$), T3 ($\alpha = 0.92$), and T4 ($\alpha = 0.90$).

2.3.5. Suicide Ideation (SI)

Due to the longitudinal nature of the study, only a single item tapping the frequency of current SI was assessed ("How often have you thought about killing yourself in the past year?"), the second item from the four-item Suicidal Behaviors Questionnaire-Revised

(SBQ-R; Ref. [40]). Several studies have used this item to assess suicidality [10,41], and there is strong evidence for a single item's predictive ability and relevance in suicidality assessment [42,43]. The SI item is presented on a 5-point Likert-type scale, ranging from 1 (*never*) to 5 (*very often*; five or more times). Higher scores indicate increased levels of suicide risk. In this study, we administered the Hebrew translation of the SBQ, which has been used in various studies (e.g., Ref. [44]). SI was assessed at all four measurement points.

2.3.6. Demographic and Suicide-Related Characteristics

In addition to the above measures, demographic and suicide loss characteristics were collected for each participant, including the age, gender, family status, the ages of the SLSs and the deceased at the time of the suicide, the time since the suicide event, and the participants' relatedness to the person who died by suicide.

2.4. Data Analysis

First, we performed a series of Pearson correlation tests and ANOVA analyses with Bonferroni correction to examine the relationships between the study variables. Then, we conducted hierarchical multiple regression analyses with depression-T4 and SI-T4 as dependent variables to further investigate the effect of interpersonal variables and hypothesized interactions beyond the effect of previous depression or SI levels. Lastly, as recommended by Aiken et al. [45], all continuous predictor variables were standardized, as were the cross-product interaction terms. To examine the nature of the interaction within a regression framework, moderation analysis was performed using the PROCESS macro (Model 1; Ref. [46]). All analyses were conducted using the Statistical Package for the Social Sciences (SPSS, v26.0 for Windows, Armonk, NY, USA). The significance level for all statistical tests was set at 0.05.

3. Results

3.1. Demographic Information of the Sample

At T4, the mean age of the sample was 45.9 (SD = 14.7). Regarding the participants' family status, 72 (47%) were married, 61 (40%) were single, nine were divorced (6%), and 10 (7%) were widowed. Most participants reported their Jewish religiosity as secular (115, 75%), with a minority (28, 18%) reporting to be religiously observant. Regarding socioeconomic status (SES), 36 (23.8%) participants reported their SES as very low, 39 (26%) as low, 38 (25%) as medium, and 38 (24%) as high. Regarding schooling, almost all participants (n = 151, 99.3%) reported completing at least 12 years, and almost 70% (n = 105) reported having a college degree. Regarding residential areas within Israel, 55% of the sample reside in central Israel, 20% in the north, and 25% in the south. In all, the participants reported 40 different cities, with the largest numbers in Tel Aviv (15%) and Haifa (7%).

3.2. Suicide-Related Characteristics

The participants reported various levels of relationship to the deceased: 29 were parents to the deceased (18.6%), 26 children (16.7%), 43 siblings (27.6%), 16 spouses (10.3%), 13 (8.4%) other family relatives, and 29 (18.6%) best friends. At T1, time since the suicide varied among the participants (M_{months} = 80), with a range of 6 to 200 months: 27 participants (17.7%) had lost their significant other within 24 months prior to T1, 38 (25%) within 24–48 months, 44 (29%) within 48–72 months, and the remainder (43; 28.2%) six years or more prior to T1. At the time of the suicide, the participants' mean age was 31.1 (SD = 15.3), ranging from 16 to 62. All participants reported being devastated by the suicide, ranging between extremely devastated (47, 30.8%), highly devastated (84, 55.8%), and devastated (20, 13.4%).

3.3. Depression and Suicide Ideation over Time

To examine SLSs' depression and SI trajectories, two repeated measure ANOVA analyses were conducted (see Figure 1). For depression, the effect of time was found to be insignificant. For SI, the effect of time was significant, $F(3, 453) = 75.02$, $p < 0.001$, $\eta 2 = 0.33$]. SI levels increased from T1 ($M = 1.74$, $SD = 1.15$) to T2 ($M = 2.85$, $SD = 1.05$) and then decreased at T3 ($M = 2.38$, $SD = 1.05$) and at T4 ($M = 1.54$, $SD = 0.59$).

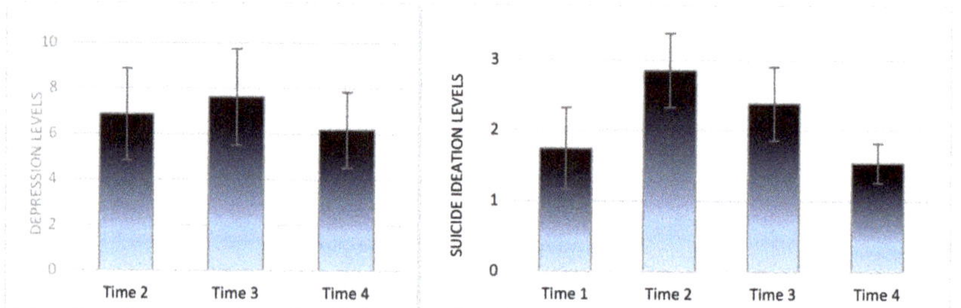

Figure 1. Depression and suicide ideation levels over time among suicide-loss survivors ($N = 152$).

3.4. Relationships between the Study Variables

Pearson correlations were calculated between the study variables to examine associations between interpersonal factors and depression/SI over time. As can be seen in Table 1, social support was negatively correlated with depression-T2 ($r_{150} = -0.37$, $p < 0.001$), but not with any other measures of depression or SI. Self-disclosure was negatively associated with depression-T3 and depression-T4, but not with depression-T2 nor with SI levels. PB-T4 was associated with depression at all time measures: PB-T4 was associated with depression-T2 ($r_{150} = 0.32$, $p < 0.001$), depression-T3 ($r_{150} = 0.26$, $p = 0.002$), and depression-T4 ($r_{150} = 0.56$, $p < 0.001$). PB was also associated with SI-T1 ($r_{150} = 0.26$, $p = 0.001$) and SI-T4 ($r_{150} = 0.31$, $p < 0.001$). Similarly, TB was associated with depression-T2 ($r_{150} = 0.19$, $p = 0.02$), depression-T3 ($r_{150} = 0.2$, $p = 0.016$) and depression-T4 ($r_{150} = 0.42$, $p < 0.001$). TB was also associated with SI-T1, ($r_{150} = 0.25$, $p = 0.002$) and SI-T4 ($r_{150} = 0.32$, $p < 0.001$).

Table 1. Inter-correlations among the study variables ($N = 152$).

Variable	1	2	3	4	5	6	7	8	9	10	11	12
1. Time since suicide	–											
2. Depression-T2	−0.111	–										
3. Depression-T3	−0.055	0.320 ***	–									
4. Depression-T4	0.005	0.426 ***	0.457 ***	–								
5. SI-T1	−0.013	0.274 ***	0.168 *	0.275 ***	–							
6. SI-T2	0.115	0.173 *	0.145	0.003	0.237 **	–						
7. SI-T3	0.040	0.246 **	0.383 ***	0.356 ***	0.205 *	0.309 ***	–					
8. SI-T4	0.150	0.166 *	0.220 **	0.524 ***	0.361 ***	0.212 **	0.336 ***	–				
9. Social Support-T4	0.121	−0.076	−0.366 ***	−0.074	−0.012	−0.095	−0.107	−0.142	–			
10. Self-Disclosure-T4	0.089	−0.015	−0.200 *	−0.180 *	0.010	0.022	0.018	0.025	0.52 1 ***	–		
11. PB-T4	−0.005	0.317 ***	0.255 **	0.551 ***	0.264 ***	0.014	0.046	0.315 ***	−0.201 **	−0.242 ***	–	
12. TB-T4	−0.055	0.189 *	0.195 *	0.421 ***	0.249 **	0.130	0.124	0.318 ***	−0.490 ***	−0.428 ***	0.709 ***	–
M	9.72	6.86	7.62	6.18	1.74	2.85	2.38	1.54	5.47	3.66	12.9	20.35
SD	9.06	4.04	4.23	3.32	1.15	1.05	1.05	0.56	0.68	0.69	3.82	5.39

Note. * $p < 0.05$, ** $p < 0.01$, *** $p < 0.001$. Time since suicide = measured in years. Depression = as assessed by the PHQ9. SI = suicide ideation = measured by the SBQ-r Item 2. Social Support = measured by the MSPSS. Self-Disclosure = measured by the DDI. PB and TB (perceived burdensomeness and thwarted belongingness) = measured by the INQ.

3.5. Effect of Interpersonal Variables on Depression at T4

To examine the contribution of interpersonal factors on depression over time, a hierarchical regression analysis was applied, with depression-T4 as the dependent variable (see Table 2). To control statistically for the time since suicide, this variable was entered into the equation in the first step. In the second step, the main effects of depression-T2 and depression-T3 were entered into the equation. Social support-T4 and self-disclosure-T4 were entered in the third step. In the final step, PB-T4 and TB-T4 were entered into the equation. This analysis enabled us to interpret the effect of interpersonal variables beyond the influence of time since suicide and previous depression levels.

Table 2. Summary of Hierarchical Regression Coefficients of Depression among SLSs by Previous Depression and Interpersonal Variables. ($N = 152$).

Predictor Variables	Step 1			Step 2			Step 3			Step 4		
	B	t	β	B	t	β	B	t	β	B	t	β
Time Since Suicide	0.002	0.058	0.005	0.024	0.864	0.060	0.023	0.828	0.057	0.014	0.588	0.035
Depression-T2				2.555	4.358	0.318 ***	2.569	4.461	0.320 ***	1.653	3.130	0.206 **
Depression-T3				2.751	4.940	0.359 ***	2.971	5.072	0.387 ***	2.807	5.333	0.366 ***
Social Support T4							−1.010	−2.289	−0.191 *	−1.495	−3.484	−0.283 ***
Self-Disclosure T4							−1.052	−2.557	−0.202 *	−0.495	−1.326	−0.095
PB-T4										0.257	2.957	0.272 **
TB-T4										0.146	2.167	0.218 *
R^2 (ΔR^2)	**0% (0%)**			**30% (30%)**			**33.6% (3.6%)**			**49.3% (15.7%)**		
***F* change**	***F*(1, 150) = 0.00**			***F*(2, 148) = 31.67 *****			***F*(2, 146) = 3.99 ***			***F*(2, 144) = 22.23 *****		
Sig.	**0.954**			**0.000**			**0.021**			**0.000**		

Note. * $p < 0.05$, ** $p < 0.01$, *** $p < 0.001$. Time since suicide = measured in years. Depression = assessed by the PHQ9. Social Support = measured by the MSPSS. Self-Disclosure = measured by the DDI. PB and TB (perceived burdensomeness and thwarted belongingness) = measured by the INQ.

Overall, the total set of variables explained 49.3% of the variance for depression-T4, $F(7, 144) = 19.98$, $p < 0.001$. As seen in Table 2, time since suicide was not found to be a significant predictor. In Step 2, a model incorporating the main effect of depression-T2 [Beta = 0.32, $t(148) = 4.36$, $p < 0.001$] and depression-T3 [Beta = 0.36, $t(148) = 4.94$, $p < 0.001$] accounted for 30% of the variance and significantly predicted depression-T4, $F(2, 148) = 31.67$, $p < 0.001$. In Step 3, the main effect of social support [Beta = −0.19, $t(146) = -2.29$, $p = 0.024$] and self-disclosure [Beta = −0.20, $t(146) = -2.56$, $p < 0.012$] significantly predicted depression-T4 and accounted for another 3.6% of the total variance, $F(2, 146) = 3.99$, $p = 0.021$. In the final step, PB-T4 [Beta = 0.27, $t(144) = 2.96$, $p = 0.004$] and TB [Beta = 0.22, $t(144) = 2.17$, $p = 0.032$] significantly and positively contributed to depression-T4 beyond all other variables, accounting for another 15.7% of the total variance, $F(2, 144) = 22.23$, $p < 0.001$].

To understand the direct effect of each one of the interpersonal variables, we performed an additional regression analysis with all of the interpersonal variables as predictors of depression at T4. Social support (Beta = −0.16, $p = 0.042$; $\Delta R^2 = 0.02$ F change = 3.55, $p = 0.042$), PB (Beta = 0.42, $p = 0.000$; $\Delta R^2 = 0.15$ F change = 40.06, $p = 0.001$) and TB (Beta = 0.27, $p = 0.007$; $\Delta R^2 = 0.05$ F change = 8.57, $p = 0.007$) were all found to be significant predictors of depression-T4, whereas self-disclosure contributed negatively but insignificantly to depression-T4.

3.6. Interpersonal Effect on Suicide Ideation at T4

To determine whether PB and TB can predict SI for SLSs, a hierarchical regression analysis was applied. A regression equation was constructed with SI-T4 as the dependent variable (see Table 3). To control for the time since suicide, the variable was entered into the equation in Step 1. In Step 2, the main effects of SI-T1, SI-T2, and SI-T3 were entered into the equation. Social support-T4 and self-disclosure-T4 were entered in Step 3. In the final step, PB-T4 and TB-T4 were entered into the equation. This analysis enabled us to interpret the effect of interpersonal variables beyond the influence of time since suicide and previous SI levels.

Table 3. Summary of Hierarchical Regression Coefficients of SI among SLSs by Previous SI and interpersonal variables ($N = 152$).

Predictor Variables	Step 1			Step 2			Step 3			Step 4		
	B	t	β	B	t	β	B	t	β	B	t	β
Time Since Suicide	0.009	1.861	0.150	0.008	1.894	0.139	0.009	2.106	0.154 *	0.009	2.083	0.148 *
SI-T1				0.145	3.969	0.300 ***	0.147	4.060	0.305 ***	0.110	2.996	0.228 **
SI-T2				0.024	0.582	0.046	0.015	0.370	0.029	0.018	0.449	0.034
SI-T3				0.135	3.305	0.255 ***	0.126	3.086	0.238 **	0.123	3.130	0.234 **
Social Support T4							−0.144	−2.086	−0.180 *	−0.094	−1.311	−0.117
Self-Disclosure T4							0.078	1.148	0.98	0.128	1.885	0.160
PB-T4										0.025	1.628	0.165
TB-T4										0.014	1.143	0.133
R^2 (ΔR^2)	**2.3% (2.3%)**			**22.5% (20.2%)**			**24.7% (2.2%)**			**30.5% (5.8%)**		
***F* change**	***F*(1, 150) = 3.5**			***F*(3, 147) = 12.763 *****			***F*(2, 145) = 2.178**			***F*(2, 143) = 5.955 ****		
Sig.	**0.065**			**0.000**			**0.117**			**0.003**		

Note. * $p < 0.05$, ** $p < 0.01$, *** $p < 0.001$. Time since suicide = measured in years. SI = Suicide Ideation as measured by the SBQ-r item 2. Social Support = as measured by the MSPSS. Self-Disclosure = as measured by the DDI. PB & TB = Perceived Burdensomeness and Thwarted Belongingness as measured by the INQ.

Overall, the total set of variables explained 30.5% of the variance for SI-T4, $F(8, 143) = 7.847$, $p < 0.001$. In Step 1 (see Table 3), time since suicide was not found to be a significant predictor. In Step 2, a model incorporating the main effect of SI-T1, SI-T2, and SI-T3, accounted for a further 20.2% of the variance in predicting SI-T4, $F(3, 147) = 12.763$, $p < 0.001$. Both SI-T1 [Beta = 0.30, $t(147) = 4.06$, $p < 0.001$] and SI-T3 levels [Beta = 0.25, $t(147) = 3.30$, $p < 0.001$] were highly correlated with SI-T4. In Step 3, the main effect of social support-T4 [Beta = −0.19, $t(145) = -2.42$, $p = 0.017$] significantly predicted lower SI-T4, but together with self-disclosure did not add a significant explanation to the SI-T4 variance. In the final step, PB-T4 and TB-T4 together accounted for 5.8% in predicting SI-T4 after all other variables had been entered, $F(2, 143) = 5.955$, $p < 0.003$.

To understand the direct effect of each interpersonal variable discretely, we performed an additional regression analysis with all the interpersonal variables as predictors of SI at T4. Social support (Beta = −0.18, $p = 0.044$; $\Delta R^2 = 0.025$ F change = 4.88, $p = 0.030$) and TB (Beta = 0.19, $p = 0.050$; $\Delta R^2 = 0.02$ F change = 3.56, $p = 0.007$) were found to be significant predictors of SI-T4, whereas self-disclosure and PB were not related significantly to SI-T4.

3.7. Moderation Analysis

Following the hierarchical regression results, we employed moderation analyses of significant interactions using the PROCESS macro (Model 1; Ref. [46]). Moderation analyses were conducted with depression-T4 as the dependent variable and depression-T3 as the independent variable. TB levels served as the moderator. The trajectory of depression (depression-T2) was entered as a covariate. As seen in Figure 2, a significant interaction was found between depression-T3 and TB in predicting depression-T4, b = −0.02, SE = 0.01, 95% CI [−0.03, −0.01], $t(147) = 1.95$, $p = 0.05$. Probing the interaction revealed that for SLSs with low/moderate/high levels of TB, depression-T3 positively contributed to depression-T4: the correlation between depression-T3 and depression-T4 was lower for low TB: b = 14.9, SE = 0.07, 95% CI [0.05, 0.34], $t(147) = 2.71$, $p = 0.001$; higher for moderate *SD*: b = 20.27, SE = 0.05, 95% CI [0.15, 0.38], $t(147) = 4.76$, $p < 0.001$, and the highest for high TB: b = 25.65, SE = 0.06, 95% CI [0.22, 0.45], $t(147) = 5.65$, $p < 0.001$.

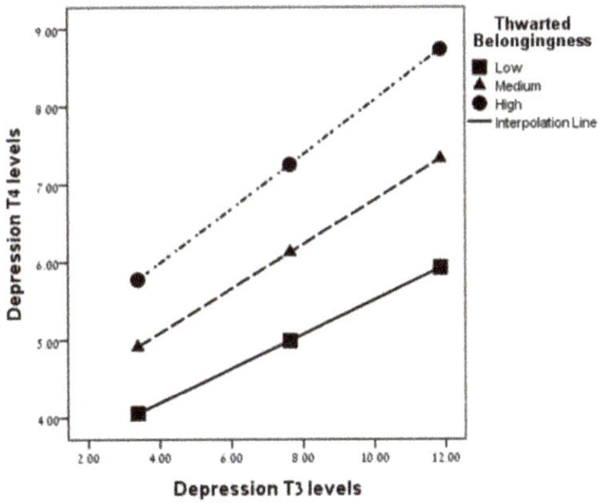

Figure 2. The moderation of thwarted belongingness on the association between depression-T3 and depression-T4 (N = 152).

3.8. DAG Analysis

To establish the correctness of the presented interaction in Figure 1, we conducted a directed acyclic graph (DAG) of an alternative moderation between the variables, in which the independent and the outcome measures switch. As seen in Figure 3, the DAG presentation shows no interaction between depression-T4 and TB when predicting depression-T3 as outcome measures (b = 0.00, SE = 0.01, 95% CI [−0.03, 0.03], $t(147) = 0.21$, $p = 0.79$). These findings help confirm the above interaction.

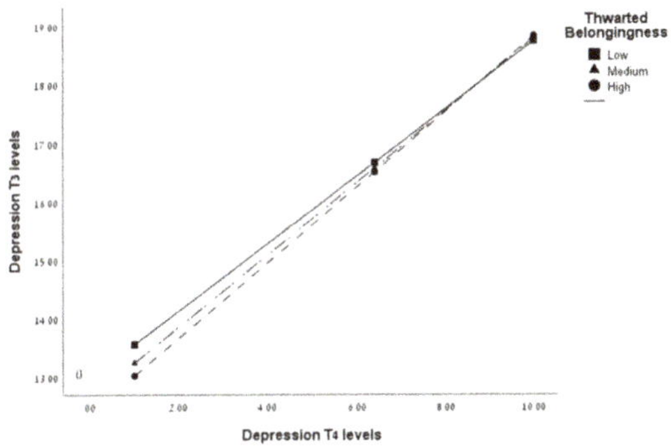

Figure 3. DAG representation of the moderation of thwarted belongingness on the association between depression-T4 and depression-T3 (N = 152).

4. Discussion

This study aimed to investigate the contribution of interpersonal factors to SLSs' course of depression and suicide ideation over time. To our knowledge, this study is the first to address the moderating role of interpersonal factors in decreasing depression and SI beyond their natural trajectories among SLSs. As expected, significant trajectories were found regarding depression and SI over time, meaning that both depression and SI in T1-T3 were strongly correlated with depression and SI at T4. However, importantly as hypothesized, the interpersonal factors of social support, self-disclosure, PB, and TB contributed to depression and SI at T4 above and beyond their natural trajectories. Thus, SLSs with higher levels of interpersonal abilities showed lower levels of depression than those with lower levels of interpersonal abilities.

Furthermore, TB was found to be a significant moderator in the link between depression at T3 and T4, as SLSs who reported a higher belongingness experience showed lower levels of depression at T4 and a lower association between depression at T3 and T4, compared with SLSs who reported moderate or low levels of a belongingness experience. Thus, it may be suggested that belongingness serves as a buffer for depression among SLSs. Taken together, these results highlight the critical role of interpersonal factors, specifically the belongingness experience, as a possible protective factor against developing depression in the aftermath of suicide loss.

What can explain the importance of belongingness and social support as a protective factor against depression among SLSs? Several explanations warrant mentioning. First, when SLSs feel thwarted belongingness and lack of social support, it may reflect a lower quality of social relationships with their surroundings. Such relationships may amplify the oppressive experience of blame and shame, which characterize many SLSs (e.g., Refs. [5,47]) and hinder their recovery from depressive symptoms. The more acute grieving process of SLSs with high TB [10] may also play a role in the association between low social relationships and depression, promoting lasting symptoms of depression for the high TB group. On the other hand, a higher sense of belongingness, viewed as one of the fundamental human psychological needs [48], may function as a buffer against the stigma and shame experienced by SLSs [5,47] and, as a result, shield SLSs from mental pain and even depression.

From another perspective, it can be suggested that the belongingness experience and better social relationships may facilitate more effective coping with depression for SLSs. Moreover, a greater sense of belongingness and social support may lead to greater prospects of self-disclosure to others, which, in turn, can promote sharing of intimate thoughts and emotions and create closer, more intimate, supportive bonds and feeling loved [24]. Together, these factors may help reduce loneliness, one of the primary characteristics of SLSs [49], closely associated with depression levels [50].

Low TB levels have also been shown to be enhanced by engaging in interpersonal activities such as disclosing intimate information and gaining support from the SLSs' surroundings [51]; both reflect feelings of being connected to and supported by significant others. It can be suggested that sharing personal information with others (reflecting a sense of belongingness) and revealing and processing emotional aspects of the trauma may facilitate intimacy and togetherness among SLSs, which are recognized as protective factors against distress. The knowledge that the individual is not bound to face loneliness and rejection from others may help alleviate the devastating emotional aspects of the suicide loss, such as depression [52]. This notion aligns with several studies highlighting the impact of social factors on depression reduction (e.g., [53,54]).

Our study had some methodological limitations. First, we used self-report questionnaires in this study, which may be less reliable and partially biased to self-presentation and inaccurate reporting of mental health-related items. Future studies should apply other types of measures. Second, most participants were members of either an SLS nonprofit organization or the Internet forum dedicated to dealing with suicide loss. Participants in these mutual help forums may be inclined to seek more support and be less isolated than other SLSs, making the current sample less representative. The relatively low levels of depression that the participants reported may be evidence of the low representativeness of the general SLS population, which is known to suffer from high distress following the suicide event. Lastly, interpersonal factors were measured in our study only at T4. Thus, these factors may have been influenced by the levels of depression and SI at T1-T3. Future studies should seek to examine these factors before the suicide loss as well, shedding light on pre-trauma characteristics that may help SLSs cope with depression and SI following their loss.

5. Conclusions and Implications

Taken together, these findings highlight the important role of interpersonal factors in decreasing SLSs' depression and SI levels. It may be suggested that when an SLS feels supported by others, senses that they belong to family and community, and can communicate pain without feeling like a burden, their healing process accelerates beyond the natural depression and SI course. Thus, it can be suggested that psychological interventions with SLSs should incorporate targeted interpersonal components that address these topics. Interventions such as interpersonal psychotherapy [55], which aims to help patients resolve interpersonal problems by employing techniques that enhance social support and reduce interpersonal stress, may be particularly effective in changing the course of coping with suicide loss [56]. Support groups for SLSs can also contribute to the healing process. They offer unique opportunities for SLSs to cope with TB, loneliness, and self-stigmatization [57] and be a place to normalize their grief experiences and share ways of coping with the suicide death [58]. Thus, it is recommended that health services proactively provide SLSs with timely and ongoing information on available support formats, including peer support groups, to minimize negative health outcomes.

More broadly, our findings suggest administering targeted postvention programs for SLSs that help them receive better social support, educating health professionals about SLSs' psychological needs, and diminishing the stigmatization of suicide loss in the general population. These programs may aid SLSs in experiencing a greater sense of belongingness in their surroundings and, thus, enable them to cope better with the distress accompanying suicide loss [59]. It is reasonable to assume that these recommended programs, when implemented broadly and nationally, have the potential to substantially improve the life of SLSs in the aftermath of suicide loss.

Author Contributions: Conceptualization, Y.L.-B.; Formal analysis, Y.L.-B. and S.B.; Methodology, Y.L.-B.; Supervision, Y.L.-B.; Validation, S.B.; Writing—original draft, S.B. All authors have read and agreed to the published version of the manuscript.

Funding: This research was funded by American Foundation for Suicide Prevention (PRG-2-083-14).

Institutional Review Board Statement: The study was conducted in accordance with the Declaration of Helsinki and approved by the Institutional Review Board of Ruppin Academic Center (protocol code 122, 5/1/2015).

Informed Consent Statement: Informed consent was obtained from all subjects involved in the study.

Data Availability Statement: Due to ethical concerns, supporting data cannot be made openly available. Further information about the data and conditions for access can be received by approaching the corresponding author.

Conflicts of Interest: The authors declare no conflict of interest.

References

1. Bartik, W.J.; Maple, M.; McKay, K. Youth suicide bereavement and the continuum of risk. *Crisis* **2020**, *41*, 483–489. [CrossRef]
2. Cerel, J.; Maple, M.; van de Venne, J.; Moore, M.; Flaherty, C.; Brown, M. Exposure to suicide in the community: Prevalence and correlates in one US state. *Public Health Rep.* **2016**, *131*, 100–107. [CrossRef]
3. Jordan, J.R.; McIntosh, J.L. Suicide bereavement: Why study survivors of suicide loss? In *Grief after Suicide: Understanding the Consequences and Caring for the Survivors*; Jordan, J.R., McIntosh, J.L., Eds.; Routledge: London, UK, 2011; pp. 3–17.
4. Maple, M.; Cerel, J.; Sanford, R.; Pearce, T.; Jordan, J.R. Is exposure to suicide beyond kin associated with risk for suicidal behavior? A systematic review of the evidence. *Suicide Life-Threat.* **2017**, *47*, 461–474. [CrossRef] [PubMed]
5. Pitman, A.; Osborn, D.; King, M.; Erlangsen, A. Effects of suicide bereavement on mental health and suicide risk. *Lancet Psychiatry* **2014**, *1*, 86–94. [CrossRef] [PubMed]
6. Camacho, D.; Pérez-Nieto, M.Á.; Gordillo, F. The role of rumination in the guilt associated with bereavement according to cause of death. *Psychiatry Res.* **2018**, *270*, 1053–1058. [CrossRef]
7. Jordan, J.R. Is suicide bereavement different? A reassessment of the literature. *Suicide Life-Threat. Behav.* **2001**, *31*, 91–102. [CrossRef] [PubMed]
8. Jordan, J.R. Lessons learned: Forty years of clinical work with suicide loss survivors. *Front. Psychol.* **2020**, *11*, 766. [CrossRef] [PubMed]
9. Erlangsen, A.; Runeson, B.; Bolton, J.M.; Wilcox, H.C.; Forman, J.L.; Krogh, J.; Shear, M.K.; Nordentoft, M.; Conwell, Y. Association between spousal suicide and mental, physical, and social health outcomes: A longitudinal and nationwide register-based study. *JAMA Psychiatry* **2017**, *74*, 456–464. [CrossRef] [PubMed]

10. Levi-Belz, Y.; Aisenberg, D. Interpersonal predictors of suicide ideation and complicated-grief trajectories among suicide bereaved individuals: A four-year longitudinal study. *J. Affect. Disord.* **2021**, *282*, 1030–1035. [CrossRef] [PubMed]
11. Williams, J.L.; Eddinger, J.R.; Rynearson, E.K.; Rheingold, A.A. Prevalence and correlates of suicidal ideation in a treatment-seeking sample of violent loss survivors. *Crisis* **2018**, *39*, 377–385. [CrossRef]
12. Kõlves, K.; Zhao, Q.; Ross, V.; Hawgood, J.; Spence, S.H.; De Leo, D. Suicide and sudden death bereavement in Australia: A longitudinal study of family members over 2 years after death. *Aust. N. Z. J. Psychiatry* **2020**, *54*, 89–98. [CrossRef] [PubMed]
13. De Groot, M.; Kollen, B.J. Course of bereavement over 8–10 years in first degree relatives and spouses of people who committed suicide: Longitudinal community-based cohort study. *Br. Med. J.* **2013**, *347*, f6649. [CrossRef]
14. Wortmann, J.H.; Park, C.L. Religion and spirituality in adjustment following bereavement: An integrative review. *Death Stud.* **2008**, *32*, 703–736. [CrossRef] [PubMed]
15. Levi-Belz, Y.; Gilo, T. Emotional distress among suicide survivors: The moderating role of self-forgiveness. *Front. Psychiatry* **2020**, *11*, 341. [CrossRef] [PubMed]
16. Wagner, B.; Hofmann, L.; Grafiadeli, R. The relationship between guilt, depression, prolonged grief, and posttraumatic stress symptoms after suicide bereavement. *J. Clin. Psychol.* **2021**, *77*, 2545–2558. [CrossRef] [PubMed]
17. Shumaker, S.A.; Brownell, A. Toward a theory of social support: Closing conceptual gaps. *J. Soc. Issues* **1984**, *40*, 11–36. [CrossRef]
18. Scocco, P.; Idotta, C.; Mareschi, T.; Preti, A.; SOPROXI Team. Do interpersonal events buffer or worsen depressive and grief related symptoms in people bereaved through suicide? *Death Stud.* **2020**, *46*, 1344–1353. [CrossRef]
19. Spino, E.; Kameg, K.M.; Cline, T.W.; Terhorst, L.; Mitchell, A.M. Impact of social support on symptoms of depression and loneliness in survivors bereaved by suicide. *Arch. Psychiatr. Nurs.* **2016**, *30*, 602–606. [CrossRef]
20. Oexle, N.; Sheehan, L. Perceived social support and mental health after suicide loss. *Crisis* **2019**, *41*, 65–69. [CrossRef]
21. Jourard, S.M. *Self-Disclosure: An Experimental Analysis of the Transparent Self*; John Wiley: New York, NY, USA, 1971.
22. Farber, B.A.; Khurgin-Bott, R.; Feldman, S. The benefits and risks of patient self-disclosure in the psychotherapy of women with a history of childhood sexual abuse. *Psychother. Theory Res. Pract. Train.* **2009**, *46*, 52. [CrossRef]
23. Harvey, J.; Boynton, K. Self-disclosure and psychological resilience: The mediating roles of self-esteem and self-compassion. *Interpersona Int. J. Pers. Relatsh.* **2021**, *15*, 90–104. [CrossRef]
24. Levi-Belz, Y.; Lev-Ari, L. Let's Talk About It: The moderating role of self-disclosure on complicated grief over time among suicide survivors. *Int. J. Environ. Res. Public Health* **2019**, *16*, 3740. [CrossRef] [PubMed]
25. Feigelman, W.; Cerel, J.; Sanford, R. Disclosure in traumatic deaths as correlates of differential mental health outcomes. *Death Stud.* **2018**, *42*, 456–462. [CrossRef]
26. Joiner, T. *Why People Die by Suicide*; Harvard University Press: Cambridge, MA, USA, 2005.
27. Van Orden, K.A.; Witte, T.K.; Cukrowicz, K.C.; Braithwaite, S.R.; Selby, E.A.; Joiner, T.E., Jr. The interpersonal theory of suicide. *Psychol. Rev.* **2010**, *117*, 575–600. [CrossRef]
28. Levi-Belz, Y.; Feigelman, W. Pulling together—The protective role of belongingness for depression, suicidal ideation and behavior among suicide-bereaved individuals. *Crisis* **2021**, *43*, 278. [CrossRef]
29. Bell, C.M.; Ridley, J.A.; Overholser, J.C.; Young, K.; Athey, A.; Lehmann, J.; Phillips, K. The role of perceived burden and social support in suicide and depression. *Suicide Life-Threat. Behav.* **2018**, *48*, 87–94. [CrossRef]
30. Nalipay, M.J.N.; Ku, L. Indirect effect of hopelessness on depression symptoms through perceived burdensomeness. *Psychol. Rep.* **2019**, *122*, 1618–1631. [CrossRef]
31. Joiner, T.E.; Van Orden, K.A.; Witte, T.K.; Selby, E.A.; Ribeiro, J.D.; Lewis, R.; Rudd, M.D. Main predictions of the interpersonal–psychological theory of suicidal behavior: Empirical tests in two samples of young adults. *J. Abnorm. Psychol.* **2009**, *118*, 634–646. [CrossRef]
32. Levi-Belz, Y. With a little help from my friends: A follow-up study on the contribution of interpersonal characteristics to posttraumatic growth among suicide-loss survivors. *Psychol. Trauma* **2019**, *11*, 895–904. [CrossRef]
33. Zimet, G.D.; Powell, S.S.; Farley, G.K.; Werkman, S.; Berkoff, K.A. Psychometric characteristics of the multidimensional scale of perceived social support. *J. Personal. Assess.* **1990**, *55*, 610–617. [PubMed]
34. Kazarian, S.S.; McCabe, S.B. Dimensions of social support in the MSPSS: Factorial structure, reliability, and theoretical implications. *J. Community Psychol.* **1991**, *19*, 150–160. [CrossRef]
35. Levi-Belz, Y.; Dichter, N.; Zerach, G. Moral injury and suicide ideation among Israeli combat veterans: The contribution of self-forgiveness and perceived social support. *J. Interpers. Violence* **2022**, *37*, 1031–1057. [CrossRef] [PubMed]
36. Slonim-Nevo, V.; Sarid, O.; Friger, M.; Schwartz, D.; Sergienko, R.; Pereg, A.; Vardi, H.; Singer, T.; Chernin, E.; Greenberg, D.; et al. Effect of social support on psychological distress and disease activity in inflammatory bowel disease patients. *Inflamm. Bowel Dis.* **2018**, *24*, 1389–1400. [CrossRef]
37. Kahn, J.H.; Hessling, R.M. Measuring the tendency to conceal versus disclose psychological distress. *J. Soc. Clin. Psychol.* **2001**, *20*, 41–65. [CrossRef]
38. Kahn, J.H.; Hucke, B.E.; Bradley, A.M.; Glinski, A.J.; Malak, B.L. The distress disclosure index: A research review and multi-trait-multimethod examination. *J. Couns. Psychol.* **2012**, *59*, 134–149. [CrossRef]
39. Kroenke, K.; Spitzer, R.L.; Williams, J.B. The PHQ-9: Validity of a brief depression severity measure. *J. Gen. Intern. Med.* **2001**, *16*, 606–613. [CrossRef]

40. Osman, A.; Bagge, C.L.; Gutierrez, P.M.; Konick, L.C.; Kopper, B.A.; Barrios, F.X. The Suicidal Behaviors Questionnaire-Revised (SBQ-R): Validation with clinical and nonclinical samples. *Assessment* **2001**, *8*, 443–454. [CrossRef]
41. Brailovskaia, J.; Teismann, T.; Margraf, J. Positive mental health, stressful life events, and suicide ideation. *Crisis* **2020**, *41*, 383–388. [CrossRef]
42. Green, K.L.; Brown, G.K.; Jager-Hyman, S.; Cha, J.; Steer, R.A.; Beck, A.T. The predictive validity of the Beck Depression Inventory suicide item. *J. Clin. Psychiatry* **2015**, *76*, 1683–1686. [CrossRef]
43. Simon, G.E.; Rutter, C.M.; Peterson, D.; Oliver, M.; Whiteside, U.; Operskalski, B.; Ludman, E.J. Does response on the PHQ-9 Depression Questionnaire predict subsequent suicide attempt or suicide death? *Psychiatr. Serv.* **2013**, *64*, 1195–1202. [CrossRef]
44. Levi-Belz, Y.; Zerach, G. Moral injury, suicide ideation, and behavior among combat veterans: The mediating roles of entrapment and depression. *Psychiatry Res.* **2018**, *269*, 508–516. [CrossRef] [PubMed]
45. Aiken, L.S.; West, S.G.; Reno, R.R. *Multiple Regression: Testing and Interpreting Interactions*; Sage: New York, NY, USA, 1991.
46. Hayes, A.F.; Montoya, A.K. A tutorial on testing, visualizing, and probing an interaction involving a multicategorical variable in linear regression analysis. *Commun. Methods Meas.* **2017**, *11*, 1–30. [CrossRef]
47. Levi-Belz, Y.; Ben-Yaish, T. Prolonged grief symptoms among suicide-loss survivors: The contribution of intrapersonal and interpersonal characteristics. *Int. J. Environ. Res. Public Health* **2022**, *19*, 10545. [CrossRef]
48. Baumeister, R.F.; Leary, M.R. The need to belong: Desire for interpersonal attachments as a fundamental human motivation. *Psychol. Bull.* **1995**, *117*, 497–529. [CrossRef]
49. Jordan, J.R. Bereavement after suicide. *Psychiatr. Ann.* **2008**, *38*, 679–685. [CrossRef]
50. Erzen, E.; Çikrikci, Ö. The effect of loneliness on depression: A meta-analysis. *Int. J. Soc. Psychiatry* **2018**, *64*, 427–435. [CrossRef]
51. Levi-Belz, Y.; Lev-Ari, L. Is there anybody out there? Attachment style and interpersonal facilitators as protective factors against complicated grief among suicide-loss survivors. *J. Nerv. Ment. Dis.* **2019**, *207*, 131–136. [CrossRef]
52. Mitchell, A.M.; Sakraida, T.J.; Kim, Y.; Bullian, L.; Chiappetta, L. Depression, anxiety and quality of life in suicide survivors: A comparison of close and distant relationships. *Arch. Psychiatr. Nurs.* **2009**, *23*, 2–10. [CrossRef]
53. Gariepy, G.; Honkaniemi, H.; Quesnel-Vallee, A. Social support and protection from depression: Systematic review of current findings in Western countries. *Br. J. Psychiatry* **2016**, *209*, 284–293. [CrossRef]
54. Teo, A.R.; Choi, H.; Valenstein, M. Social relationships and depression: Ten-year follow-up from a nationally representative study. *PLoS ONE* **2013**, *8*, e62396. [CrossRef]
55. Lipsitz, J.D.; Markowitz, J.C. Mechanisms of change in interpersonal therapy (IPT). *Clin. Psychol. Rev.* **2013**, *33*, 1134–1147. [CrossRef]
56. Cuijpers, P.; Donker, T.; Weissman, M.M.; Ravitz, P.; Cristea, I.A. Interpersonal psychotherapy for mental health problems: A comprehensive meta-analysis. *Am. J. Psychiatry* **2016**, *173*, 680–687. [CrossRef]
57. Feigelman, W.; Gorman, B.S.; Jordan, J.R. Stigmatization and suicide bereavement. *Death Stud.* **2009**, *33*, 591–608. [CrossRef]
58. Ali, F.; Lucock, M. 'It's like getting a group hug and you can cry there and be yourself and they understand'. Family members' experiences of using a suicide bereavement peer support group. *Bereave. Care* **2020**, *39*, 51–58. [CrossRef]
59. Ramchand, R.; Ayer, L.; Fisher, G.; Osilla, K.C.; Barnes-Proby, D.; Wertheimer, S. Suicide postvention in the Department of Defense: Evidence, policies and procedures, and perspectives of loss survivors. *Rand Health Q.* **2015**, *5*, 20.

MDPI
St. Alban-Anlage 66
4052 Basel
Switzerland
Tel. +41 61 683 77 34
Fax +41 61 302 89 18
www.mdpi.com

International Journal of Environmental Research and Public Health Editorial Office
E-mail: ijerph@mdpi.com
www.mdpi.com/journal/ijerph

www.ingramcontent.com/pod-product-compliance
Lightning Source LLC
Chambersburg PA
CBHW061820210926
51850CB00006B/761